# SEXUAL HARASSMENT

# RELATED TITLES

**Treatment of Rape Victims: Facilitating Psychosocial Adjustment**
Karen S. Calhoun and Beverly M. Atkeson
ISBN: 0-205-14296-6

**The Clinician's Handbook: Integrated Diagnostics, Assessment, and
    Intervention in Adult and Adolescent Psychopathology, Fourth Edition**
Robert G. Meyer and Sarah E. Deitsch
ISBN: 0-205-17181-8

**Handbook of Sexual Dysfunctions: Assessment and Treatment**
William O'Donohue and James H. Geer (Editors)
ISBN: 0-205-14787-9

**Sexual Harassment on Campus: A Guide for Administrators, Faculty,
    and Students**
Bernice R. Sandler and Robert J. Shoop
ISBN: 0-205-16712-8

**Understanding Child Abuse and Neglect, Third Edition**
Cynthia Crosson Tower
ISBN: 0-205-16814-0

# SEXUAL HARASSMENT
## THEORY, RESEARCH, AND TREATMENT

**Edited by**
**William O'Donohue**
*University of Nevada, Reno*

**Allyn and Bacon**
*Boston   London   Toronto   Sydney   Tokyo   Singapore*

Internet: www.abacon.com
America Online: Keyword: College Online

**Library of Congress Cataloging-in-Publication Data**

Sexual harassment: theory, research, and treatment / edited by
  William O'Donohue.
       p.   cm.
    Includes bibliographical references and index.
    ISBN 0-205-16412-9
    1. Sexual harassment of women.   2. Sexual harassment.
  O'Donohue, William T.
  HQ1237.S49   1996
  305.42—dc20                                           96-14379
                                                          CIP

Printed in the United States of America
10 9 8 7 6 5 4 3 2 1     00 99 98 97 96

# CONTENTS

# PREFACE

Given the human penchant for causing trouble, it is all too likely that sexual and gender harassment have been occurring for millennia. However, it is only in the 1980s and 1990s that sexual harassment has received much general attention. Part of this heightened interest may be due to a few highly publicized accusations, but another factor contributing to increased attention to sexual harassment is recent information on its startlingly high frequency and on its serious consequences.

There has been a recent surge of activity related to sexual harassment: Charges (true and false) are being leveled against individuals; these allegations are being investigated; careers and productivity are being significantly affected; individuals and institutions are being held liable by the courts; victims and harassers are seeking assessment and treatment; institutions are forming policies and offering sexual harassment prevention programs; and, most fundamentally, individuals are still interacting with one another in the workplace. However, each of these kinds of actions, if they are to be done well, must be done with accurate and complete information.

Fortunately, in the last decade, scholars from many disciplines have also turned their attention to sexual harassment. Although there has been a relative information explosion regarding sexual harassment, current scholarly interest in sexual harassment seems to be large only because sexual harassment had been virtually ignored by scholars for such a long time. This field is still quite young and there is too much that is unknown regarding sexual harassment. The unknown seriously diminishes the quality of the diverse activities regarding sexual harassment.

This is not to say that nothing is known about sexual harassment and therefore actions can be based on something other than the best current information. There are too many precedents for activities that have the potential to be influenced by information, to proceed largely divorced from the best current information. Much of contemporary psychotherapy is, unfortunately, a case in point. Accurate information collected carefully through proper methodologies can be lost because sexual harassment is a field in which strong emotions can be kindled, prejudices can come into play, political beliefs can form part of the agenda, and financial concerns can become the predominant motivation.

This edited volume attempts to draw together the best information on this important topic to help inform the diverse activities associated with the phenomenon of sexual harassment as well as to help inform future research. This book contains 16 chapters written by leading researchers in the field of sexual harassment. Our goal was to create a comprehensive text covering all major dimensions of this field. Thus, topics such as the definition of harassment, epidemiology, theories of etiology, legal issues, treatment of the victim, treatment of the harasser, prevention, sexual harassment policy, cross-cultural trends, and harassment in various specialized contexts are addressed in detail.

The field of the study of sexual harassment owes an enormous debt to the women's movement and this book's debt to the movement should be noted. Sexual harassment is, by and large, a gendered problem: Males are the harassers and women are the victims. The women's movement in the twentieth century had, regrettably, many problems to address. But its thoroughgoing insistence that gender has no relevance for the honoring of rights eventually led it to be concerned about the treatment of women at work and school. Women have as much of a right to vote, to own property, to work, and to be treated as something other than a sex object as men do. The women's movement has historically functioned, and still functions, to throw light on the injustices and prejudices encountered by women in the workplace.

This book was the product of the efforts of many individuals. I would first of all like to thank all the chapter authors. It was an honor to work with such an outstanding group of scholars. Thank you to the following reviewers for their helpful comments and suggestions: Victoria M. Follette, University of Nevada, Reno, Catherine L. Flanagan, Forensic Psychological Services; and Andrew W. Kane, Private Practice, Milwaukee, Wisconsin. I also hold a large debt of gratitude to Mylan Jaixen, who has patiently and wisely provided a guiding hand to this project. Susan Hutchinson has also provided much help at many critical junctures. Finally, I would like to thank my family, Jane and Katie, for their patience and support during this project. They have taught me, by their superlative example, how humans should treat other humans.

# ABOUT THE EDITOR
# AND CONTRIBUTORS

## ABOUT THE EDITOR

**William O'Donohue** is an associate professor of psychology at the University of Nevada, Reno. He received a doctorate in clinical psychology from the State University of New York at Stony Brook and a master's degree in philosophy from Indiana University. He has examined questions relating to the prevention of sexual harassment and the measurement of risk factors in males. He has coedited several books including *Theories of Human Sexuality*, *The Sexual Abuse of Children*, and *Handbook of Sexual Dysfunctions* (all with James Geer), *Handbook of Psychological Skills Training* and *Theories of Behavior Therapy* (with Leonard Krasner) and *Psychology and Philosophy* (with Richard Kitchener).

## ABOUT THE CONTRIBUTORS

**Jann H. Adams** received a doctorate in clinical psychology from Indiana University in 1989. Dr. Adams is an associate professor of psychology at Morehouse College, where she teaches courses in clinical, abnormal, and child/developmental psychology. Dr. Adams is the coauthor of a chapter on feminist perspectives on child sexual abuse and conducts research on the John Henryism active coping behavior pattern and health outcomes among African Americans. She is currently conducting research evaluating the effectiveness of three violence-prevention programs involving elementary- and middle-school–age children.

**Azy Barak** received his doctorate in counseling psychology from Ohio State University in 1976. Currently he is associate professor of counseling psychology at the University of Western Ontario, London (Ontario), Canada. His research interests include counseling interventions, career psychology, and various factors related to sexual harassment. Since 1987 he has been involved in research and treatment of sexual harassment in the university, workplaces, and the military in Israel, and now in Canada.

**Alba Conte** graduated summa cum laude from Douglass College of Rutgers University and received her law degree from the University of Pennsylvania Law, where she edited several publications on women and the law and received the Alice Paul Award for outstanding contributions to the status of women at the university. She is the author of *Sexual Harassment in the Workplace: Law and Practice* (Wiley, 1990 and 1994) and *Attorney Fee Awards* (Shepard's/McGraw-Hill, 1993), coauthor of *Newberg on Class Actions* (Shepard's/McGraw-Hill, 1992), and a contributor to a number of other works.

**Bonnie S. Dansky** is an assistant professor of clinical psychology at the National Crime Victims' Research and Treatment Center (NCVC) and at the Center for Drug and Alcohol Programs (CDAP) in the department of Psychiatry and Behavioral Sciences of the Medical University of South Carolina. Dr. Dansky received her doctorate in clinical psychology from Duke University in 1991 and currently is a principal investigator for a NIDA-funded scientist development award concerning substance abuse and victimization.

**Louise F. Fitzgerald** is associate professor of psychology and women's studies at the University of Illinois at Urbana-Champaign. She received her doctorate in psychology from the Ohio State University in 1979 and has held faculty positions at Kent State University and the University of California, Santa Barbara. Her major research area is sexual harassment in the workplace and academia, which she has been studying for nearly a decade. She is the 1992 recipient of the Holland Prize for Excellence in Research in Personality and Career Development and in 1991 was the psychological consultant to Professor Anita Hill's legal team during the Clarence Thomas confirmation hearings.

**James E. Gruber** is a professor of sociology at the University of Michigan, Dearborn. He is a social psychologist who has conducted programs on sexual harassment since 1980. In the early 1980s he and Lars Bjorn focused on the workplace dynamics and psychological outcomes of sexual harassment among women autoworkers. Recently he has developed typologies of and responses or reactions to sexual harassment from samples of North American and European women with colleagues Kaisa Kauppinen (Finnish Institute of Occupational Health) and the late Michael Smith (formerly of York University, Toronto).

**Elizabeth O'Hare Grundmann** is a doctoral candidate in clinical psychology at Northern Illinois University. She received her bachelor's degree from Marquette University.

**Barbara A. Gutek,** professor and head of the Department of Management and Policy at the University of Arizona, received her doctorate from the University of Michigan in 1975. She is author or editor of nine books and over 70 articles and book chapters on topics including sexual harassment and other gender issues in organizations.

**Stephanie M. Hayes** received her master's in social psychology at Howard University and is now in the doctoral program. She is also a research fellow with the Army Research Institute for Behavioral and Social Sciences.

**Kathy Hotelling,** Ph.D., ABPP, is director at the Counseling and Student Development Center at Northern Illinois University.

**Dr. Dean G. Kilpatrick** is a professor of clinical psychology and the director of the National Crime Victims' Research and Treatment Center at the Medical University of South Carolina in Charleston. Dr. Kilpatrick and his colleagues have received several grants from the National Institute of Mental Health, National Institute of Justice, and the National Institute of Drug Abuse supporting their research on the scope of violent crime and its psychological impact on victims.

**Jamie Leeser** holds a master's degree in philosophy from Northern Illinois University and a bachelor's degree from Wheaton College.

**Vicki J. Magley,** M.A., is a doctoral candidate in psychology at the University of Illinois at Urbana-Champaign. Her current substantive interests involve individual, cognitive, and behavioral factors that influence outcomes of sexual harassment, including victim gender, labeling, and coping. Methodologically, she is currently interested in the formation of indicators in testing causal models. Past research has included attributions of responsibility for date rape incidents, resolution of cognitive conflict, and group problem solving.

**Iris McQueen** is a consultant, speaker, and writer living in Northern California. She has conducted over 1,000 presentations on sexual harassment and other management topics. Because of her expertise she is used in legal proceedings and she is a frequent contributor to management journals on personnel topics.

For more information on Iris and her work, call (916) 725-3285 or write to her at 6302 Van Maren Lane, Citrus Heights, California 95621.

**Robert E. Niebuhr,** associate professor and department head of Management, Auburn University (doctorate, Ohio State University), has spent the last several years examining discriminatory climates in military settings. Additionally, he is concerned with the influence of this and other organizational/group processes on individual behavior. Dr. Niebuhr's research has been published in such journals as the *Academy of Management Journal, the Journal of Applied Social Psychology*, and *the Journal of Management*.

**Michele A. Paludi,** Ph.D., is the editor of *Ivory Power: Sexual Harassment on Campus*

(SUNY Press, 1990), coauthor of *Academic and Workplace Sexual Harassment: A Resource Manual* (SUNY Press, 1991), editor of the forthcoming *Working 9 to 5: Women, Men, Sex, and Power* (SUNY Press), and coauthor of *Educator's Guide to Controlling Sexual Harassment* (Thompson, 1993). Dr. Paludi is currently writing *Sexual Harassment of Adolescents by Teachers and Peers* for SUNY Press. She is principal of Michele Paludi & Associates, Consultants in Sexual Harassment, and offers education and training in issues related to sexual harassment at schools, colleges, and organizations. In addition, she is an expert witness for academic and court proceedings involving sexual harassment. Dr. Paludi's book *Ivory Power* received the 1992 Gustavus Myers Center Award for the Outstanding Book on Human Rights in the United States. Dr. Paludi was a member of Governor Cuomo's Task Force on Sexual Harassment.

**Scott H. Peterson** is a graduate student in clinical psychology at the University of Nevada, Reno. He received his bachelor's degree from Northern Illinois University.

**John B. Pryor** is a professor of psychology at Illinois State University. He received his doctorate in 1977 from Princeton University. His areas of interest include social psychology, human sexuality, and social cognition. In addition to his research on sexual harassment, he has worked as a consultant to the federal government on sexual harassment issues and is currently working as an expert witness for the EEOC in a hostile environment case.

**Suzanne Swan,** M.A., is a doctoral candidate in psychology at the University of Illinois at Urbana-Champaign. Her major research interests include the psychology of women, particularly sexual victimization. Currently her research examines factors that influence women's perceptions of the severity of sexual harassment experiences and how these perceptions affect subsequent coping and outcomes. Previous research includes academic climates for college women and the social cognitive aspects of perceptions of gender.

**Sandra Schwartz Tangri** is professor of psychology at Howard University. She does research on women's career development, sexual harassment, and new medical technologies.

**Nora J. Whalen** received her bachelor's degree from the University of Notre Dame in psychology. She is currently completing a master's degree in social psychology at Illinois State University. She will be continuing her graduate studies at the University of Minnesota. Her current research interests focus on interpersonal relationships.

**Barbara A. Zuber,** Psy.D., is a psychologist at the Counseling and Student Development Center at Northern Illinois University.

# SEXUAL HARASSMENT

# CHAPTER 1

# INTRODUCTION

## William O'Donohue

Sexual harassment is a problem that has a long past but a short history. For centuries, people surely have been mistreated because of their sexuality or gender, but it is only recently that there has been a label for this problem and still more recently that it has become an area of scholarly investigation.

From a historical perspective, these are quite interesting times regarding sexual harassment. Twenty years ago sexual harassment received little academic or general attention. However, with the attention generated by several well-publicized cases and with a stepped-up focus on this problem by individuals mainly concerned with women's rights, sexual harassment and questions about sexual harassment are much in the public eye. Individuals from many different positions and walks of life ask questions such as "Is this particular interaction an example of sexual harassment or not?"; "What causes sexual harassment?"; "What is the profile of a typical sexual harasser?"; "How prevalent is it?"; "How can it be prevented?"; "How can sexual harassment allegations best be investigated?"; "What is a good institutional policy regarding sexual harassment?"; "What is the best treatment for a sexual harassment victim?"; and "What are the relevant laws regarding sexual harassment?", among other questions.

It is important to recognize that these and other questions are asked from quite different positions and professional contexts because sexual harassment concerns such a wide variety of individuals. Business owners, military officers, school administrators, victims and perpetrators of sexual harassment, clinicians treating victims and perpetrators, corporate attorneys, tort attorneys, prevention programmers, feminists, and workers attempting to understand what behavior is permissible and impermissible all may be interested in certain questions regarding sexual harassment. Obviously, each of these positions has its attendant interests and thus, at times, there may be conflicts of interest. Addressing questions about sexual harassment is not a completely dispassionate enterprise.

Sexual harassment is an important topic of study because the consequences of this problem can be so significant. Sexual harassment or allegations of sexual harassment can threaten one's financial security, physical well-being, social well-being, and psychological health. It is not, as some detractors might falsely assert, a clash of different but equally valid values, nor is it a minor breach of etiquette. It is, rather, a serious infliction of injury on another.

This book contains a collection of chapters that present the best information available regarding the major dimensions of sexual harassment. In chapters 2 and 3, Fitzgerald and her colleagues and Leeser and O'Donohue address issues involved in defining sexual harassment. Like most constructs, sexual harassment is not easy to define, nor is it a homogenous set of behaviors. Sexual harassment can include diverse behaviors such as insults directed at gender, leers, inappropriate jokes, inappropriate displays of erotica, sexual bribery, and forced intercourse. However, there are also significant gray areas: When does a sustained look become a leer; when does a leer constitute sexual harassment? Fitzgerald and her colleagues review the evidence concerning legal, behavioral, and psychological definitions of sexual harassment, while Leeser and O'Donohue examine philosophical issues regarding the normative or moral dimensions of sexual harassment.

Chapter 4 discusses legal issues surrounding sexual harassment. Sexual harassment is illegal. But a thorough understanding of the legal status of sexual harassment is complex because federal guidelines, regulatory definitions, case law, statutes, and appellate decisions all bear on the legal status of sexual harassment. Conte provides a survey of the current status of the legal dimensions of sexual harassment, giving an interesting picture of an evolving area of law that is still quite unsettled. What is clear, however, is that in the past decade, courts have seen sexual harassment as a form of sexual discrimination that violates Title VII of the Civil Rights Act of 1964.

In Chapter 5, Gruber reviews epidemiological evidence regarding sexual harassment in North America and Europe. An important set of questions concerns the frequency of sexual harassment. Is it an infrequent phenomenon that simply receives a lot of attention (like serial murder)? Or is it a widespread social problem affecting millions of workers and students? Gruber makes a number of important methodological distinctions and recommendations regarding research on the frequency of sexual harassment. Epidemiological research also asks important questions about risk factors. Clearly, one of the basic facts of sexual harassment is that it is largely a gendered phenomenon: Males are the perpetrators and females are the victims.

Those involved in the women's movement have had much to do with drawing attention to the problem of sexual harassment and exposing its serious ramifications and widespread prevalence. In Chapter 6, Hotelling and Zuber argue that gendered power differentials and problematic sex roles create the context for sexual harassment, that sexual harassment is all too often an extension of problematic cultural patterns of male–female interactions, and that sexual harassment does harm to victims and potential victims by limiting their ability to live on an equal status. This chapter firmly establishes the many ways in which gender and social context relate to sexual harassment.

In Chapter 7, Tangri and Hayes review the major extant theories of sexual harassment. Natural/biological models, sex-role spillover theory, organizational power models, sociocultural models, interactionist models, and other integrative models are reviewed. These authors point to an important underlying issue that is common to most of these models, that is, that the "system of heterosexual relations is adversarial and coercive." If correct, this points to the necessity of coming to a better understanding and practice of improved heterosexual relations.

In Chapter 8, Pryor and Whalen make a very basic but nonetheless important observation. Harassers do not harass in all situations, and some situations result in more harassment than others. Thus, they argue that the interaction between person variables and situation variables needs to be considered when attempting to understand the incidence of sexual harassment. These authors construct a typology of sexual harassment based on the general psychological functions that sexual harassment can serve. They suggest that subtypes include: (1) sexual exploitation, (2) sexual attraction/miscommunication, (3) misogyny, and (4) hostile attitudes toward homosexuals. These factors produce a proclivity to sexually harass. They conclude by discussing the roles of these functions in their Person X Situation model.

Next, Dansky and Kilpatrick review evidence on the effects of sexual harassment. Although sexual harassment can be defined as a wrong without reference to its numerous sequelae (see Leeser and O'Donohue, this volume), its extensive negative consequences also point to its problematic nature. Although Dansky and Kilpatrick review the career-related, psychological, and physical effects of sexual harassment, they also point to the paucity of information and the need for more research in this area. They report evidence that the majority of harassment victims attempt to ignore the harassment, which is rarely an effective strategy for ending the harassment. These authors present some of their data indicating that the lifetime risk of Major Depression and Post-Traumatic Stress Disorder (PTSD) is higher among sexual harassment victims. The data are disturbing because they suggest that these effects can be quite long term; in some cases negative effects can be detected at least 11 years later.

Grundman and her colleagues next discuss the prevention of sexual harassment. Prevention efforts are underway in many different settings, although the extent to which these efforts actually decrease the incidence of sexual harassment is unclear. This is a serious problem because it suggests that we do not know the efficacy of various prevention efforts. It may be that a false sense of security is being produced by a reliance on ineffective prevention efforts. This chapter attempts to set prevention efforts in the context of etiological theories of sexual harassment. The authors describe some of their own research and make methodological suggestions for future outcome research in sexual harassment prevention programming.

Gutek points out in Chapter 11 that the courts have held organizations responsible for sexual harassment. Institutions as a first line of defense have formulated and adopted policies stating that they do not condone and will not tolerate sexual harassment. There has been a great deal of variety in the policies that institutions have adopted regarding sexual harassment. Gutek discusses innovations in policies, procedures, and training regarding sexual harassment in organizations and discusses the difficulties in constructing and implementing these in a way that people find satisfactory.

In Chapter 12, McQueen discusses issues relevant to conducting a sexual harassment investigation. The investigation of a sexual harassment allegation is an important and complex process. Much is at stake, much is contested, and frequently there is little or no clear definitive evidence. Most harassers know enough to harass when there are no witnesses, and most individuals making false allegations know that they should make these allegations in ways that cannot easily be disproved. McQueen discusses the roles, rights, and responsibilities of sexual harassment investigators.

In Chapter 13, Adams discusses the unique ways in which African American women experience sexual harassment. Adams's thesis is that culture and ethnic minority status affect the perception and the experience of sexual harassment. Given the historical experience of black women in the United States, the experience of sexual discrimination interacts with—and becomes compounded with—the experience of racial discrimination. As examples, she argues that the concept of raping a slave did not exist, and black women are stereotyped as promiscuous and having stronger sexual appetites. These race-related myths can have obvious impact on the experience and risk of sexual harassment for black women.

The final three chapters examine sexual harassment in particular contexts. Paludi examines sexual harassment in educational settings, Niebuhr discusses sexual harassment in the military, and Barak looks at sexual harassment in a wide variety of cultures. Each of these authors points to important differences in the nature of sexual harassment across these diverse contexts.

This book does not contain a chapter that discusses clinical issues regarding the assessment and treatment of both sexual harassment victims and sexual harassment perpetrators. Although this might be legitimately seen as an important omission, little is known at present about valid assessment devices and effective treatments. Victims can require treatment to help cope with and minimize the sequelae associated with sexual harassment. It is important to note that, as reported by Dansky and Kilpatrick, an increased risk of depression and PTSD exists, other psychological problems may also result.

Sexual harassment is not a monolithic phenomenon, and its effects should not be expected to be constant. Sexual harassment can consist of a single incident of inappropriate exposure to erotica or multiple episodes of violent rape. It would be surprising, given the wide range of individuals, behaviors, and contexts that may be involved in sexual harassment, for there to be something like a consistent "sexual harassment accommodation syndrome." It would be less surprising to see that the effects depend on many mediating variables such as the victim's relationship to the abuser, kind of harassment, length of harassment, variables relating to the disclosure and investigation, pre-abuse psychological status, social support network, attributional style of the victim, and so on.

Good assessment practices should be implemented to identify the full range of problems a particular sexual harassment victim is experiencing. Treatment would need to follow the problems uncovered in the assessment. Although there should probably be some discussion regarding whether perpetrating sexual harassment is a psychological health matter that should be treated by therapy (as opposed to being a criminal or a moral matter), currently perpetrators are seeking and receiving treatment. Assessment and treatment of a sexual harasser are complex matters, given the range of subproblems (misogyny, anger, lack of social skills, impulse-control problems, poor victim empathy, poor outcome expectancies, paraphilias) that may or may not be present. However, what is currently troubling is the scarcity of outcome data regarding how to treat either the sexual abuse victim or perpetrator. It is hoped that in the future, books on sexual harassment will be able to provide reviews of assessment validation studies and treatment outcome studies.

The purpose of this compendium of chapters is threefold: (1) Drawing together chapters written by the leading scholars of sexual harassment affords the reader a synoptic view of the entire field; (2) each chapter by thoroughly examining a major question regarding sexual harassment provides the reader with the best information currently available regarding that topic; and (3) the reader will see need for future research. Fields as emotionally laden as sexual harassment can neglect research and instead attempt to provide answers to major questions by appeals to authority, by prejudice, by political bias, or by theories that are never adequately tested. However, progress in the growth of knowledge about sexual harassment can best be achieved through well-designed research. It is hoped that this book will not only inform current practice but serve as a helpful guide for future research.

CHAPTER 2

# BUT WAS IT REALLY SEXUAL HARASSMENT? Legal, Behavioral, and Psychological Definitions of the Workplace Victimization of Women

**Louise F. Fitzgerald**

**Suzanne Swan**

**Vicki J. Magley**

> *(The) Senators agonized that sexual harassment is amorphous or hard to define, and an extraordinarily complex subject that cannot be easily understood let alone decided upon.*
> Leibman, *USC Law Review*, 1992, 1444

> *"The question is," said Alice, "whether you can make words mean different things."*
> *"The question is," said Humpty Dumpty, "which is to be master—that's all."*
> Lewis Carroll

Since its inception as an injury in law and a concept in psychology, sexual harassment has been the topic of continual controversy concerning its definition. No other psycho-legal concept, with the possible exception of pornography, has given rise to such seemingly endless debate. Like the senators of whom Leibman wrote following the confirmation hearings of Clarence Thomas, many have argued that sexual harassment is so fundamentally private and inherently ambiguous as to defy consensual understanding. Like Alice, others have questioned whether the same phrase can be applied to so many seemingly disparate experiences. And, like those trying to put Humpty Dumpty together, feminist scholars have argued that the issue is, at least in part, a political one and that, whatever the law and psychology might say, any meaningful understanding of sexual harassment must be grounded in women's experiences, the day-to-day "suchness" of our lives.

This chapter provides an analysis of empirical definitions of sexual harassment. By *empirical*, we intend not only the usual meanings of surveys, items, and scales—referred to here as *behavioral* definitions—but also legal and phenomenological meanings, the other major ways that the concept can be defined. We begin with a brief overview of the historical development of sexual harassment jurisprudence (i.e., legal definitions) and then provide a review of the frameworks that have guided survey construction (i.e., behavioral definitions) and the relationship of such instruments to legal concepts. Following a brief overview of issues of meaning and valence (i.e., the seriousness or severity issue), we explore this topic in more depth via an examination of psychological definitions of sexual harassment. We conclude with a discussion of two related issues that our analysis raises, that is, women's labeling of their experiences as sexual harassment and the controversial topic of the sexual harassment of men.

## OVERVIEW

Much of the confusion surrounding definition can be traced to a failure to distinguish sexual harassment as a *legal concept* from the *psychological experience* of workplace victimization, although it is clear that the two are not the same.

> For example, women have been shown to confront a wide range of psychologically noxious workplace experiences.... Any particular exemplar may embody behavioral instances of varying types, frequency, intensity, and duration and may or may not meet current legal criteria for sexual harassment. This is particularly so given that legal criteria evolve and change based on regulatory definitions, case law, appellate decisions and the like. (Fitzgerald, Gelfand, & Dragow, in press)

This implies that the psychological construct is appropriately conceptualized more broadly than the legal one. The law is not designed as a remedy for all offensive or even traumatic experiences, as each legal determi-

nation must take into account a variety of factors, whereas the phenomenological experience of harassment is determined solely by the experience of the victim. This distinction can be clarified by considering the analogous example of rape. Until recently, forced sexual intercourse by one's husband typically did not qualify as rape in legal terms, despite being experientially similar to sexual assault by someone to whom one is not married. Similarly, it is not uncommon for criminal complaints of rape to be considered "unfounded" by police if both individuals have been drinking heavily or there is evidence of a previous relationship between the parties, even if there is no question that the behavior (i.e., forced intercourse) occurred. In each of these examples, the woman was not raped in the legal sense; the psychological sense, of course, is another matter.

The analogy, although not exact, is illuminating. As with rape, sexual harassment law has changed over the years and will likely continue to do so for some time to come. The original decisions equating harassment with quid pro quo experiences have long since given way to recognition of the more widespread "hostile environment" situations (*Meritor Savings Bank v. Vinson*, 1986) and questions concerning the appropriate perspective (e.g., *Ellison v. Brady*, 1991; *Robinson v. Jacksonville Shipyards*, 1991), standards of severity (*Harris v. Forklift Systems, Inc.*, 1993), and welcomeness (*Carr v. Allison Gas Turbine Division, General Motors Corporation*, 1994) continue to be debated. Thus, the ultimate outcome of any particular legal decision will always depend on a variety of factors not assessed or assessable by survey instruments, that is, on the totality of the circumstances (*Meritor Savings Bank v. Vinson*, 1986; cf. *Harris v. Forklift Systems, Inc.*, 1993); the current state of the law; the characteristics of a particular jury; and, not least, a certain degree of random chance.

This is not to say that researchers have paid too much attention to legal conceptions of harassment. Indeed, the reverse appears to be the case. Several reviewers have suggested that prevalence figures are inflated by the practice of cumulating over what may be isolated minor incidents, possibly by different perpetrators and across different jobs, and thus bear little resemblance to legal conceptions of sexual harassment. Statements such as "Approximately one out of every two women will experience sexual harassment at some point during her educational or working life" (e.g., Fitzgerald, 1992; Koss et al., 1994) are properly understood to refer to women's experiences, not to legal claims.

Note that we are *not* arguing that surveys should "count" only situations that meet legal criteria, even if such a recommendation were technically feasible. After all, psychological stressors are not created by legislatures nor changed by judicial decisions; hostile work environments existed long before they were recognized by the Supreme Court and would presumably continue to do so even if that body were to reverse its ruling or Congress were to repeal Title VII. The point is not that researchers should or should not equate their measures with legal concepts, but that they should *articulate* the relationship between the two. In the sections to follow, we attempt such an articulation.

## LEGAL DEFINITIONS

Although most discussions begin with the Equal Employment Opportunity Commission guidelines (EEOC, 1980), the concept of sexual harassment had a considerable legal history throughout the 1970s. The argument that sexual harassment constituted impermissible sex discrimination did not easily prevail and, in fact, five of the first seven courts to address the issue held that quid pro quo harassment of a woman employee by a male supervisor was not actionable under Title VII. (See, e.g., *Corne v. Bausch & Lomb*, 1975; *Barnes v. Train*, 1974; *Miller v. Bank of America*, 1976; as well as Note, 1978, for a review. See also MacKinnon, 1979, for the classic argument to the contrary.)

Sexual harassment was first legally recognized as a form of sex discrimination in 1976 (*Williams v. Saxbe,* 1976). Diane Williams, an employee in the U.S. Department of Justice,

brought suit under Title VII of the 1964 Civil Rights Act, alleging that she was harassed, humiliated, and ultimately fired for refusing the sexual advances of her supervisor. The Justice Department, of which Saxbe was at that time the head, argued that Title VII did not apply because Williams was allegedly fired, not because she was female, "but rather because she decided not to furnish the sexual consideration claimed to have been demanded"—in other words, because she refused to have sex, a condition that could apply equally to men or women.

Despite finding this argument "almost persuasive," Judge Charles Ritchie ultimately rejected the analysis, noting that a finding of sex discrimination did not require that a discriminatory practice depend on a characteristic specific to one sex or the other. He noted, for example, that it was illegal to discriminate against women with pre-school children, although both men and women could be parents (*Phillips v. Martin Marietta Corporation*, 1971). Similarly, he reasoned that applying a no-marriage rule to employees of one sex but not the other was impermissible, although both sexes are capable of marriage (*Sprogis v. United Airlines*, 1971).

> The requirement of willingness to provide sexual consideration…is no different from the "pre-school age children" and "no-marriage" rules…. It was and is sufficient…to claim that the rule creating an artificial barrier to employment has been applied to one gender and not the other…. This Court concludes that plaintiff has stated a cause of action [under Title VII].

The following year the D.C. Circuit again upheld this argument; in *Barnes v. Costle* (1977), Judge Robinson confirmed that quid pro quo harassment violates Title VII, offering the now classic "but for" argument, that is, but for the plaintiff's sex, the contested behavior would not have occurred. Thus, by the end of the decade, quid pro quo claims were generally recognized as impermissible sex discrimination, although the Supreme Court, the ultimate legal arbiter, had yet to speak to this issue.

In 1980 the U.S. Equal Employment Opportunity Commission, the agency charged with enforcement of Title VII, issued its now famous guidelines, which defined sexual harassment as "unwelcome sexual advances, requests for sexual favors, and other verbal or physical conduct of a sexual nature" when cooperation or submission was an implicit or explicit condition of employment; was used as a basis for employment-related decisions; or when the conduct has the "purpose or effect of unreasonably interfering with a person's work performance or creating an intimidating, hostile, or offensive working environment" (p. 74676). This last set of conditions, originally known as *conditions of work* (MacKinnon, 1979), gave rise to the second major cause of action under Title VII, the theory generally known as *hostile environment*.

The definitive hostile environment case was also the first to reach the Supreme Court (*Meritor Savings Bank v. Vinson*, 1986). In 1974, Mechelle Vinson was hired as a teller-trainee by Sidney Taylor, vice-president of Meritor Savings Bank. She worked for him for four years, rising to the level of assistant branch manager. In 1978, she was terminated for excessive use of sick leave, whereupon she brought suit against Taylor and the bank, alleging that Taylor had subjected her to constant harassment during the years that she had worked for him. According to Vinson, Taylor made repeated demands for sexual favors, with which she complied out of fear of losing her job; he fondled her in front of other employees, followed her into the women's restroom, and even forcibly raped her on several occasions.

The D.C. District Court denied relief, ruling that "if [respondent] and Taylor did engage in an intimate or sexual relationship during the time of [respondent's] employment with [the bank], that relationship was...voluntary" (*Vinson v. Taylor*, 1985, p. 42); the D.C. Court of Appeals, architect of the pioneer quid pro quo decisions of the 1970s, disagreed. They stated that harassment that creates a hostile or offensive environment is just as impermissible as situations that condition concrete employment benefits on sexual cooperation. When the case ultimately reached the Supreme Court, that body affirmed the appellate decision, stating that

> ...the language of Title VII is not limited to "economic" or "tangible" discrimination.... Since the (EEOC) guidelines were issued, courts have uniformly held, and we agree, that a plaintiff may establish a violation of Title VII by proving that discrimination based on sex has created a hostile or abusive working environment. As the Court of Appeals...wrote in *Henson v. City of Dundee* (1982): "Sexual harassment which creates a hostile or offensive environment for members of one sex is every bit the arbitrary barrier to sexual equality at the workplace that racial harassment is to racial equality. Surely, a requirement that a man or woman run a gauntlet of sexual abuse in return for the privilege of being able to work and make a living can be as demeaning and disconcerting as the harshest of racial epithets."

In the decade since *Meritor* established the legitimacy of hostile environment claims, considerable legal attention has been devoted to examining a variety of issues raised but not settled by this decision. How hostile must an environment be to trigger the statute, and what evidence is required to demonstrate it? What determines that a behavior is sexual in nature, and whose standard of severity should be invoked? Although space precludes a full examination of these issues, we note that it is by now generally accepted that actionable behavior extends beyond traditionally sexual (i.e., seductive, suggestive) acts to include crude, offensive, and hostile behaviors directed at women simply because they are women (see *Hall v. Gus Construction Co.*, 1988, for an example, and Lindemann & Kadue, 1992, for an extended discussion). Similarly, although the appropriate severity test cannot be reduced to a mathematical formula and debates concerning the reasonable person versus the reasonable woman continue, it is becoming clear that subjective criteria (i.e., the victim's perspective) as well as objective ones are relevant to legal determinations (*Harris v. Forklift Systems, Inc.*, 1993).

As Lindemann and Kadue (1992) note drily, "In retrospect, the great question posed by the judicial history of sexual harassment is not how it came to be regarded as a form of discrimination, but why for so long it was [not]" (p. 9). Despite such judicial reluctance, the 20 years that have followed Judge Ritchey's opinion in *Williams*—and, in particular, the decade since *Meritor* was decided—have seen momentous change in the legal concept of sexual harassment. It may be difficult to remember, from the vantage point of 1996, that not so long ago, what is now considered illegal was thought to be a "natural sex phenomenon [that] plays at least a subtle part in most personnel decisions" (*Miller v. Bank of America*, 1976). As Catharine MacKinnon remarked, "Sometimes, even the law does something for the first time."

## BEHAVIORAL DEFINITIONS

In contrast to legal frameworks, behavioral definitions refer to the taxonomies and survey instruments designed to collect data on offensive sex-related experiences in the workplace. As the field has developed, a number of reviews have appeared examining these instruments and frameworks (e.g., Arvey & Cavanaugh, in press; Fitzgerald & Shullman, 1993; Gruber, 1990; Koss et al., 1994). Such critiques generally identify three concerns: *theoretical issues* of domain specification, *psychometric issues* of reliability and validity, and *psychological issues* of meaning and valence. We examine each of these in turn.

## Domain Specification

As noted by most observers, there is considerable variance in the range of behaviors assessed by harassment surveys, a state of affairs yielding conflicting frequency estimates and fluctuating prevalence rates. This situation reflects the lack of a broadly agreed upon classification system from which relevant behaviors can be sampled; measurement has taken place at the level of specific acts,

with little rationale for the inclusion or exclusion of any particular exemplar. Over the years there have been three formal attempts to chart the behavioral domain of sexual harassment: the empirically derived framework proposed by Till (1980), the rationally derived categories described by Gruber (1992), and Fitzgerald et al.'s rational-empirical system (Fitzgerald, Gelfand, & Drasgow, in press; Gelfand, Fitzgerald, & Drasgow, in press).

### Till's System

The earliest and best-known attempt to specify the domain of sexual harassment was made by Till (1980), who classified the experiences of a large sample of college women into five general categories covering a wide spectrum of behaviors from sexist comments to rape. The first of these he labeled *generalized sexist remarks and behavior*; similar in many ways to racial harassment, such behavior is not aimed at sexual cooperation, but rather conveys insulting, degrading, or sexist remarks about women. The second category consisted of *inappropriate and offensive, but essentially sanction-free sexual advances*; although such behavior is unwelcome and offensive, no penalty is attached to the woman's refusal to comply. The third category included *solicitation of sexual activity or other sex-related behavior by promise of reward*, and the fourth covered *coercion of sexual activity by threat of punishment*. Finally, Till reported instances of *sexual crimes and misdemeanors,* including rape and sexual assault.

Till noted in his discussion that "these categories are not sharply delineated, although they are arranged in a roughly hierarchical continuum [presumably of severity]. Many of the reported incidents involve several categories, as when a student is promised something in exchange for sexual favors and simultaneously threatened about noncooperation" (1980, p. 8). This work, which has the advantage of being directly derived from women's actual experiences, has been extremely influential and continues to be used as the basis for much research, training, and policy discussion, particularly in higher education (see

Riggs, Murrell, & Cutting, 1993, for a recent example).

## Gruber's Typology of Personal and Environmental Harassment

More recently, Gruber (1992) proposed a somewhat different typology, based on an analysis of court cases and the research literature. He categorized harassment in three general categories: *verbal requests, verbal remarks*, and *nonverbal displays*, each of which is further characterized by a number of subcategories. The verbal requests category, which subsumes all attempts to initiate and secure sexual cooperation, includes *sexual bribery, sexual advances, relational advances*, and *subtle pressure/advances* (this latter subcategory refers to veiled, ambiguous, or "humorous" behavior whose intent may become clear only in retrospect or after considerable time has passed). Verbal remarks include *personal remarks* (e.g., offensive and embarrassing comments, jokes, or teasing) directed *to* a particular woman; *subjective objectification*, that is, comments, rumors, or statements made *about* a woman, whether in her presence or in the workplace more generally; and *sexual categorical remarks*, that is, offensive sexual remarks about women as a social category (e.g., "All women are whores"). Finally, nonverbal displays include physical behavior (*sexual assault, sexual touching*), *sexual posturing* (e.g., body language, vulgar gestures), and *sexual materials* (e.g., graffiti, pornography, profanation of women's sexuality or bodily functions). This typology appears in Table 2-1; according to Gruber, subcategories are ordered within category in a hierarchy of increasing severity, based on the degree to which the behavior is personally and sexually focused on the recipient.

## Fitzgerald's Tripartite Model

Most recently, Fitzgerald and her colleagues have proposed a parsimonious classification of harassing behaviors consisting of three related but conceptually distinct dimensions: gender harassment, unwanted sexual atten-

**TABLE 2-1.** Gruber's (1992) Typology of Sexual Harassment

A. VERBAL REQUESTS (more to less severe)
  1. Sexual bribery—with threat and/or promise of reward *(quid pro quo)*
  2. Sexual advances—no threat, seeking sexual intimacy
  3. Relational advances—no threat, repetitively seeking social relationship
  4. Subtle pressures/advances—no threat, goal or target is implicit or ambiguous

B. VERBAL COMMENTS (more to less severe)
  1. Personal remarks—unsolicited and directed *to* a woman
  2. Subjective objectification—rumors and/or comments made *about* a woman
  3. Sexual categorical remarks—about women "in general"

C. NONVERBAL DISPLAYS (more to less severe)
  1. Sexual assault—aggressive contact involving coercion
  2. Sexual touching—brief *sexual* or contextually *sexualized*
  3. Sexual posturing—violations of personal space or attempts at personal contact
  4. Sexual materials—pornographic materials, sexually demeaning objects, profanation of women's sexuality

tion, and sexual coercion. *Gender harassment*, similar to Till's first category, refers to a broad range of verbal behavior, physical acts, and symbolic gestures that are not aimed at sexual cooperation but that convey insulting, hostile, and degrading attitudes about women. Examples include sexual epithets, slurs, taunts, and gestures; the display or distribution of obscene or pornographic materials; gender-based hazing; and threatening, intimidating, or hostile acts. *Unwanted sexual attention* is exactly that and includes both verbal and nonverbal behavior that is unwelcome, offensive, and unreciprocated; whereas *sexual coercion*, the paradigmatic example of sexual harassment, refers to the extortion of sexual cooperation in return for job-related considerations.

Fitzgerald et al. derived their model from a series of studies of survey data collected from a variety of diverse samples and settings; based on a series of confirmatory factor analyses, they argue that these categories are necessary and sufficient to categorize any particular example of sexually harassing behavior. They explicitly link their categories to parallel legal constructs, a linkage displayed in Figure 2-1, which depicts sexual coercion as isomorphic with quid pro quo and indicates that gender harassment and unwanted sexual attention constitute the two aspects of a hostile work environment. The curved arrows reflect the nonindependent nature of the categories, underscoring the fact that the great majority of harassing experiences include more than one form of behavior. Sexual coercion by definition implies unwanted sexual attention (although the reverse is generally not the case), and research confirms that gender harassment and unwanted sexual attention generally co-occur (e.g., Schneider & Swan, 1994).

### Comparison and Integration

Analysis of the three systems suggests that the tripartite model of Fitzgerald and colleagues has several advantages. First, it is more parsimonious than the Till system, whose distinction between bribery and threat is unnecessary,

as it is clear that a statement such as "If you sleep with me, I'll promote you" generally subsumes its reverse. Unlike Gruber's typology, the categories are mutually exclusive and do not conflate the legal distinction between quid pro quo and hostile environment behaviors. Gruber's (1992) system, however, has the advantage of specificity at a lower level of generality; when its subcategories are rearranged to conform to the Fitzgerald et al. model, a more completely specified taxonomy emerges. This taxonomy appears in Table 2-2.

Much as the test specifications so integral to intellective measurement are used to generate test items, ensure balanced coverage, and ascertain that no aspect of the construct is neglected, so too can such a framework provide the guidelines for developing content-valid survey instruments. It is to this topic that we now turn.

## Psychometric Considerations

Despite the existence of such frameworks, it is fair to say that the great majority of sexual harassment research rests on ad hoc instrumentation developed for a particular study with little articulated rationale for the behaviors included, no information about reliability and validity, and only passing if any attention given to issues of severity (e.g., frequency, intensity, and duration). The method of choice has typically been a brief checklist, of which Merit Systems' (1981; 1987) is probably the most well-known example.

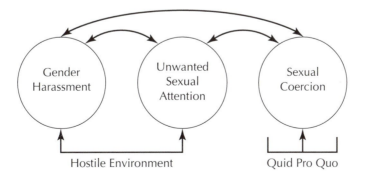

**Figure 2-1.** Fitzgerald et al.'s model of sexually harassing behaviors

**TABLE 2-2.**  An Integrated Taxonomy of Sexual Harassment and Its Relationship to Legal Concepts

| | |
|---|---|
| A.  GENDER HARASSMENT<br>    Verbal remarks<br>• personal remarks<br>• subjective objectification<br>• sexual categorical remarks<br>    Nonverbal displays (symbolic)<br>• sexual posturing<br>• sexual materials<br>  • posters, graffiti<br>  • profanation<br><br>B.  UNWANTED SEXUAL ATTENTION<br>    Verbal requests<br>• sexual advances<br>• relational advances<br>• subtle pressure/advances<br>    Nonverbal displays (physical)<br>• sexual touching<br>• sexual assault | Hostile Environment |
| C.  SEXUAL COERCION<br>    Verbal requests<br>• sexual bribery<br>• (threat) | Quid Pro Quo |

From Till (1980).

The original U.S. Merit Systems study (1981) presented respondents with a brief list of seven types of harassing behaviors, classified in three categories of severity based on the degree of agreement among respondents as to what behaviors constituted sexual harassment. In the "less severe" category, Merit Systems classified unwelcome sexual remarks, suggestive looks and gestures, and deliberate touching. The "severe" category included being pressured for dates, directly pressured for sexual favors, and receiving unwelcome letters and telephone calls. In the "most severe" category the researchers included rape and attempted rape. Items were developed based on the Office of Personnel Management's definition, that is, "deliberate or repeated unsolicited verbal comments, gestures or physical contact of a sexual nature that is considered unwelcome by the recipi-

ent" (p. 2); respondents described the frequency of each experience during the past 24 months on a 5-point scale that ranged from "Never" to "Once a week or more." Each item was analyzed separately, and no attempts to assess reliability or stability were reported.

A slightly different list was developed by Gutek (1985), who asked respondents about sexual remarks meant to be complimentary, sexual remarks meant to be insulting, sexual looks or gestures meant to be complimentary, sexual looks or gestures meant to be insulting, nonsexual touching, sexual touching, being expected to socialize as part of the job, and being expected to participate in sexual activity as part of the job. Respondents were asked, in a simple yes-no fashion, whether they had ever experienced each behavior at their present job or previously.

In contrast to the checklist approach, Fitzgerald and her colleagues (1988) developed the first inventory of sexually harassing behaviors designed to meet traditional standards of reliability and validity. They defined the domain of interest via Till's five categories and wrote multiple items to measure each one. All items were written in behavioral terms, following a standard format (i.e., "Have you ever been in a situation where..."); the words *sexual harassment* did not appear until the end of the instrument to avoid biasing the participant's response. In the original scale, participants responded to all items via a 3-point scale (never, once, more than once). Fitzgerald et al. reported excellent reliability, including alpha coefficients, corrected split-half coefficients, and two-week stability coefficients of .86.

Content validity was explicitly built into the Sexual Experience Questionnaire (SEQ) through basing item construction on Till's empirically derived categories. In addition, the authors examined the correlation of each item with the "criterion" item, that is, "I have been sexually harassed." With minor exceptions, all items were significantly positively correlated with this item; in addition, correlations of each subscale with this criterion showed the monotonic increase predicted by theory.

The SEQ was recently revised to correct base rate problems and provide methods for scale scoring, as opposed to simple frequency counts (Fitzgerald, Gelfand, & Drasgow, in press). The new instrument is based on the more parsimonious tripartite model, and the response options revised to a 5-point Likert format. This revised instrument has been shown to be sensitive to those organizational conditions thought to give rise to high levels of sexual harassment (Zickar, 1994), as well as to predict important psychological and organizational outcomes (e.g., Schneider & Swan, 1994), including anxiety, depression, job satisfaction, work-withdrawal, and—indirectly—physical health.

*Summary and Critique*

A number of reviews have appeared analyzing and critiquing the sexual harassment preva-

lence literature from a measurement perspective (Arvey & Cavanaugh, in press; Fitzgerald, 1990; Fitzgerald & Shullman, 1993; Fitzgerald, Gelfand, & Drasgow, in press) and we will not repeat those here. We note, however, with some chagrin, that previous discussions of this sort appear to have had little impact, as checklist studies continue to dominate the literature (see, for example, Morrow et al., 1995) and psychometrically sound alternatives to the SEQ have yet to appear. Although we believe, perhaps immodestly, that this instrument is the most conceptually and technically sophisticated available, it is not without its limitations, and, in any event, different organizational contexts will most certainly require different approaches. For example, gender harassment has different manifestations in a coal mine, factory, or police station than in a university or law office, although the conceptual nature of the construct remains the same. We urge researchers to thoroughly analyze their organizational context and develop items appropriate to the population of interest, rather than continue to rely on off-the-shelf checklists of unknown reliability and validity and possibly only tenuous connections to legal concepts.

## Meaning and Valence

Although domain specification and technical adequacy are necessary to any operational definition, they do not suffice because the *meaning* of any particular experience varies from person to person, depending on a variety of situational and contextual factors. Similarly, the *valence* (e.g., severity, offensiveness) of behaviors is rarely taken into account, despite statements by the EEOC, appellate courts, and even the Supreme Court noting that the victim's perspective is an important factor in any determination of whether harassment has occurred. Although by definition harassment must be unwanted and offensive, and most instruments incorporate some variety of that wording, the question of valence has yet to be systematically addressed.

Till (1980) originally suggested that his five categories could be considered as *levels*, as they appeared to him to form a rough continuum of severity from sexist remarks and behavior to sexual imposition or assault; as previously noted, simple correlations of scores on scales of the original SEQ with the statement "I have been sexually harassed" suggested that there is some validity to this formulation. For example, gender harassment correlated .15 with this criterion, whereas the correlation of sexual coercion was .37 (Fitzgerald et al., 1988). It soon became apparent, however, that this was somewhat of an oversimplification. For example, Fitzgerald and Hesson-McInnis (1989) found that *severity* of behavior and *type* of behavior were independent dimensions in their multidimensional scaling analysis of ratings of items drawn from the SEQ, suggesting that there could be more or less "serious" examples of each category. In retrospect, this seems fairly obvious; unwanted sexual attention can range from persistent, annoying, but relatively innocuous compliments and invitations, to situations that approximate stalking and assault. Similarly, gender harassment includes behaviors from subtle putdowns to the most egregious verbal, physical, and symbolic behavior, and even sexual coercion ranges from subtle to blatant.

Others have also attempted some a priori or objective classification of behaviors as more or less serious (e.g., USMSPB, 1981, 1987), the most recent efforts being those of Gruber (1992) and Lees-Haley et al. (1994). We would argue that such efforts are always doomed to failure, if only because no content-based classification can ever capture the multiple influences that determine the psychological meaning of experience. Although some situations are objectively more severe than others (e.g., assault is clearly more serious than verbal behavior, however offensive the latter may be), such examples can only capture the broadest, most obvious distinctions. Similarly, hypothetical ratings of distress obtained from research participants not actually exposed to the situations they are asked to rate have little to say about the psychological experience of individuals who are actually subject to these behaviors. As Simon (1995) has noted, "Individual perception determines

reality for the victim" (p. 51). More promising by far are attempts to assess severity by identifying objective elements common to all situations (e.g., frequency, duration, number of perpetrators), as well as identifying factors that influence outcomes and the victim's subjective evaluation of the degree to which she found the situation offensive, upsetting, frightening, and the like. We explore this topic in some detail below.

## PSYCHOLOGICAL DEFINITIONS

It is somewhat surprising that a topic mainly researched by psychologists has thus far yielded relatively little in the way of psychological theory and that those theoretical frameworks that have been proposed are mainly at the organizational rather than the individual level (e.g., Fitzgerald, Hulin, & Drasgow, 1995; Gutek, 1985; Pryor, LaVite, & Stoller, 1993). We suspect that harassment's status as a legal concept, as well as the fact that it spans fairly disparate theoretical areas (e.g., organizational psychology, sexual victimization) has a good deal to do with this state of affairs. In any event, there has been a paucity of attention to harassment as a *psychological process*, to the factors that influence that process and that interact and combine to produce or moderate outcomes for the victim. It is to this process that we address ourselves here.

Following Fitzgerald, Swan, and Fisher (in press), we define sexual harassment *psychologically* within the context of cognitive frameworks for understanding stressful life situations (Lazarus & Folkman, 1984; Carver, Scheier, & Weintraub, 1989). From this perspective, "psychological stress...is a relationship between the person and the environment that is appraised by the person as taxing or exceeding his or her resources and endangering his or her well-being" (Lazarus & Folkman, 1984, p. 21). As Kanner et al. (1981) note, "Stimuli typically experienced as stressful include both major life events (e.g., divorce), and the more frequent but less drastic [events]" (p. 124) (e.g., time pressures, interpersonal difficulties). This distinction maps smoothly onto the domain of sexual harassment, in which many experiences are of the latter type (e.g., offensive comments, annoying attention of a sexual nature), but an important minority resemble the former (e.g., sexual coercion, assaultive experiences, and the like). "*Importantly, severity of the stressor is not considered to inhere in the event itself; rather it is an individual's evaluation of the situation, as influenced by factors such as ambiguity, perceived threat, loss and so forth that is determinative*" (Fitzgerald, Swan & Fisher in press, emphasis added).

Such a conceptualization provides a heuristic framework for understanding sexual harassment from the perspective of the individual. In particular, it identifies the cognitive process of primary appraisal as the key variable in determining whether any particular situation will be experienced as stressful (i.e., harassing). Lazarus and Folkman (1984) indicate that "cognitive appraisal [is] the process of categorizing an encounter, and its various facets with respect to its significance for well being. It is not information processing, per se ... but rather largely evaluative, focused on meaning and significance, and takes place continuously during waking life" (p. 31). This process is typically dichotomized into primary and secondary appraisals, the former concerned with whether a stimulus is personally irrelevant, benign, or stressful, and the latter determining the appropriate response. Fitzgerald, Swan, & Fisher (in press) provide an extensive analysis of the role of secondary appraisal in determining coping responses to sexual harassment; here, we focus on the role of primary appraisal as a way to understand the severity issue in a more sophisticated way.

We begin by defining sexual harassment psychologically as *unwanted sex-related behavior at work that is appraised by the recipient as offensive, exceeding her resources, or threatening her well-being*. Figure 2-2 outlines the elements that influence this appraisal; we organize these into *stimulus* factors (having to do with the behavior itself), *contextual* factors (having to do with the orga-

nizational context in which it takes place), and *individual* factors (having to do with the individual woman) (Swan, in progress). We discuss each of these in turn in the following sections.

## Stimulus Factors

By *stimulus factors*, we refer to objectively defined aspects of the harassing behavior itself; for example, was it public or private, isolated or repetitive, verbal, physical, or both? Figure 2-2 suggests that such elements can be classified into three general categories: frequency, intensity, and duration. *Frequency*, of course, refers simply to the number of incidents, whereas *duration* refers to the length of time during which the woman was subjected to the harassing behavior sequence. *Intensity* refers to what is generally thought of as the magnitude of the stressor. Salisbury and Sebek (1994) identified six factors hypothesized to contribute to intensity: (1) multiple perpetrators; behavior that is (2) physical (as opposed to verbal), (3) frightening (as opposed to annoying), or (4) focused solely on the recipient; (5) a high-status or powerful perpetrator; and (6) restricted possibilities for escape. In addition, Pryor and Whalen (see Chapter 8) have found that women who experience multiple *types* of harassment have worse outcomes than those who do not.

If subjectively rated severity and perceptions of outcomes are taken as criteria, three of these predictors have so far received empirical support. In addition to Pryor's findings concerning multiple types of harassment, greater frequency of harassment has been linked to perceptions of severity and worse outcomes (Brooks & Perot, 1991; Fitzgerald & Shullman, 1993; Gutek & Koss, 1993; Schneider & Swan, 1994; Terpstra & Cook, 1985), and harassment from a supervisor tends to be perceived by victims as more severe than harassment from a peer (Gruber & Bjorn, 1986; Loy & Stewart, 1984; Pryor, 1994; Terpstra & Cook, 1985). On a related note, Merit Systems (1981) found that 56% of women harassed by a supervisor thought that various work conditions would worsen if they did not comply, as

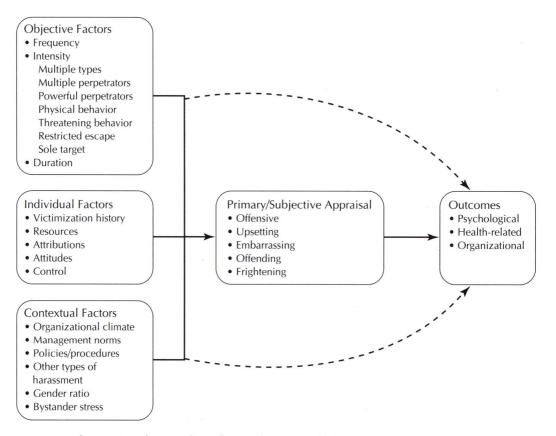

**Figure 2-2.** Elements that influence the appraisal of sex-related behavior at work

compared to 30% of those harassed by a coworker.

With respect to frightening versus annoying behavior, Gruber, Smith, and Kaupinnen-Toropainen's (in press) study of the perceived severity of different types of harassment found that sexual assault and coercion were rated by victims as the most upsetting, generally followed by "physical" types of harassment (e.g., unwanted touching, standing close) and unwanted sexual attention (e.g., advances, date requests, and sexual discussions), with offensive jokes, pornography, and staring receiving the least severe ratings.

Little is formally known concerning the impact of multiple perpetrators, harassment of an individual as opposed to a group, or restricted possibilities for escape, although the relationship between such factors and severity of appraisal and outcomes is intuitively reasonable and documented in a variety of court cases. Information is also lacking concerning how these and other stimulus variables might combine and interact to affect recipients' perceptions and outcomes. Finally, it is presently unknown whether some factors may overdetermine others or be more salient in certain situations than others; for example, can frequency and duration of "minor" incidents (e.g., pornography, sexual comments, and gestures) combine with multiple perpetrators to produce effects equivalent to those typically seen in more "severe" incidents (e.g., forceful sexual imposition)? Although formal data are lacking on this point, we would not be surprised if this were to turn out to be the case.

The first author has participated in several legal proceedings in which such a combination of factors combined to produce serious depression in plaintiffs with no previous history of psychological problems. We address this issue in some detail in the following section.

## Contextual Factors

As sexual harassment research has developed from its somewhat simplistic beginnings as a series of atheoretical prevalence studies, the importance of contextual factors has become increasingly clear. Two complementary theoretical models have appeared (Fitzgerald, Hulin, & Drasgow, 1992, 1995; Pryor, 1993) and been tested (Gelfand & Drasgow, 1994; Fitzgerald et al., in preparation; Pryor, LaVite, & Stoller, 1993; cf. McInnis & Fitzgerald, under review) that reliably link organizational tolerance and permissive management norms to higher levels of sexual harassment.

Organizational tolerance of sexual harassment is a construct identified by Hulin and his colleagues (Hulin, 1993; Hulin, Fitzgerald, & Drasgow, in press; Zickar, 1994); based on Naylor, Pritchard, and Ilgen's (1980) theory of organizational climate as shared perceptions of behavioral contingencies (i.e., rewards and punishment), they specified three characteristics of organizations that are tolerant of the existence of sexual harassment: *refusal to take complaints seriously*, *risk to the victim* for reporting, and *lack of meaningful sanctions* for the perpetrator. In an ongoing series of studies this research group has shown that organizational tolerance—as measured by the perceptions of the victims' coworkers—is reliably linked to higher levels of sexual harassment.

Our concern here is not with prevalence, however, but with seriousness and valence and the factors that predict them. Data from the same studies indicate that victims in work groups in which tolerance is greater show more serious outcomes, including depression, anxiety, and symptoms of Post-Traumatic Stress Disorder (Gelfand & Drasgow, 1994). Results from a conceptually similar study (Culbertson, Rodgers, & Rosenfeld, 1994)

indicate that the negative effects of organizational tolerance (i.e., climate) may exceed those of sexual harassment itself. Thus, it is reasonable to argue that harassing behaviors that take place in an organization tolerant of sexual harassment will be perceived as more serious and have more negative outcomes than those same behaviors occurring in a context in which there exists more support for targets and more sanctions for perpetrators.

Pryor's research supports this assertion, demonstrating that men are more likely to sexually harass women when management is perceived as tolerating or condoning such behavior (Pryor, LaVite, & Stoller, 1993). Pryor and Whalen (Chapter 8) argue that when harassment goes unpunished, a social norm is established, that is, a shared expectation among the workers that such behavior is appropriate and socially acceptable. Thus, management norms that exemplify a social context in which such behavior is acceptable should be associated with higher levels of sexual harassment and more negative outcomes for victims. Whether such norms contribute independently to a victim's perceptions of harassing behavior as offensive, distressing, humiliating, or frightening has yet to be tested empirically, although it seems a reasonable supposition and is thus included in Figure 2-2.

Closely related to the concepts of organizational tolerance and lenient management norms are weak or ineffective policies and procedures, as well as Salisbury and Sebek's (1994) contention that sexual harassment is more serious in organizational environments where other types of harassment (e.g., racial harassment, harassment due to sexual orientation, general hazing) are also present. It may be that these particular contextual factors exert their influence by their contribution to the objective factors of frequency and duration. Contextual factors more likely to account for independent variance, particularly in individual appraisal, are the gender context of the job and "bystander stress."

*Bystander stress* is a variable identified by Schneider (1995) that refers to the discomfort, apprehension, and distress felt by individuals who work in a harassing environment but themselves have thus far not been targeted for harassment. Examples include watching or hearing about female coworkers being harassed, feeling apprehensive about one's own situation, and being asked to provide information or "choose sides" in a work group after a complaint has been made. Schneider (1995) recently provided initial confirmation that bystander stress contributes variance to psychological outcomes over and above that accounted for by sexual harassment itself.

## Individual Factors

Examining individual factors shifts the lens of attention from the actual behaviors and the context in which they occur to the individual woman who is their target. Typically, such a focus implies that certain personal characteristics (e.g., financial vulnerability, previous victimization) may moderate the impact of sexual harassment, leading to more or less severe outcomes than would otherwise be the case; Fitzgerald, Hulin, and Drasgow (1995) refer to this concept as *victim vulnerability*. In the present case, we conceptualize such individual differences as independent contributors to the psychological appraisal of a particular event as stressful, while at the same time acknowledging that they bear direct links to outcomes.

What individual factors might contribute to the appraisal of an event as stressful, upsetting, or the like? Very little research has been conducted on this topic with actual victims, although analog studies abound (see Koss et al., 1994, for a recent review). Figure 2-2 suggests five areas in which pre-existing differences among women may influence perceived severity and outcomes: *victimization history, personal resources, attributions, attitudes*, and *control*. Of these, we expect victimization history to be among the most critical.

Considerable research has demonstrated that previous victimization increases the risk for subsequent abuse, although the process of re-victimization is not currently well understood; Dansky and Kilpatrick (Chapter 9) present data suggesting that previous sexual victimization may be a risk factor for some types of sexual harassment (cf. Frazier & Cohen, 1992; Salisbury et al., 1986). And it is reasonable to suppose that—as with rape, battering, and sexual abuse—the effects of such multiple victimization are likely to be more serious (Kilpatrick et al., 1987; Koss et al., 1994; Sorenson & Golding, 1990). Whether such previous victimization also affects cognitive evaluation of the harassing situation is a question that has yet to be evaluated empirically, but it is reasonable to expect that this will be the case. For example, Holgate (1989) and Junger (1987) have shown that harassment elevates women's fears of rape, as well as of crime more generally, and it well may be that the reverse is also true. This point was intuitively understood by the judge in *Ellison v. Brady*, who noted that "because women are disproportionately the victims of rape and sexual assault, women have stronger incentive to be concerned with sexual behavior…[and may perceive] the underlying threat of violence that men do not" (*Ellison v. Brady*, pp. 878–879).

Of the other four individual factors identified in Figure 2-2, *personal resources* is the most intuitively reasonable candidate for influencing both direct outcomes and perceptions of risk and stress. Women who are economically vulnerable, who are important sources of monetary support for their families, who have career goals that are particularly vulnerable to being disrupted (e.g., graduate students, untenured professors), or who are at-will employees have, in a very real and tangible sense, more at stake than women who are more securely situated, and they may well perceive harassment as more threatening. All things being equal, women with more personal, social, economic, and organizational power should be less likely to evaluate any particular event as stressful, although much depends on the nature of the event itself and the context in which it occurs.

Other individual factors that are likely to prove important are the woman's *attributions* about the event and, in particular, the *degree of control* she feels able to exert over the situation. Finally, considerable data exist suggesting that attitude and belief sets may influence victim appraisal in important ways. For example, Brooks and Perot (1991) found that victims' feminist ideology was a predictor of the perceived offensiveness of harassing behaviors, with women who identified more strongly as feminist generally finding harassment to be more offensive. Others have also found that feminists are more likely to have negative attitudes about harassment and to label harassing experiences as sexual harassment (Pryor & Day, 1988; Schneider, 1982); whether such influences also extend to other sorts of appraisals (e.g., the degree to which the behavior is upsetting, humiliating, or frightening) is currently unknown.

## The Psychological Experience and Severity of Harassment: Integration and Conclusion

To illustrate our principal thesis, that severity does not inhere solely or even primarily in the stimulus situation, consider the following two sets of circumstances, each based on an actual incident, suitably disguised. Victim A works as a waitress in a popular restaurant where the manager and other male employees routinely engage in the crudest type of sexual commentary concerning the waitresses, the female bussers, and the customers. This occurs virtually every day, all day, and has since the beginning of A's employment. A, who was raped as a young girl, was horrified to learn that the manager had recently forced one of the other waitresses to have oral sex. Although several women have complained to the owner about the behavior of the male employees, he seems unconcerned, saying, "There are always two sides to every story." The restaurant has no sexual harassment policy. Victim A, who is the sole support of her two daughters and has no salable skills besides waitressing, has no option but to remain employed. At the time she was assessed, she was seriously depressed and had suffered a recurrence of the nightmares

and flashbacks that followed her previous victimization.

In contrast, Victim B was employed as a secretary in a high-technology software firm. The firm, which had a well-developed human resources program, had an extensive sexual harassment policy and offered periodic training; the president made many public statements to the effect that harassment would not be tolerated, and the few problems that arose were dealt with immediately, usually informally, and effectively. B was thus caught off guard one night when, working late to finish a proposal, her new supervisor followed her into the women's restroom, turned out the light, locked the door, and attempted to have sex with her. Terrified, she managed to evade him, ran out of the building, and drove home; despite several frantic phone calls from her assailant protesting that he "didn't mean anything" and had thought she was interested in him, she filed a formal complaint with the director of human resources the following morning. After a brief investigation the manager was summarily fired; the company apologized to B, offered her time off with pay, and offered to pay for counseling. At the time of her assessment, B, who had never previously been victimized, was experiencing anxiety and mild phobic reactions to public restrooms. She was diagnosed with Adjustment Disorder, from which she subsequently recovered rapidly and fully.

These two sets of circumstances illuminate the perils of locating severity determinations solely in the stimulus situation, as well as the advantages of a more multidimensional, psychological approach. Victim A experienced frequent verbal (not physical) harassment for an extended period of time from a variety of coworkers as well as her manager (multiple perpetrators, powerful perpetrator). A former rape victim (previous victimization), she was embarrassed, offended, humiliated, and frightened, particularly when she heard rumors of her coworker's assault (bystander stress). Given the owner's attitude and refusal to take action (organizational tolerance, lenient management norms), the lack of policies and procedures to provide avenues for relief, and because she had few resources or options, it is not surprising that she developed extremely serious reactions, even though she personally experienced only verbal commentary (albeit ongoing and extremely crude).

Victim B, on the other hand, experienced what is, by anyone's account, a very severe episode. It was personal, physical, threatening, and perpetrated by a physically and organizationally powerful other—it was, in fact, attempted rape. Nevertheless, given her ability to escape, the immediate and supportive organizational response, and her lack of previous victimization history, Victim B survived her experience with relatively minimal psychological consequences.

We discuss these issues at some length to emphasize our contention that the issue of severity or seriousness is much more complex than is generally recognized. Attempts to develop purely "objective" definitions of severity based on cumulated ratings of research participants or even harassment victims, *absent any attention to context, vulnerability, or outcome* are not only oversimplified but misleading, and may be vulnerable to misinterpretation when used, as they invariably will be, in court. It is in this area, possibly more than in any other, that psychology should take its cue from the law, which rightly insists on taking into account the "totality of the circumstances" (*Meritor Savings Bank v. Vinson*, 1986).

We have provided an extensive discussion of the various stimulus, individual, and contextual factors that influence the psychological experience of sexual harassment, including the appraisal of any particular experience as distressing. Some of these factors (e.g., frequency, intensity, duration, organizational tolerance) are recognized as having direct importance to legal definitions and determinations, whereas the role of other, primarily individual elements is currently less relevant to that domain. Ironically, it may well be just those factors that are ultimately judged to play the most important role in individual outcomes.

## EMERGING ISSUES

Our review of empirical definitions raises a host of related issues that deserve considerably more attention than we can devote to them here. For example, what does it mean that many offensive, even vicious, situations are not defined as harassing by the women who experience them? What implications does research on definitions, meaning, and valence have for informing legal judgments of severity? Finally, how do such frameworks apply to the sexual harassment of men? Or do they? Lacking the space for the in-depth analysis such issues deserve, we content ourselves with a brief examination of two of these emerging issues.

### Labeling: The Self-Definition of Sexual Harassment

The first of what we have labeled emerging issues may perhaps be better thought of as a perennial issue—that is, is it harassment if the woman herself doesn't label it as such? In many ways this question highlights once more the interplay of psychological and legal concepts, as an affirmative response to the query "Have you been sexually harassed?" has obvious legal implications; such an answer, however, is likely to follow *only* those sorts of experiences that are appraised by the individual as threatening and stressful *and* with which she does not cope by blaming herself or reattributing the behavior (e.g., "He didn't mean to upset me"). However, this sort of attribution is far from universally the case; many women acknowledge experiencing unwanted, stressful, and even frightening situations at work but resist labeling them as sexual harassment. And, indeed, it is true that the majority of women who are "counted" by surveys as having been sexually harassed do not label their experiences in this fashion.

Lees-Haley and his colleagues (1994) have suggested that, given this lack of self-labeling by women who endorse what researchers have identified as sexually harassing behaviors, much of what research has had to say may be misleading. Referring to the original SEQ study (Fitzgerald et al., 1988), they suggest that "whether these parameters were more in the minds of researchers rather than in the perception of subjects is unclear" (p. 38). Given that the SEQ items and the Till (1980) categories from which they came were directly derived from the experiences of self-defined victims, we don't believe that this is the case. Rather, there appear to be a variety of factors that influence such self-definition; and, although an experience must obviously be self-labeled as harassment at some point to merit legal attention, it is clear that it need not be so labeled to be experienced as stressful or offensive or to have negative consequences.

### Theoretical Factors Affecting Self-Definition

Societal, organizational, and individual explanations can be made for the profound discrepancies between labeling one's experiences as sexual harassment and objectively experiencing such behaviors. Societal influence is great: Not only are women socialized to accept "nonconsensual or even offensive sexual interactions as being nonremarkable" (Fitzgerald, 1991, p. 37), but predominant sexual norms give privilege to male initiation of heterosexual activity, leading to a normalization and ultimately legitimization of sexual exploitation of women at work (Giuffre & Williams, 1994). Sexual remarks and behaviors directed toward women, although unwelcome or offensive, are normalized and thus often not perceived as harassment. This state of affairs is expressed somewhat more colloquially by the rhetorical question "Does a fish know it's in water?"

Organizational influences on self-labeling are both direct and indirect. Not only can organizations fail to explicitly state that sexual harassment is an actionable, illegal offense (Giuffre & Williams, 1994), but, as we have seen, the climate within organizations can be quite tolerant of sexual harassment (Zickar, 1994). Complaints are often not taken seriously, let alone believed, and women who report sexual harassment risk being called troublemakers, whistleblowers, and worse;

many are retaliated against and subject themselves to serious career risks (Jensen & Gutek, 1982; Riger, 1991).

Finally, women may not label various experiences as sexual harassment for more personal reasons. There are undeniable psychological costs attached to identifying oneself as a victim, including loss of the sense of control over one's life as well as the stigma that frequently comes with being victimized (Koss, 1990). Additionally, it seems reasonable to suppose that a woman might not label her experiences as sexual harassment because, since the Senate confirmation hearings of Justice Thomas, the phrase has come to bear heavy legal and political baggage. The problem that only recently had no name has now become a highly publicized target for ultraconservative attacks on "political correctness," "victimism," and the like. It seems to us not surprising that many avoid using the label of sexual harassment, given the burden of excess meaning that it has acquired.

### Research on Self-Definition

A handful of studies have attempted to capture empirically the reasons why women frequently do not label offensive experiences as harassment. Largely, these can be grouped into two categories: those that deal with objective stimulus factors and those that primarily address individual differences. To begin with the former, the most common variable believed to predict whether a woman will label her experiences as sexual harassment is what is inevitably labeled the "severity" of the experience (Barak, Fisher, & Houston, 1992; Ellis, Barak, & Pinto, 1991; Fitzgerald et al., 1988; Giuffre & Williams, 1994; Stockdale & Vaux, 1993). What is generally meant by severity in this context is the *type* of harassment, with gender harassment being considered the least severe, unwanted sexual attention moderately severe, and sexual coercion the most severe. Although the more "severe" behaviors have indeed been reported to be those most frequently labeled (Barak, Fisher, & Houston, 1992; Ellis, Barak, & Pinto, 1991; Fitzgerald et al., 1988; for an exception see Stockdale &

Vaux, 1993), virtually all respondents who have experienced the "more severe" behaviors have also experienced the "less severe" behaviors. Sexual coercion virtually never exists in the absence of unwanted sexual attention, and unwanted sexual attention and gender harassment also typically co-occur. Because these studies do not separate out the effects of such multidimensional experiences, they are unable to distinguish the effects of any "pure" type of harassment. As we have previously suggested, a cleaner "objective" interpretation of severity would be frequency and duration; indeed, increased frequency has been found to predict the labeling of one's experiences as sexual harassment (Ellis, Barak, & Pinto, 1991; Fitzgerald et al., 1988).

Three additional objective factors thought to influence labeling are the status of the harasser (Ellis, Barak, & Pinto, 1991; Guiffre & Williams, 1994), race and sexual orientation of the harasser (Giuffre & Williams, 1994), and the age of the victim (Barak, Fisher, & Houston, 1992; Fitzgerald et al., 1988). When offensive behavior is perpetrated by a supervisor or someone of a different race or sexual orientation, it is more likely to be labeled as sexual harassment; similarly, age is negatively correlated with labeling— younger women are less likely to label their experiences as harassing.

Giuffre and Williams (1994) propose a convincing interpretation of this cluster of influences: They suggest that the recognition and labeling of experiences as harassing arises primarily from the violation of predominant norms of sexual interaction. That is, it is thought to be "normal" for a coworker or someone of the same race or sexual orientation to bring sexuality into the workplace, especially when targeted at a young, single woman. Because such experiences mimic the predominant pattern of male heterosexual initiation, they are less likely to be labeled as sexual harassment. Identical behaviors exhibited by a supervisor or someone of a different race or sexual orientation are considerably more likely to be labeled because they violate predominant sexuality norms. Giuffre and

Williams's analysis is, to date, the most thoughtful approach to this issue; given their extremely limited sample size, however, it is more heuristic than definitive.

Finally, certain individual difference factors have been posited to influence the prediction of labeling. These include personal attractiveness (Ellis, Barak, & Pinto, 1991), erotophobia, sexual inexperience, repressing defensive style, and need for social approval (Barak, Fisher, & Houston, 1992), as well as normative beliefs about sexual harassment. Of these, the only significant predictor of labeling has been normative beliefs (Ellis, Barak, & Pinto, 1991; Magley, 1995). Specifically, those women who consider sexual harassment to be a serious issue are more likely to label their experiences as sexual harassment.

### The Significance and Effects of Labeling

Two studies have been conducted that assess the impact of labeling on outcomes. The results of both studies indicate that women who label their experiences as harassment do not experience different outcomes from women who do not label. The first study, conducted by Dansky and Kilpatrick, appears in Chapter 9 of this volume. The first formal examination of sexual harassment, depression, and PTSD, this study involved telephone interviews of over 3,000 women. The respondents were classified into four groups: (1) those not harassed; (2) those who experienced harassing behaviors but did not label them as such; (3) those who were harassed and labeled their experiences as harassment; and (4) those who experienced the behaviors, labeled them, and reported significant job impact. They found that overall levels of PTSD and depression differed significantly among these four groups, with at least slight monotonic increases in PTSD symptoms across the groups and increases in depression from Group 1 to Group 2 and from Group 3 to Group 4. Thus, symptoms of PTSD differed depending on whether the woman labeled her experience as sexual harassment; depression, however, was affected by labeling only when the harassment was perceived to affect the woman's job.

The second study was conducted by Magley (1995) based on a sample of 459 women from a public utility. The women were classified into categories identical to Dansky and Kilpatrick's first three groups, based on their responses to the SEQ and the criterion item "Have you been sexually harassed?" Effects of labeling on symptoms of PTSD and work-withdrawal (e.g., tardiness, absenteeism, etc.) paralleled those found by Dansky and Kilpatrick; women who experienced sexual harassment but did not label it as such had worse outcomes than women who were not harassed, but better outcomes than women who did label their experiences.

Once again, the effects of labeling were not uniform, however; for most outcome variables, both psychological and work-related, women who experienced sexually harassing behaviors experienced more negative outcomes *regardless* of whether or not they labeled the experience. If one considers only the three comparable groups in the Dansky and Kilpatrick study, this result appears to parallel their depression results. Thus, certain outcomes do not appear to be affected by the labeling process.

One final effect found in the Magley (1995) sample can be interpreted from an attribution framework (C. Mazurek, personal communication, 1995). Women who experienced sexually harassing behaviors without labeling them reported lower levels of satisfaction with their work in general than either women who were not harassed or women who labeled their experiences as sexual harassment. It may be that women who label such experiences then attribute their distress to the harasser; those who do not, attribute it to their work.

## Conclusions

As this brief review suggests, the phenomenon of labeling, or self-definition of sexual harassment, raises a variety of interesting issues. From our perspective, the main implications of this much discussed but relatively unresearched process are clearly psychological, rather than legal, as it seems obvious that

experiences not labeled as harassment will not find their way into the courts. The psychological implications may turn out to be substantial, however, if further research confirms that labeling influences outcomes over and above those attributable to the experience itself (e.g., Dansky & Kilpatrick, Chapter 9; Magley, 1995). In this situation it may be that labeling serves as a proxy variable for indicators of severity not yet detectable by our present crude measures.

On the other hand, it is already clear that such influences are not uniform, and it may be that, in some instances, labeling may serve a protective function, as suggested by our attributional explanation of the work satisfaction results in the Magley (1995) study. In other words, the process of labeling behaviors as sexual harassment may reflect a process of attributing causality to the harasser rather than oneself, in other words, a rejection of self-blame. More research on this topic is clearly needed.

## The Sexual Harassment of Men?

Finally, questions of definition and valence cast light on the current debate concerning the sexual harassment of men, an area in which very little serious conceptual work has been done. Although sexual harassment is widely agreed to be mainly a woman's problem, it has become commonplace for researchers to include men in samples and surveys, following Merit System's (1981) conclusion that 17% of men in the federal workforce had been sexually harassed. The idea that the harassment of men is more than an isolated event has gained currency with some researchers (e.g., Vaux, 1993) and caught the public imagination with the publication of Michael Crighton's novel *Disclosure* (1993), which depicts a hapless male employee at the mercy of a sexually predatory female executive.

Although it is of course quite possible for men to be sexually harassed, by women as well as by other men, we believe it is unlikely that our knowledge of this phenomenon will be enhanced by the practice of administering identical surveys to male students or employees, absent any contextual analysis or attempt to understand the *meaning* the items have for these male respondents. At the most basic level, this issue has to do with item interpretation; for example, what does it mean when a male employee endorses an item on the SEQ indicating that he has frequently been in a situation in which his coworkers or supervisor told offensive stories and jokes? After all, the overwhelming majority of sexual humor involves derogatory, crude, and vulgar remarks about *women*; it is unclear that such humor is harassing to the average man, however offensive he may find it. An analogy can be made here to a white individual who is offended by racist jokes or remarks directed at blacks or other racial or ethnic minority individuals, or a heterosexual man who is offended by homophobic humor. Although one may be offended and even outraged, it is doubtful whether it is possible to be harassed by comments directed at a group of which one is not a member.

Even when men are the direct recipients of unwanted sexual attention from women in the workplace—and there is no reason to believe that this is not sometimes the case—what are the meaning and valence of such experiences? Although it is certainly possible for such experiences to be uncomfortable and even offensive, it is clear that this is generally not the case (Gutek, 1985).

The most thorough analysis of this issue has been provided by Berdahl, Magley, and Waldo (1994, under review), who found that men report being considerably less threatened or offended by behaviors that women find harassing. This should not be surprising when one considers that sexual attention directed toward a man by a woman—even when unwanted—generally does not carry the same meaning as the reverse, given women's lesser organizational, social, and physical power. These researchers argued that the experiences men themselves find harassing may be qualitatively quite different. Their content analysis of responses from men employed at a large regulated utility indicated that, although the three basic categories were the same as those previously specified (i.e., they fit the tripartite

model portrayed in Figure 2-1), the actual behaviors identified as harassing differed in important ways. In particular, these men reported two male-specific forms of gender harassment: negative stereotyping of men and reinforcement of the male role.

Negative stereotyping of men involves comments from women that stigmatize men as a group, for example, "All men are pigs" or "Men have only one thing on their minds." Reinforcement of the male role, on the other hand, is behavior typically perpetrated by other men, for example, the expectation that a man will accept and participate in jokes and comments about women, and questioning his masculinity by calling him a "pussy" or a "fag" if he doesn't. Another poignant example was offered by a participant in the Berdahl, Magley, and Waldo study (1994, under review):

> I feel that men—not just women, can sexually harass other men.... I decided that I would take three weeks off to help my wife get adjusted to having a baby and a 19 month old. The people in my department just couldn't understand why I'd need to take that much time off—I wasn't the one who had given birth. Comments were made and my work wasn't being covered so I ended up only taking a week and two days off. It made me feel like I wasn't a "man" if I choose to stay home and take care of the kids. This same attitude manifests when I ask to take time off so I can take the kids to the doctor; after all my wife works outside the home as well and we try to share these types of chores equally.

Berdahl, Magley, and Waldo (1994, under review) suggest that, for both men and women, situations that are experienced as sexually harassing are those that signify a perceived loss of control and security in the workplace—a suggestion that parallels our psychological definition of harassment as a situation that is perceived as threatening one's well-being. They suggest, however, that the actual behaviors involved may differ for men and women, at least in part. They propose that behaviors experienced by men as sexually harassing are likely to stem from negotiations of gender (Ginsburg & Tsing, 1990) that represent challenges to current constructions of masculinity. Thus, a man who doesn't join in harassing women may be labeled a "queer," and those who want parental leave are "henpecked," "wimps," or worse. Although such experiences are somewhat far afield from current legal constructions of sexual harassment, we suggest that they are probably considerably closer to what is meant *psychologically* by the construct (and closer to the experiential reality of many women) than survey results suggesting that thus-and-such a percentage of men have been sexually harassed. It seems to us that any meaningful analysis of this issue must begin to take such factors into account.

## CONCLUSION

Our chapter has attempted an in-depth analysis of empirical definitions of sexual harassment from legal, behavioral, and psychological perspectives. Throughout the presentation we have emphasized three themes. First, it is our contention that the meaningful psychological study of sexual harassment cannot be confined solely to legal parameters because, at the level of the individual, it is a primarily *psychological* experience best understood from a cognitively grounded stress (and coping) model rather than from a strictly legal framework. We complement this assertion, however, by a second: Because of the immense potential for research to inform judicial decision making in this area, it is important to think carefully about the interface between psychological and legal frameworks, taking care to articulate where they overlap, where they diverge, and the implications that each holds for the other. Finally, we return yet again to the complexity of this topic and the need to guard against simplistic and decontextualized formulations that do justice to neither a psychological nor a jurisprudential model. The women who confront these experiences on a day-to-day basis deserve no less.

## REFERENCES

Arvey, R. D., & Cavanaugh, M. A. (in press). Using surveys to assess the prevalence of sexual harassment: Some methodological problems. *Journal of Social Issues.*

Barak, A., Fisher, W.A., & Houston, S. (1992). Individual difference correlates of the experience of sexual harassment among female university students. *Journal of Applied Social Psychology, 22*, 17–37.

*Barnes v. Costle* (1977). 561 F.2d 983, 15 FEP Cases 345 (D.C.Cir.).

*Barnes v. Train* (1974). 13 FEP Cases 123 (D.D.C.).

Berdahl, J. L., Magley, V. J., & Waldo, C. R. (under review). The sexual harassment of men? A concept in search of definition.

Brooks, L., & Perot, A. R. (1991). Reporting sexual harassment: Exploring a predictive model. *Psychology of Women Quarterly, 15*, 31–47.

*Carr v. Allison Gas Turbine Division, General Motors Corporation* (1994). 32 F.3d 1007.

Carver, C. S., Scheier, M. F., & Weintraub, J. K. (1989). Assessing coping strategies: A theoretically based approach. *Journal of Personality and Social Psychology, 36*, 267–283.

*Corne v. Bausch & Lomb* (1975). 390 F. Supp. 161, 10 FEP Cases 289 (D. Ariz.).

Culbertson, A. L., Rodgers, W., & Rosenfeld, P. (1994, August). Organizational change—the case of sexual harassment. Paper presented at the Annual Meeting of the American Psychological Association, Los Angeles.

EEOC (1980, April). "Title 29–Labor, Chapter XIV–Part 1604–Guidelines on Discrimination Because of Sex under Title VII of the Civil Rights Act, as Amended Adoption of Interim Interpretive Guideline," Washington, DC: U.S. Government Printing Office.

Ellis, S., Barak, A., & Pinto, A. (1991). Moderating effects of personal cognitions on experienced and perceived sexual harassment of women at the workplace. *Journal of Applied Social Psychology, 21*, 1320–1337.

*Ellison v. Brady* (1991). 55 FEP Cases 111 (9th Cir.).

Fitzgerald, L. F. (1990). Sexual harassment: The definition and measurement of a construct. In M. Paludi (Ed.), *Ivory power: Sexual harassment on campus* (pp. 21–44). Albany, NY: SUNY Press.

Fitzgerald, L. F. (1992). *Breaking silence: The sexual harassment of women in academia and the workplace.* Washington, DC: Federation of Cognitive, Psychological, and Behavioral Sciences.

Fitzgerald, L. F., Gelfand, M. J., & Drasgow, F. (in press). Measuring sexual harassment: Theoretical and psychometric advances. *Basic and Applied Psychology.*

Fitzgerald, L. F., & Hesson-McInnis, M. (1989). The dimensions of sexual harassment: A structural analysis. *Journal of Vocational Behavior, 35*, 309–326.

Fitzgerald, L. F., Hulin, C. L., & Drasgow, F. (1995). The antecedents and consequences of sexual harassment in organizations: An integrated model. In G. P. Keita & J. J. Hurrell, Jr. (Eds.), *Job stress in a changing workforce: Investigating gender, diversity, and family issues* (pp. 55–73). Washington, DC: American Psychological Association.

Fitzgerald, L. F., Hulin, C. L., Drasgow, F., Gelfand, M. J., & Magley, V. J. (in preparation). The antecedents and consequences of sexual harassment: A test of an integrated model.

Fitzgerald, L. F., & Ormerod, A. J. (1991). Perceptions of sexual harassment: The influence of gender and context. *Psychology of Women Quarterly, 15*, 281–294.

Fitzgerald, L. F., & Shullman, S. L. (1993). Sexual harassment: A research analysis and agenda for the 1990's. *Journal of Vocational Behavior, 42*, 5–27.

Fitzgerald, L. F., Shullman, S. L., Bailey, N., Richards, M., Swecker, J., Gold, Y., Ormerod, M., & Weitzman, L. (1988). The incidence and dimensions of sexual harassment in academia and the workplace. *Journal of Vocational Behavior, 32*, 152–175.

Fitzgerald, L. F., Swan, S., & Fisher, K. (in press). Why didn't she just report him?: The psychological and legal implications of women's strategies for responding to sexual harassment. *Journal of Social Issues.*

Frazier, P. A., & Cohen, B. B. (1992). Research on the sexual victimization of women: Implications for counselor training. *The Counseling Psychologist, 20*, 141–158.

Gelfand, M. J., Fitzgerald, L. F., & Drasgow, F. (in press). Theory and measurement of sexual harassment: A confirmatory analysis across cultures and settings. *Journal of Vocational Behavior.*

Gelfand, M. J., & Drasgow, F. (1994, April). Antecedents and consequences of sexual harassment in organizations: A test of an integrated model. Paper presented at the Ninth Annual Conference for Industrial Organizational Psychology, Nashville, TN.

Ginsburg, F. & Tsing, A. L. (1990). *Uncertain terms: Negotiating gender in American culture.* Boston: Beacon Press.

Giuffre, P. A., & Williams, C. L. (1994). Boundary lines: Labeling sexual harassment in restaurants. *Gender and Society, 8*, 378–401.

Gruber, J. E. (1990). Methodological problems and policy implications in sexual harassment research. *Population Research and Policy Review, 9*, 235–254.

Gruber, J. E. (1992). A typology of personal and environmental sexual harassment: Research and policy implications for the 1990s. *Sex Roles, 26*, 447–464.

Gruber, J. E., & Bjorn, L. (1986). Women's responses to sexual harassment: An analysis of sociocultural, organizational, and personal resource models. *Social Science Quarterly, 67*, 814–826.

Gruber, J. E., Smith, M. D., & Kauppinen-Toropainen, K. (in press). An exploration of sexual harassment experiences and severity: Results from North America and Europe. In M. Stockdale & B. Gutek (Eds.), *Women and Work, 6.*

Gutek, B. A. (1985). *Sex and the workplace.* San Francisco: Jossey-Bass.

Gutek, B., & Koss, M. P. (1993). Changed women and changed organizations: Consequences of and coping with sexual harassment. *Journal of Vocational Behavior, 42*, 28–48.

Gutek, B., & Morasch, B. (1982). Sex ratios, sex role spillover, and sexual harassment of women at work. *Journal of Social Issues, 38*, 55–74.

Gutek, B., Morasch, B., & Cohen, A. (1983). Interpreting social-sexual behavior in a work setting. *Journal of Vocational Behavior, 22*, 30–48.

*Hall v. Gus Construction Co.* (1988). 842 F.2d 1010, 46 FEP Cases 573 (8th Cir.).

*Harris v. Forklift Systems, Inc.* (1993). 114 S. Ct. 367.

*Henson v. City of Dundee* (1982). 682 F.2d 897, 29 FEP Cases 787 (11th Cir.).

Holgate, A. (1989). Sexual harassment as a determinant of women's fear of rape. *Australian Journal of Sex, Marriage, and the Family, 10*, 21–28.

Hulin, C. L. (1993, May). A framework for the study of sexual harassment in organizations: Climate, stressors, and patterned responses. Paper presented at the Annual Meeting of the Society for Industrial and Organizational Psychology, San Francisco.

Hulin, C. L., Fitzgerald, L. F., & Drasgow, F. (in press). Organizational influences on sexual harassment. In M. Stockdale & B. Gutek (Eds.), *Women and Work, 6.*

Jensen, I., & Gutek, B. A. (1982). Attributions and assignment of responsibility for sexual harassment. *Journal of Social Issues, 38*, 121–136.

Junger, M. (1987). Women's experiences of sexual harassment. *British Journal of Criminology, 27*, 358–383.

Kenig, S., & Ryan, J. (1986). Sex differences in levels of tolerance and attributions of blame for sexual harassment on a university campus. *Sex Roles, 15*, 535–549.

Kilpatrick, D. G., Saunders, B. E., Veronen, J. L., Best, C. L., & Von, J. M. (1987). Criminal victimization: Lifetime prevalence, reporting to police, and psychological impact. *Crime and Delinquency, 33*, 479–489.

Koss, M. P. (1990). Changed lives: The psychological impact of sexual harassment. In M. Paludi (Ed.), *Ivory power: Sexual harassment in academia and the workplace* (pp. 73–92). Albany, NY: SUNY Press.

Koss, M. P., Goodman, L. A., Browne, A., Fitzgerald, L. F., Keita, G. P., & Russo, N. F. (1994). *No safe haven: Male violence against women at home, at work, and in the community.* Washington DC: American Psychological Association.

Lazarus, R. S., & Folkman, S. (1984). *Stress, appraisal, and coping.* New York: Springer.

Lees-Haley, P. R., Lees-Haley, C. E., Price, J. R., & Williams, C. W. (1994). A sexual harassment–emotional distress rating scale. *American Journal of Forensic Psychology, 12*, 39–54.

Lindemann, B., & Kadue, D. D. (1992). *Sexual harassment in employment law.* Washington, DC: Bureau of National Affairs Books.

Loy, P. H., & Stewart, L. P. (1984). The extent and effects of sexual harassment of working women. *Sociological Focus, 17*, 31–43.

MacKinnon, C. (1979). *Sexual harassment of working women: A case of sex discrimination.* New Haven, CT: Yale University Press.

Magley, V. J. (1995, March). Labeling sexually harassing behaviors as sexual harassment. Paper presented at a symposium on Emerging Issues in Sexual Harassment Research at the Annual Conference of the Association for Women in Psychology, Indianapolis, IN.

Maypole, D. E., & Skaine, R. (1983). Sexual harassment in the workplace. *Social Work, 28*, 385–390.

Mazer, D. B., & Percival, E. G. (1989). Ideology or experience: The relationships among perceptions, attitudes and experiences of sexual harassment in university students. *Sex Roles, 20*, 135–170.

McInnis, M., & Fitzgerald, L. F. (under review). Modeling sexual harassment: Antecedents and outcomes.

*Meritor Savings Bank v. Vinson* (1986). 477 U.S. 57, 40 FEP Cases 1822.

*Miller v. Bank of America* (1976). 418 F. Supp. 233, 13 FEP Cases 439 (N.D. Cal.).

Morrow, et al. (1995).

Naylor, J. C., Pritchard, R. D., & Ilgen, D. R. (1980). *A theory of behavior in organizations.* New York: Academic Press.

Note (1978). Sexual harassment and Title VII: The foundation for the elimination of sexual cooperation as an employment condition, *76 Michigan Law Review*, 1007–1100.

*Phillips v. Martin Marietta Corporation* (1971). 400 U.S. 542, 3 FEP Cases 40.

Pryor, J. B. (1994, August). *The phenomenology of sexual harassment.* Paper presented at the Meeting for the American Psychological Association, Los Angeles.

Pryor, J. B., & Day, J. D. (1988). Interpretations of sexual harassment: An attributional analysis. *Sex Roles, 18*, 405–417.

Pryor, J. B., LaVite, C. M. & Stoller, L. M. (1993). A social psychological analysis of sexual harassment: The person/situation. *Journal of Vocational Behavior, 42*, 68–83.

Pryor, J. B., LaVite, C. M., & Stoller, L. M. (1993). A social psychological analysis of sexual harassment:

The person/situation. *Journal of Vocational Behavior, 42*, 68–83.

Reilly, M. E., Caldwell, D., & DeLuca, L. (1992). Tolerance for sexual harassment related to self-reported sexual victimization. *Gender and Society, 6*, 122–138.

Riger, S. (1991). Gender dilemmas in sexual harassment policies and procedures. *American Psychologist, 46*, 497–507.

Riggs, R. O., Murrell, P. H. & Cutting, J. C. (1993). *Sexual harassment in higher education: From conflict to community* (ASHE-ERIC Higher Education Report No. 2). Washington, D.C.: The George Washington University School of Education and Human Development.

*Robinson v. Jacksonville Shipyards* (1991). 760 F. Supp. 1486 (M.D. Fla.).

Salisbury, J., Ginorio, A. B., Remick, H., & Stringer, D. M. (1986). Counseling victims of sexual harassment. *Psychotherapy, 23*, 316–324.

Salisbury, J., & Sebek, M. (1994). Unpublished materials. (Available from the author at Salisbury Consulting, Boise, ID).

Schneider, B. E. (1982). Consciousness about sexual harassment among heterosexual and lesbian women workers. *Journal of Social Issues, 39*, 63–81.

Schneider, K. (1995, March). The development of a sexual harassment bystander stress scale. Paper presented at the Annual Meeting of the Association for Women in Psychology, Indianapolis, IN.

Schneider, K., & Swan, S. (1994, April). Job-related, psychological and health-related outcomes of sexual harassment. Paper presented at the Ninth Annual Conference for Industrial Organizational Psychology, Nashville, TN.

Simon, R. I. (1995). *Forensic assessment of Post-Traumatic Stress Disorder.* Washington, DC: American Psychiatric Press.

Sorenson, S. B., & Golding, J. M. (1990). Depressive sequelae of recent criminal victimization. *Journal of Traumatic Stress, 3*, 337–350.

*Sprogis v. United Airlines* (1971). 444 F.2d 1194, 1198, 3 FEP Cases, 621, 623 (7th Circ.).

Stockdale, M. S., & Vaux, A. (1993). What sexual harassment experiences lead respondents to acknowledge being sexually harassed? A secondary analysis of a university survey. *Journal of Vocational Behavior, 43*, 221–234.

Swan, S. (in progress). So what? Why did it bother her? Factors affecting women's perceptions of the severity of sexual harassment experiences.

Terpstra, D. E., & Baker, D. D. (1991). Sexual harassment at work: The psychosocial issues. In M. J. Davidson & J. Earnshaw (Eds.), *Vulnerable workers:*

*Psychosocial and legal issues*. Chichester, England: Wiley.

Terpstra, D. E., & Cook, S. E. (1985). Complainant characteristics and reported behaviors and consequences associated with formal sexual harassment charges. *Personnel Psychology, 38*, 559–574.

Till, F. J. (1980). *Sexual harassment: A report on the sexual harassment of students*. Washington, DC: National Advisory Council on Women's Educational Program.

U.S. Merit Systems Protection Board (1981). *Sexual harassment of federal workers: Is it a problem?* Washington, DC: U.S. Government Printing Office.

U.S. Merit Systems Protection Board (1987). *Sexual harassment of federal workers: An update.* Washington, DC: U.S. Government Printing Office.

Vaux, A. (1993). Paradigmatic assumptions in sexual harassment research: Being guided without being misled. *Journal of Vocational Behavior, 42*, 116–132.

*Vinson v. Taylor* (1985). 753 F.2d 141, 36 FEP Cases 1423 (D.C. Cir.).

*Williams v. Saxbe* (1976). 413 F. Supp. 654, 12 FEP Cases 1093 (D.D.C.).

Zickar, M. J. (1994). Antecedents of sexual harassment. Paper presented at the Ninth Annual Conference for Industrial Organizational Psychology, Nashville, TN.

# CHAPTER 3

# NORMATIVE ISSUES IN DEFINING SEXUAL HARASSMENT

**Jaimie Leeser**
**William O'Donohue**

The construct "sexual harassment" has a valuative or normative dimension. More specifically, the word *harass* is defined (Oxford English Dictionary, 1982) as:

1. to wear out, tire out, or exhaust with fatigue, care or trouble
2. to harry, lay waste, devastate, plunder
3. to trouble or vex by repeated attacks
4. to trouble, worry, distress with annoying labour, care, perplexity, importunity, misfortune, etc.

It can be readily seen that these words contain a pejorative dimension: something "bad" is alluded to.

Another way the implicit valuative dimension of sexual harassment can be explicated is to examine the question "Is sexual harassment bad (in some way)?" We believe that this question is not open, but rather closed in the same way the question "Is a bachelor unmarried?" is closed. The question simply asks for an explication of part of the meaning of the word or phrase contained in the subject.

However, the type of wrongness contained in the phrase is not at all clear. There are many different kinds of wrongness. Something may be wrong because it is inconsistent with a law, with a rule of etiquette, with good physical health, or with morality. Here we shall argue that sexual harassment is a moral wrong.

Arriving at an acceptable conception or definition of sexual harassment is more difficult than arriving at acceptable conceptions of many other moral phenomena. Sexual harassment is still a relatively new construct, and thus far has been defined mostly by select groups needing to formulate laws or policies on sexual harassment for schools or places of employment. Thus, definitions vary widely, and disagreement may prevail about whether a given situation is an instance of sexual harassment.

As a result, there are many controversial cases and few agreed upon cases to use as a starting point for forging a conception of sexual harassment. In addition, Christensen (1994) has argued that "sexual harassment is an ill-conceived notion that should be discarded, since, given any group of alleged cases of sexual harassment, what the cases have in common (i.e., that they have *something* to do with sexuality) has *nothing* to do with what makes the *wrong* action in each case *problematic*" (p. 1). Perhaps such a charge should be taken into account when attempting to elucidate an adequate conception of sexual harassment. For example, should we say that the sexual element in an instance of sexual harassment is a central part of the normative infraction that takes place, or is the sexual element merely an accidental property that accompanies a non-sexual wrongdoing? One's answer to this question will significantly govern the way one goes about defining sexual harassment.

Thus far, we can acknowledge that a common starting point for forging a conception of sexual harassment is the agreement that a normative infraction has occurred in instances of harassment, that is, that "something wrong" has happened, and that degree of wrongness should be made apparent in an adequate definition. But what is it about sexual harassment that some makes it subject to our disapprobation while breaches of etiquette or unprofessional or immature behavior can be equally annoying and disagreeable but do not bear the same negative moral import? On what basis do we hold the sexual harasser more deserving of moral blame than one who simply lacks etiquette, and are we justified in doing so? To date, the nature of the wrongness of sexual harassment has not been adequately explicated in the literature, nor has the significance of the wrongness been adequately justified. However, arguments over how to define sexual harassment should focus on the nature and significance of its wrongness if for no other reason than that a finding of (or even the accusation of) sexual harassment subjects the perpetrator to our moral castigation, and such castigation should be clearly justified. An acceptable conception or definition of sexual harassment should thus capture its negative moral import and also distinguish it from other annoying, but amoral phenomena like breaches of etiquette. In addition, the nature of the wrongness of sexual harassment captured in an acceptable conception should be defensible by appeal to some larger moral principles on which there is a general consensus. Ethicists throughout history have attempted to identify and defend such moral principles, and so we will turn to these philosophers later in the chapter to see how ethical principles can be applied to judge the wrongness of sexual harassment.

Our purpose here is twofold. We intend throughout most of the chapter to evaluate three major conceptions of sexual harassment based on the nature of the wrongness they identify: sexual harassment as the oppression of women, as an abuse of power, and as a violation of privacy rights. While all three fall short as acceptable conceptions, for reasons we will see later, all of these conceptions identify important aspects of the wrongness of sexual harassment and help to move us closer to a more adequate conception of the wrongness of sexual harassment. Because each of the three conceptions examined agrees that some sort of moral infraction takes place in sexual harassment, our aim in evaluating them is to do the following: to see if the severity of the infraction identified is roughly proportional to the severity of our castigation of harassment, to ensure that the moral infraction occurs in cases that we intuitively identify as sexual harassment but not in cases that are intuitively not harassive, and to see whether the moral principle that is allegedly violated is one on which there is a general consensus and for which there is some justification for why it ought not to be violated.

In the final part of the chapter, we will examine moral principles from deontological ethics, which we take to be useful in the justification of the wrongness or disvalue[1] in sexual harassment. In doing so, we will sketch our own conception of sexual harassment, which we believe encompasses and justifies the negative moral import of sexual harassment more successfully than the rival conceptions discussed in the chapter.

## THE FEMINIST CONCEPTION OF SEXUAL HARASSMENT: OPPRESSION OF WOMEN

The danger in evaluating a feminist conception of sexual harassment stems from the fact that there is no *single* feminist conception of any phenomenon. Feminists have had a central role in the study of sexual harassment. Catherine MacKinnon, a well-known feminist, published one of the first scholarly books on sexual harassment (MacKinnon, 1979). The prominence of feminist opinions on the issue of sexual harassment forces us to select one feminist standard and hope that it represents at least a large percentage of feminists. In this section we will discuss Anita Superson's article "A Feminist Definition of Sexual Harassment" and evaluate it as representative of many feminists' views.

Superson (1993) puts forth the following as a definition of sexual harassment: "Any behavior (verbal or physical) caused by a person, A, in the dominant class directed at another, B, in the subjugated class, that expresses and perpetuates the attitude that B or members of B's sex is/are inferior because of their sex, thereby causing harm to either B and/or B's sex" (p. 46). Superson remarks that the main benefit of her definition is that it pinpoints "the group harm sexual harassment causes all women, thereby getting to the heart of what is wrong with sexual harassment" (p. 61). At first glance it is unclear how one person can cause harm to all women merely by expressing to one woman that she is inferior because of her sex. Superson posits such an extreme consequence of a single case of sexual harassment in the hope that the sexual harasser will warrant equally extreme censure. But is the expression or perpetuation of a person's inferiority because of her sex what we ought to identify as the disvalue of sexual harassment? Superson engages in a rather lengthy defense and explication of her con-

ception of sexual harassment and the nature of its wrongness, so we have summarized her main points as follows:

1. Sexual harassment, a form of sexism, is at its root the domination of men over women (p. 51).
2. When A sexually harasses B, the comment or behavior is really directed at all women, not a particular woman, because many derogatory behaviors are issued at women the harasser does not even know (p. 51).
3. Only men can sexually harass women, because when a woman engages in apparently "harassive" behavior, the social impact and underlying message implicit in male-to-female harassment are missing (p. 55).
4. Though a woman may consider a man to be a sex object, all the views about domination and being relegated to certain sex roles are absent. She cannot remind him that he is inferior because of his sex, since given the way things are in society, he is not (p. 55).
5. Women cannot harm men as a group for it is impossible to send the message that one dominates (and so cause group harm) if one does not dominate (p. 55).
6. What is decisive in determining whether behavior counts as sexual harassment is whether the behavior is an instance of a practice that expresses and perpetuates the attitude that the victim and members of her sex are inferior because of their sex (p. 58).
7. The harasser's intentions are also irrelevant in assessing harassment; rather, it is the attitudes embedded *in the practice* the behavior is an instance of, not the attitudes or intentions *of the perpetrator*, that make the behavior sexual harassment (p. 59).

That Superson maintains that women cannot harass men is particularly striking, and so with that claim we will begin our evaluation of her conception of sexual harassment. Although her reason for making such a claim (that women cannot dominate men and harm them as a group given the current social structure) may be correct, the claim itself immediately clashes with our intuitions. For example, imagine a 45-year-old female professor directing sexually bothersome behavior at a 22-year-old male graduate student. Let us assume that the graduate student is poor and desperately hoping to get an assistantship and the female professor has made an implicit threat that he must tolerate her unwanted behavior in order to receive the post. Let us also assume that she is a bodybuilder and he is very thin, small, and frequently ill. He is greatly disturbed by the professor's behavior, and she recognizes this fact and enjoys the power she has over young graduate students who are so financially strained that they will be forced to drop out of school if she does not recommend them for assistantships. We hypothesize that to most people such a situation would clearly appear to be one of sexual harassment; the woman is older and is physically, financially, and professionally superior to the man. He is distressed by the behavior and she intends to distress him. Superson, however, would have to maintain that this scenario is not an instance of sexual harassment because the professor's behavior cannot result in the harm or degradation of men *as a group*.

A denial of this scenario as an instance of sexual harassment reveals two striking but popular aspects of many feminist positions. First, since Superson claims that sexual harassment is about domination and abuse of power, and since our scenario obviously seems to involve domination and the abuse of power, we notice that Superson mistakenly sees the only "real" power as that which men (in general) have over women (in general). Superson does not provide a justification for such a strong claim; it is unlikely that any adequate justification for such a claim can be provided. Many factors determine power in relationships, including race, age, financial and professional status, physical strength, physical and mental health, intelligence, and so on. Our point can be further clarified if we were also to presuppose in our scenario that the female professor is white and the male student is black. Perhaps such a position would be more plausible if one were to claim that "all other things being equal" between a male and female coworker, the male would have a certain power over the woman due to the existing social structure. In short, we have no reason to think that the power one has in virtue of one's gender outweighs the power another has in any other area of life.

Second, Superson appears not to attach any moral censure to the treatment of one individual male as a sex object. If group harm and degradation to men resulted from the preceding scenario, Superson would find fault with the actions described and label them as sexually harassive. But in the existing social structure, in which Superson maintains that no such group harm to men can occur, she does not seem to recognize that women like the professor still deserve our moral reproach. Thus, whereas Superson sees the benefit of her definition as the identification of group harm as what is wrong with sexual harassment, we see it as an obvious shortcoming insofar as it implicitly devalues the worth of an individual person. While one may be correct and even justified in proclaiming that oppression and the abuse of social power are wrong, our moral intuitions tell us that, based on our scenario, there is still an element of wrongness present in sexual harassment for which one cannot fully account by appealing to the wrongness of an abuse of social power.

The belief that the power one holds on the basis of gender overrides other types of power also leads one to conflate sexual (erotic in nature) harassment and gender (or sexist) harassment. More specifically, Superson sees sexual harassment as a subset of gender harassment but uses the phrase "sexual harassment" to denote both sexual harassment and gender harassment. The assignment of sexual harassment as a subcategory of gender harassment is typically motivated by feminist assumptions about the patriarchal nature of society. For instance, we commonly hear from feminists that rape is primarily a crime of power and domination; the male rapist wants to assert his powerful superiority over the woman, and forced sex is a convenient means by which to reinforce a woman's social inferiority. Radical feminists like MacKinnon (1979) have argued that all heterosexual sex is rape in the context of the current social structure. A belief in such an extreme tainting of individual relationships by social inequality inevitably leads to the conflation of sexual harassment and gender harassment as one accepts that sexual interactions between men and women are manifestations or mini-dramas of their social inequality and male tendencies to sexualize power differentials.

The conflation of sexual harassment and gender harassment is also a common practice insofar as both are classified as sexual discrimination, and there is frequently an overlap between the two, as we often identify both types in a single instance of harassment. Thus, although we regularly see sexual behavior linked with sexist behavior, we run into problems when we conflate the two. The first obvious problem, and one that we have already mentioned, is that if sexual harassment is a form of gender harassment and gender harassment can only be committed by males and against females, then sexual harassment cannot occur between two individuals of the same sex, nor can it be committed by women against men. The second problem is that if we do not accept the feminist social assumptions, we will see that the wrongness or disvalue in sexual harassment differs from that in gender harassment and the conflation of the two results in a loss of meaning and moral import of either one or the other. Superson seems to regard gender harassment as the more significant category since she sees harassment that is sexual (meaning erotic) as essentially sexist and therefore wrong. Although sexual harassment can be sexist in nature, there is more to the disvalue of sexual harassment than mere sexism. Later in the chapter we will argue that sexual harassment[2] involves treating persons merely as means or as objects and using their gender or sexuality as a means by which to treat them in such a way. Gender harassment, on the other hand, has as its disvalue the violation of our commonly accepted notions of fairness or equality. In cases in which both sexual and

gender harassment take place, we may then hold the perpetrator to blame for violating two different moral principles rather than one.

The third problem with conflating sexual harassment and gender harassment is that there are difficulties in forming an adequate conception of gender harassment that need not affect forming a conception of sexual harassment if the two remain separate. Specifically, in gender harassment there is ambiguity in the notion of expressing or perpetuating "the attitude that B or members of B's sex is/are inferior because of their sex, thereby causing harm to either B and/or members of B's sex" (Superson, 1994, p. 46). In addition, Superson makes no distinction between the perpetrator who expresses another's inferiority in a pejorative way and one who utters neutral expressions of another's sex-based inferiority.[3] Many neutral expressions of sex-based inferiority are also strongly justified beliefs—for example, the belief that women are inferior in some ways in physical strength because they are women. But that statement, although evidentially corroborated, could possibly harm women by discouraging them from pursuing certain careers that they find particularly enticing, such as certain roles in the military. Thus, A could express to B that she is (relatively) physically weak because of her sex and inadvertently discourage her from pursuing a career in the military. But we think it would be a mistake to allow an empirically well-corroborated belief to qualify as gender harassment. Nevertheless, such a difficulty need not concern us here as long as we remain focused on an adequate conception of sexual harassment and leave the elucidation of the nature of the wrongness of gender harassment for a separate project.

Another problem with Superson's position is its consequentialist nature; that is, her position defends the wrongness of sexual harassment based on the undesirable consequences it has. Consequentialist (or utilitarian) arguments are contrasted with deontological arguments, which we will use later to argue for the wrongness of sexual harassment. Deontological arguments maintain that the wrongness of an action is located in the action itself, because performing such an action violates a moral duty to treat others in a certain way. Superson, as a consequentialist, sees no wrongness in the action *itself* involved in sexual harassment; what she sees as wrong is the social context of patriarchy in which the action is performed. In other words, Superson sees the actions involved in sexual harassment between two individuals as neither moral nor immoral per se, but sees the context as immoral because it oppresses all women. Thus, the actions become immoral when performed in the context of patriarchy because they are seen as reinforcing patriarchy. If the actions involved in sexual harassment were not performed in a patriarchal society or did not reinforce patriarchy, they would not have the same negative moral import. In short, Superson and other feminists see sexual harassment as wrong because it has the negative consequence of reinforcing the oppression of all women.

If Superson grounds the disvalue of sexual harassment in its negative consequences, she needs to offer justification that patriarchy, or the oppression of women, is causally related to sexual harassment. If a reinforcement of patriarchy cannot be shown to be a direct result of sexual harassment, then one is left without a basis from which to defend the nature and significance of the wrongness of sexual harassment.

The task of defending the wrongness of sexual harassment from a consequentialist perspective, however, is beset with two major difficulties. First, as we mentioned earlier, it is very difficult to show how one action harms all women. Surely we can imagine a situation in which one act of sexual harassment can trigger other acts of sexual harassment and cause harm to a great number of women. For instance, if a powerful role model to American males were to sexually harass a woman and proclaim sexual harassment as a normal, masculine activity, we might expect other American men to follow the example of their role model until sexual harassment became such a widespread phenomenon that it lost its stigma and women were commonly thought of, and portrayed as, objects to be harassed. Clearly, we could then admit that one act of sexual harassment caused some group harm to many women.

However, we can also imagine a scenario in which the only woman harmed was the intended victim of the sexually harassive action. For example, imagine two coworkers, one male and one female, driving to work together. What if the man sexually harassed the woman in the car on the way to work and on that same trip, the car crashed and they both died instantly? No one had any knowledge of the harassment that had occurred before the accident except for the perpetrator and the victim, and so no one else will ever know that an instance of sexual harassment had taken place. We could not then have reason to believe that the man's action has caused harm to women as a group, and yet most of us would still maintain that such treatment of an individual woman is no less wrong. But if the consequence is not what the consequentialist claims, the moral evaluation of the action would have to change.

Second, many consequentialist arguments are also utilitarian arguments, meaning that they determine what is wrong by calculating the bad consequences (or pain) of an action against the good consequences (or pleasure). Superson, although using a consequentialist/utilitarian argument, does not consider the possibility that sexual harassment could be morally justified if the good consequences outweighed the bad. She probably does not consider that a possibility, because she goes to great lengths to enumerate the bad consequences for *all* women, and indeed doing so works to her advantage on a utilitarian scale because one would have to find a plethora of good consequences of sexual harassment to outweigh the many bad consequences. But if one defeated the claim that sexual harassment harms all women and instead found that it only harms the immediate victim (as in our car accident situation) while bringing enjoyment to scores of men, then one could plausibly argue that an instance of sexual harassment produced more pleasure than pain and was therefore morally acceptable.

The possibility of justifying intuitively immoral treatment of persons is a source of deep disagreement between deontologists and utilitarians, for deontologists hold that humans have incalculable worth and cannot be figured into a pleasure-pain formula. As a result, the deontologists argue that we have duties to treat people in certain ways and the violation of those duties cannot be justified by any amount of resulting pleasure. Since consequentialist and utilitarian arguments can justify immoral treatment of persons by its resulting pleasure, they are unlikely to provide us with an acceptable account of the inherent wrongness of sexual harassment.

Aside from consequentialist difficulties, Superson's position is in error for several other reasons. Superson appears inconsistent on whether she wants to appeal to the mental state of the perpetrator as evidence of sexual harassment. On the one hand, she claims that "it is the attitudes embedded and reflected *in the practice* the behavior is an instance of, not the attitudes or intentions *of the perpetrator*, that makes the behavior sexual harassment" (p. 59). Such a claim leads one to believe that we need not concern ourselves with the intentions of particular perpetrators. But, on the other hand, Superson's conception of sexual harassment relies heavily on the untestable assumption that sexual harassers intend their behavior to send a message to all women. Consider the following reasoning by Superson:

> When A sexually harasses B, the comment or behavior is really directed at the group of all women, not just a particular woman, a point often missed by the courts. After all, many derogatory behaviors are issued at women the harasser does not even know (e.g., scanning a stranger's body). Even when the harasser knows his victim, the behavior is directed at the particular woman because she happens to be "available" at the time, though its message is for all women. For instance, a catcall says not (merely) that the perpetrator likes a woman's body but that he thinks women are at least primarily sex objects and he—because of the power he holds by being in the dominant group—gets to rate them according to how much pleasure they give him. (p. 51)

The passage quoted here makes obvious use of a harasser's intentions, as Superson cannot

help but refer to the perpetrator's intentions when attempting to argue that a harasser's comment is really meant for all women. Not only is such a claim extremely presumptuous; it is also inconsistent, for Superson at that same time claims that the harasser's intentions are irrelevant and points to the harasser's intentions as *evidence* of the group harm sexual harassment causes all women. In addition, her reasoning is flawed in assuming that because men harass women they do not even know, they intend to send a message to all women. We can easily conceive of a man who makes a catcall to an unknown tall, blonde-haired woman carrying a lap dog simply because he holds the unusual, false belief that tall, blonde-haired women carrying lap dogs enjoy being the objects of catcalls. The man may have an otherwise favorable, nonsexist view of women but somehow came to believe strangely that such "blonde, lap dog–carrying" women enjoy this sort of attention. While we may think it odd that a man would behave in such a way, it is certainly possible. Also, we know that many men would make catcalls to some women and not to others, thinking that some women, by the way they walk or dress, invite such behavior and actually enjoy it. Such behavior, while blameworthy on some level, does not *necessitate* an unfavorable attitude toward women as a group and is thus blameworthy for a reason other than because it reveals an unfavorable attitude toward women as a group. In short, establishing that a harassive message is "really" directed at all women is extremely difficult to corroborate, and most of us would hold that a legitimate instance of harassment ought to be punished regardless of whether a few or all women were the objects of the harassive behavior.

In summarizing what is wrong with Superson's conception of sexual harassment, we find it confusing to neglect the distinction between sexual harassment and gender harassment because, as we will argue, the two incur moral blame for different reasons. In reducing sexual harassment to gender harassment, one cannot pass a negative moral judgment on same-gender sexual harassment or female-to-male sexual harassment. Finally, a reliance on a consequentialist argument to attempt to demonstrate the wrongness of sexual harassment does not locate the wrongness of sexual harassment in the action itself, but instead locates the wrongness in the negative consequences of the action.

The conclusion we can draw here is that Superson's conception of the wrongness of sexual harassment is fraught with spurious assumptions and is justified only by consequentialism. But consequentialism is too shaky a ground from which to proclaim our disapproval of the sexual harasser, for if the consequences of his actions are not what we predict, we are left without a reason to condemn sexual harassment. Thus, we are forced to turn elsewhere for adequate conception and justification of the wrongness of sexual harassment.

## THE WRONGNESS OF SEXUAL HARASSMENT AS ABUSE OF POWER

In the preceding section we criticized Superson for claiming that power is at the heart of sexual harassment and recognizing only the power men have over women in virtue of their being men. The abuse of power, on the other hand, can be identified in female-to-male sexual harassment and same-sex sexual harassment as well as male-to-female sexual harassment. Thus, we need to examine whether the abuse of power in general is the essential factor resulting in the disvalue in sexual harassment. Let us begin by acknowledging that "abuse of power" is a muddy notion despite its frequency in common parlance. As we mentioned earlier, power is a difficult thing to define and identify; one individual may have power over another in numerous ways. Being someone's supervisor or professor is only one way of having power, and it can indeed be overridden by other means of power. For instance, we normally think that in a university setting it is the professor who harasses the student, because the professor has professional power over the student. But what if the professor is a young, petite female just out of graduate school and the student is an older, physically large male?

If we say that an abuse of power must occur in order for sexual harassment to occur, we must have some idea of which individual is in a more powerful position in any allegedly harassive situation. Being able to make such judgments would require that we have some sort of scale by which we can rank different types of power that one individual may have over another, which seems extremely cumbersome. Thus, the first problem with identifying the abuse of power as that which bears negative moral import in sexual harassment is that the task of identifying and placing power is extremely difficult since thus far we have no standard to which we can refer in the classification and ranking of different types of power.

Although the task of consistently determining power in relationships is a formidable one, that presents only a practical difficulty and not a philosophical objection to the position that the abuse of power is the central disvalue in sexual harassment. Thus, we need to look at cases in which it is fairly simple to discern which individual is in the position of power and then decide if an abuse of that power with sexual overtones constitutes sexual harassment. Consider the following scenario put forth by Crosthwaite and Swanton (1986) as an example in which there is a clear case of an abuse of power and the abuse is motivated by sexual attraction:

> Consider a lecturer whose passions are so excited by a student that he loses his sense of professional responsibilities. Out of excessive concern for her interests, and neither requesting nor expecting any response from her, he gives her an unwarranted pass in the subject. This is wrong, but it is hardly harassment. The woman concerned need know nothing at all of his motivation, and may be only favorably affected by his action. (p. 99)

Crosthwaite and Swanton are correct in their assessment that this example qualifies as an abuse of power but does not qualify as an instance of sexual harassment. What this tells us is that abuse of power, even when exercised for sexual reasons in some sense, is not a sufficient condition for sexual harassment; that is, there are cases that are intuitively not sexually harassive in which sexually motivated abuses of power do occur. As Crosthwaite and Swanton claim, "There are clear cases of misuse of power which are not harassment" (p. 99). The Crosthwaite-Swanton scenario also seems to lack the negative moral import that is often present in sexual harassment; the lecturer's behavior is certainly unprofessional but not exactly deserving of the extreme censure that sexual harassers deserve. And as we stated at the beginning of the chapter, we want the disvalue in sexual harassment to enable us to differentiate it from instances of immature and unprofessional behavior. While an instance of unprofessional behavior may be immoral, the severity of the moral infraction in the lecturer case does not match the severity of blame we typically assign to sexual harassers. Also, the wrongness of an abuse of power is difficult to justify since it is not clear what moral principle an abuser of power violates. One can even abuse power for some perceived "greater good," calling into question whether the abuse of power is *necessarily* wrong. Thus, it seems that the wrongness of sexual harassment cannot be found solely, if at all, in the abuse of power; something with greater negative moral import must be missing from the assessment, and perhaps it is something that is very similar to, or commonly associated with, an abuse of power.

Although we realize that an abuse of power cannot be sufficient for determining what is wrong with sexual harassment, some philosophers have also argued that it is not even necessary. For example, Crosthwaite and Swanton maintain that male coworkers who use pornography as decorations for their offices or who engage in lewd conversation can be said to be sexually harassive without misusing any power. Dodds and colleagues (1988) posit the example of "Bill C" and "Mary C" in an attempt to argue that the abuse of power is not necessary for sexual harassment:

Bill C and Mary C are coworkers in the office, and Bill C lacks formal power over Mary C. He sexually harasses her—with sexual innuendoes, touches, leers, jokes, suggestions, and unwanted invitations. To many women Bill C's actions would be unpleasant. But Mary C is a veteran—this has happened to her so many times before that she no longer responds. It is not that she desires or wants the treatment, but it no longer produces the unpleasant mental attitude it used to produce—it just rolls off her. She gives the negative responses automatically, and goes on as though nothing has happened.... [W]hat power has Bill C misused against Mary C? He has not used even some informal power which has caused her some significantly unpleasant experience. (p. 116)

While we agree that this example illustrates that an abuse of power is not a necessary condition for sexual harassment, the example is flawed in that it unnecessarily includes Mary C's mental state apparently as further evidence that no misuse of power is taking place. Were everything else the same in the example, there is no reason one would have to assert that a misuse of power is occurring even if Mary C were not so nonchalant about Bill C's behavior. Nevertheless, the example illustrates the difficulty in determining whether power exists and is being misused in any given social situation. Too often the temptation exists to posit the existence of power in a relationship after a situation seems a clear-cut case of sexual harassment, rendering the meaning of power totally empty. Thus, when we make declarations such as that all men have power over all women or that rich people have power over poor people in an effort to confirm that misuse of power exists in sexual harassment, we end up saying nothing informative. In short, the abuse of power is neither necessary nor sufficient to the wrongness of sexual harassment, so there must be something more illustrative than the misuse of power that is central to the wrongness of sexual harassment.

Perhaps the illustrative element we are looking for is that which is also similar to and closely associated with an abuse of power—namely, coercion. Part of the reason that the example of Crosthwaite and Swanton lacked negative moral import is that the scenario failed to identify specific *harm* committed by the perpetrator. Coercion, however, can be defined in terms of harm, since what often occurs in an instance of coercion is that the victim commits an action she would not otherwise commit with the belief that doing so will spare her some sort of threatened harm from the perpetrator. Thus, an element of harm in cases of coercion is illustrative regardless of the existence of power in a relationship. When one individual coerces another, we frequently assume that such a coercion could not have taken place without one having power over the other. However, we do not need to verify the existence of power between two or more individuals in order to determine whether coercion has taken place. Rather, we can simply use an objective standard to determine whether coercion has taken place and evaluate the wrongness of coercion and its relationship to sexual harassment, happily ridding ourselves of the bewildering search for a misuse of power.

Before going any further with our discussion of coercion, it will be helpful to explain what we mean by coercion so that we may see why it is or is not essential to the wrongness of sexual harassment. Let us first examine Edmund Wall's (1988) necessary and sufficient conditions for defining coercion:

1. X threatens Y, that is, X intentionally attempts to create the belief in Y that X will be responsible for harm coming to Y should Y fail to do A. X's motive for attempting to create this belief is his desire to bring about a state of affairs in which Y's recognition that this possible harm to himself influences Y to do A.
2. X successfully creates the belief in Y that Y may be harmed if he fails to do A, that is, X is successfully causing Y to recognize that harm may come to him should he fail to do A.
3. Y intends to do A, and Y's motive for doing A is Y's desire to avoid harm to himself.
4. Y does A. (p. 75)

Further explanation of Wall's conditions and what is meant by coercion will be necessary before we can determine if sexually moti-

vated coercion is either a necessary or sufficient condition of sexual harassment. First, a striking feature of Wall's conditions is his excessive reference to "intentions." What might Wall mean by "intentions"? Have we stumbled upon another notion as perplexing and indiscernible as that of an "abuse of power"? Although later in the chapter we will discuss the advantages and disadvantages of referring to mental states such as intentions, let us here briefly propose how we might understand these mental states and why reference to them is common when describing moral phenomena. The obvious reason one talks about an individual acting intentionally is, as Hampshire and Hart (1972) point out, "to rebut a *prima facie* suggestion that he was in some way ignorant of, or mistaken about, some element involved in the action" (p. 661). In other words, reference to an action being *intentional* can draw a moral distinction between two cases of apparently similar action (e.g., brushing up against a woman's body) if we say that one action was done "accidentally," while the other was done "on purpose." Hampshire and Hart specify that two kinds of requirements be satisfied in order for an action to be considered intentional:

> First, the agent must have ordinary empirical knowledge of certain features of his environment and of the nature and characteristics of certain things affected by his movements. Precisely what knowledge of this sort he must have will depend upon precisely what action is ascribed to him. If, for example, he is said intentionally to have shot at a bird, he must know, in the ordinary sense of "know," that what he has in his hands is a gun, and that there is a bird in the line of fire. He must also have certain types of general knowledge, for example, of the consequences of pulling the trigger of a loaded gun.... Second ... the agent must know what he was doing in some sense which would differentiate his shooting at the bird from other nonaccidental actions performed at the same time, such as making the cartridge explode. (p. 662)

This analysis, while not without controversy, can give us a working definition of intentional action and provide a brief justification of the usefulness of referring to mental states when analyzing moral phenomena. However, as we proceed, we will examine whether we can simply discard reference to intentions and include only references to knowledge as the unavoidable mental element in our analysis of coercion and, eventually, of sexual harassment.

In Wall's article "Intention and Coercion," he claims, "Both the perpetrator and the victim are thinking, feeling beings who can purposefully direct their actions. Without these features which make human beings what they are, coercion would not be possible" (p. 75). Elsewhere, Wall states that coercion is "essentially an interpersonal relationship between individuals" (p. 76). Such statements are directly applicable to sexual harassment since it seems to us that sexual harassment is also essentially an interpersonal relationship between individuals who can purposefully direct their actions, and that sexual harassment would not be possible if humans did not have the capacity to think, feel, and purposefully direct their actions.

The reason that coercion or sexual harassment would not be possible if humans did not have the specified capacities is that in cases of both coercion and sexual harassment the perpetrator attempts to treat the victim as something other than a thinking, feeling, purposeful being. Rather, the perpetrator treats the victim as an object or as a mere means to accomplish the perpetrator's goal. Of course, there would be nothing wrong with treating people as objects if they actually *were* objects. But since people are thinking, feeling, purposeful beings, we see it as wrong to treat them as if they are not. When one person coerces another, there is a clear disregard for the interests of the person; the goal of coercion is to make an individual act against his or her own will, to commit an act the individual would not otherwise do. In addition, as Wall points out, the victim's motivation for committing the act is to avoid greater harm to himself. The threat of harm in coercion is what distinguishes it from more common situations in which one commits an act one would not have done otherwise for the benefit of another. In cases of coercion the perpetrator knows that commit-

ting the act is against the victim's interests and still attempts to get the victim to believe that harm will come to him if he fails to commit the act.

As we mentioned, Wall's emphasis on the intention of the perpetrator might be both illuminating and problematic for our attempt to forge an adequate conception of sexual harassment. First, let us examine how Wall's emphasis on intention is helpful in alerting us to the fact that some sort of role allotted to cognitive states of perpetrators can illuminate subtle differences in culpability that purely behavioral accounts cannot. Consider the following scenario, which Wall uses to stress the importance of the perpetrator's intentions in determining whether a situation is coercive:

> P is a homeless individual who happens to be a very large man. P approaches another man, Q, seeking some money for that night's meal. P goes about his request in a polite fashion. However, unknown to P, Q was once the victim of a serious and unprovoked assault. Similar to P, the assailant was a very large man dressed in soiled clothing. The thought of this terrible incident is recalled by Q when P approaches him, evoking a feeling of fear in Q. As a result of fear, Q feels threatened into performing the action (A) that P requests. He does, indeed, perform A. But, do we want to conclude that Q was coerced by P into doing A? I think not. (p. 76)

How does this example relate to sexual harassment? First of all, Wall mentions that although Q feels threatened, he is not actually threatened. Such a distinction applies to sexual harassment, as we often hear that sexual harassment is whatever makes the victim feel uncomfortable, or that we must define sexual harassment from a victim's point of view. While it may be perfectly normal for Q to feel threatened given his having previously been an assault victim, the proposition *Q was coerced by P* remains false. In Wall's example we can say that Q's reaction is normal or even justified and yet still maintain that coercion, or a moral infraction, did not occur.

The same attitude must be brought to instances of alleged sexual harassment. Too often those asked to judge whether sexual harassment has occurred are forced into a false dichotomy of deciding whether the victim's feelings are normal or abnormal and on that basis deciding whether sexual harassment did or did not occur. In brief, the victim's feelings are not ultimately decisive in ascertaining whether sexual harassment occurred, but they are a part of that decision, just as they are in coercion. Both coercion and sexual harassment have subjective elements to them; the victim must have a certain cognitive state or respond in a specific way, otherwise we would have only a *thwarted attempt* at coercion or sexual harassment. On the other hand, both of these concepts have an objective element to them since they both have negative moral import, and the *moral* status of an act does not fluctuate with the reaction of the victim of the act. Thus, even if the victim of an attempted sexually harassing action is not bothered by the action, we ought to still assign moral blame to the perpetrator. Again, because both coercion and sexual harassment are subject to our moral disapprobation, we must make sure we can point to a breach of a moral principle in such cases, and we must make sure that the perpetrator is a thinking, feeling, purposeful being who is at least *capable* of knowing the moral principle he violates.

If we do not include *any* cognitive state of the perpetrator and look only to his behavior, we will incorrectly identify cases of coercion and sexual harassment and misassign moral blame. For instance, let us assume that in Wall's example, P knows that Q had been assaulted by a large man in soiled clothing because P's brother, R, committed the assault and looks very much like P. Let us also assume that P knows that Q has a certain tendency toward paranoia, and knows that Q is very likely to be frightened when approached by men like P and will honor P's request immediately for fear of being mugged. Although in such a situation P may *act* exactly the same way as in Wall's example, we would tend to say that P coerced Q. P's *knowledge* of Q's fear of being assaulted by large men in soiled clothing *changes his culpability,* although his external behavior remains the

same. In the revised scenario, P has knowledge of his resemblance to Q's attacker and believes that Q will give P money without P having to show any external signs of threatening behavior. Hence, P knows the effect that his appearance and actions will have on Q and uses it to his advantage. Even though no *verbal* threat is made, Wall would say that P does attempt to create the belief in Q that P will cause harm to come to Q if Q fails to do action A. Also, Wall would say that P's motive for attempting to create this belief is his desire to bring about a state of affairs in which Q's recognition of this possible harm to himself influences him to do A. Thus, Wall's first condition is met. In addition, P's attempt succeeds and Q does A to avoid harm to himself, and so all of Wall's necessary conditions for coercion are satisfied.

It is relatively easy for us to set up an analogous situation in sexual harassment and thus realize the relevance of our discussion of coercion for sexual harassment. Imagine a place of work with Y, a male superior, and Z, a female subordinate. Z is relatively new on the job and shy because the workplace is almost entirely male. Y, her superior, has been in his position for a long time and is respected and liked by all the other men at the workplace. Z came from a previous workplace in which she was asked out by her superior and when she refused, her superior and the other men at the workplace who were friends with her superior shunned her. They excluded her from company picnics, ignored her in the lunchroom, and so on. Because the workplace was almost entirely male at her previous job, Z finally felt that her rapport with coworkers and superiors was so poor that she had no chance for advancement, and she left.

Z's present employment situation appears similar to her previous one in that it is almost entirely male, her coworkers are close friends with her superior, and building rapport with others in the company is crucial for advancement. Y then properly and politely asks Z out on a date, and Z fears that if she refuses to go out with him, she will be shunned as she was at her last job. So Z agrees to go out with Y in order to avoid the harm that befell her at her last job. Y, however, is unaware of Z's past experience and her present mental state and would not ask her out had he known that she would feel pressured into going out with him. Thus, although Z's feelings are reasonable in light of her previous employment experience, Y is not guilty of any wrongdoing. However, had Y *known* of Z's previous employment experience and her fear of that experience repeating itself, then his mere request for a date could be viewed as an attempt to create the belief in Z that her previous employment experience would repeat itself if she did not acquiesce. Were that the case, Y might then be guilty of coercion and quid pro quo sexual harassment and deserving of our moral blame.

A final aspect of Wall's conception of coercion that has implications for a conception of sexual harassment is his condition that "Y's motive for intending to do A is Y's desire to avoid harm to himself." Wall posits this condition in order to include situations like the following as instances of coercion:

> Suppose that Y wants to give his pocket-money to a beggar in the hope that the poor fellow will eat something. Now suppose that the beggar takes out a gun and points it at Y demanding that Y give him all his money....[I]f Y gives the beggar money with the intention to avoid the beggar's threat, then Y is genuinely coerced here. (p. 82)

Wall's condition enables one to include cases like this as coercion whereas many definitions of coercion would not. Other definitions of coercion, such as Robert Nozick's (1972), focus on whether the victim would have chosen to perform the action *had the threat not been made*. But, as Wall's example demonstrates, one may decide to perform a certain action before the threat is made, but still ultimately perform the action to avoid harm coming to oneself and be coerced. However, we should notice that, regardless of the victim's previous decision to give money to the beggar, we would most likely recognize the example as an instance of coercion because of the overtly threatening behavior of the beggar (i.e., using a gun in his demand for money).

Also, and again without looking at the victim's intention for actually giving money to the beggar, we might recognize coercion in the example because although the victim was initially inclined to give the beggar money, the beggar had *no knowledge* of the victim's initial inclination and showed an obvious disregard for whatever wishes or inclinations the victim possessed by demanding money at gunpoint.

The implication of this situation for sexual harassment is that in instances of quid pro quo sexual harassment we frequently hear of cases of alleged harassment in which the victim had shown a sexual interest in the perpetrator before the sexually threatening or harassing behavior occurred. The victim's sexual interest is then sometimes incorrectly used as evidence that no sexual harassment could have occurred. However, the perpetrator may not *know* about the victim's interest and so may still attempt to coerce her into a sexual relationship. The perpetrator may threaten the victim with diminished promotional opportunities should she refuse to undertake a sexual relationship with him. In such cases the perpetrator deserves moral blame regardless of whether the victim had a previous sexual interest in him. Such a statement should not come as a surprise since we are accustomed to hearing about similar instances in cases of date rape. In short, a general sexual interest in the perpetrator does not entail a sexual interest or sexual willingness at any given time or place; therefore, an initial inclination to commit a certain action does not obviate the possibility that coercion or (sexual harassment) has occurred. The perpetrator may still either fail to consider the victim's interests at that time or knowingly act contrary to them.

Again, Wall's emphasis on intentions in his conception of coercion is, although helpful in illuminating subtle differences in culpability, also problematic insofar as intentions are difficult both to define and to measure. Furthermore, giving a central role to the intentions of the perpetrator will make determining guilt in cases of sexual harassment largely a matter of weighing what the perpetrator claims his intentions were against what the victim supposes the perpetrator's intentions to be. There-fore, looking to intentions to determine guilt does not have much practical merit. However, many of the conclusions we drew in the pre-ceding cases as to whether one was guilty of coercion can still be reached without a specific appeal to intentions, although we do have to appeal to the perpetrator's background knowl-edge in order to reach the same conclusion in determining guilt. Although determining background knowledge will also be somewhat imprecise, the definition of knowledge is much less perplexing than that of intention, and we do frequently (and at least somewhat accurately) assess the degree of the back-ground knowledge a perpetrator has of a vic-tim, while assessing a perpetrator's intentions involves much more guesswork. For example, in the case of Y and Z, although Z feels pres-sured into going out with her superior because of her previous employment experience, she may not think that Y is attempting to coerce her into a date if she knows that he has no access to the confidential files describing her previous experience and reason for leaving her former job. Also, if Z charged Y with sexual harassment, we might think it normal for Z to feel uncomfortable given her previous experi-ence, but not find Y blameworthy since, with-out such background knowledge, he could not reasonably be expected to foresee that Z would feel pressured into going out with him. Admit-tedly, whether one has the requisite back-ground knowledge of the victim in certain cases can also be disputed, although the dis-putes will not typically be of the "he said, she said" variety as disputes over intentions are likely to be. To some extent, there are external "clues" to the knowledge an individual has about another individual. For instance, we might look at an employee's access to files revealing personal information about a victim-ized employee that could be exploited in an attempt to coerce the victim into doing some-thing against her interests, or we might have witnesses who claim to have told a perpetrator, like Y, about the experience that made a vic-tim, like Z, leave her previous job. In grappling with these issues, we might conclude that

some sort of mental state information about the perpetrator will always be the proverbial monkey wrench in a sexual harassment case; if we look only to the empirically measurable and ignore mental states altogether, we will lose important but subtle clues in determining guilt or innocence. As long as we appeal to mental states, we will have to tolerate an ele-ment of imprecision and immeasurability. As a compromise, we ought to appeal to one's mental state (such as one's background knowl-edge) sparingly, and when doing so, we ought to rely as much as possible on external indica-tors of the mental state, in hopes of keeping the "he said, she said" disputes to a minimum.

Despite the attention we have shown to coercion, a moment's reflection makes us real-ize that it is not a necessary condition for sex-ual harassment because many cases that strike us as intuitively harassive simply involve a man subjecting the victim to an overtly sexual environment, without attempting to force her to perform any action whatsoever. Cases of hostile environment sexual harassment typi-cally do not involve coercion unless we were to construe coercion broadly enough to include a forcible exposure to a certain envi-ronment. However, coercion is readily appar-ent in quid pro quo sexual harassment, and when coercion of a sexual nature occurs, we will almost certainly declare that action to be sexually harassive. Thus, sexual coercion is a sufficient condition for sexual harassment, although it is not a necessary one. Notice that the wrongness in quid pro quo sexual harass-ment lies primarily in the coercive nature of the phenomenon; the sexual aspect does not appear to play a role in the wrongness but is merely an accidental feature. That is, this harassment is wrong because it is coercion, not because it is sexual coercion. Whether coer-cion of a sexual nature is somehow more wrong than coercion of a financial nature is not something we are justified in believing at this point. The frequency of coercive behavior in cases of sexual harassment brings us closer to identifying its wrongness since coercion involves one thinking, purposeful human being forcing his interests and desires upon another and in violation of the other person's interests. Sexual harassment as a violation of the victim's interests or rights is another popular conception, one that brings us to the next section of the chapter.

## THE WRONGNESS OF SEXUAL HARASSMENT AS A VIOLATION OF PRIVACY RIGHTS

In the previous section we examined Wall's conception of coercion in an attempt to identify the disvalue in sexual harassment. In this section we will evaluate what Wall (1991) and others identify as the wrongness in sexual harassment. Although we found much of what Wall says about coercion applicable to at least some forms of sexual harassment, Wall makes no mention of coercion in his defense of the wrongness of sexual harassment; instead, he locates the disvalue of sexual harassment in a violation of the victim's privacy rights. In "The Definition of Sexual Harassment," Wall (1991, p. 374) sets up his own necessary and sufficient conditions for sexual harassment, which are as follows:

1. X does not attempt to obtain Y's consent to communicate to Y, X's or someone else's purported sexual interest in Y.
2. X communicates to Y, X's or someone else's purported sexual interest in Y. X's motive for communicating this is some perceived benefit that he expects to obtain through the communication.
3. Y does not consent to discuss with X, X's or someone else's purported sexual interest in Y.
4. Y feels emotionally distressed because X did not attempt to obtain Y's consent to this discussion and/or because Y objects to the content of X's sexual comments.

The first strength of Wall's set of conditions is that most of us agree that the right to privacy is a basic human right, and so the violation of it is likely to warrant moral censure. However, Wall's first condition seems overly stringent in requiring that X attempt to obtain Y's consent merely to communicate one's

sexual interest in X. Of course, it depends on what Wall means by "sexual interest," which he does not make clear in his article. But since sexual interest is usually understood to include attraction, the condition seems too stringent. Most of us would not want to say that X would be violating Y's privacy rights merely by not attempting to obtain Y's consent to express to Y, X's or *someone else's* sexual attraction to Y. Asking someone out for a date, for example, could be a way of expressing sexual attraction/sexual interest. Under Wall's condition, however, X would be required to attempt to obtain Y's consent simply to *ask* Y out for a date. It is difficult to get permission to express sexual interest without inadvertently expressing one's interest in the process of asking for permission. A failure to obtain an individual's consent before asking her out for a date is not even severe enough to qualify as a breach of etiquette, much less a moral infraction.

The reason Wall makes the first condition so inclusive is to capture those cases in which Y has an interest in X but still objects to X's sexual behavior. As Wall (1991) notes, "Y may actually agree to a sexual proposition made to her by X and still be sexually harassed by X's attempting to discuss it with her.... Y might not feel that it is the proper time or place to discuss such matters" (p. 375). Again, Wall holds that a failure to obtain consent to a certain type of communication (in this case, to discuss sexual matters with an individual) is a violation of one's privacy rights and is central to sexual harassment. He goes on to elaborate about the wrongness of sexual harassment in the following passage:

> What is inherently repulsive about sexual harassment is not the possible vulgarity of X's sexual comment or proposal, but his failure to show respect for X's rights. It is the obligation that stems from privacy rights that is ignored. Y's personal behavior and aspirations are protected by Y's privacy rights. The intrusion by X into this moral sphere is what is so objectionable about sexual harassment. If X does not attempt to obtain Y's approval to discuss such private matters, then he has not shown Y adequate respect. (p. 375)

Although Wall's conception of sexual harassment is too broad, he makes an important point: that vulgarity is less central to sexual harassment than the failure to show respect for X's rights. If coworkers, or even supervisors and subordinates, have an agreement that sexual joking and teasing is harmless and enjoyable, then it is not sexually harassive even though it may be unprofessional. However, less vulgar sexual joking directed at someone whom the perpetrator knows is distressed by such language can be sexually harassive.

The areas in which Wall's conception can be shown to be too broad are what he means by a victim's privacy rights and by "some perceived benefit" in the second condition. For instance, we know that Wall maintains that failure to gain consent to a certain type of communication violates a victim's privacy rights, but such communication is not only verbal; it includes "gestures, noises, stares, etc. that violate its recipient's privacy rights. Such behavior can be every bit as intrusive as verbal remarks" (1991, p. 375). We do not typically think of an individual's privacy rights as something that can be violated by noises, stares, and so on. It sounds as though Wall's idea of the right to privacy is more like a right to be left alone from all disturbances. The problem with such a broad conception of an individual's privacy rights is that it encroaches on other individuals' rights to free expression.

Also, Wall appears inconsistent in qualifying a failure to attempt to obtain consent as a *violation* of a victim's privacy rights. If one fails to attempt to gain consent, then it is more fitting that we should say he perhaps has been insensitive, negligent, or has *failed to show proper respect* to the victim's privacy rights. A *violation* of privacy rights should occur only if the perpetrator *acts against* (and, hence, violates) the victim's wishes. Briefly, the moral judgment Wall pronounces on perpetrators is too severe; there is an imbalance between the severity of the action and the severity of the judgment on that action.

Finally, Wall mentions in his second condition that X's motive for communicating to Y

someone's interest in Y is some perceived benefit that he expects to obtain through the communication. Wall maintains that in X's attempt to obtain the perceived benefit, he violates his victim's rights. But Wall's conception of "some perceived benefit" to X is also so broad that it fails to be informative. Wall characterizes a benefit as anything from X's increased chance of having sexual relations with Y, the satisfaction of disturbing Y, and decreased sense of inferiority by controlling Y's feelings, to conformity to what he believes to be parental and/or peer standards for males. Such an inclusive understanding of "benefit" leaves us hard to put to find any individual who is *not* motivated by some perceived benefit in *most* of his communications with other people.

## THE WRONGNESS OF SEXUAL HARASSMENT AS TREATING PERSONS AS MERE SEX OBJECTS

Although we have not yet settled on a firm conception of what sexual harassment is, we have, it seems, come closer to deciding what is wrong with sexual harassment, and once we discover the wrongness of sexual harassment, we have at least one necessary condition in its definition. What is central to the wrongness of sexual harassment, we propose, is that it involves using another individual as a means only. The wrongness of using a human being as a means is a much defended and easily accepted principle in moral philosophy that first gained popularity as the principle of humanity in the categorical imperative of Immanuel Kant (1964): "Act in such a way that you always treat humanity, whether in your own person or in the person of any other, never simply as a means, but always at the same time as an end" (*Groundwork of the Metaphysic of Morals*, pp. 32–33). It is important to notice in Kant's imperative that he does not prohibit treating someone as a means; he prohibits treating someone *merely* as a means. Thus, when a student uses her professor as a means of getting an education, she does not violate Kant's imperative because she does not treat her professor merely as a means. The student still recognizes her professor as an end in himself; she does not treat him as if his only worth was as a means to her getting an education. Kant's principle essentially tells us that it is wrong to "use" people, a moral judgment we usually take for granted. Kant maintains that it is wrong to treat people merely as means because people are in fact ends in themselves. Because they are ends in themselves (and not mere means to our pleasure, for example) they deserve to be treated as such.

Kant's argument for the principle of humanity, however, is somewhat obscure and beyond the scope of this chapter. Contemporary moral philosophers have developed their own versions of Kant's principle of humanity and have explained them less obscurely. Robert Nozick (1981), for instance, admitting his kinship with Kant, cites the following as the fundamental ethical principle: "Treat someone [who is a value-seeking I] as a value-seeking I" (p. 462). He explains his fundamental ethical principle as follows:

> What is it to treat someone as a value-seeking I? Suppose that in order to break a window I pick up a sleeping person and hurl him through it. I am treating him as an object. My behavior utilizes his mass, size, center of gravity, and other characteristics the physicist speaks of, but it is not cued in to his being a person, to his being a value-seeking I. My behavior is in no way dependent upon his possession or nonpossession of that characteristic. For me to treat someone as a value-seeing I, something about my behavior...must depend upon his having that characteristic: that characteristic must (actually or subjunctively) make some difference to me. (p. 462)

Nozick arrives at the fundamental ethical principle by first identifying what he takes to be the basic moral characteristic: being a value-seeking self. A value-seeking self is like a moral agent, one who is capable of moral judgment and action and is capable of discerning value, that is, discerning what is good or important and seeks that which is of value. The basic moral characteristic, or moral basis, is

the characteristic of people "in virtue of which they are owed moral behavior" (Nozick, 1981, p. 451). According to Nozick, this characteristic exerts a moral claim on us, which he refers to as an "ethical pull." In short, the notion that a basic characteristic exerts a moral claim on us means simply that a value-seeking self, because it is a value-seeking self and not an automaton, ought to *elicit* certain behavior from us and ought to *prohibit* certain behavior; the basic moral characteristic thus deserves or warrants appropriate behavior from others.

Richard Peters (1986) also defends a Kantian theory on the treatment of others known as "respect for persons." Respect for persons is a popular theory within deontological ethics that arose in an attempt to make Kant's principle more personal. Peters and other respect for persons defenders maintain that Kant's imperative to treat people as ends in themselves seems based on a respect for the moral law, or equates respect for persons and respect for moral law whereas it ought to emphasize a respect for persons *qua* persons. Thus, one may treat someone as an end in himself while maintaining an attitude of indifference or even contempt toward that person. Peters and others place more stress on consideration of persons' interests and wishes as part of the respect for persons. Peters claims that what we mean when we say that someone shows a lack of respect for persons is that:

> he does not treat others seriously as agents or as determiners of their own destiny, and that he disregards their feelings and view of the world. He either refuses to let them be in a situation where their intentions, decisions, appraisals, and choices can operate effectively, or he purposely interferes with or nullifies their capacity for self-direction. He denies them the dignity which is the due of a self-determining agent who is capable of valuation and choice and who has a point of view of his own future and interests. (pp. 45–46)

The notion of respect for persons is relatively straightforward. As one would expect, respecting persons as persons entails respecting those characteristics about persons that make us persons as opposed to animals or automatons. For instance, persons make rational and moral judgments and act on the basis of those judgments, so we have a duty to respect a person's liberty to make such judgments and actions. A deliberate violation of another's liberty to decide and act as she chooses would violate her autonomy and show a lack of respect for her as a volitional person.

Philosophers have identified many different, although similar, characteristics of human beings that make them worthy of respect and ought to shape our behavior toward them. For instance, R. S. Downie and Elizabeth Telfer (1970) identify self-determination and rule following as the two characteristics of the rational will that make human beings worthy of respect. In identifying these two traits as pivotal, Downie and Telfer attempt to explain how those characteristics shape our behavior toward persons, for in order to show respect for persons, we must know what it means to respect someone *as* a self-determining, rule-following person. In other words, our behavior toward a person must be affected in a positive way by the fact that the person possesses the characteristics of being self-determining and rule-following. For example, if we want to sit in a particular chair and that chair has books on it, we simply pick up the books and move them elsewhere so that we can sit down. If, however, we want to sit in a particular chair and another person is presently occupying that chair, we do not simply pick up the person and move her elsewhere. Instead, we ask her if she would mind moving elsewhere in order to leave the chair unoccupied. In doing so, we both recognize and act according to the fact that she is capable both of selecting where she wants to sit and of responding to our request. Hence, we show consideration of her interests and respect her as a person, while the books warrant no such consideration.

One may select a variety of attributes that make human beings worthy of respect; it is not our aim at this point to defend one basic moral characteristic over another. It is important to recognize that persons, being what they are, *deserve* to be treated in some *favorable* ways and *deserve not* to be treated in some *unfavorable* ways. The ways in which persons are to be treated are governed by the fundamental ethical principles of showing respect for persons as persons and treating people as ends in themselves rather than merely as means.

While such statements seem to coincide with our strongest moral intuitions, it is on the notion of respect for persons that the deontologists part with the utilitarians and consequentialists most drastically. Deontologists claim that utilitarians cannot recognize respect for persons as a fundamental ethical principle, because utilitarians cannot accept humans as having incalculable intrinsic worth. Rather, utilitarians weigh actions in terms of the pleasure or pain they produce; thus, if showing a lack of respect for persons produced a great deal of pleasure for a great number of people, such an action may be morally acceptable. Deontologists maintain that such a fundamental ethical duty as respect for persons cannot be violated in order to produce greater pleasure, because the "rightness" of such a duty is linked to the intrinsic worth of human beings rather than to the consequences of performing such a duty. As a result, deontological theories have greater explanatory and justificatory power for the wrongness of sexual harassment, since according to deontological theories, sexual harassment, insofar as it displays a lack of respect for persons, is always wrong, while in some utilitarian theories an act of sexual harassment may be justifiable.

Now that we have described what it means to show respect for persons and to treat people as ends in themselves, we can see that sexual harassment involves treating someone as a means or not showing her the respect that is morally required of us. These are the fundamental ethical principles that are violated in the act of sexual harassment and that are the basis on which we are justified in passing a negative moral judgment on those who sexually harass. A violation of such principles, then, is a *necessary condition* of sexual harassment; that is, it is what we ought to look for as a minimum requirement in determining whether sexual harassment has occurred in a given situation.

The disvalue of sexual harassment, on our view, is that when A sexually harasses B, he displays a lack of respect for her as a person. We may say that he treats her as less than a person, and he uses her sexuality *as a means* of treating her as less than a person. Therefore, a second necessary condition of sexual harassment is that the *vehicle* for violating these ethical principles is something sexual. Put simply, we may say that sexual harassment involves treating someone as a sex object rather than as a sexual person. Let us examine briefly what it means to treat someone as a sex object by contrasting the meaning of "sex object" with the meaning of "a sexual person."

As we explained earlier, persons have certain attributes that make them worthy of respect and favorable treatment, and those attributes ought to shape our behavior toward persons in certain ways. Thus, if we want to show respect for persons, we must show respect especially to those attributes that make persons unique, such as the capacity to choose one's own destiny, seek after value, and so on. What makes sexual persons worthy of respect, are, quite simply, many of the same attributes that make persons in general worthy of respect; but now we apply those attributes to the sexual domain of a person's life. Hence, sexual persons seek after valuable sexual interactions, are capable of following rules or principles to which they have assented as guides for their sexual conduct, and have the ability to choose their sexual partners and the timing of their sexual interactions. There are, of course, other attributes that make sexual persons worthy of respect and distinguish them from animals or objects, but these are some of the basic differences. We do not ordinarily think of animals as making conscious, deliberate choices over when, where, and with whom to engage in sexual interaction. Instead, they operate largely on instinct, mating with anything, anywhere when the sexual instinct strikes them. Such a sexual trait is no doubt valued by animal breeders. But humans, being rational and moral agents, are capable of choosing their own sexual interactions, and that characteristic makes them worthy of

respect. In showing respect for that characteristic of humans, we do not try to breed persons as we do animals, since we respect the ability of persons to make choices regarding their sexual fate. To respect someone as a sexual person, then, would entail respecting her sexual principles, and not coercing her to act contrary to the principles she has consciously chosen to guide her actions.

Also, if A respects B as a sexual person, he respects her right to choose when, where, and with whom she engages in sexual interaction by presenting her with sexual choices (e.g., asking B out for a date) without attempting to intimidate or infringe on her freedom to choose her desired course of action in that situation. As a general rule for treating someone as a sexual person rather than a sex object, we propose the following principle: *For any quality x, where x is a characteristic making a sexual person, P, worthy of respect, do not act in such a way that you treat P as if P does not possess x, nor in such a way that you infringe upon or attempt to diminish P's possession of x.* Ways in which one might treat a sexual person as if she did not possess characteristics making her, *qua* sexual person, worthy of respect would include many of the cases already discussed, such as any type of action in which one individual coerces another into a sexual relationship, thereby not respecting the victim's ability to choose his or her own sexual interactions. In addition, a man who subjects a woman, against her interests, to listening to detailed reports of sexual fantasies he has about her would be in violation of these principle because we may construe one's ability to choose his or her own sexual interactions to include sexual conversation.

This construal of sexual interactions to include sexual conversation must be qualified, however, since it is not designed as a puritanical prohibition against innocuous compliments on one's appearance. On the contrary, innocuous compliments should not be considered "sexual conversation." However, sexual conversation can frequently be a form of verbal foreplay, and, because of this, can be included within sexual interaction. Thus, engaging in sexual conversation against the interests of one's interlocutor can constitute a violation of our principle. Finally, an example of treating a person, P, in such a way as to infringe upon or attempt to diminish P's possession of x would be secretly giving P any sort of chemical substance for the purpose of impairing her ability to be self-determining about her sexual interactions. The point of saying "secretly" giving P a chemical substance is to rule out a case of offering a woman a glass of wine as a violation of the principle. Presumably, the effects of alcohol can be taken to be common knowledge; nevertheless, putting some sort of tasteless alcohol or other drug in a woman's soft drink without informing her and with the hope of eventually seducing her would obviously show a lack of respect for the woman as a self-determining, sexual person.

Our proposed principle is not put forth as a necessary or sufficient condition of sexual harassment but is proposed as a general principle that tends to be violated in many instances of sexual harassment. As a result, we maintain that those forging conceptions of sexual harassment should include a violation of this principle in their conceptions. When our proposed principle is violated by A, and B is distressed by A's violation of the principle, sexual harassment has probably occurred. The advantage of such a simple conception of sexual harassment is that it is defined largely by its disvalue; if we accuse someone of sexual harassment, we can immediately point to a moral principle that has been violated to justify our moral disapproval of the harasser. In addition, our proposed principle is based on the commonly accepted moral imperatives that we ought not to treat people as means only or that we ought to show persons the respect that is due them in virtue of their being persons. Our proposed principle also identifies a wrongful interaction between two individuals regardless of sex or social status, locating the wrongness in the action itself as opposed to its consequences or the social context in which it occurs.

## CONCLUSION

In the foregoing examination of various conceptions of the disvalue of sexual harassment, we have attempted to make several important points. First, an adequate conception of sexual harassment must make explicit what it posits the disvalue or wrongness in sexual harassment to be. Second, the wrongness identified in sexual harassment should coincide with our fundamental moral intuitions, or the principle that one claims is violated in sexual harassment should be a principle on which there is a general consensus. Third, deontological ethical theories give us a stronger basis than utilitarian or consequentialist theories from which to argue for the necessary wrongness of sexual harassment because deontological theories stress the incalculable worth of human beings and locate the wrongness of actions in the moral duty that is violated rather than in the contingent consequences of the action. Fourth, the principle that one claims is violated in sexual harassment must have the moral significance to enable us to differentiate cases of sexual harassment from cases of poor etiquette or mere unprofessional behavior. We have used these four points as a standard by which to evaluate the various conceptions of the disvalue of sexual harassment discussed in the chapter, and we hope to have convinced the reader of the need for a clearly articulated disvalue in one's conception of sexual harassment in order to justify our accompanying moral censure when we identify an interaction as sexually harassive.

## ENDNOTES

1. For the purpose of the present chapter, we will use the terms *wrongness* and *disvalue* interchangeably as that which makes sexual harassment deserving of our reprehension.

2. Henceforth we will use *sexual harassment* to refer to harassment that has some kind of erotic overtone and *gender harassment* to refer to harassment that is without erotic overtones but is sexist and meant to distress someone by deprecating her on the basis of her gender.

3. An example of a neutral expression of one's sex-based inferiority would be something like the following: "In an open competition, you are less likely to be a successful pole vaulter because you are a woman and women lack the upper body strength that enables men to be successful pole vaulters."

# REFERENCES

Christensen, F. M. (1994). "Sexual harassment" must be eliminated. *Public Affairs Quarterly, 8,* 1–17.

Crosthwaite, J., & Swanton, C. (1986). On the nature of sexual harassment. *Australian Journal of Philosophy, 64,* 91–106.

Dodds, S., Frost, L., Pargetter, R., & Prior, E. (1988). Sexual harassment. *Social Theory and Practice, 14,* 111–130.

Downie, R. S. & Telfer, E. (1970). *Respect for persons.* New York: Schocken Books.

Hampshire, S., & Hart, H. L. A. (1972). Decision, intention, and certainty. In H. Feigl, W. Sellars, & K. Lehrer (Eds.), *New readings in philosophical analysis.* New York: Appleton-Century-Crofts.

Kant, I. (1964). *Groundwork of the metaphysic of morals* (trans. H. J. Paton). New York: Harper & Row.

MacKinnon, C. A. (1979). *Sexual harassment of working women.* New Haven, CT: Yale University Press.

Nozick, R. (1972). Coercion. In P. Laslett, W. G. Runcimann, & Q. Skinner (Eds.), *Philosophy, politics, and society: Fourth series.* Oxford: Blackwell.

Nozick, R. (1981). *Philosophical explanations.* Cambridge, England: Belknap Press.

Peters, R. S. (1986). Respect for persons and fraternity. In C. Hoff Sommers (Ed.), *Right and wrong: Basic readings in ethics.* New York: Harcourt Brace Jovanovich.

Superson, A. M. (1993). A feminist definition of sexual harassment. *Journal of Social Philosophy, 24,* 46–64.

Wall, E. (1988). Intention and coercion. *Journal of Applied Philosophy, 5,* 75–85.

Wall, E. (1991). The definition of sexual harassment. *Public Affairs Quarterly, 5,* 371–385.

# CHAPTER 4

# LEGAL THEORIES OF SEXUAL HARASSMENT

## Alba Conte, Esq.

Sexual harassment law, while unsettled, has evolved into a significant facet of the employment discrimination bar. Early claims of sexual harassment found little acceptance by judges who were unwilling to deem the "personal proclivit[ies]" of supervisors sexual harassment (*Corne v. Bausch & Lomb, Inc.*, 1975), and even those who were sympathetic to the concept that such conduct was discrimination had trouble integrating that notion into existing law. In the mid-1970s, more enlightened opinions began to surface in the federal circuit courts, but the disparity in judicial construction lingered. Sexual harassment takes on many forms, but it usually falls into one or both of two categories: quid pro quo or hostile environment harassment. *Quid pro quo*, or sexual harassment for tangible benefit, involves the exchange of employment benefits by a supervisor or employer for sexual favors from a subordinate employee. *Hostile*

*environment harassment* consists of verbal or physical conduct that unreasonably interferes with one's work or creates an intimidating, hostile, or offensive working environment. Although most victims of sexual harassment are women, men have also charged female superiors with sexual harassment, and a number of cases have involved harassment by members of the same sex. Not until 1986 did the U.S. Supreme Court rule in *Meritor Savings Bank v. Vinson* that, "without question," sexual harassment is a form of sex discrimination and that hostile environment as well as quid pro quo harassment violates Title VII of the Civil Rights Act of 1964. Unresolved questions regarding scope, employer liability, and evidentiary issues remain, however, to concern employers, employees, supervisors, unions, personnel staffs, and employment attorneys. Nevertheless, in this decision the Supreme Court took an important step toward legitimizing this elusive area of law for complainants and putting employers and harassers on notice that unwelcome sexual conduct will not be tolerated in the workplace. In *Harris v. Forklift Systems, Inc.* (1993) the Court addressed the issue of hostile environment again, holding that a plaintiff need not demonstrate psychological injury to prove sexual harassment. This chapter addresses the evolution of sexual harassment law generally and the range of legal theories and remedies available to the victim of sexual harassment.

## TYPES OF SEXUAL HARASSMENT

### Quid Pro Quo

Quid pro quo is the most obvious form of sexual harassment, involving the conditioning of employment benefits on sexual favors. As in traditional Title VII sex discrimination suits, the plaintiff must demonstrate that she was otherwise qualified to receive the relevant job benefit and that the job benefit was actually withheld or altered because of sexual harassment. The harassment may take several forms. Benefits may be withheld until a subordinate complies with sexual demands, a superior may retaliate against a subordinate for refusing to acquiesce, or a subordinate may comply with sexual demands and not receive a promised job benefit. Noncompliance has resulted in termination, transfer, denial or delay in receiving job benefits, and negative performance reviews. Underlying sexual harassment and other sexual discrimination claims is the requirement that, but for the sex of the complainant, the offending conduct would not have occurred (*Boyd v. James S. Hayes Living Health Care Agency*, 1987).

A plaintiff charging quid pro quo sexual harassment must prove by a preponderance of the evidence that she was denied an employment benefit because she refused to grant sexual favors (*Bundy v. Jackson*, 1981). In response an employer must show some legitimate motive for the adverse employment action, such as poor work performance, excessive absenteeism, lack of credentials, insubor-

dination, dishonesty, personality conflicts, violation of company policy, or lack of work. If the employer adequately supports its argument, the plaintiff must then demonstrate by a preponderance of the evidence that the proffered explanation was not the real reason for the employment decision (*Texas Dep't. of Community Affairs v. Burdine*, 1981). There are a number of ways in which a plaintiff may rebut the defendant's case, such as the employer failed to warn the plaintiff of poor work performance, failed to uncover the basis for the deterioration of work performance, or did not follow company policy in making the employment decision.

Unlike hostile environment harassment, a quid pro quo harassment claim may be based on a single incident. Almost all lower federal courts have held employers strictly liable for the quid pro quo sexual harassment of an employee by a supervisor, based on the agency doctrine of respondeat superior. An employer is generally liable for the torts committed by its employees who are acting within the scope of their employment. The doctrine breaks down in this context when sexual harassment occurs outside the scope of employment. Although the dynamics and potential for coercion remain outside the workplace or without delegated functions, courts have found employer liability in such situations. A policy prohibiting sexual harassment cannot insulate an employer from liability in quid pro quo cases, particularly when the complainant must report any grievances to her supervisor, the alleged offender, in order to invoke internal procedures.

Evidence of sexual advances made to other employees may be admitted on the issue of motive, intent, or plan in making the sexual advances toward the plaintiff.

### Hostile Environment

The concept of hostile environment sexual harassment has challenged courts to broaden their notions of sexual discrimination and offensive conduct. Hostile environment claims challenge workplace practices, rather than tangible job benefits, and consist of "verbal or physical conduct of a sexual nature" that unreasonably interferes with the employee's work or creates an "intimidating, hostile or offensive working environment" (EEOC Guidelines, 1993, §1604.11[a][3]). In *Meritor* the Supreme Court noted that the requirement that "a man or woman run a gauntlet of sexual abuse in return for the privilege of being allowed to work and make a living can be as demeaning and disconcerting as the harshest of racial epithets," and that requiring a victim of sexual harassment to demonstrate the loss of a tangible economic benefit would undermine the purpose of Title VII, which was to prevent discrimination against an employee with respect to "terms, conditions or privileges of employment." This type of harassment is both more pervasive and more elusive. Courts have acknowledged its debilitating emotional consequences:

> Victims of sexual harassment suffer stress effects from the harassment. Stress as a result of sexual harassment is recognized as a specific, diagnosable problem by the American Psychiatric Association.... Among the stress effect suffered is "work performance stress," which includes distraction from tasks, dread of work, and an inability to work.... Another form is "emotional stress," which covers a range of responses, including anger, fear of physical safety, anxiety, depression, guilt, humiliation, and embarrassment.... Physical stress also results from sexual harassment; it may manifest itself as sleeping problems, headaches, weight changes, and other physical ailments.... A study by the Working Women's Institute found that ninety-six percent of sexual harassment victims experience emotional stress, forty-five percent suffered work performance stress, and thirty-five percent were afflicted with physical stress problems.
>
> Sexual harassment has a cumulative, eroding effect on the victim's wellbeing.... When women feel a need to maintain vigilance against the next incident of harassment, the stress is increased tremendously.... When women feel that their individual complaints will not change the work environment materially, the ensuing sense of despair further compounds the stress. (*Robinson v. Jacksonville Shipyards, Inc.*, 1991, pp. 1506–1507)

## Conduct Constituting a Hostile Environment

Hostile environment harassment takes many forms, including repeated requests for sexual favors, demeaning sexual inquiries and vulgarities, offensive language, and other verbal or physical conduct of a sexual or degrading nature. Offensive conduct need not be sexual to contribute to a hostile environment. The First Amendment does not protect sexually harassing language in a hostile environment case. The regulation of such conduct in the workplace "constitutes nothing more than a time, place, and manner regulation of speech" (*Robinson v. Jacksonville Shipyards, Inc.*, 1991, p. 1535). In *Robinson* the court held that the First Amendment guarantee of freedom of speech did not impede the remedy of injunctive relief for verbal harassment and the pervasive use of pinups. The court noted that (1) the defendant disavowed that it sought to express itself through the sexually oriented pictures or the verbal harassment of its employees, (2) the pictures and verbal harassment were regulable because the eradication of workplace discrimination is a compelling governmental interest, (3) female workers are a captive audience in relation to the speech that constituted the hostile environment, and (4) the cleansing of the workplace of impediments to the equality of women is a compelling interest that permits the regulation of the speech and the regulation is narrowly drawn to serve this interest.

The physical work environment can be offensive when sexually offensive explicit or sexist signs, cartoons, calendars, literature, or photographs are displayed in plain view. In *Robinson* a female welder successfully asserted sexual harassment claims stemming from the extensive, pervasive posting of pictures depicting nude women and from sexual conduct by male coworkers. In *Sanchez v. City of Miami Beach* (1989) a district court concluded that a sexually harassing work environment was created by male police officers who subjected a female patrol officer to verbal abuse, "a plethora of sexually offensive posters, pictures, graffiti, and pinups placed on the walls throughout the Police Department" (*Sanchez*, p. 977).

Offensive graffiti may demean and intimidate an employee to the point that it affects her job performance. In *Danna v. New York Telephone Co.* (1990), graffiti and vulgar comments on workplace walls were at least partially responsible for the plaintiff seeking a demotion. The plaintiff's failure clearly to adduce specific harm did not relieve the defendant from liability when the graffiti remained on the walls for at least 2 years and the plaintiff was advised to not make "a stink about it" (*Danna*, p. 609).

An employer or supervisor also can alter working conditions by, for example, denigrating the employee in front of other workers, constantly picking on her, monitoring the plaintiff's work more closely than others', threatening her job security, or giving the employee different work assignments or less desirable physical facilities.

Whether the sexual conduct complained of is sufficiently pervasive to create a hostile or offensive work environment must be determined by a totality of the circumstances (*Vinson v. Meritor Savings Bank*, 1986; *Harris v. Forklift Systems, Inc.*, 1994). In *Ross v. Double Diamond, Inc.* (1987) the District Court for the Northern District of Texas noted that a short duration of sexual harassment does not obviate a Title VII claim if the harassment is frequent and/or intensely offensive, finding that it would be inconsistent with this new awakening to allege that someone who has been intensely sexually harassed at the workplace does not have a claim under Title VII because he or she did not stay on the job for a longer period of time and subject himself or herself to further degradation.

Incidents of sexual harassment directed at employees other than the plaintiff may be used to establish a hostile work environment, and the alleged offensive conduct need not be purely sexual.

African American women face unique patterns of harassment. In *Hicks v. Gates Rubber Co.* (1987), for example, the Tenth Circuit held that although the employer's work environment was not openly hostile to African Americans, evidence of racial treatment could be combined with that of sexual harassment to establish a hostile work environment toward an African American woman employee. "[A]n employer who singles out black females for less favorable treatment does not defeat plaintiff's case by showing that white females or black males are not so unfavorably treated" (*Graham v. Bendix Corp.*, 1984, p. 1047).

## Liability

While quid pro quo sexual harassment can only be committed by someone with authority to change the employee's job status, employers, supervisors, coworkers, customers, or clients can create a hostile work environment. Generally, employers are liable for the conduct of their employees in hostile environment cases only when they knew or should have known of the offensive behavior. Actual knowledge may be obtained through firsthand observations, an internal complaint to other management employees, or a formal complaint of discrimination. Evidence of the pervasiveness of the conduct may establish constructive knowledge. The Supreme Court in *Meritor* declined to issue a definitive rule on employer liability, noting that the record was insufficient to decide the issue, but it concluded that the court of appeals erroneously applied a strict liability standard to employers whose supervisors have created a hostile environment. Rejecting the views of both the EEOC guidelines and the court of appeals, the Court stated that it was "wrong to entirely disregard agency principles and impose strict liability on employers for the acts of their supervisors, regardless of the circumstances of the particular case." The Court felt that in defining "employer" under Title VII to include any "agent" of the employer, Congress intended to limit the scope of employer liability (*Meritor*, p. 73).

Unlike quid pro quo sexual harassment cases, in which a supervisor has actual or apparent authority to affect the employee's job status, the creation of a sexually hostile environment is less clear-cut in terms of whether a supervisor is acting within the scope of his or her employment. In quid pro quo cases, employers are strictly liable because agency principles impute notice of supervisory harassment to the employer. In a typical hostile environment action the harassers may be coworkers who do not act as the employer's agents, and thus the employer should not be liable without notice and an opportunity to remedy the situation. But the power enjoyed by supervisors over employees would seem to leave no room for a liability distinction between quid pro quo and hostile environment cases. The legal relationship between an employer and a supervisor should be such that an employer is on notice of liability for all of its supervisors' actions. In his concurrence, Justice Marshall noted that a supervisor's responsibilities do not begin and end with the power to hire, fire, and discipline employees, or with the power to recommend such actions; rather, a supervisor is charged with the day-to-day supervision of the work environment and with ensuring a safe, productive workplace, and there was no reason why abuse of the latter authority should have different consequences than abuse of the former.

Although the majority in *Meritor* rejected the notion of strict liability in hostile environment cases, it recognized that agency principles "may not be transferable in all their particulars to Title VII" and appeared to reject an absolute requirement of notice as well, stating that "absence of notice to an employer does not necessarily insulate that employer from liability" (*Meritor*, 1986, p. 72). Nor does the existence of a grievance procedure and a policy against discrimination preclude a finding of liability.

## Conduct Must Be Unwelcome

"The gravamen of any sexual harassment claims is that the alleged sexual advances were 'unwelcome'" (*Meritor*, 1986, p. 68). The plaintiff must show she was actually offended by the conduct and suffered some injury from it. A number of courts have focused on the plaintiff's participation in allegedly offensive conduct or other workplace behavior. In *Meritor* the Supreme Court

held that the court of appeals erred in concluding that testimony regarding the plaintiff's "provocative dress and publicly expressed fantasies" had no place in the litigation (*Meritor*, 1986, p. 69). The Court rejected the bank's contention that it could not be held liable for the alleged sexual conduct because Vinson participated in the acts voluntarily, concluding that the district court had improperly focused on Vinson's compliance. The correct inquiry was whether Vinson by her conduct indicated that the alleged sexual advances were unwelcome, not whether her actual participation was voluntary, and that evidence such as dress and fantasies was "obviously relevant" in determining whether sexual harassment occurred (*Meritor*, 1986, p. 69). So, although voluntary participation is not an absolute defense to a claim of sexual harassment, it is a factor in deciding whether sexual advances were unwelcome. Because the alleged harasser maintained that the alleged sexual incidents never occurred, not that the plaintiff welcomed his advances, the Court could have declined to consider whether the plaintiff's fantasies and clothing supported a finding that the sexual advances were welcome. By admitting such evidence, courts turn the plaintiff into the accused and shift the focus from the conduct of the harasser to the nature of the harassed. While employers still should be able to argue that the plaintiff welcomed sexual advances, such a showing should be made without introducing highly charged and subjective evidence. Courts may now feel compelled to consider this type of evidence whether or not they consider it appropriate to do so. For example, in *Jones v. Wesco* (1988) the Eighth Circuit stated that a court must consider any provocative speech or dress of the plaintiff in a sexual harassment case and observed from the record that the plaintiff "wore non-provocative clothing." In *Weiss v. Amoco Oil Co.* (1992), a wrongful termination action by a male employee fired for sexual harassment, the plaintiff sought to engage in discovery concerning the alleged victim's sexual history. According to the plaintiff, the alleged victim had cards pinned up at her workstation that were of a sexual nature, sent another male employee a birthday card that showed the torso of an adult female wearing a bikini, made sexual jokes with other employees, and discussed her sexual activities while at work. The court held that the alleged victim, a nonparty witness, failed to meet her burden of showing that information concerning her sexual history was irrelevant and not reasonably calculated to lead to discovery of admissible evidence. The court noted that the material sought was relevant in assessing the thoroughness of Amoco's investigation into Streebin's complaint of sexual harassment. Weiss alleged that he and Streebin were social friends who dated occasionally, and that Streebin dated other fellow employees. Weiss alleges that a thorough investigation into Streebin's complaint against him would have disclosed these facts, facts that would be necessary in any analysis of Streebin's sexual harassment complaint against Weiss.

The fact that the plaintiff had a consensual relationship with her alleged harasser does not welcome harassment that occurs after the relationship ends. In *Shrout v. Black Clawson* (1988) a consensual relationship of 3 years between the plaintiff and the defendant was followed by 4 years of sexual advances and comments and refusals to give the plaintiff pay raises and performance evaluations because she refused to continue the relationship. The court concluded that the plaintiff had been subjected to quid pro quo as well as hostile environment sexual harassment. In *Babcock v. Frank* (1990), allegations that the plaintiff's supervisor begged her to love him again, along with his subsequent issuance of a disciplinary letter against her, were more than sufficient to raise an inference in a reasonable person that the defendant used his supervisory authority to blackmail the plaintiff into accepting his sexual advances. After ending the relationship, the plaintiff had the right, like any other worker, to be free from a sexually abusive environment and to reject sexual advances without the threat of punishment. Some courts, however, have refused to find sexual harassment in cases involving prior consensual relationships because of the requirement that the plaintiff must have been

discriminated against because of membership in a particular class. In *Huebschen v. Department of Health and Social Services* (1983) the Seventh Circuit reversed the trial court's finding of sexual harassment when there was no evidence that a female supervisor who had started insulting the plaintiff after they had had a "one-night stand" intentionally discriminated against the plaintiff because he was a man or that she had attempted to discriminate against other men in the workplace. In *Keppler v. Hinsdale Township High School District 86* (1989) the court construed *Huebschen* to preclude quid pro quo claims by plaintiffs who had had consensual relationships with their alleged harassers and distinguished the type of quid pro quo claims stemming from the conditioning of job benefits on the receipt of sexual favors from those stemming from retaliatory conduct, concluding that retaliatory claims create a presumption against a finding of sexual harassment. The court noted that an employee who chooses to become involved in an intimate affair with her employer removes an element of her employment relationship from the workplace, and in the realm of private affairs, people have the right to react to rejection, jealousy, and other emotions that Title VII says have no place in the employment setting.

Victims of sexual harassment often tolerate offensive conduct in fear of retribution. Failure to report incidents of harassment, however, may suggest to the court that the conduct was not so severe or pervasive as to alter the plaintiff's condition of employment. Courts almost always consider whether the plaintiff complained of the challenged conduct in making a determination of hostile environment.

## Psychological Impact of Harassment

In *Harris v. Forklift Systems* (1993), in which the plaintiff alleged that she was constructively discharged from her manager position because of a sexually hostile environment created by the company president, the trial court found that although the plaintiff "was the object of a continuing pattern of sex-based derogatory conduct from Hardy," including sexual innuendos about clothing worn by the plaintiff and other female employees; throwing things on the ground in front of the plaintiff and other female employees and asking them to pick them up; asking the plaintiff and other female employees to retrieve coins from his front pockets; stating to the plaintiff, "Let's go to the Holiday Inn and negotiate your raise," "You're a woman, what do you know," "You're a dumb ass woman," and "We need a man as the rental manager," the plaintiff was not able to prove that the president's conduct was so severe as to create a hostile work environment when the court found that the alleged harasser's comments could not be characterized as much more than annoying and insensitive. The trial court did not believe that the plaintiff was subjectively so offended that she suffered injury, when she repeatedly testified that she loved her job, she and her husband socialized with Hardy and his wife, and she herself drank beer and socialized with Hardy and her coworkers.

In a unanimous opinion the Supreme Court rejected the standard adopted by the lower courts and held that psychological harm is one factor among many that the courts may weigh in a sexual harassment case. Federal law "comes into play before the harassing conduct leads to a nervous breakdown." Writing for the Court, Justice O'Connor stated that Title VII as applied to sexual harassment is violated when, for any of a variety of reasons, "the environment would be perceived, and is perceived, as hostile or abusive" and that "no single factor is required."

> As we made clear in *Meritor Savings Bank v. Vinson*, (1986), [Title VII's] language "is not limited to 'economic' or 'tangible' discrimination. The phrase 'terms, conditions, or privileges of employment' evinces a Congressional intent 'to strike at the entire spectrum of disparate treatment of men and women' in employment," which includes requiring people to work in a discriminatorily hostile or abusive environment. When the workplace is permeated with "discriminatory intimidation, ridicule, and insult" that

is "sufficiently severe or pervasive to alter the conditions of the victim's employment and create an abusive working environment," Title VII is violated.

> This standard, which we reaffirm today, takes a middle path between making actionable any conduct that is merely offensive and requiring the conduct to cause a tangible psychological injury. As we pointed out in *Meritor*, "mere utterance of an ... epithet which engenders offensive feelings in an employee" does not sufficiently affect the conditions of employment to implicate Title VII. Conduct that is not severe or pervasive enough to create an objectively hostile or abusive work environment, an environment that a reasonable person would find hostile or abusive, is beyond Title VII's purview. Likewise, if the victim does not subjectively perceive the environment to be abusive, the conduct has not actually altered the conditions of the victim's employment, and there is no Title VII violation.

> But Title VII comes into play before the harassing conduct leads to a nervous breakdown. A discriminatorily abusive work environment, even one that does not seriously affect employees' psychological well-being, can and often will detract from employees' job performance, discourage employees from remaining on the job, or keep them from advancing in their careers. Moreover, even without regard to these tangible effects, the very fact that the discriminatory conduct was so severe or pervasive that it created a work environment abusive to employees because of their race, gender, religion, or national origin offends Title VII's broad rule of workplace equality. The appalling conduct alleged in *Meritor*, and the reference in that case to environments " 'so heavily polluted with discrimination as to destroy completely the emotional and psychological stability of minority group workers,' " merely present some especially egregious examples of harassment. They do not mark the boundary of what is actionable.

> We therefore believe the District Court erred in relying on whether the conduct "seriously affect(ed) plaintiff's psychological well-being" or led her to "suffe(r) injury." Such an inquiry may needlessly focus the factfinder's attention on concrete psychological harm, an element Title VII

does not require. Certainly Title VII bars conduct that would seriously affect a reasonable person's psychological well-being, but the statute is not limited to such conduct. So long as the environment would reasonably be perceived, and is perceived, as hostile or abusive, there is no need for it also to be psychologically injurious.

This is not, and by its nature cannot be, a mathematically precise test. We need not answer today all the potential questions it raises, nor specifically address the E.E.O.C.'s new regulations on this subject. But we can say that whether an environment is "hostile" or "abusive" can be determined only by looking at all the circumstances. These may include the frequency of the discriminatory conduct; its severity; whether it is physically threatening or humiliating, or a mere offensive utterance; and whether it unreasonably interferes with an employee's work performance. The effect on the employee's psychological well-being is, of course, relevant to determining whether the plaintiff actually found the environment abusive. But while psychological harm, like any other relevant factor, may be taken into account, no single factor is required (*Harris*, pp. 370–371).

Justice Ginsburg concurred, stating that Title VII's critical issue is whether members of one sex are exposed to disadvantageous terms or conditions of employment to which members of the other sex are not exposed, and that, as the EEOC as amici curiae emphasized, "the adjudicator's inquiry should center, dominantly, on whether the discriminatory conduct has unreasonably interfered with the plaintiff's work performance" (*Harris*, p. 372), and that to show such interference, the plaintiff need not prove that her or his tangible productivity has declined as a result of the harassment but only that the harassment so altered working conditions as to make it more difficult to do the job.

Justice Scalia concurred as well, noting that although he knew of no alternative to the course taken by the Court, he was concerned that the term "abusive" did not seem to be a very clear standard and that clarity was not increased by adding the adverb "objectively"

or by appealing to a "reasonable person's" notion of what the "vague" word means:

Today's opinion does list a number of factors that contribute to abusiveness, but since it neither says how much of each is necessary (an impossible task) nor identifies any single factor as determinative, it thereby adds little certitude. As a practical matter, today's holding lets virtually unguided juries decide whether sex-related conduct engaged in (or permitted by) an employer is egregious enough to warrant an award of damages.

One might say that what constitutes "negligence" (a traditional jury question) is not much more clear and certain than what constitutes "abusiveness." Perhaps so. But the class of plaintiffs seeking to recover for negligence is limited to those who have suffered harm, whereas under this statute "abusiveness" is to be the test of whether legal harm has been suffered, opening more expansive vistas of litigation. (*Harris*, p. 372)

## THE REASONABLE WOMAN STANDARD

*Robinson v. Jacksonville Shipyards* (1991) was the first case to delve into the issue of whether sexually harassing conduct should be measured by its impact on a reasonable woman, rather than a reasonable person or victim. The Ninth Circuit advanced the reasonable woman standard in *Ellison v. Brady* (1991) to determine whether conduct is sufficiently pervasive to alter the conditions of employment and create a hostile working environment. A female revenue agent for the IRS had alleged that a male coworker's amorous attention frightened her, and even though he was subsequently transferred, he returned to her office and wrote her another love letter. The court held that it is the harasser's conduct that must be pervasive or severe, not the alteration in the conditions of employment, and that in evaluating the severity and pervasiveness of sexual harassment, a court should focus on the perspective of the victim. The court adopted the perspective of a reasonable woman primarily because it believed that a sex-blind reasonable person standard tends to be male-biased and to systematically ignore the experiences of women. If courts only examined whether a reasonable person would engage in allegedly harassing conduct, they would run the risk of reinforcing the prevailing level of discrimination. Harassers could continue to harass merely because a particular discriminatory practice was common, and victims of harassment would have no remedy. A thorough understanding of the victim's view requires, among other things, an analysis of the different perspectives of men and women. For example, because women are disproportionately victims of rape and sexual assault, women have a stronger incentive to be concerned with sexual behavior. Women who are victims of mild forms of sexual harassment may understandably worry whether a harasser's conduct is merely a prelude to violent sexual assault. Men, who are rarely victims of sexual assault, may see sexual conduct in a vacuum without a full understanding of the social setting or the underlying threat of violence that a woman may perceive.

The court noted that in order to shield employers from having to accommodate the idiosyncratic concerns of the rare hypersensitive employee, it would hold that a female plaintiff states a prima facie case of hostile environment sexual harassment when she alleges conduct that a reasonable woman would consider sufficiently severe or pervasive to alter the conditions of employment and to create an abusive working environment.

In *Andrews v. City of Philadelphia* (1990), in which the plaintiff police officers alleged a hostile work environment created by abusive language, sexually explicit pictures at the workplace, the destruction of the plaintiffs' private property and work product, physical injury, and anonymous telephone calls at home, the court of appeals reversed the trial court's ruling against the plaintiffs and held that to prove a hostile environment, a plaintiff must demonstrate that the discrimination would detrimentally affect a reasonable person of the same sex in that position, thus protecting the employer from an oversensitive employee but still serving the goal of equal opportunity by removing the walls of discrim-

ination that deprive women of self-respecting employment. The court noted that men and women have different perspectives on obscene language and pornography: "Although men may find these actions harmless and innocent, it is highly possible that women may feel otherwise" (*Andrews*, p. 1486).

In *Austin v. State of Hawaii et al.* (1991) the district court cited *Ellison* with approval in ruling in favor of the plaintiff English professor in an action alleging sexual harassment by the male chair of the English department, noting that the chair referred to her in ways that reasonable women consider to be typical of males who consider women inferior.

The court certified a class of women employees alleging sex discrimination including sexual harassment in *Jenson v. Eveleth Taconite Co.* (1991), noting that the common question of law was not how an individual class member reacted, but whether a reasonable woman would find the work environment hostile.

Several state courts have also applied the reasonable woman standard. In *Lehmann v. Toys 'R' Us, Inc.* (1993), the New Jersey Supreme Court carefully considered the basis for such a test, noting that an objective reasonableness standard better focuses the court's attention on the nature and legality of the conduct rather than on the reaction of the individual plaintiff, which is more relevant to damages, and that as community standards evolve, the standard of what a reasonable woman would consider harassment will also evolve. In *Radtke v. Everett* (1991), however, in which the plaintiff alleged that her employer forcibly held her down, caressed and attempted to kiss her, the Supreme Court addressed the elements of a prima facie case of a hostile work environment under the Michigan Civil Rights Act and held that the reasonable woman standard violated the legislative intent of the Act, concluding that if the Legislature intended a departure from that standard, it would have explicitly mandated that alteration, and that the reasonable person standard should be utilized because it is sufficiently flexible to incorporate gender differences.

## THIRD-PARTY EMPLOYEES

### Quid Pro Quo

Otherwise qualified employees who lose employment opportunities because job benefits went to those who submitted to sexual harassment may have discrimination claims under Title VII. Both men and women may be entitled to bring such a claim. A qualified male may lose a potential job benefit on the basis of sex, or a qualified woman who was not approached sexually by a supervisor may lose a job benefit to a less qualified woman who submitted unwillingly to sexual advances. In *Broderick v. Ruder* (1988) a female attorney who refused to participate in workplace sexual conduct successfully challenged a work environment in which compliance with sexual advances brought career advancement and other employment benefits to other employees.

Although romantic relationships between a supervisor and an employee sometimes result in the woman subordinate's enjoying certain unique job benefits, some courts have held that such preferential treatment is not gender-based discrimination (*Miller v. Aluminum Co. of Am.*, 1988). But in *Piech v. Arthur Andersen & Co.* (1994) the plaintiff asserted a claim that a less qualified, single female coworker was promoted to manager instead of her because of the "favored" female's knowledge of inappropriate male partner sexual conduct and her amorous relationship with a partner in the decision-making process, but did not allege that she suffered an adverse employment decision because of her sex. The plaintiff did allege that it was generally necessary for women to grant sexual favors to decision makers for professional advances and that because she did not grant sexual favors she was denied a promotion, fitting the classic definition of quid pro quo harassment. Plaintiff's allegations "regarding the favored female co-worker who received a promotion while involved romantically with a decision-maker may be considered simply circumstantial evidence that her employer conditioned employment benefits on the granting of sexual favors" (*Piech*, pp. 442–443). And in *Dirksen v. City of Springfield* (1994) a demoted female secretary for the city police department claimed that a police officer made numerous nonconsensual sexual advances toward her that included attempts to kiss and touch her body; offensive placement of his hands on her body; forcing the placement of her hands on his body; attempted sexual assault, during which the alleged harasser stated that if the plaintiff wanted to be promoted to his personal secretary, she had to submit to sexual intercourse with him; and that when she went on medical leave, she was replaced by a worker who was having sexual relations with him. The complainant stated a claim for quid pro quo sexual harassment, despite the defendant's argument that the plaintiff was not discriminated against on the basis of sex but because her boss allegedly favored his paramour. This was not a single instance of favoritism; plaintiff alleges that it was generally necessary for *women* to grant sexual favors to the officer to obtain professional advancement.

When such romantic involvement and its job-related implications are a matter of common knowledge, however, the work atmosphere may be tainted in violation of Title VII, and thus a hostile environment claim may be appropriate.

### Hostile Environment

A hostile work environment is most likely experienced by other employees besides the complainant. Even a woman who was never herself the object of harassment might have a Title VII claim if she were forced to work in an atmosphere in which such harassment was pervasive. This type of harassment includes situations in which male supervisors have romantic relationships with female subordinates and afford them job benefits to the detriment of other employees. In *Broderick v. Ruder* (1988) an attorney for the Securities and Exchange Commission was awarded $120,000 in back pay and interest and previously denied promotions for proving that her office supervisors created a hostile work environment by engaging in sexually offensive conduct. Such conduct included rewarding employees who complied with sexual advances with promotions and other employment benefits to the detriment of Broderick, who had refused such requests. Despite the fact that few of the alleged incidents of harassment had been directed at Broderick herself, the environment "poisoned any possibility of plaintiff's having the proper professional respect for her supervisors and, without any question, affected her motivation and her performance of her job responsibilities" (*Broderick*, p. 1273). Although Broderick had complained to higher management, no one was ever disciplined for conduct that was common knowledge, and management made no serious effort to enforce guidelines prohibiting sex discrimination.

Broderick clearly established a violation of Title VII through her testimony and that of coworkers. Not only were her working conditions "poisoned" to the extent that she suffered psychologically, but she was denied tangible work benefits as a result of her supervisors' flagrant sexual conduct. The hybrid nature of Broderick's hostile environment claim, which included allegations that employment benefits were bestowed upon compliant employees to Broderick's detriment, gave the case that quid pro quo element that courts have embraced. However, it is unclear how far the courts will take Title VII.

Preferential treatment not only undermines an employee's motivation and work performance but also deprives her of job opportunities. Some courts have argued that because women and men are in the same position with respect to lost employment opportunities, such conduct cannot form the basis of a sex discrimination charge (*Miller v. Aluminum Co. of Am.*, 1988). While it is true that women and men both may suffer the loss of similar benefits, the bases for their respective charges differ. Because the qualified man is an unlikely candidate for an office romance with a presumably heterosexual supervisor, he relinquishes a job opportunity to the less qualified but involved woman on the basis of his sex, and thus he may bring an employ-

ment discrimination action. The qualified woman who loses job benefits to a less qualified but involved woman or who is exposed to male supervisors having affairs with subordinates and showering them with attention is undermined. She is made to feel that, among other things, merit and hard work by women are irrelevant, women get ahead by sleeping with their superiors, sexual objectification is a byproduct of employment, and women have no control over their professional destinies short of submitting to sexual advances. This sense of loss of control may be enhanced when the plaintiff is also subjected to sexual advances or fears physical violence. Clearly, these elements create a hostile work environment in violation of Title VII.

An employee who protests the sexual harassment of other employees may bring a retaliation action if adverse personnel actions are taken in response to such complaints. For such a claim to survive judicial scrutiny, the plaintiff must give the employer a fair opportunity to remedy the situation.

## CONSTRUCTIVE DISCHARGE

An employee is constructively discharged when the employer deliberately makes that employee's working conditions so onerous that a reasonable person would find them intolerable. In *EEOC v. Gurnee Inn Corp.* (1988), for example, the decision of a female employee to quit her job amounted to a constructive discharge when in addition to rebuffing a supervisor's advances, she was forced to observe sexual conduct in her workplace and watch employees who tolerated it receive better treatment by the supervisor. She was unable to help her subordinates avoid the supervisor's advances because management refused to take action.

Sexual harassment may force a person to quit her job, giving rise to a separate constructive discharge claim in addition to claims of sexual harassment, although someone who leaves a position need not prove constructive discharge in order to obtain relief for sexual harassment under Title VII. Intent may be inferred from circumstantial evidence, including a failure to act in the face of known intolerable conditions. Either type of harassment, quid pro quo or hostile environment, may form the basis for a constructive discharge claim. Constructive discharge will not be established, however, merely by demonstrating that sexual harassment occurred. Nor will constructive discharge be established if the incidents of harassment are too remote in time from the resignation. Constructive discharge also will not be found if resignation occurred for reasons other than alleged sexual harassment, or if the employer did not receive actual or constructive notice of the alleged harassment or was not given sufficient time to remedy the situation. The Sixth Circuit has required some inquiry into the employer's intent and the reasonably foreseeable impact of its conduct on the employee. A reasonable woman standard should be applied to determine whether the harassed employee quit because of sexual harassment. In *Radtke v. Everett* (1991) the Michigan Court of Appeal held that the constructive discharge claim of a female veterinary technician who was caressed and kissed by her supervisor during a break and who subsequently ended her employment and sought counseling should have survived summary judgment. A single incident of sexual harassment could be sufficiently severe under some circumstances to support a finding that a reasonable woman's employment was substantially affected or that a hostile environment was created. In some cases the mere presence of a harasser may create a hostile environment. The proper perspective to view the offensive conduct from was that of a reasonable woman. Most courts have applied a reasonable person standard, and the reasonable person "in the plaintiff's position" test may imply a reasonable woman standard.

Coworkers and nonemployees as well as supervisors may create conditions giving rise to a constructive discharge claim. The failure by supervisors to take immediate remedial action after notice of harassment by coworkers may constitute constructive discharge.

An employee need not quit her job to raise a claim of constructive discharge. For example, forced medical leave without pay may be deemed a constructive discharge for purposes of back pay liability. Nor does an employee have to resign immediately after the harassing conduct has occurred in order to plead constructive discharge.

## RETALIATION

Title VII prohibits discrimination against an employee who has either opposed an employment practice made unlawful under Title VII or made a charge or participated in any manner in an investigation, procedure, or hearing under Title VII. To determine whether an action is protected by Title VII, the court must consider whether the employee's conduct was reasonable in light of the circumstances. The trial court also should balance the employer's right to run a business with the right of employees to express their grievances.

Sexual harassment complaints often include claims of retaliation, and such claims may succeed despite a finding that no violation of Title VII has occurred. A prima facie case of retaliation is established by proof that (1) the plaintiff engaged in statutorily protected opposition or participation, (2) an adverse employment action occurred, and (3) there was a causal link between the opposition or participation and the adverse employment action.

The opposition clause of Title VII protects a variety of forms of expression. In addition to the filing of charges, protected activity includes resisting advances; registering internal complaints of sexual harassment; testifying on behalf or supporting the claims of another employee; picketing; or, when appropriate, notifying law enforcement authorities.

The most common form of retaliatory action is dismissal. Other adverse employment actions may include demotion, transfer, negative evaluation, and verbal misconduct. Temporary transfers or demotions that reduce an employee's duties and responsibilities but maintain salary and benefits may not constitute adverse employment actions.

The causal link element requires only that the plaintiff establish that the protected activity and the adverse action "were not wholly unrelated" (*Petrosky v. Washington-Greene County Branch Pa. Assoc. for the Blind*, 1987, p. 825). "Essential to a causal link is evidence that the employer was aware that the plaintiff had engaged in the protected activity" (*Miller v. Aluminum Co. of Am.*, 1988, p. 504). A plaintiff may establish this link when only a short period of time has passed between the protected activity and the adverse personnel action, as well as by circumstantial evidence. For example, the employee may have received favorable evaluations before engaging in the protected activity but negative evaluations afterward.

An employee may not use her right to oppose unlawful activity to undermine legitimate interests of the employer. In *Jones v. Flagship International* (1986) the court of appeals affirmed the district court's decision that a former equal employment opportunity manager who encouraged other employees to file discrimination charges and who sought to maintain a class action clearly engaged in protected activity when she filed a discrimination charge with the EEOC. Her subsequent suspension and termination were adverse employment actions, but she failed to establish the causal link between the two. The district court found that the defendant suspended the plaintiff to avoid the "conflict of interest inherent in Jones's representation of Flagship before the agency to whom she made the complaint" and because she planned to initiate a class action suit against the company. The court considered the evidence of Jones's solicitation of other employees to sue or join the class suit and concluded that Jones's actions "not only rendered her ineffective in the position for which she was employed, but critically harmed Flagship's posture in the defense of discrimination suits brought against the company."

As in disparate treatment cases, the plaintiff meets the initial burden by establishing facts sufficient to permit an inference of retaliatory motive. Once this burden is met, the defendant must articulate a legitimate, nondiscriminatory reason for the personnel action. The employer must show by clear and convincing evidence that the plaintiff would not have been treated differently if she had not opposed the harassment. The reason for this different rule in sexual harassment cases is that once a plaintiff establishes that she was harassed, it is difficult to see how an employer can justify the harassment. The plaintiff will prevail if she then demonstrates by a preponderance of the evidence that the proffered reason was but a pretext for retaliation or by persuading the court that the desire to retaliate more likely motivated the employer.

## EMPLOYER RESPONSE TO COMPLAINTS OF SEXUAL HARASSMENT

An employer's liability for sexual harassment often turns on the response to complaints of sexual harassment. The response must be reasonably calculated to prevent further harassment (*Juarez v. Ameritech Mobile Communications*, 1990). In *Robinson v. Jacksonville Shipyards, Inc.* (1991) the court measured the effectiveness of employer response in two ways. First, the total response may be evaluated on the basis of the circumstances as then existed. It is ineffective if the employer delayed unduly and the action taken, however promptly, was not reasonably likely to prevent the harassment from recurring. Second, an employer can show that the conduct brought to the company's attention was not repeated after the employer took action. In *Watts v. New York Police Department* (1989) the court held that Title VII imposes an affirmative duty on the employer to investigate charges, even if the harassment stops after the complaint is made. Here a probationary police officer who filed a sexual harassment charge against her instructor was subsequently subjected to further harassment in the form of verbal attacks and ostracism by her coworkers and supervisors, but not her instructor. The court concluded that the employer has an obligation to investigate whether acts conducive to the creation of an atmosphere of hostility do in fact occur, and, if so, it must attempt to dispel workplace hostility by taking prompt remedial steps. For that reason, the fact that the plaintiff, after apprising the police department of concerns about harassment by one officer, instead became the victim of harassment by another did not provide the department with a shield against its duty to take reasonable measures to enforce the federal policy that sexual harassment will not be tolerated in the workplace.

The prompt investigation of a sexual harassment complaint followed by appropriate action will usually prevent a finding of liability against the employer. In *Carmon v. Lubrizol Corp.* (1994) the district court determined that an employer took prompt and remedial action in response to a female employee's two sexual harassment complaints when the employer sprang into action immediately: met with the plaintiff on the same day as her first complaint, questioned the alleged harasser, interviewed six witnesses, found that the alleged harasser and the plaintiff had used foul language, reprimanded the alleged harasser, and transferred him to another shift. A similar investigation was conducted the next year following another complaint of sexual harassment. Similarly, in *Saxton v. American Tel. & Tel. Co.* (1993), the employer took appropriate corrective action upon notice of sexual harassment when the department head promptly began a thorough investigation of the employee's charges, interviewing principals as well as witnesses; recommended the separation of the parties; began the process of transferring the supervisor after learning that the employee did not want a transfer; and allowed the employee to work at home during the entire process.

Allegations of harassment that are investigated only to the extent that the alleged harasser denies the charges may be insufficient (*Mays v. Williamson & Sons, Janitorial Servs.*, 1985). In *Heelan v. Johns-Manville Corp.* (1978), management's response to complaints of sexual harassment by a supervisor consisted only of calling the accused harasser on the phone for verification or denial and hardly satisfied the company's obligation under Title VII. And in *Hansel v. Public Service Co.* (1991), merely discussing the issue with four of the perpetrators was

insufficient to stop harassment of female machine operators that had been occurring over an 8-year period when, although physical harassment ceased, other forms continued. The court noted that a hostile environment "is like a disease. It can have many symptoms, some of which change over time, but all of which stem from the same root" (*Hansel*, p. 1132). The court went so far as to hold that Title VII imposes an affirmative duty on employers to seek out and eradicate a hostile work environment. "An employer simply cannot sit back and wait for complaints. The very nature of sexual harassment inhibits its victims from coming forward because of fear of retaliation" (*Hansel*, p. 1133).

Termination of an alleged harasser usually is not required; other forms of discipline such as suspension, demotion, or transfer may be appropriate. A warning may suffice in certain cases if more severe discipline is imposed for subsequent misconduct (*Bigoni v. Pay 'n Pak Stores*, 1990), but one court has held that an employer's knowledge of previous sexual harassment could render the employer liable for the harasser's subsequent conduct (*Paroline v. Unisys Corp.*, 1989). The transfer of the complainant is usually not appropriate, but in *Nash v. Electrospace System, Inc.* (1993) the defendant employer adequately responded to an employee's claim of sexual harassment by a supervisor, thus precluding liability under Title VII, when the employer immediately began an investigation of the supervisor, and, when the charges could not be corroborated because the supervisor denied them and coworkers had not experienced offensive behavior by him, the plaintiff was transferred to another department with no loss of pay or benefits. The investigation and transfer occurred within a week of the plaintiff's first complaint, and the record indicated that the transfer was successful as the plaintiff got along well with her new boss and soon was eligible for a raise.

The existence of an effective grievance procedure and the enforcement of a sexual harassment policy can help an employer avoid liability.

## FEDERAL REMEDIES FOR SEXUAL HARASSMENT

### Title VII

Most sexual harassment suits are brought under Title VII of the Civil Rights Act of 1964. Title VII provides in part:

> It shall be an unlawful employment practice for an employer (1) to fail or refuse to hire or to discharge any individual, or otherwise to discriminate against any individual with respect to [her or] his compensation, terms, conditions, or privileges of employment, because of such individual's...sex...; or (2) to limit, segregate, or classify [her or] his employees or applicants for employment in any way which would deprive or tend to deprive any individual of employment opportunities or otherwise adversely affect [her or] his status as an employee, because of such individual's ... sex. (Title VII, Civil Rights Act §2000e-2(a))

Title VII was passed to provide equal opportunity through the removal of artificial barriers to employment. To accomplish the congressional purpose of giving an effective voice to victims of employment discrimination, Title VII also prohibits employers from retaliating against employees who initiate complaints. In 1972, Congress extended the protections of Title VII to federal employees. With little legislative history available to assist the courts, judicial interpretation of the prohibition against sex discrimination has been largely a self-guided process. Indeed, the addition of the provision prohibiting sex discrimination apparently was a last-minute attempt to defeat Title VII's passage. However, the 1972 amendments to Title VII indicate a clear congressional intent to eliminate sex discrimination.

Title VII has been broadly construed. In *Sprogis v. United Airlines, Inc.* (1971) the Seventh Circuit stated that Congress intended to strike at the entire spectrum of disparate treatment of men and women resulting from sex stereotypes. Ten years after the enactment of Title VII, sexual harassment claims became an important part of the discrimination spectrum.

### The Civil Rights Act of 1991

In the aftermath of the Clarence Thomas hearings, former President Bush signed the Civil Rights Act of 1991 on November 21, 1991, thus ending a two-year political battle. The Act amends Title VII of the Civil Rights Act of 1964, section 1981 of the Civil Rights Act of 1866, the Attorney's Fees Awards Act of 1976, the Age Discrimination in Employment Act of 1967 (ADEA), and the Americans with Disabilities Act of 1990 (ADA). The Act has a significant impact on sexual harassment cases by providing damage awards in federal court as well as expert witness fees and jury trials. The Act is particularly beneficial to sexual harassment plaintiffs who live in states where damages for such conduct are not available under state law or in jurisdictions unsympathetic to such claims. Under prior law, damages were available only to victims of intentional racial or ethnic discrimination. The Civil Rights Act of 1991 (CRA) corrects the inadequate remedial provisions of Title VII by extending compensatory and punitive damages to victims of employment discrimination based on sex, religion, and disability as well as race under Title VII, the ADA, and the Rehabilitation Act of 1973. Compensatory damages are available from private employers and federal, state, and local governments. Punitive damages, however, may only be recovered from private employers when the employer acted with malice or with reckless indifference to the rights of the victim. Under the 1991 law, punitive damages are capped at $50,000 for companies of 100 or fewer workers and at $100,000 for companies with 101 to 200 employees, $200,000 for employers with 201 to 500 employees, and $300,000 for employers of over 500 employees. Sexual harassment plaintiffs who sought monetary relief for their injuries previously had to resort to state court or append state law claims to their federal claims. Federal courts must agree to assert jurisdiction over the pendent state law claims. A major deterrent to the litigation of sexual harassment claims has been the financial investment necessary to obtain elusive remedies. Reinstatement is often not an option, as the victim of sexual harassment may be unwilling to return to a hostile environment or has found other employment during what can be years of litigation. An injunction provides only prospective relief, and back pay may be offset by subsequent earnings in a new job. Under the Civil Rights Act of 1991, victims of sexual harassment can recover compensatory damages for medical bills or psychiatric treatment necessary as a result of harassment. Compensatory damages include future pecuniary losses, emotional pain, suffering, inconvenience, mental anguish, loss of enjoyment of life, and other nonpecuniary losses. Punitive damages may be recovered when the plaintiff can demonstrate that the employer acted with malice or with reckless indifference to the individual's federally protected rights.

The number of state court actions or pendent state claims for damages may diminish as a result of an enhanced federal law. Courts will not allow double recovery. In *Bristow v. Drake Street* (1992) the court declined to award compensatory damages to a sexually harassed female employee when a jury awarded her $30,000 for intentional infliction of emotional distress and to award compensatory damages would be to issue duplicative judgments.

Experts play an important role in sexual harassment cases. In *Robinson v. Jacksonville Shipyards, Inc.* (1991), as well as a number of other cases, the court relied on the testimony of expert witnesses on sexual harassment and sexual stereotyping to conclude that pinups of nude and partially nude women, demeaning sexual remarks, and other harassment created a hostile working environment. The Civil Rights Act reversed the Supreme Court decision in *West Virginia University Hospitals, Inc. v. Casey* (1991), in which the Court held that expert witness fees were not part of the "reasonable" attorney fees awarded under the Civil Rights Attorneys Fees Awards Act or

Title VII and thus recovery for such fees was limited to $30.00 per day. Under the Act, prevailing parties should be able to recover fees for expert consultation throughout the course of litigation, as the Act provides for "expert fees," not only expert witness fees.

Jury trials are seldom allowed under Title VII. Under the 1991 Act, any party to a discrimination action may demand a jury trial when compensatory or punitive damages are sought. In addition, the court may not inform the jury about the cap on damages.

## Section 1983

Section 1983 has formed the basis for many sexual harassment claims against government bodies, both alone and in conjunction with a Title VII claim. To establish liability under §1983, a plaintiff must demonstrate that the defendant's actions deprived her of the rights, privileges, or immunities granted by the Constitution and that the defendant acted under color of state law (*Gomez v. Toledo*, 1980). In contrast to Title VII, "section 1983 is not a statute with any substantive content but merely the conduit through which individuals may obtain redress for violations to rights protected by the federal constitution or by federal law" (*Monell v. Department of Social Servs.*, 1978, pp. 690–691). Section 1983 may not be used to sustain an action for violation to Title VII only, however. Similarly, a plaintiff may not bring a §1983 action based on Title VII against a defendant who could not be sued directly under Title VII.

Any injured person may sue under §1983, and any person who acts under color of state law may be sued. The "person" who acts under color of state law has been broadly construed, and includes cities, counties, and other local governmental entities. Private persons may be liable under §1983 if the nexus between the action and the state is close enough to satisfy the state action requirement of the 14th Amendment. Section 1983 covers actions of federal officials done under color of state law, but not actions under color of federal law.

The 11th Amendment bars a suit against the state unless the state expressly waives sovereign immunity or injunctive relief is sought.

Supervisors are not vicariously liable for the §1983 violations of their subordinates unless the supervisor knew or should have known of the misconduct and could have prevented future harm but did not. Furthermore, municipalities and other local government entities may not be sued for the acts of their employees unless the unconstitutional conduct stems from governmental "custom" or a "policy statement, ordinance, regulation, or decision officially adopted and promulgated by the body's officers," and the government entity has notice of the custom or policy.

A plaintiff need not exhaust state administrative procedures before bringing a §1983 action, but if the plaintiff has sought a state administrative review, the findings of fact are binding in the federal action.

A plaintiff in a §1983 action for damages is entitled to a jury trial. No such entitlement exists when the plaintiff seeks only equitable relief. If both damages and equitable relief are sought, a jury will decide the damages claim initially and the court alone will hear the claim for equitable relief.

The plaintiff asserting a §1983 claim must prove its elements by a preponderance of the evidence. In proving a violation of equal protection under the 14th Amendment, the plaintiff must demonstrate intentional discrimination based on a class characteristic.

A prevailing plaintiff suing for violations of §1983 may recover a court award of reasonable attorneys' fees under 42 U.S.C. §1988, the Civil Rights Attorney's Fees Awards Act, payable by the losing defendant. Such fees generally are awarded to prevailing plaintiffs unless such an award would be unjust.

## Section 1985(3)

Section 1985(3) of 42 U.S.C. provides that if two or more persons conspire to deprive another person of equal protection, the victim of the conspiracy may recover damages against any one or more of the conspirators. In order to succeed in a §1985(3) claim, a sexual harassment plaintiff must demonstrate that a conspiracy existed to deprive her of her rights to equal treatment with members of the opposite sex. She is not required to allege that the discriminatory treatment was classwide in its application by the defendant. A plaintiff may demonstrate that the employer and/or supervisors were aware of her grievance, discussed it among themselves, and either did nothing or themselves participated in the harassment.

## Title IX

Title IX of the 1964 Civil Rights Act prohibits sex discrimination in any educational program receiving federal financial assistance. Several courts have applied the standards governing Title VII to Title IX cases, at least when the action involved employment discrimination, but few sexual harassment victims have sought relief under this statute. In *Alexander v. Yale University* (1977) a district court held that quid pro quo harassment was a justifiable claim under Title IX but that a claim based only on allegations of a hostile environment was not viable. The Second Circuit affirmed without addressing the issue of hostile environment when it determined that the issue was moot. In *Moire v. Temple University* (1986) the court recognized the hostile environment claim but did not find such an environment in the case before it.

The First Circuit addressed the issue in *Lipsett v. University of Puerto Rico* (1988). Following the reasoning in *Meritor*, the court held that an educational institution is liable for hostile environment sexual harassment by its supervisors or coworkers upon employees if an institutional official knew, or should have known, of the harassment, unless the official can show that he or she took appropriate steps to halt it. In this action by a female surgical resident the constant attack by male residents on the capabilities of the plaintiff and other female residents and frequent sexual comments created a hostile environment so blatant that it put the defendants on constructive notice that sex discrimination permeated the residency program. In *Duron v. Hancock* (1993) the former owners of an unincorporated hairstyling school could be found directly liable for a supervisor's alleged sexual harassment of an instructor in a Title IX action when the former owners delegated authority to the supervisor to run the school and could fire or promote the plaintiff.

## RICO Actions

The Racketeer Influenced and Corrupt Organizations Act (RICO), 18 U.S.C. §§1961–1968, provides a private civil action to recover treble damages for injury to a person in her or his business or property for a violation of §1962. That section prohibits the use of income derived from a "pattern of racketeering activity" (RICO, 18 U.S.C. §19612) to acquire an interest in, establish, or operate an enterprise engaged in or affecting interstate commerce; the acquisition or maintenance of any interest in an enterprise through a pattern of racketeering activity; conducting or participating in the conduct of an enterprise through a pattern of racketeering activity; and conspiring to violate any of these provisions. Allegations of a prolonged pattern and practice of sexual harassment may be sufficient to demonstrate a pattern of racketeering activity. In *Hunt v. Weatherbee* (1986), allegations regarding the union shop steward's use of sexual harassment to coerce a female journeyman carpenter into purchasing raffle tickets for a union "political action fund" and of a pattern of sexual harassment against the plaintiff and other female union members gave rise to a RICO claim when the union business agent allegedly condoned and ratified the harassing conduct.

## STATE REMEDIES FOR SEXUAL HARASSMENT

### State Fair Employment Practice Laws

Most states have employment statutes that prohibit discrimination based on race, color, sex, religion, national origin, age, or handicap. Some states have distinct provisions related to sexual harassment, and such provisions may

provide the exclusive statutory remedy. In *Bergeson v. Franchi* (1992) a former employee who was subjected to conduct by her employer including sexual advances; touching; threats; attempts to kiss her; discussion of rape and infidelity; begging her to fly to Florida with him and stay at his house there; and attempts to bribe her to accept his advances with a raise, a fur coat, money to finance her restaurant business, and medical expenses could not bring an independent cause of action under both the Massachusetts civil rights act and the Massachusetts discrimination statute based on a claim for sexual harassment when to permit such duplication of remedies would allow claimants to bypass the procedural prerequisites defined by the legislature, crippling the effectiveness of this specific statutory remedy.

State antidiscrimination statutes generally are similar to Title VII, but differences in coverage, exhaustion of jurisdictional requirements, applicable statutes of limitation, the range of possible remedies, or the availability of attorneys' fees may render one or the other preferable in a particular situation. Those statutes that parallel the prohibitions of Title VII have been interpreted similarly (*Gallagher v. Witton Enterprises*, 1992).

Although most statutes cover public and private employers, some apply to state workers only. A number of statutes follow Title VII in requiring that the defendant employ at least 15 people before the antidiscrimination statute applies. However, many have no such minimum requirement and in others the minimum number of employees ranges from 2 to 12.

Exhaustion of administrative requirements is required by almost half of the state antidiscrimination statutes. Like Title VII, some state antidiscrimination statutes also prohibit retaliation against persons who have asserted their rights under the relevant law.

A jury trial is available under almost half the state statutes. A number of state antidiscrimination statutes provide for a range of relief beyond Title VII's provisions, including actual damages; incidental damages for pain and suffering; compensatory damages; treble damages; damages for pain, humiliation, mental anguish, and embarrassment; and punitive damages. Some limit damage awards to $1,000 to $6,000.

More than half of the state antidiscrimination statutes provide for an award of attorneys' fees, at least to prevailing plaintiffs. In some states, prevailing defendants are entitled to fees if the action was brought in bad faith or if the complaint was frivolous. Attorneys' fee awards are available under Title VII. In the absence of a fee provision in the state statute, a contingent fee arrangement is possible if damages are available under the state statute.

## State Equal Rights Amendments

"The equal protection guaranty and a fortiori an equal rights amendment condemn discrimination on grounds of sex" (*Attorney General v. Massachusetts Interscholastic Athletic Ass'n*, 1979, p. 351). In *O'Connell v. Chasdi* (1987) the Massachusetts Supreme Court construed the state equal rights amendment to prohibit sexual harassment in the workplace. State equal rights amendments seldom are asserted as grounds for a sexual harassment suit, perhaps because of the success of state and federal antidiscrimination laws and the availability of damages under state common law. Courts have also attempted to resolve state statutory and/or common law issues without addressing constitutional claims.

## Pendent or Supplemental Jurisdiction

Pendent state claims often are included in Title VII sexual harassment complaints. Courts may assert supplemental jurisdiction over pendent claims that arise out of "a common nucleus of operative fact" with the Title VII action (*United Mine Workers v. Gibbs*, 1966, p. 725). Tort theories that have been asserted include intentional infliction of emotional distress, assault and battery, tortious interference with an employment contract, false imprisonment, and negligence.

In *United Mine Workers v. Gibbs* (1966) the Supreme Court established a two-pronged standard for pendent state claims. A court must first determine whether it has jurisdiction over the state law claims, and then it must decide whether it should hear them. Jurisdiction may be asserted over state claims if (1) there exists a federal claim with substance sufficient to confer subject matter jurisdiction on the court, (2) the state and federal claims derive from a common nucleus of operative fact, and (3) the claims are such that the plaintiff would ordinarily be expected to try them all in one proceeding. Gibbs set out a number of factors that courts have considered in deciding whether to exercise jurisdiction over pendent state claims:

1. Judicial economy, convenience, and fairness to the litigants
2. Whether the pendent state claims present unsettled questions of state law
3. Whether state issues predominate in terms of proof, scope of issues raised, or comprehensiveness of remedies sought
4. Whether the existence of divergent state and federal claims and theories would confuse a jury

Courts have declined to exercise pendent jurisdiction over related state claims when the only substantial federal claim arose under Title VII (*Bouchet v. National Urban League, Inc.*, 1984), when state law claims invoke undecided issues of state law (*Guzman Robles v. Cruz*, 1987), or when the defendant would be unduly prejudiced if the claims were tried in one proceeding (*Swanson v. Elmhurst Chrysler/Plymouth, Inc.*, 1987).

Plaintiffs may also plead state civil rights claims under state human rights or fair employment acts. In *Bridges v. Eastman Kodak Co.* (1992) the court exercised pendent jurisdiction over the plaintiff's state human rights act claims despite the defendants' contention that both jury confusion and predomination of state issues were likely to result because of the disparity in damages awarded under state and federal laws and different standards of employer liability. The CRA provides that the jury not be informed of damages limitations, and juries are instructed regularly on different theories of relief, even when only federal claims are present. "The mere existence of one difference in legal theory does not create a sufficient likelihood of jury confusion to justify dismissing plaintiffs' HRL claims" *(Bridges*, p. 1179).

A court may refuse to hear state law claims if doing so would complicate the trial and result in the predominance of state issues. Jury confusion may result if state law standards for proving sex discrimination are stricter or broader than under Title VII. If the federal claims are dismissed before trial, state claims may be dismissed as well. "The district court, of course, has the discretion to determine whether its investment of judicial energy justifies retention of jurisdiction ... or if it should more properly dismiss the claims without prejudice" (*Otto v. Heckler*, 1986, p. 338).

## Liability under Common Law Theories

Under common law theories applicable to sexual harassment an employer may be directly or indirectly liable for its own conduct or that of its employees. The doctrine of respondeat superior extends liability to the employer for acts of its agent when the agent's act is expressly authorized by the principal, when the act is committed within the scope of employment and in furtherance of the principal's business, or when the act is ratified by the principal (Restatement [Second] of Agency, 1958). Obviously, sexual harassment is seldom officially authorized by the employer or committed in furtherance of the principal's business, except perhaps in cases involving revealing dress requirements. Conduct is implicitly ratified when it involves quid pro quo sexual harassment. In *Lehmann v. Toys 'R' Us, Inc.* (1993) the New Jersey Supreme Court noted that in cases of quid pro quo sexual harassment the employer is strictly liable for all equitable damages and relief, including hiring or reinstating the victim, disciplining, transferring or firing the harasser, proving back or front pay, and taking preventative and remedial measures at work. In cases of hostile environment sexual harassment,

employers are vicariously liable if the supervisor acted within the scope of his or her employment, and, if the supervisor acted outside the scope of employment, the employer will be vicariously liable if the employer contributed to the harm through its negligence, intent, or apparent authorization of the harassing conduct, or if the supervisor was aided in the commission of the harassment by the agency relationship. The employer may be vicariously liable for compensatory damages stemming from a supervisor's creation of a hostile work environment if the employer grants the supervisor the authority to control the working environment and the supervisor abuses that authority to create a hostile environment. An employer may also be held vicariously liable for compensatory damages for supervisory sexual harassment occurring outside the scope of the supervisor's authority if the employer had actual or constructive notice of the harassment, or even if the employer did not have actual or constructive notice, if the employer negligently or recklessly failed to have an explicit policy that bans sexual harassment and that provides an effective procedure for the prompt investigation and remediation of such claims.

The employer may be liable for punitive damages only in the event of actual participation or willful indifference. In *Monge v. Superior Court* (1989) the plaintiff pleaded facts sufficient to demonstrate oppression and malice for purposes of punitive damages when she alleged that corporate officers conspired to display the message "How about a little head?" on her computer terminal, then retaliated against her when she complained.

## Tort Claims Based on Sexual Harassment

In *Kerans v. Porter Paint Co.* (1991) the Ohio Supreme Court created a common law tort remedy for sexual harassment, holding that workplace sexual harassment could be a tort in and of itself for which the victim could file suit not only against the offending employee, but also against the employer. To hold the employer liable, the plaintiff must prove that the alleged harasser had a past of sexually harassing behavior and the employer knew or should have known about it. In *Kerans* a store employee was molested by a supervisor five separate times in one day. As a result of this conduct, the plaintiff suffered severe emotional injury, including nightmares, flashbacks, and stomach cramps, and was in psychiatric care for at least two years. The employer took no immediate action when she finally complained, even though the alleged harasser had engaged in similar conduct on at least eight other occasions with five other female employees and the employer knew or should have known about these incidents. The company had responded to other complaints with a "boys will be boys" attitude.

The state supreme court concluded that at least a genuine issue of fact existed for a jury as to whether employer liability could be imposed in this case when the employer had put the alleged harasser in a supervisory position where he could exert control over the victim and cause her to believe that she would have to endure the harassment to keep her job. The court also held liability may be imposed for sexual harassment for failing to take appropriate action against an offending employee when the employer knows or has reason to know that the alleged harasser poses an unreasonable risk of harm to other employees.

Tort law has been recognized repeatedly as a proper remedy for the sexual harassment victim. Actions have been brought under the theories of assault and battery, intentional infliction of emotional distress, invasion of privacy, tortious interference with contractual relations, and others. However, because sexual harassment does not fit neatly into the traditional grounds for relief, and because the courts are unclear about what sexual harassment is, the application of these theories has been inconsistent. Although it is clear that the standards for tortious conduct are connected to the relative authority of the parties, courts are sometimes unwilling to find liability for the abuse of authority if there is no physical injury or loss of a tangible work benefit. Others acknowledge the unique economic coer-cion inherent in workplace sexual harassment in sustaining claims for intentional infliction of emotional distress. Conceptual distinctions based on the unique character of the relationship between superior and subordinate are proper and necessary. Economic considerations affect coworker relationships as well. Although a coworker harasser may not have the means to alter the victim's work status, her economic dependence on her job may limit her options.

## Workers' Compensation Statutes

State workers' compensation statutes generally provide an exclusive remedy for workplace injuries. Many states, however, have developed exceptions to the exclusivity provision of these laws. In *Gantt v. Sentry Insurance* (1992) the court declined the invitation to retreat from its long-held view that employees discharged in violation of fundamental public policy may bring a tort action against their employers and held that the exclusive remedy provisions of the state workers' compensation act did not preempt the plaintiff's wrongful discharge claim in an action charging that the plaintiff was constructively discharged in retaliation for supporting a coworker's claim of sexual harassment. The court rejected the defendant's contention that there was something anomalous in restricting the recovery of an employee who incurs a standard industrial injury, while extending a tort remedy to one who suffers similar injuries from sexual or racial discrimination.

Although the scope of injuries covered by state workers' compensation laws varies, most courts have held that common law tort claims arising from sexual harassment are not barred by the statutes. Some courts have found sexual harassment to fall within the willful physical assault or intentional wrong exceptions to exclusivity provisions. Under the doctrine of ratification an employee who was harassed by a supervisor or coworker may state a sexual harassment claim against an employer by alleging that the employer knew of the conduct but did nothing to discipline the offender. Even if a claim is barred against the employer by the state workers' compensation law, a plaintiff may still be able to assert claims against individual harassers. In *Dickert v. Metropolitan Life Ins. Co.* (1993) the state workers' compensation act provided the exclusive remedy in a sexual harassment claim against an employer, but a coworker could be held individually liable for an intentional tort committed while acting within the scope of employment.

One point of contention in these cases is whether sexual harassment arises out of employment for purposes of workers' compensation statutes, as illustrated by cases under Missouri law. In *Pryor v. United States Gypsum Co.* (1984), an assault and battery action, the District Court for the Western District of Missouri could not conclude that as a matter of law the plaintiff's injuries from sexual harassment arose out of her employment, even though the alleged incidents occurred in the workplace during normal working hours. "The court is simply not prepared to say that a female who goes to work in what is apparently a predominately male workplace should reasonably expect sexual harassment as part of her job, so as to bring any such injuries under the Workers' Compensation Law." However, in *Miller v. Lindenwood Female College* (1985), an action charging intentional infliction of emotional distress, the District Court for the Eastern District of Missouri noted that it would be inconsistent to deem sexual harassment by a supervisor as outside the course of employment for purposes of the workers' compensation law but within the course of employment when establishing vicarious liability against the employer for the wrongful acts of its agent. The Eastern District also held that the workers' compensation law barred an action for assault and battery and intentional infliction of emotional distress arising from sexual harassment in *Harrison v. Reed Rubber Co.* (1985), when the alleged injuries occurred at the place of employment and arose out of, and in the scope of, the plaintiff's employment. The Missouri State Court of Appeals held in *Hollrah v. Freidrich* (1982) that an

employee could properly assert tort claims against her employer and a coworker when the record did not indicate that the conduct arose in the course of, and out of, the employment.

In *Cox v. Chino Mines/Phelps Dodge* (1993) an employee's injury from three instances of sexual harassment in the workplace did not arise out of employment for purposes of workers' compensation. The incidents included being accosted on the job twice by a coworker who attempted to hug and kiss her and stated that he wanted to take her to bed and hearing a comment by a coworker to several other coworkers that another employee had obtained a job "because he sucked cock." All three incidents were reported, and the coworker who accosted her was threatened with discharge after the second incident. The claimant subsequently saw a psychiatrist and complained of anxiety, gastric pain, depression, sleeplessness, lack of energy, crying spells, and feelings of despair, all due to the incidents of sexual harassment. Her subsequent workers' compensation claim was dismissed, and the court of appeal affirmed, noting that the plaintiff admitted in her testimony that she had experienced no incidents of sexual harassment in approximately nine years of previous employment with her employer and that she was unaware of any other female employee who had previously been sexually harassed at this workplace.

Some courts frame the issue in terms of whether the conduct was employment-related or "personal." In *Fernandez v. Ramsey County* (1993), an action by a county employee against supervisors and the county alleging sexually motivated assault and battery stemming from acts including the touching of breasts, massaging of shoulders and neck, dropping paper clips down her blouse, fluffing her hair, and standing so close as to touch her body, the court of appeals held that whether such a common law action arising from employment was barred by the exclusivity provisions of the workers' compensation statute turned on whether the alleged intent to injure was for personal reasons or directed against the employee as an employee; summary judgment was not appropriate when fact issues existed as to whether the alleged acts were for personal reasons or directed against the plaintiff as an employee.

## Intentional Infliction of Emotional Distress

The tort of intentional infliction of emotional distress is the most widely asserted state common law claim in sexual harassment actions. A full range of tort remedies, including punitive damages, is available for successful claims of intentional infliction of emotional distress. The potential for significant damages has steered many victims of sexual harassment toward this remedy. Damages are available under Title VII, but plaintiffs may still prefer to bring suit in state court or find a pendent tort action against a particular party viable. In most states, in order to prove intentional infliction of emotional distress, a plaintiff must demonstrate that:

1. The defendant acted outrageously.
2. The defendant intentionally caused or should have known that his conduct would cause plaintiff's emotional distress.
3. The defendant actually and proximately caused plaintiff's severe or extreme emotional distress.
4. The plaintiff suffered severe or extreme emotional distress. (Restatement [Second] of Torts §46, 1965; *Fletcher v. Western Nat'l Life Ins. Co.*, 1970)

Because the relative nature of the parties' power creates the potential for abuse, the tort of intentional infliction of emotional distress clearly applies to sexual harassment cases. The power of sexual harassment is staggering and often affects not only the victim's job, but her health, relationships, and mental stability. Although many states have heard claims for intentional inflictions of emotional distress, the standard for "outrageous" conduct is unclear. The *Restatement (Second) of Torts* (1965) offers this circular explanation:

> Liability has been found only where the conduct has been so outrageous in nature, and so

extreme in degree, as to go beyond all possible bounds of decency and to be regarded as atrocious, and utterly intolerable in a civilized community. Generally, the case is one in which the recitation of the facts to an average member of the community would arouse [her or] his resentment against the actor, and lead [her or] him to exclaim, "Outrageous!" (*Restatement (Second)* §46 comment d)

The notion that women may be more offended by or sensitive to certain behavior may work in the plaintiff's favor in a determination of outrageousness but may be based on an antiquated notion of women's roles. Although the plaintiff failed to show that a cartoon drawn by a coworker in which she was depicted in a "sexually compromising" position with a male coworker was gender-oriented or that the posting of the cartoon created a hostile environment in *Linebaugh v. Sheraton Michigan Corp.* (1993), the trial court erred in granting summary disposition to the defendant coworker with respect to the claim of intentional infliction of emotional distress.

> Once having viewed the cartoon at issue, a reasonable factfinder could conclude that the depiction of plaintiff engaged in a sexual act with a co-worker constitutes conduct so outrageous in character and so extreme in degree that it goes beyond all bounds of common decency in a civilized society. We note that a number of plaintiff's co-workers testified that the cartoon was offensive. Furthermore, Herring's creation of the cartoon and his delivery of it to Shorkey may well constitute reckless behavior. (*Linebaugh*, pp. 588–589)

The Restatement also notes that the distress must be "so severe that no reasonable man could be expected to endure it. The intensity and the duration of the distress are factors to be considered in determining its severity" (*Restatement (Second)* §46 comment j), as well as the response by management to complaints of harassment. In *Laughinghouse v. Risser* (1992) the plaintiff proved that her supervisor's conduct was extreme and outrageous for purposes of her outrage claim when during the 18 months following the plaintiff's refusal of her supervisor's sexual advance, he was constantly critical, cursed, called the plaintiff "stupid," attacked her personal life, threatened to fire her, screamed, threw things, constantly engaged in sexual overtones, and said that he tried to "squeeze" employees until they "popped" if he wanted employees to leave. In *Bustamento v. Tucker* (1992) a female employee was harassed almost daily over a two-year period by a coworker who cursed at her; made sexual comments, innuendos and advances; invaded her privacy by asking her about her marital affairs and sexual relationship with her husband; and threatened her with physical violence, including rape, running her out of the plant, and running her over with his forklift. He also used his forklift to terrorize her by driving it at her, attempting to run her over and pinning her against the walls of the plant. The Supreme Court held that in an action for intentional infliction of emotional distress resulting from sexual harassment, when the acts or conduct are continuous on an almost daily basis, by the same action, of the same nature, and the conduct becomes tortious and actionable because of its continuous, cumulative, synergistic nature, a one-year prescription does not commence until the last act occurs or the conduct is abated. But in *Hendrix v. Phillips* (1993) the state court properly held that conduct by an employee, including showing the plaintiff a hole in the crotch of his pants and asking her in the presence of coworkers if she would like to staple the hole closed, showing her a drawing he made depicting fecal matter moving through a colon, a lewd gesture referring to sexual activity he supposed she engaged in with her husband on a vacation trip, a verbal confrontation during which he cursed her, and a series of complaints he filed against her with her supervisor, was "tasteless and rude social conduct" but did not rise to the level necessary to inflict emotional distress. The trial court could grant summary judgment without first ruling on the sufficiency of affidavits from the plaintiff's treating psychiatrist and psychologist tending to show that she suffered severe depression and anxiety as a result of the

harassment when the plaintiff failed to establish a prima facie case of liability.

The court should consider the context in which the acts were committed as well as the severity of the acts themselves. In *Dias v. Sky Chefs* (1990) the jury properly found for the plaintiff on her intentional infliction of emotional distress claim. The plaintiff's injury was distinguishable from ordinary employment abuses because it was carried out in the context of an allegedly sexually abusive work environment intentionally established by Sky Chef's local general manager; the jury was entitled to consider that context and look behind the manager's specific acts in its determination of outrageousness.

In *Underwood v. Washington Post Credit Union*, an action alleging sexual harassment and intentional infliction of emotional distress by a female credit union employee who had broken off an affair with the chair of the board of the credit union and was subsequently subjected to hostile treatment, a district court held that a finding by the jury that the plaintiff had not been sexually harassed did not mean that the employer and its chair could not be found liable for intentional infliction of emotional distress, despite the defendants' argument that sexual harassment has a lower threshold than intentional infliction of emotional distress. Jury verdicts may be inconsistent, and because the elements of sexual harassment and intentional infliction of emotional distress differ somewhat, it was at least theoretically possible on the facts of this case for the jury to have reached different verdicts on the two claims. The court noted that while general mental distress was not a covered injury, when the emotional distress has as its consequence physical disability, the administrative agency and the courts have both ruled that the injury is a covered one.

Other courts have held that a claim for intentional infliction of emotional distress requires more than what is required for sexual harassment. In *Piech v. Arthur Andersen & Co.* (1994) the court noted that the plaintiff's most extreme allegation was that she was subjected to one isolated proposition or advance over four years, and other allegations included being subjected to sexual humor, references to female anatomy, and general discriminatory conduct; such allegations lacked the required elements of being systematic and intentional actions designed to humiliate the plaintiff.

The testimony of treating physicians or psychiatrists may play an important role. In *Benavides v. Moore* (1993) the plaintiff did not state a claim for intentional infliction of emotional distress when, although she testified that she felt stress and anguish from her termination because her income decreased and she did not know why she was fired, she admitted that she consulted no psychologists or psychiatrists and had no plans to do so and offered no evidence that directly showed the severity of her distress. Severity of distress is an element of a cause of action for intentional infliction of emotional distress, not only of damages. But in *Hackney v. Woodring* (1993), an action by a female employee against her employer alleging assault, battery, false imprisonment, and intentional infliction of emotional distress stemming from acts including touching, fondling, spanking and holding her down in his lap, threatening her life while ripping off her clothes and exposing himself, the court of common pleas improperly granted the employer's motion for judgment notwithstanding the verdict in favor of the plaintiff for the intentional infliction of emotional distress claim and for $15,000 in compensatory damages on the ground that the plaintiff, by failing to introduce expert medical testimony, had not sustained her burden of proof as to damages. The court concluded that expert testimony was not necessary to explain the issues in this case and would have only served the purpose of buttressing plaintiff's credibility, thus usurping the province of the jury.

Because employment status entitles a person to greater protection from insult and outrage, sexual harassment in employment, as defined under Title VII and state antidiscrimination statutes, should be deemed outrageous per se. In *Retherford v. AT&T Communications* (1992), a sexual harassment and retaliation action by a former employee against her employer, supervisors, and coworkers, allegations that after she complained about sexual harassment, coworkers followed her around and intimidated her with threatening comments and looks and manipulated circumstances at her work in ways that made her job markedly more stressful were sufficient to satisfy the objective conduct requirement of the tort of intentional infliction of emotional distress. The court noted that any other conclusion would amount to an intolerable refusal to recognize that our society has ceased seeing sexual harassment in the workplace as a playful inevitability that should be taken cheerfully and has awakened to the fact that sexual harassment has a corrosive effect on those who engage in it as well as those who are subjected to it, and that such harassment has far more to do with power than it does with sex.

The per se approach has found acceptance in some state courts. In *Howard University v. Best* (1984) the District of Columbia Court of Appeals rejected the notion that appears to form the basis for much of the disparity in sexual harassment decisions and recognized that women suffer sexual harassment in the workplace based on outmoded sexual stereotypes and male domination of subordinate female employees. The court thus rejected the view, articulated by the trial court, that, as a matter of law, the degrading and humiliating behavior in this case was at worse a "social impropriety" that did not amount to the intentional infliction of emotional distress.

Although in most states a plaintiff need not have suffered a physical injury to recover for intentional infliction of emotional distress, some courts seem to distinguish between verbal harassment and conduct that includes physical contact. In *Class v. New Jersey Life Insurance Co.* (1990) the court held that the conduct of a male supervisor would not have been sufficiently outrageous had it remained verbal, even though he subjected the plaintiff to an eight-week period consisting of daily sexual jokes, personal stories of group sex, invitations to visit his home, asking if she swallowed during oral sex, describing the size of his penis, and commenting that he enjoyed anal sex with women. What made the difference for the court was that the alleged harasser retaliated against the plaintiff for complaining about his conduct. The Restatement supports a distinction between verbal and physical conduct. One court has held that verbal harassment alone is not outrageous conduct unless tangible work benefits are at stake. Another deemed the absence of overt propositions determinative. In *Kinnally v. Bell of Pennsylvania* (1990) a phone company engineer was subjected to a "regime of misogynous comments"; one defendant made "vulgar and suggestive comments in her presence, some of which were directed toward plaintiff, and showed a videotape of rabbits mating at a meeting where she was the only female present" (*Kinnally*, p. 1138). Another defendant unnecessarily singled her out as a woman on a memorandum recording attendance rates and repeated to the plaintiff comments made by the defendant and others regarding the ability of women to work as engineers. After a history of superior work performance the plaintiff received an unjustifiably poor work evaluation from one defendant. Plaintiff subsequently suffered a mental breakdown. "However disturbing" the allegations were, "the regime of derision and intimidation" fell short of the state prescription for intentional infliction of emotional distress. "Plaintiff does not claim to be either the recipient or the victim of any overt propositions. Accordingly, her claim of intentional infliction of emotional distress must be dismissed" (*Kinnally*, p. 1145). Several courts have found at least a stated claim for intentional infliction of emotional distress when the challenged conduct included unwelcome touching. When appropriate, an accompanying claim for assault and battery may bolster an emotional distress claim. Allegations of retaliation also may support such a claim. In *Pommier v. James L. Edelstein Enterprises* (1993) a female former employee stated a claim for intentional infliction of emotional distress when the plaintiff alleged repeated acts of sexual harassment and a pattern of retaliation in response to her internal complaint of sexual harassment—the defendants allegedly withheld information necessary to perform her job, sabotaged programs she had implemented to ensure she would fail, and interfered with her customer contacts in order to ruin her professional reputation and credibility.

Employment has been considered a property right, and both tangible and hostile environment harassment interfere with the enjoyment of that right. The notion that in the absence of accompanying trespass or assault there was "no harm in asking" (Magruder, 1936) has given way to a heightened societal sensitivity regarding the "bounds of decency." Although the injuries generated by a threat to job security or retaliatory conduct may appear to present a clearer case of intentional infliction of emotional distress, harassment engendered by words, looks, and gestures may in fact be more emotionally debilitating. In the tangible harassment situation an employee may feel wronged and angry because the nature of the injury is straightforward. An employee who is subjected to a hostile work environment and whose job is not directly threatened, however, may be more likely to live with the degradation longer and suffer more far-reaching consequences. Physical symptoms are common; sexual harassment victims experience a range of stress-related ailments including high blood pressure, nausea, chest pains, nervous tics, weakness, insomnia, and headaches.

As in the federal sexual harassment context, courts should analyze the facts from the perspective of a reasonable woman in an employment situation because only this standard can capture the essence of sexual harassment. Some courts have not agreed. In *Garcia v. Andrews* (1993) a Texas court rejected the plaintiff's attempt to use the reasonable woman standard to determine what constituted conduct that was extreme and outrageous in cases of intentional infliction of emotional distress, concluding that existing policy is concerned not only with safeguarding freedom of expression, but also with the even-handed disposition of all claims without regard to whether the plaintiff is a woman or a man, is young or old, or is a member of any one of numerous and varied subgroups in our society, each, possibly, with its own standard of decency.

A claim of intentional infliction of emotional distress may be brought against an employer, a supervisor, or a coworker. An employer may be responsible for failing to respond to complaints of sexual harassment by a supervisor or coworker. A showing of intent may not be necessary in this situation; a reckless disregard of the harassing conduct may be sufficient. Generally, the more attenuated the employment relationship between the parties, the greater the injury must be to establish a claim.

## Assault and Battery

Assault occurs when a person "acts intending to cause a harmful or offensive contact with the person of the other or a third person or an imminent apprehension of such conduct and... the other is thereby put in such imminent apprehension" (Restatement [Second] of Torts §21, 1965, §31). Verbal harassment alone without a threat of physical harm thus may not constitute assault. This threat may be in the form of a gesture or movement toward the plaintiff. Liability for battery results from intentional unwelcome physical contact, which may include touching, kissing, embracing, or rubbing up against the body of the plaintiff. In *Waltman v. International Paper Co.* (1988) an employee stated claim for battery when she alleged subjection to unwelcome touching and pinching of breasts and thighs and placing of an air hose between her legs. Damages have been awarded for assault and battery based on sexual advances and unwelcome touching. In *Troutt v. Charcoal Steak House, Inc.* (1993) an award of $50,000 as punitive damages for sexual battery was made in an action for sexual harassment and assault against a former employer. After the plaintiff's first month at work as a waitress, her supervisor began to make sexually suggestive remarks that escalated into physical contact including putting his hands on her waist and breast, grabbing her buttocks, kissing her on the neck, reaching under her skirt, and grabbing her crotch. The supervisor's conduct caused the plaintiff to suffer extreme emotional distress, sleeplessness, and depression, and she quit her job.

Although touching need not be of sexual areas to be actionable, the plaintiff usually must show that the touching incident itself, apart from previous harassment, caused an injury. Mental suffering is an injury for which damages may be awarded. Evidence of repeated physical contact, however, is more likely to sustain a claim of battery.

Damages available for assault and battery include those for humiliation and fright.

## Tortious Interference with Contracts

A plaintiff may recover compensatory and punitive damages from a defendant who "intentionally acts to deprive another of an economic benefit" (*Kyriazi v. Western Elec. Co.*, 1978, p. 950). Under this theory, a victim of sexual harassment may recover damages directly from the person who harassed her. In order to state a claim for tortious interference with an employment contract, a plaintiff must prove that:

1. A valid contract existed at the time of the harassment.
2. The defendant, who was not a party to the contract, had knowledge of the contractual relationship.
3. The defendant intentionally interfered with the contract for an improper purpose or by an improper means.
4. The plaintiff suffered damages as a result of the interference. (Restatement [Second] of Torts §§766–767, 1979)

Many state courts have recognized actions brought under this theory even when the employment involved is at will. Because the action may not be brought against a party to the employment contract and the plaintiff must demonstrate the loss of an economic benefit, this theory may have limited value. However, it may be useful when supervisors or coworkers force an employee to quit by making her work environment intolerable, or when a supervisor or coworker retaliates against an employee who has rejected his advances by maligning that employee to his superior, who discharges the harassed employee or otherwise alters her employment status. For example, in *Favors v. Alco Mfg. Co.* (1988) the plaintiff alleged that her supervisor tortiously interfered with her employment contract when he facilitated her discharge after she rejected his sexual advances. In *Lewis v. Oregon Beauty Supply Co.* (1987), punitive damages were warranted when a male coworker's threats, insults, and intimidation forced the plaintiff to leave her job. In *Fisher v. San Pedro Peninsula Hospital* (1989), however, a plaintiff nurse did not prove that a doctor's sexual harassment of other nurses negatively affected her employment relationship with the hospital when the court found no evidence that the doctor intended to disrupt the plaintiff's employment relationship through the sexual harassment of others.

A female former employee who alleged, in *Gruver v. Ezon Products* (1991), that during the course of her employment she was subjected to various forms of sexual harassment by her supervisor that though reported went unpunished could not argue that, by allowing the harassment to go unpunished, the defendant breached a provision of an employment contract established by the antiharassment terms of the employee handbook. Common law requires that for a policy to become part of an employment contract, it must be part of the offer of employment—an inducement to join the company—and nowhere in the complaint did the plaintiff state that she accepted employment by the defendant because of the antiharassment section of the handbook or that the definite terms of the policy were made known to her prior to her acceptance.

When the employer is the alleged harasser, a breach of contract action may be appropriate. A supervisor cannot be liable for intentional interference with an employment contract if he is acting within the legitimate scope of authority, so a plaintiff must argue that the defendant acted out of improper personal reasons.

In order to establish a claim for intentional interference with an employment contract, the plaintiff must show that the alleged harasser acted intentionally, but a finding of malice is not required for liability. Proof of an interference claim also may require that "the interference either be in pursuit of an improper or wrongful motive or involve the use of an improper or wrongful means" *Lewis v. Oregon Beauty Supply Co.*, 1987, p. 434). The motives or means may be defined as improper in a statute or other regulation or a recognized rule of common law, but it is unnecessary to prove all the elements of another tort.

A range of remedies, including punitive damages, is available for intentional interference with an employment relationship.

## Defamation, Libel, and Slander

A sexual harassment plaintiff may sue for defamation when the employer makes false statements about the employee to coworkers or to a prospective employer. A plaintiff must establish that:

1. The defendant made a false or defamatory statement.
2. The defendant made that statement in an unprivileged communication to a third party.
3. The defendant was at least negligent in communicating the statement.
4. The communication either proximately caused plaintiff special harm or was actionable irrespective of special harm or proximately. (Restatement [Second] of Torts, 1977)

Written defamatory matter has traditionally been considered libel, while oral defamation constitutes slander. An individual may prove libel without any proof of special harm. In *Linebaugh v. Sheraton Michigan Corp.* (1993), although the plaintiff failed to show that a cartoon drawn by a coworker in which she was depicted in a "sexually compromising" position with a male coworker was gender-oriented or that the posting of the cartoon created a hostile environment, the drawing of the cartoon was actionable as libel irrespective of special harm because the cartoon could be interpreted as depicting the plaintiff in a sexual act with a man other than her husband, thus imputing want of chastity to the plaintiff. Proof of actual damage is required in slander cases unless the slander involves the plaintiff's business, trade, or profession; the commission of a crime by the plaintiff; the contraction of a "loathsome" disease; or the unchasteness of a female plaintiff. In *Garcia v. Williams*, 704 F. Supp. 984 (N.D. Cal. 1988) the plaintiff sustained a slander claim when she alleged that her former employer, a judge, had told other people that she was romantically interested in him. In *Chamberlin v. 101 Realty* (1985) the plaintiff who was discharged for allegedly resisting her employer's sexual advances stated a claim for defamation when the employer made statements implying that the plaintiff had improperly removed property from the employer's office.

## Invasion of Privacy

There are several different types of torts under the general heading of invasion of privacy. Applicable to sexual harassment are intrusion, public disclosure of private facts, and false light publicity.

### Intrusion

Sexual harassment may constitute the tortious invasion of privacy called intrusion when, for example, an alleged harasser badgers an employee by following her into her office, telephoning her in her office or at home, making sexually related inquiries, or putting her in fear of sexual contact. Under the Restatement (Second) of Torts a plaintiff usually can establish intrusion by showing that:

1. The defendant committed an intentional intrusion, physical or otherwise, upon the solitude or seclusion of the employee's private affairs or concerns.
2. This intrusion would be highly offensive to a reasonable person.

3. The plaintiff suffered damages as a result of this intrusion. (Restatement [Second] of Torts, 1977)

In the employment context, intrusion usually involves an invasion by the employer or supervisor into an area in which the employee had a reasonable expectation of privacy to elicit personal information from the employee. This tort "is directed to protecting the integrity and sanctity of physical areas a person would naturally consider private and off limits to uninvited, unwelcomed, prying persons" (*Cummings v. Walsh Constr. Co.*, 1983, p. 884). Although in some instances physical location may be a factor in determining whether the alleged intrusion is actionable, the challenged conduct may be so offensive that it would be actionable no matter where it occurred. The actions of the defendant must be unwanted, uninvited, and unwarranted. Sexual touching and propositions may support a claim of intrusion. In *Waltman v. International Paper Co.* (1988) the plaintiff stated a claim for invasion of privacy when the plaintiff alleged that a coworker placed a high-pressure air hose between her legs.

The right to privacy may be waived by discussing the relevant issues in the workplace. In *Moffett v. Gene B. Glick Co.* (1985) the plaintiff's open discussions about her interracial relationship waived a privacy claim based on racial comments and threats by supervisory personnel. Privacy rights may also be waived by acquiescing to the challenged conduct. In *Cummings v. Walsh Construction* (1983) the court held that a plaintiff waived her right to privacy when she yielded to her supervisor's sexual advances.

### Public Disclosure of Private Facts

Generally, there are four elements to a claim of unauthorized disclosure of private facts:

1. The defendant publicized a private matter about the plaintiff.
2. The publicity would be highly offensive to a reasonable person.
3. The disclosed matter was not of legitimate concern to the public.

4. The plaintiff suffered injury from the publicity. (Restatement [Second] of Torts, 1977, §652D)

A plaintiff may negate the effect of a challenged publication by communicating the events herself to third persons.

### False Light Publicity

A sexual harassment plaintiff may recover damages for publicity that places her in a false light in the public eye. Publicity requires "communicati[on] to the public at large, or to so many persons that the matter must be regarded as substantially certain to become one of public knowledge" (Restatement, 1977, §652D comment a). The false light must be objectionable to a reasonable person, but need not be defamatory. For example, in *Tomson v. Stephan* (1988) a federal district court held that a female employee could seek damages for injuries arising from her employer's failure to keep the terms of a sexual harassment settlement confidential by discussing it at a news conference and declaring the lawsuit "without merit" and "totally unfounded."

## False Imprisonment

Acts of sexual harassment often include conduct that falls within the parameters of the tort of false imprisonment. False imprisonment involves an act by a person who intends to confine another person "within the boundaries fixed by the act" that results in a confinement of which the confined person is aware. A plaintiff may state a cause of action for false imprisonment when one party restrains another's freedom of movement, such as when a supervisor calls an employee into an office and subsequently blocks the entrance or locks the door. In *Priest v. Rotary* (1986) a restaurant owner was guilty of false imprisonment when he picked up a waitress and carried her across the room and later trapped her while he fondled her. Employees who have been forced to remain in supervisors' hotel rooms while on business also may claim false imprisonment. Physical force is not necessary as long as the plaintiff demonstrates unwelcome restraint. Despite the physical nature of the tort, the injury is in large part a mental one, and a successful plaintiff may recover damages for injuries including mental suffering and humiliation.

## Loss of Consortium by Partner of Victim

The spouse of a person alleging sexual harassment may bring an accompanying claim for loss of consortium. In several reported opinions, courts have heard loss of consortium claims from husbands whose wives became nervous, depressed, and withdrawn and suffered physical symptoms as a result of sexual harassment at work. Although an injury need not be physically disabling to form the basis of a loss of consortium claim, plaintiffs have suffered physical injuries that gave rise to assault and battery charges or physical symptoms of emotional stress, such as headaches and nausea. In *Bowersox v. P.H. Glatfelter Co.* (1988) the court noted that the manifestations of sexual harassment, including depression, severe emotional distress, headaches, and nausea, clearly may result in the deprivation of society and companionship.

## Wrongful Discharge

Historically, courts generally considered employment contracts to be "at will" unless otherwise specified, making them terminable with or without cause by either party at any time. Over the years, however, construction of this doctrine has narrowed, and employees have enjoyed an increasing number of implied rights notwithstanding the absence of a formal contract. In a wrongful discharge action a victim of sex discrimination may argue that she has an implied right to be free from conduct that violates public policy, or that the employer has an implied good faith duty to refrain from acting maliciously or arbitrarily when discharging employees. In *Monge v. Beebe Rubber Co.* (1974), for example, the New Hampshire Supreme Court ruled in favor of a female employee who was given different duties and ultimately discharged when she refused to submit to her supervisor's sexual advances, noting that "a termination by the employer of a contract of employment at will which is motivated by bad faith or malice or based on retaliation is not in the best interest of the economic system or the public good and constitutes a breach of the employment contract" (*Monge*, p. 551). In *Chamberlin v. 101 Realty, Inc.* (1985) the district court of New Hampshire noted that the state supreme court had narrowed the scope of *Monge* somewhat by requiring the plaintiff in a wrongful discharge action to show that the defendant was motivated by bad faith, malice, or retaliation and that he or she was discharged for performing an act that public policy would encourage or for refusing to do something that public policy would condemn. The court was convinced, however, that public policy would condemn the endurance of sexual harassment as a means of retaining employment. Evidence that conduct violates Title VII or state antidiscrimination law supports a finding that the conduct was in contravention of an express public policy.

A wrongful discharge action must stem from conduct by a party who has authority to participate in personnel actions against the plaintiff.

In states whose courts have held that the state employment discrimination statute is the exclusive remedy for those claims predicated on the policies or provisions of the state law a wrongful discharge claim may not be viable.

## Negligent Hiring, Retention, and Supervision

A number of sexual harassment cases have asserted claims of negligent hiring, retention, and/or supervision. To find negligent hiring or retention, the court generally must find that the employer knew or should have known of the employee's offensive conduct. In *Geise v. Phoenix Company of Chicago, Inc.* (1993) the district court improperly dismissed the plaintiff's claims for the negligent hiring and retention of a manager who was sexually harassing her by attempting to kiss and touch her body, placing his hands on her body and objects

down the front of her dress. The court recognized a duty on the part of the employer to make a prehiring inquiry into an applicant's history of workplace harassment, given the serious harm that sexual harassment has been legislatively deemed to constitute, the foreseeable hazard of that harm's occurring upon hiring a new manager of a staff comprised primarily of persons not of the manager's gender, the plaintiff's allegation that the employer could have but failed to learn through investigation that the manager had a predisposition to female coworkers, and the plaintiff's allegation of her proximate injuries from the employer's failure to act. The judgment fell short of a declaration of a specific duty to investigate and fully learn potential management employees' sexual harassment history; the court's conclusion was merely that the plaintiff's pleadings support her cause of action, considering the Illinois courts' long-held view that an employer has a duty to exercise ordinary and reasonable case in the employment and selection of careful and skillful co-employees and to discharge that duty with care commensurate with the perils and hazards likely to be encountered in the employee's performance of her job.

> With reference to the serious concern now afforded the issue of sexual harassment in the workplace, we find that the plaintiff sufficiently pleaded a cause of action based on whether the company negligently breached its duty of diligent and cautious hiring in consideration of co-workers…. In our judgment, that duty can comprise a need to make the sort of investigation urged by the plaintiff here, and even with that inclusion, it imposes no inappropriate administrative or economic burden for employers…. We also find that in being sufficiently broad to address the harm of sexual harassment, that duty serves a prophylactic role in the interest of today's ethical or moral thinking and in the general interest of justice. (*Geise*, p. 1185)

The plaintiff properly stated a claim for negligent retention when she alleged that she suffered proximate injury after she repeatedly informed the company of the manager's sexually harassing conduct toward her and that the company took no action. The plaintiff's complaint was not rendered insufficient by her acknowledgment that the manager's sexual harassment ended after the company verified her complaints; the complaint alleged that before the harassing conduct ended, she complained of it to the company and that the company took no responsive action.

Some courts have held that the tort of negligent supervision or retention requires a showing of bodily injury. In *Laughinghouse v. Risser* (1992) the physical harm requirement for emotional distress damages in a negligent retention suit against the employer was satisfied by evidence that the employee suffered life-threatening hives, high blood pressure, angina, fatigue, depression, and posttraumatic stress disorder as a result of her supervisor's harassment.

The exclusivity provisions of state workers' compensation laws may bar negligent hiring, supervision, or retention claims. In *Byrd v. Richardson-Greenshields Securities* (1989), however, the Florida Supreme Court held that workers' compensation laws were never intended to address acts of sexual harassment and thus declined to apply the exclusivity provisions to claims of negligent hiring and retention, noting that state and federal policies are strongly committed to eliminating sex discrimination in employment.

## CONCLUSION AND FUTURE TRENDS

Although the Supreme Court's recent ruling in *Harris* played an important role in the refinement of sexual harassment law by holding that a plaintiff need not show psychological injury to prove sexual harassment, the court left a number of questions unanswered. Unsettled is whether the objective standard in sexual harassment cases should be the reasonable person or the reasonable woman or victim. While all the opining justices used the reasonable person language, the Court did not explicitly reject the reasonable woman standard.

Because of the availability of damages in Title VII cases under the Civil Rights Act of 1991, more sexual harassment cases may be litigated in federal court. The *Harris* court did not address how compensatory damages, available under the Civil Rights Act of 1991, can be measured and awarded in light of its decision that proof of psychological injury is not required to prove sexual harassment.

Finally, also in dispute is the scope of employer liability in hostile environment cases. The issue was not relevant in *Harris*, but in *Kauffman v. Allied Signal* (1992) the Supreme Court refused to review a decision by the Sixth Citcuit holding that the proper standard for determining employer liability for a supervisor's actions is whether the supervisor's conduct was foreseeable and within the scope of employment.

## REFERENCES

*Alexander v. Yale University,* 459 F. Supp. 1 (D. Conn. 1977), *aff'd,* 631 F.2d 178 (2d Cir. 1980).

*Andrews v. City of Philadelphia,* 895 F.2d 1469 (3d Cir. 1990).

*Attorney General v. Massachusetts Interscholastic Athletic Ass'n,* 378 Mass. 343, 393 N.E.2d 284 (1979).

*Austin v. State of Hawaii et al.,* 759 F. Supp. 612 (D. Haw. 1991), *affd,* 967 F.2d 583 (9th Cir. 1992).

*Babcock v. Frank,* 729 F. Supp. 279 (S.D.N.Y. 1990).

*Benavides v. Moore,* 848 S.W.2d 190 (Tex. Ct. App. 1993).

*Bergeson v. Franchi,* 783 F. Supp. 713 (Tex. Ct. App. 1992).

*Bigoni v. Pay 'n Pak Stores,* 746 F. Supp. 1 (D. Or. 1990).

*Bowersox v. P.H. Glatfelter Co.,* 677 F. Supp. 307 (M.D. Pa. 1988).

*Bouchet v. National Urban League, Inc.,* 730 F.2d 799 (D.C. Cir. 1984).

*Boyd v. James S. Hayes Living Health Care Agency,* 671 F. Supp. 1155, 1165 (W.D. Tenn. 1987).

*Bridges v. Eastman Kodak Co.,* 800 F. Supp. 1172 (S.D.N.Y. 1992).

*Bristow v. Drake Street,* 57 Fair Empl. Prac. Cas. (BNA) 1367 (N.D. Ill. 1992).

*Broderick v. Ruder,* 685 F. Supp. 1269 (D.D.C. 1988).

*Bundy v. Jackson,* 641 F.2d 934 (D.C. Cir. 1981).

*Bustamento v. Tucker,* 607 So.2d 532 (La. 1992).

*Byrd v. Richardson-Greenshields Securities,* 552 So.2d 1099 (Fla. 1989).

*Canada v. Board Group, Inc.,* 1992 WL 387581 (D. Nev. Oct. 27, 1992).

*Carmon v. Lubrizol Corp.*, 64 Fair Empl. Prac. Cas. (BNA) 481 (5th Cir. 1994).

*Chamberlin v. 101 Realty, Inc.*, 626 F. Supp. 865 (D.N.H. 1985).

The Civil Rights Act of 1964, 42 U.S.C. §1983.

The Civil Rights Act of 1964, Title VII, 42 U.S.C. §2000e *et. seq.*

The Civil Rights Act of 1964, §42 U.S.C. 1985.

Civil Rights Attorney's Fees Awards Act, 42 U.S.C. §1988.

*Class v. New Jersey Life Insurance Co.*, 746 F. Supp. 776 (N.D. Ill. 1990).

*Corne v. Bausch & Lomb, Inc.*, 390 F. Supp. 161 (D. Ariz. 1975), *vacated*, 562 F.2d 55 (9th Cir. 1977).

*Cox v. Chino Mines/Phelps Dodge*, 850 P.2d 1038 (N.M. Ct. App. 1993).

*Cummings v. Walsh Constr. Co.*, 561 F. Supp. 872 (S.D. Ga. 1983).

*Danna v. New York Telephone Co.*, 752 F. Supp. 594 (S.D.N.Y. 1990).

*Dias v. Sky Chefs*, 919 F.2d 1370 (9th Cir. 1990), *vacated on other grounds*, 111 S. Ct. 532, *on remand*, 948 F.2d 532 (9th Cir. 1991), *cert. denied*, 112 S. Ct. 1294 (1992).

*Dickert v. Metropolitan Life Ins. Co.*, 428 S.E.2d 700 (S.C. 1993).

*Dirksen v. City of Springfield*, 64 Fair Empl. Prac. Cas. (BNA) 116 (C.D. Ill. 1994).

*Drinkwater v. Union Carbide Corp.*, 904 F.2d 853 (3d Cir. 1990).

*Duron v. Hancock*, 64 Fair Empl. Prac. Cas. (BNA) 81 (D. Kan. 1993).

*EEOC v. Gurnee Inn Corp*, 48 Fair Empl. Prac. Cas. (BNA) 871 (N.D. Ill. 1988), *aff'd*, 914 F.2d 815 (7th Cir. 1990).

*Ellison v. Brady*, 924 F.2d 872 (9th Cir. 1991).

Equal Employment Opportunity Guidelines on Discrimination Because of Sex, 29 C.F.R. §1604.11 (1993)

*Favors v. Alco Mfg. Co.*, 186 Ga. App. 480, 367 S.E.2d 328 (1988).

*Fernandez v. Ramsey County*, 495 N.W.2d 859 (Minn. Ct. App. 1993).

*Fisher v. San Pedro Peninsula Hospital*, 214 Cal. App. 3d 590, 262 Cal. Rptr. 842 (1989).

*Fletcher v. Western Nat'l Life Ins. Co.*, 10 Cal. App. 3d 376, 89 Cal. Rptr. 78 (1970).

*Gallagher v. Witton Enterprises*, 59 Fair Empl. Prac. Cas. (BNA) 1251 (1st Cir 1992).

*Gantt v. Sentry Insurance*, 1 Cal. 4th 1083, 4 Cal. Rptr.2d 874, 824 P.2d 680 (Cal. 1992).

*Garcia v. Andrews*, 867 S.W.2d 409 (Tex. Ct. App. 1993).

*Geise v. Phoenix Company of Chicago, Inc.*, 615 N.E.2d 1179 (Ill. Ct. App. 1993).

*Gomez v. Toledo*, 446 U.S. 635 (1980).

*Graham v. Bendix Corp.* 585 F. Supp. 1036 (N.D. Ind. 1984).

*Greenland v. Fairtron Corp.*, 500 N.W.2d 36 (Iowa 1993).

*Gruver v. Ezon Products*, 64 Fair Empl. Prac. Cas. (BNA) 270 (M.D. Pa. 1991).

*Guzman Robles v. Cruz*, 670 F. Supp. 54 (D.P.R. 1987).

*Hackney v. Woodring*, 622 A.2d 286 (Pa. Super. Ct. 1993).

*Hansel v. Public Service Co.*, 778 F. Supp. 1126 (D. Colo. 1991).

*Harris v. Forklift Systems, Inc.*, 114 S. Ct. 367 (1993).

*Harrison v. Chance*, 797 P.2d 200 (Mont. 1990).

*Harrison v. Reed Rubber Co.*, 603 F. Supp. 1457 (E.D. Mo. 1985).

*Heelan v. Johns-Manville Corp.*, 451 F. Supp. 1382 (D. Colo. 1978).

*Hendrix v. Phillips*, 207 Ga. App. 394, 428 S.E.2d 91 (Ga. Ct. App. 1993).

*Henson v. Dundee*, 682 F.2d 897 (11th Cir. 1982).

*Hicks v. Gates Rubber Co.*, 833 F.2d 1406 (10th Cir. 1987).

*Hollrah v. Freidrich*, 634 S.W.2d 221 (Mo. Ct. App. 1982).

*Howard University v. Best*, 484 A.2d 958 (D.C. 1984).

*Huebschen v. Department of Health and Social Services*, 716 F.2d 1167 (7th Cir. 1983).

*Hunt v. Weatherbee*, 626 F. Supp. 1097 (D. Mass. 1986).

*Jenson v. Eveleth Taconite Co.* 139 F.R.D. 657 (D. Minn. 1991).

*Jones v. Flagship International*, 793 F.2d 714 (5th Cir. 1986), *cert. denied*, 479 U.S. 1065 (1987).

*Jones v. Wesco*, 846 F.2d 1154 (8th Cir. 1988).

*Juarez v. Ameritech Mobile Communications*, 746 F. Supp. 798 (N.D. Ill. 1990).

*Kauffman v. Allied Signal*, 970 F.2d 178 (6th Cir. 1992), *cert. denied*, 113 S. Ct. 831 (1992).

*Kerans v. Porter Paint Co.*, 575 N.E.2d 428 (Ohio 1991).

*Keppler v. Hinsdale Township High School District 86*, 715 F. Supp. 862 (N.D. Ill. 1989).

*Kinnally v. Bell of Pennsylvania*, 748 F. Supp. 1136 (E.D. Pa. 1990).

*Kyriazi v. Western Elec. Co.*, 461 F. Supp. 894 (D.N.J. 1978), *modified*, 473 F. Supp. 786 (D.N.J. 1979), *affd*, 647 F.2d 388 (3d Cir. 1981).

*Laughinghouse v. Risser*, 786 F. Supp. 920 (D. Kan. 1992).

*Lehmann v. Toys 'R' Us, Inc.*, 133 N.J. 587, 626 A.2d 445 (N.J. 1993) (Garibaldi, J.).

*Lewis v. Oregon Beauty Supply Co.*, 302 Or. 616, 733 P.2d 430 (1987).

*Linebaugh v. Sheraton Michigan Corp.*, 198 Mich. App. 335, 497 N.W.2d 585 (1993).

*Lipsett v. University of Puerto Rico*, 864 F.2d 881 (1st Cir. 1988).

Magruder, C. (1936). *Mental and emotional disturbance in the law of torts*, Harv. L. Rev., *49*, 1033, 1055.

*Mays v. Williamson & Sons, Janitorial Servs.*, 591 F. Supp. 1518 (E.D. Ark. 1984), *aff'd*, 775 F.2d 258 (8th Cir. 1985).

*Meritor Savings Bank v. Vinson*, 477 U.S. 57 (1986).

*Miller v. Aluminum Co. of Am.*, 679 F. Supp. 495, 502 ((W.D. Pa.), *aff'd*, 856 F.2d 184 (3d Cir. 1988).

*Miller v. Lindenwood Female College*, 616 F. Supp. 860 (E.D.Mo. 1985).

*Moffett v. Gene B. Glick Co.*, 621 F. Supp. 244 (N.D. Ind. 1985).

*Moire v. Temple University*, 613 F. Supp. 1360 (E.D. Pa. 1983), *aff'd*, 800 F.2d 1136 (3d Cir. 1986).

*Monell v. Department of Social Servs.*, 436 U.S. 658 (1978).

*Monge v. Beebe Rubber Co.*, 114 N.H. 130, 316 A.2d 549 (1974).

*Monge v. Superior Court*, 176 Cal. App.3d 503, 222 Cal. Rptr. 842, 860 (1989).

*Nash v. Electrospace System, Inc.*, 9 F.3d 401 (5th Cir. 1993).

*O'Connell v. Chasdi*, 400 Mass. 686, 511 N.E.2d 349 (1987).

*Otto v. Heckler*, 802 F.2d 337 (9th Cir. 1986).

*Paroline v. Unisys Corp.*, 879 F.2d 100 (4th Cir. 1989).

*Petrosky v. Washington-Greene County Branch Pa. Assoc. for the Blind*, 663 F. Supp. 821 (1987).

*Piech v. Arthur Andersen & Co.*, 64 Fair Empl. Prac. Cas. (BNA) 439 (N.D. Ill. 1994).

*Pommier v. James L. Edelstein Enterprises*, 816 F. Supp. 476 (N.D. Ill. 1993).

*Priest v. Rotary*, 634 F. Supp. 571 (N.D. Cal 1986).

*Pryor v. United States Gypsum Co.*, 47 Fair Empl. Prac. Cas. (BNA) 159 (W.D. Mo. 1984).

Racketeer Influenced and Corrupt Organizations Act (RICO), 18 U.S.C. §1961–1968.

*Radtke v. Everett*, 56 Fair Empl. Prac. Cas. (BNA) 923 (Mich. Ct. App. 1991).

Restatement (Second) of Torts (1977).

Restatement (Second) of Torts (1965).

Restatement (Second) of Agency (1958).

*Retherford v. AT&T Communications*, 844 P.2d 949 (Utah 1992).

*Robinson v, Jacksonville Shipyards, Inc.*, 760 F. Supp. 1486 (M.D. Fla. 1991).

*Ross v. Double Diamond, Inc.*, 672 F. Supp. 261 (N.D. Tex. 1987).

*Sanchez v. City of Miami Beach*, 720 F. Supp. 974 (S.D. Fla. 1989).

*Saxton v. American Tel. & Tel. Co.*, 785 F. Supp. 760 (N.D. Ill. 1992), *aff'd*, 10 F.3d 526 (7th Cir. 1993).

*Shrout v. Black Clawson*, 689 F. Supp. 774 (S.D. Ohio 1988).

*Sprogis v. United Airlines, Inc.*, 444 F.2d 1194 (7th Cir.), *cert. denied*, 404 U.S. 991 (1971).

*Swanson v. Elmhurst Chrysler/Plymouth, Inc.*, 43 Fair Empl. Prac. Cas. (BNA) 399 (N.D. Ill. 1987).

*Texas Dep't. of Community Affairs v. Burdine*, 450 U.S. 248 (1981).

*Tomson v. Stephan*, 696 F. Supp. 1407 (D. Kan. 1988).

*Troutt v. Charcoal Steak House, Inc.*, 835 F. Supp. 899 (W.D. Va. 1993).

*Underwood v. Washington Post Credit Union*, 59 Fair Empl. Prac. Cas. (BNA) 952 (D.C. Sup. Ct. 1992).

*United Mine Workers v. Gibbs*, 383 U.S. 715 (1966).

*Waltman v. International Paper Co.*, 47 Fair Empl. Prac. Cas. (BNA) 671 (W.D. La. 1988), *rev'd on other grounds*, 875 F.2d 468 (5th Cir. 1989).

*Watts v. New York Police Department*, 724 F. Supp. 99 (S.D.N.Y. 1989).

*Weiss v. Amoco Oil Co.*, 142 F.R.D. 311 (S.D. Iowa 1992).

*West Virginia University Hospitals, Inc. v. Casey*, 111 S. Ct. 1138 (1991).

# CHAPTER 5

# AN EPIDEMIOLOGY OF SEXUAL HARASSMENT: EVIDENCE FROM NORTH AMERICA AND EUROPE

## James E. Gruber

This chapter explores the parameters of sexual harassment in terms of its overall occurrence in the United States as well as in Canada and Europe, the relative frequency of different forms of harassment, and the demographic and work-related characteristics of women who are the targets of harassment. Greater certainty, or at least more complete information, about each issue—overall level, relative occurrence, and correlates or predictors—has developed over nearly two decades. A brief overview highlights the issues and problems of sexual harassment research that recent discussions have addressed. This is followed by a more detailed discussion of current research on each issue.

### SEXUAL HARASSMENT THEORY AND RESEARCH: PRE-1987

The first attempts to define sexual harassment used general and often ambiguous terms. It was defined as sexually oriented behavior by men (often meaning supervisors) in the workplace that was used to dominate and/or denigrate women (e.g., Working Women's Institute, 1979; Farley, 1978). The first attempts to determine "what happened to how many women" relied either on case studies (e.g., Bernstein, 1976) or used nonrandom samples (Safran, 1976; Lindsey, 1977) as the basis of their evidence. As a result of definitional and sampling problems, the early reports of the percentage of women who had experienced harassment were quite high, often in excess of 70%.

The first nationwide study of harassment was published in 1981 by the U.S. Merit Systems Protection Board (USMSPB, 1981). It collected survey data from a representative sample of more than twenty thousand federal employees. Forty-two percent of the women federal employees indicated that they had experienced at least one of six forms of sexual harassment presented in the survey. The survey gave researchers in the field a model—and a challenge—for their own endeavors.

In a review of 18 research studies of sexual harassment conducted between 1979 and 1986 that included Americans and Canadians, public and private employees, and university students, the percentage of women who were found to have experienced sexual harassment ranged from 28% to 75% (Gruber, 1990b). In order to determine the sources of variability in the percentages of women who reported harassment, six methodological factors were analyzed: sample size, survey response rate, sample diversity, harassment frame of reference (i.e., harassment during a time period or harassment on a particular job), number of harassment categories, and the wording used to elicit responses. The surveys were compared in light of these factors on the basis of whether the percentage of women who had experienced sexual harassment in each study was at or near the median figure (44%) for the 18 studies, below the median, or above. The analyses showed that surveys with low response rates tended to have harassment rates that were above the median. Samples drawn from homogeneous populations had below-median levels of harassment. These surveys varied considerably in response rates. While several studies were noteworthy for their high response rates (e.g., USMSPB 1981, with 85%; Gutek, 1985, with 75%; CHRC, 1983, with 88%), others had rates under 40% (e.g., Hayler, 1979; LaFontaine & Tredeau, 1986; Cammaert, 1985). Also, most studies, even those with a fairly large sample size, were drawn from fairly homogeneous populations. For example, surveys typically restricted their samples by focusing upon specific occupations (e.g., Gruber & Bjorn, 1982; Maypole, 1986), occupational sectors (e.g., Hayler, 1979; McIntyre, 1982), or geographic areas (e.g., Gutek, 1985; Loy & Stewart, 1984), or populations (e.g., Verba, DiNunzio, & Spaulding, 1983). The number of explicit categories of sexual harassment was a significant factor. Surveys that offered respondents a checklist of behaviors or experiences and asked them to

indicate which they had experienced but offered them less than six alternatives (e.g., Maypole, 1986) and studies that generated harassment categories from open-ended questions (e.g., Gruber & Bjorn, 1982) tended to report harassment percentages below the median figure. Finally, the critique noted what Fitzgerald (1994) has stressed: that harassment research has often not included women in nontraditional or blue-collar jobs.

The derivation of categories or measures of harassment has been problematic. Measurement development has rarely included tests of validity and reliability (Fitzgerald, 1990). Also, measures that tapped similar types of harassment experiences were seldom employed by different researchers (Gruber, 1990). For example, the term "sexual bribery" found in two surveys referred to the experience labeled as "verbal negotiations" in one study and as "expected social activity" in another. The wording of survey items was often ambiguous and open to several interpretations (Fitzgerald, 1990). Finally, the survey items were often not exhaustive or else included items that were not clearly in the realm of sexual harassment (Fitzgerald, 1990; Gruber, 1990). In particular, hostile environment forms of sexual harassment were underarticulated in most harassment studies (Gruber, 1992). Fitzgerald and Shullman (1993) proposed that such measurement problems could be addressed by assessing the full range of behaviors that are considered to be harassing; creating survey items that ask respondents if they have experienced specific types of behaviors; avoiding the use of the term "sexual harassment" when asking them about these experiences; and using supplementary scales to assess frequency, duration, and offensiveness of specific behaviors.

## OLD PROBLEMS AND NEW APPROACHES

Early attempts to elicit information from respondents about their experiences with sexual harassment involved either asking women if they had experienced "sexual harassment" or, as in the case of the Merit Systems study, presenting respondents with a list of experiences (e.g., sexual propositions, touching) that had been derived from formal or legal definitions. Conceptualizations and measurements of sexual harassment were aided substantially by research on *perceptions* of sexual harassment that began to emerge in the early 1980s (e.g., Rossi & Weber-Burdin, 1983). This substantial body of research (see Stockdale, 1993, for an overview) provided a research foundation for the development of sexual harassment categories and assessment of the seriousness or severity of sexual harassment experiences. As discussed earlier, surveys that tapped sexual harassment experiences often presented lists or categories that were not exhaustive or which subsumed more than one form of experience in a single category.

The research on perceptions of harassment (e.g., Pryor & Day, 1988; Weber-Burdin & Rossi, 1982; see also Chapter 2) facilitated a refinement of our understanding by discriminating separate types of sexual harassment and enlarging the scope of what we defined as sexual harassment. Specifically, perceptions research expanded our understanding of the factors that affect judgments of a simulation or scenario as being one of sexual harassment—for example, the source of the act, sexual explicitness of verbal comments, type of verbal request—and the factors that influence judgments of severity of different experiences. The Merit Systems study (1981) gauged harassment experiences and seriousness of harassment by employing 6 items; Terpstra and Baker (1987), in contrast, developed 18 scenarios to tap different aspects of harassment. Research on perceptions of sexual harassment spurred the development of two comprehensive sexual harassment experience inventories in the latter half of the 1980s: Gruber's Inventory of Sexual Harassment (1990), and Fitzgerald's Sexual Experiences Questionnaire (1985).

Gruber's development of a comprehensive typology of sexual harassment experiences included personal as well as environmental forms organized in terms of severity within three general forms of harassment—verbal comments, verbal requests, and nonverbal displays (1992b). Eleven categories of sexual harassment were developed from a content analysis of four types of material: the categories used in 17 sexual harassment surveys between 1979 and 1986; harassment recipients' accounts of their experiences reported in scholarly publications; court decisions, or interpretations of these decisions; and the categories described in the EEOC's (1988) guidelines. A content analysis and subsequent validity checks produced 11 categories.

The severity ranking of each type within a general form of harassment (i.e., remarks, requests, nonverbal displays) was determined by adapting the results of analyses by Fitzgerald and Hesson-McInnis (1989) and Baker, Terpstra, and Larntz (1990). Verbal requests were ranked on the basis of directness, explicitness, and threat (see Gruber, 1992a, for a discussion of severity dimensions). Sexual bribery was considered to be the most severe because it affected a woman's job and usually originated from someone with supervisory power. This was followed by sexual propositions, relational advances, and subtle hints/pressures (offensive but not direct, and generally not threatening). Three types of sexual remarks were distinguished, largely on the basis of directness and threat. Personal remarks were direct and often threatening (e.g., comments about sexual anatomy or expressions of sexual desire). Subjective objectification—such a man openly talking about a target in sexual terms while pretending to ignore her presence, or a male coworker spreading sexual rumors about her—is a form that has received little attention from researchers. Sexual categorical remarks, or statements about "women in general," women's sexual anatomy, or sexual acts, are the least serious form of sexual remarks because they are less direct and less threatening than remarks that reference or explicitly include the target. Finally, four types of nonverbal displays were ranked. Sexual assault (first) and sexual touching were highly severe. Sexual posturing (e.g., feigning intercourse or masturbation) was often direct but did not involve contact and was less threatening. Sexual materials were least severe. These 11 categories formed the basis for the construction of Gruber's Inventory of Sexual Harassment (1990).

The Inventory of Sexual Harassment was first used in a cross-national survey of American and European women in nontraditional jobs in 1989 through 1991. It was directed by Kaisa Kauppinen-Toropainen of the Finnish Institute of Occupational Health. A slightly modified version was included in a cross-national survey of Canadian women conducted by Michael Smith of York University in Toronto. A confirmatory factor analysis provided statistical evidence that the items fell into three dimensions, as articulated earlier (1992a).

Fitzgerald's Sexual Experiences Questionnaire (1985) was prompted by Till's (1980) categorization of five types of sexual harassment that was developed through a content analysis of responses to open-ended questions in a survey of college women. The five types were gender harassment (sexist remarks or behavior), seductive behavior (sexual advances or propositions), sexual bribery (sexual advances with a promise of reward), sexual coercion (sexual advances with a threat of punishment), and sexual imposition (sexual assault or sexual touching). A 28-item survey that was developed to tap each type of harassment was found to be stable and internally consistent (Fitzgerald et al., 1988). The SEQ advanced sexual harassment research because of its rigorous empirical bases: Scale items were dropped or modified on the basis of testing and retesting, and the scale was tested for reliability and validity. Also, the harassment types reflect levels of severity: bribery and coercion are most severe and gender harassment is least severe.

## SEXUAL HARASSMENT IN A CROSS-NATIONAL CONTEXT

The perception of sexual harassment as a workplace issue in Europe followed developments in the United States. Official policy definitions in northern Europe, for example, closely paralleled the EEOC's (1980) distinctions of sexual bribery (quid pro quo) and hostile environment. The first survey ("FRIDA") of working women in Sweden in 1986 used items to tap sexual harassment that were nearly identical to those in the Merit Systems survey (Hagman, 1992). Seventeen percent of respondents indicated that they had experienced at least one form of harassment. A 1986 survey of Finnish women in nontraditional jobs that also used the six items from the Merit Systems study to measure sexual harassment found that 34% had been sexually harassed (Hogbacka et al., 1987). In France a study commissioned by the Secretary of State for Women's and Consumer's Rights in 1991 found that 21% of respondents had experienced at least one form of harassment (Rubenstein, 1992). A survey of former Soviet (Russian and Estonian) professional and blue-collar women revealed that 36% had been sexually harassed during the previous two years (Kauppinen-Toropainen & Gruber, 1993b).

Other European studies found much higher rates of harassment, most probably because of many of the same methodological problems found in a number of American surveys, such as small or unrepresentative samples, ambiguous survey items, or the use of lifetime prevalence rates (Gruber, 1990). For example, 58% of the women in the Netherlands, 62% of working women in Madrid, 73% of British women in a survey conducted by the Labour Research Department, and 63% of Norwegian women were found to have been sexually harassed (Rubenstein, 1992).

Since many European and American surveys did not sample similar types of occupations or use similar types of survey items, it is difficult to compare sexual harassment rates internationally. However, given the few studies that used comparable methods and survey items (e.g., Hagman, 1986) or which actually used the same survey instruments on European and American samples (e.g., Kauppinen-Toropainen & Gruber, 1993a), it appears that Americans have somewhat higher rates of harassment than Europeans, in particular those in the Baltic countries. This may be because Scandinavia has the highest overall gender equality in the modern world, and Scandinavian women have had greater labor force participation and income parity than American women for several decades (Kauppinen-Toropainen & Gruber, 1993a).

## THE UNIVERSALITY OF SEXUAL HARASSMENT: TYPES AND CORRELATES

Do women across the United States and internationally experience similar forms of harassment in roughly similar proportions? Are similar types of women or work situations vulnerable to sexual harassment across occupational and international boundaries? The answers to both of these questions seems to be affirmative. It does not appear that women of a particular occupational status, region, or country are more vulnerable to distinct forms of harassment than others. Nor does it appear that the types of women or the types of occupations or work situations that are most vulnerable to harassment vary internationally. These commonalities suggest a universality of sexual harassment experiences. Specifically, while more women in some countries or some

occupations may experience more harassment than other women, it appears that the types of experiences and the characteristics of women and work situations that predict sexual harassment are essentially the same.

## Types of Sexual Harassment

One of the first attempts to work through the morass of research studies that employed different sampling strategies, survey procedures, and survey items to elicit information about sexual harassment critically evaluated the sexual harassment categorizations of 18 harassment surveys conducted before 1987 (Gruber, 1990). When categories that were similar across these surveys were compared (see Table 5-1), it was found that sexual comments were most frequent, followed (in order) by sexual posturing (staring, following, gesturing), sexual touching, pressure for social and/or sexual relationships, and sexual assault. This order persisted in spite of large differences among these surveys in the percentages of women who indicated that they had been sexually harassed. The results from European surveys provide additional evidence of this ranking, again, in spite of differing methodologies. Surveys conducted in France, Spain, and England found that verbal comments, "verbal abuse,"

**TABLE 5-1.** Percentages of Women Who Experienced Sexual Harassment from Four Representative Surveys[a]

| TYPE OF HARASSMENT | PERCENTAGE RANGE ACROSS FOUR SURVEYS | MEDIAN PERCENTAGE |
| --- | --- | --- |
| Pressure for dates/relationships | 9–22 | 13 |
| Sexual commentary | 27–35 | 28 |
| Sexual posturing | 8–26 | 24 |
| Sexual touching | 12–27 | 17 |
| Sexual assault | 1–2 | 1 |

[a]The four surveys were conducted by: U.S. Merit Systems Protection Board, 1981; Canadian Human Rights Commission, 1983; McIntyre, 1982; and Verba, DiNunzio, and Spaulding, 1983.

Source: J. E. Gruber (1990). Methodological problems and policy implications in sexual harassment research. *Population Research and Policy Review, 9*, 235–254. Table 4.

or suggestive comments were the most frequent forms of harassment, followed by nonverbal harassment (touching, following, leering) and relational or sexual pressures (Rubenstein, 1992). Two surveys that used the same items as the Merit Systems study revealed comparable results. Verbal commentary was the most frequent form of harassment, followed by sexual posturing, sexual touching, sexual bribery, and sexual assault, respectively (Hagman, 1988; Hogbacka et al., 1987).

Research results from comprehensive inventories of sexual harassment experiences provide more concise information about the relative frequencies of sexual harassment types. In a survey of students and working women, Fitzgerald et al. (1988) found verbal comments of a sexual nature (e.g., suggestive jokes, discussions of personal or sexual matters, sexual insinuations) to predominate, while nonverbal harassment (touching, ogling) and pressures for a sexual/social relationship followed. Their research also confirmed what others had found, namely, that sexual bribery and sexual assault were relatively infrequent among both students and workers.

Survey results from women in different occupations and different countries who were queried about sexual harassment using the Inventory of Sexual Harassment provide additional evidence about the universality of harassment experiences. Two surveys that tapped the sexual harassment experiences of women in Canada (Smith, 1992), the United States, Russia, and Estonia (Kauppinen-Toropainen & Gruber, 1993b) provide comparative evidence about specific forms of sexual harassment. Two forms of verbal comments—sexual categorical remarks (sexual comments about women in general or about women other than the target) and personal remarks (sexual jokes or remarks directed at the target) were the most prevalent forms of harassment among white- and blue-collar women (Gruber, Smith, & Kauppinen-Toropainen, 1996). Sexual posturing (staring, leaning or following, and gesturing) was the second most prevalent form. Sexual touching and inappropriate questions about a woman's

sex life ranked third, followed by pressures for dates or sexual liaisons and subjective objectification (e.g., spreading sexual rumors). Sexual bribery and sexual assault were reported by less than 5% of the international sample.

Evaluations of severity of different forms of sexual harassment have been drawn from the perceptions of general populations of research participants. Information about what people perceive to be sexual harassment has come from three sources. One source is surveys that asked respondents to judge whether a specific behavior constituted sexual harassment and then used the extent of agreement among respondents to determine severity (e.g., Terpstra & Baker, 1987; USMSPB, 1981). A second source used written scenarios to elicit judgments from survey participants about the degree of seriousness, offensiveness, or threat of a particular situation (e.g., Fitzgerald & Hesson-McInnis, 1989; Gutek, 1985). The third and largest body of research used written or visual scenarios in which the content was carefully manipulated in order to determine the impact of individual factors (e.g., harasser behavior, power differential between harasser and target, target's behavior) on judgments of severity (e.g., Pryor, 1992; Reilly et al., 1982; Weber-Burdin & Rossi, 1982).

A recent analysis of the relative severity of different forms of sexual harassment used actual targets in workplace settings to determine impact (Gruber, Smith, & Kauppinen-Toropainen, 1996). Women in white-collar and blue-collar occupations in the United States and Canada were asked to describe the personal impact of sexual harassment experiences. The analyses revealed that sexual assault and sexual bribery were the two most impacting forms of harassment, followed by touching and leaning (i.e., violations of personal space, cornering). Inappropriate questions about a woman's sex life, spreading sexual rumors behind a woman's back (subjective objectification), and persistent date requests were of moderate severity. Two forms of harassment that are not usually targeted at the victim herself, sexual materials and sexual categorical remarks, were least severe. Sexual jokes or comments of a personal nature were somewhat more severe than materials or categorical remarks.

## Correlates of Sexual Harassment

One of the most useful ways of conceptualizing the occurrence of sexual harassment was developed in the early 1980s by Sandra Tangri and her colleagues. According to their research, sexual harassment was a function of two forms of power differentials: sociocultural power and organizational power (Tangri, Burt, & Johnson, 1982). Sociocultural power includes attitudes, expectations, and roles that create culturally legitimated differences of power and influence between men and women. Differences in age, marital status, and education reinforce gender differences in power and status in society. A consistent finding in American and European research is that single and/ or young women tend to be targets of sexual harassment more frequently than others (Baker, 1989; CHRC, 1983; Gruber & Bjorn, 1982; Gutek, 1985; Haavio-Mannila, Kauppinen-Toropainen, K., & Kandolin, I., 1991; Hagman, 1992; Hogbacka et al., 1987; Rubenstein, 1992). Women with low education are often the targets of harassment, but educational differences are apparently not as significant in predicting harassment as are differences in age or marital status (Fain & Anderton, 1987; CHRC, 1983; Hogbacka et al., 1987; Stringer-Moore, 1982; USMSPB, 1981). As potent as sociocultural factors are, however, it seems that the most important factors that explain sexual harassment are related to work. This can be seen when the impact of sociocultural variables is compared to that of organizational factors in a single multivariate analysis.

Organizational power, defined as the amount of influence members have in affecting their mobility or their attainment of scarce resources or in influencing the behavior of others or the functioning of the organization (Fitzgerald, Hulin, & Drasgow, 1995; Haavio-Mannila, 1992; Kanter, 1977), generally includes occupation or occupational status, gen-

der of supervisory personnel, organizational climate, seniority, sex ratio of an occupation or workplace, and seniority or job tenure.

Women in male-dominated workplaces report more experiences of harassment than women in other work settings (Gutek, Cohen, & Konrad, 1990; Izraeli, 1983; Hagman, 1988; Hogbacka et al., 1987). Similarly, women in male-dominated occupations both in North America and Europe report higher rates of harassment than women in either traditionally female or gender-balanced occupations (Baker, 1989; Gutek, 1985; LaFontaine & Tredeau, 1986; Rubenstein, 1992). It appears that women who work in male-dominated positions are victimized more frequently because of male cultural norms that influence work-related and social activities. Specifically, male-dominated workplaces or occupations generally emphasize sexual aggression, sexual bravado and posturing, or denigration of that which is defined as "soft" or feminine (Kauppinen-Toropainen & Kandolin, 1992). Normative male culture may also affect women who are low in seniority or function in low-status positions in an organization, and women in these positions report high rates of harassment (Gruber & Bjorn, 1982; Martin, 1980; Rubenstein, 1992; USMSPB, 1981).

Organizational climate has also been found to be related to women's experiences with sex discrimination and sexual harassment. Work situations in which women were regarded in terms of cultural stereotypes or as sex objects were typified by frequent harassment (Gutek, 1985; Haavio-Mannila, 1992). Even when the climate of workplaces was not sexualized specifically but rather was typified by petty bickering, rivalry, and unprofessional behavior, reports of sexual harassment tended to be high (Kauppinen-Toropainen & Gruber, 1993a).

Finally, policies against sexual harassment and leadership by organizational officials in the implementation and enforcement of such policies are important in predicting the sexual harassment experiences. Specifically, workplaces with explicit policies about sexual harassment or with officials who are proactive with regard to the problem have fewer problems with sexual harassment (Hesson-McInnis & Fitzgerald, 1992; Pryor, LaVite, & Stoller, 1993) and encourage women to respond more assertively to their harassers (Gruber & Smith, 1994).

In addition to questions about the characteristics of targets or work situations and the experiences of sexual harassment, there is the issue of severity of harassment. Are some women or work situations more vulnerable to severe sexual harassment than others? One of the few studies that used multivariate analyses to determine the predictors of several types of harassment (of varying severity) found that the size and significance of the predictors varied considerably from one form of harassment to another (Fain & Anderton, 1987). A similar outcome was found recently in a survey of American and European women (Gruber & Kauppinen-Toropainen, 1994). The predictors of sexual touching were generally stronger than those of sexual jokes and comments. Also, organizational variables were better at predicting sexual touching than jokes or comments. Marital status but not age was similar in this respect.

## THE LOCUS OF SEXUAL HARASSMENT: HARD FACTS AND UNANSWERED QUESTIONS

### How Many Women Have Been Harassed?

The median rate of harassment for 18 surveys discussed by Gruber (1990) was 44%. Given the fact that sexual harassment surveys have generally presented respondents with no more than six alternatives (types of harassment), it is reasonable that this figure is a somewhat conservative estimate of women who have experienced harassment during a two-year time period. A survey that used the seven categories employed in the Merit Systems studies (USMSPB, 1981, 1988) found that 46% of the women had experienced harassment (Pryor, LaVite, & Stoller, 1993). A national sample of Canadian women that used the

Inventory of Sexual Harassment found that 51% had experienced at least one form of harassment. The latter also revealed that the typical target had experienced four different forms of harassment, and women who had experienced the more severe forms of harassment encountered a significantly greater variety of other harassment forms than those who were recipients of less severe forms.

## What Are the Forms and Severity of Harassment?

An evaluation of the types of harassment that emerge from research and which are presented in legal guidelines (e.g., EEOC, 1990) suggests that there are 11 forms of sexual harassment. This figure includes types discussed by only a few researchers, such as "rumoring," or spreading sexual gossip behind a target's back (e.g., Fitzgerald et al., 1988); sexual graffiti or materials (e.g., Terpstra & Baker, 1987); or "bystander harassment" (women who routinely witness the sexual harassment of female coworkers), a type that is part of federal policy (EEOC, 1990) but is not explicitly measured by most research scholars.

Less severe forms of harassment occur more frequently in workplaces than those of greater severity. It appears that 2–5% of North American and European women have been sexually assaulted at their jobs, and 3–7% have experienced sexual bribery (Gruber, 1990; Gruber, Smith, & Kauppinen-Toropainen, 1996; Fitzgerald et al., 1988). On the other hand, sexual jokes or comments about women or women's bodies or sexuality were experienced by 46% of Canadian women (Gruber, Smith, & Kauppinen-Toropainen, 1996), a figure quite close (44%) to that found in Fitzgerald's (1988) survey of working women. Also, personal questions or comments of a sexual nature directly to a woman are experienced by approximately one-sixth to one-fifth of North American and European respondents (Fitzgerald et al., 1988; Gruber, Smith, & Kauppinen-Toropainen, 1996). Women are apt to experience repeated incidents of less severe harassment, and, as the EEOC (1990) guidelines indicate, these forms have higher thresholds of impact. The impact of some low-severity forms increases significantly only after three incidents (Gruber & Kauppinen-Toropainen, 1994).

## For Whom and Where Is Sexual Harassment a Problem?

### Youth and Singleness

Young and single women tend to be the targets of sexual harassment cross-nationally. While this is hardly a new or surprising finding, it is probably one that is overstated. Despite the considerable volume of current research on sexual harassment, studies based on surveys that employ multivariate techniques in an analysis of experiences are somewhat sparse. Such analyses have the advantage of isolating the unique impact of a single predictor on a dependent variable, in contrast to descriptive or bivariate analyses that do not account for what are often complex interrelationships among the predictors themselves. When the impact of age and marital status is analyzed simultaneously with other variables—workplace characteristics, for example—their significance diminishes considerably. This is most evident for "environmental" forms (e.g., sexual categorical remarks, sexual materials) of harassment. Age and marital status differences are not very important in predicting which women are likely to hear demeaning sexual comments about women or women's bodies or to see pornographic posters displayed in the workplace. In addition, these variables are often not as predictive of interpersonal forms (e.g., touching, date requests) of sexual harassment as are workplace or organizational factors (Gruber, Smith, & Kauppinen-Toropainen, 1995).

It appears that women's deficits in sociocultural power (i.e., youth, singleness) are often transformed into deficits of organizational power. An important research question for the future is: Which types of workplaces or occupations increase the vulnerability of young and single women? In general, the climate or normative context of a workplace or occupation may accentuate women's visibility *as women*.

### Sex Role Spillover

Workplaces or occupations where women have less status or authority or are paid significantly less than men create an "atmosphere of inequality" (Faley, 1982). These types of positions legitimize sexist attitudes toward women and visibly mark and reinforce women's cultural status. Sexual harassment is a frequent outcome of such work situations. Most traditionally female occupations, especially those where there is a great deal of "sex-role spillover" (Gutek & Morasch, 1982) or an infusion of cultural stereotypes about women (e.g., sexual availability, submissiveness, nurturance), fit this description. The primacy of cultural roles and definitions over organizational roles may be a factor in "contra-power" sexual harassment, or harassment by someone with less organizational power than the target (McKinney, 1990, 1992).

### Male Preserves

Nontraditional workplaces and occupations create similar problems of discrimination and harassment for women, but for somewhat different reasons. Women in nontraditional situations experience more sexual harassment (Gutek & Dunwoody, 1987), especially environmental forms (Gruber, Smith, & Kauppinen-Toropainen, 1996). It has become apparent since Kanter's (1977) thesis on the impact of workplace or occupational sex ratios on gender relationships was first articulated that numerically skewed situations create normative dominance by men. The normative male dominance of a workplace or occupation varies on the basis of two factors that "gender" an organization or occupation (Collins, 1990). First, the length of time a position has been predominately male may be a good indicator of the dominance of male norms, rituals, and behavioral and linguistic expressions. Specifically, the depth and texture of a male "subculture" arises only after a long period of time when several generations of men, who have been privileged by access to educational programs, professional licensure, union acceptance, or apprenticeship training, have marked the territory as theirs (Bergman,

1986). Also, the extent of normative male dominance is influenced significantly by the degree to which a workplace or occupation stresses highly stereotypical male traits, such as aggression, risk taking, manual dexterity, or technical or analytical problem-solving skills. Highly gendered male environments often deliberately debase womanhood or femininity as a means of reinforcing their unique claims to masculinity (Sanday, 1991). Thus, a woman entering such a field or workplace is not only "invading" male territory but is threatening the bases of male solidarity.

Research on male team sports, military and paramilitary groups, and male-only social organizations provides an understanding of male normative dominance. Evidence from very different cultural and social situations— tribal societies, police stations, military bases, and American college fraternities—reveals that violence against women is an important vehicle for creating and reinforcing male bonding (Martin, 1980, 1990; Martindale, 1990; Sanday, 1981, 1991). Indeed, exclusively male groups create a sense of identity and forcefulness of shared purpose by distancing themselves socially and psychologically from the ever-present Other (Messner, 1992). Pryor has shown that men with a high likelihood to sexually harass fuse dominance and sexuality (Pryor & Stoller, 1992); they tend to hold adversarial beliefs about sexual relations, endorse traditional sex role stereotypes, and score low on empathy and high on authoritarianism (Pryor, 1987). "Local norms" that encourage sexist and aggressive behavior are reinforced both by high-status persons within a setting (e.g., managers, commanding officers) and through interaction with like-minded peers (see Pryor, Giedd, & Williams, 1995). Koss and Dinero (1988) find that membership in college peer groups that reinforce highly sexualized beliefs about women predicts sexually aggressive behavior by individual males.

The data on women in the military and police work provide additional evidence of the impact of male normative and numerical dominance. Martindale (1990) reported that *64% of women in the military* had experienced sex-

ual harassment during a two-year period. This figure is significantly larger than the survey of Canadian women (51%), which uses a comparable number of categories, as well as those from large American surveys (e.g., USMSPB, 1981, 1988; Pryor, LaVite, & Stoller, 1993). A Navy-wide survey in 1991 found that 44% of enlisted women had been sexually harassed during a *one-year* period. Problems of harassment are widespread in police departments. Martin (1990) reported that two-thirds of women police officers who had been on the force for less than three years had been harassed. A similar figure—62%— was found in a survey of Florida women police officers (Robinson, 1994). Martin (1980, 1990) and Balkin (1988) provide an analysis of male police culture. According to the latter, male resentment of women police officers is premised on the beliefs that they (the women) are less competent and capable. These beliefs fly in the face of a considerable volume of research literature that shows few major differences between policemen and -women in job performance and competence. It appears that a "change-threatened" personality typical of policemen is reinforced by a police subculture based on mutual trust of fellow officers who have similar backgrounds, attitudes, and values (Balkin, 1988). Balkin's findings are strikingly parallel to Pryor's person X situation research, which reveals that high-LSH (likelihood to sexually harass) men have distinct attitudinal profiles and are apt to sexually harass when they are in a group of like-minded (high-LSH) peers (see Pryor, Giedd, & Williams, 1995). Invasion of the male "clubhouse" exacts a heavy toll on policewomen. In a job noted for stress and burnout, women experience an additional stressor: discrimination and harassment. Balkin (1988) found sexual harassment to be the single greatest source of stress among policewomen. When Martin (1990) asked rookies to describe the sources of the problems they experienced as police officers, two-thirds of the men cited work-related problems (e.g., having too much to learn, unfamiliarity with the area to which they were assigned), while less than 10% listed harassment by a supervisor or peer; in contrast, in a similar survey, women officers cited work-related difficulties (39%) and harassment (35%) as problems.

## Workplace Sexualization

Workplaces in which sexual comments, displays, and materials are prominent have problems with sexual harassment. While it is evident that negative stereotypes about women or hostile treatment of women is often conveyed sexually—or, as MacKinnon (1979) puts it, "sex is the medium of power"—there is also evidence that "positively" sexualized environments foster sexual harassment. That is, work environments in which a number of women and men pursue romantic relationships, engage in friendly sexual bantering, or infuse their conversations with discussions of sex or sexuality *also* report a high incidence of sexual harassment (Haavio-Mannila, 1992). This finding suggests two interpretations. A general interpretation is that a positively affected sexualized environment creates daily "reminders" of women's subordinate cultural status as objects of pursuit. A second possibility is that the men displaying the appropriate or flattering sexual attention are not the same ones who are doing the harassing, although both are reacting to sexual currents in the environment. These interpretations suggest that policies that discourage persons of both sexes from pursuing romantic relationships at work may have some merit. The fact that such policies are strongly—and often passionately—debated should provide a stimulus to further research on this matter.

## Unprofessional Behavior

Gutek (1985) speculated that unprofessional work environments are apt to create a number of problems, including sexual harassment. Recently this hypothesis was tested using a sample of American and European women who held nontraditional blue- and white-collar jobs (Kauppinen-Toropainen & Gruber, 1993a). Unprofessional environments—those in which there was a steady current of bickering, petty rivalry, and favoritism—were char-acterized by high levels of sex discrimination and sexual harassment. A reasonable corollary of this finding, though as of yet an untested one, is that work environments in which *alienation* is high—for example, where the work is stressful, the routine is tedious, the schedule is arduous or inflexible, or the input or creativity of employees is minimal—are likely to show problems with sexual harassment. The aforementioned study found that American autoworkers, in comparison to American engineers and to their European blue-collar counterparts, worked in the least congenial or professional environments and reported the most experiences of discrimination and harassment. These experiences were, in turn, related to the fact that they also had the highest levels of work and psychological stress and the lowest level of job satisfaction.

It is well established that work alienation is stressful and creates workplace turmoil. What the Kauppinen-Toropainen and Gruber study (1993) suggests is that in an alienating work environment, conflict is routed along power dimensions. Consequently, women are targeted not only because their work roles reproduce cultural sexual roles, or because they are intruders on male territory, but also because they are convenient scapegoats for frustrated, unhappy workers. Researchers may consider giving greater scrutiny to the dimensions of work alienation in future endeavors that focus on the relationship between different aspects of organizational climate and sexual harassment.

## Policies and Leadership

Although sexual harassment policies are widespread across the United States, Canada, and most of the European Community, there is a dearth of research on their impact. In the last decade several studies have shown encouraging results with regard to the effects of training or sensitization procedures on attitudes toward, or definitions of, sexual harassment (see Chapter 8 for a review). The impact of policies or procedures on *behavioral* change, however, has only recently received attention from researchers, with research based on three quite different samples—active duty U.S. military personnel, employees in a private-sector organization with branches across the United States, and a nationwide stratified sample of working women in Canada. Analyses conducted by John Pryor and his colleagues (see Pryor, LaVite, & Stoller, 1993; Pryor, Giedd, & Williams, 1995) on the first two samples found that the attitudes of commanding officers or management toward sexual harassment (encouraged, were indifferent to, or discouraged it), as perceived by male and female rank-and-file members of these organizations, were significantly related to the incidence of harassment. In brief, organizations whose leaders were perceived as discouraging harassment had a lower incidence of harassment.

A national sample of Canadian women were queried about their experiences with public and workplace harassment. In one section of the interview they were asked if they had seen or otherwise had knowledge of these policies or procedures concerning sexual harassment: written policy, official procedure for handling complaints, company or union poster, company or union pamphlet, or presentation by a company or union representative. Women in workplaces with a variety of policies or procedures on sexual harassment were more apt to respond assertively to harassment (e.g., speaking to a supervisor, filing a complaint) than others (Gruber & Smith, 1995). Also, these women experienced less sexual harassment (Gruber, in preparation).

## A Final Word

Sexual harassment is a workplace problem that has probably affected about half of all working women in the United States, Canada, and some European countries in the 1990s. Comparative research suggests that there is a "universality" to the experience: The types and relative frequency of harassment are similar, as are women's ways of handling, or responding to, harassment. Also, similar types of organizational factors predict harassment in North America and in Europe. Organizations in which men and women work in sex-segregated units or workplaces and/or where women's economic rewards and organizational power are considerably less than men's are likely to create harassment problems for women. Organizations in which men and women do not behave appropriately—for example, where sexualized conduct is widespread in the workplace, or where morale is low and employees engage in a wide range of unprofessional activities—seem to be environments in which women frequently become targets of harassment. Organizations or occupations in which there is a strong male culture seem to be especially problematic for women. It seems unlikely that the introduction of women into such work environments (e.g., changing the sex ratio) is sufficient to change the sexist climate. Ideally, the problem of male culture should be dealt with before the introduction or substantial increase in the number of women. Finally, organizations (and organizational leaders) that do not take sexual harassment seriously create problems for women. Work units that have leaders who do not actively discourage sexual harassment have more problems with harassment than those that take a stand. Organizations that have a variety of policies on sexual harassment encourage more assertive responses to harassment from women, and, overall, have a lower incidence of harassment.

## REFERENCES

Baker, D., Terpstra, D., & Larntz, K. (1990). The influence of individual characteristics and severity of harassing behavior on reactions to sexual harassment. *Sex Roles, 22*, 305–326.

Baker, N. L. (1989). Sexual harassment and job satisfaction in traditional and nontraditional industrial occupations. Unpublished doctoral dissertation, California School of Professional Psychology, Los Angeles.

Balkin, J. (1988). Why policemen don't like policewomen. *Journal of Police Science and Administration, 16*, 29–37.

Bergman, B. R. (1986) *The economic emergence of women*. New York: Basic Books.

Bernstein, P. (1976, August). Sexual harassment on the job. *Harper's Bazaar*, p. 33.

Cammaert, L. (1985). How widespread is sexual harassment on campus. *International Journal of Women's Studies, 8*, 388–397.

Canadian Human Rights Commission (CHRC) (1983). *Unwanted sexual attention and sexual harassment.* Montreal: Minister of Supply and Services of Canada.

Collins, E., & Blodgett, T. (1981). Sexual harassment: Some see it, some won't. *Harvard Business Review, 59* (March/April), 77, 95.

Collins, R. (1990). Conflict theory and the advance of macrohistorical sociology. New York: Columbia University.

Culbertson, A., Rosenfeld, P., Booth-Kewley, S., & Magnusson, P. (1992). *Assessment of sexual harassment in the Navy: Results of the 1989 Navy-wide survey.* TR–92–11. San Diego, CA: Navy Personnel Research and Development Center.

Equal Employment Opportunity Commission (EEOC). (1988). *Guidelines on discrimination because of sex.* EEOC Policy Guidance. N–915.035.5168, October 25.

Fain, T., & Anderton, D. (1987). Sexual harassment: Organizational context and diffuse status. *Sex Roles, 16,* 291–311.

Faley, R. (1982). Sexual harassment: Critical review of legal cases with general principles and preventive measures. *Personnel Psychology, 35,* 583–600.

Farley, L. (1978). *Sexual shakedown: The sexual harassment of women on the job.* New York: McGraw-Hill.

Fitzgerald, L. F. (1990). Sexual harassment: The definition and measurement of a construct. In M. Paludi (Ed.), *Ivory power: Sexual and gender harassment in academia.* Albany, NY: SUNY Press.

Fitzgerald, L. F. (1994). No safe haven: Violence against women in the workplace. In APA Taskforce on Male Violence Against Women (Eds.), *No safe haven: Violence against women at home, at work, and in the community.* Washington, DC: American Psychological Association.

Fitzgerald, L., & Hesson-McInnis, M. (1989). The dimensions of sexual harassment: A structural analysis. *Journal of Vocational Behavior, 35,* 309–326.

Fitzgerald, L. F., Hulin, C. L., & Drasgow, F. D. (1995). The antecedents and consequences of sexual harassment in organizations: An integrated model. In G. Keita & J. J. Huvvell, Jr. (Eds.), *Job stress in a changing workforce: Investigating gender* (pp. 53–73). Washington, DC: American Psychological Association.

Fitzgerald, L. F., & Shullman, S. L. (1985). The development and validation of an objectively scored measure of sexual harassment. Paper presented to the annual meetings of the American Psychological Association, Los Angeles.

Fitzgerald, L., & Shullman, S. (1993). Sexual harassment: A research analysis and agenda for the 90's. *Journal of Vocational Behavior, 42,* 5–29.

Fitzgerald, L., Shullman, F., Bailey, N., Richards, M., Swecker, J., Gold, A., Ormerod, A., & Weitzman, L.

(1985). The incidence and dimensions of sexual harassment in academia and the workplace. *Journal of Vocational Behavior, 32,* 152–75.

Fitzgerald, L., Weitzman, L., Gold, Y., & Omerod, M. (1988). Academic harassment: Sex and denial in scholarly garb. *Psychology of Women Quarterly, 12,* 329–340.

Gruber, J. E. (1990a). Inventory of sexual harassment: Survey items for measuring eleven types of sexual harassment. Unpublished paper.

Gruber, J. E. (1990b). Methodological problems and policy implications in sexual harassment research. *Population Research and Policy Review, 9,* 235–254.

Gruber, J. E. (1992). A typology of personal and environmental sexual harassment: Research and policy implications for the 1990's. *Sex Roles, 26,* 447–464.

Gruber, J. E. (1993, March). The sexual harassment experiences of women in nontraditional jobs: Results from cross-national research. *Proceedings* of Conference on Sex and Power Issues in the Workplace, Seattle, WA.

Gruber, J. E. (in preparation). Organizational policies and sexual harassment experiences: Do policies reduce the incidence of sexual harassment?

Gruber, J., & Bjorn, L. (1982). Blue-collar blues: The sexual harassment of women autoworkers. *Work and Occupations, 9,* 271–298.

Gruber, J., & Bjorn, L. (1986). Women's responses to sexual harassment: An analysis of sociocultural, organizational, and personal resource models. *Social Science Quarterly, 67,* 814–825.

Gruber, J., & Kauppinen-Toropainen, K. (1994, August). Sexual harassment experiences and outcomes: A comparison of American and European women. Paper presented at the Annual Meetings of the American Psychological Association, Los Angeles.

Gruber, J., & Smith, M. (1995). Women's responses to sexual harassment: A multivariate analysis. *Basic and Applied Social Psychology, 17* (4), 543–562.

Gruber, J., Smith, M., & Kauppinen-Toropainen, K. (1995, August). Sociocultural and organizational antecedents of sexual harassment in the United States, Canada, and Europe. Paper presented at the Annual Meetings of the American Sociological Association, Washington, DC.

Gruber, J., Smith, M., & Kauppinen-Toropainen, K. (1996). Sexual harassment types and severity: Linking research and policy. In M. Stockdale (Ed.), *Women and work V: Sexual harassment* (pp. 151–173). Newbury Park, CA: Sage.

Gutek, B. A. (1985). *Sex and the workplace: The impact of sexual behavior and harassment on women, men and organizations.* San Francisco: Jossey-Bass.

Gutek, B. A., Cohen, A. G., and Konrad, A. M. (1990). Predicting social-sexual behavior at work: A contact hypothesis. *Academy of Management Journal, 33*, 560–577.

Gutek, B. A., & Dunwoody, V. (1987). Understanding sex in the workplace. In A. H. Stromberg, L. Larwood, & B. A. Gutek (Eds.), *Women and work: An annual review,* Vol. 2 (pp. 249–69). Newbury Park, CA: Sage Publications.

Gutek, B. A. and Morasch, B. (1982). Sex ratios, sex-role spillover, and sexual harassment of women at work. *Journal of Social Issues, 38*, 55–74.

Gutek, B. A., Morasch, B., and Cohen, A. G. (1983). Interpreting socio-sexual behavior in a work setting. *Journal of Vocational Behavior, 22*, 30–48.

Haavio-Mannila, E. (1992). *Work, family, and well-being in five North- and East-European capitals.* Helsinki: Soumalainentiedeakatemia.

Haavio-Mannila, E., Kauppinen-Toropainen, K., and Kandolin, I. (1991). Gender system of the working life. *People and Work, 5*, 185–196.

Hagman, N. (1988). *Sexual harassment on the job.* Helsinki: Wahlstrom & Widstrand.

Hagman, N. (1992). *Measures taken in Sweden to combat sexual harassment at work.* Geneva: International Labour Office.

Hayler, B. (1979, March 4). Report of Illinois Task Force on sexual harassment: Testimony before the State of Illinois State Judiciary Committee.

Hesson-McInnis, M., & Fitzgerald, L. F. (1992, November). *Sexual harassment: A preliminary test of an integrative model.* Paper presented at the Second Annual APA/NIOSH Conference on Stress in the Workplace, Washington, DC.

Hogbacka, R. Kandolin, I., Haavio-Mannila, E., & Kauppinen-Toropainen, K. (1987). *Sexual harassment in the workplace: Results from a survey of Finns.* Helsinki: Ministry for Social Affairs and Health.

Izraeli, D. (1983). Sex effects or structural effects? An empirical test of Kanter's theory of proportions. *Social Forces, 62*, 153–165.

Kanter, R. M. (1977). *Men and women of the organization.* New York: Basic Books.

Kauppinnen-Toropainen, K., & Gruber, J. (1993a). The antecedents and outcomes of women-unfriendly behavior: A study of Scandinavian, former Soviet, and American women. *Psychology of Women Quarterly, 17*, 431–456.

Kauppinen-Toropainen, K., & Gruber J. (1993b). Sexual harassment of women in nontraditional jobs: Results from five countries. *Working papers.* Ann Arbor, MI: Center for the Education of Women.

Kauppinen-Toropainen, K., & Kandolin, I. (1992). Women in non-traditional occupations: International comparisons. To appear in a book ed. by G. Goodale. Geneva: International Labour Office.

Koss, M., & Dinero, T. (1988). Predictors of sexual aggression among a national sample of male college students. In R. A. Prentky & V. Quinsey (Eds.), *Human sexual aggression: Current perspectives. Annals of the New York Academy of Sciences, 528*, 133–146.

LaFontaine, E., & Tredeau, L. (1986). The frequency, sources, and correlates of sexual harassment among women in traditional male occupations. *Sex Roles, 15*, 433–442.

Lindsey, K. (1977). Sexual harassment on the job. *Ms.*, November, 46–48.

Loy, P., & Stewart, L. (1984). The extent and effect of the sexual harassment of working women. *Sociological Focus, 17*, 31–43.

MacKinnon, C. (1979). *Sexual harassment of working women: A case of sex discrimination.* New Haven, CT: Yale University Press.

Martin, S. (1980). *Breaking and entering: Policewomen on patrol.* Berkeley: University of California Press.

Martin, S. (1990). *On the move: The status of women in policing.* Washington, DC: Police Foundation.

Martindale, M. (1990). *Sexual harassment in the military: 1988.* Arlington, VA: Defense Manpower Data Center.

Maypole, D. (1986). Sexual harassment of social workers at work. *Social Work, 31*, 29–34.

Mazer, D., & Percival, E. (1989). Ideology or experience? The relationships among perceptions, attitudes, and experiences of sexual harassment in university students. *Sex Roles, 20*, 135–147.

McIntyre, D. (1982). *Sexual harassment in government: The situation in Florida and the nation.* Tallahassee: Florida State University.

McKinney, K. (1990). Sexual harassment of university faculty by colleagues and students. *Sex Roles, 23*, 7/8, 421–438.

McKinney, K. (1992). Contrapower sexual harassment: The effects of student sex and type of behavior on faculty perceptions. *Sex Roles, 27*, 11/12, 1–17.

Messner, M. (1992). *Power at play: Sports and the problem of masculinity.* Boston: Beacon Press.

Pryor, J. (1987). Sexual harassment proclivities in men. *Sex Roles, 17*, 269–290.

Pryor, J., & Day, J. (1988). Interpretations of sexual harassment: An attributional analysis. *Sex Roles, 18*, 405-417.

Pryor, J., Giedd, J., & Williams, K. (1995). A social psychological model for predicting sexual harassment. *Journal of Social Issues, 51*, 69–84.

Pryor, J., LaVite, C., & Stoller, L. (1993). A social psychological analysis of sexual harassment: The person/situation interaction. *Journal of Vocational Behavior, 42*, 68–81.

Pryor, J. B., & Stoller, L. M. (1992). Sexual cognition processes in men who are high in the likelihood to sexually harass. Unpublished manuscript, Illinois State University.

Rielly, M. E., Carpenter, S., Dull, V., & Bartlett, K. (1982). The factorial survey: An approach to defining sexual harassment on campus. *Journal of Social Issues*, *38*, 99–110.

Robinson, G. (1994). Sexual harassment in Florida law enforcement: Problem or Pandora's Box? Unpublished manuscript. Ocala Police Department: Ocala, FL.

Rossi, P., & Weber-Burdin, E. (1983). Sexual harassment on the campus. *Social Science Research*, *12*, 131–158.

Rubenstein, M. (1987). *The dignity of women at work: A report on the problems of sexual harassment in the member states of the European community*. Geneva: International Labor Organization.

Rubenstein, M. (1992). Combating sexual harassment at work. *Conditions of Work Digest*, *11*, 1, 7–285.

Safran, C. (1976). What men do to women on the job: A shocking look at sexual harassment. *Redbook*, *149* (Nov.), 217–224.

Sanday, P. R. (1981). The socio-cultural context of rape: A cross cultural study. *Journal of Social Issues*, *37*, 5–27.

Sanday, P. R. (1990). *Fraternity gang rape: Sex, brotherhood, and privilege on campus*. New York: New York University Press.

Smith, M. (1992). Questionnaire: Sexual harassment in the workplace. Project 743. Institute of Social Research: York University, Toronto.

Stringer-Moore, D. (1982). *Sexual harassment in the Seattle city workforce*. Seattle, WA: Office of Women's Rights.

Stockdale, M. (1993). The role of sexual misperceptions of women's friendliness in an emerging theory of sexual harassment. *Journal of Vocational Behavior*, *42*, 84–101.

Tangri, S., Burt, M., & Johnson, L. (1982). Sexual harassment at work: Three explanatory models. *Journal of Social Issues*, *38*, 33–54.

Terpstra, D., & Baker, D. (1987). A hierarchy of sexual harassment. *The Journal of Psychology*, *121*, 599–605.

Terpstra, D., & Baker, D. (1989). The identification and classification of reactions to sexual harassment. *Journal of Organizational Behavior*, *10*, 1–14.

Till, F. (1980). *Sexual harassment: A report on the sexual harassment of students*. Washington, DC: National Advisory Council on Women's Education.

U.S. Merit Systems Protection Board (1981). *Sexual harassment in the federal workplace: Is it a problem?* Washington, DC: U.S. Government Printing Office.

U.S. Merit Systems Protection Board (1988). *Sexual harassment in the federal workplace: Is it a problem?* Washington, DC: U.S. Government Printing Office.

Verba, S., DiNunzio, J., & Spaulding, C. (1983). *Unwanted attention: Report on a sexual harassment survey*. Report to the Faculty Council, Harvard University.

Weber-Burdin, E., & Rossi, P. (1982). Defining sexual harassment on campus: A replication and extension. *Journal of Social Issues*, *38*, 111–120.

Working Women's Institute (1979). *The impact of sexual harassment on the job: A profile of the experiences of 92 women*. New York: Working Women's Institute Research Series.

# CHAPTER 6

# FEMINIST ISSUES IN SEXUAL HARASSMENT

**Kathy Hotelling**
**Barbara A. Zuber**

Feminist paradigms of inquiry have provided scholars with the opportunity to address scientific questions and societal issues from viewpoints that formulate new questions to be answered, reconstruct prevailing theories, and develop new theories from which the world and human behavior can be viewed. Feminist thought has contended that traditional paradigms of understanding have not only been slow to address issues that face women in society, but also that they have not understood these problems adequately. Within this chapter, feminist thought is applied to the issue of sexual harassment. Following a summary of the assumptions about sexual harassment from the point of view of traditional paradigms, feminist theory specific to sexual harassment is delineated, studies incorporating feminist factors are reviewed, and implications for prevention are discussed from a feminist viewpoint.

While sexual harassment is not a problem exclusively of women, it is overwhelmingly so. It is highly likely from a feminist perspective that the meaning of sexual harassment by women of men is different than that by men of women. Thus, because of this difference in context, effects, and attitudes, only the sexual harassment of women is discussed here.

## TRADITIONAL PARADIGMS OF INQUIRY

Kuhn (1962) described a paradigm shift as the alteration of viewpoints that occurs when new data or phenomena cannot be accommodated by traditional perspectives. Paradigm shifts were described not merely as extensions of the old, but rather as representing changes that shake fundamental beliefs and ways of looking at the world. New paradigms present new assumptions, new values, and new methods in generating and testing theories. The development of feminist paradigms was necessary because of the plethora of ways in which sex bias has been evidenced in scientific thought and research (in theoretical models, the formulation of questions, the choice of subjects, experimenter effects, observer effects, and bias in interpretations) and, therefore, how it has affected the understanding of both women and men and their experiences and behavior (Hyde & Rosenberg, 1985).

## Assumptions of Traditional Paradigms

Traditional psychological philosophy has viewed behavior exclusively as a manifestation of individual dynamics and pathology. When considering sexual harassment and other forms of victimization, one assumption has been that perpetrators are psychologically disturbed (Brownell, 1986); that is, they are the "exception" rather than the "rule." This was operationalized in early legal opinion in which sexual harassment was viewed as a personal phenomenon characterized as "egregious, in frequent behavior engaged in by powerful individuals who should know better than to use their power to extort sexual concessions" (Harvard Law Review, 1984, p. 1452); in order to be found guilty of sexual harassment under this belief system, an individual had to be especially flagrant in his violations of the law (e.g., termination of an employee for refusal to submit to sexual advances). A variation of the perspective that perpetrators are pathological is that men have a high sex drive and cannot control themselves (Martin, 1989). Another assumption has been that victims precipitate the perpetrator's behavior (Brownell, 1986); this assumption has been evident in both general comments about sexual harassment and in courtroom questioning about a woman's dress or behavior, presumably flirtatious or provocative. A third assumption has been that victims enjoy being victimized, also demonstrated in the courtroom by questions regarding victims' sexual fantasies, previous relationships, et cetera.

Not straying from traditional paradigms has meant that these assumptions have been given credibility and perpetuated as fact regardless of the lack of support from research. Prevalence statistics belie the assumption that sexual harassment is rare or unique; estimates indicate that 40% or more of women workers have been sexually harassed (Lach & Gwartney-Gibbs, 1993; see Chapter 5 in this volume for additional epidemiological information), while 20–30% of women students have been victimized in the same way (Sandler, 1990). The first major survey of sexual harassment (Renick, 1980), as well as subsequent studies and personal accounts of harassment (Anonymous, 1991), have indicated that women are unwilling participants in sexual harassment. In regard to the assumption that victims enjoy harassment, studies as early as 1980 found that an extremely low percentage of women were even flattered by sexual attention in the workplace (Renick, 1980). The far-reaching effects of sexual harassment on its victims, including physical problems (insomnia, headaches, digestive problems, neck and headaches, etc.; MacKinnon, 1979), emotional problems including injury to self-esteem and confidence (Jensen & Gutek, 1982); and behavioral changes such as avoidance of perpetrators (Dziech & Weiner, 1984) have been devastating beyond the immediate situation. In the long run, sexual harassment in academic settings can "reduce the quality of education, diminish academic achievement, and ultimately may lower earning power" (Hotelling, 1991, p. 500). In the work arena, sexual harassment can lead women to experience attitude changes such as loss of self-confidence and negativity toward work (Safran, 1976; Silverman, 1976–77) that can result in poor performance, loss of positions through resignations or firings, and lower wages (due to lack of raises or lack of longevity in positions).

## What Is Missing?

According to feminist scholars, traditional psychological paradigms of inquiry and attendant assumptions fail to examine the social context of behavior and to acknowledge the effects of sex role socialization. Specifically in regard to sexual harassment, the saliency of gender vis-à-vis sexual harassment and the imbalance of power between men and women (which is compounded by the power relationship between employer and employee and professor and student) have not been recognized or studied through traditional paradigms (Harvard Law Review, 1984). Traditional paradigms do not recognize that sexual harassment discriminates against women by limiting their ability to establish equality, thus resulting in harm to victims of sexual harassment. Kitchener (1984) has called the principle of "do no harm" the most fundamental ethical obligation in professions committed to helping others and benefitting society through practice and research. This ethical principle requires one to consider both the intentional and unintentional harm and the direct and indirect harm that is inflicted on others through theories and corresponding actions, such as treatment of victims of sexual harassment. Brownell (1986) has suggested that the harmful effects of traditional paradigms provide a compelling reason to implement feminist paradigms.

## FEMINIST PARADIGMS OF INQUIRY

With this background of the development of feminist paradigms for the understanding of sexual harassment, the specifics of feminist conceptualizations of this issue are delineated below.

### Saliency of Gender

All conceptualizations of sexual harassment by feminist scholars have included the saliency of gender. Sexual harassment is not a peculiarity of human behavior, but rather a manifestation of the cultural patterns of male–female interactions: an extension of "normal behavior" that is taught and expected from an early age. Gutek and Morasch (1982) termed the carryover of expectations based on gender into the workplace as "sex role spillover." According to Gutek (1985), this phenomenon occurs regardless of the direction of the gen-

der skew in the workplace: The gender role of the predominant group influences the workplace expectations for that job and the treatment of women within the work group. In a workplace of primarily women, then, the jobs themselves often have assumed the characteristics of female sex roles; those that hold these jobs are expected to be nurturing, supportive, and helpful (Nivea & Gutek, 1981). When men are dominant, the jobs are characterized as ones requiring assertiveness, rationality, and competitiveness (Gutek & Dunwoody, 1987). These expectations are in force regardless of job requirements or skills. Also, when there are more men than women in the workplace, Gutek (1985) asserted that women are treated first as women and secondarily as workers. That is, gender is "the classifying variable in men's perceptions of women" (Glass, 1988, p. 64).

Since gender itself represents a hierarchy with men on the top and women underneath, the sexual harassment of women occurs not only when women are on the bottom of the formal hierarchical ladder, but also when they are in lateral positions or even on top of the hierarchy (MacKinnon, 1987). According to MacKinnon, men have had the experience of needing to act in certain ways or fear repercussions, which is what occurs in sexual harassment when the harasser is in a more powerful position than the victim; because of this personal experience of men, they can understand hierarchical sexual harassment. But since the inherent hierarchy between the sexes is often overlooked, lateral and reverse hierarchical sexual harassment are often not understood by men; this leads in part to its perpetuation. This issue will be discussed further in the next section regarding power.

The potential for miscommunication that is fostered as a result of culturally induced sex role behavior has been explicated by Glass (1988). A degree of stereotypical sexual interaction between men and women can be considered "normal" in our society. Traditionally, men have been expected to be the aggressors in all realms, especially the sexual. Women, on the other hand, are taught to be asexual since sexual interest on their part is equated with promiscuity. Passivity and silence are also part of the female role. So, women's nonresponsiveness or "no" could be interpreted as the women being good at their role and not have anything to do with their interest level. In addition, women's friendliness, another culturally induced trait, can be misperceived by men as indicative of interest in sex (Abbey, 1991). The dysfunctional quality of this socialization of men and women is further exemplified by the fact that an advance may become harassment only after the man doesn't respond to evidence from the woman that she is not interested. The "boys will be boys" motto indicates both women's resignation about the existence of unwanted sexual advances and the inescapable nature of sex role socialization (Leidig, 1981).

It is also gender roles that perpetuate sexual harassment once it occurs because women have been taught to avoid conflict and to doubt their perceptions, which means that they often do not report such behavior (Stockard & Johnson, 1992). Additionally, the importance to the self-concept of women of establishing and maintaining relationships is learned by females at a very young age and remains predominant throughout their lives (Gilligan, 1982). In the workplace this is exemplified by women's dependence on relationships for mobility (Kanter, 1975), which reinforces passivity, again leading to the underreporting of sexual harassment.

In summary, gender identity is more powerful than work identity or social identity. No matter what the job requirements, the academic requirements, or the social situation, women are seen as women first and are treated on the basis of sex role stereotypes.

## Gender Stratification, Sexuality, and Power

As a feminist theorist and attorney, Catherine MacKinnon has written extensively about the social, political, and economic underpinnings of the problem of sexual harassment and has extended the effect of the saliency of gender described above in her writings. She has pointed out that the feminist concept of the personal as political is not a metaphor, but rather refers to the experience of sexual objectification (MacKinnon, 1982): "The substantive principle governing the authentic politics of women's personal lives is pervasive powerlessness to men, expressed and reconstituted daily as sexuality" (p. 535). It is because of this viewpoint regarding women's lives that MacKinnon argues that gender and sexuality are inseparable and that the home and the marketplace become the same; at work, women's role is sexualized as it is in the family.

As early as 1980, sexual harassment was viewed as more endemic than epidemic because of women's economic vulnerability (Renick, 1980). MacKinnon (1982) characterized work as potentially allowing women to gain independence, to extend abilities demonstrated in the home, and to survive economically. Because money is an exchangeable commodity, women can gain control by working outside of the home even if they are doing the same tasks as they do in the home. But, according to MacKinnon, sexual harassment in the workplace furthers social inequality because it undermines women's ability to achieve work equality; women are again dependent on men financially. When one group has been allocated fewer advantages and less power and wealth than another group, a social context is created to support this disproportionate distribution. Renick and MacKinnon agree that this is the environment within which sexual harassment flourishes.

In the academic world, the lack of clarity about the nature of formal relationships, such as the student/professor relationship, has allowed professors to determine the importance of gender and, therefore, the degree to which sexuality has entered into interactions with students (Thorne, as quoted by Benson & Thomson, 1982) and can be used selectively to obligate students to behaviors required or encouraged by professors (Blau, 1964). Lach and Gwartney-Gibbs (1993) asserted that to whatever extent sexuality is present in a given interaction, it could be expected that women would receive more uninvited attention of a sexual nature than men.

In summary, from a feminist perspective, sexual harassment both emanates from and reinforces the traditional sex roles of men and women.

## Power, Sexual Victimization, and Sexual Harassment

Power, a multifaceted construct, has been defined as "the ability to achieve ends through influence" (Huston, 1983, p. 170). As pointed out earlier, power most commonly has been understood as emanating from authority or position. According to Tangri, Burt, and Johnson (1982), organizations may provide an opportunity structure that makes sexual harassment possible because people use their power and position to influence behavior. Individuals who occupy a high-status role or position are believed to have the right to make demands of those in lower-status positions; harassing behaviors may be viewed by some high-status individuals as simple extensions of that right and that lower-status individuals are expected to comply with these demands (Eagly, 1982). This reality, coupled with the fact that a gender differential has existed and currently exists in who holds organizational power (as evidenced by the 1994 Bureau of Labor statistics indicating that men hold 88.1% of upper-management positions) results in the harassment of female subordinates by male supervisors. But, as already indicated, gender also determines power: Males are more powerful in American society than women, and harassment also occurs among coworkers.

The power of the male perpetrator over the female victim and the element of coercion in sexual harassment have led many scholars to examine the similarities between sexual harassment and other forms of sexual victimization, such as domestic violence and rape. McCormack (1979) compared academic women to battered wives in that they both are embarrassed and worried about retaliation if they were to talk openly about the violations. MacKinnon stated that "economic power is to sexual harassment as physical force is to rape" (1979, pp. 217–218). Rape is now accepted not as a crime of sex, but rather of violence; in

the same vein, MacKinnon argued that sexual harassment is the abuse of "hierarchical economic (or institutional) authority, not sexuality" (p. 218). Both of these crimes, sexual harassment and rape, according to MacKinnon, reinforce women's lack of power as a gender. Just because sexual harassment is representative of "normal" relationships between the sexes, and because these relationships have as their base unequal social power, does not mean that the existence of such behavior is justified; in essence, such behavior only grows out of these societal realities and, therefore, results in systematic disadvantagement based on group status. Because of this, MacKinnon has not tolerated the "differences" doctrine as a defense of sexual harassment. This doctrine allows courts to determine whether there are adequate reasons supporting the treatment of one category of persons differently from another. Except for the Japanese detention during World War II, the courts have not found compelling reasons to support the differences doctrine in regard to race, but when differences in treatment have been argued on the basis of sex, this differential treatment often has been justified. Thus, power equality is assumed, when in reality women have been subordinate in our society at the same time as they are distinct. Therefore, MacKinnon (1979) has argued that if sexuality were set within analyses of gender, equality (e.g., women as distinct and "fully human" [p. 221]) would be guaranteed.

In summary, both sexual harassment itself and the potential or threat of sexual harassment create discrimination and deny women the opportunity for full participation in society as workers, as students, and as individuals. Sexual harassment is a complex phenomenon that is a social, and only derivatively a personal, problem.

## RESEARCH RELATED TO SEXUAL HARASSMENT

Research related to a feminist perspective of sexual harassment has been organized around gender, perceptual, and organizational variables.

## Gender Variables

As previously noted, men and women do not experience the same levels of sexual harassment. Forty-two percent of the women and 15% of the men reported having been sexually harassed at work within two years of the 1981 United States Merit System Protection Board survey. In regard to students, women are also much more likely to be harassed than men (Hotelling, 1991). The gender variables explored here both define and set the stage for the environments within organizations and institutions that perpetuate the sexual harassment of women by men.

Hill (1980) and Wolf and Fligstein (1979) found that men had more power over the pay and promotions of others than women; even when men and women occupy the same positions with the same job titles and supervisory responsibilities, women are given less decision-making discretion and less latitude for exercising influence than men (Wolf & Fligstein, 1979). Harlan and Weiss (1982) found that men had greater control than women over access to materials, money, and resources needed to meet goals and to reward employees.

There also is evidence that promotion within organizations has implications for a power differential between men and women. Heilman, Martell, and Simon (1988) found consistent bias favoring men for selection and promotion. Women were found to need a greater number of promotions than men to reach the same rank (Flanders & Anderson, 1973). Also, Stewart and Gundykunst (1982) showed that women with comparable credentials did not acquire the status and influence comparable to male counterparts in the organization. Findings such as these have indicated that a person's formal position within an organization may be a poor indicator of actual power and that gender represents a hierarchy and is an important determining factor of perceived and actual power.

## Perceptual Variables

Differential perceptions have been found to be influenced by gender, the severity of the behavior, the behavior of the victim, and the attitudes of the perceiver (Fitzgerald & Ormerod, 1993). Gender has been demonstrated to be the most influential factor in determining whether incidents are defined as sexual harassment, with women universally more likely to view certain behaviors as sexual harassment (Gutek, 1985; Gutek, Morasch, & Cohen, 1983; Fitzgerald & Ormerod, 1991; Powell, 1986). Gutek et al. (1980) found that women were more likely than men to consider sexual comments, looks, or gestures that were meant to be complimentary to be sexual harassment. Women also are more likely to consider ambiguous situations, such as sexual teasing or sex-typed jokes, as sexual harassment (Kenig & Ryan, 1986). Men are more likely than women to perceive sexual propositions at work as complimentary (Gutek, 1985). All of these findings are consistent with the fact that men are more accepting of sexually harassing behaviors and more likely to perceive sexual behaviors at school as natural and less problematic than women (Lott, Reilly, & Howard, 1982). Thus, it should not be surprising that men more than women tend to blame the victim, believe that people should not take offense so quickly about sexual attention at work, and believe that individuals should deal with harassment on their own as opposed to seeking help (Kenig & Ryan, 1986; USMSPB, 1981).

For both men and women, perceptions of the behaviors that constitute sexual harassment are defined by more severe behavior, such as explicit requests for sexual favors (Fitzgerald & Ormerod, 1991; Reilly et al., 1986), by the negative response of the victim (Gutek, 1985), and by the existence of a prior relationship and any suggestive behavior on the part of the victim (Reilly et al., 1986).

Attitudes and sex role stereotypes are additional factors in the tolerance of sexual harassment. Pryor (1987) has found that men with a proclivity to sexually harass hold attitudes and beliefs similar to men who are predisposed to sexually victimize women; specifically, such men have been found to accept stereotypical myths about rape, hold traditional sex role attitudes, perceive relationships between men and women as adversarial, condone violence against women, and report a likelihood to rape if they are assured of no consequences (Koss et al., 1985; Muehlenhard & Linton, 1987; Reilly et al., 1991). Reilly et al. (1991) and Murrell and Dietz-Uhler (1993) showed that men who held rape-supportive belief systems were more accepting of sexually harassing behavior. Profeminist attitudes increased the likelihood that behaviors will be perceived as sexual harassment by both men and women (Brooks & Perot, 1991; Pryor & Day, 1988; Schneider, 1982).

## Organizational Variables

The organizational factors of gender ratios, sexualized atmospheres, and organizational power have been found to influence both the incidence and maintenance of sexual harassment in the workplace and in academia. Negative views of women both reinforce and underlie these organizational factors supporting sexual harassment and have been discussed as a backdrop for the other research.

### Stereotypes

Studies have demonstrated that stereotypes of women foster negative attitudes in the workplace, lending support for the sex role spillover theory of Gutek and Morasch (1982). While it is beyond the scope of this chapter to review all studies relevant to this concept, two studies (Harlan & Weiss, 1982; Pleck, 1976) are highlighted here to symbolize the tenor of work environments that support the sexual harassment of women. Harlan and Weiss (1982) found that male managers preferred male supervisors and reported that it was an "insult to their intelligence" to be supervised by a woman. Pleck (1976) reported that men were threatened by women's competence, and, when placed in competitive positions with women, men elevated their performance and avoided future task interactions with female partners. In a study of male and female managers, women were perceived as working only to supplement the family income, not because they were committed to a career (Har-

lan & Weiss, 1982). The negative attitudes described in these studies create environments that support the sexual harassment of women.

### Gender Ratios

The influence of gender ratios in the workplace on the incidence of sexual harassment has been demonstrated by several researchers. Fain and Anderton (1987) found that equal and predominantly female groups tend to experience more sexual harassment than predominantly male groups. It is important to note, however, that the severity of sexual harassment was greater for women in predominantly male groups (e.g., assault and pressure for sexual favors) than for women in equal or predominantly female groups (who experienced sexual harassment in the form of gesturing, pressure for dates, touching and joking). A similar finding in higher education was that women faculty and students in traditional fields (e.g., education, liberal arts, and nursing) were more likely to experience harassment than those in nontraditional fields (e.g., agricultural sciences, architecture, commerce and industry sciences, forests and recreational resources, and engineering) (Ryan & Kenig, 1991). To the contrary, the studies of Schneider (1982), Gutek (1985), and Gutek and Cohen (1987) have shown that the likelihood of sexual harassment increases as a function of having a greater proportion of men in a work group. These latter, predominant findings are consistent with the literature indicating that women in nontraditional jobs experience more of almost all kinds of sexual harassment than women in traditional jobs or in jobs that have an equal representation of men and women (Gutek & Dunwoody, 1987; Lafontaine & Tredeau, 1986; Tangri, Burt, & Johnson, 1986). Martin (1989) attributed these findings to both the larger proportion of men in jobs that are nontraditional for women and resentment from the men about the presence of the women in these jobs. Lafontaine and Tredeau (1986) added to these attributions by pointing out that in these situations women's minority status highlighted the incongruity between their feminine sex role and their masculine work role and that these women were more apt to identify harassment as such than women in traditional occupations.

### Sexualized Atmospheres

The research of Gutek (1985), Haavio-Mannila, Kauppinen-Toropainen, and Kandolin (1988), and Tangri et al. (1982) indicated that a sexualized atmosphere (defined by frequent sexual talking and joking) in an organization increased the incidence of sexual harassment. When this type of atmosphere was not permitted or accepted by management, sexual harassment occurred less often than in situations where management was either indifferent or encouraging of such behavior (Ellis, Barak, & Pinto, 1991; Pryor, Lavite, & Stoller, 1993).

### Organizational Power

Cleveland and Kerst (1993) used the term "organizational power" to refer to the structure of occupations within an organization, who occupies these positions, and who has access to vital resources. From a feminist perspective, organizational power is difficult to differentiate from gender power because gender is seen as hierarchical and therefore confounds the effect of organizational power. Nonetheless, numerous studies have operationalized this concept as it relates to sexual harassment. Subordinates were much more likely to experience harassment than supervisors (Fain & Anderton, 1987). The same researchers found that lower-status service workers were more likely to be harassed than higher-status professionals.

The status or power of the harasser has also been found to have an impact on the perception of sexual harassment, both in academic and work settings. In general, power inequality between the harasser and the person being harassed increases the likelihood that an interaction will be viewed as harassment by the person being harassed (Bursik, 1992; Gutek, Morasch, & Cohen, 1983; USMSPB, 1981, 1987). Both male and female students perceived behaviors performed by instructors as more harassing than similar actions from peers (Lester et al., 1986; Pryor & Day, 1988).

## PREVENTION

With the examination of the dynamics of sexual harassment from a feminist perspective and related research as background information, the final portion of this chapter is devoted to applying feminist paradigms to the prevention of sexual harassment. Prevention from this perspective is necessarily broader than prevention from a traditional perspective whereby sexual harassment training programs have focused on education regarding what behaviors constitute sexual harassment and dealing with harassment once it occurs (see Chapter 3). Awareness of what constitutes sexual harassment may not be enough to change a problem situation (Popovich & Licata, 1987). Furthermore, grievance procedures and discipline are reactive measures and do not address the underlying dynamics of sexual harassment. Shullman (1992) has argued that if harassment is conceptualized as a result of cultural roles and organizational hierarchy, then prevention and training should focus on sociocultural and organizational interventions. This contention also has been supported by Fitzgerald (as reported by Custer, 1994), who argued that sexual harassment prevention must be conceptualized as ecological and proactive rather than individual and reactive. In this section on prevention, sex role socialization is given primary attention. The traditional, yet necessary, prevention strategies of organizational initiatives and the enforcement of policies and law also are outlined.

### Socialization

From a feminist perspective, the occurrence of sexual harassment is fostered by cultural factors that intertwine power, gender, and sexuality as described above. By changing the cultural factors (sex role socialization, media portrayals of the objectification and victimization of women, the sex-segregated nature of the work force, and the acceptance of interpersonal violence) that essentially promote and condone sexual harassment, true prevention can be achieved. Because sex role socialization is considered to be a precursor to the other factors, this section focuses on this aspect of culture specifically.

Early socialization teaches males to be aggressive and dominant and women to be submissive and passive (Chodorow, 1989), which contributes to the development of women's secondary social and cultural status and sexually coercive attitudes and behaviors. Because the socialization process begins early in life, alternative parenting strategies (Chodorow, 1989) are essential in decreasing women's subordinate status and ultimately in developing equality between men and women. Chodorow recommended that parents replace traditional messages wherein boys are encouraged to be achievement oriented and self-reliant, while girls are socialized to be nurturing and obedient by teaching children that both sexes are of value; for example, fathers and mothers can model behavior representative of such messages by sharing child care and household responsibilities. This may decrease the stereotypes of "women's work" and "men's work" and give children less restrictive conceptions of masculinity and femininity than they currently hold, as well as symbolizing respect for the opposite gender as a group.

The educational system is another powerful gender socialization agent because formal curriculum and other activities convey values that shape students' perceptions of themselves and the world (Renzetti & Curran, 1989). Researchers have found that girls are short-changed in their educational experiences by the type of attention they receive from teachers and as a consequence of segregation. In the classroom, teachers tend to give more time and more esteem-building encouragement to boys than girls (AAUW, 1992). For example, boys are provided remediation and challenge to achieve the best possible academic performance, praise for the intellectual quality of work, and attention when answers are called out. Teachers, however, provided less assistance with problem solving to girls than boys, praised the neatness of girls' work, and completed complex tasks for girls as opposed to giving more detailed instructions for independent completion, as they did with the boys

(AAUW, 1992; Sadker & Sadker, 1985). Furthermore, teachers often used various subtle forms of sex segregation, such as seating girls and boys on opposite sides of the room and by organizing tasks by gender (Sadker & Sadker, 1985). As Renzetti and Curran (1989) pointed out, these practices have far-reaching implications for the lives of children:

> First, sex segregation in and of itself prevents boys and girls from working together cooperatively, thus denying children of both sexes valuable opportunities to learn about and sample one another's interests and activities. Second, it makes working in same-sex groups more comfortable than working in mixed-sex groups—a feeling that children may carry into adulthood and which may become problematic when they enter the labor force. And finally, sex segregation reinforces gender stereotypes, especially if it involves differential work assignments. (p. 81)

While these educational practices continue into middle school and high school, it is imperative that the issues outlined here be addressed as early as possible to improve gender relations. Specifically, teacher training to recognize gender inequity in the classroom and to remedy these inequities, through such measures as the elimination of gender segregation in work and play groups and the structuring of activities to encourage cooperation between the sexes, is necessary to achieve the type of change that is advocated to proactively address the workplace problems that females experience later in life.

## Organizational Initiatives

Until such societal changes occur, organizations must continue to establish policies, procedures, and climates that reinforce the prohibition against sexual harassment. The thoughtful crafting of sexual harassment policies and procedures by clearly defining sexual harassment (including examples of blatant and subtle forms of harassment, as well as recognition of harassment by peers), procedures for filing complaints, investigation procedures, consequences of harassment, and victim rights is necessary. As demonstrated in the research reviewed here, men and women have different perceptions of the appropriateness of behavior within the workplace; therefore, because women are the victims, the perspectives of women should be reflected in harassment policies and procedures. To encourage the reporting of harassment, policies and procedures must protect the confidentiality of both the victim and the alleged harasser and clearly condemn retaliatory action against complainants. Many institutions of higher education already have in place sexual harassment policies but fail to directly address amorous relationships between faculty and student. Since the power differential between faculty and student cannot be eliminated and because such relationships can never be truly consensual relationships, institutions need to develop clear policies and procedures that educate faculty about and discourage them from establishing such relationships with students.

Institutional and organizational policies and procedures are not sufficient and must take place in the broader context of "institution-wide efforts to create an educational and workplace environment that does not disadvantage women" (Hoffmann, 1986, p. 117). This involves creating an environment that is affirming and valuing of women through a commitment from managers and administrators that a sexualized work environment will not be tolerated, through the promotion of nonsexist behavior and affirmative action policies, through an examination of the issue of comparable worth and the remedying of salary inequities, through the promotion of women into faculty and management positions, and through education about the dynamics of sexual harassment.

## Enforcement of Policies and Law

Policies and procedures are necessary, but not sufficient, for addressing sexual harassment. Institutions and organizations must protect the rights of students and employees, instead of protecting perpetrators, by following through with remedies and disciplinary actions for proven charges of sexual harassment. It is imperative that disciplinary or other actions do not focus on the victim (e.g., encouraging a student to leave a class or transferring a worker to another department to avoid the situation) but on the harasser and his inappropriate behavior (Biaggio, Watts, & Brownell, 1990). Disciplinary actions must be more than a "slap on the wrist" or a letter in a personnel file and be a factor in receiving tenure, salary increases, and promotions.

The use of the reasonable person legal standard, which is male-biased and fails to take into account the discrepancy between the views of men and women about appropriate sexual conduct, must be replaced by the standard of reasonable woman (Shoop, 1992) as a means for determining a hostile work environment (see Chapter 4). Using this standard when investigating internal or legal charges of sexual harassment will guarantee victims of harassment greater protection than is often afforded them and takes into account their perception of the offensive behavior.

## SUMMARY

Utilizing feminist paradigms to examine the problem of sexual harassment clearly has provided scholars and researchers with alternative theories, new questions to be answered, and suggestions for prevention. This perspective has promoted a broader view of the underlying dynamics and the remedies for the long-standing problem of the sexual harassment of women by men than traditional perspectives. A feminist perspective challenges us to restructure gender roles in society to address the underlying causes of sexual harassment in our institutions of higher learning and workplaces and will enhance environments and relationships for both men and women.

## REFERENCES

Abbey, A. (1991). Misperception as an antecedent of acquaintance rape: A consequence of ambiguity in communication between women and men. In A. Parrot & I. Bechhofer (Eds.), *Acquaintance rape: The hidden crime* (pp. 96–111). New York: Wiley.

Anonymous (1991). Sexual harassment: A female counseling student's experience. *Journal of Counseling and Development, 69*(6), 502–506.

American Association of University Women (1992). *How schools shortchange girls: Executive summary.* Washington, DC: American Association of University Women.

Biaggio, M. K., Watts, D., & Brownell, A. (1990). Addressing sexual harassment: Strategies for prevention and change. In M. Paludi (Ed.), *Ivory power: Sexual harassment on campus* (pp. 213–230). Albany: SUNY Press.

Blau, P. (1964). *Exchange and power in social life.* New York: Wiley.

Brooks, L., & Perot, A. R. (1991). Reporting sexual harassment: Exploring a predictive model. *Psychology of Women Quarterly, 15,* 31–47.

Brownell, A. (1986, August). *Re-visions of psychology: Feminism as a paradigm of scientific inquiry.* Paper presented at the Meeting of the American Psychological Association, Washington, DC.

Bursik, K. (1992). Perceptions of sexual harassment in an academic setting. *Sex Roles, 27,* 401–412.

Chodorow, N. J. (1989). *Feminism and psychoanalytic theory.* New Haven, CT: Yale University Press.

Cleveland, J. N., & Kerst, M. E. (1993). Sexual harassment and perceptions of power: An under-articulated relationship. *Journal of Vocational Behavior, 42,* 49–67.

Custer, G. (1994, October). In sexual harassment cases, psychologists still have a role. *APA Monitor, 10,* 48.

Dziech, B. W., & Weiner, L. (1984). *The lecherous professor: Sexual harassment on campus.* Boston: Beacon Press.

Eagly, A. H. (1983). Gender and social influence. *American Psychologist, 38*(9), 971–981.

Ellis, S., Barak, A., & Pinto, A. (1991). Moderating effects of personal conditions on experienced and perceived sexual harassment of women in the workplace. *Journal of Applied Social Psychology, 21,* 1320–1337.

Fain, T. C., & Anderton, D. L. (1987). Sexual harassment: Organizational context and diffuse status. *Sex Roles, 5/6,* 291–311.

Fitzgerald, L. F., & Ormerod, A. J. (1993). Breaking silence: The sexual harassment of women in academia and the workplace. In F. L. Denmark & M. A. Paludi (Eds.), *Psychology of women: A handbook of issues and theories* (pp. 553–581). Westport, CT: Greenwood Press.

Fitzgerald, L. F., & Shullman, S. L. (1993). Sexual harassment: A research analysis and agenda for the 1990s. *Journal of Vocational Behavior, 42,* 5–27.

Flanders, D. P., & Anderson, P. E. (1973). Sex discrimination in employment: Theory and practice. *Industrial Relations, 26,* 938–955.

Gilligan, C. (1982). *In a different voice.* Cambridge, MA: Harvard University Press.

Glass, B. L. (1988). Workplace harassment and the victimization of women. *Women's Studies International Forum, 11*(1), 55–67.

Gutek, B. A. (1985). *Sex and the workplace: Impact of sexual behavior and harassment on women, men and organizations.* San Francisco: Jossey-Bass.

Gutek, B. A., Nakamura, C. Y., Gahart, M., Handschumacher, I., & Russe, D. (1980). Sexuality in the workplace. *Basic and Applied Social Psychology, 1,* 255–265.

Gutek, B. A., & Cohen, A. G. (1987). Sex ratios, sex role spillover, and sex at work: A comparison of men's and women's experiences. *Human Relations, 40,* 97–115.

Gutek, B. A., & Dunwoody, V. (1987). Understanding sex in the workplace. In A. Stromberg, L. Larwood, & B. A. Gutek (Eds.), *Women and work: An annual review* (vol. 2, pp. 249–269). Newbury Park, CA: Sage.

Gutek, B. A., & Morasch, B. (1982). Sex ratios, sex-role spillover, and sexual harassment of women at work. *Journal of Social Issues, 38,* 55–74.

Gutek, B. A., Morasch, B., & Cohen, A. G. (1983). Interpreting social-sexual behavior in a work setting. *Journal of Vocational Behavior, 22,* 30–48.

Harlan, A., & Weiss, C. L. (1982). Sex differences in factors affecting managerial career advancement. In P. A. Wallace (Ed.), *Women in the workplace* (pp. 59–96). Boston: Auburn House.

Haavio-Mannila, E., Kauppinen-Toropainen, K., & Kandolin, I. (1988). The effect of sex composition of the workplace on friendship, romance, and sex at work. In B. A. Gutek, A. Stromberg, & L. Larwood (Eds.), *Women and work: An annual review* (vol. 3, pp. 123–137). Beverly Hills, CA: Sage.

Harvard Law Review (1984). *Sexual harassment claims of abusive work environment under Title VII, 97,* 1449–1467.

Heilman, M. E., Martell, R. F., & Simon, M. C. (1988). The vagaries of sex bias: Conditions regulating the undervaluation, equivaluation, and overvaluation of female job applicants. *Organizational Behavior and Human Decision Processes, 41*(1), 98–110.

Hill, M. S. (1980). Authority at work: How men and women differ. In G. J. Duncan & J. N. Morgan (Eds.), *Five thousand American families: Patterns of economic progress* (vol. 7, pp. 107–146). Ann Arbor: University of Michigan, Survey Research Center, Institute for Social Research.

Hoffmann, F. L. (1986). Sexual harassment in academia: Feminist theory and institutional practice. *Harvard Educational Review, 56*(2), 105–121.

Hotelling, K. (1991a). Introduction to special feature. *Journal of Counseling and Development, 69*(6), 495–496.

Hotelling, K. (1991b). Sexual harassment: A problem shielded by silence. *Journal of Counseling and Development, 69*(6), 497–500.

Huston, T. (1983). Power. In H. Kelly, E. Berscheid, A. Christensen, J. H. Harvey, T. L. Huston, G. Levinger, E. McClintock, L. A. Peplau, & D. R. Peterson (Eds.), *Close relationships* (pp. 169–219). New York: Freeman.

Hyde, J. S., & Rosenberg, B. G. (1985). *Half the human experience* (3d ed.). Lexington, MA: Heath.

Jensen, I. W., & Gutek, B. A. (1982). Attributions and assignment of responsibility in sexual harassment. *Journal of Social Issues, 38*(4), 121–136.

Kanter, R. M. (1975). Women and the structure of organizations: Explorations in theory and behavior. *Sociological Inquiry, 4*(2–3), 34–50.

Kenig, S., & Ryan, J. (1986). Sex differences in levels of tolerance and attribution of blame for sexual harassment on a university campus. *Sex Roles, 15*, 535–548.

Kitchener, K. (1984). Intuition, critical evaluation and ethical principles: The foundation for ethical decisions in counseling psychology. *The Counseling Psychologist, 12*, 43–55.

Koss, M. P., Leonard, K. E., Beezley, D. A., & Oros, C. (1985). Nonstranger sexual aggression: A discriminant analysis of the psychological characteristics of undetected offenders. *Sex Roles, 12*(9/10), 981–992.

Kuhn, T. S. (1962). *The structure of scientific revolutions*. Chicago: University of Chicago Press.

Lach, D. H., & Gwartney-Gibbs, P. A. (1993). Sociological perspectives on sexual harassment and workplace dispute resolution. *Journal of Vocational Behavior, 42*, 102–115.

Lafontaine, E., & Tredeau, L. (1986). The frequency, sources, and correlates of sexual harassment among women in traditional male occupations. *Sex Roles, 15*(7/8), 433–442.

Leidig, M. W. (1981). Violence against women: A feminist-psychological analysis. In S. Cox (Ed.), *Female psychology* (pp. 190–205). New York: St. Martin's Press.

Lester, D., Banta, B., Barton, J., Elian, N., Mackiewicz, L., & Winkelreid, J. (1986). Judgments about sexual harassment: Effects of the power of the harasser. *Perceptual and Motor Skills, 63*(2, pt. 2), 990.

Lott, B., Reilly, M. E., & Howard, D. R. (1982). Sexual assault and harassment: A campus community case study. *Signs, 8*, 296–319.

MacKinnon, C. (1979). *Sexual harassment of working women*. New Haven, CT: Yale University Press.

MacKinnon, C. (1982). Feminism, Marxism, method, and the state: An agenda for theory. *Signs, 7*(3), 515–544.

MacKinnon, C. A. (1987). *Feminism unmodified*. Cambridge, MA: Harvard University Press.

Martin, S. E. (1989). Sexual harassment: The link joining gender stratification, sexuality, and women's economic status. In J. Freeman (Ed.), *Women: A feminist perspective* (4th ed., pp. 57–75). Mountain View, CA: Mayfield.

McCormack, T. (1979). *Sexual harassment of working women*. New Haven, CT: Yale University Press.

McKinney, K. (1990). Sexual harassment of university faculty by colleagues and students. *Sex Roles, 23*(7/8), 421–438.

Muehlenhard, C. L., & Linton, M. A. (1987). Date rape and sexual aggression in dating situations: Incidence and risk factors. *Journal of Counseling Psychology, 34*(2), 186–196.

Murrell, A. J., & Dietz-Uhler, B. L. (1993). Gender identity and adversarial sexual beliefs as predictors of attitudes toward sexual harassment. *Psychology of Women Quarterly, 17*, 169–175.

Nivea, V., & Gutek, B. A. (1981). *Women and work: A psychological perspective*. New York: Praeger.

Pleck, J. H. (1976). Male threat from female competence. *Journal of Consulting and Clinical Psychology, 44*, 608–613.

Popovich, D., & Licata, B. (1987). A role model approach to sexual harassment. *Journal of Management, 13*, 149–161.

Powell, G. N. (1986). Effects of sex role identity and sex on definitions of sexual harassment. *Sex Roles, 14*, 9–24.

Pryor, J. B. (1987). Sexual harassment proclivities in men. *Sex Roles, 17*, 269–290.

Pryor, J. B., & Day, J. D. (1988). Interpretations of sexual harassment: An attributional analysis. *Sex Roles, 18*, 405–417.

Pryor, J. B., LaVite, C. M., & Stoller, L. M. (1993). A social psychological analysis of sexual harassment: The person/situation interaction. *Journal of Vocational Behavior, 42*, 68–93.

Reilly, M. E., Lott, B., Caldwell, D., & DeLuca, L. (1991). Tolerance for sexual harassment related to self-reported sexual victimization. *Gender and Society, 6*(1), 122–138.

Reilly, T., Carpenter, S., Dull, V., & Bartlett, K. (1986). The factorial survey technique: An approach to defining sexual harassment on campus. *Journal of Social Issues, 38*, 99–110.

Renick, James C. (1980). Sexual harassment at work: Why it happens, what to do about it. *Personal Journal, 59*(8), 658–662.

Renzetti, C. M., & Curran, D. J. (1989). *Women, men, and society* (2d ed.). Boston: Allyn and Bacon.

Ryan, J., & Kenig, S. (1991). Risk and ideology in sexual harassment. *Sociological Inquiry, 61*, 231–241.

Safran, C. (1976, November). What men do to women on the job: A shocking look at sexual harassment. *Redbook, 149*, 217–223.

Sandler, B. R. (1990). Sexual harassment: A new issue for institutions. *Initiatives, 52*(4), 5–10.

Sadker, M., & Sadker, D. (1985). Striving for equity in classroom teaching. In A. Sargent (Ed.), *Beyond sex roles* (pp. 442–455). St. Paul, MN: West.

Schneider, B. E. (1982). Consciousness about sexual harassment among heterosexual and lesbian women workers. *Journal of Social Issues, 38* (4), 75–98.

Shoop, R. J. (1992, April 23). The reasonable woman in a hostile work environment. *72 Ed. Law Rep.*

Silverman, D. (1976–77, Winter). Sexual harassment: Working women's dilemma. *Quest: A Feminist Quarterly, 3*, 15–24.

Stewart, L. P., & Gundykunst, W. P. (1982). Differential factors influencing the hierarchical level and number of promotions of males and females within an organization. *Academy of Management Journal, 25*, 586–597.

Stockard, J., & Johnson, M. M. (1992). *Sex and gender in society.* (2d ed.). Englewood Cliffs, NJ: Prentice-Hall.

Tangri, S. S., Burt, M. R., & Johnson, L. B. (1982). Sexual harassment at work: Three explanatory models. *Journal of Social Issues, 38*(4), 33–54.

U.S. Bureau of Labor Statistics (1994). *Handbook of Labor Statistics* (Report No. L 2.5/5). Washington, DC: U.S. Government Printing Office.

U.S. Merit Systems Protection Board (1981). *Sexual harassment in the federal workplace: Is it a problem?.* Washington, DC: U.S. Government Printing Office.

U.S. Merit Systems Protection Board (1988). *Sexual harassment in the federal workplace: An update.* Washington, DC: U.S. Government Printing Office.

Wolf, W., & Flipstein, N. (1979). Sex authority in the workplace: The cause of sexual inequality. *American Sociological Review, 44* (April), 238–252.

# CHAPTER 7

# THEORIES OF SEXUAL HARASSMENT

**Sandra Schwartz Tangri**
**Stephanie M. Hayes**

In the 1980s and early 1990s, sexual harassment has been transformed from a woman's private trouble to a president's political nightmare. Correspondingly, the research and theory have become increasingly diverse, complex, and, often, sophisticated. Explanations for why sexual harassment occurs run the gamut from species wide evolutionary adaptation to personality configurations. As we become increasingly sophisticated about the inadequacy of single and sovereign theories about any realm of social behavior, it is perhaps inevitable that a comprehensive theory of sexual harassment will require incorporating factors operating at several levels of social life. In some cases the same explanatory construct appears at several levels of analysis, the prime example being "power" that operates at cultural, organizational, and individual levels. Previous research (Brewer & Berk, 1982; Cleveland & Kerst, 1993; Tangri, Burt, & Johnson, 1982) suggests that no one explanation covers the full range of phenomena labeled sexual harassment. None of the literature has demonstrated that any one "cause" is both necessary and sufficient.

Furthermore, how one defines sexual harassment will of course determine how apt a given theory will be. For example, if sexual harassment is defined as something that men do to women (Backhouse & Cohen, 1981; Bularzik, 1978; Farley, 1978; MacKinnon, 1979; Studd & Gattiker, 1991), a theory that rests on the premise that sexual harassment is the abuse of organizational power will encompass incidents not included in the definition (female bosses harassing male subordinates) and exclude other incidents (street harassment). Definitions that specify the sex of the harasser and of the victim invoke either sociobiological or sociocultural explanations. On the other hand, defining sexual harassment as the abuse of organizational power (Dzeich & Weiner, 1984; Gutek & Morasch, 1982; MacKinnon, 1979; May & Hughes, 1992; Nieva & Gutek, 1981) incorporates causal assumptions into the definition and excludes theories that would explain "contrapower" harassment. Definitions that include negative consequences for the individual or the organization (Gutek & Koss, 1993) will not produce theories that easily explain female-on-male harassment or contrapower harassment.

To organize this review of theories about sexual harassment, we suggest the following model of the various levels of analysis, organized like the layers of an onion: The "deep structure" or innermost layers represent specieswide evolutionary behavioral adaptations and other biological processes; the next layers represent sociocultural norms, values, and institutions; the next layers represent organizational structures and arrangements; and the outermost layer represents idiosyncratic individual and dyadic characteristics, the most outwardly visible variables.

Other classifications are possible. Terpstra and Baker (1986b) organize the factors associated with sexual harassment into *Environmental*-level variables (the ratio of men to women in the population and sex-role attitudes, socioeconomic inequalities, labor market and economic conditions, and legal sanctions), *Organizational*-level variables (technology, task design, worker proximity, organizational climate, employee composition, organization and work roles, sex ratios and formal status or power differentials), and *Individual*-level variables (motivation, attitudes, personality, physiology, demographic characteristics, and information-processing styles). Because this is a classification of variables rather than theories, it does not offer an account of how variables at the various levels are related to each other, or about harassment outside of the work context.

The model proposed by Fitzgerald and Shullman (1993) offers an integration of most of the variables classified by Terpstra and Baker (1986a), showing how they relate to each other and where they enter the chain of cause and effect. Given a sufficiently large data set, their model could be tested for the strength of those relationships. However, it too is descriptive. Although it may account for much of the variance in the incidence and consequences of sexual harassment, it does not ultimately explain why sexual harassment occurs in the first place. That is, it describes covariates but not causes. This model will be more fully presented at the end of the chapter, where its integrative utility will be more fully appreciated.

We begin with the innermost layer of our own scheme, two sociobiological arguments: that sexual harassment results either from evolutionarily adaptive sociosexual behavior that is dimorphic with respect to gender, or from hormones and intellectual defenses against nature's vagaries. Previous writers, including the first author, have used the term "natural/biological model" (e.g., Tangri, Burt, & Johnson, 1982) to classify these theories, and we continue that convention here.

## THE NATURAL/BIOLOGICAL MODELS

A growing number of social behaviors have come under the scrutiny of sociobiological theorists. Sexual harassment is a prime candidate for such an interpretation, given its dual signification as both sex and aggression—two of the most basic human drives. Some of these theories emphasize evolutionary adaptations, whereas others emphasize current hormonal forces. When this view of sexual harassment was first described in a review of theories of sexual harassment (Tangri, Burt, & Johnson, 1982), the authors worried that readers would view it as a "straw man" and defensively cited its use in legal briefs to show that it was not our own creation. Today, sociobiological positions are argued in the academic literature, with varying degrees of claim to scientific support.

### The Hormonal Model

Of the several versions of the argument that sexual harassment is a normal expression of men's stronger sex drive, one stands out for its dramatic rendering: "Men are in a constant state of sexual anxiety, living on the pins and needles of their hormones.... They must quest, pursue, court, or seize...by concentration and insistence [they] may carry the day" (Paglia, 1992, pp. 117–118). This version also argues that objectifying women as sex objects is just another expression of humans' highest faculty—conceptualization—and will never disappear. The behavior is simply another expression of humans' "struggle to fix and stabilize nature's dreadful flux."

We note that female humans presumably share this faculty (of conceptualizing) and the same dreadful state of nature, yet do not seem to engage in sexual harassment to nearly the degree that male humans do. Further, if raging hormones were the cause, we should find younger men and older women whose sex drives are at their peak more often culpable, whereas the reverse (older men and younger women) is found much more often (Gutek, 1985; Pryor, 1987; Reilly et al., 1982; Schneider, 1991; Tangri, Burk, & Johnson, 1982). This argument appears so weak as to not warrant further evaluation. We move on to a much more elaborate argument: that sexual harassment is the result of evolutionary adaptation to reproductive cost-benefit ratios.

## The Evolutionary Adaptation Model

Studd and Gattiker (1991) present the proposition that because reproduction entails different cost-benefit calculuses for men and women, they have evolved different reproductive strategies and the psychological mechanisms to support them. Specifically, men should aggressively compete for access to sexually receptive women of reproductive age, establish long-term mateship in which confidence of paternity is maximized (i.e., be primarily monogamous), and expend parental investment to increase the success of offspring produced (i.e., provide for the survival and flourishing of offspring). This is not, however, a scenario that would lead to sexual harassment.

The alternative reproductive strategy for men is the "pursuit of short-term, low-cost, and low-commitment sexual liaisons" (Studd & Gattiker, 1991, p. 253), which presumably maximizes reproductive success for the male not by ensuring survival of offspring, but simply by increasing the probability of impregnating females. It is the "evolved psychology" of this strategy that accounts for sexual harassment of women by men according to this theory. Women, on the other hand, because their reproductive investments (of time, energy, and risk) are much higher than men's (but only under the second strategy), should be more sexually cautious and choosier than men, selecting those "who have at least the potential to provide economic resources or parental effort over the long-term in exchange for sexual access" (p. 253). Therefore, "women... have evolved a generally negative emotional response to unsolicited sexual attention from men" (p. 256). Actually, this is not the logical conclusion to draw from the argument. It would be more logical to conclude that women should welcome any sexual attention, thus increasing their choices, and exercise the right to choose among suitors. On the other hand, if women have evolved a generally negative emotional response to unsolicited sexual attention from men, then normal mating behavior should usually be initiated by women, not men; but this is not the conclusion drawn by Studd and Gattiker.

This theory therefore posits a psychosexual system of reproduction that inherently produces conflict of interests between the parties seeking to reproduce themselves. One wonders whether this makes evolutionary sense. One could also question whether in the "Environment of Evolutionary Adaptiveness (EEA)" (p. 252), human females—whose *sexual* interest is not cyclical (unlike other mammals)—would have been averse to enjoying "casual" sexual encounters when risk of pregnancy was low, that is, when pregnant or lactating, which was most of their adult life. Nor does the theory explain why women wouldn't harass men as much as men harass women: If women must be "choosier," then active pursuit of the most attractive candidates makes sense.

Furthermore, the EEA was not a nuclear family context for the nurturing of children, but a cooperative, clan social structure in which the welfare of all children was in the interest of all clan members; food and shelter were shared. Therefore, the female's criteria for mate selection would not have had to include a male's individual ability to provision or protect her and her young, but only his potential for producing healthy offspring. Her selection criteria, therefore, should have evolved to focus on youth, health, and attractiveness as signifiers of reproductive viability. Males, on the other hand, given the uncertainties of paternity and ubiquity of environmental and health hazards to the newborn, should have evolved criteria for mate selection that include stability (or monogamy) and wisdom, along with fertility. Thus, mature, "smart" females who could keep themselves and their infants healthy should be preferred. This reading of the EEA produces profiles of the mating desiderata of men and women that are nearly the reverse of what the authors posit. It is not clear what data might be used to support or refute either one, since there is no way to control for the influence of present-day circumstances on mating choices: the nuclear family structure and significant disparities between the sexes in economic resources, that is, structural economic dependence of women on men for supporting children. These contemporaneous conditions appear to be as capable as the evolutionary alternative of explaining the dimorphic patterns of assortative mating among contemporary men and women.

The fact that quite opposite predictions about male and female psychology and behavior can be derived from the theory means that the theory is underspecified, and any refutation of one derivation could simultaneously be considered support of the other. The authors do indeed conclude that existing research findings support both predictions even though they predict opposite behaviors. Therefore, it is not falsifiable.

Furthermore, this theory predicts that humans will "react and behave *as if* these perceived or potential fitness costs and benefits

are real, even if this is no longer true in the current environment" (p. 254). Therefore, any evidence about current behavior or circumstances that argues against the reproductive viability of such strategies (such as nonpossibility of having intercourse, use of contraceptives, harassing postmenopausal women or married women—whose offspring would not necessarily be the harasser's) is considered by the authors to be irrelevant.

There are also two conceptual confusions in the argument's construction. The first is revealed in a footnote (#2, p. 256) in which the authors ask us to "assume that sexual advances in the workplace and sexual harassment are, at least to begin with, sexually motivated rather than motivated by the desire...to exercise power." Yet this proposition/assumption is precisely what is at issue, and what the theory attempts to explain. The second confusion is the failure to distinguish sexual motivation from reproductive motivation. Although this distinction may not be possible in other species, it is certainly important for humans (and not just since the invention of oral contraception). The noncyclical nature of women's sexuality requires that theories of human sexuality take into account women's sexuality as distinct from reproductive functions, a reality that this theory ignores.

A more general problem with this theory is that even if it is true, and evolutionary adaptation to "modern" environments must be slow, learning adaptation can be very fast, if necessary. The question remains, why has it not been necessary? The answer is that much of our society accepts Studd and Gattiker's underlying assumption about the "natural place" of men and women in the social order that they reveal in their recommendations for remedies. They suggest that since men are evolutionarily adapted to sexually harassing women, the remedy lies in separating men and women in the workplace "to reduce the stimulus and opportunity for evolved male sexual psychology to motivate the initiation of sexual advances" (p. 287)—readers should note the similarity to the rationale for purdah in Muslim countries and segregated prayer spaces for women in Orthodox Judaism—and to "allow women more freedom to change jobs or change the working environment as they feel necessary" (p. 287). Although the first phrase suggests that men as well as women might be quarantined, the second makes clear that the workplace belongs to men, and it is women who should leave if they are uncomfortable.

This is exactly what happens now, most of the time. (If women had the power to change the work environment, sexual harassment would not be the problem it is.) Such a remedy would use "evolutionary adaptation" to justify further institutionalization of occupational segregation by gender, thus reinforcing the status quo. Putting such a "remedy" into practice would exaggerate the imbalance of sex ratios in the workplace and exacerbate the very conditions that Gutek (1982) argues increase the likelihood that sexual harassment will occur, and which research has documented (Fain & Anderton, 1987; Kanter, 1977).

It is worth noting, as we review the broad range of theories about sexual harassment, that there is an odd concurrence on two important points between conservative theories like that of Studd and Gattiker (1991) and the most radical feminist theories like that of Schacht and Atchison (1993). Although the former argument is based on evolutionary adaptation with its conservative implications for human change and the latter is based on a social constructionist view with the implication that social constructs can be reconstructed, both agree that heterosexual relationships are systemically adversarial and coercive: In the former theory, heterosexual relationships, including sexual harassment, are driven by reproductive strategy; in the latter theory the system of heterosexual relationships, including the ideology that supports those relationships and sexual harassment, is the fundamental mechanism for the maintenance of male dominance. Schacht and Atchison's theory of heterosexual instrumentalism is dealt with in detail in the section on sociocultural theories.

Studd and Gattiker also agree with many feminist writers that "sexual harassment" reported by males isn't really harassment at all

in the sense of it being a negative or damaging experience. For instance, Malovich and Stake (1990) and Konrad and Gutek (1986) report that men, rather than feeling harassed, report having enjoyed the experience and feeling flattered (although alternative interpretations of these findings have been offered, cf. Reilly & Lott, 1986).

Studd and Gattiker conclude that evidence from prior research largely supports the predictions derived from their theory. However, there remain the two difficulties that (1) there is at least one alternative derivation from evolutionary considerations, and (2) the current findings have at least one alternative interpretation. At best, we can only conclude that the evidence for the natural/biological model, with its contradictory derivations, is mixed and, worse, not falsifiable.

## THE ORGANIZATIONAL MODELS

There are several explanations of sexual harassment that focus on various aspects of organizational structure or process. Most of these are included and described in Terpstra and Baker's (1986b) classification. Most of these are conditions that make it easier or more likely for sexual harassment to occur, such as requirements for night work or travel out of town with coworkers, or organizational norms that require women to act "sexy." But none of them explains why workers take advantage of these opportunities, or why men disproportionately do things to women that women don't like.

### Sex-Role Spillover Theory

One theory that does provide an explanation for why workers sexually harass other workers is the sex-role spillover theory by Gutek and Morasch (1982). Sex-role spillover is defined as the carryover into the workplace of gender-based expectations for behavior that are irrelevant or inappropriate to work. According to this theory, this occurs because in most cultures, gender identity is more salient than work identity, and because men and women fall back on sex-role expectations when they (as men) are unused to women carrying out work roles or (as women) are prevented from, or resented for, carrying out work roles. This is most likely to occur when the gender ratio is heavily skewed in either direction, that is, when those in the workplace are either predominantly male or predominantly female.

In the first situation, nontraditionally employed women with predominantly male colleagues are treated differently than their (male) colleagues, are aware of this differential treatment, are likely to report a high frequency of social-sexual behaviors that are not part of the work role in general, and to feel that sexual harassment is a problem at work. In the second situation, traditionally employed women occupy jobs in which the job itself takes on aspects of the female sex role and, depending on the job (e.g., cocktail waitress, actress), this may include the sexual aspects of the female sex role. Yet, because the job description heavily overlaps with gender-role prescriptions, women may attribute how they are treated to the nature of the job, rather than to their gender.

Some of the predictions from this theory have been tested and supported (cf. Gutek & Morasch, 1982): that nontraditionally employed women in male-dominated work settings perceive they are treated differently from male colleagues, that this differential treatment is directed at them as women, and that such women consider such treatment to be discriminatory (in general) and harassment (when the content is sexual). Traditionally employed women surrounded by other women who do the same work and who are all treated similarly, but whose role partners (e.g., supervisors) are men are less likely to perceive their treatment as discriminatory or as harassment. Finally, women who work in integrated work settings (i.e., having nonskewed sex ratios) are least likely to report experiencing sexual harassment at work (Gutek & Morasch, 1982; Sheffey & Tindale, 1992).

Theories that emphasize structural factors over gender are supported by research that finds symmetrical outcomes (such as inci-

dence rates of sexual harassment or seriousness of outcomes for victims of sexual harassment) for men and women under symmetrical conditions (such as skewness of sex ratios in opposite directions, or positional authority held by either sex). The difficulty has been finding the contexts in which such symmetry occurs. Sexualized female occupations far outnumber sexualized male occupations. The number of women working for male bosses is far greater than the number of men working for female bosses. It is therefore difficult to test half of the derivations from these models. When these hypotheses can be tested, the evidence is strained. The enormous size of the sample used in the U.S. Merit Systems Board (USMSPB, 1981) study of sexual harassment in the federal workforce (n = 23,964) generated a sufficient number of men working in female-dominated workplaces to test whether they were more subject to sexual harassment than men working in other sex-ratio contexts. This did, indeed, turn out to be the case. However, this reversal of the sex ratio did not generate nearly the incidence rate of harassment that women in male-dominated workplaces reported (USMSPB, 1981). It is not, therefore, a sufficient explanation for sexual harassment at work.

So it is not surprising that Gutek (1985) added a "gender hypothesis" to the sex-role spillover model, arguing that men more than women sexualize the environments they work in, and therefore, other things being equal, they make more sexual comments and suggestions than women do, women receive such remarks more than men do, and women experience more sexual harassment than men do. Gutek suggests that this sex difference is rooted in sex-role socialization for sexual behavior that prescribes the role of initiator and pursuer to men, and nay-sayer and limit setter to women. But what is the origin of these sex-role definitions? And why are other kinds of "inappropriate and irrelevant" behaviors in the workplace (such as wearing sloppy clothing or pushing one's political opinions) often perceived as funny, pathetic, or more damaging to the actor than to the perceiver, while inappropriate and irrelevant sexual behaviors are often intimidating? Sociobiologists would argue that gender roles reflect evolutionary or hormonal sex differences. Others argue that their origins lie in the dominance system of patriarchy that is reproduced in all relations between the sexes, whether at work, on the street, or in the home. This argument falls under the sociocultural theory of sexual harassment, which is discussed in the next section.

## Organizational Power

The earliest writings about sexual harassment were about men abusing their organizational power to sexually coerce or intimidate women (Backhouse & Cohen, 1981; Bularzik, 1978; Farley, 1978; MacKinnon, 1979). This also remains the focus of most research and legal developments. Later writings and policy statements emphasize a gender-neutral version of organizational power, arguing that where there is formal power that derives from the hierarchical structure of an organization, it can and will be abused (although not by everyone who could) to extort sexual gratification (Crocker, 1983; EEOC, 1980; Nieva & Gutek, 1981; Zalk, 1991). Thus, although men typically harass women, in principle it is possible for women to sexually harass men. It is less likely only because women tend to be employed in positions subordinate to men (Evans, 1978).

However, the interpretation of sexual harassment as an abuse of organizational power appeared to be challenged by findings that peers rather than supervisors are the most frequent harassers (Gutek, 1985; Phillips, Stockdale, & Joeman, 1989; USMSPB, 1981), and by documentation of contrapower harassment (McKinney, 1992)—that is, the harassment of superiors by subordinates. These findings raise the question of what constitutes organizational power, and whether formal authority is the only kind of power that can be used this way.

Drawing on a substantial body of organizational theory and research, Cleveland and Kerst (1993) explicate the various kinds of power that are used in organizations, how they

are used, by whom, and to what end. They also show how these are often linked to gender and help explain sexual harassment. This explication does not exclude the role of other sources of power (societal and interpersonal), but may be seen as an extension of these.

Formal organizational power, in this analysis, derives from the structure of occupations within the organization (the levels of hierarchy and how they are related vertically and horizontally), who occupies what positions, and who has access to the most important resources of the organization. In each of these respects, women are generally positioned at a disadvantage to men, occupying positions of less formal authority and in departments that are not central to the mission of the organization (Kanter, 1977). We do not need to describe the power disadvantage deriving from formal subordinacy and how this increases women's vulnerability to sexual harassment—these implications are obvious enough (Collins & Blodgett, 1981; Lipman-Blumen, 1984; Little-Bishop, Seidler-Feller, & Opalach, 1982; Schneider, 1982). Even without formal subordinacy, however, women's organizational power is also eroded by their being excluded from the informal structures of influence, information, and opportunities created by alliances with mentors, peers, and subordinates (Kanter, 1977). Studies of selection, promotion, and perceived causes of performance also find systematic sex bias against women (Heilman, Martell, & Simon, 1988; Stewart & Gundykunst, 1982). Thus, formal differences in status are not the only source of power within organizations; informal dynamics also operate against women at all status levels.

Among coworkers, organizational power differences are created through informal networks, differential support from peers, and differences among peers in how much latitude in decision making they are granted by supervisors. That these differences are often linked to gender is demonstrated by studies that show why a woman who occupies the same position as a man often does not have the same level of authority or influence (DiTomaso, 1989;

Kanter, 1977; Ragins & Sundstrom, 1989; Pleck, 1976; Wolf & Fligstein, 1979). In a sexist organizational culture, sexual harassment from colleagues is just another expression of the undervaluing and undermining of women at work. It is a particularly effective tool for countering the threat of women invading previously male-dominated domains (Benson & Thomson, 1982; LaFontaine & Tredeau, 1986).

Sexual harassment by subordinates has been documented mostly in academic settings, where significant numbers (almost half) of female professors report being harassed by male students (Grauerholz, 1989). Subordinate and peer harassers use sexual or sex-role assertion to gain power or minimize power differentials. It should also be noted that contrapower harassment is the rarest form of harassment and is nearly always perpetrated by men against women (Benson, 1984; Grauerholz, 1989; McKinney, 1992).

Cleveland and Kerst (1993) point out that explaining sexual harassment as an attempt to gain power or as an expression of a sense of entitlement granted either by organizational power or by societal gender stratification does not address the question of why all men do not harass all women. Although this question might be referred to research on individual differences, they attempt to answer it by adding two elements: Gutek's (1982) sex-role spillover thesis and the "misperception" hypothesis, which is that behavior intended and perceived by women as friendly is perceived by men as sexy. As previously noted, Gutek has incorporated a gender hypothesis into the sex-role spillover model to account for the fact that under symmetrical sex-ratio conditions, there is still a gender difference in the incidence and nature of sexual harassment. Gutek assumes that the underlying basis for this difference is differential sex-role socialization— a sociocultural interpretation. The misperception findings are interpreted as possible support for a natural/biological model of sexual harassment presumably based on men's stronger sex drive. Since there is no way to prove that men in general have a stronger sex drive

absent greater societal permission for sexual activities of all kinds, an alternative interpretation of the misperception findings is that the perceptions of both men and women are embedded in sex-role socialization for dimorphic patterns of sexual behavior.

In both of these adjustments to their analysis of the role of power in sexual harassment, as well as in their own discussion of sociocultural power, Cleveland and Kerst (1993), along with others (Finigan, 1982; Izraeli, 1983; Kanter, 1977; Sokoloff, 1980), recognize that organizational explanations alone, though robust, are an insufficient explanation for sexual harassment in organizations. More comprehensive explanations must also incorporate elements from another layer of the onion, the sociocultural milieu.

In one of the few direct comparisons of the explanatory power of three different models of sexual harassment, Fain and Anderton (1987) found support for all three: power differentials deriving from organizational structure, numerical minority status of victims resulting from skewed sex ratios, and "diffuse master status characteristics" (i.e., age, ethnicity, marital status, and education). Although their analyses support the significance of all three models, master status characteristics were the most pronounced, particularly marital status and age. (Although gender is also a master status characteristic, it was not part of the equation since these analyses were performed only on women, and most scholars agree that women are harassed more than men. For an alternative argument, however, see Vaux, 1993.) We are therefore led once again to examine the source of these "master" or "diffuse" status characteristics (Fain & Anderton, 1987; Lockheed & Hall, 1976; Meeker & Weitzel-O'Neill, 1977), the sociocultural system.

## THE SOCIOCULTURAL MODEL

There are two ways to think about how the broader sociocultural context relates to sexual harassment. One is to consider how individuals bring their gender status and sex-stereotypical responses with them into the organization, and how this shapes their positions and experiences within it (Sokoloff, 1980). From this perspective, sexual harassment at work is an extension of the male dominance that thrives in the larger society. Another approach is to examine the sociocultural system itself and address the questions of how and why it assigns status the way it does. From this perspective, sexual harassment is not a consequence of an unfortunate but remediable aspect of relations between the sexes in the larger society, but is the organizing principle of our system of heterosexuality.

Both perspectives have validity. But they make different assumptions about how anomalous sexual harassment is: In the first view it is systemic deviance, an aberration unleashed by male dominance, much as criminal behavior might be viewed as an aberrant but systemic response to poverty. In the second view, dominance and its expression in sexual harassment are not deviant, but a "normal"—both normatively and statistically—consequence of the ideology of heterosexuality, that is, heterosexual instrumentalism. According to Schacht and Atchison (1993): "Heterosexual instrumentalism refers to the behaviors which reflect and sustain the expectation that all heterosexuality is to be practiced with explicit requirements of dominance and subordination.... The ultimate goal...is the maintenance of pre-existing gender inequalities" (p. 39).

We begin with a general characterization of gender status, describe the specific characteristics assigned to gender, and discuss how these help us understand sexual harassment.

According to Pryor (1987), "sexual harassment may be better understood in the general context of heterosexual relationships in our society" (p. 288) than within the confines of intraorganizational structures. MacKinnon (1979) proposes that sexual harassment be understood as one among several expressions of, and mechanisms for, perpetuating beliefs, attitudes, and actions that devalue women because of their sex and enforce male dominance—in short, a social system defined by patriarchy. Other practices serving the same

purpose are rape, prostitution, incest, and pornography (Schacht & Atchison, 1993). It does not affect this analysis to note that not all members of one class oppress all members of another class, just as it does not require that all Americans be capitalists to accept that the United States is an economy based on capitalism.

Another power-based sociocultural explanation of sexual harassment is offered by Vaux (1993). Vaux agrees with many feminists that male entitlement rights, sexual access rights, and coercion are inherent in our culture and suggests that the dynamic at work in sexual harassment belongs to a broader class of attitudes and behaviors known as "moral exclusion" (Opotow, 1990). Thus, Vaux sees sexual harassment as "an instance of moral exclusion, whereby members of a relatively powerful group conduct their lives in their own interest, sometimes at the expense of a relatively less powerful group, in such a way that any harm is denied, diminished, or justified" (p. 132).

This theory is consistent with other power-based theories and describes a psychological mechanism operating at both the individual and cultural level that facilitates victimization. In this version the ultimate explanation for using this mechanism is the more powerful group members' desire to maintain their position of privilege.

A closely related version of this perspective is one that emphasizes social identity processes rather than power per se yet sees the use of status, prestige, authority and power as central to men's agentic style of identity construction. In this view, sexual harassment is a "corollary of the agentic style of identity construction whereby men define themselves as different from and better than women" (Stockdale, 1991, p. 58). This begs the question of why more men than women use this style and why men but not women define themselves as better than members of the other sex.

There is general agreement in the literature about the characteristics of the sex stratification system and the socialization patterns that maintain it. Men are expected to exercise, and are socialized for, dominance, leadership, sexual initiative and persistence, and self-interest. Women are expected to exercise, and are socialized for, submissiveness, nurturing, sexual gatekeeping, and self-abnegation. These attributes and behaviors are verbal and nonverbal, explicit and implicit, coerced and persuaded (Blumberg, 1984; Finigan, 1982; Henley, 1977; Henley & Freeman, 1975; Korman & Leslie, 1982; Lottes, 1991; Saal, Johnson, & Weber, 1989; Weitzman, 1979).

The relationship of this pattern of sex-role definitions to sexual harassment is spelled out in Tangri, Burt, and Johnson (1982):

> Society rewards males for aggressive and domineering sexual behaviors and females for passivity and acquiescence. Members of each sex are socialized to play their respective and complementary roles. Because women, more than men, are taught to seek their self-worth in the evaluation of others, particularly of men (Bardwick, 1971), they are predisposed to try to interpret male attention as flattery, making them less likely to define unwanted attention as harassment. Their training to be sexually attractive, to be social facilitators and avoid conflict, to not trust their own judgment about what happens to them, and to feel responsible for their own victimization, contributes to their vulnerability to sexual harassment. According to this model, the function of sexual harassment is to manage ongoing male–female interactions according to accepted sex status norms, and to maintain male dominance occupationally and therefore economically, by intimidating, discouraging, or precipitating removal of women from work. (p. 40)

Socialization for these patterns occurs throughout the life span and across institutions (Fain & Anderton, 1987), including the family, heterosexual dating, work, and training for work.

Both versions of the sociocultural model have the advantage over the organizational model of explaining not only why sexual harassment is endemic in social life, occurring outside as well as inside organizations, but also how it is linked to other kinds of sexual coercion. The natural/biological model has these same advantages.

Each of these models contributes another layer to our understanding, and all of them taken together probably account for most of the variation in incidence, type, severity, and consequences of sexual harassment. Nevertheless, given the strong associations among gender, power, and harassment, we must still return to the question of why all men or all powerholders do not harass and why the same behaviors are perceived and experienced by some men and women as harassment and not by others.

## INDIVIDUAL DIFFERENCES

In this section we deal with those individual differences that do not derive from organizational structure or culturally defined status. For the most part this means personality differences. Whether these characteristics are socially constructed or not is a matter of disagreement or not specified.

There have been two general approaches to individual differences in research on sexual harassment. Our primary focus here is framed by the question "What characteristics distinguish harassers from nonharassers, and what characteristics distinguish victims from nonvictims?" The other approach asks, "What characteristics of perceivers (and of incidents) influence the perception of sexual harassment, that is, whether a certain behavior is considered sexual harassment, and how serious it is?" (See Chapter 2.)

The search for individual-level characteristics of harassers and victims does not negate any of the other levels of explanation and often invokes diffuse status characteristics such as gender, age, race, or marital status as the context in which personal motives are satisfied (Defaur, 1990; LaFontaine & Tredeau, 1986; Mansfield, Koch, & Henderson, 1991; Neibuhr & Boyles, 1991; Schneider, 1982, 1991). As Zalk (1991) aptly argues:

> The fact that misogyny is rampant in most societies and that these societies provide for and promote its expression does not explain why men hate women. Concluding that men hate wome n because they *can* is nonsensi-

cal. Just as hating women is not simply an expression of many individuals' idiosyncratic psychological histories existing in a societal vacuum, neither is sexual harassment the acting out of isolated individuals' emotional irritants.

Not all men sexually harass women, but it is pervasive enough in most societies to indicate that the social structure nurtures a male psychology that finds gratification in this behavior...[and] reflects a pattern of shared experience. (p. 142)

Zalk (1991) uses a psychodynamic model to adapt and interpret profiles suggested by Dziech and Weiner (1984) describing five professional roles that male professors may play vis-à-vis the female students they harass. These are the Counselor-Helper, who plays the role of nurturer and caretaker; the Confidante, who treats students as friends and equals; the Intellectual Seducer, who impresses students and encourages their awe; the Opportunist, who uses various opportunities to harass students; and the Power Broker, who uses promises of rewards or threats of punishment (subtle or not) to extract sexual compliance. Although these roles vary in the extent to which the harassment is public or private, the harasser is the initiator or the willing noninitiator, assumes entitlement, or is himself infatuated. "The theme which appears to characterize almost all men who have sex with female students is anger toward women" (p. 166). Since the evidence for these profiles rests for now on qualitative data, no quantitative conclusions about their explanatory power can be made at the present time. Yet these profiles are recognizable to anyone who has spent time in academia, and they are probably not limited to that setting. Similar types may be found in the corporate and governmental world.

Research on the distinguishing characteristics of those likely to sexually harass has profited from research on rape proclivities (Burt, 1978, 1980; Field, 1978; Malamuth, 1981). Using scenarios that present male subjects with opportunities to sexually harass a hypothetical woman, Pryor (1987) developed a scale that measures the likelihood of sexually

harassing (the LSH). He found that scores on this scale were most strongly correlated with the Likelihood to Rape scale (Malamuth, 1981), adversarial sexual beliefs (Burt, 1980), acceptance of rape myths (Burt, 1980), sex-role stereotyping (Burt, 1980), and less feminist attitudes (Smith, Feree, & Miller, 1975). Also, people who reported a higher likelihood of sexually harassing also tended to report that they had difficulties in perspective taking or "putting themselves in another person's shoes" (part of the IRI scale by Davis, 1980). Thus,

The profile of a person who is likely to initiate severe sexually harassing behavior...is one that emphasizes sexual and social male dominance.... These belief structures seem to contribute to the likelihood of sexual harassment...and seem coupled with a basic insensitivity to other's perspectives. (p. 277)

Pryor also found that high-LSH men are more likely than low-LSH men to be high in authoritarianism and low in Machiavellianism, have negative feelings about sexuality, describe themselves in socially undesirable masculine terms or masculine terms that strongly differentiate them from stereotypical femininity, and have a tendency to behave in sexually exploitive ways when their motives can be disguised by situational excuses. In light of this profile, it becomes harder to argue that sexual harassment is simply the result of perceptual or communication errors, and not coercive in intent.

Other research has focused on the characteristics of victims of harassment. According to Vaux (1993), this research suffers from two difficulties: Victim incidence is assessed by self-reports, which are influenced by both "false consciousness" (unwillingness or inability to identify harassing behavior as such) and "victim sensitivity" (the same behaviors being harassment to some persons and not to others). We, however, do not consider these a validity problem, since the target's perception is a part of the definition of the phenomenon (see previous discussion).

Some research acknowledges these issues by separating reports of uninvited and unwelcome sexual experiences ("objectively defined sexual harassment") and subjective perceptions that one has been sexually harassed. Barak, Fisher, and Houston (1992) found a large gap between these two ways of defining incidence, the "objective" incidence being much higher than the subjective one. The incidence of uninvited and unwelcomed sexual experiences among female university students was associated with lower scores on erotophobia, less need for social approval, and less repression of defenses. That is, women who depart from the sex-role script for female sexuality (Laws & Schwartz, 1977) are subjected to more uninvited and unwelcome sexual experiences. On the other hand, the base rate of subjective perceptions that one had been sexually harassed was low and unassociated with individual differences. The gap is interpreted by the researchers as either a methodological problem ("overdefining" sexual harassment relative to women's own definitions) or motivated by the high emotional cost of acknowledging one's victimization. Their data do not permit one to choose between these interpretations, and both may be true. One might also interpret these findings in light of the description of female socialization given above, which encourages women to be self-abnegating and put others' interests first.

One clue to the gap between incidence rates of "objectively" and "subjectively" defined sexual harassment lies in attitudinal characteristics of the perceiver. Several researchers report that traditionality of sex-role attitudes is a stronger determinant of reactions to hypothetical scenarios than gender. Men and women with more traditional sex-role attitudes are slower to label behaviors harassment and underplay the seriousness of the behavior and the consequences (Jensen & Gutek, 1982; Malovich & Stake, 1990). The fact that men generally report no negative reactions to personal experiences of being "harassed" is explained by attitudinal differences associated with gender, men generally having more traditional sex-role attitudes than women (Powell, 1986). If this is true, we should expect that

men's and women's consciousness of and reports of sexual harassment will increase as (and if) nontraditional attitudes become more prevalent.

Although we have focused primarily on the question of what characteristics distinguish harassers from nonharassers and victims from nonvictims, it is important to note that the literature on what characteristics of perceivers and of incidents influence the perception of sexual harassment reveals an interesting disjuncture with the literature on sex differences in perceptions of *non*harassing behavior. That is, behaviors that women are more likely to interpret as friendly, men are more likely to interpret as expressing sexual intent or interest (Abbey, 1982; Gutek, Morasch, & Cohen, 1983; Johnson, Stockdale, & Saal, 1991; Saal, Johnson, & Weber, 1989). On the other hand, the sexual harassment research consistently shows that women have a lower threshold than men for perceiving (interpreting) sexual behavior as harassment (Adams, Kottke, & Padgett, 1983; Gutek, 1985; Powell, 1986; Rossi & Weber-Burden, 1993). We thus encounter at the level of perceptions a dilemma similar to that created by different a priori definitions of sexual harassment. That is, depending on whose perceptions or definitions are operative, the phenomena being explained, and therefore the explanations, will vary. As noted by MacKinnon (1979), the law on sexual harassment for the first time gives women and other victims the power to define the situation. However, since men and women have different thresholds for labeling certain behaviors as sexual harassment, one explanation for the problem is that men and women misinterpret each other's behavior; that is, behavior intended as friendly, humorous, or romantic by men is often perceived by women as harassing.

The misperception findings are interpreted differently in different models. In the sociocultural model, men's "misperceptions" are interpreted as "motivated errors" that fit the larger picture of a male-dominance structure. In the organizational model these misperceptions are interpreted as the result of gender salience under conditions of skewed sex ratios. In the natural/biological model, men's misperceptions are interpreted as evidence of their stronger sex drive. But whichever interpretation one prefers, the operational question remains: Whose definition of the situation should prevail? The combination of women having higher thresholds for perceiving (non-harassing) behavior as sexual and lower thresholds for perceiving sexual behavior as harassing means that women tend to make finer distinctions among possible sociosexual behaviors than men, while men generally have more difficulty distinguishing friendly from sexual, and sexual from harassing, behavior. It is therefore reasonable to give the power to define to those whose ability to distinguish is greater. This line of reasoning and evidence supports the reasonable woman standard that has been proposed in courts of law (see Chapter 4). However, we should note that this operationalization departs from the definition that sexual harassment is not in the eye of the beholder, but of the target, and makes a material difference when the target is either a man (not a frequent occurrence) or can be portrayed as not a reasonable woman (perhaps a very common occurrence).

## SYNTHESES AND CONCLUSIONS

There have been two notable attempts at integration of the diverse body of research and theory on sexual harassment. An early synthesis by Brewer (1982) proposed that each model described by Tangri, Burt, and Johnson (1982) best explained one of three types of sexual harassment and was associated with one of three work environments described by Gutek and Morasch (1982). Brewer suggested that the organizational model best explains sexual harassment that is coercive, such as quid pro quo harassment, and is most likely to occur in traditional work settings where women in low-status jobs outnumber men in higher-status jobs and the organizational climate promotes sexual joking and other forms of sexualization. The sociocultural model

might best explain gender harassment, that is, sexist behavior that may or may not be sexual in content, which is most likely to occur in nontraditional jobs in which men outnumber women and use harassment to reassert their sex-role expectations over "out-of-role" behavior by women. The biological model might best explain harassment that resembles courting behavior and is most likely to occur in gender-balanced work settings. This synthesis nicely integrated most of the research at that time.

Since 1982, empirical work has produced findings that must be taken into account. The most comprehensive of these attempts to do so is by Fitzgerald and Shullman (1993), whose model also incorporates a smaller model developed by Pryor (1992; Pryor, Lavitte, & Stoller, 1993). These integrative models are not strictly theoretical, but attempt to describe the growing body of empirical evidence on the incidence, context, and consequences of sexual harassment in organizations.

Fitzgerald and Shullman's model begins with two exogenous variables: the organizational context, which includes the level of tolerance for sexual harassment and the policies and procedures for dealing with sexual harassment; and the job context, which includes the sex ratio of the work force in the job and the degree to which the work requirements resemble traditional sex-role expectations. These predict the incidence and type of sexual harassment. The consequences of sexual harassment with respect to job-related outcomes, psychological outcomes, and health outcomes for the victim are influenced by the victim's personal vulnerability and response style. Personal vulnerability is determined by diffuse status characteristics, such as age, race, marital status, and sexual orientation, and "personal tolerance" such as may be determined by their sex-role attitudes. Response styles may be passive and therefore more internally focused, or active and therefore more externally focused. Further, the three classes of outcomes (job, psychological, and health) interact to produce the overall degree of impact on the victim.

Fitzgerald and Shullman's model succeeds in describing much of the empirical work on sexual harassment at work but does not incorporate most theories about why sexual harassment occurs in the first place—Gutek's sex-role spillover explanation is the exception. Nor does the model address the question of why, in the same work environment, some men do and others do not harass, but from the standpoint of designing organizational remedies, this may not be important. If Zalk (1991) is right that the underlying motivation for male harassment of women is anger at women, which is consistent with Pryor's findings on the Likelihood to Sexually Harass scale, the obvious remedy—psychotherapy—is not one that organizations could implement, although other kinds of interventions (mostly training) are being used.

The Fitzgerald and Shullman model also does not attempt to address the issue of sexual harassment in nonorganizational contexts (e.g., street harassment, harassment among school children [cf. Orenstein, 1994], or harassment—including rape—by dating partners and acquaintances). Again, these may be tangential to instituting organizational remedies, but the lack of data leaves our understanding of the broader phenomenon incomplete.

If the natural/biological theory is correct—that sexual harassment is an extension of normal male courting behavior and only becomes harassment when men's attraction is not reciprocated—then the remedy would lie in something like sensitivity training to enable men to more clearly perceive negative signals from women and to enable women to more clearly send such signals. This approach has, in fact, been adopted in some organizations, and may help in some cases, but it does not address what's at stake when such failures of communication, on both sides, are not simply mistakes but are often motivated by self-interest, that is, by men wishing to retain their privilege and by women wishing to protect their jobs by being "good girls."

To the extent that the sociocultural model is correct, organizational remedies will be fighting an uphill battle against the larger issues of misogyny, instrumental heterosexuality (see p. 120 and Schacht & Atchison, 1993) and patriarchy.

Although all of these models contribute something to our understanding of the causes of sexual harassment, it is important to recognize that the two most opportune points of intervention are in the policies, procedures, and commitment to change in organizations and in the educational system.

When we pull together the most strongly supported arguments about the causes of sexual harassment, an intriguing consensus emerges across all of the theories presented. When it comes to heterosexual interactions, women experience a narrower range of male behavior that is acceptably sexual. This has been used to characterize women's sexual tastes as constricted, prudish, or inhibited. Such a characterization implies that there is nothing "wrong" with the behaviors outside this range and that heterosexual interactions would be better if women would enjoy these behaviors. This, of course, reflects the male point of view that what is good for men should be good for (or accepted by) women. Much traditional sex counseling has been based on this assumption. But the alternative view is that women's range of acceptable or enjoyable behaviors is not narrower, but simply different, and may be "better" in a sense that is explicated by the theories on sexual harassment.

The most puzzling question to be answered by these theories is why men's sexual behavior is so often experienced by women as harassing even when there is no explicit or implicit threat of sanctions or promise of rewards, and even when men do not have a formal power advantage. The answer appears to lie in the point on which the most conservative and most radical theories agree: The *system* of heterosexual relations is adversarial and coercive. Even the middle-of-the-road theories (which focus primarily on organizational structure or sex-role socialization) acknowledge that some of the asymmetry in men's and women's initiation of and reactions to unwanted sexual attention is based on the asymmetry in power relations between the sexes that exists outside of organizations.

We conclude with this succinct statement by McKinney and Maroules (1991) about the causes of sexual harassment:

> If there is any common feature to the many factors suggested as variables influencing sexual harassment by researchers in this area, it is the factor of power or status. Whether formal or informal, organizational or diffuse, real or perceived, status differences between victims and offenders are the root of the problem of sexual harassment. (p. 35)

## ENDNOTE

1. The *Journal of Social Issues* (Spring, 1995), Vol. 51, No. 1, "Gender Stereotyping, Sexual Harassment, and the Law" was published after this chapter was submitted and is recomended to the reader as an excellent source of theoretical and empirical information about sexual harassment.

## REFERENCES

Abbey, A. (1982). Sex differences in attributions for friendly behaviors: Do males misperceive females' friendliness? *Journal of Personality and Social Psychology, 42,* 830–838.

Adams, J. W., Kottke, J. L., & Padgett, J. S. (1983). Sexual harassment of college students. *Journal of College Student Personnel, 24,* 484–490.

Backhouse, C., & Cohen, L. (1981). *Sexual harassment on the job: How to avoid the working woman's nightmare.* Englewood Cliffs, NJ: Prentice-Hall.

Barak, A., Fisher, W., & Houston, S. (1992). Individual difference correlates of the experience of sexual harassment among female university students. *Journal of Applied Social Psychology, 22,* 17–37.

Bardwick, J. (1971). *The psychology of women.* New York: Harper and Row.

Benson, K. (1984). Comment on Crocker's "An analysis of university definitions of sexual harassment," *Signs, 9,* 377–397.

Benson, D. J., & Thomson, G. E. (1982). Sexual harassment on a university campus: The confluence of authority relations, sexual interest, and gender stratifications. *Social Problems, 29,* 236–251.

Blumberg, R. L. (1984). A general theory of gender stratification. *Sociological Theory, 2,* 23–101.

Brewer, M. B., & Berk, R. A. (1982). Beyond nine to five: Introduction. *Journal of Social Issues, 38,* 1–4.

Bularzik, M. (1978). Street harassment at the workplace: Historical notes. Reprinted in pamphlet from *Radical American,* MA: New England Free Press.

Burt, M. (1978, January 10–12). *Attitudes supportive of rape in American culture* (pp. 277–322). House committee on Science and Technology, Subcommittee on Domestic and International Scientific Planning Analysis and Cooperation, Research in Violent Behavior: Sexual Assaults. Hearing, 95th Congress, Second Session, Washington, DC: Government Printing Office.

Burt, M. (1980). Cultural myths and supports for rape. *Journal of Personality and Social Psychology, 38,* 217–230.

Cleveland, J., & Kerst, M. (1993). Sexual harassment and perceptions of power: An under-articulated relationship. Special issue: Sexual harassment in the workplace. *Journal of Vocational Behavior, 42,* 49–67.

Collins, E. G., & Blodgett, T. B. (1981). Sexual harassment: Some see it…some won't. *Harvard Business Review, 59(2),* 76–95.

Crocker, P. L. (1983). An analysis of university definitions of sexual harassment. *Journal of College Student Personnel, 24,* 219–224.

Davis, M. H. (1980). Measuring individual differences in empathy: Evidence for a multidimensional approach. *Journal of Personality and Social Psychology, 49,* 113–126.

Defaur, D. C. (1990). The interface of racism and sexism on college campuses. In M. A. Paludi (Ed.), *Ivory power. Sexual harassment on campus.* New York: SUNY.

DiTomaso, N. (1989). Sexuality in the workplace: Discrimation and harassment. In J. Hearn, D. L. Sheppard, P. Tancred-Sheriff, & G. Burrell (Eds.), *The sexuality of organizations* (pp. 71–90). Newbury Park, CA: Sage.

Dzeich, B. W., and Weiner, L. (1984). *The lecherous professor. Sexual harassment on campus.* Boston: Beacon Press.

Equal Employment Opportunity Commission (EEOC). (1980). Guidelines on discrimination because of sex. *Federal Register, 45,* 74676–74677.

Evans, L. J. (1978). Sexual harassment: Women's hidden occupational hazard. In J. R. Chapman & M. Gates (Eds.), *The victimization of women* (pp. 203–223). Beverly Hills, CA: Sage.

Fain, T. C., & Anderton, D. L. (1987). Sexual harassment: Organizational context and diffuse status. *Sex Roles, 17,* 291–311.

Farley, R. L. (1978). *Sexual shakedown: The sexual harassment of women on the job.* New York: Warner Books.

Field, H. S. (1978). Attitudes toward rape: A comparative analysis of police, rapists, crisis counselors, and citizens. *Journal of Personality and Social Psychology, 36,* 156–179.

Finigan, M. (1982). The effects of token representation on participation in small groups and decision making groups. *Economic and Industrial Democracy, 3/4,* 531–550.

Fitzgerald, L. F., and Shullman, S. L. (1993). Sexual harassment: A research analysis agenda for the 1990s. Special issue: Sexual harassment in the workplace. *Journal of Vocational Behavior, 42,* 5–27.

Grauerholz, E. (1989). Sexual harassment of women professors by students: Exploring the dynamics of power, authority, and gender in a university setting. *Sex Roles, 21,* 789–801.

Gutek, B. A. (1985). *Sex and the workplace.* San Francisco: Jossey-Bass.

Gutek, B. A., & Koss, M. P. (1993). Changed women and changed organizations: Consequences of and coping with sexual harassment. Special issue: *Journal of Vocational Behavior, 42,* 28–48.

Gutek, B. A., & Morasch, B. (1982). Sex-ratios, sex-role spillover, and sexual harassment of women at work. *Journal of Social Issues, 38,* 55–74.

Gutek, B. A., Morasch, B., & Cohen, A. G. (1983). Interpreting social sexual behavior in a work setting. *Journal of Vocational Behavior, 22,* 30–48.

Heilman, M., Martell, R. F., & Simon, M. C. (1988). The vagaries of sex bias: Conditions regulating the undervaluation, equivalation, and overvaluation of female job applicants. *Organizational Behavior and Human Decision Processes, 41,* 98–110.

Henley, N. M. (1977). *Body politics: Power, sex and nonverbal communication.* Englewood Cliffs, NJ: Prentice-Hall.

Henley, N. M., & Freeman, J. (1975). The sexual politics of interpersonal behavior. In J. Freeman (Ed.), *Women: A feminist perspective* pp. (391–401). Palo Alto, CA: Mayfield.

Izraeli, D. N. (1983). Sex effects or structural effects? An empirical test of Kanter's theory of proportions. *Social Forces, 62,* 153–165.

Jensen, I. W., & Gutek, B. A. (1982). Attributions and assignment of responsibility in sexual harassment. *Journal of Social Issues, 38,* 121–136.

Johnson, C. B., Stockdale, M. S., & Saal, F. E. (1991). Persistence of men's misperceptions of friendly cues across a variety of interpersonal encounters. *Psychology of Women Quarterly, 15,* 463–475.

Kanter, R. M. (1977). Some effects of the proportions on group life: Skewed sex ratios and responses to token women. *American Journal of Sociology, 82,* 965–990.

Konrad, A. M., & Gutek, B. (1986). Impact of work experiences on attitudes toward sexual harassment. *Administrative Science Quarterly, 31,* 422–438.

Korman, S. K., and Leslie, G. R. (1982). The relationship of feminist ideology and date sharing to perceptions of sexual aggression in dating. *The Journal of Sex Research, 18,* 114–129.

LaFontaine, E., & Tredeau, L. (1986). The frequency, sources, and correlates of sexual harassment among women in traditional male occupations. *Sex Roles, 15,* 433–442.

Laws, J. L., & Schwartz, P. (1977). *Sexual scripts: The social construction of female sexuality.* Hinsdale, IL: Dryden Press.

Lipman-Blumen, J. (1984). *Gender roles and power.* Englewood Cliffs, NJ: Prentice-Hall.

Little-Bishop, S., Seidler-Feller, D., & Opalach, P. E. (1982). Sexual harassment in the workplace as a function of initiator's status: The case of airline personnel. *Journal of Social Issues, 38,* 137–148.

Lockheed, M. E., & Hall, K. P. (1976). Conceptualizing sex as a status characteristic. Applications to leadership training strategies. *Journal of Social Issues, 32,* 111–124.

Lottes, I. L. (1991). The relationship between nontraditional gender roles and sexual coercion. *Journal of Psychology and Human Ecology, 4,* 89–109.

MacKinnon, C. A. (1979). The social causes of sexual harassment. In E. Wall (Ed.), *Sexual harassment. Confrontations and decisions.* Buffalo, NY: Prometheus Books.

Malamuth, N. (1981). Rape proclivity among males. *Journal of Social Issues, 37,* 138–157.

Malovich, N. J., & Stake, J. E. (1990). Sexual harassment on campus: Individual differences in attitudes and beliefs. *Psychology of Women Quarterly, 14,* 63–81.

Mansfield, P. K., Koch, P. B., & Henderson, J. (1991). The job climate for women in traditionally male blue-collar occupations. *Sex Roles, 25,* 63–79.

May, L., & Hughes, J. C. (1992). Is sexual harassment coercive? In E. Wall (Ed.), *Sexual harassment. Confrontations and decisions.* Buffalo, NY: Prometheus Books.

McKinney, K. (1992). Contrapower sexual harassment: The effects of student sex and type of behavior on faculty perceptions. *Sex Roles, 27,* 627–643.

Meeker, B. F., & Weitzel-O'Neill, P. A. (1977). Sex roles and interpersonal behavior in task-oriented groups. *American Sociological Review, 42,* 91–105.

Neibuhr, R. E., & Boyles, W. R. (1991). Sexual harassment of military personnel. *International Journal of International Relations, 15,* 445–457.

Nieva, V. F., & Gutek. B. A. (1981). *Women and work: A psychological perspective.* New York: Praeger.

Opotow, S. (1990). Moral exclusion and injustice: An overview. *Journal of Social Issues, 46,* 1–20.

Orenstein, P. (1994). Schoolgirls: Young women, self-esteem, and the confidence gap. *In association with the American Association for University Women.* New York: Doubleday.

Paglia, C. (1992). Sexual aggression and nature. In E. Wall (Ed.), *Sexual harassment: Confrontations and decisions.* Buffalo, NY: Prometheus Books.

Paludi, M. A. (Ed.) (1990). *Ivory power. Sexual harassment on campus.* Albany, NY: SUNY.

Phillips, C. M., Stockdale, J. E., & Joeman, L. M. (1989). *The risks in going to work. The nature of people's work, the risks they encounter, and the incidence of sexual harassment, physical attack and threatening behaviour.* London: The Suzy Lamplugh Trust.

Pleck, J. H. (1976). Male threat from female competence. *Journal of Consulting and Clinical Psychology, 44,* 608–613.

Powell, G. N. (1986). Effects of sex roles identity and sex on definitions of sexual harassment. *Sex Roles, 14,* 81–95.

Pryor, J. B. (1987). Sexual harassment proclivities in men. *Sex Roles, 17,* 269–290.

Pryor, J. B. (1992). The social psychology of sexual harassment: Person and situation factors which give rise to sexual harassment. *Proceedings of the First National Congress on Sex and Power in the Workplace.* Bellevue, WA.

Pryor, J., Lavite, C., & Stoller, L. (1993). A social psychological analysis of sexual harassment: The person/situation interaction. Special issue: Sexual harassment in the workplace. *Journal of Vocational Behavior, 42,* 68–83.

Ragins, B. R., & Sundstrom, E. (1989). Gender and power in organizations: A longitudinal perspective. *Psychological Bulletin, 105,* 51–88.

Reilly, J., & Lott, B. (1986). Sexual harassment of university students. *Sex Roles, 15,* 333–358.

Reilly, T., Carpenter, S., Dull, V., & Bartlett, K. (1982). The factorial survey technique: An approach to defining sexual harassment on campus. *Journal of Social Issues, 38,* 99–110.

Rossi, P. H., & Weber-Burden, E. (1993). Sexual harassment on the campus. *Social Science Research, 12,* 131–158.

Saal, F. E., Johnson, C. B., & Weber, N. (1989). Friendly or sexy? It may depend on whom you ask. *Psychology of Women Quarterly, 13,* 263–276.

Schacht, S. P., & Atchison, P. H. (1993). Heterosexual instrumentalism: Past and future directions. *Feminism and Psychology, 3,* 37–53.

Schneider, B. E. (1982). Consciousness about sexual harassment among heterosexual and lesbian women workers. *Journal of Social Issues, 38,* 75–98.

Schneider, B. E. (1991). Put up or shut up: Workplace sexual assault. *Gender and Society, 5,* 533–548.

Sheffey, S., & Tindale, R. S. (1992). Perceptions of sexual harassment in the workplace. *Journal of Applied Social Psychology, 22,* 1502–1520.

Smith, E. R., Feree, M. M., & Miller, F. (1975). A short scale of attitudes towards feminism. *Representative Research in Social Psychology, 6,* 51–56.

Sokoloff, N. J. (1980). *Between money and love: The dialectics of women's home and market work.* New York: Praeger.

Stewart, L. P., & Gundykunst, W. P. (1982). Differential factors influencing the hierarchial level and number of promotions of males and females within an organization. *Academy of Management Journal, 25,* 586–597.

Stockdale, J. E. (1991). Sexual harassment at work. In E. C. Viano (Ed.), *Critical issues in victimology: International perspectives.* New York: Springer.

Stockdale, M. (1993). The role of sexual misperceptions of women's friendliness in an emerging theory of sexual harassment. Special issue: Sexual harassment in the workplace. *Journal of Vocational Behavior, 42,* 84–101.

Studd, M. V., & Gattiker, U. E. (1991). The evolutionary psychology of sexual harassment in organizations. *Etiology and Sociobiology, 12,* 249–290.

Tangri, S., Burt, M., & Johnson, L. (1982). Sexual harassment at work: Three explanatory models. *Journal of Social Issues, 38(4),* 33–54.

Terpstra, D. E., & Baker, D. D. (1986a). Psychological and demographic correlates of perception of sexual harassment. *Genetic, Social and General Psychology Monographs, 112,* 459–478.

Terpstra, D. E., & Baker, D. D. (1986b). A framework for the study of sexual harassment. *Basic and Applied Social Psychology, 7,* 17–34.

U.S. Merit Systems Protection Board (USMSPB). (1981). *Sexual harassment in the federal workforce: Is it a problem?* Washington, DC: U.S. Government Printing Office.

Vaux, A. (1993). Paradigmatic assumptions in sexual harassment research: Being guided without being misled. Special issue: Sexual harassment in the workplace. *Journal of Vocational Behavior, 42,* 116–135.

Weitzman, L. J. (1979). *Sex role socialization: A focus on women.* Palo Alto, CA: Mayfield.

Wolf, W. C., & Fligsten, N. D. (1979). Sex and authority in the workplace. A policy-capturing approach. *Academy of Management Journal, 32,* 830–850.

Zalk, S. R. (1991). Men in the academy: A psychological profile of harassment. In M. A. Paludi (Ed.), *Ivory power: Sexual harassment on campus* (pp. 141-145). Albany, NY: SUNY.

# CHAPTER 8

# A TYPOLOGY OF SEXUAL HARASSMENT
## Characteristics of Harassers and the Social Circumstances under Which Sexual Harassment Occurs

John B. Pryor
Nora J. Whalen

Sexual harassment can be defined as unwelcome sexual behavior that significantly interferes with a recipient's work. The *American Heritage Dictionary* defines the verb *harass* as "to irritate or torment persistently." Thus *harassment* implies behavior that occurs repeatedly. While legal and policy analyses of sexual harassment recognize that single, isolated behaviors sometimes can have a negative impact on a recipient's work (EEOC, 1993), most often sexually harassing behavior occurs over time. For example, in a survey of over 20,000 military personnel, Martindale (1992) found that, with the exception of attempted rape or sexual assault, most recipients of sexual harassment reported having experienced such behavior more than once. Similarly, in a study of sexual harassment complaints investigated by the U.S. Air Force, Popovich (1988) found that 86% of the confirmed cases involved multiple incidents.

While legal definitions of sexual harassment are not gender-specific, in practice, sexual harassment is most often a problem experienced by working women. According to practically every survey to date on the subject, the most common perpetrator of sexual harassment is male and the most common recipient is female (cf. Culbertson et al., 1992; Culbertson, Rosenfeld, & Newel, 1993; Fitzgerald et al., 1988; Martindale, 1990; USMSPB, 1980, 1987). In this chapter we will examine a fundamental question about this often controversial phenomenon: Why do some men engage in persistent, unwelcome sexual behavior toward women in the workplace? Further, under what circumstances is such behavior likely to occur?

One basic assumption of our analyses is that both person and situational factors are important contributors to sexual harassment (Pryor, Giedd, & Williams, in press; Pryor, LaVite, & Stoller, 1993). Some men may have proclivities for certain types of sexual harassment. Various forms of sexually harassing behavior may be more likely to occur in some social situations than in others. Implied in these statements is the added assumption that sexual harassment is not a monolithic phenomenon. There are, no doubt, different forms of sexual harassment with different psychological and social antecedents. In this chapter we will develop a typology of sexual harassment based on an analysis of the social and psychological factors that can produce such behavior.

Within our typology we assume there are two general psychological functions that may be served by sexual harassment. First, sexual harassment can be an expression of sexual feelings. As we will see later, such feelings may be either invidious or relatively innocuous; however, the intent is nevertheless sexual. Second, sexual harassment can be an expression of hostility toward a recipient perceived as an outgroup member. Here the sexual nature of the behavior is secondary. As detailed later, other nonsexual forms of harassment are likely to co-occur when the behavior is of this type. Our typology further distinguishes two subtypes of sexual harassment with sexual intent: (1) sexual exploitation and (2) sexual attraction/miscommunication and two subtypes of sexual harassment with outgroup hostility intent: (3) misogyny, and (4) homo-anathema (our term for hostile attitudes and behaviors toward homosexuals). While there is empirical evidence to support the existence of each of these types of sexual harassment in the workplace, the first type, sexual exploitation, has been the subject of previous *Person X Situa-*

*tion* analyses (cf. Pryor, Giedd, & Williams, in press). Thus, our discussion will begin with this type of sexual harassment and use the analyses developed in the study of sexual exploitation as a model for subsequent analyses. We assume that person factors, such as those to be described with regard to sexual exploitation, constitute a proclivity or readiness for certain sexually harassing behaviors. However, research has led us to conclude that situational factors represent *necessary conditions* for such behaviors to occur repeatedly in the workplace. Thus, for each type of sexual harassment we will describe both the psychological factors that produce such unwelcome sexual behavior and the social or situational factors that facilitate its repeated occurrence.

## SEXUAL EXPLOITATION

Some accounts of sexual harassment cast the phenomenon wholly as an exertion of male power over women. For example, power is an important issue in the analyses of many feminist scholars who have written about sexual harassment. Along these lines, the National Council for Research on Women (1991) states the following "fact" about sexual harassment: "Sexual harassment is about power, not sex." One problem inherent in such sweeping generalizations is that they cast sexual harassment as a monolithic phenomenon. In contrast, our typology distinguishes different kinds of sexually harassing behavior with potentially different antecedents. Another problem with this particular generalization is that it does not recognize the possibility of sex and power having dual roles. Sometimes sexual harassment is about sex *and* power.

When one thinks of how interpersonal power functions in work settings, images of formal authority come to mind: the exploitive boss and the vulnerable underling. However, from a social psychological standpoint there are several different potential bases of power that could be relevant for understanding sexual harassment (Barak, Pitterman, & Yitzhaki, in press). *Organizational power* refers to the power that someone holds by virtue of the person's formal standing in some sort of organizational hierarchy. This is the boss–subordinate stereotype. Characteristics associated with higher status in society may also infuse someone with a sense of *status power* (Fain & Anderton, 1987). For example, men typically hold a higher status in society than women and thus sheer maleness may render a basis for power. In addition, men are typically stronger physically than women. Such *physical power* differences could serve to make men's actions seem threatening to women. *Situational power* is created by the interdependence that people sometimes develop in work situations. For example, people often depend on their coworkers for cooperation in getting a job done and for making work a congenial environment. Also, situational power can arise from privileged knowledge in certain social circumstances. For example, knowing that a coworker has been stealing from the company can endow the knower with certain power over the thief. Thus, as Cleveland and Kerst (1993) point out, the role of power in sexual harassment is not necessarily confined to organizational or authority power issues. It potentially encompasses all of these bases of power, which each provide some basis for leverage of one person over another. In other words, all provide the possibility of one person's will being imposed upon another. When this imposition involves sexual ends, we describe this as *sexual exploitation*.

Sexual exploitation is not only a factor in the business world; it is also a type of sexual harassment that can occur in the academic community as well. Although not always given the same attention as other social issues on college campuses (Barickman et al., 1990), sexual harassment is increasingly recognized as a problem that can importantly influence women's academic experiences (Benson & Thomson, 1982; Fitzgerald et al., 1988). *Ivory Power: Sexual Harassment on Campus* (Paludi, 1990) contains several compelling stories of students who have been sexually harassed in some way by their professors. These perpetrators of sexual harassment differ in their personalities and use different ways of getting access to their victims. Dziech and

Weiner (1984) developed a typology of some different types of sexual harassers in academia. They discuss the counselor/helper type, the confidante, the intellectual seducer, the opportunist, and the power broker. Zalk (1990) contends that while these types of sexual harassers use different means to achieve their goals, the basic cornerstone upon which their motivation lies is power and the denial of power. The professors have it and the students do not. Some of the professorial perpetrators of sexual harassment wield their power like a club, using blatant quid pro quo demands on their students, while others are more subtle in their abuse of power for sexual ends. The professor–student relationship is analogous to the relationships described here as examples of organizational power in business settings. Some researchers (e.g., McKinney, 1992) have begun to explore how other power relationships are also evident in the sexual harassment found in academic settings.

Our conception of sexual exploitation involves the dual roles of sex and power. Men who have a tendency for sexual exploitation may see some inherent connection between sexuality and the use of power. In other words, some men may possess a readiness to use power for sexually exploitive ends. Across an extensive series of studies, Pryor and his colleagues examined the hypothesis that a proclivity for sexual exploitation may be one psychological factor underlying some forms of sexual harassment. These studies began with the development of the Likelihood to Sexually Harass (LSH) scale (Pryor, 1987). In the LSH scale, men are asked to imagine themselves in 10 different social situations in which they have opportunities to sexually exploit women with relative impunity. In each scenario, men are asked to rate the likelihood of their using power for sexual gain. Although the term "sexual harassment" never appears in the LSH, respondents' ratings essentially represent the likelihood of their performing acts of quid pro quo sexual harassment. Here is an example scenario from the LSH:

> Imagine that you are the owner of a modeling agency. Your agency specializes in sexy female models used in television commer-

cials. One of your models, Amy T., is a particularly ravishing brunette. You stop her after work one day and ask her to have dinner with you. She coldly declines your offer and tells you that she would like to keep your relationship with her "strictly business." A few months later you find that business is slack and you have to lay off some of your employees. You can choose to lay off Amy or one of four other women. All are good models, but someone has to go. How likely are you to do the following things in this situation?

The key item for this scenario is: "Assuming that you are unafraid of possible reprisals, would you offer to let Amy keep her job in return for sexual favors?" Respondents are asked to rate the likelihood of their performing this behavior on a 1–5 scale where 1 is labeled "not at all likely" and 5 is labeled "very likely."

Across a series of studies the LSH has consistently demonstrated high reliability, with coefficient alphas around .90. Pryor, Giedd, and Williams (in press) summarized the findings from studies that examined the correlations between the LSH and other established self-report scales. These can be divided into three categories: (1) scales related to sexual violence, (2) scales related to gender roles, and (3) scales related to sexual behavior. This research shows that men who score high in LSH tend to score high on measures related to proclivities for sexual violence like the Rape Myth Acceptance Scale (Burt, 1980) and the Attraction to Sexual Aggression Scale (Malamuth, 1989). With regard to gender roles, high-LSH men tend to identify with hypermasculine stereotypes, scoring high on such measures as the antifemininity, desire for status, and toughness subscales from the Brannon and Junni (1984) scale of stereotypic masculinity. Finally, high-LSH men have been found to describe their own sexual behavior as motivated by a desire for dominance, scoring high on the dominance subscale of the Nelson (1979) Functions of Sexuality Inventory (Pryor & Stoller, 1994).

Two key studies have examined the social cognitive processes characteristic of how high-LSH men view sexuality. First, using an illusory correlation methodology, Pryor and Stoller (1994) found that ideas of social power and sexuality are cognitively linked in men who score high in LSH. In this study, subjects were asked to remember pairs of words that were projected sequentially onto a screen. Among these were words relating to sexuality (e.g., "intercourse"), words relating to social dominance (e.g., "authority") and control words that did not relate to either of these two concepts, with equal pairings of all of the different types of words. Afterwards subjects were asked to estimate the number of times they saw each specific pair of words. Men who scored higher in LSH tended to report that they saw sexuality words paired with dominance words more often than men who scored lower on the LSH. Furthermore, high-LSH men rated greater confidence in their estimates of dominance/sexuality pairs than low-LSH men. Phi analyses of the frequency estimates (modeled after Hamilton & Gifford, 1976) indicate that high-LSH men tended to detect an illusory correlation between dominance and sexuality words. This study demonstrates that high-LSH men tend to cognitively link concepts of sexuality and power.

Further evidence of this link can be seen in a study by Bargh et al. (in press). In this research, prime words were presented below the threshold of conscious awareness (90 ms) to subjects on a computer screen, followed by a brief visual mask. Subsequently subjects were asked to pronounce target words presented on the same screen. When high-LSH men were primed with words concerning power (e.g., "boss"), they were faster in pronouncing sexuality words (e.g., "bed"). Sexuality words also served to prime power words for high-LSH men. Low-LSH men did not evidence these priming effects. This research demonstrated that thoughts of power can trigger ideas of sexuality relatively automatically for men who score high on the LSH scale.

Three studies have demonstrated that high-LSH men behave in a sexually harassing way in certain social situations (Pryor, 1987; Pryor, LaVite, & Stoller, 1993; Pryor, Giedd,

& Williams, in press). In Pryor, LaVite, and Stoller (1993), college men were given a position of authority over a female confederate. They were asked to teach her a word-processing task on a computer and to evaluate her performance. Half of the men were exposed to a harassing role model. In this condition a graduate student who served as the experimenter treated the confederate trainee in a sexist and sexually harassing manner. The other half of the men were exposed to a professional role model. In this condition the graduate student treated the trainee in a courteous and friendly manner. In both conditions the graduate student role model was essentially an authority figure whose function was to define the local social norms for interaction in the experimental situation. Half the men in each condition were preselected by high scores on the LSH and half with low scores (upper and lower quartiles were used). Results indicated that high-LSH men tended to emulate the behavior of the harassing role model. Low-LSH men treated the confederate professionally even in the harassing role model condition. Neither the high- nor the low-LSH men tended to sexually harass in the professional role model condition.

In addition to providing evidence for the behavioral validity of the LSH, the Pryor, LaVite, and Stoller (1993) study demonstrates the importance of situational factors in predicting sexual harassment. High-LSH men only seemed to act upon their proclivities for sexual harassment when the local social norms condoned or permitted such behavior. Research by Pryor, Giedd, and Williams (in press) showed that social norms permitting sexual harassment also can develop in cohesive groups of peers as well as emanating from authority figures. Pryor, Giedd, and Williams (in press) found that high-LSH men who witnessed their male peers sexually harass a female confederate tended to follow suit. They tended to harass her as well. Sexual harassment was measured by the verbal and physical behaviors of these men toward the confederate, for example, the degree to which without invitation they spoke in a sexual way and

touched the confederate sexually. The relative cohesion of the groups of men was an important mediator of this behavior. The behavioral contagion of sexually harassing behavior tended to happen only when groups of high-LSH were made to feel some sense of group cohesion.

Both of these studies demonstrate that exposure to another man who sexually harasses can influence the behavior of men who already have a proclivity for sexual harassment. One way to understand this phenomenon is through a normative influence analysis. *Norms* can be defined as agreed-on informal rules that guide behaviors (Greenberg & Baron, 1995). Cialdini, Reno, and Kallgren (1990) suggest that norms have both descriptive and injunctive functions. Observations of others' behaviors tell us what is typical or normal in a social situation—what everybody else is doing. This is the descriptive function. Observations of others' behaviors also tell us what is morally approved or disapproved conduct—what we should or should not do. This is the injunctive function. Cialdini, Reno, and Kallgren suggest that norms primarily guide behaviors when they are activated or made salient. Thus, the function of a model may be to make salient pro or anti sexual harassment norms. We speculate that exposure to a harassing model could influence the perception of both descriptive and injunctive norms—everybody's doing it and it's okay to do it. The exposure to a professional or nonharassing model could similarly evoke both descriptive and injunctive norms.

People's perceptions of social norms are known to be important determinants of a wide variety of social behaviors (Ajzen & Fishbein, 1980). In this context it is not surprising that sexually exploitive behaviors also should be related to social norms. Using a diverse sample of Canadian college men, community male volunteers, and male sex offenders, Denton (1993) found that LSH scores, ratings of the appeal of sexual harassing behaviors, the frequency of contemplating sexually harassing behaviors, and self-reports of having actually performed acts like those depicted in the LSH were correlated with men's estimates of the extent to which other men would make similar ratings. While correlation findings like this give rise to alternative causal interpretations, they further attest to a connection between this form of sexual harassment and the perception of social norms.

To summarize, sexual exploitation is a form of sexual harassment in which some form of social power is used for sexual gain. Sexual gain can be broadly defined as some sort of sexual access to another person. It does not necessarily have to be sexual intercourse. Any behavior that results in some kind of sexual gratification may qualify as resulting in sexual gain. The studies by Pryor and his colleagues demonstrate that some men possess a readiness to use power for sexual gain. However, these proclivities are more likely to be manifested in actual behavior in some social situations than in others. So, it cannot be assumed that sexual exploitation is solely the result of deviant personality tendencies. Men who want to sexually exploit do so when the circumstances or local social norms permit such behavior. Such behavior seems unlikely to occur when the social situation is not ripe for sexual exploitation and does not provide support for sexual exploitation (Pryor, Giedd, & Williams, in press). We speculate that for sexual exploitation to occur repeatedly, facilitative local norms *must* exist. We base this assertion on the commonsense notion that most forms of exploitation are generally viewed as socially unacceptable behavior and seem likely to occur only when the would-be exploiter believes he can get away with them.

## SEXUAL ATTRACTION/ MISCOMMUNICATION

In the preceding section we argued that the desire to sexually exploit is one factor that may produce unwelcome sexual behavior in the workplace. In addition, social norms permitting or condoning such behavior make it more likely to occur. Not all unwelcome sexual behavior need be motivated by a desire to sexually exploit. A variety of other motives could also be behind such behavior. Reports of sex-

ual harassment victims give support to this idea. In a recent survey of over 2,600 employees from a government agency, Pryor (1994) found that 46% of the women in the survey claimed to have been subjected to unwelcome sexual behavior at work in the last two years. Women who were sexually harassed were asked why they were bothered by the unwelcome sexual behavior they had experienced in their most recent or significant episode. Only 26% reported that they were bothered because the perpetrators were trying to exploit power over them. So, almost three-fourths of women who were recipients of unwelcome sexual behavior were not concerned with sexual exploitation.

In this survey the three most commonly endorsed reasons for women being bothered by sexual behavior at work were: (1) "The behaviors I observed were unprofessional" (75%), (2) "The individual(s) involved was insensitive to my feelings" (61%), and (3) "I was not attracted to the person" (55%). In being bothered by unprofessional behaviors, women seem to be suggesting that they hold certain expectations about the appropriateness of social sexual behavior for people in work roles. Perhaps women expect men and women at work to treat each other as coworkers, not as potential mates or sex partners (cf. Gutek, 1985). Of course, norms about professionalism could entail a variety of social sexual behaviors (e.g., the appropriateness of sexual "horseplay," telling sexual jokes, displays of sexual materials, etc.). The two other reasons, insensitivity on the part of the perpetrator and not being attracted to the perpetrator, suggest a possible breakdown in communication between the perpetrator of the unwelcome sexual behavior and the recipient. The perpetrator fails to grasp that the behavior is unwelcome or that such behavior might be welcome from someone else, but not this perpetrator.

Several years ago Brewer (1982) speculated that sometimes sexual harassment could be the result of insensitive or awkward sexual advances from men with intentions of establishing sexual relationships with women at work. Sometimes such inept overtures may be terminated after women openly express their lack of mutual interest. However, if the simple strategy of just saying "no" were always effective, then this form of sexual harassment would present substantially fewer problems for working women. Unfortunately, the perpetrators of this form of sexual harassment sometimes do not seem to take "no" for an answer even when they have been continually rebuffed in no uncertain terms.

The case of *Ellison v. Brady* (1992) provides a vivid example of this extreme. As an agent for the Internal Revenue Service in San Mateo, California in the mid-1980s, Kerry Ellison was continually bothered by a fellow agent who attempted to establish a romantic relationship with her. Although Ellison made her rejection of these advances abundantly clear, her would-be suitor (a married man 14 years her senior) persisted. Ellison's male supervisors dismissed her complaints about these behaviors as exaggerated. An incident that finally resulted in Ellison's filing a petition with the EEOC involved the harasser's tracking her down when she was on a business trip in St. Louis. Although few people knew her whereabouts, a three-page letter from her harasser was waiting for her when she arrived in her hotel room. While the EEOC initially rejected Ellison's petition, the Ninth U.S. Circuit Court of Appeals in San Francisco ruled that a "reasonable woman" could view such letters differently than a man would and feel threatened by them. This case helped set a new gender-conscious standard in sexual harassment cases ("When love letters become hated mail," 1991).

Stockdale (1993) suggests that one factor that contributes to men's persistence in unwelcome sexual behavior may be the tendency of many men to misperceive women's friendliness as conveying sexual intent. Based upon original research by Abbey (1982), numerous studies have found that men tend to rate women as trying to behave more sexually than women rate themselves or other women rate them (Saal, Johnson, & Weber, 1989; Shotland & Craig, 1988). In studies of naturally occurring misperceptions, Abbey (1987)

found that 72% of college women had experienced incidents in which their intentions had been misperceived by men to be sexual. In over 70% of these incidents the misunderstood women did something to overtly signal that misperception had occurred. For example, half simply told the misperceiver they were not interested. Interestingly, only 24% of the misperceivers were reported as reacting with understanding. Twenty-six percent "kept trying" and 30% were angry or upset.

Abbey's (1982) original misperception study involved ratings made of college women and men in casual get-acquainted interactions. Subsequent work by Saal, Johnson, and Weber (1989) extended this to videotaped interactions of women and men in working roles. Shotland and Craig (1988) point out that the crux of this misperception phenomenon is that men tend to rate many social behaviors of both men and women as having more sexual intent than women rate them. It is not that men just rate *women's* behaviors as implying more sexual intent. This finding seems consistent with trends seen in a recent national survey in which men were almost three times more likely than women to report that they they think about sex every day or several times a day (54% vs. 19%) (Michael et al., 1994). Perhaps many men see sex in numerous places because they often have sex on their minds. Such behaviors as eye contact, standing or sitting close, touching, wearing revealing clothing, and using alcohol are all more likely to be interpreted as implying sexual availability by men than by women (Stockdale, 1993). Stockdale, Dewey, and Saal (1992) found that the tendency to view friendly behavior as sexy behavior was correlated with measures of traditional sex-role orientation, greater tolerance for sexual harassment, and beliefs that women generally display sexual interest by acting friendly.

Work by Shotland (1989, 1992) has suggested that misperceptions about sexual intent may contribute to some forms of courtship rape. Research by McDonel and McFall (1991) found that men with deficits in the ability to interpret or decode women's affective cues tend to perceive more justification for persistence in sexual advances when women resist. Similar heterosocial decoding deficits have been found to be higher in samples of incarcerated rapists than in nonrapist comparison groups (Lipton, McDonel, & McFall, 1987). Murphy, Coleman, and Haynes (1986) found that men's rape-supportive attitudes were correlated with less ability to distinguish between friendliness and seductiveness and between assertiveness and hostility in videotapes of a man and a woman interacting in a bar. This research points to some possible individual differences in social skills that also may contribute to misperceptions leading to sexual harassment.

One personality construct that has been related to social skill or the ability to interpret interpersonal cues is *self-monitoring* (Snyder, 1987). Research has indicated that high self-monitors have a more extensive knowledge base than low self-monitors about other people and the sort of behavior others will usually exhibit in a given situation (Snyder & Cantor, 1980). Furthermore, high self-monitors tend to form impressions of others they meet more quickly than low self-monitors (Berscheid et al., 1976). In heterosexual interactions, high self-monitors tend to speak first, initiate subsequent conversation, tailor their behavior to their partners, and be more directive in guiding the interaction than low self-monitors (Ickes & Barnes, 1977). Finally, there is evidence that high self-monitors tend to have more extensive sexual experience than low self-monitors (Snyder, Simpson, & Gangstead, 1986). Due to their social assertiveness, high self-monitors have had more opportunities to meet others and typically have a larger pool of potential sexual partners. While research has yet to explore the possible connections of this construct to sexual harassment, some research has begun to examine possible connections of self-monitoring to heterosocial misperception. For example, Harnish, Abbey, and DeBono (1990) examined the relationship of self-monitoring to inferences of sexual intent made in get-acquainted interactions between men and women like those studied by Abbey in 1982. While men who were high self-monitors tended to rate themselves as behaving more flirtatiously and seductively

than men low in self-monitoring, they did not rate their female partners' behavior as having more or less sexual intent than did low self-monitors. An important issue for sexual harassment research unexamined by this study is whether self-monitoring might relate to sensitivity in interpreting negative cues. Of course, post hoc decoding of interpersonal cues represents only part of the social skills that are potentially relevant for avoiding sexual harassment. Anticipating how people are likely to react to specific sexual advances in different social situations is perhaps even more important. Given the connection of self-monitoring to heterosocial experience, future research might find that high-monitoring men are more likely to recognize and avoid making unwelcome sexual advances.

Consistent with this individual difference analysis, Stewart (1982) has suggested a possible distinction between *nonsexist* (naive) and *sexist* sexual harassers. According to this analysis, nonsexist sexual harassers do not commit their offenses out of prejudice or hatred of women, nor do they necessarily feel that women should be sexually subservient to men. Instead, the harassment is committed out of ignorance or social pressure. Stewart suggested that the way to intervene with these harassers is either by making them aware of the fact that they are committing sexual harassment or by eliminating the functional value of the harassment—that is, by reducing the reinforcement they are receiving from their peers for the actions.

Obviously, more research is needed to explore the person factors or individual differences that contribute to this form of sexual harassment. Situational factors may also contribute to the sexual attraction/miscommunication form of sexual harassment. Gutek (1985) and others (Haavio-Mannila, Kaupinen-Toropainen, & Kandolin, 1988) have found that sexual harassment is more likely to occur in highly sexualized work environments. To state this another way, in environments where other nonharassing sexual behaviors are more common, sexual harassment is more common too. A highly sexualized environment potentially creates confusion about the separation of work life and private life. In extreme situations, work and gender roles may blend into unity. It is in such situations that the socially unskilled probably commit many acts of sexual harassment (Gutek, 1985). When work life becomes intermingled with private life, eventually the sexual harasser cannot tell the difference, and since he cannot readily detect the romantic disinterest of another, some women are subjected to repeated unwanted overtures. Workplaces that harbor a nonprofessional atmosphere in which men and women dress and act in sexually provocative ways could unintentionally contribute to sexual miscommunication. If there is an abundance of sexual offers transpiring among the workers, sheer numbers would indicate that some of those offers will be unwelcome. The socially unskilled man has difficulty in differentiating welcome from unwelcome sexual advances and will thus persists until his behavior becomes harassing.

In sum, sexual attraction coupled with miscommunication is a combination that could lead to sexual harassment. Unlike exploitive sexual harassers, the harassers of this type are typically men possessing no coercive or exploitive intentions. However, they persist in expressing attraction for another without the social skills to understand when this attraction is not reciprocated. As with all the sexual harassers within our typology, situational factors are critical to the undertaking of sexual harassment by these perpetrators. Some environments compound the problem and some alleviate it. It is vitally important, however, that the men who commit these transgressions not be lumped together with other sexual harassers. The reasons for their behavior and, as we will see later, the potential interventions that might alleviate it are different.

## MISOGYNY

One of the most common forms of sexual harassment is what Fitzgerald and her colleagues term *gender harassment* (Fitzgerald & Hesson-McInnis, 1989; Fitzgerald, Hulin, & Drasgow, in press; Fitzgerald, Swan, & Fischer, in press; Fitzgerald et al., 1988). Gelfand, Fitzgerald, and Drasgow (in press)

suggest: "This category encompasses a wide range of verbal and nonverbal behaviors not aimed at sexual cooperation; rather, they convey insulting, hostile, and degrading attitudes about women" (p. 8). When such behaviors are so pervasive as to alter the working conditions of women, they fall under the legal category of what the EEOC (1993) terms hostile environment sexual harassment (cf. *Robinson v. Jacksonville Shipyards*, 1991). Common examples of this kind of sexual harassment include the public distribution or display of pornographic materials demeaning to women; sexual epithets, slurs, gestures, or taunts aimed at offending women; and gender-based hazing. Like sexual exploitation, the expression of misogyny or hostility toward women in the workplace may be strongly influenced by local social norms or work group climate. Recent research by Zickar (1994) found that the incidence of gender harassment was higher in work groups in which there was a general perception of organizational tolerance toward sexual harassment.

While working as a consultant in a governmental organization, the first author came upon an example of gender-based hazing that exemplifies some essential qualities of this kind of harassment. New female workers in a predominantly male office were given a computer disk on their first day of work and told to insert it into a computer that occupied a work carrel for a tutorial. When inserted into the computer, the program on the disk produced a loud orgasmic sound and a feminine voice exclaimed, "Oh-h-h-h, that's a big one." Men from the office were huddled around the periphery of the carrel observing the reactions of the unsuspecting female and laughing. One social psychological function of this sophomoric prank seemed to be to reinforce the *ingroup identification* of the male workers. In addition, this initiation ceremony marked the female's status as an outsider to the all-male club.

According to *social identity theory* (Tajfel & Turner, 1987), even arbitrary interpersonal differences can result in the categorization of people into ingroups and outgroups. Research has shown that outgroup members are rewarded less, perceived to have fewer positive attributes, and perceived to be more homogeneous than ingroup members (Brewer, 1979; Gaertner et al., 1989; Hamilton & Sherman, 1994; Judd & Park, 1988; Linville, Fischer, & Salovey, 1989; Quatrone & Jones, 1980). Turner et al. (1987) argue that ingroup favoritism is the result of people defining themselves and their self-esteem in relation to their ingroup associates. Dovidio and Gaertner (1993) maintain that ingroup-outgroup categorizations may automatically activate evaluational structures that can influence expectations about and perceptions of group members. In their research, subliminal priming with terms like "we" and "they" influenced people's expectations of how pleasant interactions with unknown target persons would be. So, even subtle cognitive factors that increase the probability of categorizing someone as an outgroup member can lead to devaluation.

We suggest that certain situational and person factors can increase the probability of using gender as a categorical schema. In other words, these factors can increase the likelihood of men thinking of their female coworkers in we/they terms. When women are categorized by men as an outgroup, conditions are ripe for the form of sexual harassment we term *misogyny*. One factor that has been found to encourage the use of gender-based categorizations is the token status of women (Kanter, 1977; Taylor et al., 1977). When women are solo members of a work group or in a numeric minority, their gender is particularly salient. In other words, they stand out as *the women* of the group. This enhances the use of gender-based categorizations and can lead to exaggerated and often stereotypical evaluations of their characteristics. Such reactions seem particularly likely when women have jobs in "typically" male professions and are in the minority. Consistent with this analysis, Rosenberg, Perlstadt, and Phillips (1993) found that female lawyers who held "token" positions in a workplace and women who worked in a solo practice were more often the victims of discrimination and harassment.

While the numeric infrequency of women would seem sufficient to invoke gender-based categorizations, additional factors may contribute to the intensity of negative affect felt for women as an outgroup. Gruber and his colleagues (Gruber & Smith, in press; Gruber & Bjorn, 1985) suggest that women may be more likely to experience sexual harassment in workplaces where they represent a "threatening minority" (i.e., less than half, but more than just a token few). In other words, when women are perceived as on the verge of taking over numeric dominance in a workplace, male workers may react with hostility or harassment. Research has found that perceived competition for limited resources often enhances the hostility expressed to outgroup members (Sherif et al., 1961).

Research by Bem (1986) has found that some people may manifest a greater readiness to use gender as a basis of categorization than others. For example, both men and women who are more traditional in their sex-role orientations seem to readily divide the social world into male and female categories and to view the self as strongly associated with maleness or femaleness, respectively. Such a readiness to categorize by gender would seem to facilitate men's viewing women in a we/they framework. However, gender-based harassment would seem to additionally imply a strong negative attitude associated with the category of women.

A variety of individual difference scales have been developed to assess misogynist or sexist attitudes. Some earlier examples include the Attitudes Toward Women Scale (Spence, Helmreich, & Stapp, 1974) and the FEM Scale (Smith, Feree, & Miller, 1975). Recent research by Swim and her colleagues (Swim et al., in press) has developed a scale to measure "Modern Sexism" as contrasted to "Old-Fashioned Sexism" in a way parallel to recent efforts in measuring modern and old-fashioned racism (McConahay, 1986; Sears, 1988). Paralleling problems in assessing racism, Swim and her colleagues suggest that more sensitive measures are needed to assess sexism in contemporary society because people are reluctant to admit to openly sexist opinions. The Modern Sexism (MS) scale measures three constructs: denial of continuing discrimination, antagonism toward women's demands, and resentment about special favors for women. Higher MS scores are correlated with overestimation of the percentage of women in male-dominated occupations. More-sexist MS scores also are correlated with higher ratings of the importance of biological factors, lower ratings for socialization factors, and lower ratings for discrimination factors as reasons for sex segregation in the work force. Measures like the MS scale seem to hold promise for predicting men's reactions toward women as an acrimonious outgroup. Further measures of sexism are being developed that also take into consideration people's reluctance to admit such attitudes (Glick & Fiske, 1994).

Hostile reactions to women as an outgroup often involve nonsexual as well as sexual harassment. For example, in an ethnographic study of the experiences of female coal miners, Yount (1991) described a general pattern of abuse, harassment, and exclusion. The male coal miners, by their own admission, treated these women as outsiders. These men purposely tried to make it hard for the women to remain on the job because they did not feel that the women were up to the work, and they resented their presence. In the short time that Yount was doing her study, several women quit and one had to be treated for emotional distress due to a very malicious form of harassment by the male miners. (She was stripped and smeared with grease.) To deal with the difficult situation in the mine, these female coal miners took on different roles in interacting with the men. Some of the women accepted their roles as outsiders and tried to distance themselves from the men as "ladies." Others tried to play along with the constant sexual banter by flirting with the men. Still others sought acceptance by assuming the role of "tomboy." The tomboys tried to become "one of the guys" by participating in male activities and being just as crude and harassing as the men in the mine. While these women seemed to feel that acting in this way

made the men respect them more, when the men were interviewed, they claimed to harbor the same resentment toward these women. There were times when the men felt that the tomboys crossed the line in their counter harassment of the men. When this occurred, the men felt it was necessary to put the woman "back in her place" and make certain that she understood that she was still just a woman and, therefore, an outsider.

There seem to be two general patterns characteristic of how women respond to holding an outsider status in the workplace. They either seek accommodation or they try to assimilate. Accommodation implies some sort of acceptance of women as distinct from men. Interestingly, the female coal miners who sought to be treated as "ladies" were attempting this strategy. Accommodation also could be a strategy that recognizes the unique problems faced by women in the workplace. In some very male-dominated workplaces, accommodation strategies may be easier and evoke less hostility than assimilation strategies. When female lawyers were studied (Rosenberg, Perlstadt, & Phillips, 1993), it was discovered that women who were labeled as having a more "feminist" orientation were less likely to be sexually harassed than those women who were labeled as having a "careerist" orientation. The women with a feminist orientation were those women who made a point of supporting women's causes and voting for public officials who support women's causes and who, in general, were very open in their acknowledgment of the handicaps women face in the workplace. Careerist women, on the other hand, were those who were reluctant to admit there is sexism at work. They felt that they would be assessed based on their value as a lawyer and they would not be the victims of discrimination in the workplace.

Why would women who possess a careerist orientation be more likely to suffer from sexual harassment? Rosenberg, Perlstadt, and Phillips suggest that perhaps male lawyers felt that careerist women had more to lose by reporting the sexual harassment, especially because they were so reticent to vocalize opinions on workplace sexism. Therefore, the men may have felt more freedom in harassing these women because they felt safe in the knowledge that these women probably would not report them. Men may have been less likely to harass the women who had the feminist orientation because they felt that these women would not hesitate to report the harassment and take a stand on the issue. It is also possible that these men experienced more threat from the women who ignored the sex differences in the workplace and just concentrated on their careers as lawyers, not as female lawyers. Perhaps these men resented the fact that careerist women not only saw themselves as equal to the men, but also disregarded suggestions that inequalities do exist. When the potential sexual harasser saw this behavior, he could have felt the need to assert the fact that there are differences in the workplace and acting as if men and women have equal footing in the corporation in question does not negate these differences.

In summary, *misogyny* in our typology refers to reactions to women as an outgroup. A Person X Situation analysis suggests that men who hold sexist opinions or who readily divide the social world into male and female categories are more likely to manifest hostility toward women in the workplace. This form of sexual harassment is typically part of a larger pattern of outgroup hostility. In workplaces or occupations traditionally dominated by men, women are more likely to stand out and be perceived as a threatening outgroup. In such workplaces, women are particularly likely to be subjected to sexual harassment. As we will see in the next section, other sex-relevant characteristics may also serve as a basis for ingroup/outgroup distinctions.

## HOMO-ANATHEMA

Both men and women may be targeted for sexual harassment because they are assumed to be homosexual. Accusations of homosexuality also may be used to harass heterosexuals. *Homo-anathema*, the reaction to homosexuals as a hated and feared outgroup, begins early in American socialization. In a survey of 1,632 public school students from grades 8–11 conducted by the American Association of University Women (1993), respondents were asked their reactions to 14 different types of sexual harassment. None provoked as strong a negative reaction in boys as being called "gay." Eighty-five percent of the boys said they would be "very upset" by such harassment. Although other kinds of sexual harassment also were upsetting to girls, they too were deeply bothered by this kind of harassment. Eighty-seven percent said that they would be "very upset" at being accused of being a lesbian. Twenty-three percent of the boys and 10% of the girls surveyed said that they had actually experienced such harassment.

Research from a number of large-scale surveys documents the scope of sexual harassment based upon sexual orientation as a social problem. For example, a survey conducted by the National Gay and Lesbian Task Force in 1986 (described in Herek, 1989) found that 20% of gay men and lesbians reported that they had been victims of sexual harassment. Eighty-six percent also reported they had been the victims of verbal abuse, although it is not clear whether this abuse happened in work contexts. Most of the perpetrators of these acts seem to be men (Herek & Berrill, 1992).

There are several indications in the sexual harassment literature that male-to-male sexual harassment may be a relatively common problem for working men. For example, in the 1980 survey of federal workers conducted by the U.S. Merit Systems Protection Board (1981), 42% of the women and 15% of the men reported having experienced sexual harassment in a two-year period. While only 3% of the women who were harassed reported having experienced harassment from females, 22% of the men who were harassed reported having experienced harassment from males. Male-to-male sexual harassment may be even more common in male-dominated work contexts. In a 1988 Department of Defense (DoD) survey of active-duty military personnel, approximately 64% of the women and 17% of the men reported having experienced sexual harassment from someone at work during the last year (Martindale, 1992). About 3% of the women and 37% of the men who reported sexual harassment in the DoD survey described incidents involving perpetrators of their own gender. Similarly, a Navy-wide survey conducted in 1989 found that 0.5% of the women and 40% of the men had experienced same-gender harassment (Culbertson et al., 1992). The most common experience reported by men who were harassed by other men in the DoD survey was "sexual teasing, jokes, remarks, or questions." More than 70% reported this form of harassment, which seems typical of the sort often perpetrated on homosexuals (or those suspected of being homosexuals) by heterosexuals (Herek, 1989).

While women are not often targeted for harassment by their female peers, it seems reasonable to assume that some portion of the male-to-female sexual harassment reported in surveys like those conducted by the MSPB and the DoD reflect men harassing women they suspect or simply accuse of being homosexual (see Herek & Berrill, 1992, for examples of this form of sexual harassment). Several strands of evidence point to this conclusion especially in the military context. For example, retired Air Force general Jeanne M. Holm once observed: "The military lives by all these shibboleths. One of the ways the culture has kept women in their place is to say that anyone who'd join is either a nympho or a lesbian" (Boodman, 1980, p. A6). Consistent with Gen. Holm's observation, a 1987 report from the Defense Advisory Committee on Women in the Services (DACOWITS) noted that the female barracks in naval installations inspected by DACOWITS were often referred to by military men as "Lessy Land" (Davis, 1987). Military women who participated in focus groups on the issue of homosexuality in the military conducted by the National Defense Research Institute (1993) described how this nympho-or-lesbian stereotype often puts military women in a no-win situation. If they experience unwanted sexual advances from their male coworkers and refuse, they risk being accused of homosexuality. Thus,

the stigma of the outgroup label "homosexual" is often used as a weapon to harass both lesbian and straight women.

Other evidence that women who are perceived to be lesbian may be targeted for sexual harassment from males comes from research by Schneider (1982). Schneider surveyed 192 lesbian and 121 heterosexual women about their experiences of sexual behaviors in the workplace. Lesbians were more likely to report that they had been the targets of jokes about their appearance, asked for dates, pinched or grabbed, and sexually propositioned at work than heterosexual women. In this study, 83% of lesbians and 69% of heterosexual women reported having experienced at least one of these incidents at work. Although lesbians occasionally reported harassment from other women, the vast majority of the perpetrators of these acts were men. Lesbians also were more likely than heterosexual women to report that they had been targeted for actual or attempted sexual assault at work. Harassment of lesbians was over four times more common in male-dominated workplaces ($\geq 80\%$ men) than in female-dominated workplaces ($\geq 80\%$ women). In summary, sexual harassment based on sexual orientation seems to be a pervasive problem in the American workplace.

Despite the apparent ubiquity of sexual harassment based on sexual orientation, discrimination based on sexual orientation is not prohibited by the 1964 Civil Rights Act. Thus, sexual harassment related to sexual orientation is not subject to the same legal sanctions as sexual harassment linked to gender-based discrimination in federal law. However, some protection from this sort of harassment is afforded by certain state and local statutes. Nine states, beginning with Wisconsin in 1982, have passed gay and lesbian rights legislation forbidding employment discrimination. However, many such ordinances cover only public-sector employment. More than 120 municipalities have passed similar ordinances (National Defense Research Institute, 1993). In 1975 the U.S. Civil Service Commission dropped its long-standing policy of not hiring homosexual people for government jobs (Byer & Shainberg, 1994). The Civil Service Reform Act of 1978 prohibits discrimination for or against any employee on the basis of conduct that does not adversely affect the performance of the employee or applicant or the performances of others. Notwithstanding this, homosexual orientation is still used as a criterion in judging whether people are eligible for security clearances in many federal jobs (Herek, 1990b). Homosexuals are considered a security risk because of their supposed vulnerability to blackmail. The current policy in the U.S. military is "don't ask, don't tell." While homosexual conduct is still prohibited under a DoD directive of 1981, gay men and lesbians are accepted by the military provided they remain closeted about their sexual orientation. Officers are expected not to pry. As of 1992, 23 states had sodomy laws prohibiting homosexual intercourse. Of these states, 6 had laws that pertain only to homosexual sodomy. Interestingly, in two states (Massachusetts and Minnesota) such sodomy laws remain on the books even though state law also bans discrimination on the basis of sexual orientation (National Defense Research Institute, 1993).

Our Person X Situation analysis of sexual harassment suggests that social norms contribute importantly to all forms of sexual harassment. The varying legal status of antihomosexual discrimination across American life is one aspect of this normative climate. According to Herek (1990a), the legal status of homosexuality in the United States reflects a general "heterosexist" ideology in American society. American culture supports an ideological system that disowns, denigrates, and stigmatizes any nonheterosexual form of behavior, identity, relationship, or community. Organized religion in the United States, Herek points out, has all but completely denounced homosexuality. The law has not protected homosexual citizens the way it would protect any other victimized group. Finally, the media have added to the negative stigma attached to homosexuality through biased portrayals of gay men and lesbians.

Despite the widespread heterosexism in American culture, without doubt local social norms regarding the acceptability of expressing homo-anathema vary widely. A fascinating study of how prejudice and harassment based on sexual orientation vary across different social milieus in the United States was reported by the National Defense Research Institute (1993). This study examined police and fire departments across six major urban centers that varied widely in employment policies about homosexuals. At one end of the continuum, most municipalities studied had some sort of nondiscrimination policy; some of the police departments even actively recruited homosexuals (in Seattle and New York City). At the other end of the continuum were municipalities where there was no official antidiscrimination policy at the time of the study and sometimes open antagonism toward homosexuals. For example, in Houston until 1990 there had been aggressive attempts to screen homosexuals out of the police department. Adding to the antihomosexual climate in Houston, Texas is also a state with a relatively strong homosexual sodomy law.

Variations in the fear of potential harassment clearly were related to these municipal departments' policies on nondiscrimination in the National Defense Research Institute study (1993). While most homosexual respondents kept their sexual orientation private, more people were found to openly declare their sexual orientation in departments that assertively pursued a policy of nondiscrimination than those "characterized by pervasive hostility or benign neglect" (pp.124–125). Some of the most serious instances of harassment and abuse occurred in situations in which a homosexual had been "outed" by others, in other words, where the person's sexual orientation had become public knowledge through others' malicious revelations. In this study, differences also were found between the police and fire departments in almost all cities. Police departments generally evidenced more tolerance than fire departments. The researchers attributed these differences to the strong pressures toward conformity associated with firehouse culture and to the political pressures often exerted upon police departments to better serve homosexual communities. In deference to these political pressures, police officers were more likely to have received diversity training. This study also found that in departments in which hostility toward homosexuality was particularly strong the harassment of individuals suspected of homosexuality was more frequent. In some instances this harassment was targeted to individuals who were not homosexual.

The person X situation model suggests that some people are more likely to commit sexual harassment based on sexual orientation than others. One set of person factors that surely contributes to this form of sexual harassment are attitudes toward homosexuality. While national surveys of the American public indicate antihomosexual attitudes are common (Davis & Smith, 1991), considerable variation exists in the magnitude of these feelings. One of the strongest predictors of antihomosexual attitudes is general political conservatism (Seltzer, 1992). Those who hold antihomosexual views also tend to be male, more religiously devout, less educated, and from Southern states. Antihomosexual attitudes also are related to a tendency to view men and women stereotypically (Dunbar, Brown, & Amoroso, 1973). Therefore, we might expect that those most likely to perceive homosexuals as an outgroup also might be very likely to perceive heterosexual women in nontraditional roles as trespassing over the bounds of male entitlements.

Why do people hold negative attitudes about homosexuals? Research by Herek (1987) suggests that such negative attitudes can serve at least three different possible psychological functions. First, for some people these attitudes can serve an *experiential-schematic function*, in which experiences with specific outgroup members are generalized to the whole social category. When this experience is positive, positive regard may be generalized and the ingroup/outgroup boundary may be weakened. When the experience is negative, the opposite may happen. Second, attitudes

toward homosexuals can serve a *value-expressive* function. For example, many people cite specific religious values as the source of their negative feelings about homosexuality. Finally, negative attitudes toward homosexuals can serve a *defensive function*. Expressing hostility toward homosexuals can be a way of affirming heterosexual ingroup identification and denying one's own homosexual feelings. Research on hate crimes (Berrill, 1990; Comstock, 1991; Herek, 1989) suggests that perpetrators of antihomosexual violence tend to be young males, often acting in groups. Thus, more extreme instances of such outgroup hostility seem most likely to occur when males are at an age of establishing their own sexual identities. Further, "gay-bashing" may be more likely to occur when there is an audience of one's male peers.

In summary, homo-anathema is essentially an expression of outgroup hostility. Antihomosexual attitudes serve to demarcate the boundary of this outgroup and may be the basis of sexually harassing both men and women in the workplace. Those who are the victims of this form of sexual harassment are not necessarily homosexual; such antihomosexual epithets as "queer" and "faggot" are sometimes weapons used to harass heterosexuals as well. Traditionally masculine work settings where males dominate in numbers seem to foster the expression of homo-anathema. More research is needed to document the scope and effects of this kind of sexual harassment as well as the person and social factors that give rise to its occurrence.

## SUMMARY OF THE PERSON X SITUATION MODEL

The person X situation model suggests that sexual harassment is a behavior some people do some of the time. As a conceptual tool this model helps to focus research on understanding those factors that predict the occurrence of sexual harassment. One test of the usefulness of such analyses is to be able to identify people who are likely to perform some sort of sexual harassment and then create conditions in the laboratory under which such behavior may be directly observed. At present, research of the sort that directly supports the person X situation analysis of sexual harassment comes only from studies of sexual exploitation (cf. Pryor, Giedd, & Williams, in press). Laboratory investigations of the other three categories in the typology await future research. However, indirect evidence of the meaningfulness of these categories can be found in studies of victims' experiences of sexual harassment.

A widely used assessment tool in academic and business settings is the Sexual Experiences Questionnaire (SEQ) (Fitzgerald et al., 1988). Numerous analyses of the SEQ have found three general factors underlying women's experiences of sexual harassment: gender harassment, unwanted sexual attention, and sexual coercion (Fitzgerald, Gelfand, & Drasgow, in press). We have already discussed the nature of gender harassment. Unwanted sexual attention includes repeated requests for dates and persistent attempts to establish unwanted sexual relationships. Sexual coercion includes the use of threats or bribes to solicit sexual involvement. What the research of Fitzgerald and her colleagues demonstrates about these behaviors is a covariance structure in their occurrence. In other words, women who experience one form of sexual coercion, for example, are likely to experience another. Experiences of behaviors within the same category tend to covary more than experiences of behaviors between categories. There are at least three possible reasons why victims would report experiences that covary within these three categories: (1) The three categories reflect equivalence classes in the perceptions of the recipients of sexual harassment (i.e., these behaviors are seen as functionally similar by those who are subjected to the behaviors), (2) the categories reflect the behavior patterns of the harassers (i.e., these behaviors covary in the way individual harassers interact with the recipients), and (3) the social circumstances that give rise to the behaviors within a particular equivalence class (e.g., gender harassment) might be similar. Obviously, these are not mutually

exclusive reasons; all could contribute to the noted covariation patterns in Fitzgerald's research.

These three categories from the SEQ bear some similarity to the first three types of sexual harassment described in our taxonomy: Sexual coercion is similar to what we term sexual exploitation, unwanted sexual attention may sometimes reflect the sexual attraction/ miscommunication type of sexual harassment, and gender harassment represents many of the kinds of behaviors our typology terms misogyny. Furthermore, reasons 2 and 3 for this covariance structure are consistent with our analysis of the person and situational factors that contribute to repeated sexual harassment in the workplace. The final category of our taxonomy has not received as much attention in surveys of sexual harassment as the other three. Harassment related to homosexuality was not assessed in the SEQ, nor has it been directly assessed in any of the large-scale scientific studies of sexual harassment (Culbertson et al., 1992; Culbertson, Rosenfeld, & Newel, 1993; Martindale, 1992; USMSPB, 1980, 1987). (An exception is the AAUW [1993] study. However, factor analyses of these data have not been reported yet.) Of course, we suspect that future studies will find that different manifestations of homo-anathema also covary in victims' experiences.

Our taxonomy attempts to categorize sexual harassment through an analysis of its social psychological causes. However, we do not assume that manifestations of the four types of sexual harassment are entirely independent. For example, both misogyny and homo-anathema represent reactions to outgroups in which the contrasting ingroup is most often traditional males. Factors that promote a sense of an all-male club are likely to increase both forms of sexual harassment. Similarly, workplace norms that foster sexual relationships among coworkers may provide opportunities for socially unskilled men to persist in unwelcome sexual advances and, at the same time, may give those with proclivities for sexual exploitation a more easily accessed selection of potential targets. Furthermore, some of the sexist attitudes that underlie misogyny are related to desires to sexually exploit (Pryor, 1987). Despite these interconnections, we believe that it is important to try to understand the different reasons that men sexually harass.

Too often confusion is created by assuming that common outcomes imply common causes. A common outcome of sexual harassment on a societal level is the hindrance of women's achievement of social and economic equality with men. According to Hoffman (1987), sexual harassment is "a pattern of interpersonal behavior that functions at the social structural level to reinforce and perpetuate the subordination of women as a class" (p. 107). Hoffman goes on to assert that "sexual harassment is more closely tied to structural conditions and historical patterns of sex-role interaction than to individual attitudes and behaviors" (p. 107). We do not argue with Hoffman's conclusions regarding the general effects of sexual harassment on women as a class. However, we contend that successful attempts to ameliorate sexual harassment problems in the workplace are best guided by a recognition that there are different types of sexual harassment with potentially different causes.

## INTERVENTIONS

Popovich (1988) offers the following advice for organizations in dealing with sexual harassment. First, establish a policy and circulate it to all employees. Second, establish a grievance procedure. Third, educate all employees. Part of the recommended education should simply be directed at making the employees aware of the policy, the grievance procedures, and the potential costs to the company of sexual harassment. Education also should include some attempts to make employees aware of what constitutes sexual harassment. Presumably, the idea that men and women sometimes have different views of what constitutes sexual harassment should be addressed. Additionally, Popovich suggests that organizations set up programs to provide support for those who have been harassed on the job.

Education is often perceived as the panacea to many social ills. Many authors, like Popovich (1988), have suggested that educational training can ameliorate sexual harassment in the workplace (some recent examples include: Barak, 1992; Bingham, 1991; Brooks & Perot, 1991; Phillips & Schneider, 1993; Terpstra & Baker, 1992). However, very few reported studies have attempted to evaluate the effects of educational efforts. Indeed, Fitzgerald and Shullman (1993) noted that this represents a glaring omission in sexual harassment research.

We have been able to locate only four attempts to evaluate educational training efforts, and only three of these are published. The first and perhaps most widely cited is the work of Beauvais (1986). In this study, resident advisors in dormitories at the University of Michigan were given a two-hour training session that included viewing and discussing "trigger tapes" that depicted all possible combinations of gender in sexual harassment. Participants also discussed societal and personal values on sexual harassment, reviewed alternative courses of action and resources for victims, and learned university policies. Data were collected immediately before and two weeks after the sessions. Men tended to evidence more change after these sessions than women. Changes were found in men's opinions regarding certain issues stressed in the workshops. For example, after the workshop, men tended to show less agreement with the statement "Sexual harassment has little to do with power." However, statistical significance was obtained on only 4 out of 18 opinion measures. Men also tended to recognize more appropriate courses of action for victims after the workshop. While Beauvais is to be commended for a pioneering effort, the pre-post design of this study makes demand explanations for these results difficult to rule out. Male subjects could well have been responding in a way they thought met the researcher's expectations. A similar study reported by Thomann, Strickland, and Gibbons (1989) found similar results but also suffered from reliance upon a prepost design.

A third study by Maurizo and Rogers (1992), while not suffering from the same design problems of the Beauvais and Thomann, Strickland, and Gibbons studies, seems to have been directed primarily at potential victims. Ninety-five percent of the subjects in this study were women. So, this study seems to have very little potential for telling us how training might affect men.

The fourth evaluation study, by Moyer and Nath (1994), is perhaps the most methodologically sophisticated of the lot. However, the scope of what the educational training set out to accomplish in this study was much more limited than the other three. Moyer and Nath tried to establish whether and how men and women differed in their ability to discriminate descriptions of sexually harassing behavior from those of non–sexually harassing behavior and whether any gender differences could be ameliorated by training. Experts were used to categorize a series of short vignettes as examples—or not—of sexual harassment (under Maine law). Male and female subjects (undergraduate volunteers) were randomly assigned to either a no-training control condition or a training condition in which they learned specifics about the legal definition of sexual harassment in Maine and the university's policies. In some conditions a film depicting examples also was used. Afterward, both groups judged whether the scenarios constituted sexual harassment. A signal-detection analysis was used in comparing women's and men's responses (MacMillan & Creelman, 1991). Without training, women were found to be both more biased (they more often judged sexual harassment when it was not there) and more accurate (they better discriminated harassment from nonharassment) than men. Moyer and Nath found a convergence in women's and men's judgments after training. This was due to men adopting a response bias similar to that of women.

None of these studies went beyond tests concerning the knowledge, opinions, and perceptions of workshop participants. To our knowledge, there has never been an experimental or quasi-experimental study of how

educational efforts have affected the incidents of sexual harassment in an organization. Furthermore, attempts to examine a possible correlation between the amount of training offered in an organization and the rate of sexual harassment have come up empty handed (USMSPB, 1988).

Obviously, educational interventions designed to reduce sexual harassment might have different goals. Most we have examined take a "shotgun" approach of trying to combine as many different strategies as possible. One of the advantages offered by our theory of sexual harassment is that we may now be in a position of understanding how interventions might work. Here are some suggestions about how some possible educational interventions might work based upon our four-part typology and person X situation analysis. First, our analysis of sexual exploitation suggests that men who have a tendency to sexually exploit may perceive an integral link between power and sexuality. While we do not speculate about the origins of this cognitive linkage, the automaticity of these links suggest that they are overlearned and might be very difficult to change. So, interventions aimed at altering how these men view sex and power would appear to be unlikely to be successful. On the other hand, men who sexually exploit do seem sensitive to normative variations in the social acceptance of sexually exploitive behavior. For this reason, we suggest that interventions that make the policies prohibiting sexual harassment clear and which outline concrete punishments for those who violate such policies might be an effective deterrent for such men. Also, attempts to convey the seriousness of management's resolve in eliminating sexual harassment could help to deter these potential harassers (Pryor, Giedd, & Williams, in press). Second, men who harass out of miscommunication might benefit from training focused on improving their heterosocial skills. Specifically, training that conveys the notion that men and women often have different views about the potential unwelcomeness of social sexual behaviors might be beneficial. Third, both misogyny and homo-anathema might be reduced by exercises designed to break down some of the ingroup/outgroup barriers at the root of this sexual harassment. Research from the race relations literature seems to hold promise for some models of how this might be accomplished (Cook, 1984; Smith, 1990).

# REFERENCES

Abbey, A. (1982). Sex differences in attributions for friendly behavior: Do males misperceive females' friendliness? *Journal of Personality and Social Psychology, 42,* 830–838.

Abbey, A. (1987). Misperceptions of friendly behavior as sexual interest: A survey of naturally occurring incidents. *Psychology of Women Quarterly, 11,* 173–194.

Ajzen, I., & Fishbein, M. (1980). *Understanding attitudes and predicting social behavior.* Englewood Cliffs, NJ: Prentice-Hall.

American Association of University Women (1993). *Hostile hallways: The AAUW survey on sexual harassment in America' schools.* Annapolis, MD: Author.

Barak, A. (1992). Combating sexual harassment. *American Psychologist, 47,* 818–819.

Barak, A., Pitterman, Y., & Yitzhaki, R. (in press). An empirical test of the role of power differential in originating sexual harassment. *Basic and Applied Social Psychology.*

Bargh, J. A., Raymond, P., Pryor, J. B., & Strack, F. (in press). The attractiveness of the underling: An automatic power sex association and its consequences for sexual harassment. *Journal of Personality and Social Psychology.*

Barickman, R., Korn, S., Sandler, B., Gold, Y., Ormerod, A, & Weitzman, L. M. (1990). An ecological perspective to understanding sexual harassment. In M. Paludi (Ed.), *Ivory power: Sexual harassment on campus (pp. xi–xix).* Albany, NY: SUNY Press.

Bem, S. L. (1985). Androgyny and gender schema theory: A conceptual and empirical integration. In T. B. Sonderegger (Ed.), *Nebraska Symposium on Motivation: Psychology and gender* (pp. 179–226). Lincoln: University of Nebraska Press.

Benson, D. J., & Thomson, G. (1982). Sexual harassment on a university campus: The confluence of power relations, sexual interest and gender stratification. *Social Problems, 29,* 236–251.

Berrill, K. (1990). Anti-gay violence and victimization in the United States: An overview. *Journal of Interpersonal Violence, 5,* 274–294.

Berscheid, E., Graziano, W., Monson, T., & Dermer, M. (1976). Outcome dependency: Attention, attribution and attraction. *Journal of Personality and Social Psychology, 34,* 978–989.

Beauvais, K. (1986). Workshops to combat sexual harassment: A case of studying changing attitudes. *Signs, 12,* 130–145.

Bingham, S. G. (1991). Communication strategies for managing sexual harassment in organizations: Understanding message options and their effects. *Journal of Applied Communication Research, 19,* 85–115.

Boodman, S. G. (1980, Jan. 29). Women cite GI's sexual harassment at Army bases. *The Washington Post,* p. A6.

Brannon, R., & Junni, S. (1984). A scale for measuring attitudes about masculinity. *Psychological Documents, 14,* 6–7.

Brewer, M. B. (1979). In-group bias in the minimal group situation: A cognitive-motivational analysis. *Psychological Bulletin, 86,* 307–324.

Brewer, M. (1982). Further beyond nine to five: An integration and future directions. *Journal of Social Issues, 38,* 149–158.

Brooks, L., & Perot, A. R. (1991). Reporting sexual harassment: Exploring a predictive model. *Psychology of Women Quarterly, 15,* 31–47.

Burt, M. (1980).Cultural myths and supports for rape. *Journal of Personality and Social Psychology, 38,* 217–230.

Byer, C.O., & Shainberg, L.W. (1994). *Dimensions of human sexuality.* Dubuque, IA: Brown Communications.

Chapman, L. J. (1967). Illusory correlation in observational report. *Journal of Verbal Learning and Verbal Behavior, 6,* 151–155.

Cialdini, R. B., Reno, R. R., & Kallgren, C. A. (1990). A focus theory of normative conduct: Recycling the concept of norms to reduce littering in public places. *Journal of Personality and Social Psychology, 58,* 1015–1026.

Cleveland, J., & Kerst, M. (1993). Sexual harassment and perception of power: An under-articulated relationship. *Journal of Vocational Behavior, 42,* 49–67.

Cohen, A. F., & Gutek, B. A. (1985). Dimensions of perceptions of social-sexual behavior in a work setting. *Sex Roles, 13,* 317–327.

Comstock, G. D. (1991). *Violence against lesbians and gay men.* New York: Columbia University Press.

Cook, S. W. (1984). Cooperative interactions in multiethnic contexts. In N. Miller & M. Brewer (Eds.) , *Groups in contact: The psychology of desegregation* (pp.156–186). New York: Academic Press.

Culbertson, A. L., Rosenfeld, P., & Newel, C. E. (1993). Sexual harassment in the active-duty Navy. *Assessment of sexual harassment in the Navy: Results of the 1989 Navy-wide survey.* San Diego, CA: Navy Personnel Research and Development Center.

Culbertson, A. L., Rosenfeld, P., Booth-Kewley, S., & Magnusson, P. (1992). *Assessment of sexual harass-*

*ment in the Navy: Results of the 1989 Navy-wide survey.* San Diego, CA: Navy Personnel Research and Development Center.

Davis, J. A., & Smith, T. (1991). *General social surveys, 1972–1991: Cumulative data.* Storrs: University of Connecticut, Roper Center for Public Opinion Research.

Davis, J. K. (1987). *Memorandum: 1987 WestPac visit of the Defense Advisory Committee on Women in the Services.* Cambridge, MA: Institute for Foreign Policy Analysis, Tufts University.

Denton, K. J. (1993). *Sexual harassment: Expansion of the Likelihood of Sexually Harassing questionnaire and the positive relationship between sexual harassment and sexual aggression.* Masters thesis, Saint Mary's University, Halifax, Nova Scotia.

Dovidio, J. F., & Gaertner, S. L. (1993). Stereotypes and evaluative intergroup bias. In D. M. Mackie & D. L. Hamilton (Eds.), *Affect, cognition and stereotyping: Interactive processes in group perception* (pp. 167–193). San Diego, CA: Academic Press.

Dunbar, J., Brown, M., & Amoroso, D. M. (1973). Some correlates of attitudes toward homosexuality. *Journal of Social Psychology, 89,* 271–279.

Dziech, B., & Weiner, L. (1984). *The lecherous professor.* Boston: Beacon Press.

*Ellison v. Brady , 924 F. 2d 872 (CA9 1991).*

Equal Employment Opportunity Commission (EEOC) (1980). Guidelines and discrimination because of sex (Sec. 1604.11). *Federal Register, 45,* 74676–74677.

Equal Employment Opportunity Commission (EEOC) (1993). Guidelines on harassment based upon race, color, religion, gender, national origin, age or disability. (Sec. 1609.1–1609.2). *Federal Register, 58,* 51268–51269.

Fain, T. C., & Anderton, D. L. (1987). Sexual harassment: Organizational context and diffuse status. *Sex Roles, 17,* 291–311.

Fitzgerald, L., & Hesson-McInnis, M. (1989). The dimensions of sexual harassment: A structural analysis. *Journal of Vocational Behavior. 35,* 309–326.

Fitzgerald L., Hulin, C. L., & Drasgow, F. (1994). The antecedents and consequences of sexual harassment in organizations: An integrated model. In G. P. Keita & J. J. Hurrell, Jr. (Eds.), *Job stress in a changing workforce: Investigating gender, diversity, and family issues* (pp. 55–74). Washington, DC: American Psychological Association.

Fitzgerald, L., & Ormerod, A. J. (1991). Perceptions of sexual harassment: The influence of gender and context. *Psychology of Women Quarterly, 15,* 281–294.

Fitzgerald, L. F., & Shullman, S. L. (1993). Sexual harassment: A research analysis and agenda for the 1990s. *Journal of Vocational Behavior, 42,* 5–27.

Fitzgerald, L., Shullman, S. L., Bailey, N., Richards, M., Swecker, J., Gold, Y., Ormerod, A. J., & Weitzman, L. (1988). The incidence and dimensions of sexual harassment in academia and the workplace. *Journal of Vocational Behavior, 32,* 152–175.

Fitzgerald, L. F., Swan, S., & Fischer, K. (1995). Why didn't she just report him? The psychological and legal implications of women's responses to sexual harassment. *Journal of Social Issues, 51* (1), 117–138.

Gaertner, S. L., Mann, J., Murrel, A., & Dovidio, J. F. (1989). Reducing intergroup bias: The benefits of recategorization. *Journal of Personality and Social Psychology, 57,* 239–249.

Gelfand, M. J., Fitzgerald, L. F., & Drasgow, F. (in press). The structure of sexual harassment: A confirmatory analysis across cultures and settings. *Journal of Vocational Behavior.*

Glick, P., & Fiske, S. T. (1994). *The Ambivalent Sexism Inventory: Differentiating hostile and benevolent sexism.* Unpublished manuscript, Lawrence University, Appleton, WI.

Greenberg, J., & Baron, R. A. (1995). *Behavior in organizations: Understanding and managing the human side of work (5th ed).* Englewood Cliffs, NJ: Prentice-Hall.

Gruber, J. E., & Bjorn, L. (1982). Blue-collar blues: The sexual harassment of women autoworkers. *Work and Occupations, 9,* 271–298.

Gruber, J. E. & Bjorn, L. (1986). Women's responses to sexual harassment: An analysis of sociocultural, organizational, and personal resource models. *Social Science Quarterly, 67,* 814–825.

Gruber, J. E., & Smith, M. D. (in press). Women's responses to sexual harassment: A multivariate analysis. *Basic and Applied Social Psychology.*

Gutek, B. (1985). *Sex and the workplace.* San Francisco: Jossey-Bass.

Haavio-Mannila, E., Kaupinen-Toropainen, K., & Kandolin, I. (1988). The effect of sex composition of the workplace on friendship, romance and sex at work. In B.A. Gutek, A.H. Stromberg, & L. Larwood (Eds.), *Women and work (vol. 3).* Beverly Hills, CA: Sage.

Hamilton, D. L., & Gifford, L. (1976). Illusory correlation in interpersonal perception: A cognitive basis of stereotypic judgments. *Journal of Experimental Social Psychology, 12,* 392–407.

Hamilton, D. L., & Sherman, J. W. (1994). Stereotypes. In R. S. Wyer & T. K. Srull (Eds.), *Handbook of social cognition* (2d ed.). Hillsdale, NJ: Erlbaum.

Harnish, R., Abbey, A., & DeBono, K. (1990). Toward an understanding of the "Sex Game": The effects of gender and self-monitoring on the perceptions of sexuality and likability in initial interactions. *Journal of Applied Social Psychology, 20,* 1333–1344.

Herek, G. M. (1986). The instrumentality of attitudes: Toward a neofunctional theory. *Journal of Social Issues, 42,* 99–114.

Herek, G. M. (1989). Hate crimes against lesbians and gay men: Issues for research and policy. *American Psychologist, 44,* 948–955.

Herek, G. M. (1990a). The context of anti-gay violence: Notes on cultural and psychological heterosexism. *Journal of Interpersonal Violence, 5,* 316–333.

Herek, G. M. (1990b). Gay people and government security clearances: A social science perspective. *American Psychologist, 45,* 1035–1042.

Herek, G M., & Berrill, K. T. (1992). *Hate crimes: Confronting violence against lesbians and gay men.* Newbury Park, London: Sage.

Hoffman, F. L. (1987). Sexual harassment in academia: Feminist theory and institutional practice. *Harvard Educational Review, 56,* 105–120.

Ickes, W. J., & Barnes, R. D. (1977). The role of sex and self-monitoring in unstructured dyadic interactions. *Journal of Personality and Social Psychology, 35,* 315–330.

Judd, C. M., & Park, B. (1988). Out-group homogeneity: Judgments of variability and the individual and group levels. *Journal of Personality and Social Psychology, 54,* 778–788.

Kanter, R. M. (1977). *Men and women of the corporation.* New York: Basic Books.

Larwood, L., Szwajkowski, E., & Rose, S. (1988). Sex and race discrimination resulting from management–client relationships: Rational bias theory of management discrimination. *Sex Roles, 18,* 9–29.

Larwood, L., Szwajkowski, E., & Rose, S. (1989). When discrimination makes sense: The rational bias theory of discrimination. In B.A. Gutek, A.H. Stromberg, & L. Larwood (Eds.), *Women and work* (vol. 3). Beverly Hills, CA: Sage.

Lewin, K. (1951). *Field theory in social science: Selected theoretical papers.* New York: Harper and Row.

Linville, P. W., Fischer, G. W., & Salovey, P. (1989). Perceived distributions of the characteristics of in-group and out-group members. *Journal of Personality and Social Psychology, 57,* 165–188.

Lipton, D., McDonel, E. C., & McFall, R. M. (1987).Heterosocial perception in rapists. *Journal of Consulting and Clinical Psychology, 55,* 17–21.

MacMillan, N. A., & Creelman, C. D. (1991). *Signal detection theory: A user's guide.* Cambridge, England: Cambridge University Press.

Malamuth, N. M. (1989). The Attraction to Sexual Aggression Scale: Part one. *Journal of Sex Research, 26,* 26–49.

Martindale, M. (1992, August). Sexual harassment in the military: 1988. *Sociological Practice Review, 2,* 200–216.

Maurizio, S. J., & Rogers, J. L. (1992). Sexual harassment and attitudes in rural community care workers. *Health Values, 16,* 40–45.

McConahay, J. (1986). Modern racism, ambivalence and the Modern Racism scale. In J. F. Dovidio & S. L Gaertner (Eds.), *Prejudice, discrimination and racism* (pp. 99–125). Orlando, FL: Academic Press.

McDonel, E. C., & McFall, R. M. (1991). Construct validity of two heterosocial perception skill measures for assessing rape proclivity. *Victims and Violence, 6,* 17–30.

McKinney, K. (1992). Contrapower sexual harassment: The effects of student and type of behavior on faculty perceptions. *Sex Roles, 27,* 267–243.

Michael, R. T., Gagnon, J. H., Laumann, E. O., & Kolata, G. (1994). *Sex in America: A definitive survey.* Boston: Little, Brown.

Moyer, R. S., & Nath, A. (1994). *Gender and training influence bias and accuracy in perceptions of sexual harassment.* Unpublished manuscript, Bates College, Augusta, Maine.

Murphy, W. D., Coleman, E. M., & Haynes, M. R. (1986). Factors related to coercive sexual behaviors in a nonclinical sample of males. *Violence and Victims, 1 (4),* 255–278.

National Council for Research on Women (1991). *Sexual harassment: Research and resources.* New York: Author.

National Defense Research Institute (1993). *Sexual orientation and U. S. military personnel policy: Options and Assessment.* Santa Monica, CA: RAND.

Nelson, P. A. (1979). *A sexual functions inventory.* Doctoral dissertation, University of Florida, Gainsville, Florida.

Paludi, M. A. (Ed.) (1990). *Ivory power: Sexual harassment on campus.* Albany, NY: SUNY Press.

Paludi, M. A., & Barickman, R. B. (1991). *Academic and workplace sexual harassment.* Albany, NY: SUNY Press.

Phillips, S. P., & Schneider, M. S. (1993). Sexual harassment of female doctors by patients. *New England Journal of Medicine, 329,* 1936–1939.

Popovich, P. (1988a). *An examination of sexual harassment complaints in the Air Force for FY 1987.* Patrick Air Force Base, FL: Defense Equal Opportunity Management Institute.

Popovich, P. (1988b). Sexual harassment in organizations. *Employee Responsibilities and Rights Journal, 1,* 273–282.

Pryor, J. B. (1987). Sexual harassment proclivities in men. *Sex Roles, 17,* 269–290.

Pryor, J. B. (1994, August). *The phenomenology of sexual harassment.* Paper presented at the Meeting of the American Psychological Association. Los Angeles.

Pryor, J. B., Giedd, J. L., & Williams, K. B. (in press). A social psychological model for predicting sexual harassment. *Journal of Social Issues.*

Pryor, J. B., LaVite, C., & Stoller, L. (1993). A social psychological analysis of sexual harassment: The person/situation interaction. *Journal of Vocational Behavior (Special issue),* 42, 68–83.

Pryor, J. B., & Stoller, L. (1994). Sexual cognition processes in men who are high in the likelihood to sexually harass. *Personality and Social Psychology Bulletin, 20,* 163–169.

Quatrone, G., & Jones, E. E. (1980). The perception of variability within ingroups and outgroups: Implications for the law of small numbers. *Journal of Personality and Social Psychology, 38,* 141–152.

Riger, S. (1991). Gender dilemmas in sexual harassment policies and procedures. *American Psychologist, 46,* 497–505.

*Robinson v. Jacksonville Shipyards, Inc.* (1991). 59 LW 2470 (DC M Fla).

Rosenberg, J., Perlstadt, H., & Phillips, W. R. (1993). Now that we are here: Discrimination, disparagement and harassment at work and the experience of women lawyers. *Gender and Society, 7,* 415–433.

Saal, F. E., Johnson, C. B., & Weber, N. (1989). Friendly or sexy? It depends on whom you ask. *Psychology of Women Quarterly, 13,* 263–276.

Schneider, B. A. (1982). Consciousness about sexual harassment among heterosexual and lesbian women workers. *Journal of Social Issues, 38,* 75–97.

Sears, D. O. (1988). Symbolic racism. In P. A. Katz & D. A. Taylor (Eds.), *Eliminating racism: Profiles in controversy* (pp. 53–85). New York: Plenum.

Seltzer, R. (1992). The social location of those holding antihomosexual attitudes. *Sex Roles, 26,* 391–398.

Sherif, M. (1936). *The psychology of social norms.* New York: Harper and Row.

Sherif, M., Harvey, O. J., White, B. J., Hood, W. R., & Sherif, C. (1961). *Intergroup conflict and cooperation: The robber's cave experiment.* Norman: University of Oklahoma Press.

Shotland, L. (1989). A model of the causes of date rape in developing and close relationships. In C. Hendrick (Ed.), *Close relationships* (pp. 247–270). Newbury Park, CA: Sage.

Shotland, L. (1992). A theory of the causes of courtship rape: Part 2. *Journal of Social Issues, 48,* 127–143.

Shotland , L., & Craig, J. (1988). Can men and women differentiate between friendly and sexually interested behavior? *Social Psychology Quarterly, 34,* 990–999.

Smith, A. (1990). Social influence and anti-prejudice training programs. In J. Edwards, R. S. Tindale, L. Heath, & E. J. Prosavac (Eds.), *Social influence processes and prevention* (pp. 183–196). New York: Plenum.

Smith, E., Feree, M., & Miller, F. (1975). A short scale of attitudes toward feminism. *Representative Research in Social Psychology, 6,* 51–56.

Snyder, M. (1974). The self-monitoring of expressive behavior. *Journal of Personality and Social Psychology, 30,* 526–537.

Snyder, M., & Cantor, N. (1980). Thinking about ourselves and others: Self-monitoring and social knowledge. *Journal of Personality and Social Psychology, 39,* 222–234.

Snyder, M., Simpson, J., & Gangstead, S. (1986). Personality and sexual relations. *Journal of Personality and Social Psychology, 51,* 125–139.

Spence, J. T., & Helmreich, R. (1978). *Masculinity and femininity: Their psychological dimensions, correlates, and antecedents.* Austin: University of Texas Press.

Spence, J. T., Helmreich, R., & Stapp, J. (1973). A short version of the Attitude Toward Women scale. *Bulletin of Psychonomic Society, 2,* 219–220.

Stewart, L. P. (1982, October). *Sexual harassment as discrimination: Guidelines for effective responses.* Paper presented at the Fifth Annual Meeting of the Communication, Language, and Gender Conference, Athens, OH.

Stockdale, M. S. (1993). The role of sexual misperceptions of women's friendliness in an emerging theory of sexual harassment. *Journal of Vocational Behavior, 42,* 84–101.

Stockdale, M. S., Dewey, J. D., & Saal, F. E. (1992). *Evidence that misperception tendencies relate to a sexual belief system.* Unpublished manuscript, Southern Illinois University, Carbondale, IL.

Swim, J. K., Aiken, K. J., Hall, W. S., & Hunter, B. A. (in press). Sexism and racism: Old fashioned and modern prejudices. *Journal of Personality and Social Psychology.*

Tajfel, H., & Turner, J. C. (1986). The social identity theory of intergroup conflict. In W. G. Austin & S. Worchel (Eds.), *The social psychology of intergroup relations* (pp. 33–47). Monterey, CA: Brooks/Cole.

Taylor, S. T., Fiske, S. E., Close, M., Anderson, C., & Ruderman, A. (1977). *Solo status as a psychological variable: The power of being distinctive.* Unpublished manuscript, Harvard University, Cambridge, MA.

Terpstra, D. E., & Baker, D. D. (1992). Outcomes of federal court cases on sexual harassment. *Academy of Management Journal, 35,* 181–190.

Thomann, D. A., Strickland, D. E., & Gibbons, J. L. (1989). An organizational development approach to preventing sexual harassment. *CUPA Journal, 40,* 34–43.

Thompson, E. H., & Pleck, J. H. (1986). The structure of male role norms. *American Behavioral Scientist, 29,* 531–543.

Turner, J. C., Hogg, M., Oakes, P. J., Reicher, S. D., & Wetherell, M. (1987). *Rediscovering the social group: A self-categorization theory.* Oxford, England: Basil, Blackwell.

U.S. Merit Systems Protection Board (USMSPB) (1981). *Sexual harassment in the federal workplace: Is it a problem?* Washington, DC: Government Printing Office.

U.S. Merit Systems Protection Board (USMSPB) (1988). *Sexual harassment in the federal government: An update.* Washington, DC: Government Printing Office.

When love letters become hated mail. (Oct. 21, 1991). *Time,* p. 63.

Yount, K. R. (1991). Ladies, flirts and tomboys: Strategies for managing sexual harassment in an underground coal mine. *Journal of Contemporary Ethnography, 19,* 396–422.

Zalk, S. R. (1990). Men in the academy: A psychological profile of harassment. In M. Paludi (Ed.), *Ivory power: Sexual harassment on campus* (pp. 141–176). Albany, NY: SUNY Press.

Zickar, M. J. (1994, April). *Antecedents of sexual harassment.* Paper presented at the Society for Industrial/Organizational Psychology Meeting, Nashville, TN.

# CHAPTER 9

# EFFECTS OF SEXUAL HARASSMENT

**Bonnie S. Dansky**
**Dean G. Kilpatrick**

As can be seen from the research discussed in Chapter 5, sexual harassment is a common form of sexual victimization, which may touch the lives of approximately 50% of all women who were ever employed and about 30% of women attending four-year colleges (Adams, Kottke, & Padgitt, 1983; Dziech & Weiner, 1984; Fitzgerald & Ormerod, 1993; Fitzgerald & Shullman, 1993; Gutek et al., 1980). In the first large-scale study of sexual harassment in the workplace, the United States Merit Systems Protection Board (USM-SPB, 1981) sampled 23,964 federal workers and found that 42% of female participants reported some type of sexual harassment. A slightly higher rate of sexual harassment (53%) was documented by Gutek (1985) in a random sample of employed women in Los Angeles, and it was estimated, based on a study conducted by staff at the National Crime Victims Research and Treatment Center (Dansky et al., 1992; Kilpatrick, 1992; Saun-

ders, 1992), that approximately 10 million women have experienced sexual harassment incidents in the workplace that meet all criteria outlined in Title XII of the Civil Rights Act of 1964 ("EEOC Guidelines"). Since research has demonstrated that an overwhelming majority of victims of sexual harassment are women with men as the perpetrators, the language used in this chapter will reflect this. However, this should not be interpreted as suggesting that women are always the victims and that men are always the perpetrators.

Despite the widespread nature of sexual harassment, public awareness of this major social issue was not apparent until news of cases such as the Anita Hill/Clarence Thomas allegations and Tailhook forced the topic into the homes of most Americans. In both cases, victims were repeatedly questioned about (1) their initial responses to the sexual harassment and (2) subsequent effects sexual harassment had on their lives, which are the two central topics of this chapter. An underlying assumption of many individuals, including some U.S. senators at the Thomas hearings, was that victims who experience "real" sexual harassment immediately protest and take action against the harasser (Fitzgerald et al., in press; Fitzgerald & Swan, in press). Research has demonstrated that people view victims as culpable unless strong resistance is displayed (Bularzik, 1978; Burt & Katz, 1985). Failing to display resistance is often regarded as an admission that the offensive behaviors are not really problematic. Furthermore, the fact that some victims of sexual harassment, such as Anita Hill, may continue on their career paths receiving raises and/or promotions and showing no visible signs of distress adds doubts about whether the identified behaviors actually constituted sexual harassment. Such assumptions about common responses to and effects of sexual harassment can only be supported or refuted with empirical research.

In contrast to the abundance of research conducted on the definition and prevalence of sexual harassment, few researchers have studied responses to and effects of sexual harassment. Koss (1990), cautioned in her chapter on the psychological impact of sexual harassment: "The empirical database is too small to provide the basis for this chapter." Gutek and Koss (1993) also noted the paucity of research and outlined pros and cons of conducting such research. They questioned whether research pertaining to psychological or health-related outcomes may influence the definition of sexual harassment. They raised the possibility that victims of sexual harassment would be given the responsibility to prove that the harassment led to deleterious psychological or physical outcomes, in order for the offending behaviors to be considered harassment. Such a process is parallel with the rape laws that formerly existed in many states, wherein a rape victim had to sustain physical injuries in order to "prove" that the sexual contact was nonconsensual. Fortunately, such rape laws have been replaced, since empirical research demonstrated that a majority of rape victims sustain few, if any, physical injuries.

A recent ruling by the U.S. Supreme Court may assauge Gutek and Koss's (1993) concern about the implications of research documenting mental health impairment subsequent to sexual harassment. In December 1993 the Supreme Court, in overturning the District Court of Tennessee's ruling in *Harris v. Forklift Systems, Inc.*, ruled that "to be actionable as 'abusive work environment' harassment, conduct need not 'seriously affect [an employee's] psychological well-being' or lead the plaintiff to 'suffer injury.'" Justice O'Connor delivered the court's opinion and stated, "So long as the environment would reasonably be perceived, and is perceived, as hostile or abusive...there is no need for it also to be psychologically injurious." Thus, researchers investigating the psychological consequences of sexual harassment currently need not be impeded by the concern that victims of sexual harassment will be forced to prove that the harassment led to deleterious psychological or physical outcomes in order to be considered harassment.

The potential benefits of research concerning the outcomes of sexual harassment are unmistakable. Understanding career-related, psychological, and physical effects of sexual harassment might enable victims to receive necessary resources to facilitate coping with the aftermath of harassment. Further understanding of sexual harassment outcomes also can affect the frequency and content of educational efforts directed at sexual harassment prevention. Furthermore, the apparently false assumptions held by many people concerning the "typical" sexual harassment victim and "typical" responses to sexual harassment would be replaced with accurate information, which may impact coworker relationships and attitudes of individuals involved in the judicial system. Finally, understanding the effects of sexual harassment can influence legislation, which can be enacted to not only assist with prevention but also to serve the needs of victims.

Researchers who have studied effects of sexual harassment primarily focused on the effects for the individual victim, although some work has been done concerning effects at an organizational level. A majority of the sexual harassment outcomes research falls into one of four categories: responses to sexual harassment, work-related effects, psychological effects, and physical or somatic effects. Most of the studies outlined here used samples of convienence or special populations, utilized terms that were not operationally defined, and contained nonstandardized measures of psychological or physical distress. In other words, few well-controlled investigations in this area have been conducted. The work by Fitzgerald and her colleagues (in press, in preparation, 1993, 1991, 1989, 1988), Koss (1990), and Gutek and her colleagues (1980, 1982, 1985, 1993) are notable exceptions. Furthermore, the majority of investigations to date have been exploratory studies that generated descriptions of sexual harassment phenomena. Few have involved hypothesis testing based on theory.

Despite the fact that most studies of the effects of sexual harassment have been atheoretical, possible theoretical explanations to account for work-related, psychological, and health-related effects of sexual harassment will be presented first, followed by the presentation of empirical findings. For the reasons just outlined, the findings from these empirical studies need to be considered preliminary and useful as guidelines for future research.

## THEORETICAL EXPLANATIONS FOR THE EFFECTS OF SEXUAL HARASSMENT

Since sexual harassment occurs in a multitude of forms with varying degrees of physical, psychological, and financial threat, it is impossible to identify one model or theoretical framework as being "the" way to account for responses to and outcomes of sexual harassment. Providing explanations for the phenomenon of sexual harassment is particularly challenging due to the wide variety of behaviors that constitute harassment. Till (1980) identified five types of sexual harassment: (1) *gender harassment*—sexually discriminatory remarks, gestures, and behavior; (2) *seductive*

*behavior*—unwanted sexual behavior that is inappropriate but does not involve direct threats or sanctions; (3) *sexual bribery*—promise of rewards for engagement in sexual conduct; (4) *sexual coercion*—nonconsensual sexual conduct obtained by threat of punishment; and (5) *sexual assault*—nonconsensual sexual conduct obtained by threat or use of force. Fitzgerald and her colleagues (1988) created a scale (the Sexual Experiences Questionnaire) based on Till's work and used factor analysis to derive three relatively stable factors: "gender harassment," "unwanted sexual attention," and "sexual coercion." The degree of stress produced by gender harassment may differ enormously from that of unwanted sexual attention, which may differ from the stress of sexual coercion. Thus, certain theoretical frameworks may be more applicable to certain types of sexual harassment. The following four models are presented as possible frameworks for understanding the various types of sexual harassment.

## Learned Helplessness

The learned helplessness model predicts that people in uncontrollable situations will begin to perceive that their responses are ineffective in obtaining reinforcement, positive or negative (Klein, Fencil-Morse, & Seligman, 1976; Miller & Seligman, 1975). The process that is thought to take place in producing learned helplessness is as follows: Individuals first learn that response-outcome contingencies are out of their control. Then, people make causal attributions (Abramson, Seligman, & Teasdale, 1979), which are followed by the development of expectancies about the relationship between responses and outcomes for future situations. Depression and helplessness result when a person develops expectancies that bad outcomes are probable and/or desired outcomes are improbable.

Sexual harassment can be seen as a situation during which victims learn that all attempts (passive/avoidant or active) to end the harassment are futile and that the harassment will nonetheless continue. Experiencing no connection between responses and outcomes leads victims to tolerate harassment; feel helpless; and/or experience depression, a decline in self-esteem, or other psychological sequelae. Thus, the learned helplessness model can be used to account for many of the responses exhibited by victims of prolonged harassment and the psychological distress that many victims experience during and following harassment.

## Conditioning

Based on learning theory principles posited by Mowrer (1960a; 1960b), fear and anxiety resulting from sexual victimization can be explained in terms of both classical and instrumental conditioning (Kilpatrick, Veronen, & Resnick, 1982; Kilpatrick, 1985a, b; Kilpatrick & Veronen, 1984). It has been proposed that negative emotions produced during a violent crime become associated via classical conditioning to the stimuli present during the crime (conditioned stimuli). In addition to the original conditioned stimuli themselves, other stimuli *similar* to those present during the crime also acquire the capacity to evoke high levels of fear and anxiety as a result of stimulus generalization when the victim encounters them. Possible cues include thoughts, feelings, stimuli in the environment, and characteristics of the victim and the assailant (Kilpatrick, Veronen, & Resnick, 1982).

Once the cues have evoked anxiety or fear, a major way to reduce anxiety is to engage in avoidance behavior. If one avoids what makes one anxious, one feels better in the short run. The reduction in anxiety by avoidance constitutes instrumental conditioning, which operates by negative reinforcement. Since anxiety reduction is reinforcing, the pattern of avoidance prevents the anxiety associated with trauma-related cues from ever diminishing.

It is likely that this process can be triggered by harassment, particularly harassment that can be classified as sexual coercion or assault. For instance, a patient in our clinic reported that on a daily basis her supervisor would grab her "rear end" and attempt to follow her into the bathroom, in order to touch her breasts and genitals and kiss her. The woman responded to this by trying to avoid the harasser, making

excuses to use other bathroom facilities, and pushing him away. The woman found that she experienced fear and anxiety in the presence of men who resembled the harasser, became fearful of all sexual contact, and experienced intrusive thoughts about work and the harasser continually throughout the day.

While a conditioning model may be used to account for more intrusive or violent forms of sexual harassment, alternative explanations appear more appropriate to account for victims' symptoms associated with gender discrimination or harassment that is not perceived as being threatening to the victims' physical integrity. A number of researchers (e.g., Fitzgerald & Hesson-McInnis, 1989; Frieze, Hymer, & Greenberg, 1984; Janoff-Bulman & Frieze, 1983; Koss, 1990; Perloff, 1983; Wortman, 1983) have employed stress and coping or attribution models to account for victim *responses* to sexual harassment. In addition, these models can be used to explain psychological and physical *outcomes* of sexual harassment.

## Attribution

Attribution theorists have made substantial contributions to facilitating understanding of why victims of crimes experience psychological problems (e.g., Frieze, Hymer, & Greenberg, 1984; Janoff-Bulman & Frieze, 1983; Perloff, 1983; Wortman, 1983). A major thrust of attribution theory is that individuals have a compelling need to understand their experience and are constantly interpreting environmental events and attaching meaning to them. Attempts to understand behavior and events must involve attributions, or explanations, that people ascribe to events. It is thought that people feel more comfortable believing that the universe is predictable and lawful, and having a "reason" for why an event occurred enables a victim to feel more control over his/her environment than believing that events happen randomly and unpredictably. The whole attributional process can be viewed as a cognitive coping process by which individuals attempt to achieve some perceived control over events and their own self-perceptions.

It is thought that prior to a victimization experience most individuals have core assumptions: They are invulnerable to serious harm, they are worthwhile individuals, and the world is a place in which justice prevails (Janoff-Bulman & Frieze, 1983; Janoff-Bulman, 1989). Direct experiences with victimization can lead to a shattering of victims' core assumptions about the world and themselves, which, in turn, can result in considerable psychological distress. A sexual harassment victim's sense of invulnerability, as well as a sense that there is order in the world, is challenged by the harassment. Further, it is not uncommon for the harasser to be someone the victim respected, which can lead to feelings of betrayal and a general questioning of one's ability to judge people. Initial efforts to cope indirectly with sexual harassment, by joking about it or trivializing it, can be viewed as attempts to safeguard core assumptions about invulnerability or the world being a safe place. Explaining the harasser's motives in terms of his own personal unhappiness may constitute a "reason" for the harassment, which makes its occurrence appear less random.

If attempts to ignore sexual harassment do not lead to its cessation, victims may begin to feel increased vulnerability and helplessness. Psychological symptoms such as intrusive thoughts or nightmares and somatic symptoms result from victims' inability to assimilate the sexual harassment into their core asssumptions (Horowitz, 1986). Until a victim accommodates her core assumptions to incorporate the sexual harassment, she will remain symptomatic, experiencing intrusions of trauma-related stimuli and making efforts to avoid "triggers" for reexperiencing such symptoms (Horowitz, 1986; McCann & Pearlman, 1990). Victims' future beliefs and ways of interpreting the world are affected by the accommodation process. According to attribution theory, if core assumptions are altered in unhealthy ways—such as believing that all people are untrustworthy or that the victim was to blame—then it is hypothesized that victims may experience more long-term symptomatology associated with the harassment.

## Conservation of Resources

The conservation of resources (COR) model is particularly relevant in accounting for sequelae of sexual harassment, because victims of harassment typically suffer losses in many areas of life including financial, social, psychological, and health. Hobfoll (1989) has conceptualized stress as a loss of resources, a threat of loss of resources, and/or a lack of gains in resources following an "investment" of resources. As he states (1991), "individuals strive to obtain, retain, and protect that which they value" (p. 187). Resources are considered to be "objects, personal characteristics, conditions, or energies that are valued by the individual or that serve as a means for attainment of these objects, personal characteristics, conditions, or energies" (Hobfoll, 1989, p. 516). "Conditions" include secure work and marriage, whereas "energies" encompass knowledge and money.

Sexual harassment can be seen as a threat to an individual's resources by threatening financial resources, status at work or in the family, self-esteem, and belief systems. Losses can occur in terms of a lost job, lost status among coworkers, failure to gain a raise or promotion, lost interpersonal supports, and lost esteem regarding one's work or judgment about people. According to this model, victims of sexual harassment respond to the harassment in ways to protect against losses. The model also suggests that, once losses in resources begin to occur or gains are not achieved, psychological or somatic symptomatology may set in.

Sexual harassment that involves sexual coercion or sexual assault or is perceived to be a serious threat by the victim can be considered a "traumatic stressor." Traumatic stressors are hypothesized as leading to a rapid loss of resources that typically are of the highest value to the victim (Hobfoll, 1991). Hobfoll (1991) outlined five reasons for the rapid loss of resources following a traumatic stressor: The stressor disrupts victims' basic values, it is unexpected, it demands more from victims' systems than they are equipped to handle, no proper resource utilizations strategies were developed prior to the occurrence of the stressor, and the stressor is of a nature that mental images are created that can be triggered by several types of cues. Sexual harassment, as mentioned in the discussion of the attribution model, may threaten core belief systems; in many cases, sexual harassment is completely unexpected; many victims' resources are taxed by the experience of sexual harassment; an individual plan of action is rarely conceived prior to the occurrence of harassment; and, depending on the nature of sexual harassment, it may be associated with many trauma-related stimuli in the environment and internally, as described in the discussion of conditioning. Therefore, incidents of sexual harassment may constitute traumatic experiences through which individuals experience losses in resources.

## Summary

Regardless of which theoretical framework is applied to explain sexual harasssment outcomes, it is apparent that each of the aforementioned theories would predict various negative outcomes for women who have been sexually harassed. Conducting empirical research that directly tests hypotheses derived from these theories would probably advance current knowledge substantially. It is possible that the effects of different forms of harassment (i.e, gender harassment vs. sexual assault) can be better explained by different theoretical frameworks. Alternatively, it is possible that similar mechanisms function for all types of harassment, and it is the chronicity that is an important factor.

## RESPONSES TO AND EFFECTS OF SEXUAL HARASSMENT

### Responses by the Victim

When attempting to classify victim responses to sexual harassment, most researchers have categorized responses mainly in terms of the extent to which the victim responded assertively to the unwanted sexual advances or discrimination (Gruber & Bjorn, 1986; Gutek & Koss, 1993; Maypole, 1986; Terpstra & Baker, 1989). Victims' verbal, nonverbal, and behavioral responses were considered as "direct" versus "indirect" or "passive" versus "active."

### Indirect Responses by the Victim

The most common response to sexual harassment, at least initially, is to ignore it (Benson & Thomson, 1982; Gutek, 1985; Fitzgerald, in press; Fitzgerald et al., 1988; Fitzgerald & Swan, in press; McKinnon, 1979; Lindsey, 1977; Loy & Stewart, 1984). Benson and Thomson (1982) discussed how sexual harassment victims in a university setting attempted to "manage the trouble" of harassment by ignoring it or responding in a number of indirect ways such as redirecting conversation away from personal topics, bringing a friend to meetings, leaving the door open during meetings, mentioning the existence of a spouse or boyfriend, and sitting far enough away to prevent physical contact. Avoiding contact with the harasser may entail avoiding contact at work or elsewhere (Culbertson et al., 1992), avoiding taking a class with the harasser (Benson & Thomson, 1982), or even quitting the job (Loy & Stewart, 1984).

Numerous researchers described the way many victims conceptualized sexual harassment benignly or trivialized it by viewing it as joking/playing around or by believing that the harasser was just voicing interest in their social lives (Benson & Thomson, 1982; Dziech & Weiner, 1984; Gutek, 1985; Reilly, Lott, & Gallogly, 1986). Koss (1990) described trivializing a victimization experience as a self-protective measure to maintain a sense of invulnerability. Other victims attributed the harasser's behavior to some external factor such as the victim's dress or the harasser's unhappiness in his personal life. Some victims responded passively to the harassment simply because they were unaware that it was possible to file a formal complaint (Reilly, Lott, & Gallogly, 1986). They also feared that the harasser would lose his job and his family would suffer (Alliance Against Sexual Coercion, 1981; Dziech & Weiner, 1984). Finally, many victims tolerated harassment because they did not believe that anything could or would be done about it (Allen & Erickson, 1989; Fitzgerald, Gold, & Brock, under review; Fitzgerald & Swan, in press).

Fear of retaliation or reprisals may be the principal reason why students and workers respond indirectly to sexual harassment (Alliance Against Sexual Coercion, 1981; Benson & Thomson, 1982; Dziech & Weiner, 1984). Regardless of the internal explanations that victims provide themselves, a majority of them hope that the harassment will go away if they ignore it (Benson & Thomson, 1982; Gutek, 1985; Fitzgerald, in press; Fitzgerald et al., 1988; Fitzgerald & Swan, in press; McKinnon, 1979; Lindsey, 1977; Loy & Stewart, 1984). However, there is little empirical research that supports the idea that harassers stop harassing if the victim tries to ignore it. Rabinowitz (1990) concluded: "The preponderance of research on harassment is clear in indicating that most harassers are persistent; harassment rarely ends spontaneously, and often escalates in the absence of direct action" (p. 106). However, as will be seen below, direct action does not necessarily lead to a cessation of the sexual harassment.

## Direct Responses by the Victim

The research outlined above demonstrates that responding directly to sexual harassment, as was expected of Anita Hill in the Thomas hearings, is not typical. Furthermore, filing a formal complaint or reporting the harassment to an authority appears to be a very uncommon occurrence (Fitzgerald et al., 1988; Gutek, 1985; Kilpatrick, 1994; Livingston, 1982). Only 18% of the harassment victims in Gutek's (1985) sample, 7% of the women in Gruber and Bjorn's (1982) sample, and less than 5% of the victims in Fitzgerald et al.'s (1988) sample reported the harassment to an authority. Similarly, only 15% of the victims in Kilpatrick, Dansky, and Saunders's (1994) sample, 5% of the female victims in the USM-SPB (1987) sample, and 12% of the enlisted victims in the Navy sample (Culbertson et al., 1992) filed a formal complaint.

There are a number of implications of the low formal reporting rate among sexual harassment victims. First, it demonstrates that women, for a multitude of reasons, do not feel that taking such direct action is advisable. The second implication is that generalizing findings based on victims who file complaints is probably of limited value, since 80–95% of victims are not captured in such studies. It has been documented that sexual harassment victims who reported their harassment experienced more "offensive" forms of harassment than those who did not file a complaint (Brooks & Perot, 1991; Jensen & Gutek, 1982). Therefore, caution is necessary when interpreting results from studies in which the samples consisted of victims who reported their harassment.

Several explanations have been provided by victims for their choice of whether or not to report the harassment. A study conducted by Brooks and Perot (1991) with a sample of female faculty and graduate students demonstrated that likelihood to report gender harassment was significantly predicted by the extent to which the victim perceived the behavior to be "offensive." Another factor that influenced reporting rates was that some victims, particularly those who held themselves responsible for the harassment, were concerned that the harasser and/or his family would suffer as a result of reporting the harassment (Alliance Against Sexual Coercion, 1981; Gutek, 1985; Jensen & Gutek, 1982). Other victims were too embarrassed to report the harassment, believed that reporting it would not have an impact on the situation, feared retaliation for reporting, feared being labeled a "troublemaker," or feared not being believed (Culbertson et al., 1992; Fitzgerald et al., 1988; Gutek, 1985; Jensen & Gutek, 1982). Unfortunately, sexual harassment victims' beliefs that reporting the harassment may have no impact on the situation or worsen it is supported by research.

Although it appears that the public expects direct responses to sexual harassment to be more effective than indirect responses, the empirical literature does not support this expectation. About one-third of the victims who actually filed a formal complaint reported that such action resulted in a worsening of their situation (Hesson-McInnis & Fitzgerald, 1992; Livingston, 1982). Similarly, researchers found that a majority of the victims who complained directly to the harasser continued to be harassed (Benson & Thomson, 1982;

Kilpatrick et al., 1994). Specifically, of the 15 women in the survey by Benson and Thomson (1982) who complained to the harasser, 13 continued to experience harassment. Kilpatrick et al. (1994) reported that in 75% of the cases in which the victim requested that the harassment stop, the harassment continued.

In addition to experiencing continued harassment, many victims experience reprisals (real or perceived) as a result of asking the harasser to stop. Benson and Thomson (1982) and Crull (1982) observed in their samples that a majority of victims who asked the harasser to stop the harassment experienced reprisals for refusing to comply sexually. One-quarter of the women in the Crull sample, consisting of women who had asked for assistance from the Working Women's Institute, indicated that they had been fired or laid off for refusing to comply with harassment. About 25% of the victims in the Kilpatrick et al. (1994) survey who informed someone about the harassment felt that the harasser took action against them because they requested that the sexual harassment stop. Glaser and Thorpe (1986) sampled female clinical psychologists about their experiences of sexual harassment during graduate school. They found that 30% of the victims of sexual harassment responded directly to the harassment, and 45% of those reported punitive treatment from faculty members as a result.

Not only do many women who report the harassment experience a worsening of their situation at work or school; they also appear to be at higher risk for mental and physical health–related consequences. Livingston (1982) documented that, in contrast to women who did not file a compliant, those who filed a formal complaint or sought legal services were much more likely to experience psychological and somatic symptoms. Consistent with this finding, a reanalysis of the Merit Systems Protection Board data by Hesson-McInnis and Fitzgerald (1992) revealed that more direct responses by the victim, such as requesting that the harassment stop, were associated with more deleterious job-related and health-related consequences. Therefore, it appears that direct, assertive behaviors by the victim to cope with the sexual harassment are typically responded to with continued harassment and/or retaliation, and the victims often experience heightened distress. However, an alternative explanation is that victims are more likely to respond directly to more "severe" harassment, and such harassment is more likely to be associated with psychological distress. This explanation is challenged by Hesson-McInnis and Fitzgerald's (1992, under review) analysis, which showed that the association between direct responding and negative outcomes was present even after the influence of harassment severity was statistically controlled. Additional research in this area is necessary to clarify these findings.

Several researchers examined factors that mediate or moderate the types of responses sexual harassment victims use to cope with harassment. Gruber and Bjorn (1986) analyzed responses of female, blue-collar auto plant workers to sexual harassment. They found that although women of lower socioeconomic status (SES) were more likely to be victims of sexual harassment than women of higher SES, no differences in *responses* to sexual harassment were found on the basis of SES. Furthermore, women who occupied low-status, high-visibility positions (e.g., receptionists) were often targets of sexual harassment, and such women were more likely to respond passively to harassment. Finally, the authors reported that women with lower self-esteem and less life satisfaction were more likely to respond passively to sexual harassment than women who felt better about themselves and their life in general. However, the causal sequence of this relationship is open to question. It is equally plausible that passive responses to sexual harassment may lead to lowered self-esteem and less life satisfaction.

Other researchers found that the degree of traditional sex-role attitudes (Jensen & Gutek, 1982), "severity" of the harassment (Loy & Stewart, 1984), or the extent to which a victim blames herself (Jensen & Gutek, 1982) influenced the degree to which the victim responded assertively. Women who were more traditional, more "mildly" harassed (e.g., gender harassment or seductive behavior), and who blamed themselves for the harassment were less likely to respond directly than women who were less traditional, experienced more severe types of harassment (e.g., sexual bribery or coercion), or who blamed themselves less for the harassment.

### Victim Responses Considered Within a Stress and Coping Framework

Turning away from the previously described method of classifying sexual harassment victims' responses in terms of level of assertiveness/directness, Fitzgerald and Swan (in press) used a stress and coping framework, based on work of Lazarus and Folkman (1984), to provide a cognitive conceptualization of victims' responses to sexual harassment. They analyzed descriptions provided by actual sexual harassment victims who participated in a large sexual harassment prevalence study. A coding system was devised consisting of 10 response strategies that are either internally focused (attempts to manage emotions or cognitions) or externally focused (attempts to problem solve or alter the situation; Fitzgerald et al., 1988). In creating this coding system, Fitzgerald and her colleagues rejected the notion that victims who respond assertively, as opposed to ignoring the harassment or managing emotions, have necessarily responded with greater competence. Instead, they viewed coping as a process that results in a variety of outcomes, which include both direct (externally focused) and indirect (internally focused) responses to the harassment.

## Work-Related/School-Related Effects

### Work-Related Effects

Negative job ramifications for individual victims include decreased job satisfaction (Baker, 1989; Culbertson et al., 1992; Gruber & Bjorn, 1982; O'Farrell & Harlan, 1982), declines in job performance (Crull, 1982; Gutek, 1985; USMSPB, 1981, 1987), decreased motivation (Jensen & Gutek, 1982), interrupted careers

(Coles, 1986; Livingston, 1982), decreased morale, increased absenteeism (Gosselin, 1986; USMSPB, 1981, 1987), lowered productivity (USMSPB, 1981, 1987), and impaired relationships between coworkers (Bandy, 1989 as cited in Fitzgerald, 1993; Culbertson et al., 1992; DiTomaso, 1989; Gutek, 1985; O'Farrell & Harlan, 1982). Specifically, a decline in job performance was reported by 75% of the women in the Crull (1982) sample, which consisted of women who had sought assistance from the Working Women's Institute. Decreased self-confidence in work-related skills was observed, as well as diminished work motivation. More than 25% of the women were fired or "laid off." A similarly high number of firings was observed by Coles (1986), who sampled women who had filed complaints with the California Fair Employment and Housing Department. She found that one-half of all complainants had been fired and another 25% had quit their job. Of course, it is possible that women who had adverse reactions to harassment on the job were more likely to file complaints.

Schneider and Swan (1994) measured job-related outcomes in a sample of 447 women employed at a public utilities company in the U.S. Northwest. Complete data were obtained from 371 women, and they were divided into four groups: no harassment (33%), low frequency of harassment (14%), moderate frequency of harassment (26%), and high frequency of harassment (13%). Women in the no harassment group scored significantly higher on a measure of work satisfaction, satisfaction with coworkers, and satisfaction with supervisors than women who had experienced harassment. Harassment victims also were less committed to their organization, and victims in the high frequency of harassment group were significantly more likely to withdraw from their job as evidenced by considering or actually quitting (Schneider & Swan, 1994).

There also are subtle effects of sexual harassment on job performance. Sexual harassment in the form of gender discrimination may prevent women from benefiting from informal social interactions with coworkers (DiTomaso, 1989; Ragins & Scandura, 1992).

Such interactions sometimes provide "inside" information that can influence promotions, raises, and other job-related outcomes.

Despite the fact that studies in the area of sexual harassment have been conducted for the past 20 years, until the 1990s virtually no investigators had researched *organizational responses* to sexual harassment, and questions such as how sexual harassment affects professional relationships or how the public identification of sexual harassment influences the work environment still remain unanswered. It appears that organizations may experience several outcomes that resemble individual outcomes, such as lower productivity and a damaged reputation (Bravo & Cassedy, 1992). Fitzgerald and Shullman (1993) asserted that sexual harassment includes many emotional factors that create difficulties when victims "reintegrate" in their workplace. They mentioned a rise in retaliatory actions at the workplace when a sexual harassment victim is identified and noted a pressing need for research in this area.

Recently, organizational effects of sexual harassment such as forced early retirement or other types of "organizational withdrawal" have been discussed (Hanisch & Hulin, 1990, 1991). Hanisch and Hulin identified two types of organizational withdrawal: one type was called "work withdrawal" and involved avoidance by an *individual* of work duties, whereas the second type was labeled "job withdrawal" and encompassed job turnover, retirement, et cetera. The authors proposed that "job attitudes" mediate the influence of sexual harassment on organizational withdrawal (Fitzgerald, Hulin, & Drasgow, in preparation). Understanding the impact of sexual harassment at an organizational level can lead to improved public/organizational policy regarding filing and processing sexual harassment complaints and help shape prevention programs.

## Effect at an University Level

Research has documented that the effect of sexual harassment at an university level can be a disrupted academic experience due to changes in class schedule, major, program, institution, or career intentions (Adams, Kot-tke, & Padgitt, 1983; Benson & Thomson, 1982; Fitzgerald, 1990; Lott, Reilly, & Howard, 1982). Benson and Thomson (1982) stated: "The male prerogative to define the terms of the relationship—to use sexual rather than official criteria to evaluate a woman's worth in academia—remains unchecked" (p. 247). The authors discussed how female students may purposefully avoid contact with individuals whom they perceive to be potential harassers, which can lead to substandard education due to "missed opportunities." Similar to what can occur in the workplace, distrust may develop between students and faculty and create an environment wherein women do not have access to informal informational channels and relationships that sometimes result in academic advancements.

The effect of sexual harassment can also be observed in women's dress and office conduct. Dziech and Weiner (1984) describe how women may "dress down" in order to appear less sexual or attractive, avoid contact with the harasser, or purposefully disclose personal information about a spouse or boyfriend in an effort to divert the harasser's attention. Although these tactics were utilized by women attempting to cope with actual sexual harassment, it is likely that even when sexually harassing behaviors have not been perpetrated, women's choices of clothing, gestures, and topics of conversation may be guided by a desire to avoid potential sexual harassment "before it starts."

Sexual harassment at colleges and universities may be a major contributor to lower earning power of women in the work force. Research has demonstrated that sexual harassment can compromise the quality of education, and this, in turn, may lead to lowered academic achievement (Hotelling, 1991). With lower-quality education, women are likely to have lower earning power. This is then added to the problem of sexual harassment in the workplace, which has a direct impact on women's earning power.

## Economic Effects

The costs of sexual harassment to the U.S. economy are alarming. For instance, it has been estimated that the monetary cost of sexual harassment per company, excluding costs of litigation, averages $6.7 million annually (Wagner, 1992). Wagner attributed these costs to declines in morale and productivity, increased medical claims for missed work, and job turnover. It was estimated in the study conducted by the Merit Systems Protection Board that sexual harassment cost the federal government more than $250 million over a two-year period (USMSPB, 1987). A job turnover rate of 10% was documented in the USMSPB (1981) sample, which results in added costs of job recruitment and training (Gosselin, 1986).

## Psychological Effects

Despite that fact that few researchers have examined the relationship between psychiatric/psychological *disorders* and sexual harassment, reports can be found in the literature dating back 20 years regarding *psychological symptoms* reported by sexual harassment victims in surveys by Brodsky (1976), Redbook (Safran, 1976), and the Working Women's United Institute in New York (Silverman, 1976–77). Although the sexual harassment victims in these surveys were either self-selected (Redbook) or those who filed a formal report (WWUI), their responses clearly indicated that sexual harassment victims can experience numerous negative emotions, including anger, fear, guilt, and helplessness.

A central difficulty in studying mental health consequences of sexual harassment is that outcomes can be multiply determined (Gutek & Koss, 1993). Often a victim of sexual harassment not only is affected by the sexual harassment itself, but can experience other related stress such as office "gossip," lower pay, and disrupted work history. Furthermore, since a majority of sexual assault victims experience their first assault during childhood, it is likely that a significant proportion of sexual harassment victims may have a previous assault history (Dansky et al., 1994). The psychological impact of a sexual harassment experience may be compounded by a resurfacing of affect and cognitions associated with a prior victimization. Additionally, sexual

harassment victims who respond to the harassment by denying its existence or importance are a difficult group to capture with standardized instruments; measurement of psychological symptomatology connected with sexual harassment is an arduous task.

A majority of the current research, most of which is anecdotal, suggests that victims of harassment experience a wide variety of symptoms, including decreased self-esteem (Gruber & Bjorn, 1986) and self-confidence (Benson & Thomson, 1982), depression (Pendergrass et al., 1976; Institute for Research on Women's Health, 1988; Hamilton et al., 1987), anxiety, fear of rape (Holgate, 1989), and increased fear of crime in general (Junger, 1987). Based on survey data from student victims, Tong (1984) identified a "sexual harassment syndrome," which is a constellation of psychological symptoms including depression, helplessness, isolation, irritability, fear, anxiety, and substance abuse.

Similar patterns of symptoms—anger, fear, depression, anxiety, irritability, lowered self-esteem, alienation, shame, helplessness, and vulnerability—were reported by other investigators (Gutek, 1985; McCormack, 1985; Safran, 1976; Silverman, 1976–77). Ninety percent of the women in Crull's (1982) sample reported psychological symptoms resulting from the sexual harassment, with "tension" or "nervousness" being the most frequently reported symptoms, along with anger and fear. Paludi and Barickman (1991) asserted that the psychological effects of sexual harassment can be long-term, although at present there are no empirical data to support this contention.

Sexual harassment may be regarded by the victim as a shameful experience, which may lead to social isolation/alienation from coworkers who may have experienced similar harassment (Fitzgerald, 1993). Gutek (1985) observed that sexual harassment at times influenced women's relationships with other men, and victims in Benson and Thomson's (1982) sample reported difficulties with trust. Furthermore, Gosselin (1986) described how victims of sexual harassment may display seemingly "contradictory" emotional responses to the harassment. She pointed out that victims may feel angry at the harasser, yet hesitate in reporting the harassment for fear of reprisals. Victims may feel that stopping the harassment is not within their power, yet they also may hold themselves responsible for its occurrence. Victims may dislike their feelings of alienation, yet at the same time they may isolate themselves from their peers. These seemingly contradictory emotions are considered to play a large part in victims' mental health outcomes.

Although research including an evaluation of all symptom criteria necessary to make a diagnosis of Post-Traumatic Stress Disorder (PTSD) has not yet been published (see discussion below), symptoms such as emotional numbing, restricted affect, and flashbacks were observed in a sample of harassment victims (Institute for Research on Women's Health, 1988). Koss (1990) and Gutek and Koss (1993) have advocated a PTSD model for understanding the mental health consequences of sexual harassment. Furthermore, Hamilton and colleagues (1987) described sexual harassment victims as suffering from a "post-trauma syndrome" characterized by flashbacks, sleep disturbance, emotional numbing, and anxiety.

## The National Women's Study: Sexual Harassment, Prior Assault, and Psychological Outcomes

The research team at the Crime Victims Research and Treatment Center at the Medical University of South Carolina conducted the first systematic examination of sexual harassment, depression, and PTSD at the diagnostic level (Dansky et al., 1992, 1994; Kilpatrick, 1992; Saunders, 1992). Information regarding sexual harassment was collected from a national sample of 3,006 female adults. This sample was derived from an original sample (Wave 1) that included a national probability household sample of 2,008 women and an oversample of 2,000 women age 18 to 34. The original survey design included an oversample of younger age cohorts to ensure an adequate sample of sexual assault victims, since younger age groups are overrepresented among recent sexual assault victims.

The Wave 1 sample was generated by multistage geographic sampling procedures that produced stratified samples in four regions of the United States. Random digit dialing was used to target households within each stratum. To ensure random selection within a household, the female adult with the most recent birthday was interviewed. Completed Wave 1 telephone interviews were obtained from 85% of the women with whom telephone contact was achieved. Of the Wave 1 sample, 3,006 women (75% of Wave 1 participants) were located in the Wave 3 of the study (which occurred two years after the Wave 1 interviews) and completed the telephone interview. Interviews averaged approximately 40 minutes in length. Since the original sample was derived in 1989, the data were weighted according to estimates of the 1989 U.S. Census figures for age and race.

### Instruments

*Sexual harassment.* To measure sexual harassment, seven potentially sexually harassing behaviors were listed one at a time (see Table 9-1). Respondents first indicated whether a boss or supervisor had behaved in the manner described. Respondents who answered "yes" were then asked whether they had felt that they were "being sexually harassed" by the particular behavior. After responding to the behavioral probes, participants who reported that they had experienced at least one of seven behaviors *and* had perceived the behavior as harassing were asked:

a. "Did you think that if you complained or didn't go along that would hurt you with respect to hiring, firing, promotions, or pay raises?"

b. "Did your boss or supervisor ever say that if you complained or didn't go along that it would hurt you with respect to hiring, firing, promotions, or pay raises?"; and

c. "To what extent did the unwanted sexual advances or comments interfere with your ability to do your job?"

The guidelines outlined in Section 703 of Title VII of the Civil Rights Act of 1964 (EEOC criteria) were utilized to identify sexual harassment *victims*. To be classified as a victim of sexual harassment, a respondent: (1)

indicated that she had experienced at least one of the potentially sexually harassing behaviors *and* perceived it to be harassment, *and* (2) believed or was told by the harasser that complaining or failure to comply would result in negative job consequences, *or* (3) the harassment interfered with the respondent's ability to perform her job (Table 9-2). If a respondent was classified as a sexual harassment victim, she was asked a series of questions about the "worst" or most serious time this had occurred.

Among respondents who indicated that they had been employed at some point during their lives ($n = 2,941$), four mutually exclusive groups were constructed:

*Group 1*: No Sexual Harassment ($n = 2,114$; 71.8%)

*Group 2*: Potentially Sexually Harassing Behaviors Only ($n = 314$; 10.7%)

*Group 3*: Potentially Sexually Harassing Behaviors + Perception of Harassment but without a deleterious impact on the job ($n = 175$; 6.0%)

*Group 4*: Sexual Harassment that met EEOC criteria (Behavior + Perception + Job Impact – Sexual Harassment Victims, ($n = 337$; 11.5%)

It should be noted that the method of classifying sexual harassment victims listed here may be more stringent than methods employed by other researchers (e.g., Fitzgerald and her colleagues, Gutek, Koss, etc.) in that the more subtle or nonverbal types of sexual harassment or instances of harassment perpetrated by coworkers (which can create a hostile work environment) were not captured in this survey. It is likely that incidents of coworker sexual assault were captured in the complete trauma screening protocol described below. Also, the *National Women's Study (NWS)* did not assess sexual harassment in educational settings. Therefore, it is likely that the data presented are conservative estimates of the mental health consequences of sexual harassment.

*Post-Traumatic Stress Disorder.* PTSD was assessed using the *NWS* PTSD module (Kilpatrick, et al., 1989). The *NWS* PTSD module was modified from the Diagnostic Interview Schedule (DIS) used in the National Vietnam Veterans Readjustment Study (NVVRS;

**TABLE 9-1.** Possible Sexually Harassing Behaviors and Perceptions of Those Behaviors

| BOSSES' OR SUPERVISORS' BEHAVIOR | PREVALENCE | FELT HARASSED[a] | FELT HARASSED[b] |
|---|---|---|---|
| Told stories about their sexual attributes or behavior | 16.8% | 54.6% | 8.9% |
| Said things to you, or in your hearing, about your body | 16.9% | 64.6% | 10.5% |
| Made repeated unwanted requests for you to go out with them "socially" or on dates | 10.5% | 70.7% | 7.2% |
| Touched you in a sexual way when you had not encouraged them | 7.2% | 90.1% | 6.3% |
| Tried to kiss or fondle you when you had not encouraged them | 6.2% | 89.5% | 5.4% |
| Promised to help you on the job if you were nice to them | 7.0% | 82.5% | 5.7% |
| Promised to make trouble for you if you were not nice to them | 4.2% | 85.1% | 3.5% |

[a] Base: Number of participants having experienced the behavior.

[b] Base: Entire weighted sample of women who had ever worked ($n = 2,941$).

**TABLE 9-2.** Questions Addressing Part 2 of Section 703 of Title VII

| | PREVALENCE AMONG THOSE WHO FELT HARASSED | PREVALENCE AMONG ALL WORKERS |
|---|---|---|
| Did you think that if you complained or didn't go along that it would hurt you with respect to hiring, firing, promotions, or pay raises? | 56.7% | 9.8% |
| Did your boss or supervisor ever say that if you complained or didn't go along that it would hurt you with respect to hiring, firing, promotions, or pay raises? | 16.5% | 2.8% |
| To what extent did the unwanted sexual advances or comments interfere with your ability to do your job? | 70.1% | 12.1% |

Kulka et al., 1990). Participants were screened for symptoms of PTSD (using DSM-III-R criteria) regardless of whether they had experienced an event that met PTSD Criterion A (an event outside of range of usual human experience that would produce marked distress in almost anyone).

As part of the *complete trauma screening* designed to target events that met PTSD Criterion A, participants were asked about *completed rape*, which included any unwanted penetration of the vagina or anus (with a finger, object, tongue, or penis) that occurred as the result of force or threat of force; *sexual molestation*, which included unwanted contact with breasts or genitals without penetration due to force or threat of force; *attempted sexual assault*, which included any unwanted physical contact excluding breasts or genitals wherein the victim perceived intended forced sexual contact; and *aggravated assault*, which included physical assault with or without a weapon but during which the victim perceived the assailant as intending serious injury or killing. For data-analysis purposes a category of *direct assault* was created to capture any type of sexual or aggravated assault.

The remaining PTSD symptom criteria were obtained via a structured interview schedule to assess intrusive symptoms, symptoms of avoidance, and symptoms of increased arousal. Respondents were not required to link their symptoms to a specific

traumatic event (non–event-specific), which would necessitate a level of insight concerning symptom–event correspondence that most respondents likely did not possess. *Lifetime PTSD* was assigned if a respondent met the DSM-III-R criteria by having the necessary number of Criterion B (one reexperiencing symptom), C (three avoidance symptoms), and D (two increased arousal symptoms). (See Resnick et al., 1993 for more information about the PTSD screening instrument.)

*Major Depressive Disorder.* The screening instrument for major depression was based on DSM-III-R criteria. Respondents were asked the following probes: "Have you ever had a period of two weeks or longer when you were feeling depressed or down most of the day or nearly every day?" and "Has there been a time of two weeks or longer when you were uninterested in most things or unable to enjoy things you used to do?" Respondents who endorsed either of the two probe questions were asked about the following symptoms (which were required to have lasted for at least two weeks): changes in weight, changes in sleep patterns, restlessness, lethargy, feelings of worthlessness or guilt, problems with concentration, and thoughts about hurting themselves. Participants were classified as having *Lifetime Depression* if they had experienced a major depressive episode at some point during their lifetime, whereas respondents with *Cur-*

*rent Depression* met criteria for depression during the six months prior to the interview.

## Results

A series of chi-square analyses were calculated to compare respondents in the four sexual harassment groups with respect to rates of PTSD and depression. The prevalence of Lifetime PTSD differed among the four sexual harassment groups in that it was lowest among respondents who reported that they had never experienced any potentially harassing behavior (9.0%), slightly higher among women classified in the Behavior Only group (12.1%), higher among women in the Behavior + Perception group (20.2%), and highest among women in the Sexual Harassment Victim group (29.7%). $X^2(3) = 125.34$, p < 0.001; see Figure 9-1. A similar pattern of prevalence rates was observed for Current PTSD with more than 1 in 10 sexual harassment victims experiencing current symptoms of PTSD.

Sexual harassment victims also were significantly more likely to have experienced a major depressive episode than women who had encountered less intrusive or no sexual harassment. Specifically, the prevalence of Lifetime Depression was lowest among women who had experienced no sexual harassment (12.3%), higher among women in the Behavior Only group (19.4%) and the Behavior + Perception Only group (20.1%), and highest among women classified as Sexual Harassment Victims (28.8%). $X^2(3) = 68.98$, p < 0.001; see Figure 9-2. As can be seen in Figure 9-2, a similar pattern of prevalence rates was obtained for Current Depression—$X^2(3) = 76.57$, p < 0.001. The high rate for Current Depression (21.9%) among sexual harassment victims is particularly noteworthy.

In order to assess the extent to which current symptoms of PTSD or depression could be explained by sexual harassment group membership, two hierarchical multiple logistic regression equations were calculated. In the first equation, Current PTSD was the dependent variable and whether the respondent had a history of a direct sexual or physical assault was entered on the first step ($n = 947$ direct assault victims and 1,993 nonvictims), fol-

lowed on the second step by whether or not participants met full EEOC criteria for being a sexual harassment victim ($n = 337$ victims and 2,604 nonvictims). This order of entry was selected in order to evaluate whether being a victim of sexual harassment makes an independent contribution in predicting PTSD status beyond the effect of other types of victimization. The results indicate that being classified as a victim of sexual harassment was a significant predictor of Current PTSD, even after the effect of other direct assaults was taken into account [−2 Log Likelihood = 1002.15; Model Improvement $X^2(1) = 10.17$, p < 0.001]. Examination of the odds ratios indicate that the odds of meeting criteria for Current PTSD were 4.6 times greater for participants who had experienced some type of sexual and/or physical assault as compared with nonvictims and were 1.2 times greater among victims of sexual harassment than among women who were not classified as victims of sexual harassment (Table 9-3).

Similar results were obtained in the second hierarchical multiple logistic regression predicting current depression. Being classified as a sexual harassment victim was a significant predictor of current depression, even after the influence of assault history was taken into account [−2 Log Likelihood = 1785.22; Model Improvement $X^2(1) = 22.28$, p < 0.001]. Respondents with a history of sexual and/or physical assault were 2.9 times more likely to have Current Depression than respondents without such an assault history, and respondents who were victims of sexual harassment were 1.2 times more likely to have Current Depression than respondents who were not classified as sexual harassment victims (see Table 9-3).

## Discussion

The results clearly suggest that the lifetime risk of PTSD or major depression is significantly higher among sexual harassment victims than among women who never experienced sexual harassment, as defined by EEOC guidelines. This increased risk of PTSD or depression associated with being a victim of sexual harassment was present even

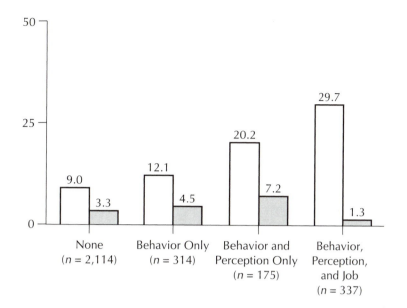

**Figure 9-1.** Prevalence of Lifetime and Current PTSD by harassment groups (from data collected by the National Women's Study, Crime Victims Research and Treatment Center, Department of Psychiatry and Behavioral Sciences, Medical University of South Carolina, Charleston)

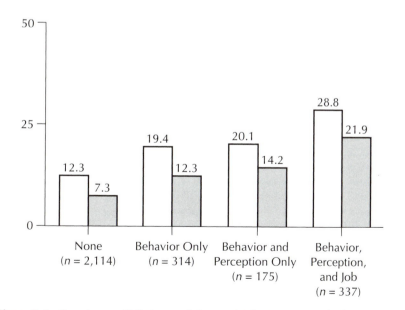

**Figure 9-2.** Prevalence of Lifetime and Current Major Depression by harassment groups (from data collected by the National Women's Study Crime Victims Research and Treatment Center, Department of Psychiatry and Behavioral Sciences, Medical University of South Carolina, Charleston)

after any effect due to other types of victimizations was accounted for. In addition, the findings that 1 in 10 sexual harassment victims had Current PTSD and 1 in 5 had Current Depression illustrate that the negative effects of this type of sexual victimization can be long-term, since the average amount of time that elapsed since the sexual harassment incident occurred was approximately 11 years (SD = 9.82; range 0–50 years). This highlights the incredible psychological cost of sexual harassment.

Of course, there are a number of methodological limitations of this study. First, participants made their own subjective judgments concerning whether the behaviors constituted "harassment," although a woman's perception as to whether a sexual advance or behavior is unwanted is a key factor in legal definitions of sexual harassment. Second, certain types of sexual harassment were not measured, such as gender harassment, which typically involves sexist comments, public display of materials denigrating women, or harassment perpetrated by coworkers. Third, the investigation was retrospective and therefore suffers from the typical difficulties associated with such methodology. Fourth, this study did not measure sexual harassment in educational settings. However, the findings are from a national, representative sample of women (not just those who have reported their experience) and clearly support the need for further research in

this area, since sexual harassment victims appear to be at high risk for current psychiatric disorders.

## Health-Related Effects

In addition to studying psychological sequelae of sexual harassment, several researchers have documented a variety of somatic complaints in their samples of sexual harassment victims. Crull (1982), in her sample of women seeking assistance from Working Women Institute, found that physical complaints were reported by 63% of the sample and included headaches, gastrointestinal disturbances, and tiredness. Other researchers also have documented negative health consequences of sexual harassment such as gastrointestinal disturbance, dental-related problems, headaches, sleep disturbance, fatigue, nausea, weight loss, and loss of appetite (Gutek, 1985; Lindsey, 1977; Loy & Stewart, 1984; Safran, 1976; Salisbury et al., 1986). MacKinnon (1979) noted reports of sleep disturbance, headaches, gastrointestinal distress, neck pain, and back pain among victims of sexual harassment. Although several researchers such as those just cited have mentioned health-related consequences of sexual harassment, as of 1995, no one had made a systematic study of this issue. Future research efforts in this area should include the use of standardized measures of health-related problems with large samples of women.

**TABLE 9-3.** Logistic Regression: Direct Crime, Sexual Harassment, Current PTSD, and Current Depression

| INTERVAL | ODDS RATIO | CONFIDENCE INTERVAL (95%) |
|---|---|---|
| Criterion: Current PTSD | | |
| Step 1—Direct Crime | 4.6 | 3.12–6.78 |
| Step 2[a]—Sexual Harassment Victim | 1.2 | 1.07–1.32 |
| Criterion: Current Depression | | |
| Step 1—Direct Crime | 2.9 | 2.23–3.73 |
| Step 2[b]—Sexual Harassment Victim | 1.2 | 1.12–1.31 |

[a]Model chi-square improvement $X^2(1) = 10.17$, $p < 0.001$
[b]Model chi-square improvement $X^2(1) = 22.28$, $p < 0.001$

## Summary

Empirical studies of responses to and outcomes of sexual harassment have revealed important information about the sequelae of sexual harassment. First, it is apparent that a majority of victims of sexual harassment, at least initially, attempt to ignore the offensive behavior. It is also apparent that ignoring sexual harassment rarely leads to its termination, yet more direct or assertive efforts to respond to sexual harassment may not be more effective. Many victims respond to harassment by attempting to avoid contact with the harasser, which may entail dropping a class, changing positions, or even quitting a job. In a sizable proportion of cases, direct requests to the harasser to stop the harassment can lead to a worsening of the situation. Sexual harassment victims fear reprisals for their noncompliance, and many experience retaliation if they resist. Fewer than 15% of sexual harassment victims file formal complaints about the harassment.

Sexual harassment victims suffer a multitude of work-related consequences, including interrupted careers from quitting or being fired, declines in job performance, decreased job satisfaction, decreased motivation, decreased morale, increased absenteeism, and impaired relationships with coworkers. Impaired relationships may prevent women from benefiting from informal social interactions with coworkers, which can provide information that is important for promotions, raises, and other job-related outcomes. Ramifications of school-related sexual harassment include a disrupted academic experience due to changes in class schedule, major, program, institution, or career intentions. Similar to what can occur at work, distrust between students and faculty can create an environment wherein victims of harassment no longer have access to the informal informational channels and relationships that may lead to academic advancements.

Effects of sexual harassment on an organization may include work withdrawal, or avoidance by an individual of work duties, and job withdrawal, or job turnover or retirement. Research also has shown that harassment victims may be less committed to their organization and more likely to withdraw from their job by considering or actually quitting. The economic cost of sexual harassment is enormous, averaging $6.7 million per company annually and about $250 million for the federal government.

The psychological and physical costs of sexual harassment are manifold. Sexual harassment is associated with numerous psychological complaints, including decreased self-esteem, depression, isolation, irritability, anxiety, anger, fear, guilt, helplessness, fear of rape, increased fear of crime in general, sexual dysfunction, and substance abuse. In addition, sexual harassment victims are more likely to have experienced other types of victimization, and their risk of post-traumatic stress disorder and/or depression is significantly higher than that of women who never were harassed. Somatic complaints that have been reported by victims of sexual harassment include gastrointestinal disturbance, headaches, sleep disturbance, fatigue, neck pain, back pain, nausea, weight loss, and loss of appetite. Although not all victims of sexual harassment necessarily experience all symptoms, the range of difficulties is broad and the likelihood is high that many victims experience at least some distress associated with their experience.

## Research Directions

Given that the study of effects of sexual harassment is a relatively new area of inquiry, there remain a number of gaps in scientific knowledge. First, the majority of studies have included samples of convenience or special populations. Therefore, the effects of sexual harassment among people of varying ages, races, socioeconomic backgrounds, and employment histories have not been well documented. Second, researchers have either allowed respondents to use their own subjective interpretations of the term "sexual harassment" or have provided definitions that vary across research teams. Third, many surveys assessed only workplace sexual harassment *or* sexual harassment in an educational setting. This practice is problematic since it is likely that employed women also attend school or have attended school in their lifetimes and that college students also have a work history. Assessing only one type of harassment fails to take into account the complex work/school histories of many people. Fourth, the potential impact of other forms of victimization/discrimination or major life events typically was not assessed. Without such information it is impossible to draw conclusions regarding the specific effects of sexual harassment. A woman who appears to be suffering from PTSD as a result of sexual harassment may actually have a long and complex assault history, which may account for or contribute to her current symptomatology. Fifth, when measuring outcomes, few researchers have included standardized measures of psychological or physical distress. Most often, respondents were asked to generate their own list of symptoms or were provided with a broad list of symptoms not pertaining to any particular diagnostic category.

To address these gaps in the research literature, we propose the following attributes of an "ideal" study:

1. An ideal study of the effects of sexual harassment should use probability sampling techniques, since there are reasons to believe that samples of self-identified victims may be biased toward more "severe" forms of sexual harassment or that the minority of individuals who ever report harassment differ from the majority who never do. Probability samples where respondents are interviewed at home (in person or by telephone) would provide a diverse sample that includes ethnic/racial minorities, individuals in both traditional and nontraditional job settings, students from all types of institutions of higher learning, and individuals who have dropped out of school or left work.

2. An ideal study also should be prospective in design so that new incidents of sexual harassment that occur over the course of the investigation could be detected and the limitations of retrospective reporting would be avoided.

3. Additionally, sexual harassment should be operationally defined using behaviorally specific questions. All forms of sexual harassment, from gender discrimination to sexual assault, should be measured. Some researchers already have begun to utilize standardized measures of sexual harassment (e.g., Fitzgerald et al.'s [1988] Sexual Experiences Questionnaire) and victim responses (e.g., Fitzgerald, Gold, & Brock [under review]).

4. Theory should drive research protocols. Although descriptive data are beneficial, the field soon must move toward theory-driven hypothesis testing, including factors that mediate/moderate the relationship between sexual harassment and negative outcomes.

5. Respondents' perceptions of the harassing behavior should be evaluated, along with details of the harassment—e.g., duration, relationship to the perpetrator, type of sexual activity, etc.

6. Incidents that involve potential harassment (e.g., a boss asking a subordinate to go on a date, a teacher making sexual comments to a student) that were *not* perceived as harassment by the individual should be compared with those viewed as harassment. Since it is increasingly common for people to become romantically involved with individuals with whom they work, it would be beneficial to examine the nature of consensual relationships between bosses and employees, coworkers, and students and teachers. For example, if a boss asks a subordinate for a date and that person is pleased with the invitation, then the boss's behavior does not constitute sexual harassment, since it was not unwanted. An important research question involves teasing apart interactions that are perceived to be sexual harassment and those that are not. (Of course, many would view relationships between teacher and students as problematic because of the power differential between the two parties, irrespective of whether the advance was wanted or not.)

7. A complete assessment of respondents' trauma history would enable researchers to understand how previous traumatic events influence the way in which individuals cope with sexual harassment experiences and the degree to which symptomatology can be attributed to the harassment.

8. An ideal study should include an instrument (like Holmes and Rahe's [1967] social readjustment rating scale) to assess the "stressfulness" of sexual harassment relative to other major events in a person's life.

9. An ideal study also should use standardized instruments to evaluate multiple outcomes of sexual harassment, which would enable researchers to determine the relative impact of sexual harassment experiences on different domains of functioning, i.e., physical, psychological, economic, etc. In most instances, clinical psychologists have studied psychological effects of sexual harassment, industrial/organizational psycholo-gists have focused on work-related outcomes, and social psychologists have concentrated on issues such as the definition of sexual harassment and perceptions of it. The use of a multidisciplinary team of researchers might facilitate measurement of multiple outcomes of sexual harassment, since each outcome area would be represented by a researcher with specialized training.

Of course, the likelihood is low that any one survey could contain all of the elements listed here. However, with improved research methodology many of the remaining questions concerning the effects of sexual harassment could be answered with as much accuracy as possible. The next step after such information is available would be to construct primary, secondary, and tertiary prevention policies to reduce the incidence of sexual harassment, reduce its negative impact if it does occur, and reduce the severity of the suffering that some victims withstand.

# REFERENCES

Abramson, L. Y., Seligman, M. E. P., & Teasdale, J. D. (1979). Learned helplessness in humans: Critique and reformulation. *Journal of Abnormal Psychology, 87,* 49–74.

Adams, J. W., Kottke, J. L., & Padgitt, J. S. (1983). Sexual harassment of university students. *Journal of College Student Personnel, 24,* 484–490.

Allen, D., & Erickson, J. (1989). *Sexual harassment of faculty at the University of Illinois.* Champaign: Union of Professional Employees, University of Illinois at Urbana-Champaign.

Alliance Against Sex Coercion (1981). *Fighting sexual harassment: An advocacy handbook.* Boston: Alyson.

Baker, N.L. (1989). *Sexual harassment and job satisfaction in traditional and nontraditional industrial occupations.* Doctoral dissertation, California School of Professional Psychology, Los Angeles.

Bandy, N. (1989). *Sexual harassment and job satisfaction in traditional and nontraditional industrial occupations.* Doctoral dissertation, California School of Professional Psychology, Los Angeles, as cited in L. F. Fitzgerald (1993), Sexual harassment: Violence against women in the workplace. *American Psychologist, 48,* 1070–1076.

Benson, D.J., & Thomson, G.E. (1982). Sexual harassment on a university campus: The confluence of authority relations, sexual interest, and gender stratification. *Social Problems, 29,* 236–251.

Bravo, L. & Cassedy (1992). *The 9 to 5 guide to combating sexual harassment.* New York: Wiley.

Brodsky, C.M. (1976). *The harassed worker.* Lexington, MA: D.C. Health and Co.

Brooks, L., & Perot, A.R. (1991). Reporting sexual harassment: Exploring a predictive model. *Psychology of Women Quarterly, 15,* 31–47.

Bularzik, M. (1978). Sexual harassment at the workplace: Historical notes. *Radical American, 12,* 25–43.

Burt, M.R., & Katz, B.L. (1985). Rape, robbery, and burglary: Responses to actual and feared criminal victimization with special focus on women and the elderly. *Victimology: An International Journal, 10,* 325–358.

Coles, F.S. (1986). Forced to quit: Sexual harassment complaints and agency response. *Sex Roles, 14,* 81–95.

Crull, P. (1982). Stress effects of sexual harassment on the job: Implications for counseling. *American Journal of Orthopsychiatry, 52,* 539–544.

Culbertson, A.L., Rosenfeld, P., Booth-Kewley, S., & Magnusson, P. (1992). *Assessment of sexual harassment in the Navy: Results of the 1989 Navy-wide survey, TR–92–11.* San Diego, CA: Naval Personnel Research and Development Center.

Dansky, B.S., Kilpatrick, D.G., Saunders, B.E., Resnick, H.S., Best, C.L., Hanson, R.F., & Saladin, M.E. (1992, August). Sexual harassment: I can't define it but I know it when I see it. Poster presented at the Annual Meeting of the American Psychological Association.

Dansky, B.S., Best, C.L., Saunders, B.E., Resnick, H.S., & Kilpatrick, D.G. (1994, March). Sexual harassment and victimization history: The National Women's Study. Poster presented at the Annual Meeting of the Southeastern Psychological Association, New Orleans, LA.

DiTomaso, N. (1989). Sexuality in the workplace: Discrimination and harassment. In J. Hearn, D.L. Sheppard, P. Tancred-Sherif, & G. Burrell (Eds.), *The sexuality of organizations* (pp. 71–90). London: Sage.

Dziech, B.W., & Weiner, L. (1984). *The lecherous professor*. Boston: Beacon Press.

Fitzgerald, L. F. (1990). Sexual harassment: The definition of a construct. In M. Paludi (Ed), *Ivony Power*, Albany, New York: SUNY Press. 21-44.

Fitzgerald, L.F. (1993). Sexual harassment: Violence against women in the workplace. *American Psychologist, 48*, 1070–1076.

Fitzgerald, L.F. (in press). Violence at work. In APA Taskforce on Male Violence Against Women (Eds.), *No safe haven: Violence against women at home, at work, and in the community*. Washington, DC: American Psychological Association.

Fitzgerald., L.F., Gefland, M.J., & Drasgow, F. (in press). Measuring sexual harassment: Theoretical and psychometric advances. *Basic and Applied Social Psychology*.

Fitzgerald, L.F., Gold, Y., & Brock, K. (under review). *Women's responses to victimization: Validation of an objective inventory for assessing strategies for responding to sexual harassment*.

Fitzgerald, L.F., & Hesson-McInnis, M. (1989). The dimensions of sexual harassment: A structural analysis. *Journal of Vocational Behavior, 35*, 309–326.

Fitzgerald, L.F., Hulin, C.L., & Drasgow, F. (1993). The antecedents and consequences of sexual harassment in organizations: An integrated model. In APA/NIOSH volume (Eds.) *Stress in the workplace*. Washington, D.C: American Psychological Association.

Fitzgerald, L.F., Hulin, C.L., & Drasgow, F. (in preparation). The antecedents and consequences of sexual harassment in organizations. In G. Keita & S. Sauter (Eds.), *Job stress 2000: Emergent issues*. Washington, DC: American Psychological Organization.

Fitzgerald L. F., & Ormerod, M. (1993). Breaking silence: The sexual harassment of women in academia and the workplace. In F. Denmark & M. Paludi (Eds.),

*Handbook of the psychology of women*. New York: Greenwood.

Fitzgerald, L.F., & Shullman, S.L. (1993). Sexual harassment: A research analysis and agenda for the 1990's. *Journal of Vocational Behavior, 42*, 5–27.

Fitzgerald, L.F., Shullman, S.L., Bailey, N., Richards, R., Swecker, J., Gold, Y., Ormerod, M., & Weitzman, L. (1988). The incidence and dimensions of sexual harassment in academia and the workplace. *Journal of Vocational Behavior, 32*, 152–175.

Fitzgerald, L.F., & Swan, S. (in press). Why didn't she report him? The psychological and legal implications of women's responses to sexual harassment. *Journal of Social Issues*.

Fitzgerald, L.F., Weitzman, L.M., Gold, Y., & Ormerod, M. (1988). Academic harassment: Sex and denial in scholarly garb. *Psychology of Women Quarterly, 12*, 329–340.

Frieze, I. H., Hymer, S., & Greenberg, M. S. (1984). Describing the victims of crime and violence. In A.S. Kahn (Ed.), *Final report of the American Psychological Association Task Force on the Victims of Crime and Violence*. Washington, DC: American Psychological Association.

Glaser, R.D., & Thorpe, J. (1986). Unethical intimacy: A survey of sexual contact and advances between psychology educators and female graduate students. *American Psychologist, 41*, 43–51.

Gosselin, H.L. (1986). Sexual harassment on the job: Psychological, social and economic repercussions. *Canadian Mental Health, 32*, 21–24.

Gruber, J.E., & Bjorn, L. (1982). Women's responses to sexual harassment: An analysis of sociocultural, organizational, and personal resource models. *Social Science Quarterly*, 814–825.

Gruber, J.E., & Bjorn, L. (1986). Women's responses to sexual harassment: An analysis of sociocultural, organization, and personal resource models. *Social Science Quarterly, 67*, 815–826.

Gutek, B. (1985). *Sex and the workplace*. San Francisco: Jossey-Bass.

Gutek, B.A., & Koss, M.P. (1993). Changed women and changed organizations: Consequences of and coping with sexual harassment. *Journal of Vocational Behavior, 42*, 28–48.

Gutek, B.A., & Morasch, B. (1982). Sex ratios, sex role spillover, and sexual harassment of women at work. *Journal of Social Issues, 38*, 55–74.

Gutek, B.A., Nakamura, C.Y., Gahart, M., Handschumacher, I., & Russell, D. (1980). Sexuality in the workplace. *Basic and Applied Social Psychology, 1*, 255–265.

Hamilton, J. A., Alagna, S.W., King, L.S., & Lloyd, C. (1987). The emotional consequences of gender-based abuse in the workplace: New counseling programs for sex discrimination. *Women and Therapy, 6,* 155–182.

Hanisch, K.A., & Hulin, C.L. (1990). Job attitudes and organizational withdrawal: An examination of retirement and other voluntary withdrawal behaviors. *Journal of Vocational Behavior, 37,* 60–78.

Hanisch, K.A., & Hulin, C.L. (1991). General attitudes and organizational withdrawal: An evaluation of a causal model. *Journal of Vocational Behavior, 39,* 110–128.

Hesson-McInnis, H., & Fitzgerald, L.F. (1992, November). Modeling sexual harassment: A preliminary analysis. Paper presented at the APA/NIOSH Conference on Stress in the 90's: A Changing Workforce in a Changing Workplace, Washington, DC.

Hesson-McInnis H., & Fitzgerald, L. F. (under review). *Sexual harassment: A preliminary test of an integrative model.*

Hobfoll, S.E. (1989). Conservation of resources: A new attempt at conceptualizing stress. *American Psychologist, 44,* 513–524.

Hobfoll, S.E. (1991). Traumatic stress: A theory based on rapid resource loss. *Anxiety Research, 4,* 187–197.

Holgate, A. (1989). Sexual harassment as a determinant of women's fear of rape. *Australian Journal of Sex, Marriage, and the Family, 10,* 21–28.

Holmes, T. H., Rahe, R. H. (1967). The social readjustment rating scale. *Journal of Psychosomatic Research, 11,* 213–218.

Horowitz, M.J. (1986). *Stress response syndromes.* New York: Jason Aronson.

Hotelling, K. (1991). Sexual harassment: A problem shielded by silence. *Journal of Counseling and Development, 69,* 497–501.

Institute for Research on Women's Health (1988). *Sexual harassment and employment discrimination against women: A consumer handbook for women who are harmed, and those who care.* Bethesda, MD: Feminist Institute Clearinghouse.

Janoff-Bulman, R. (1989). Assumptive worlds and the stress of traumatic events: Applications of the schema construct. *Social Cognition, 7,* 113–136.

Janoff-Bulman, R., & Frieze, I. H. (1983). A theoretical perspective for understanding reactions to victimization. *Journal of Social Issues, 38,* 1–17.

Jensen, I., & Gutek, B. (1982). Attributions and assignment of responsibility for sexual harassment. *Journal of Social Issues, 38,* 121–136.

Junger, M. (1987). Women's experiences of sexual harassment. *British Journal of Criminology, 27,* 358–383.

Kilpatrick, D. G. (1985a, March). Research on long-term effects of criminal victimization: Scientific, service delivery, and public policy perspectives. Paper presented at a colloquium sponsored by the National Insti-

tute of Mental Health with the cooperation of the National Organization for Victim Assistance, Washington, DC.

Kilpatrick, D. G. (1985b). The sexual assault research project: Assessing the aftermath of rape. *Response to the Victimization of Women and Children, 8,* 2024.

Kilpatrick, D.G. (1992, June). Treatment and counseling needs of women veterans who were raped, otherwise sexually assaulted, or sexually harassed during military service. Invited testimony provided to the Senate Committee on Veteran's Affairs.

Kilpatrick, D.G., Dansky, B.S., & Saunders, B.E. (1994). Sexual harassment in the workplace: Results from the National Women's Study. Charleston, SC: Crime Victims Research and Treatment Center, Department of Psychiatry and Behavioral Sciences, Medical University of South Carolina

Kilpatrick, D.G., Resnick, H.S., Saunders, B.E., & Best, C.L. (1989). *The National Women's Study PTSD Module.* Unpublished instrument. Charleston, SC: Crime Victims Research and Treatment Center, Department of Psychiatry and Behavioral Sciences, Medical University of South Carolina.

Kilpatrick, D. G., & Veronen, L. J. (1984). *Treatment of fear and anxiety in victims of rape* (Final Report, Grant No. RO1 MH29602). Rockville, MD: National Institute of Mental Health.

Kilpatrick, D.G., Veronen, L.J., & Resnick, P.A. (1982). Psychological sequelae to rape: Assessment and treatment strategies. In D.M. Doleys, R.L. Meredith, & A.R. Ciminero (Eds.), *Behavioral medicine: Assessment and treatment strategies* (pp. 473–497). New York: Plenum.

Klein, D.C., Fencil-Morse, E., & Seligman, M.E.P. (1976). Learned helplessness, depression, and the attribution failure. *Journal of Personality and Social Psychology, 33,* 508–516.

Koss, M.P. (1990). Changed lives: The psychological impact of sexual harassment. In M. Paludi (Ed.) *Ivory power: Sex and gender harassment in academia* (pp. 73–92). Albany, NY: SUNY Press.

Kulka, R.A., Schlenger, W.E., Fairbank, J.A., Hough, R.L., Jordan, B.K., Marmar, C.R., & Weiss, D.S. (1990). *Trauma and the Vietnam War generation.* New York: Brunner/Mazel.

Lazarus, R.S., & Folkman, S. (1984). *Stress appraisal and coping.* New York: Springer.

Lindsey, K. (1977, November). Sexual harassment on the job. *MS,* 47–48.

Livingston, J.A. (1982). Responses to sexual harassment on the job: Legal, organizational, and individual action. *Journal of Social Issues, 38,* 5–22.

Lott, B., Reilly, M.E., & Howard, D.R. (1982). Sexual assault and harassment: A campus community case study. *Signs: Journal of Women in Culture and Society, 8*, 296–319.

Loy, P.H., & Stewart, L.P. (1984). The extent and effects of sexual harassment of working women. *Sociological Focus, 17*, 31–43.

MacKinnon, C. (1979). *Sexual harassment of working women.* New Haven, CT: Yale University Press.

Maypole, D. (1986). Sexual harassment of social workers at work. *Social Work, 31*, 29–43.

McCann, L., & Pearlman, L. (1990). *Psychological trauma and the adult survivor: Theory, therapy, & transformation.* New York: Guilford.

McCormack, L. (1985). The sexual harassment of students by teachers: The case of students in science. *Sex Roles, 13*, 21–32.

Miller, W.R., & Seligman, M.E.P. (1975). Depression and learned helplessness in man. *Journal of Abnormal Psychology*, 228–238.

Mowrer, O.H. (1960a). *Learning theory and behavior.* New York: Wiley.

Mowrer, O.H. (1960b). *Learning theory and symbolic processes.* New York: Wiley.

O'Farrell, B., & Harlan, S.L. (1982). Craftworkers and clerks: The effects of male coworker hostility on women's satisfaction with nontraditional jobs. *Social Problems, 29*, 252–264.

Paludi, M.A. (Ed.) (1990). *Ivory power: Sexual harassment on campus.* Albany, NY: SUNY Press.

Paludi, M.A., & Barickman, R.B. (1991). *Academic and workplace sexual harassment: A manual of resources.* Albany, NY: SUNY Press.

Pendergrass, V.E., Kimmel, E., Joesling, J., Petersen, J., & Bush, E. (1976). Sexual discrimination counseling. *American Psychologist, 31*, 36–46.

Perloff, L.S. (1983). Perceptions of vulnerability to victimization. *Journal of Social Issues, 39*, 41–61.

Rabinowitz, V.C. (1990). Coping with sexual harassment. In M. Paludi (Ed.), *Ivory power: Sexual harassment on campus* (pp. 103–118). Albany, NY: SUNY Press.

Ragins, B.R., & Scandura, T.A. (1992). Antecedents and consequences of sexual harassment. Paper presented at the 1992 Society of Industrial/Organizational Psychology Conference, Montreal.

Reilly, M.E., Lott, B., & Gallogly, S. M. (1986). Sexual harassment of university students. *Sex Roles, 15*, 333–358.

Resnick, H., Kilpatrick, D.G., Dansky, B.S. Best, C.L., & Saunders, B.E. (1993). Prevalence of civilian trauma and Post-Traumatic Stress Disorder in a representative national sample of women. *Journal of Consulting and Clinical Psychology, 61*, 984–991.

Safran, C. (1976). What men do to women on the job: A shocking look at sexual harassment. *Redbook, 10*, 148–149.

Salisbury, J., Ginoria, A.B., Remick, H., & Stringer, D.M. (1986). Counseling victims of sexual harassment. *Psychotherapy, 23*, 316–324.

Saunders, B.E. (1992, October). *Sexual harassment of women in the workplace: Results from the National Women's Study.* Presentation at the Eighth Annual North Carolina/South Carolina Labor Law Seminar, Asheville, NC.

Scheidner, K.T., & Swan, S. (1994). *Job-related, psychological, and health-related outcomes of sexual harassment.* Paper presented at the Ninth Annual Conference of the Society of Industrial and Organizational Psychology, Nashville, TN.

Silverman, D. (1976–1977). Sexual harassment: Working women's dilemma. *Quest and Feminist Quarterly, 3*, 15–24.

Terpstra, D.E., & Baker, D.D. (1989). A framework for the study of sexual harassment. *Basic and Applied Social Psychology, 7*, 17–34.

Till, F.J. (1980). Sexual harassment: A report on the sexual harassment of students. Washington, DC: National Advisory Council on Women's Educational Programs. Cited in Fitzgerald et al. (1989), The dimensions of sexual harassment: A structural analysis. *Journal of Vocational Behavior, 35*, 309–326.

Tong, R. (1984). *Women, sex, and the law.* Totowa, NJ: Rowman & Allanheld.

U.S. Merit Systems Protection Board (USMSPB) (1981). *Sexual harassment of federal workers: Is it a problem?* Washington, DC: Government Printing Office.

U.S. Merit Systems Protection Board (USMSPB) (1987). *Sexual harassment of federal workers: An update.* Washington, DC: Government Printing Office.

Wagner, E.J. (1992). *Sexual harassment in the workplace: How to prevent, investigate, and resolve problems in your organization.* New York: AMACOM.

Wortman, C. B. (1983). Coping with victimization: Conclusions and implications for future research. *Journal of Social Issues, 39*, 195–221.

# CHAPTER 10

# THE PREVENTION OF SEXUAL HARASSMENT

**Elizabeth O'Hare Grundmann**
**William O'Donohue**
**Scott H. Peterson**

Research indicating the high prevalence of sexual harassment (Chapter 5; Gutek, 1985; USMSPB, 1981) and the detrimental and sometimes severe consequences both to individuals and the organizations in which sexual harassment is prominent (Chapter 9; Gutek & Dunwoody, 1987; Loy & Stewart, 1984; USMSPB, 1981) highlights the need for interventions aimed at the prevention of sexual harassment. Prevention interventions could occur at three levels: (1) *Primary prevention* efforts would be aimed at preventing new cases of harassment by targeting causal and risk factors; (2) *secondary prevention* would be aimed at identifying existing problems that might lead to sexual harassment and correcting them at the earliest possible stage to prevent further negative consequences; and (3) *tertiary prevention* would focus on providing service to perpetrators to minimize the occurrence of further harassment. In this chapter we will concentrate on primary and secondary prevention. Currently preventive interventions and research on prevention are in their preliminary stages due to a number of issues, which we will discuss here.

Prevention efforts at all levels first require an awareness and appreciation of the problem. It is only recently that sexual harassment has been recognized as a widespread problem in need of remediation. Despite this recognition by some, research suggests that many individuals (particularly males) hold the following beliefs: The issue of sexual harassment has been exaggerated, reports of harassment are generally attempts to cause trouble, victims who are harassed have usually "asked for it" (USMSPB, 1981), and much "so-called" harassment is simply normal sexual interaction between men and women (Lott, Reilly, & Howard, 1982). Although the extent to which these attitudes currently prevail is unclear, it seems apparent that such beliefs would stifle prevention interventions. It is often difficult to obtain the necessary resources for prevention of widely recognized problems, and therefore, it seems that the resources required to address a problem about which there is such ambivalence would be even more difficult to obtain.

## CURRENT STATUS OF SEXUAL HARASSMENT REDUCTION PROGRAMS

Considering the well-documented negative effects of sexual harassment on victims, one might ask what is being done to eliminate sexually harassing behaviors in the workplace and academic settings. Many businesses, academic institutions, the military, and other institutions have been implementing programs to address the issue of sexual harassment in their environments for several years (Feldman, 1987), although the percentage of institutions utilizing sexual harassment prevention programs is unclear. Two major questions arise from these efforts: What types of programs to address sexual harassment are these institutions using, and how effective are these prevention programs?

Many institutions have devised policies against harassment and have begun to offer training and awareness programs within the institution (Feldman, 1987; Hotchkiss, 1994). Institutional policies usually include statements on how the institution is committed to providing an environment free from sexual harassment, a legal definition of sexual harassment, and descriptions of disciplinary actions for individuals engaging in sexually harassing behaviors (Chapter 11; Flynn, 1991; Hotchkiss, 1994). Training typically includes educating employees and managers on the company policies as well as workshops that give individuals direction on how to confront a harasser and how to report sexual harassment (Flynn, 1991).

Unfortunately, none of these programs has been shown to reduce the incidence of sexual harassment or to reduce the likelihood that individuals will sexually harass. An extensive search of the literature fail to reveal one study of the effectiveness of any program treating the likelihood to sexually harass. As previously mentioned, a number of individuals advocate various procedures to reduce the likelihood of sexual harassment in the workplace. However, no one has published an empirical evaluation of the effectiveness of any company policy or educational program to reduce sexually harassing attitudes or behaviors.

Another potential problem with the current status of sexual harassment programs in business is their motivation. Many extant harassment prevention programs may exist for the purpose of limiting the institution's legal liability (Flynn, 1991; Bresler & Thacker, 1993). We hope that insititutions will not cynically implement "prevention" programs simply to reduce their liability and the chance that they will be subjected to lawsuits. This would fail to take advantage of an opportunity to actually have a significant impact upon an important social problem.

## PRIMARY PREVENTION

The primary prevention of sexual harassment requires knowledge of specific causal or risk factors. Prevention is predicated upon intervening in the causal network that results in sexual harassment. Prevention efforts may target: sufficient causes, necessary causes, or, in a probabilistic model, any risk factors or contributory causes. However, little empirical work has been done to identify the causes of sexual harassment, leaving prevention designers with questions about what variables any intervention should address. A number of theoretical models have been proposed that could guide prevention efforts. These models include the natural/biological model (Tangri, Burt, & Johnson, 1982), the organizational model (Tangri, Burt, & Johnson, 1982), the sociocultural model (Farley, 1978; MacKinnon, 1979) the sex-role spillover model (Gutek & Morasch, 1982), and the four-factor model (Grundmann & O'Donohue, 1995). Each model implicates different causes for sexual harassment and therefore each would have different implications for prevention efforts.

## Implications of the Natural/ Biological Model

The natural/biological model assumes that men have stronger sex drives than women and that they are therefore more often the sexual aggressor both in the workplace and other settings. According to the model, behaviors that are perceived as sexual harassment are simply the result of the natural interaction between men and women, and the men involved have no intent to harass the women they pursue. It is often inferred from this model that because the behavior is "natural" and does not involve any harmful intent, behaviors are not actually harassing, do not have any harmful consequences for women, and are not sexist or discriminatory. Because the harmful consequences of harassment have been clearly demonstrated (Chapter 9; Gutek & Dunwoody, 1988; Loy & Stewart, 1984; USMSPB, 1981), this model is often dismissed as invalid and accordingly is seen as having no implications for prevention. However, it could be argued that it is the inferences drawn from the model that are invalid rather than the basic tenet of the model itself. Because the basis of the harassing behavior is considered natural or because there is no harmful intent does not entail that the behavior is not harmful. In terms of prevention, it follows from this model that interventions aimed at increasing men's awareness of how their "courtship" behavior is experienced by women in the workplace might be a fruitful starting point. Victim empathy training or social skills training also might be helpful, as these might increase the probability that males would court more appropriately.

## Interventions Based on the Organizational Model

The organizational model holds that organizations facilitate sexual harassment through the power differentials created by their hierarchical structures. In addition, other organizational characteristics, including contact with the opposite sex on the job, ratio of males to females in the workplace, occupational norms (e.g., work schedule, overtime, travel, working on weekends), job alternatives, availability of grievance procedures, privacy of work space, "sexy" atmosphere, and unresponsive management, may also influence the incidence of sexual harassment in a particular organization. According to this model, it is these characteristics of the work environment that should be the targets for change in any sort of a prevention effort. An ideal work environment would be one in which there are equal numbers of men and women in the various levels of authority. Job roles would be clearly stated with expected duties and limits of authority explicitly defined. Communication across levels of power would be open, with management receptive and responsive to complaints of sexual harassment or other inappropriate behaviors including other types of unprofessional and sexist behavior. Official grievance procedures would also be clearly defined, with consequences to offenders widely known. The physical work environment would be open, providing little opportunity for a harasser to approach a victim unseen. Prevention interventions based on this model would target the situations in which the harassment occurs. While such a focus would appear to be a necessary part of the prevention of harassment, it would not be sufficient. This approach ignores factors related to the individuals who harass as well as those related to the victims of harassment.

## Changes Based on the Sociocultural Model

The sociocultural model holds that sexual harassment is a reflection of a patriarchal system in which men dominate and assert power over women. According to this model, harassment is one mechanism for maintaining male dominance over women, both occupationally and economically. Males can accomplish this end by limiting women's growth in the work force or by intimidating them to leave the work arena. This model holds that men and women are socialized in ways that maintain this structure of dominance and subordination. Males are rewarded for aggressive and assertive behavior, while women are socialized to be passive, to avoid conflict, to be sexually attractive, and to feel responsible for their own victimization. According to the sociocultural model, the prevention of sexual harassment would require changes in the structure of society and in attitudes toward men and women and their respective roles. This would include changes in the socialization of young boys and girls. Ideally, boys and girls would be introduced to the same opportunities for developing various skills. Assertive behavior by both genders would be equally valued, while overly aggressive and passive behaviors would not be encouraged or endorsed for either. Obviously, changing the way children are socialized is not a simple task nor one that could be accomplished in any short time period. While these goals may be desirable, it does not seem appropriate to rely on changes that could require generations to be fully realized. Further, such an approach focuses on the broader context in which harassment occurs, ignoring both the immediate context (i.e., the organizational environment) and factors related to the individuals who harass.

## Equalizing According to the Sex-Role Spillover Model

The sex-role spillover model attributes sexual harassment to the carryover into the workplace of gender-based expectations that are irrelevant to and inappropriate for work. According to this model, sexual harassment is most likely to occur in work environments in which the sex ratio is skewed in either direction. In the male-dominated work place a woman's gender is a salient feature because of her singularity and distinctiveness. Women in the male-dominated work place stand out and are recognized in their sex role over and above recognition in their work role. In the female-dominated work place, sex role and work role overlap. Traditional female jobs tend to emphasize aspects of the female sex role (e.g., the nurturing role of teachers and nurses; the sex-object role of waitresses in revealing cos-

tumes; the helper role of administrative, dental, or research assistants). This results in the job itself acquiring aspects of the sex role. Based on this model, sexual harassment could be prevented by equalizing the numbers of men and women who hold any particular job. However, it does not seem likely that sex-role spillover would automatically be eliminated with equal representation of men and women in any particular job. The attitudes that contribute to sex-role spillover are based on widely held stereotypical beliefs about men's and women's roles, and therefore change also would have to occur at the sociocultural level. As stated earlier, such change would require a great deal of time, and therefore more immediate interventions also seem to be called for.

## Changing Situations and Person Factors

While each of these models has its strengths, they all tend to oversimplify sexual harassment by focusing too narrowly on one aspect of the phenomenon. Therefore, prevention efforts based on any of these models would also be too narrow. In another model that appears to better account for the complexity of determining the causes of sexual harassment, Pryor (1993) suggests that harassment occurs within the framework of an interaction of person and situation. This model suggests that situational factors and individual factors both contribute to the incidence of sexual harassment. Pryor states that sexual harassment is much more prevalent in some organizational contexts than in others and that some individuals are more likely to harass than others. In addition, those men who possess the proclivity to sexually harass do not do so in all situations. Rather, they only harass when the social norms allow such behavior to occur. Pryor (1992) found that men who are more likely to sexually harass have the tendency to relate sexuality to social dominance. Based on this model, prevention efforts should address the situational norms that facilitate harassment as well as individual factors related to the harasser. Organizational and sociocultural variables such as those discussed above would be appropriate targets for addressing the situational factors. The individual factors implicated by this model would be the harasser's or potential harasser's cognitive schema relating sexuality and social dominance. Thus, cognitive therapy and/or education about healthy sexual and social relationships would be possible prevention approaches.

## A Four-Factor Approach to Changing Preconditions

Another model, the four-factor model (Grundmann & O'Donohue, 1995), combines relevant aspects of the models discussed here and further emphasizes the multidimensional nature of sexual harassment and thereby the multidimensional approach that would appear to be appropriate for prevention. This model, based on Finkelhor's (1984) four-precondition model of sexual abuse, groups the factors related to sexual harassment into four "preconditions" that must be met for harassment to occur: motivation of the harasser, the ability to overcome internal inhibitions that act to prevent the offender from acting on his motivation, opportunity to overcome inhibitors in the external environment, and the opportunity or ability to overcome resistance by the potential victim.

The first precondition addresses the motivation to sexually harass. Sexual harassment may be motivated by a number of factors, including the need for power and control, or sexual attraction toward a woman. Sexual harassment may also result from the uncertainty that exists with men and women now entering into new working relationships (Stringer et al., 1990). For the traditional role relationships (e.g., daughter/father, wife/husband, student/teacher, secretary/boss) there exist sets of rules and expectations that establish both the power and any sexual relationship that may or may not exist. However, there are no established rules for dealing with many of these new relationships. It is possible that sexual harassment can occur when a man clumsily attempts to show acceptance of a female new to the work setting through behavior that is considered inappropriate by the woman, such as sexual jokes, comments, touching, or other sexual behavior. Although little is known about the actual motivations for sexual harassment, researchers have suggested that the following factors may motivate males to commit sexual offenses against women: unusual power needs, deviant sexual arousal, sexist beliefs, adversarial sex role beliefs, and anger toward women. More research is needed to investigate the role of these motivators in sexual harassment, as well as research into methods of changing any motivating factors.

The second precondition, overcoming internal inhibitors, concerns the ability of the potential harasser to overcome any internal inhibitors that would otherwise prevent him from acting on the motivation to sexually harass. Most members of society are taught to respect the rights and dignity of others and therefore would have some inhibitions to overcome in attempting to exploit, degrade, or hurt another as is the case in sexual harassment. Fear of reprisals such as a tarnished reputation or the loss of a job may also act as internal inhibitors. When the harassment is aimed at establishing a sexual relationship, and either individual is involved in another exclusive relationship, overcoming inhibitions against being unfaithful could come into play. General inhibitions about sexuality or about expressing sexual interest may also have to be overcome for harassment to occur.

For some individuals, such as those with antisocial personality disorder, inhibitions against sexually harassing behavior may not even exist. In other cases, when the harassing behavior is motivated by sexual attraction toward a woman and there is no intent to degrade the woman, this precondition may not be necessary. However, for individuals who do have such inhibitions, motivation alone is not sufficient for harassment to occur. The inhibitions must first be overcome. Victim empathy training, clarification of the moral wrongness of the action (see Chapter 3), and changing harassment myths (O'Donohue & Dubois, 1995) and outcome expectancies (O'Donohue & Peterson, 1995) may increase internal inhibitions.

The third precondition, overcoming external inhibitors, addresses the situational factors that may either facilitate or inhibit harassment incidents. External inhibitors and facilitators can exist at three different levels: the sociocultural context, the organizational context, and the immediate work environment. One of the situational variables that has been demonstrated to inhibit sexual harassment is the existence of explicit grievance procedures within the organization. One study has shown that women who are more aware of the grievance procedures in their workplace are less likely to have experienced sexual harassment (Grundmann & O'Donohue, 1995). It appears that, in an organization where sexual harassment is recognized as a problem, victims have a clear means of filing complaints, the consequences of harassment are explicit, and offenders are punished appropriately, potential harassers are more likely to be deterred from harassing. Thus, establishing such a procedure and making it widely known to employees appear to be simple and straightforward steps that could be taken in any prevention intervention (see Chapter 7).

Grundmann and O'Donohue (1995) also showed that a professional environment acts as an external inhibitor. Women who worked in environments that they perceived as unprofessional reported experiencing more harassment than women who perceived their environments as more professional. Unprofessional environments included those where there was frequent use of obscene language and/or alcohol on the job, employees were expected to perform menial activities not formally a part of their job, and employees engaged in inappropriate displays of emotion (e.g., crying, losing their temper) and/or frequently used company time and resources for their personal use. It appears that, in environments in which such unprofessional behavior is prominent, a general attitude of disrespect toward employers and coworkers may facilitate harassment. Such environments may also reflect a lack of control on the part of the employer such that employees do not expect to be held accountable for their actions and there-fore are more likely to engage in sexually harassing behavior. This suggests that employers can take steps to prevent sexual harassment by promoting professional work environments. This might involve supervisors modeling professional behavior and making job duties and expectations of acceptable and unacceptable behavior explicitly stated, with clear disciplinary action taken for inappropriate behavior.

A second variable that has been demonstrated to act as an external inhibitor is the unacceptability of sexist behavior in the workplace. In an organization where such behavior is not tolerated, sexual harassment is less likely to occur than in one where sexist behavior is accepted. It may be that in environments in which women have not been accepted as equally capable as men or in which hiring and/or job assignment practices are not comparable between women and men a climate that is conducive to the domination and denigration of women through sexual harassment is created. This variable operates both at the level of the organization and more widely at the sociocultural level. Laws against gender-based discrimination in employment begin to address this factor at a more molar level. However, such laws do not preclude differing expectations held in society for men and women, boys and girls. It is still frequently the case that while more young boys are given a doctor's bag to play with, more young girls are given a nurse's cap, and while more boys are taught to be aggressive and to be leaders, more girls are taught to be passive and to be followers. Thus, while men and women have the same opportunities according to the law, societal practices perpetuate the disproportionate numbers of men and women in many professions and in supervisory or management roles. According to the sex-role spillover model, it is this imbalance that causes sexual harassment. This suggests that organizations can begin to counteract such beliefs by providing opportunities for women that have traditionally been provided for men. Any of the situational variables discussed here could operate to inhibit the occurrence of sexual harassment. Any individual who meets the first two preconditions must also overcome these external inhibitors if sexual harassment is to take place. Thus, strengthening any of these factors should operate to reduce the likelihood of sexual harassment.

The fourth precondition, overcoming victim resistance, addresses the fact that the attitudes, behaviors, and occupational positions of women play a significant role in whether or not they are targets of sexual harassment. It may be that women who reject the stereotypical feminine role, which is passive and as a sex object, who are knowledgeable about sexual harassment, and/or who have high-status positions within their organization are less likely to be harassed than are other women. These women may be more able to recognize harassment and to assert themselves to more effectively counteract or resist any harassing behavior. They may also be more able to recognize premonitory behavior that might lead to harassment and so be more able to avert it. Also, women's resistance to sexual harassment may be subtle. Simply because of their position of power, or because of the attitude of personal power and control that they project, a potential harasser may avoid such women as "targets."

It follows that women could take a number of steps to be active in reducing their likelihood to be sexually harassed. By learning more about sexual harassment, they could learn to avoid situations in which harassment is more likely to occur. They could learn to recognize inappropriate behaviors that might lead to sexual harassment. They can also increase their ability to effectively deal with precursors to harassment or with actual harassment by learning assertiveness skills. Women can also take individual responsibility for maintaining professional atmospheres and for preventing sex-role spillover in their work environments. For example, women who dress professionally versus provocatively might be less likely to be sexually harassed. (It should be noted that even if a woman dresses "provocatively," she is not to blame for any subsequent sexual harassment. But, just as it is prudent to not leave one's key in the car, there are prudent actions a woman can take to decrease her risk of victimization.) In addition, women could reduce sex-role spillover by not expecting to be given any special treatment on the job based on their gender. This would include not avoiding duties of the job that might be uncomfortable or dirty or require travel or time away from the family.

The four-factor model addresses multiple variables that may be involved in sexual harassment, including those relevant to the potential harasser, the potential victim, and the situation in which the sexual harassment occurs. In order for sexual harassment to occur, all four preconditions must be satisfied. The implications for prevention efforts are that interventions targeted at any or all of the preconditions would be effective in reducing the likelihood of sexual harassment. Thus, prevention efforts could focus on the potential harasser by targeting his/her motivation to harass to be reduced or by targeting his/her internal inhibitors to be strengthened. In addition, external inhibitors could be strengthened in the workplace and at the societal level, and individual women's abilities to actively resist and cope with early indications of harassment could be enhanced. Ideally, multiple variables within each precondition would be targeted in order to maximize the probability of reducing the prevalence of sexual harassment. However, according to the model, this would not be necessary. Because all four preconditions are required for harassment to exist, targeting any one area should reduce the likelihood of harassment. Because it seems improbable that any one precondition could be completely controlled, preventionists are left with the option of targeting the more malleable variables within each precondition. Thus, this model allows for more flexibility in designing prevention interventions.

## OUTCOME EVALUATION OF PREVENTION PROGRAMS

Thus far we have focused on the task of choosing variables that may serve as promising targets for prevention efforts. However, identifying promising variables is only part of the problem when attempting to identify effective sexual harassment prevention strategies. The other major piece of the problem is utilizing proper investigatory methodologies to accurately identify the impact of prevention efforts.

To date, this part of the problem has received relatively little attention. It appears that various institutions and individuals offer diverse prevention programs but seem much less concerned with systematically evaluating these programs. In fact, despite an extensive literature search, we could find no published outcome study on the effectiveness of a sexual harassment prevention program. Stated differently, there currently is no evidence that these efforts are actually having a beneficial effect.

The lack of outcome research is a potentially dangerous state of affairs for two reasons. First, it shouldn't be assumed that interventions based on good intentions can only have neutral or beneficial effects. Negative or iatrogenic effects are also possible. For example, a prevention program that gives the message that many women are sexually harassed but that harassment is underreported might give certain males the message that the likelihood is good that they can get away with harassing females. Second, when a prevention program is being offered, it gives the impression that "something is being done." However, the reality is that it is unclear whether the program makes any difference. If ineffective, a program may actually lull individuals into a false sense of complacency and security. Ineffective programs can cause significant harm because they may meet an institution's burden of doing something about sexual harassment without having any effect on the bottom line: reducing the incidence of sexual harassment. Indeed, the negative effects of sexual harassment may be heightened when individuals working in a hostile or harassing environment are placed in a more difficult position because there are sexual harassment prevention programs in place (albeit ineffective) that putatively address their problem. The issue is not simply having a program that ostensibly decreases the rate of sexual harassment; rather, it is to have a demonstrably effective program.

We suggest that the following methodological considerations be taken into account when evaluating prevention programs:

1. Representative sampling of subjects (and trainers if used)
2. Random assignment of subjects to conditions (and trainers if used)
3. Adequate cell size to ensure sufficient statistical power
4. Appropriate control groups, such as no treatment, placebo control (with appropriate credibility checks), and post-test only control groups
5. Use of double-blind procedures
6. Treatment fidelity checks and other relevant manipulation checks
7. Use of relevant and psychometrically sound measures of an array of dependent variables
8. Assessment of potential negative effects
9. Assessment of social validity of the intervention and use of consumer satisfaction measures
10. Measurement of subject and work environment variables
11. An analysis of potential subject–treatment interactions (this necessitates measurement of certain subject characteristics and is based on the view that treatments will have differential effects on certain types of clients)
12. Measurement of generalization across settings and time (long-term follow-ups and clear measurement of the extent of transfer from training setting to actual work setting are essential)
13. Conducting some research so that process variables can be understood (e.g., the use of treatment dismantling designs)

These design characteristics are essential for accurately and unambiguously arriving at responses to our initial question. We suggest that organizations at this early stage of sexual harassment prevention programming practice a healthy skepticism regarding the effectiveness of any program and adopt an experimental attitude in which programs are rigorously evaluated. This experimental attitude is critical for the growth of knowledge about how to effectively intervene to decrease the incidence of sexual harassment.

Fitzgerald (personal communication, May 14, 1995) has described what is to our knowledge the best-designed evaluation of a prevention program. Employees were randomly assigned to either a training or no-training condition in a modified Solomon four-group design. The program contained both cognitive (knowledge) and affective (experiential) components. The results indicated a significant and substantial increase in knowledge of the company's policies and procedures and improved attitudes toward sexual harassment (e.g., employees took it more seriously and thought it was a more serious problem following training). However, employees who were trained also rated the organizational climate as significantly more tolerant of sexual harassment (e.g., more risk to victims for reporting, less likelihood that they would be taken seriously, less likelihood that significant sanctions would be levied on the perpetrator). The investigator interpreted this to be a logical outcome of the fact that intervention sensitized the employees to the problem and its seriousness. She also suggested that the pattern of results provides support for the argument that training cannot be a "one-shot deal," but rather must be embedded in an ongoing process of organizational change; otherwise, employees will simply become cynical and the training possibly will do more harm than good.

In an effort to address some of the methodological considerations of evaluating a treatment prevention program, O'Donohue and Peterson (1995) have developed a prototypical treatment prevention program. The evaluation of the effectiveness of this program will take into account each of the 13 methodological considerations listed here.

The prevention program to be tested addresses educational issues, victim empathy, outcome expectancy, and sexual harassment myths. A previous study that assessed the effectiveness of a rape prevention program dealt with similar issues (Schewe & O'Donohue, 1993). The results of that program support the efficacy of utilizing these variables in a treatment program for sexual harassment.

This prevention program focuses on the potential harasser by targeting his (the program is aimed at males only) motivation to harass by challenging sexual harassment myths. Myths such as "Women ask to be sexually harassed by the way they dress" are challenged throughout the program. In addition, an educational component targets the potential harasser's motivation to harass by defining sexual harassment for him and educating him about it.

This program also targets the potential harasser's internal inhibitors and attempts to strengthen them through the use of victim empathy and outcome expectancy manipulations. Victim empathy is utilized to sensitize the potential harasser to the effects of sexual harassment on the victim. Increasing the empathy of the potential harasser should, in turn, increase his internal inhibition (Miller & Eisenberg, 1988). Increased awareness of potential outcomes for the perpetrator of sexual harassment is the goal of outcome expectancy treatment. This is accomplished by informing the potential harasser of the potential personal outcomes of sexual harassment. These outcomes could include loss of job, lawsuits, and other negative personal and professional consequences.

The goal of this treatment prevention program is not only to have a treatment that decreases the rate of sexual harassment, but also to have a demonstrably effective program that takes into account the methodological considerations discussed in this chapter.

## SUMMARY

For obvious reasons, prevention of a problem is more desirable than post hoc treatment or other kinds of after-the-fact remediation efforts. However, the prevention of sexual harassment requires knowledge about the causes of sexual harassment. Currently there are several models of the causes of sexual harassment, but the evidence supporting any of them is quite meager. Further research into the causes of sexual harassment is needed.

There seems to be a trend to implement prevention programs without rigorously assessing their effects. We have discussed problems with this state of affairs and have offered methodological suggestions for evaluation research. We hope all interested parties insist upon sexual harassment prevention programming that has been shown to be effective and that is subject to ongoing evaluation, rather than programming that is simply assumed to work because of its face validity or because of the poorly substantiated claims of its promoters.

## REFERENCES

Bresler, S. J., & Thacker, R. (1993). Four-point plan helps solve harassment problems. *HR Magazine, 38*, 117–124.

Farley, L. (1978). *Sexual shakedown: The sexual harassment of women on the job*. New York: McGraw-Hill.

Feldman, D. (1987). Sexual harassment: Policies and prevention. *Personnel, 64*, 12–17.

Finkelhor, D. (1984). *Child sexual abuse: New theory and research*. New York: Free Press.

Flynn, K. (1991). Preventive medicine for sexual harassment. *Personnel, 68*, 17.

Grundmann, E. O., & O'Donohue, W. (1995). Sexual harassment: Identifying risk factors. Master's thesis, Northern Illinois University, Dekalb, IL.

Gutek, B. A. (1985). *Sex and the workplace*. San Francisco: Jossey-Bass.

Gutek, B. A., & Dunwoody, V. (1988). Understanding sex and the workplace. In A. H. Stromberg, L. Larwood, & B. A. Gutek (Eds.), *Women and work: An annual review* (vol. 2), Newbury Park, CA: Sage.

Gutek, B. A., & Morasch, B. (1982). Sex-ratios, sex-role spillover, and sexual harassment of women at work. *Journal of Social Issues, 38*, 55–74.

Hotchkiss, J. (1994). Ridding the workplace of sexual harassment. *Management Review, 83*, 57.

Lott, B., Reilly, M. E., & Howard, D. (1982). Sexual assault and harassment: A campus community case study. *Signs, 8*, 296–319.

Loy, P. H., & Stewart, L. P. (1984). The extent and effects of the sexual harassment of working women. *Sociological Focus, 17*, 31–43.

MacKinnon, C. (1979). *Sexual harassment of working women: A case of sex discrimination*. New Haven, CT: Yale University Press.

Miller, P., & Eisenberg, N. (1988). The relation of empathy to aggressive and externalizing/antisocial behavior. *Psychological Bulletin, 103* (3), 324–344.

O'Donohue, W. & Dubois, A. (in preparation). *A sexual harassment myth scale*.

O'Donohue, W. & Peterson, S. H. (in preparation). *The prevention of sexual harassment*.

Pryor, J. B., LaVite, C. M., & Stoller L. M. (1993). A social psychological analysis of sexual harassment: The person/situation interaction. *Journal of Vocational Behavior, 42*, 68–83.

Pryor, J. B., & Stoller, L. M. (1992). Sexual cognition processes in men who are high in the likelihood to sexually harass. Unpublished manuscript, Illinois State University, Bloomington, Illinois.

Schewe, P. A., & O'Donohue, W. (1993). Sexual abuse prevention with high-risk males: The roles of victim empathy and rape myths. *Violence and Victims, 8*, 339–351.

Stringer, D. M., Remick, H., Salisbury, J., & Ginorio, A. B. (1990). The power and reasons behind sexual harassment: An employer's guide to solutions. *Public Personnel Management, 19*,(1), 43–69.

Tangri, S. S., Burt, M. R., & Johnson, L. B. (1982). Sexual harassment at work: Three explanatory models. *Journal of Social Issues, 38*, 33–54.

U.S. Merit Systems Protection Board (USMSPB). (1981). *Sexual harassment in the federal workplace: Is it a problem?* Washington: DC: Government Printing Office.

# CHAPTER 11

# SEXUAL HARASSMENT POLICY INITIATIVES

**Barbara A. Gutek**

The Equal Employment Opportunity Commission (EEOC) sexual harassment guidelines and other government guidelines have had the effect of making organizations and their agents responsible for providing a harassment-free work or educational environment. This chapter reviews the major initiatives taken by organizations to deal with this responsibility. In general, they have established sexual harassment policies, procedures for handling allegations of harassment, and training to inform people about the law and the organizations' policies and procedures. Together, policies, procedures, and training (PPT) constitute the major components of many organizations' system for handling sexual harassment. In this chapter, I first provide some background to explain how employers came to be responsible for providing workers with a harassment-free environment, and then I review the initiatives taken by organizations in response to this new responsibility.

## A NEW RESPONSIBILITY FOR EMPLOYERS

In 1979, Catharine MacKinnon, now a law professor at the University of Michigan, wrote a book, *Sexual Harassment of Working Women*, that sought a legal mechanism for handling sexual harassment and compensating its victims. A worker who is sexually harassed is placed at a disadvantage relative to other workers and therefore does not have equal opportunity with other, nonharassed employees. In a strong and compelling argument, MacKinnon contended that sexual harassment was primarily a problem for women, that it rarely happened to men, and therefore that it should be viewed as a form of sex discrimination. Viewing sexual harassment this way would make available to harassment victims the same legal protection afforded victims of sex discrimination. In 1980 EEOC established guidelines consistent with MacKinnon's position and defined sexual harassment under Title VII of the 1964 Civil Rights Act as a form of unlawful sex-based discrimination. Several states have passed their own increasingly strong laws aimed at eliminating sexual harassment, and legal scholars have sought additional avenues to recover damages inflicted by sexual harassment.

The various guidelines and regulations define sexual harassment broadly. For example, the EEOC guidelines (1993) state:

> Unwelcome sexual advances, requests for sexual favors, and other verbal or physical conduct of a sexual nature constitute sexual harassment when (1) submission to such conduct is made either explicitly or implicitly a term or condition of an individual's employment or academic advancement, (2) submission to or rejection of such conduct by an individual is used as the basis for employment decisions or academic decisions affecting such individual, or (3) such conduct has the purpose or effect of reasonably interfering with an individual's work or academic performance or creating an intimidating, hostile or offensive working or academic environment.

Enough cases have worked their way through the judicial system that we have developed a set of legal practices and procedures for dealing with sexual harassment. No doubt, legal theory and practice with respect to sexual harassment will continue to develop. So far one of the most important developments in sexual harassment policy has been to make organizations responsible for sexual harassment. Organizations and their agents (i.e., executives and managers) are responsible for any sexual harassment that occurs in the organization or to an employee or customer of an organization in the course of conducting business, whether or not the harassment actually takes place within the organization. Thus, organizations are not only responsible if a supervisor sexually harasses a subordinate or a colleague at work, but an organization can also be held responsible if, for example, an employee of the company harasses a receptionist or secretary of another company to

which he is selling the first company's products. A technician who harasses an employee of another company while repairing a photocopy machine or a salesperson who harasses a receptionist in the course of trying to make a sale of textbooks or office equipment can precipitate a harassment charge against that person and against the organization for which he or she works.

Given this reality, organizations cannot afford to remain ignorant, as headlines like "End sexual harassment of employes [sic] or your board could be held liable" (Underwood, 1987) remind them. Are the dire warnings warranted? How likely is it that a company will be charged with sexual harassment and how does a company protect itself and its agents against a lawsuit? First, it is worth noting that, although organizations are responsible for preventing sexual harassment, only a small minority of people who are sexually harassed ever inform someone in their organization about the harassment (Bremer, Moore, & Bildersee, 1991; Dunwoody-Miller & Gutek, 1985; Fitzgerald, 1993; Gutek & Koss, 1993; Gwartney-Gibbs & Lach, 1992). Nevertheless, various public and private agencies as well as the courts have seen a steady if uneven increase in sexual harassment complaints since the early 1980s (e.g., *USA Today*, 1992). For example, in the years between 1984 and 1988 the number of sexual harassment complaints filed with the EEOC generally rose, dropping only twice (from 4,953 in 1985 to 4,431 in 1986 and from 5,336 in 1987 to 5,215 in 1988) (Budhos, in press 1995). A total of 5,557 complaints were filed in 1990 (Clark, 1991), but there are now over 10,000 cases filed with the EEOC annually, and there is every reason to think that the number will continue to increase. Although few targets of harassment make formal complaints, it is also true that many, if not most, large organizations have had to deal with formal charges of sexual harassment and/or have been involved in a court case. At 10,000 or more cases a year, it is doubtful that many of the Fortune 1000 companies or major government agencies have escaped a formal charge. Thus, in many large organizations in North America today, one or more human resource specialists have of necessity become knowledgeable about the legal guidelines and their company's legal liability. Smaller organizations often have much less knowledge about sexual harassment. All too often, even in the more enlightened organizations, too few human resource specialists, not to mention general managers, understand the origins of sexual harassment and the workplace factors that contribute to it. Thus, the organizations are ill-prepared for preventing sexual harassment from occurring in the future, and they may be ill-prepared to handle allegations when they arise. In general, most managers still have little experience with sexual harassment despite the amount of media attention and the growing number of complaints and court cases.

In general, in an effort to avoid lawsuits and prevent sexual harassment, organizations have learned that several steps are desirable. In particular, they learned which steps are most useful in defending themselves in a court case. The first line of defense is a sexual harassment policy that states that the company does not condone and in fact will not tolerate any sexual harassment. A policy may simply state the organization's position, or it may also include steps to be taken should an allegation of sexual harassment arise. Many organizations simply repeat the EEOC guidelines as their policy statement, but others go much further. For companies really interested in eradicating sexual harassment, instead of merely reducing legal liability, additional steps are usually necessary. Thus, the second line of defense is typically a set of procedures for handling sexual harassment. This may involve the creation of a new position in the organization or adding a new task to someone's job responsibilities, typically someone in human resources (HR). If the policy and procedures are not known, then victims of harassment may not come forward at all or may not come forward until they already have been severely harassed (see Bremer, Moore, & Bildersee, 1991; Gutek & Koss, 1993). Thus, the third step that organizations typically take is to establish some kind of training to be sure that everyone concerned is aware of harassment, knows the organization's policy, and knows what to do in case of a sexual harassment allegation.

In short, what many organizations do today to combat sexual harassment is (1) establish a policy, (2) establish a set of procedures for handling sexual harassment complaints, and (3) establish a training program to be sure that sexual harassment is understood by all relevant parties. These major initiatives taken by organizations in response to sexual harassment together constitute the "system for handling sexual harassment" (SHSH) in many large organizations. The three steps together are intended to show that the organization is serious about sexual harassment and is taking reasonable steps to eliminate it. More specifically, these three steps are intended to eliminate sexual harassment from the organization and protect the organization in case a sexual harassment charge is filed.

The remainder of this chapter reviews the SHSH adopted by organizations to deal with sexual harassment and the threat of being sued. Today many policies incorporate procedures in them, but I will discuss policies and procedures separately. The chapter then focuses briefly on training, its goals and effectiveness. In general, these topics have not been subject to much research. For example, although having a sexual harassment policy is viewed as important in a court case, it is not clear what are the effects of having a policy. Does having a policy, per se, encourage sexual harassment targets to come forward? Does it discourage potential harassers? We do not know. Do procedures intended to resolve sexual harassment disputes work? We do not know much about that either (see Lach & Gwartney-Gibbs, 1993). Similarly with training. What does training do? Is it effective in teaching people about sexual harassment? If so, what about it makes it effective? Establishing policies, procedures, and training is widely recommended (e.g., Bingham, 1991; Paludi & DeFour, 1989; Terpstra & Baker, 1992; Underwood, 1987), but relatively little is actually known beyond testimonials (e.g., Spann, 1990; but see Blax-all, Parsonson, & Robertson, 1993 and Moyer & Nath, 1994). In this chapter, I rely on my own experience as an expert witness for both plaintiffs and defendent organizations and on my consulting experience in the area of sexual harassment, as well as on the research litera-ture.

In focusing on policies, procedures, and training (PPT), I do not mean to imply that an organization is necessarily legally negligent or even remiss in its responsibilities to its employees if it does not have all three, or even necessarily any of them. What I want to do is focus on what we know, or at least believe, about PPT aimed at eradicating sexual harass-ment from organizations, keeping in mind that what appears to be good practice today may be considered inappropriate or ineffective tomor-row.

## SEXUAL HARASSMENT POLICIES

Today most large corporations have sexual harassment policies and procedures for deal-ing with allegations of harassment. According to one report (Bureau of National Affairs, 1987), 97% of the companies in their study had sexual harassment policies, but the major-ity of these were established well after 1980, the year the EEOC publlished guidelines on sexual harassment. When the *Harvard Busi-ness Review* conducted a survey in 1981 (Col-lins & Blodgett, 1981), only 29% of respondents said they worked in companies where top executives had issued statements to employees disapproving of sexual conduct.

The goals of sexual harassment policies seem to be to: (1) take a stand on sexual harass-ment, that is, to show the organization cares; (2) make the stance public knowledge; (3) dis-courage employees from engaging in harass-ing behavior; (4) encourage targets of harassment to come forward and inform man-agement; (5) educate people about sexual harassment; (6) provide guidelines for dealing with allegations of harassment; and (7) be able to defend the organization in the event that it

is taken to court in a sexual harassment case. It is unlikely, however, that any policy can actually achieve all seven of these goals. Indeed, most policies are probably not that ambitious, and some organizations probably adopt a policy because they heard it is the thing to do or because their comparison organiza-tions all have such policies. There are undoubtedly many good policy statements in place today; one that achieves many of the goals listed here and meets many of the other criteria discussed in this chapter is the policy adopted by the University of Southern Califor-nia in April, 1994 (USC Policy on Sexual Harassment, 1994).

## Policy Content

The simplest form of policy merely restates the EEOC guidelines, supplemented with a statement saying that the organization sup-ports and/or will enforce the guidelines. Among the strengths of this simple policy statement are the facts that it is short and therefore quick and easy to read, it takes little effort to prepare (e.g., no task forces or com-mittees are necessary to set up such a policy), and it provides the organization with consider-able flexibility and discretion in handling real cases of harassment because it does not try to specify matters in detail.

Its strengths also contribute to its weak-nesses. One weakness is that unless there is some other evidence that the organization takes sexual harassment seriously, the policy statement does not send a strong statement that the organization is concerned about harass-ment. It does not take much work for an orga-nization to repeat the EEOC's words about harassment. If there is no evidence that the organization has put forth any real effort to establish a policy, there is little reason to think it really cares about harassment. In short, it is easy to dismiss a short policy statement as window dressing and/or a quick attempt to defend against a lawsuit. In addition, a policy consisting of the EEOC guidelines cannot achieve many of the goals that a policy state-ment could achieve. For instance, the EEOC guidelines are themselves a little vague, especially the third clause. The guidelines do not define what makes a work environment intimidating or hostile, and a policy statement that contains only the EEOC guidelines may leave some readers uncertain whether they have been harassed or whether the person making a complaint to them has been harassed.

It is not necessary, of course, to have all detailed information in a policy statement if that information is readily available elsewhere (for example, from the HR department) and if it is regularly covered in training. Under these circumstances it is helpful if the policy lists some places where interested parties can obtain more information about sexual harassment. Not surprisingly, today many policies do more than restate the EEOC guidelines. But before discussing additions to a policy that are intended to be beneficial, it is worth asking, "Is it possible to make a minimum policy less effective by adding to it?" The answer is yes. It is possible to discourage people from coming forward if the policy, for example, tells them they must be able to prove any allegation they make or informs them that people who make unsubstantiated charges will be reprimanded and/or terminated. I have seen one such policy statement in use, and it is probably not the only one of its kind.

In general, the more a policy attempts to accomplish, the longer it is likely to be. A good example of a long policy that achieves multiple goals is the policy of the University of Southern California that was published in a campus newspaper accompanied by a letter by the president of USC, Steven B. Semple (USC Policy on Sexual Harassment, 1994). A policy that aims to educate readers will probably be longer than one that has more limited goals. Many policies include specific examples of sexual harassment and/or otherwise expand on the types of behavior that constitute sexual harassment by listing categories or classes of behavior that might be defined as sexual harassment. Many policies tell where to go for more information or where to go to file a complaint. Some policies list multiple avenues for making a complaint. Among the options sometimes listed are the person's immediate super-

visor; someone else in the chain of command; someone in personnel or HR, either locally or at another site such as corporate headquarters; an ombudsperson; a counselor in an employee assistance program or career planning; any supervisor with whom the person feels comfortable; and an anonymous hotline. Some policies explain why they provide multiple avenues; some differentiate between reporting sexual harassment and filing a formal complaint. Some list the specific titles of people who have been trained and authorized to receive complaints and respond to questions about sexual harassment. For example, USC lists the following designated offices for staff members who have complaints: Senior Vice President for Administration, Executive Director of Personnel Services, Director of Affirmative Action, Manager of Employee Relations, and Office of the General Counsel.

Some policies also list rights and responsibilities of complainants and defendants. Some list the range of sanctions that can be applied to someone who is found guilty of sexual harassment. Balancing the rights of the complainant with the rights of the accused is a concern in many organizations (see Rowe, in press). "Overemphasis" on the rights of the accused and the responsibilities of the complainant, as in the preceding example of a policy in which the only additional information warns complainants about making unsupportable accusations, is likely to have the effect of reducing or even eliminating any complaints. Neglect of the rights of the accused and the responsibilities of the complainants may lead to backlash and a policy that is viewed as lacking in objectivity.

## Disseminating the Policy

Targets of harassment are often deterred from complaining because they do not know their company's policy on harassment or where to file a complaint (Bremer, Moore, & Bildersee, 1991). In one study in 1985, only about half the employees were aware of their department's policy on sexual harassment (Dunwoody-Miller & Gutek, 1985). A policy cannot be effective unless it is known. If it is buried in a policy manual that resides on the HR manager's desk and nowhere else, it is not likely to be effective. Where dissemination is taken seriously, policies are often posted prominently, for example, on bulletin boards along with other information of interest to employees. Some organizations include a copy of the sexual harassment policy in an employment package given to all new employees. One grocery store chain included their updated sexual harassment policy along with employees' paychecks or direct deposit notices. The policy can be included in the organization's newsletters or along with an annual statement from the president (see for example, the policy statement of USC published in the university newspaper). The policy can also be incorporated into the performance appraisal of all managers and supervisors so that they are evaluated on how well they know and implement the policy.

## Does the Perfect Policy Exist?

As more information is learned about sexual harassment, opinion about what constitutes a good policy changes. Thus, a good policy can become outdated rather quickly. For example, although it seems like a good idea to promise a person who makes a complaint that she or he will remain anonymous, it may be impossible to do so. Once the alleged harasser is confronted with the information that someone has lodged a complaint, he or she can often guess correctly who made the complaint. If it is not possible to guarantee anonymity, then it makes no sense to promise it. It can also cause additional anguish for the complainant, who is probably suffering enough already.

Guidelines exist for devising an effective policy (see, for example, appendix D in Budhos, in press), but experts (e.g., Klein, cited in Budhos, in press; Rowe, in press) suggest that policies should be tailored to the requirements of particular organizations and they express concern over organizations' penchant for adopting boilerplate policies aimed at reducing their legal liability rather than reducing the amount of harassment.

## Is No Policy an Option?

Given the problems of setting up a good policy, is it possible to make a case for not having a policy? I believe there is, especially if the organization is fairly small and is confident that it can limit sexual harassment through other mechanisms like company norms that emanate consistently and directly from the top. If an organization has a policy on harassment, it looks very bad in court if it did not follow its own policy and procedures, even if the deviation can be justified. Furthermore, it undermines its own policy if the policy is not consistently followed. Thus, if an organization is setting up its own policy and procedures, the failure to establish a just and workable policy may get the organization in greater trouble or cause more anguish and grief for victims than either no policy or a simple policy. Policies need to be updated regularly as new information and policy developments emerge. Not having a policy may save some time. This may be an illusion, though, as the organization without a policy will need to defend not having a policy to a government agency or court if a case arises. Thus, the organization will still need to rely on some knowledgeable person or persons inside or outside the organization from time to time and maintain a strong cultural intolerance of sexual harassment in the meantime. Furthermore, it is generally believed that where sexual harassment is condoned, the likelihood of its occurring increases, and without a policy prominently displayed the organization will have to take extra steps to demonstrate to its own employees or students as well as to the courts that sexual harassment is, in fact, not tolerated.

## PROCEDURES FOR DEALING WITH SEXUAL HARASSMENT

Having a policy is only a first step, and a toothless one at that if there is no procedure or set of procedures for implementing the policy. But devising a workable procedure  or set of procedures is not easy. Further- more, because most targets of harassment never report sexual harassment, organizations should supplement their own formal and/or informal procedures with suggestions for how targets can try to handle sexual harassment on their own. This may be as simple as suggesting reading materials that advise victims on steps they can take (e.g., Rowe, 1981; VanHyning, 1993). It might also include telling victims how to gather information and prepare a complaint in the event they want to come forward and make a formal charge, and providing information about what is involved and what to expect if the person wishes to pursue formal or informal institutional channels (see VanHyning, 1993). Giving targets of sexual harassment options is generally recommended (cf. Budhos, in press; Rowe, in press). For example, at the University of Waikato in New Zealand, contact persons are trained to inform harassment targets about seven different options: (1) self-help, (2) getting academic work re-marked, (3) Human Rights Commission mediation, (4) university mediators and grievance procedures, (5) trade union and professional association grievance procedures, (6) legal action, and (7) counseling. Providing options and information can benefit the organization; for example, the organization's task of performing an investigation is greatly expedited if the complainant has clear documentation, a diary, witnesses, and corroborating information rather than vague perceptions and impressions with little corroboration.

In the early days of sexual harassment policies and procedures a common recommendation was for the employee to go see the person charged with handling most of the employee's problems—his or her boss or immediate supervisor (see Coles, 1986, appendix, for an example of such a policy). A policy recommending that the only appropriate place to lodge a sexual harassment complaint is with one's boss is a flawed policy because approximately half of all sexual harassers are the direct supervisors of the target persons (Gutek et al., 1980; Gutek, 1985). If the harasser is a boss and the usual company policy is to go to one's boss with any problem, the victim may feel she has little recourse and will receive little support from her organization.

## Formal Procedures

In some organizations the logical outcome of a policy is a formal procedure for enforcing it. Rowe (in press) contends that several stakeholders support formal procedures, notably institutional lawyers whose interest lies in protecting the employer, and sometimes certain groups in the organization, one group of whom have experienced sexual harassment (and may be concerned with punishing harassers), and another group of whom are primarily concerned with the rights of the alleged harassers (and want to be sure that the accused have an opportunity to face the accuser and mobilize resources to protect themselves). Under a formal system a person who is harassed is expected to come forward and make a complaint that she or he signs. The accuser may be promised confidentiality or anonymity, but this is typically impossible to ensure. The accused is informed of the accusation and may or may not have an opportunity to confront the accuser. An investigation is conducted, sometimes by a person whose formal work responsibilities include investigating formal complaints, sometimes by a person on special assignment, and sometimes by a person hired from outside the organization because of special expertise in sexual harassment. In any case, it helps if the investigation is conducted by someone viewed by both sides as impartial—if such a person can be found. The person who conducts the investigation, or another person or a group of persons such as the board of directors, personnel committee, a specially appointed panel or hearing board makes a determination on whether the organization's policies have been violated. If so, sanctions may be applied, according to the policy if the policy includes this information. Often there is an appeals process, so no matter in whose favor the case is decided, the other side can prolong the formal process by appealing, often through several layers of the institution or beyond. Formal procedures are costly in money, time, energy, good will, and just about any other relevant factor. In a formal system there is usually a declared winner and a declared loser, although people involved with court cases and other formal systems often point out that, because the costs are so high, there are no "real winners," only "real losers."

Formal procedures in themselves are fine as one avenue that complainants can take. But today formal procedures are generally regarded as inadequate as the only method of recourse. This is so for several reasons. First, the majority of sexual harassment targets want the sexual harassment to stop, but they are not willing to file a formal grievance. Many victims of harassment are understandably reluctant to come forward and accuse a more powerful harasser and an even more powerful institution, both of whom can often marshall considerable resources for a defense. Furthermore, in the spirit of the belief that "the best defense is a strong offense," both the institution and the alleged harasser may be willing and have the resources to launch a full-scale attack on the professional, personal, and sexual life of the complainant (Schultz & Woo, 1994). Second, many targets have no interest in punishment or even determining blame; they just want the harassment to stop. Formal methods, in a sense, provide more than they want—or something other than they want. Third, many targets rightfully fear retaliation for making a formal complaint because it is almost impossible to keep a formal complaint from becoming public knowledge. This can not only hurt the accuser in her or his organization, but also may follow the person elsewhere. The accuser may be labeled a troublemaker or an overly sensitive person. Particularly if the occupation or speciality in which a person works is small and "everyone knows everyone else," the accusation will not be limited to the complainant's organization but will likely permeate her or his professional network. Rowe (in press) suggests that some employers adopt only a formal procedure in order to discourage people from coming forward with complaints. Consistent with that contention, the U.S. Merit Systems Protection Board (1981) study of sexual harassment found that only 2.5% of women who were harassed used formal complaint channels.

Formal procedures may themselves do a poor job of providing recourse for targets of sexual harassment. A recent Office of Civil Rights review of the procedures used at the University of California, Santa Cruz exposed their investigative procedures as highly inadequate. The university's grievance procedures were confusing and discouraged students from coming forward for fear of the "hassle" of the process. Recordkeeping was inconsistent; an inordinate amount of attention was placed on the procedural rights of the accused, while the Title IX rights of the complainants were ignored; hearings were delayed; adequate steps were not taken to provide safety for victims; and disciplinary sanctions were inadequate (reported in Budhos, in press).

## Informal Procedures

Informal procedures often have different goals than formal procedures. Informal procedures are typically aimed at stopping the offensive behavior rather than determining culpability or intent. The outcomes can range from an apology to a change in behavior or policy, a transfer of one or both parties, a voluntary resignation of one or both parties, or something else. Informal procedures are less public, less intimidating, and less litigious and confrontational (Budhos, in press). There may not be an announced winner and loser, and the potential for a "win-win" situation exists. Informal procedures, however, typically do not allow disciplinary sanctions against the accused unless the accused agrees. In addition, because they are not as public as formal procedures, exclusive reliance on them may lead targets of harassment to think they are the only persons to be sexually harassed. Believing that no one else is being harassed may discourage the target from coming forward (Rowe, in press).

Informal procedures may be centralized or decentralized (Rowe, in press); that is, they can be handled in one central location such as the HR department, or the responsibility can be delegated to local units such as heads of departments. Both centralized and decentralized options may be available simultaneously. Complainants may be provided the option of going to a direct supervisor if they feel comfortable talking to their supervisor versus going to a central location for either a formal complaint (e.g., the HR department) or an informal process (e.g., the organization's employee assistance plan if there is one).

One disadvantage of informal systems is that they make it easy to do a slipshod job. In several court cases on which I have worked, the informal investigation consisted of someone in HR or a higher-level supervisor asking the alleged harasser if he had done the things alleged by the complainant and believing him when he said he did not. In one case he was asked to prepare a brief statement to the effect that he denied all allegations. That was the sum and substance of that particular procedure for handling a complaint.

## Is No Procedure an Option?

While under certain circumstances some organizations may be able to get by without a policy, it may be less feasible to have no procedures for handling allegations of harassment. Waiting until a serious case arises without a set of procedures in place can seriously delay the handling of a complaint and exacerbate the problem. It also increases the possibility of mishandling the complaint. Many court cases for which I have consulted resulted in legal action because the organization bungled the investigation of a complaint that it was ill-prepared to handle or in some cases, lacking a set of procedures, chose instead to ignore the complaint or retaliate against the complainant in an effort to discourage her efforts.

## Is There an Ideal Set of Procedures?

No single procedure seems to be ideal in satisfying complainants. According to the 1992 *Working Woman* survey, only 20% of women believe that most complaints are handled justly, although over 70% of personnel managers surveyed believe they are (reported in Budhos, in press). In addition, it is frequently alleged that companies may not implement the policies they have on the books: "Manage-ment may publicly endorse the company policy condemning sexual harassment while personally practicing it. Such a situation conveys the expectation that sexual harassment is a behavior that is done by those who can get away with it" (Pryor, LaVite, & Stoller, 1993, p. 80). In a survey of women who used their job problems hotline, the Women Employed Institute found that of the 18 cases in which women reported sexual harassment internally, employers took effective action in only 2 cases (Budhos, in press).

In the case of sexual harassment procedures, the more the better. Rowe (in press), who estimates that she has handled or been consulted on between 8,000 and 9,000 complaints of sexual harassment, discrimination, and other workplace mistreatment, recommends that complainants be able to pursue both formal and informal paths. Making available multiple procedures has the effect of providing choice to the complainant rather than forcing the complainant to accept the method imposed by the organization. The more options available, the more complainants will find one of them to their liking. Thus, more complaints will surface and the organization can deal effectively with them.

One minor problem with providing many options is that it will be difficult for the organization to assess the number of complaints of harassment and their outcomes. It might not be a good idea, however, to confound a data collection system with a system for handling sexual harassment. Information about harassment, number and kinds of complaints, outcomes, and satisfaction with the organization's response can be collected through surveys or some other method if the organization desires this information.

## TRAINING

Training is the third prong of many organizations' system for handling sexual harassment. Training is widely recommended (e.g., Paludi & DeFour, 1989; Terpstra & Baker, 1992), but although I know of no data on the amount and extent of harassment training in organizations, it is likely to be less common than the existence of sexual harassment policies. It is more expensive than establishing a policy. There is not only the cost of buying or producing training materials, but also the cost of lost work time for all employees who participate in training. An education or training component may be incorporated in the policy (for example, by discussing what constitutes sexual harassment or providing a brief review of the major sexual harassment laws and court decisions) or in the procedures. For example, training may be a voluntary or mandatory step for people who are accused of sexual harassment.

Training may be designed mostly for managers and focus narrowly on the laws and the organization's legal liability, or it may be broader in scope in attempting to explain why it exists, to change men's thinking about women at work, or to alter both men's and women's behavior. Regardless of whether it is broad or narrow in scope, it may be required for senior managers only, for all supervisors, or all workers. Some organizations, for example the Bureau of Mines and Department of the Army (1984), have slightly different training programs for supervisors and workers.

## Content of Training

Coverage of the law is typically included in sexual harassment training; so are the organization's policy and procedures. Training may also include information about the various sanctions that can be imposed by the organization. For example, IBM informs managers that employees can be terminated for performance problems only after they are given a warning and an opportunity to improve, but they can be terminated immediately for illegal or other inappropriate conduct such as hitting someone at work. Sexual harassment comes under the latter category. Other organizations provide a series of steps, like a warning and/or voluntary or mandated counseling, before termination.

Rather than providing specific information, some training is aimed more at sensitizing workers to inappropriate behavior and/or treats sexual harassment primarily as a form of miscommunication. For example, the 1982 film *Shades of Grey*, produced by the Xerox

Corporation but used by other organizations as well, provided a series of examples of misunderstanding. When the offending employees were informed that their seemingly (to them) inocuous behavior was offensive to a fellow employee, they graciously changed their behavior. A more recent film produced by KCET television in Los Angeles (*Sex, Power, and the Workplace*) provided information about real cases that were much more egregious examples of harassment. It also followed the cases, showing that even winning in court did not necessarily solve the problem.

A training program may or may not include an evaluation component. In fact, it is not clear what are the indicators of successful training: knowledge of laws, behavior change, increased sensitivity, increased assertiveness, more or fewer complaints, attitude change (cf. Beauvais, 1986), something else? In an area generally bereft of research, Moyer and Nath (1994) showed in a careful experimental study that training had several effects: (1) It increased perceptual accuracy in men (but not in women, whose perceptions of harassment were more accurate then men's without training) and (2) both men's and women's knowledge levels increased. They focused on the definition of sexual harassment as an indicator of successful training. In another study, Blaxall, Parsonson, and Robertson (1993) evaluated a sexual harassment training program used at the University of Waikato in New Zealand. The training was aimed at contact persons, that is, those to whom a sexual harassment target would make a complaint. Using a pretest/posttest design, the researchers found that after training (which averaged 11.2 hours per trainee), the six contact persons were better able to identify sexual harassment, showed an increased level of knowledge, and were more confident in their assessments.

## Forms of Training

Training may be conducted using lectures, role playing, skits with professional actors, exercises, audiovisuals, handouts and reading, or some combination. It may simply consist of watching a training film or listening to a lecture that involves no active participation by individuals. It may involve exercises, homework, and/or tests. It can be conducted in groups or individually, as part of an organization's regular training schedule (e.g., as part of annual management training on HR issues) or as a special initiative. Training has been mandated as part of court action in some cases.

Training materials can be devised specifically by the organization for itself, materials developed by others can be adapted, or an off-the-shelf training program may be used. The trainer, if there is one, may be an attorney, an expert from outside the organization, someone from the organization's HR department, the organization's designated sexual harassment expert, or the line manager of the department. The organization might go to one of an increasing number of training companies that profess expertise in sexual harassment.

Training may be required for certain employees or it may be made available for any employees or units desiring it. One problem with voluntary training is that those most in need of training often do not attend; one problem with mandatory training is that it creates resentment and may result in very little learning. In some universities and other organizations, departments or other units that have a problem with harassment may request training. Someone from HR or an affirmative action unit might provide a training program customized to that department's concerns.

## Other Issues

Organizational policies and training are influenced by the belief that sexual harassment is in the eye of the beholder (see Chapter 2). As sexual harassment training has become more common in large corporations and some universities, a key component of much of the training is the subjective nature of sexual harassment. An emphasis on the fuzziness of the sexual harassment construct and sex differences in definition of sexual harassment feeds into people's fears that they or their organization could be charged with sexual harassment for some seemingly innocent deed (see for example, Slade, 1994). This fear is exacer-

bated by the fact that the management of an organization is responsible for the actions of its employees. Thus, it is conceivable (although not likely) that a sexual joke or mildly sexual comment could be interpreted as sexual harassment by a bystander, who in turn could sue the organization (assuming she or he could find an attorney to handle the case). The fears generated by such scenarios may be good business for those who are in the business of sexual harassment training, but it is not clear that they accurately reflect the social science research findings or legal reality.

## DISCUSSION

The federal and state policy guidelines and the policy initiatives adopted by organizations in response to legal developments have had the effect of increasing the *rights* of sexual harassment complainants and increasing the *responsibilities* of organizations (Gutek, 1993). In the past, targets of sexual harassment had few rights and it was their responsibility to prevent sexual harassment from happening to them. Now the organization and its agents are responsible for providing a harassment-free work or educational environment. In general, in order to do so, organizations have relied on establishing policies, procedures, and training. No easy formula exists so far for establishing these in a way that necessarily helps victims of harassment, much less provides a handling system that satisfies all parties involved: the organization, the individual(s) accused, and the complainant(s).

Rowe (in press) contends that it is impossible to devise a single best sexual harassment handling system, even for a short period of time. One reason is because different people have, based on their knowledge of sexual harassment and the own experience, very different and constantly changing ideas about what constitutes a good system. New research findings and legal developments contribute to shifts in what constitutes a good system for handling sexual harassment. Second, Rowe contends that it is "nearly impossible to build a complaint system that users will think is genuinely satisfactory" (p. 2). Once harassment occurs, it is unlikely that it can be resolved to everyone's satisfaction. It may be difficult to resolve it to *anyone's* satisfaction. Thus, implementing any policy is likely to lead to some dissatisfaction. So, of course, is not having a policy and failing to implement a policy in force. Even implementing a state-of-the-art system may fail to eliminate dissatisfaction. Third, there can be no one correct system of handling sexual harassment because organizations differ. Universities, the armed forces, corporations, and volunteer organizations have different missions, are responsible to different constituents, and are subject to somewhat different laws. Following the chain of command is likely to take higher priority in the armed forces than in a volunteer organization, and the military may be reluctant to set a precedent in implementing procedures that violate hierarchical norms. Nevertheless, in-house intervention and resolution are crucial because legal recourse is costly for everyone concerned and typically involves considerable anguish for the plaintiffs even if the court rules in their favor.

It is also likely that there is no one right set of procedures for handling complaints. Having a centralized complaint-handling procedure has advantages and disadvantages. So does having a decentralized system. Likewise, formal and informal procedures both have advantages and disadvantages. Having multiple avenues for seeking relief does seem to be helpful, at least for increasing reporting of harassment and providing options for victims of harassment. Providing advice that empowers victims may be helpful to them, but an organization may then feel it is remiss in protecting their workers and customers. Tailoring any system to the organization's mission and goals seems to be a good strategy. For example, in the post-Tailhook Navy, Rowe has been developing an "integrated dispute resolution structure" that offers a range of help options to victims while it remains anchored in the core values of the Navy and Marine Corps (Rowe, 1993).

Another issue is that the effectiveness of training has not been determined, although the scant research to date is promising (see Blaxall, Parsonson, & Robertson, 1993; Moyer & Nath, 1994). This is complicated by the fact that there is money to be made on sexual harassment training, and it is not clear that everyone offering training is very knowledgeable about harassment. In their eagerness to show that they are doing something, organizations may not be very discriminating in selecting trainers, the number of whom has mushroomed. Several years ago, for example, when the U.S. Geological Survey issued a "request for contract" for sexual harassment training, they received 200 responses, an order of magnitude more than they expected (Gunn, personal communication, 1992).

## SOME PROBLEMS ASSOCIATED WITH CURRENT PPT

In general, the current set of policies, procedures, and training used in organizations has not solved the problem of sexual harassment. Nor is there any evidence that they have or will lead most targets of harassment to come forward and make formal complaints or that they are greatly inhibiting would-be sexual harassers. While they *may* be having a positive impact and are probably leading more victims to come forward and are restraining some harassers, such effects have not been documented so far. Furthermore, creating better, more effective PPT does not promise to lessen the number of complaints. In fact, the number of complaints is likely to rise, given that it is widely believed that targets of harassment are more likely to come forward when they believe their organization will be supportive of them. In addition, the adversarial nature of the formal complaint procedures has had the effect of polarizing men and women in the workplace. Many men (and some women) seem to feel that attempts to eradicate sexual harassment constitute an attack on men in general. (For example, in a 1994 survey about sexual harassment and other topics conducted at the University of Arizona, 10% of the men from the faculty and staff who responded to the survey felt strongly enough to write in negative comments about the survey; most contended that the survey was a waste of time, the problem of sexual harassment was blown out of proportion, and/or it was an exercise in "male bashing.") Some people are concerned that organizations are responding to sexual harassment by policing personal choices that are none of their business and that they are "taking all the fun out of work" by, for example, forbidding dating and touching of others under any circumstances. A pat on the back, an arm around the shoulder—should these be categorically forbidden activities? There is also a great deal of concern about false accusations and the cost associated with dealing with sexual harassment. Some organizations and individual defendants are fighting back with a viciousness that is likely to make the most hardy plaintiff blanch (Schultz & Woo, 1994), as part of an effort to stem the rising tide of expensive lawsuits and what is believed to be increasingly large awards to plaintiffs. While it appears that only a minority of plaintiffs prevail in court (Terpstra & Baker, 1988, 1992), it is obvious that court cases are a considerable expense regardless of who wins. Some of the accused are fighting back in court. Some, for example, are suing the charging party for defamation of character. Men fired for sexual harassment are suing their former employers, claiming that they were fired without due process, that others who still hold their jobs engaged in more frequent or more serious sexual harassment, or that they are victims of discrimination. It is possible for an organization to be sued by both parties, for example, by a woman charging sexual harassment and later by the man accused, contending that the punishment meted out by the organization exceeded his crime.

Finally, an organization might provide PPT that completely fail in meeting their mandate to provide workers with a harassment-free work environment or students with a harass-ment-free learning environment. Policy and procedures that emphasize the rights of the accused over the rights of the complainants, a single rigidly prescribed system for handling allegations, and training that presents sexual harassment as a trivial issue or just a misunderstanding may provide some protection from legal liability but actually increase the probability that workers or students will be sexually harassed. Organizations interested in establishing PPT that are effective have many sources from which to gather ideas and information (e.g., Brandenburg, 1982; Paludi & Barickman, 1991; Wagner, 1992; Webb, 1991). A particularly rich source of information in itself and a good source of further information is the National Council for Research on Women's third edition (or an earlier edition) of *Sexual Harassment: Research and Resources* (Budhos, in press).

## REFERENCES

Beauvais, K. (1986). Workshops to combat sexual harassment: A case study of changing attitudes. *Signs, 12,* 130–145.

Bingham, S. (1991). Communication strategies for managing sexual harassment in organizations: Understanding message options and their effects. *Journal of Applied Communication Research, 19,* 85–115.

Blaxall, M. D. C., Parsonson, B. S., & Robertson, N. R. (1993). The development and evaluation of a sexual harassment contact person training package. *Behavior Modification, 17*(2), 148–163.

Bremer, B. A., Moore, C. T., & Bildersee, E. F. (1991). Do you have to call it "sexual harassment" to feel harassed? *College Student Personnel Journal, 25,* 258–268.

Budhos, M. (in press). *Sexual harassment: Research and resources* (3d ed., based on 1st and 2d ed. by D. Siegel, edited by M. E. Capek). New York: National Council for Research on Women.

Bureau of National Affairs (1987, June). Sexual harassment: Employer policies and problems.

Clark, C. S. (1991). The issues. *Congressional Quarterly Researcher, 1*(13), 539–545.

Collins, E. G. C., & Blodgett, T. B. (1981). Sexual harassment: Some see it ... Some won't. *Harvard Business Review, 59*(2), 76–95.

Department of the Army (1984a). *Training in the prevention of sexual harassment: Employee training.* Washington, DC: Government Printing Office.

Department of the Army (1984b). *Training in the prevention of sexual harassment: Supervisory training.* Washington, DC: Government Printing Office.

Dunwoody-Miller, V., & Gutek, B. A. (1985). *S.H.E. Project report: Sexual harassment in the state workforce: Results of a survey.* Sacramento, CA: Sexual Harassment in Employment Project of the California Commission on the Status of Women.

Equal Employment Opportunity Commission (EEOC) (1993). 29 CFR 1609.1.

Fitzgerald, L. (1993). Sexual harassment: Violence against women in the workplace. *American Psychologist, 48,* 1070–1076.

Gutek, B.A. (1985). *Sex and the workplace: Impact of sexual behavior and harassment on women, men and organizations.* San Francisco: Jossey-Bass.

Gutek, B. A. (1993). Sexual harassment: Rights and responsibilities. *Employee Rights and Responsibility Journal,* 6(4), 325–340.

Gutek, B. A., & Koss, M. P. 1993. Changed women and changed organizations: Consequences of and coping with sexual harassment. *Journal of Vocational Behavior, 42,* 28–48.

Gutek, B. A., Nakamura, C. Y., Gahart, M., Handschumacher, I., & Russell, D. (1980). Sexuality in the workplace. *Basic and Applied Social Psychology, l,* 255–265.

Gwartney-Gibbs, P. A., & Lach, D. H. (1992). Sociological explanations for failure to seek sexual harassment remedies. *Mediation Quarterly,* 9(4), 365–373.

Lach, D. H., & Gwartney-Gibbs, D. H. (1993). Sociological perspectives on sexual harassment and workplace dispute resolution. *Journal of Vocational Behavior,* 42(1), 102–115.

MacKinnon, C. (1979). *Sexual harassment of working women.* New Haven, CT: Yale University Press.

Moyer, R. S., & Nath, A. (1994). Gender and training influence bias and accuracy in perceptions of sexual harassment. Unpublished paper available from Robert S. Moyer, Department of Psychology, Bates College, Lewiston, ME 04240.

Paludi, M. A., & Barickman, R. B. (1991). *Academic and workplace sexual harassment: A resource manual.* Albany, NY: SUNY Press.

Paludi, M. A., & DeFour, D. (1989). Research on sexual harassment in the academy: Definitions, findings, constraints, responses. *Initiatives, 52,* 43–49.

Pryor, J. B., LaVite, C. M., & Stoller, L. M. (1993). A social psychological analysis of sexual harassment: The person/situation interaction. *Journal of Vocational Behavior, 42,* 68–83.

Rowe, M. (forthcoming). Harassment: A systems approach. In M. Stockdale (Ed.), *Sexual harassment: A volume in the Women-and-Work series.* Newbury Park, CA: Sage.

Rowe, M. (1993). The post-Tailhook Navy designs an integrated dispute resolution system. *Negotiation Journal, 12,* 1–16.

Rowe, M. (1981). Dealing with sexual harassment. *Harvard Business Review, 59,* 42–46.

Schultz, E. E., & Woo, J. (1994, September 19). Plaintiffs' sex lives are being laid bare in harassment cases. *Wall Street Journal,* A1, A9.

*Sex, power, and the workplace.* Video produced by KCET Television, 4401 Sunset Blvd., Los Angeles, CA 90027.

Spann, J. (1990). Dealing effectively with sexual harassment: Some practical lessons from one city's experience. *Public Personnel Management, 19,* 53–69.

Slade, M. (1994, March 27). Sexual harassent: Stories from the field. *New York Times,* Section 4, pp. 1 & 6.

Terpstra, D. E., & Baker, D. D. (1988). Outcomes of sexual harassment charges. *Academy of Management Journal,* March, 185–194.

Terpstra, D. E., & Baker, D. D. (1992). Outcomes of federal court decisions on sexual harassment. *Academy of Management Journal, 35,* 181–190.

*U.S.A. Today* (1992, October 2). Sexual harassment charges rise, 6A.

U.S. Merit Systems Protection Board (USMSPB) (1981). *Sexual harassment in the federal workplace: Is it a problem?* Washington, DC: Government Printing Office.

Underwood, J. (1987). End sexual harassment of employes[sic], or your board could be held liable. *American School Board Journal,* April, 43–44.

———(1994). University of Southern California policy on sexual harassment. *University of Southern California Chronicle,* June 13, 12–14.

VanHyning, M. (1993). *Crossed signals: How to say no to sexual harassment.* Los Angeles: Infotrends Press.

Wagner, E. J. (1992). *Sexual harassment in the workplace: How to prevent, investigate, and resolve problems in your organization.* New York: American Management Association.

Webb, S. L. (1991). *Step forward: Sexual harassment in the workplace: What you need to know.* New York: MasterMedia Limited.

# CHAPTER 12

# INVESTIGATING SEXUAL HARASSMENT ALLEGATIONS: THE EMPLOYER'S CHALLENGE

**Iris McQueen**

With respect to widespread forms of job-related discrimination, the contemporary employer faces a serious challenge.

In February 1988 the challenge presented itself in violence when a gunman, terminated two years prior on sexual harassment charges, entered a Sunnyvale, California defense contractor's plant and killed 8 people including himself, injuring 28 others in his quest to kill the woman who rejected his attention. In May 1988 a retired police officer killed a federal judge and committed suicide after his daughter's sexual harassment suit was dismissed. The case was over seven years old. The challenge continued through charges against both the president of the United States, Bill Clinton, and popular TV game show host Bob Barker. The impact was felt in the nomination of Supreme Court justice Clarence Thomas and the congressional inquiry into staff allegations against Oregon senator Bob Packwood.

Although sexual harassment is first recorded in the Old Testament (Genesis 39), the employer's responsibility in maintaining order and professional decorum has only recently been established relative to social/sexual behaviors exhibited in the workplace. In traditionally male-dominated workplaces such as the military, public safety, manufacturing, construction, forestry, and trucking these behaviors are very visible and should be expected until workforce parity occurs.

Absent established policies and procedures for employees to report behavioral violations of policies, the organization stands without proper defense both administratively and legally. This chapter is designed to help individuals and organizations cope and manage more effectively in an obviously difficult situation. No one wins in discrimination complaints but an organization may minimize its risk exposure by investigating competently, confidently, and credibly.

## IMPORTANCE AND COMPLEXITY OF THE ISSUES

There is no single cause for the complex set of discriminatory behaviors discovered in the sexual harassment investigation. The wide gap between traditional beliefs about the roles for males and females as well as the changing paradigms of social, economic, and political realities are the roots of the problem.

For the investigator the message conveyed is compelling. There is a substantial risk for the firm or agency. The savvy investigator will make a critical assessment of the organization before undertaking any investigation. Not to do so enlarges the potential arena for liability and forestalls a successful conclusion to an in-house remediation.

A female child learns how to be a girl in her parents' home; that learning is reinforced in school and church; as an adult it affects her career choices in open competition with male contemporaries as well as in awkward and unresolved hostilities that may affect relationships with coworkers. In applying these concepts to sexual harassment, the investigator should recall that the nature of work itself in our postagrarian and postindustrial social structure has changed. The 1990s present a substantial paradigm shift for men and women.

Work is no longer as physically demanding as it used to be, making it possible for females to perform many if not most jobs traditionally reserved for males. Old, untested myths and assumptions about men and women at work compound workplace social dynamics as well as an investigation's facts.

## DISTINGUISHING SEXUAL HARASSMENT

Sexual harassment can be informally defined as unwanted and unreciprocated sexual attention (mating or dating behaviors) focused on someone who is not in a position to accept, correct, or reject these sexual advances with-

out consequence. Sexual harassment is power displayed in a sexual/social manner. Sexual harassment is always a form of gender discrimination but may also replicate other prohibited personnel practices.

Broadly, the Equal Employment Opportunity Commission guidelines (published in 1978) hold the employer responsible for acts of its supervisors and the behavior of coworkers. The responsibility extends even to some nonemployees when they create a hostile or abusive work environment.

Sexual harassment victims frequently fail to report incidents because they don't know how to or they are unaware that the behavior is forbidden. They are afraid of reprisal or escalation when it is investigated. They agonize over being excluded or ridiculed by the work group. They hope for it to go away. They expect to be blamed and that things will deteriorate into an unpleasant atmosphere, up to and including losing their job or getting a bad recommendation if they elect to leave.

The competent investigator will remain cautious about blaming the victim. Compounding the predicament is that victims frequently will excuse the harasser's conduct rather than confront it. This occurs when victims feel guilty and blame themselves ("bad things only happen to bad people"); when victims and witnesses excuse objectionable behavior with phrases like *S/he doesn't mind when X does it, S/he didn't really know what they were doing, They could have stopped it if they really wanted to, That is just the way men/women are, S/he must have given him/her cause, S/he does that to everyone,* or *S/he doesn't mean it that way;* when managers and coworkers fail to support or assist the worker who has been sexually harassed; or when victims do not attempt to resist sexual harassment when it happens to them (reinforces guilt feelings).

An essential role of the investigator is to determine *if* and *when* sexual harassment occured. It is also crucial to the quality and credibility of the resolution for the investigator to distinguish the level of inappropriate conduct, using specific work performance standards prohibiting it or the fact that it is not commensurate with conservative business practices (such as sexually stimulating or graphic posters).

## ROLES, RIGHTS, AND INVESTIGATORS' RESPONSIBILITIES

In every incident of sexual harassment there are four crucial role players for the investigator to become familiar with—the victim, the alleged harasser, the supervisor(s), and the observers (who will become the witnesses).

The *victim* of sexual harassment, of course, is the person making the allegation. The victim charges facts that construct a plausible suspicion that such an event occurred. While the victim is not required to make an internal allegation with the employer, it is to the advantage of both to do so. It alerts the firm to potential snags in interpersonal relationships as well as potential litigation. Such an act of trust also gives the company a chance to respond, to make amends, and to restore order.

The *alleged harasser* is accused by the victim, but the accusation remains only an allegation until the investigative report and findings are published. If the allegation is supported, there has been a *substantive finding* that may require disciplinary action.

The *supervisor* involved in the incident may be involved just because s/he supervises one of the principal parties. If investigative activity can be worked through the line supervisor, it reinforces the supervisor's position of authority .

An important role played out in every investigation is the *witness*. Coworkers must know that the company relies on their cooperation to get to the facts and effect a reasonable and timely resolution.

## The Role of the Investigator

While not all complaints will require a formal investigation, experience recommends that the employer assign a competent and thoroughly trained investigator to each case. The litigation record is replete with cases of bungled investigations. If employers are to be successful, investigators must be competent, credible, and capable of a proper and prompt inquiry into the allegations.

The investigator is the fact finder and objective reporter. His or her responsibility is to assemble sufficient information to determine whether the behavior occurred and constituted sexual harassment under the lawful definition.

The investigator must never act so as to leave an impression of personal interest in the outcome of the investigatorial process. The investigator must be empathetic enough to put interviewees at ease, but, the investigator must also be extremely careful not to communicate to the interviewee any personal opinion or judgment on the merits of the complaint.

## Choosing a Competent Investigator

In any work assignment as sensitive and potentially controversial as the investigation of a sexual harassment complaint, employers must select a person with appropriate training, experience, abilities, and personal characteristics. Above all else, the investigator must be able to maintain objectivity throughout data identification, data gathering, and report preparation. The perceived credibility, competence, and objectivity of the investigator will influence the complainant's feeling of being fairly treated.

The competent investigator should have some training in investigative skills (collection, analysis, and preservation of evidence gathered from interviewing). The investigator should also be familiar with applicable personnel laws, rules, and practices (as well as any contractual obligations under collective bargaining agreements). An investigator should be thoroughly familiar with the basic tenets of civil rights. In addition, the individual should have a good understanding of particular employment problems encountered by women and ethnic minorities.

The following are the desirable qualities an employer should look for in the recruitment and selection of an investigator from within the existing work force:

- Ability to communicate effectively with persons of different races, sexes, nationalities, ages, and economic, cultural, and educational backgrounds
- Ability to communicate with persons at different levels within the organization, including those who hold key managerial positions
- Ability to listen actively and recall effectively
- Ability to gather and analyze a variety of information from a variety of sources concerning sensitive or controversial issues
- Abiity to exercise mature judgment and self-control when exposed to personal criticism or emotional expressions
- Ability to produce clear and concise reports
- Willingness to leave interpretive decisions to someone else's authority

Fairness, impartiality, objectivity, neutrality, and a nonjudgmental attitude are vital to the professional credibility of the employer's designated investigator.

## PLANNING AND ORGANIZING THE INVESTIGATION

Investigating is applied problem solving. The steps involve identifying the problem, gathering information about the problem, evaluating the information, identifying possible courses of action, and solving the problem. That is a familiar and fundamental problem-solving cycle. In cases of sexual harassment the investigator's role is gathering and evaluating information relating to the problem defined—a sexual harassment behavior.

After the complaint has been filed, the investigator's first step is planning and organizing the investigation.

## Planning

Planning is an important step in any undertaking, but it is crucial in this endeavor. It is best done in a quiet location with all available tools immediately accessible. The planning should be done free of distractions and interruptions so that no important detail is overlooked.

The investigator's *goal* is to develop sufficient evidence to make a determination on the allegation—a finding of merit or no merit. The astute investigator will seek evidence from sources that may be in conflict. This evidence will lead to a balanced record. A balanced and objective investigation is almost impossible without sufficient time in the planning stage.

In developing the plan, the investigator must first consider the number of allegations, the issues involved, and the specific basis for discrimination (in addition to sexual harassment, are there other charges as well?). A complaint that alleges multiple charges translates into a multitiered investigation. The investigator is charged with collecting evidence to produce findings on each allegation.

## Evidence

*Evidence* is critical to a competent investigation. Direct and material evidence are the best forms, and the investigator must consciously try to find these kinds of evidence, or others if these are lacking.

*Direct evidence* is any proof in the form of testimony from a witness who actually saw or heard the alleged incident (i.e., an "eye witness"). Direct evidence, if believable and believed, tends to prove the existence of a fact at issue without presumption or inference. A problem with direct evidence is the reliability and integrity of the witness. In contrast, problems of relevancy arise with circumstantial evidence.

*Circumstantial evidence* is not based on actual observation and personal knowledge but on other facts from which deductions or inferences are drawn, indirectly showing the fact(s). Although it is necessary to make inferences from circumstantial evidence, it can still be a valid, reliable, and useful form of evidence lacking direct evidence. In fact, when there is conflict within the direct testimony, great weight may be given to circumstantial evidence.

There are four sources of evidence. *Documentary evidence* is all written information and is considered to be the best form of evidence. An investigation normally requires information to be extracted from procedures manuals, employee files, correspondence, printouts, and records. Questions are less likely to be raised about the reliability of these sources since they preexisted the complaint incident in question.

*Testimony* is the evidence provided by a witness in the form of a statement. All testimony should be supported by one additional source—this is *corroboration*.

*Statistical evidence* is used only to document trends or support broad statements and is considered generally weak for sexual harassment cases.

*Personal observation* is information gained through the investigator's personal experiences. Recording the composition or adequacy of the work site, working conditions, or treatment of a specific group or individual is considered valuable in providing a framework for the investigation and to validate other evidence. Personal observation should be used to validate testimony but should not be used as the cornerstone because of its inherent potential for false conclusions.

It is important that investigators recognize the limits and distinctions of each type of evidence.

## Inference and Assumptions

Inference and assumptions are to the skilled investigator like hammer and nails to the skilled carpenter. When drawing conclusions from limited information, one uses assumption and inference skills. While the terms are used interchangeably, they are actually quite different, and the investigator must be aware of the distinct usage.

When making *assumptions*, we depend on intuition, past experience, feelings, attitudes, values, prior experiences, and education. We lump these together to formulate a conclusion rather than working through an analytical process. Therefore, our conclusion becomes more of a statement about who we are than an expression that can stand the scrutiny of cross-examination.

An *inference*, however, is a systematic, analytical approach to conclusion development.

For the common person the concept of inference is that "given this set of facts, a reasonable person could draw a predictable conclusion...." The key concept is *reasonable*—an inference is a leap of faith into logic. All inferences involve a theory and a set of tests to validate the set of facts relative to the theory.

In an administrative process the complainant must present a "cause to believe" statement that poses reasonable suspicion that an incident did occur. The rules of administrative inquiry are not the same as the rules of litigation in open court but should be parallel in propriety and integrity so that the inquiry results can represent the interests of the employer should litigation become inevitable.

To make the inference that the incident occurred as charged, the investigator can ask three test questions:

- Are there precedents for the conclusion? Has anyone else presented similar facts to infer a similar conclusion?
- Can any other conclusion be drawn from the same set of facts?
- Can the same conclusion be drawn from another set of facts?

## Determining Jurisdiction

While planning, the investigator must determine jurisdiction, or the authority of the employer to intervene in the complaint, to investigate, and to enact remedy. Although in most cases the issue of jurisdiction will be determined prior to assignment to the specific investigator, the sharp investigator will watch for unresolved issues of jurisdiction that may compromise the remedy enacted later. Four areas that may be helpful in determining jurisdiction are that the complaint incident involved the employer's work activity, premises, and time or was within the employer's sphere of influence or control.

## The Case File

Organizing the investigative file will form the basis for making a determination at the close of the investigation. The file's contents and completeness will make the findings more credible. Although there is no "right" way to organize a file, a complete method should ensure that no evidence is lost. The file should be assigned a case name or number and be housed within a legal-sized folder that will accommodate all entries and documents of evidence. The actual file may become several file folders before completion, but the general organizational structure should include the following:

- Table of contents (or chronology of events)
- Statement of complaint/allegation
- Time frames, deadlines, etc.
- Jurisdictional items
- Complainant's statement and witnesses
- Complainant's records and documents
- Statement of alleged harasser and witnesses
- Alleged harasser's documents and records
- Statement of employer and witnesses
- Employer's records and documents
- Work site location description, rules, etc.
- Investigator's observations and analysis
- List of witnesses/persons contacted, with addresses
- Other relevant information (cases, research, etc.)

## Limiting Scope Of Inquiry

The *scope of inquiry* restricts the investigation to the specific allegation(s) at issue and the immediate environment where the complaining party suffered the injury. Limiting the scope will create a solid basis for a clear and concise investigation. The following steps will assist in limiting the scope of inquiry:

1. Examine the charge of discrimination. Determine and clarify the specific allegations by reviewing the statement of the complainant and any supporting evidence.
2. Contact the complainant to verify that all allegations are included and to request additional information if needed.
3. Identify any issues that are not in dispute.
4. Identify any and all issues that have already been investigated.

5. Identify charges that are not relevant to employment discrimination or are not material to the investigation.
6. Isolate remaining issues, which will be the subject of the investigation.

Failure to limit the scope of inquiry by following these steps can result in a long, drawnout, and confusing process that makes it difficult to reach a well-reasoned conclusion.

## CONDUCTING THE INVESTIGATION

While the role of the investigator may vary from one organization to another, the investigations are fundamentally the same. It is the investigator's duty to ensure a prompt, thorough, and competent investigation with clear, concise findings.

### Special Investigative Considerations

*Criminal Charges*

Charges may be brought in sexual harassment cases that may be unfamiliar to an investigator through other discrimination investigations. Criminal charges, such as sexual assault, rape, attempted rape, assault and battery, may be filed with local law enforcement agencies.

*Countercharges*

Sometimes the alleged harasser will file a countercharge (such as defamation) when first advised of the complaint. Such an action may constitute reprisal for filing the complaint. In some cases presiding judges have denied the defamation filings in favor of the sexual harassment victim's right to freedom of adjudication without threat of additional legal action under differing legal standards. In such instances the investigator's strict adherence to the rules of confidentiality and fairness may avoid such a precarious situation.

*Volatility*

Sexual misconduct of any kind is a volatile and sensational issue. The investigator should anticipate the strong feelings and polarity of workers about the intentions and impact of the behavior of the involved parties. People take sides, blaming and skewing evidence to meet their values and beliefs about the guilt or innocence of the parties.

## Focus

Investigators can fall into the trap of examining the alleged harasser's *intent* rather than focusing on the *impact* of the behavior on the victim and the workplace integrity. Many incidents are, in fact, unintentional and unwitting. If a work environment is tedious, pressured, and repetitive, there may be a pattern of teasing, pranks, and raucous humor to alleviate the tedium and unrelenting boredom or pressure. While the intent may be to have fun, the effects on a single individual may be offensive. (In one organization a crew member on a manufacturing floor showed up for work with a sanitary napkin for a sweatband. In another an executive gave the secretaries a penis-shaped eraser for Christmas. While many see these actions as generally harmless, particular individuals may be offended.)

## Past Complaints

Investigators must avoid the temptation to review or consider complaints from the same complainant that do not relate to the current incident under investigation. If a victim has filed previously under the same policy, it may seem easy to consider the victim a "gold digger," especially if some tangible "reward" was extended as consideration. The past case(s) and its resolution should have no bearing on the present inquiry. Review of precedents serves to introduce unnecessary, irrelevant bias. The only time the investigator should consider such a review is if the past complaints and remedy have involved the same accused individual(s) and there is a pattern of repetition or reprisal.

It is important to review the history of the alleged harasser for prior letters of instruction (warnings) or other remediation. In cases in which the same alleged harasser shows up in differing cases, the investigator and the employer must consider if retaining the

employee is warranted. Certainly, the consequences of a meritorious finding would be more severe based on such a history and previous warnings and counseling.

## Special Effects

The investigator must consider whether performance (attendance, injury, errors, etc.) is attributable to the sexual harassment incident(s). Harassment is an unsettling incident even in its less severe forms; however, the victim may start encountering a deterioration in performance before filing the complaint. When reviewing work history and job performance indicators, the investigator will encounter the possibility that poor job performance may be a direct result of the sexual harassment. Further, the victim may not have even been aware of poor performance or at least reluctant to discuss it (hoping it would go away). Victims who are unable to be timely in filing and provide sketchy evidence may be suffering extreme stress. Their limited cooperation may be all that they can contribute. The investigator is under greater pressure to get corroborating evidence *without* penalty or compromise to the victim's complaint.

## Victim's Reputation

A major pitfall for the investigator is the victim's reputation within the work force and within the community, particularly if there are no eye witnesses. While some investigators are swayed by a "bad" reputation, it is just as likely to be distracted by a particularly "good" reputation. Investigators must guard against those prejudices being introduced into the investigation.

## Confidentiality

Incidents of sexual harassment involve behaviors of sexual assault or other allegations that would embarrass the complainant and the alleged harasser if widely known among the company's work force. When an investigation is under way, some "well-intentioned" person may leak details to the press, which brings discomfort to the firm and all its employees. In routine cases the investigator must respect the rules of confidentiality until the completion of the investigation and publication of findings by management. Any premature disclosure may wrongfully damage both the complainant and the alleged harasser when there is inadequate evidence to substantiate a meritorious finding.

The final report is also confidential after the remedy has been enacted. The investigator should not discuss the specific investigation or the evidence with anyone after closure of the case. The access to the investigator's files and notes should remain very limited and, then, only on an absolute need-to-know basis.

### Prima Facie

Prima facie establishes a requirement to shift the burden of proof for the allegation from the complainant to the employer. To establish prima facie, the investigator should examine the complaint for:

- A representation of specific opportunity
- A representation of why the complainant was affected by this opportunity (to accept or refuse)
- A representation of how and why the complainant was affected by the conduct or act (substantial interference with work performance or hostile environment)
- A rationale for the adverse effect (the connection between the behavior and the harm or injury to victim)

When all of these issues are addressed, the complaint is said to be perfect for investigation and remediation. If the complainant is unclear about any of these, the investigator must interview the complainant to collect sufficient information to incorporate into the allegation (amending).

## Interviewing Skills

A successful investigation depends on a successful series of interviews and the clever collection of evidence through testimony. The success of the interview depends on some basics, including planning the interview;

developing questions; and conducting the interview, with special attention to dealing with the principals and witnesses.

### Planning the Interview

The investigator should select the proper time, place, and an appropriate series of questions; decide how to record the interview; and be mentally alert. The interview should be planned for a place that offers privacy, off-site if possible. The investigator should make certain that the conversation cannot be overheard or interrupted during the interview. Distractions (visual and audio) should be kept to a minimum. The interview should be scheduled for the earliest possible convenience. As the investigator develops the interview plan, there are five cues to keep in mind as the plan develops:

1. How will I open the interview? What can I do that will set up a relaxed, cordial environment?
2. What information do I plan to give to the witness within this investigation?
3. What information do I need to get from the witness to complete the investigation?
4. How will I record/document the course of the interview and the presented facts?
5. How will I close the interview?

### Developing Questions

In a sexual harassment complaint there are basic questions that should be answered in the course of the interview sequence.

Did harassment of a sexual nature occur? Who is purportedly the responsible (charged) party? Was the harassment of a sexual nature? Does evidence indicate that the alleged incident occurred? Did the harassment substantially interfere with the employee's work performance or create a hostile or intimidating environment? Are there any witnesses? Did the victim tell anyone about the behavior? Did s/he do anything at the time to advise the harasser that the conduct was unwelcome? Was the alleged harasser aware of the behaviors that constitute sexual harassment within the workplace? Is there a policy and procedural remedy for behaviors? Is there evidence of a pattern of similar incidents that indicates the allegation occurred as presented? Has the charged party harassed others? Does the employer have substantial control over the charged party? Have any prevention measures been taken? If harassing behavior was known, was immediate and appropriate corrective action taken at the time? Is there evidence that the employer (or its agent) exercised the ability to intervene to prevent or eliminate sexual harassment or other forms of discrimination? Was the alleged act(s) within the scope of employment or within the confines of the employer's direct interest in the employee's work performance (if the employer had no knowledge of the event)? What does the victim want to remedy the injustice? Is the remedy within the resources of the employer? Are there other legal considerations in the allegation that require consultation with a law enforcement agency?

In cases of *termination or any disciplinary action*, the investigator must know if the job action actually occurred or was threatened. Is the stated reason for the adverse condition factually accurate? Does the treatment of similarly situated individuals indicate the adverse action occurred because the complainant refused, resisted, or objected to sexual harassment? What has happened to others in similar situations under the same decision maker? Determine if they were subjected to the same or similar acts. Exactly who made the adverse action decision and what role(s) did the alleged harasser play in that decision?

In *constructive discharge*, did the employer force the complainant to resign? Is there evidence indicating an intolerable work environment? Were any corrective actions timely and appropriate, and did working conditions improve as a result, making resignation effectively unnecessary? Did the employer have actual or constructive knowledge that resignation would be likely? Did the complainant inform the employer or an agent of the pressure to resign? (It is the employer that is expected to be aware of how a reasonable woman would react in similar circumstances.)

For both the *adverse action and constructive discharge*, use the patterns for both the termination and constructive discharge situations.

For cases where *selection* is the issue, did the employer fail to hire (select) the complainant because the complainant refused, resisted, or objected to the sexual advances? Was there a vacancy? Did the complainant formally apply or otherwise demonstrate interest in the vacancy? Did the employer reject the complainant for the position? Is any rebuttal by the employer for nonselection valid? Is the employer's reason for rejecting the applicant factually accurate and clearly job-related? How were other applicants in similar situations treated? Is there a pattern for other applicants? Does the employer's treatment of the applicant/complainant before and after the allegation indicate that the failure to select was either directly or indirectly related to the act of sexual harassment?

## Conducting the Interview

- A competent, professional investigator keeps the goal and objectives of each interview in mind and keeps track of information needed from each source. During the interview the investigator is mindful of these directives:

- Keep your talking to a minimum (less than 30%) and allow the witness to dominate interview time. Use active listening techniques and attend to the speaker at all times with visual, verbal, and body posture behaviors. Don't interrupt the witness unless it is to clarify a specific point central to the allegation. Keep notes but don't become tied to them—keep looking at the witness.

- Always be polite and courteous to each witness, but act in a professional, clinical manner. Any inappropriate joviality or personal remarks can be seen as bias or preconceived findings.

- Do not record any information concerning anyone's personal activity unless such activity is directly related to the case issues.

- Select appropriate and reliable pieces of information to synthesize into the investigative plan and support determination processes.

## Interviewing The Victim

The investigator should interview the complainant first. Winning the complainant's confidence maintains an atmosphere that will foster open and candid communications. Using the following checklist, the investigator should take a statement from the complaining party. Although some of this information is already provided via the complaint itself, it should appear again in the complainant's statement.

- Name and business or home address of the complainant (and phone numbers)
- Title and classification of the complainant's position within the organization
- Name and location of the department and unit involved in this complaint
- Nature of the action, decision, or condition giving rise to the complaint
- Date or time period for the alleged discrimination
- Kind of discrimination (any and all should be noted)
- Identity of charged party(ies) if known to be responsible
- Specific relief sought by the complainant
- Information known to the charging party in support of the allegation of sexual harassment (or other forms of discriminatory practices)
- Identity of individuals known to the complainant to have information or evidence relevant to the alleged matter(s) (Avoid committing to interview all individuals listed.)
- Information essential to the review of the specific matter giving rise to the complaint and whatever assessment of the general work environment or working conditions that may foster such conduct

During this initial interview and with all subsequent interviews the complainant should have the right of representation and advice by someone of her or his choosing, including a family member or an attorney. The investigator should be familiar with all facets of the complaint-processing system in order to answer any and all questions submitted by either the complainant or the complainant's representative.

If during the course of the interview the complainant submits new issues for redress, the investigator should advise that, if the complainant wants to pursue them, these issues either be amended to this complaint or be submitted as a new complaint utilizing the same system. All allegations of restraint, interference, coercion, discrimination or reprisal resulting from the pending complaint should immediately be brought to the attention of the CEO and the investigative team.

## Interviewing The Harasser

When the complaint subject is identified, the investigator should inform the individual of the full nature of the allegation and the charging party. The investigator should immediately take a statement from this individual giving the facts as that person knows them to be, relevant to the specific complaint.

Fairness, impartiality, and objectivity must be absolutely apparent at every step. The investigator must be thoroughly familiar with the allegation by the complainant in order to construct queries that will clarify the source of the conflict. This contact with the target should be used to develop leads to other information sources.

## Interviewing Witnesses

*Choosing Interviewees.* Choosing witnesses is based on the employee's known or presumed ability to furnish information that is both material and relevant to the allegation. To obtain the information, the investigator asks the witness a series of questions and, based on the responses, formulates other clarifying or probing questions. It is essential that during this process the investigator keep the issues in the complaint clearly in mind to avoid discussion of irrelevant matters. The investigator must remain in control of the interview with traditional interview techniques, such as being candid and concise, asking open-ended questions, allowing silence as the witness formulates a response, and avoiding leading the witness. It is the investigator's responsibility to keep the interview focused and goal-oriented.

*Interacting with the Witness.* An investigator should never give information to a witness that allows the witness to guess what answer the investigator expects to hear. The witness should not be able to anticipate what s/he thinks the investigator wants to hear. With few exceptions, the investigator must refrain from posing questions that can be answered "yes" or "no." The investigator must not promise the witness that s/he will not have to testify further. In a punitive action hearing the witness may be required again to offer evidence, such as in a tort action or even a criminal proceeding. The investigator should not give the impression that s/he either believes or disbelieves the witness's testimony nor ever reveal any biases about the facts or the merit of the complaint.

Heading the list of witnesses for interview are, of course, the complainant(s) and the subject(s) of the complaint if one has been clearly identified. To the extent reasonable and feasible, all witnesses suggested by the complainant should be given an opportunity to make a statement for the record. Further need for statements may develop as the investigation progresses; however, it is the investigator that will decide which witnesses will make statements. Selection will depend directly upon the investigator's estimate of the relevancy of the evidence available through each witness.

Ideally, witnesses should be interviewed personally and privately at some off-site location. Attendance at the interview can be considered within the scope of employment requirements and the employer's right to know about the work environment. The investigator should always make a personal contact and not use the mails or any third-party to relay information about the meeting or the content for discussion. In advance of the interview the investigator should only inform the witness that the interview is confidential and not subject to discussion.

*Uncooperative Witness.* Discrimination in employment is prohibited. Therefore, the investigation of an allegation of discrimination is an important matter of official business. A letter of authority should be issued to the investigator(s) stipulating that all employees are required to cooperate with the process and furnish information if they have knowledge regarding the allegation. If this strategy fails, a note should be made in the investigative file and the investigator should ascertain if the relevant information can be obtained from any other source.

## Other Components of the Investigation

### Statements

In taking statements, the investigator will get all the essential information and reduce it to writing. After it is in print, the statement should be submitted to the witness to make any necessary corrections. If corrections or changes are made, they must be in ink and initialed by the witness and the investigator. For ease in reading and reference, statements should be typed, but this is not essential if they are legibly written. If not, a typewritten version should be rendered and attached to the handwritten original. Since this information is highly sensitive, it is advised that the investigator hire the services of a typist who is not associated with the firm and has no interest in the content of the investigation or its outcomes.

### Site Tour

The investigative process may require an on-site visit to properly deal with the facts. The bearing and conduct of the investigator are important factors influencing the success of the tour. It must be conducted in a thoroughly professional manner, projecting the image of an impartial fact finder determined to identify all facts related to the charge(s).

The visit should occur as soon as possible after the initiation of the investigation. The tone of this planned visit should be low-key; it should not be a formal visit accompanied by the manager. The investigator should not interview any employees during the tour, but concentrate on seeing as much as possible. Observations should not be shared with anyone at the facility until there has been opportunity to analyze and research all conditions observed. While on tour the investigator should keep in mind all details related to the allegation, including the need for facts and records from the site for consideration on the alleged violations.

The investigator should not rely totally on memory and personal observation for obtaining information, but, rather, should carry a notebook. Photos, plans, and the like may assist in reconstructing the unit layout later. The thorough investigator strives to obtain an understanding of the unit's overall operations—the movement of materials, machinery, goods, people, and management practices within the setting.

## Closing the Investigation

Closing the investigation begins by analyzing the evidence and developing findings consistent with the corporate personnel rules and regulations. The competent investigator follows these steps:

### Step One: Reviewing the Evidence

Review all the evidence, including the documentary, statistical, and testimonial evidence. From these sources, the investigator should be able to discern whether a law was violated and where the responsibility lies.

Distinguish between fact and opinion. A fact can be objectively verified; an opinion cannot be verified and remains subjective. The source of data may be the clue—for example, photocopies of agency documents versus someone's oral testimony. In the review the investigator should highlight any conflicting evidence and attempt to corroborate each version of the facts presented.

### Step Two: Analyzing the Charge and Explanations

Analyze the charge and the plausible explanation for the behavior. Articulate all possible explanations, including any differences between policy and practice. For instance, if the sexual harassment policy clearly prohibits sexually graphic posters but the employees on the delivery dock have posted several "beefcake" posters and the crew leader has not objected and instructed them to remove the offending posters, the investigator is faced with a dilemma because standards of practice have set a new performance norm that is counter to the company's established policy.

### Step Three: Reviewing Similar Cases

Review similar cases for similar constructs of logic and accusation. The more similar the cases, the more aid the investigator will get in determining the risk of selected outcomes. Cull from these cases the ones most relevant to the current set of facts and available evidence. Review the opinion at length to determine if any conditions are attached to the opinion or judgment. Extract and highlight these cases and append the extracts into the case file for reference.

### Step Four: Determining Options and Risks

Map the determination and remedy options with attendant risk scenarios (e.g., alleged harasser files libel or wrongful firing suit). Using a numeric problem-solving technique (a Likert scale of 1–5 is useful), affix a risk quotient to the options (using criteria such as urgency, legality, frequency, seriousness, and history).

The federal Equal Employment Opportunity Commission recommends the following *minimum* remedies:

1. Persons who commit acts of intimidation and harassment should be admonished in writing to discontinue such conduct and should be disciplined in proportion to the severity of the case. Make sure due process considerations are met.

2. The employer should develop and disseminate a clear and direct policy forbidding intimidation and harassment and providing for disciplinary action against all offenders.

3. The victim's employment records should be cleansed where an adverse personnel action has taken place as part of the sexual harassment or in retaliation for filing a charge. Other corrective action should be taken as necessary.

4. An immediate offer of rehire with no loss of seniority, wages, or other benefits should be made by the employer when there has been an actual or constructive discharge due to sexual harassment or in retaliation for filing a charge.

Other suggestions from the EEOC compliance manual are reprisal protection, established policy and procedures, file purging for complainant, hiring and reinstatement or promotion, restoring sick leave or vacation credits, reinstating back wages, training, and compensatory or punitive damages or attorneys' fees and costs.

### Step Five: Writing the Report

The investigative work is complete. But perhaps the most challenging task is writing the report of findings. The report is a carefully designed summary of complaint issues and findings as well as recommendations for remedy. It is a diplomatic document and must be absolutely devoid of any personal bias or unsupported contentions. It is a decision-making tool and it becomes the permanent record. It may also become court evidence, so one should be cautious about details.

While writing styles and corporate writing standards vary, these are the essentials of a well-presented report of investigative findings: The report must be clear, concise, accurate, and complete. The report includes all necessary details but excludes the many unnecessary details not specifically related to the findings of merit. The goal is to be brief. It should be written in terms that any reader will understand. Jargon and acronyms should be kept to a minimum.

The report's audience includes the victim and the alleged harasser (and their representatives or attorneys), the company CEO, and any outside agencies with an interest in the case. Investigative reports and supporting documents are not for public record since they contain sensitive personnel information. The reader(s) should be able to understand the investigative report and to rely on the information contained within it. Any inaccuracy, however small, will cause question as to the reliability and credibility of the entire report and the investigation—as well as the investigator—that it represents.

Typically the report is produced with an executive summary page succinctly presenting the allegation, the findings, and the recommendations for the decision maker's quick reference. It is a digest of the who, what, where, when, why, and how issues.

The report must contain the following:

- The name of the investigator and the names of the involved principals, the accuser and the accused as well as the witnesses.
- A finding and conclusion for each specific allegation. The findings are represented as "with merit" or "with no merit" as to the specific allegation.
- A discussion of appropriate jurisdiction and any limits or boundaries (such as for nonemployees).
- The evidence and rationale for each conclusion. Contains factual, material, and related evidence, including the investigator's observations.
- Any findings related to other violations (may or may not be discriminatory) such as improper personnel transactions, inadequate training, prohibited personnel practices, conduct unbecoming, inept supervision, or generally poor management practices. (Frequently a thorough investigation will unveil a myriad of other management problems that also need addressing but are outside the scope of the inquiry.)
- The investigator's recommendations on remedy, if the charge of sexual harassment has been found "with merit."

While the investigative report is a summary of activity, the investigative file contains *all* material relevant to the investigative process. The investigator should keep no other personal notes. The official file is kept secure and is subject to only limited access under the policies of the company.

## SUMMARY

The employer's challenge when a sexual harassment complaint is made can be summarized by the following points:

- Employers must design and deliver a defensible investigation that examines the facts to determine if a violation of policy and law has occurred.
- Employers must select and train competent investigators with the proper knowledge, skills, and abilities to conduct sensitive investigations.
- Investigators must document the course of investigative activity so that the employer's official record supports their applied consequence of disciplinary action *or* their decision not to pursue more formal remediation.

# CHAPTER 13

# SEXUAL HARASSMENT AND BLACK WOMEN: A HISTORICAL PERSPECTIVE

## JANN H. ADAMS

Sexual harassment negatively impacts women's professional development and personal esteem and integrity. This phenomenon has been studied primarily in the workplace and in academic settings. Because sexual harassment may include behaviors that are prevalent and condoned under certain social circumstances, clarifying the damaging effects of these behaviors is difficult.

The impact of race on the experience or reporting of sexual harassment is unclear. The historical experience of ethnic women in the United States is quite varied, and the unique circumstances associated with the immigration and life circumstances of these women may strongly influence their experience of all types of sexual abuse, including sexual harassment.

## THE IMPORTANCE OF CULTURE AND RACE

Culture and ethnic minority status may impact the perceptions and experiences of individuals in the United States and elsewhere. *Culture* refers to the common beliefs, expectations, values, and rituals shared by people. These people may or may not belong to the same ethnic group. Therefore, culture and ethnic group identification should be discussed separately.

Culture may be tied to ethnic group identification or may be provided by an organization, school, or other type of environment. According to Hotelling (1991), both "the sociocultural expectations and the view of women and the organizational climate" (p. 498) of a university are important factors in the makeup of the cultural climate. Dziech and Weiner (1984) argue that the socialization of American women and perceptions of college women specifically provide a cultural climate in which sexual harassment is allowed to occur and go unchallenged by the victims of this harassment.

The extent to which ethnic minority women experience different rates of sexual harassment and report this harassment at different levels than white women is unclear. Specific circumstances present in the United States may contribute to a cultural climate that results in an experience of sexual harassment that may be both more severe and more difficult to report for minority women. The increased risk for sexual harassment among black women is difficult to test. Results of studies that have compared differences in rates of sexual harassment among women of differing ethnic backgrounds may be influenced by cultural norms regarding the perception of, tolerance for, and prohibitions against reporting of these behaviors. Results of these studies provide equivocal support for the increased risk of sexual harassment of black women (see Chapter 16).

The historical experience of ethnic minority groups in the United States is quite varied. Most minority group members immigrated to the United States with the expectation that status as citizens receiving the full benefits of the United States was available to them. In most cases, recent immigrants have been forced to work in jobs of low esteem and have encountered a number of economic and discriminatory hardships. However, the circumstances of black Americans are unique in that the arrival of the vast majority of this group's members was as slaves. Additionally, a number of social customs and laws have been enacted over time to limit black Americans' access to economic opportunity and social status. These circumstances were accompanied by social customs that supported the sexual exploitation of black women in a manner different from that experienced by any other ethnic minority group.

Numerous authors have argued that the experience of slavery will always distinguish blacks from other ethnic minorities in the United States. Hacker (1992) argued that in the United States the separation between blacks and whites "is pervasive and penetrating...it surpasses all others—even gender—in intensity and subordination" (p. 3). Hacker wrote that the stigma of slavery and the association of blacks with Africa and the negative conditions associated with it continue to influence the perceptions of black Americans in the United States. He argued that after slavery the ideology that rationalized slavery did not disappear and continued to function through legal mechanisms and socially sanctioned behaviors. According to Hacker, blacks continue to be perceived as an inferior group for these and other reasons. Likewise, Lerner (1972) noted the legal, economic, and social mechanisms evident before, during, and after slavery designed to demean black Americans and maintain their vulnerability.

This chapter will limit its discussion to the historical experience of black women in the United States and the implications of this experience for sexual harassment today.

## BLACK WOMEN'S HISTORICAL EXPERIENCE IN THE UNITED STATES

Accepted definitions of sexual harassment are consistent in their proposal that sexual harassment often results from an abuse of power in relationships and falls along a continuum from gender harassment, including sexist statements and behaviors, to sexual assault. An examination of the historical abuse of power against black women demonstrates the extent to which the experience of sexual vulnerability and abuse impacts black women's current experience of sexual harassment.

Numerous black female scholars have argued that it is impossible to separate racism and sexism in the experience of black women (Giddings, 1984; Hooks, 1981). However, a historical review of the experience of black women in the United States must begin with racism and its impact on the lives of these women.

According to many historical texts (Franklin, 1969; Davis, 1981), the experiences of black men and women during slavery were similar in most ways. Male and female slaves were the legal property or chattel of their owners. Both men and women were expected to plow, plant, and harvest crops. Most women assumed the same responsibilities as men and were considered laborers just as men were. The value of slaves was often based on their productivity on the plantation (Davis, 1981). A small number of female slaves worked as nurses, cooks, seamstresses, washerwomen, and maids. However, it can be argued that the most significant difference in the slavery experience of black men and women was the sexual exploitation of black women. Hooks (1981) argued that the sexism of colonial males protected black males' sexuality and socially legitimized sexual abuse of female slaves. Lerner (1972) wrote:

> The sexual exploitation of black women by white men was so widespread as to be general....Many were assaulted both by their masters and by overseers, neighboring youth or the master's sons. The point here is that such exploitation was always possible and could in no way be fought or avoided— it was yet another way in which the total helplessness of the slave against arbitrary authority was institutionalized. (p. 46)

According to Brownmiller (1975), "the concept of raping a slave simply did not exist. The rape of one man's slave by another white man was considered a mere 'trespass' in the eyes of plantation law. The rape of one man's slave by another slave had no official recognition at all" (pp. 162–163). According to Brownmiller (1975) and other authors, abolitionists voiced moral objections to the sexual involvement of white men with female slaves, but they presented their arguments under the guise of "miscegenation, amalgamation, degradation and lust" (Brownmiller, 1975, p. 163). This early characterization of the sexual abuse of black women by white men was misleading and failed to acknowledge the exploitation of female slaves. It may also have contributed to the perception that black women were consensual partners in their sexual exploitation.

## Purposes of Rape Within the Institution of Slavery

Many authors disagree with the view that sexual exploitation of female slaves resulted simply from the lust of white men (Davis, 1983; Hooks, 1981; Brownmiller, 1975; Lerner, 1972). The views of these authors are consistent with that supporting the effect of the power drive in creating or contributing to the occurrence of sexual harassment. "Power drive" refers to a motivation to degrade and control as the major determinant of behavior. According to the authors just cited, two important functions of sexual exploitation of female slaves were (1) rape as a weapon of domination and (2) rape for the purpose of breeding slaves.

Davis (1981) argued:

> It would be a mistake to regard the institutionalized pattern of rape during slavery as an expression of white men's sexual urges, otherwise stifled by the specter of white womanhood's chastity. That would be far too simplistic an explanation. Rape was a weapon of domination, a weapon of repression, whose covert goal was to extinguish slave women's will to resist, and in the process, to demoralize their men. (pp. 23–24)

Brownmiller (1975) agreed and argued that rape of female slaves was an institutionalized crime. The multiple roles of female slaves as laborers, concubines, and breeders produced a psychological control and subjugation of female slaves that was a method of domination and control.

The use of female slaves for the purpose of breeding slaves became even more important when the African slave trade was banned in 1807. After the influx of new slaves into the United States was halted, the value of female slaves was determined not only by their work productivity, but also by their ability to produce healthy slaves. Paternity of female slaves' offspring was considered irrelevant and was rarely noted in records of births. Pregnancy could be caused by any number of individuals, ranging from the owner or his male family members or friends to males within the hierarchy of the plantation system, including white overseers and male slaves. Access to female slaves was often offered as a reward to males working on the plantation. The use of female slaves for breeding is well documented. Frances Kemble (1961), wife of a slave owner, wrote about the resulting condition of female slaves on her husband's plantation in her *Journal of a Residence on a Georgian Plantation in 1838–1839:*

> Fanny has had six children; all dead but one, she came to beg to have her work in the field lightened....
> Sally, Scipio's wife, has had two miscarriages and three children born, one of whom is dead. She came complaining of incessant pain and weakness in her back. This woman was a mullato daughter of a slave called Sophy, by a white man of the name of Walker who visited the plantation. (p. 42)

The mass sexual exploitation and rape of female slaves by white men was often termed prostitution by abolitionists. Frederick Douglass, the orator and ex-slave, was highly criticized for his involvement and support of the women's movement. He fought to align the women's rights movement with the abolition movement. In a speech given in 1850, Douglass argued that slaveholders were responsible for the prostitution of their female slaves. He stated that this forced prostitution was legal and that the slaves involved had no recourse and no rights to prevent this abuse (Douglass, 1969).

Hooks (1981) argued that the application of the term "prostitution" to the coerced sexual activity of black females by white males was a result of the language of the Victorian ethos. However, she also argued:

> ...the use of the word prostitution to describe the mass sexual exploitation of enslaved black women by white men not only deflected attention away from the prevalence of forced sexual assault, it lent further credibility to the myth that black females were inherently wanton and therefore responsible for rape. (p. 34)

The belief that black women were responsible for their sexual exploitation was widely held. The abolitionist William Wells Brown wrote, "...the greater portion of the colored women, in the days of slavery, had no greater aspiration than that of becoming the finely dressed mistress of some white man" (Christian, 1982, p. 14). Clearly, the view that black women were willing partners in their sexual exploitation was held long after slavery and, combined with other social factors, resulted in one of the current myths regarding the sexuality of black women.

## The Impact of Industrialization

Industrialization resulted in continued changes in the roles of women in the United States. By the middle of the nineteenth century, affluent women's roles as caretakers, nurturers, and housewives were firmly established. Most of the work previously performed by these women was completed in factories. Many historians argue that the status of middle-class women declined during this period because their economic survival depended solely on males and they were no longer important contributors to the economic survival of the family (Lerner, 1979). During this period the work of women outside of the home was generally of low prestige and was provided primarily by poor immigrant women. In most cases, black Americans who were skilled in trades were not allowed to work in these skilled professions, but were restricted to menial work of all types (Franklin, 1969). Black women were excluded from factory work, which resulted in their continued dependence on domestic work as a means of economic survival. The continued presence of black women in the homes of white people as well as their economic reliance on whites resulted in continued availability and vulnerability to sexual abuse.

By the middle of the nineteenth century the influence of Victorian views of womanhood increased in importance, as middle-class women continued to be viewed as pure and above the sexual temptations of men. This view of women was tied to the attributes of femininity associated with leisure, a luxury limited to middle-class women. As womanhood and femininity became defined by commitment to home, family, and the pursuit of leisure activities, black women were excluded from the status of most white women based on the circumstance that black women did not engage in the behaviors consistent with this Victorian view of womanhood (Davis, 1981). Although it can be argued that this view of womanhood devalued white women and placed them in a more subordinate role in the family and society, this view of femininity served to support the sexual vulnerability of black women in a number of ways. The majority of black women were still required to work in the homes of white people as a means of economic survival. Further, because of their work status, they were not perceived as feminine or chaste. The availability of black women and the perception that they were sexually promiscuous provided conditions consistent with their continued sexual violation. According to Lerner (1979), working-class women, and especially black women, were perceived as available for the sexual exploitation of affluent men. Clearly, the status of black women had changed very little since the end of slavery.

## Black Women and the Women's Movement

According to Davis (1981), industrialization and the resulting decline in the status of white women due to their lack of productivity and economic contribution to the family resulted in an organized political movement among women to establish greater rights and esteem. Davis (1981) and Giddings (1984) argued that white women felt an identification with black men and women and used slavery as an analogy for their oppressive existences as middle-class wives and mothers, and as factory workers. Both groups of women were essential to the organization of the antislavery movement. Davis (1981) argued that the "anti-slavery movement offered women of the middle class the opportunity to prove their worth according to standards that were not tied to their role as wives and mothers. In this sense, the abolitionist campaign was a home where they could be valued for their concrete works" (p. 39).

Numerous women abolitionists linked slavery to the women's movement and argued that the status and circumstances of black Americans and women were intertwined. Two of the most well known of these abolitionists were Sarah and Angelina Grimke. Their lectures on the evils of slavery were attacked by abolitionist and nonabolitionist males. The work of these sisters was important and influential. Other women's rights leaders understood the relation between suffrage rights for black Americans and women's suffrage rights. However, a major turning point in the relationship between individuals working for these goals occurred when the passage of the 15th Amendment became imminent. The 15th Amendment prohibited disenfranchisement on the grounds of race, color, or previous condition of servitude, thereby allowing black men to vote. In 1865, in response to the proposed amendment, leading women's rights advocate Elizabeth Cady Stanton wrote a letter to the *New York Standard* that included the following passage:

> ...the black man is still, in a political point of view, far above the educated white women of the country. The representative women of the nation have done their uttermost for the last thirty years to secure freedom for the negro; and as long as he was lowest in the scale of being, we were willing to press his claims; but now, as the celestial gate to civil rights is slowly moving on its hinges, it becomes a serious question whether we had better stand aside and see "Sambo" walk into the kingdom first. (Stanton, Anthony & Gage, 1881, pp. 49–95)

In spite of these views, in 1866, delegates to a women's rights meeting in New York City voted to establish the Equal Rights Association. This association was to integrate the issues of black Americans, including the right to vote, with the women's suffrage movement. Susan B. Anthony, a leader of the women's suffrage movement, argued for unifying these two struggles to enhance the success of both causes. However, as passage of the 15th Amendment neared, white women struggled with the decision of whether to support the right of black males to vote before white women had obtained this right.

In 1869, while black abolitionists Frederick Douglass and Sojourner Truth lobbied for the Equal Rights Association to make a unified effort to support passage of the 15th Amendment, Stanton and Anthony argued for the dissolution of the association. The organization was dissolved, and Stanton and Anthony organized the National Woman Suffrage Association. Simultaneously the American Woman Suffrage Association was organized; it included members who supported the passage of the 15th Amendment and women's suffrage (Giddings, 1984). This series of events highlights the difficulty experienced by many women's suffrage workers in their effort to promote women's suffrage by linking their plight to that of black Americans. Whether the dissolution of the Equal Rights Association resulted from a strategy designed strictly to promote issues related to white women or from racist attitudes is not completely clear. However, it is most likely that both entered into the decision of Anthony and other women's suffrage leaders to work toward their goals independently.

## Post-Slavery

After slavery the vast majority of black women continued to work in the same capacity as during slavery. Many worked as sharecroppers, tenant farmers, and farmworkers. Others worked as domestic servants, which required that they work in the homes of white Americans and face many of the working conditions that existed during slavery. The continuation of the pattern of relationships between black women and white Americans provided an opportunity for the myths regarding black women to continue.

Most scholars of American history fail to discuss the existence of sexual exploitation of black women after slavery. However, the relatively rare historical accounts that focus on black women document their continued sexual abuse long after the end of slavery (Lerner, 1972). A number of factors contributed to this exploitation, including the continuation of certain myths and stereotypes of black women and the devaluation of black Americans through legal prohibitions, lack of legal protection, and lack of access to professional advancement.

Numerous stereotypes of black women exerted a strong influence on the perceptions of these women and continue to serve as biases used by white Americans and other ethnic minority group members to assist in their understanding of the culture and behavior of black women. Arguably, three of the most pervasive and widely held stereotypes are that of the "Mammy," the "Sapphire," and the "Jezebel." These stereotypes have their bases in slavery. The Mammy stereotype was immortalized in the book and movie *Gone with the Wind* with the character known only by that name. This stereotype is characterized by an overweight black woman with complete loyalty to her white "family." The Mammy stereotype is asexual. The second stereotype, the Sapphire, refers to the manipulative and evil troublemaker who has no morals and no loyalty. The third stereotype, the Jezebel, is a promiscuous female with an irrepressible sexual appetite. Bell (1992) argued that this stereotype has its foundation in the sexual exploitation of black women during and after slavery. It results from the belief that black women were consensual partners in the sexual abuse they suffered during and after slavery. Lerner (1972) argued that the creation of the Jezebel stereotype helped to support a social system that included the sexual exploitation of black women. This author wrote (1972):

> After slavery ended, the sexual exploitation of black women continued, in both the North and the South, although in different forms and with somewhat greater risk to the white man involved. To sustain it…a complex system of supportive mechanisms and sustaining myths was created. One of these was the myth of the "bad" black woman. By assuming a different level of sexuality for all blacks than that of whites and mythifying their greater sexual potency, the black woman could be made to personify sexual freedom and abandon. A myth was created that all black women were eager for sexual exploits,

voluntarily "loose" in their morals and, there-fore, deserved none of the consideration and respect granted white women…therefore, to assault her and exploit her sexually was not reprehensible and carried with it none of the normal communal sanctions against such behavior. (p. 163)

Lerner (1972) further argued that legal interventions were designed to support social prohibitions and stereotypes of black women as unworthy of the status afforded to white women and as sexually promiscuous.

A wide range of practices reinforced this myth: the laws against intermarriage; the denial of the title "Miss" or "Mrs." to any black woman; the taboos against respectable social mixing of the races; the refusal to let black women customers try on clothing in stores before making a purchase; the assign-ing of single toilet facilities to both sexes of blacks; the different legal sanctions against rape, abuse of minors and other sex crimes when committed against white or black women. (p. 164)

The Jezebel stereotype is essential to main-taining the sexual exploitation of black women in the United States. Its influence on perceptions of black women and behavior of both white men and men of other ethnic back-grounds toward black women may continue to result in their increased vulnerability to sexual abuse of all kinds.

Feminist authors disagree on the effect of the sexual exploitation of black women on their families and on black males. However, it is clear that the perception of black women in their own community has been affected by their constant contact with white Americans through domestic work. Numerous myths operate to support the contention that black women's access to white people empowers them to serve as mediators and liaisons between the black and white communities. Moreover, the misconception that black women enjoy greater access to economic opportunities and success than black men may result from the greater access of black women to white people.

The sexual exploitation of black women after slavery serves the same major functions of that behavior during slavery. It serves to solidify the inferiority of black Americans and degrades both the women who are abused and black males.

Giddings (1984) argued that the status of black males in the family was diminished by their inability to adequately provide for their wives and children due to economic circum-stances and restriction from skilled work. Therefore, the continued work of black women at the most menial levels necessarily resulted in the perception of them as accessi-ble for the sexual advances of white men. The power differential between the white employer and the black employee provided another factor resulting in the abuse of black women and discouraged them from reporting the abuse.

Lerner (1972) wrote of black women:

…ever since slavery, they have been sexu-ally exploited by white men through rape or enforced sexual services. These sexual mores, which are characteristic of the rela-tionship of colonizers to the women of the conquered group, function not only symbol-ically but actually to fasten the badge of infe-riority onto the enslaved group. The black man was degraded by being deprived of the power and right to protect his women from white men. The black woman was directly degraded by the sexual attack and, more pro-foundly, by being deprived of a strong black man on whom she could rely for protection. This slavery pattern was carried into the post-slavery period and has only in this cen-tury begun to yield to the greater strength and high militancy of the black community. (pp. xxii–xxiii)

Clearly, the sexual exploitation of black women has diminished greatly over time. However, the prevailing attitudes and beliefs regarding black women continue to be rein-forced through limitations in opportunities for economic advancement among black women and through the media, which continue to por-tray black women as counselors, maids, and nannies with undivided loyalty to a white fam-ily, or as promiscuous, sexually unrepressed Jezebels. The continued reliance of white Americans on stereotypes of black women is clear and may serve to increase the vulnerability of black women to all forms of sexual exploitation, including sexual harassment.

According to Lerner (1992),

The essence of black and white relations in United States history up to the present time has been the oppression of blacks by whites, based entirely on arbitrary definitions of white superiority. Essential to the functioning and perpetration of this racist system of oppression has been the special victimization of black women. This has taken several forms: (1) black women share in all aspects of the oppression of blacks in general; (2) black women are objects of exploitative sex by white men; (3) the rape of black women is employed as a weapon of terror directed against the entire black community; (4) when black men are prevented, through social taboos and violence, from defending their own women, the oppression of all Blacks is heightened and institutionalized; (5) when black men are oppressed economically to the extent that they cannot secure steady employment at decent wages, many black women are deprived of the support of a male breadwinner and must take on added economic burdens. The psychological effects of the symbolic castration of black males is also borne by black women. (p. 149)

Lerner's (1992) explanation of relations between black and white individuals in the United States implicates an institutionalized system of racism that involves the intertwined role of limited economic opportunities, sexual exploitation, and devaluing of relationships of black men and women. In this context, sexual exploitation is one tool used in a system of oppressive forces designed to oppress black Americans economically and psychologically.

## IMPLICATIONS FOR SEXUAL HARASSMENT TODAY

As members of an oppressed ethnic group, black women may experience sexual harassment that is substantially different than that experienced by white women. Several black female scholars have argued the impossibility of separating race from gender in issues of sexual harassment. Therefore, the sexual harassment of black women results in the racialization of this form of harassment. The stereotypes of black women that have functioned to increase their vulnerability to sexual exploitation may influence the form this harassment takes. The perception of black women as available and sexually promiscuous combines with sexist views of women in general to result in harassment that includes both racial and sexual connotations (McKay, 1992). According to McKay (1992), "black women's struggle against their oppression occurs at the intersection where the sexual and racial sources of this oppression come together" (p. 279). The implications of this harassment may be different for black women, who may understand that historically sexual aggression against black women was viewed differently than that same behavior perpetrated against white women. Crenshaw (1992) argued that cases of rape and assault against white women are widely publicized, while similar cases involving black women do not receive the same level of media attention or public response. This may be indicative of the devalued status of black women and the extent to which a tolerance of violence against them has been established.

## Perception and Reporting of Sexual Harassment by Black Women

A unique case that highlights some of the difficulties inherent in the reporting of sexual harassment for black women is that of the sexual harassment reported by Anita Hill during the Senate confirmation hearings of Clarence Thomas. The factors that result in fear of reporting this behavior among black women include those experienced by white women, as well as additional factors relevant to the experiences of black women and apparent in the response to Hill's report of Thomas's sexual harassment.

First, white women and black women may expect different responses to their reports of sexual harassment, resulting from differing stereotypes and perceptions of the two groups of women. The Jezebel and Sapphire stereotypes are most relevant in this case and result in attributions that the purpose of the report of harassment is to gain revenge for some slight against the accuser or that the accuser provoked the harassment by her own sexually charged behavior. Additionally, the status of black and white women and the tolerance of their abuse may vary and influence perception of their honesty and credibility. For black women the factors that contribute to the underreporting of sexual harassment among white women are compounded by recognition that their status and other perceptions of them will mediate responses to their charges of sexual harassment.

## Harassment of Black Women by Black Men

Additional barriers to addressing sexual harassment are experienced by black women who are victims of sexual harassment by black men. Crenshaw (1992) argued that one of these barriers is a connection between black men and women based on a "common social history of social exclusion" (p. 426). This shared history results in expectations that a system of mutual support will protect black Americans from many dangers posed by white America. This set of mutual expectations creates serious dilemmas for black women who experience sexual harassment by black men and must negotiate their most appropriate response based on conflicting expectations that they protect their male comrades and prevent sexual advances of those same individuals. These expectations may result in the disapproval of black women by both black men and women when they expose black male sexual harassers.

Other authors revise this argument to suggest that black males expect black females to subordinate their own needs to those of black men. Bell (1992) argued that the treatment afforded Hill was representative of the treatment given to black women in this country historically. She concluded that if Thomas was a victim of a "high-tech lynching," then Hill was a victim of a high-tech rape. She further argued

that many of the stereotypes applied to black women were applied to Hill. According to Bell (1992), attempts were made to portray Hill as a sexually promiscuous woman (Jezebel) and a scorned woman seeking revenge (Sapphire). By identifying with Hill, black women were forced to confront the stereotypes and "mythologies" attributed to all black women. According to Bell (1992), observing the treatment of Hill during the hearings left her and other black women with a profound sense of defenselessness and powerlessness.

Painter (1992) argued that while Thomas effectively used stereotypes to control the behavior of the Senators judging him, Hill did not use established myths to develop her own identity or to characterize the proceedings. Further, Hill did not easily fit into any established stereotypes of black women. As a well-educated, articulate black woman, Hill was difficult to pigeonhole by the American public, while Thomas created his identity using stereotypes understood by the public.

Bell (1992) further argued that, historically, issues related to sexism have been secondary to issues related to racism in the black community. She attributed this phenomenon to the "Black Men's Club." Bell (1992) argued that the Black Men's Club allows black men to:

> maintain a privileged position when it comes to power, prestige and status. For Black men, however, the Black Men's Club fulfills the need for them to assert their authority within the Black community because they are deprived of the full power of their masculinity within the White power structure. (p. 366)

Bell (1992) contended that the pattern of black men representing the black community and prioritizing the advancement of issues related to black people against racism, but not sexism, is well established. These behaviors have been reported in historical accounts of the initial lack of support received by black women from black men during the suffrage rights movement and the civil rights movement (Davis, 1981; Giddings, 1984).

Finally, Bell (1992) argued that the Black Men's Club serves to protect and support its members, even if defense involves extreme measures designed to undermine the credibility of others or relies on a misunderstanding of practices that are assumed as normal in the black community. Bell argued that the treatment afforded Thomas by black leaders was provided due to his membership in the Black Men's Club. According to Bell (1992),

> ...[Thomas] got away without having to disclose anything about himself relevant to Anita Hill's accusations. He did not watch her testimony. He placed himself above the situation by refusing to have any aspects of his life examined. Anita Hill had none of these rights. Many aspects of her professional and personal life were made open for public scrutiny. Although Anita Hill and Clarence Thomas share the same racial identity, Hill had none of the privileges of membership in the Black Men's Club. (p. 367)

Additional evidence of Thomas's preferred status is given by the response of leaders called upon to represent the black community. These leaders, all of whom were male, either supported the nomination of Thomas to the Supreme Court of the United States or maintained a neutral status during the Senate hearings.

Wooley (1992) argued that there are mainstream social influences that create greater discomfort at the sight of a man experiencing pain or anguish than at a women experiencing these feelings. Wooley posited that protecting Thomas from discomfort became the major objective of the hearings; a similar response was not provided to Hill. Again, the extent to which American society tolerates abuse of women and their suffering prevented an outpouring of sympathy or support for Hill.

Finally, Bell (1992) argued that the historical and current experience of oppression serves to bond black men and women around the issue and effects of racism. This is a shared experience resulting in the perception that black men receive the brunt of the abuse by oppressive and racist forces. Therefore, black women willingly operate within a code of silence that is designed to protect black men and help to maintain their status in the black community. Black women who break this code of silence are viewed as coconspirators with the oppressors and are punished by both black men and women who believe that the evils in the black community should not be exposed for public review.

It can be concluded that Hill's testimony was an affront to the social expectations of the majority of black Americans, who at the time of her testimony reported believing that her accusations were false.

## CONCLUSIONS

Numerous factors operate to increase the experience and underreporting of sexual harassment among black women in the United States. A historical experience of sexual exploitation and oppression, myths that support perceptions of promiscuity of black women, institutionalized mechanisms designed to suppress the status of black women, and cultural norms and expectations that prohibit black women from reporting sexual harassment perpetuated by white and black men function to increase the vulnerability of black women to sexual exploitation. Additionally, the disproportionate representation of black women in poverty results in economic dependence, which may increase the risk for sexual harassment.

Studies documenting the prevalence of sexual harassment of black women and rates of reporting sexual harassment by these women are essential to understanding the vulnerability of black women to sexual harassment. Studies that explore the perceptions of perpetrators and women who experience sexual harassment are also needed to clarify the extent to which race influences the specific circumstances and methods of harassment, as well as the target of the abuse. This work will also help to clarify the most effective strategies for reducing sexual harassment of black women and increasing victims' willingness to report harassment.

Qualitative research methods may be the first step to developing working hypotheses regarding the beliefs and perceptions of black women. In-depth interviews and focus groups with black women that allow them to explore and honestly relate their experiences of harassment and their motivations for remaining silent may clarify the cultural norms that guide black women's behavior and identify other behavioral determinants. This is especially relevant in light of possible culture-bound determinants of reporting behavior and beliefs regarding what behaviors constitute sexual harassment. Measures must assess women's perceived vulnerability and perceptions of institutional support for their reports of harassment, as well as the coping styles used by black women who experience sexual harassment. Measures of black women's experiences will be inadequate if they fail to account for the influence of culture and beliefs, or if they make assumptions about the impact of culture on behavior. Further, measurements including individuals from only one social class group may result in results that are not generalizable. Qualitative methods may be used to assess contextual, cultural, and perceptual experiences of black women that influence what they believe sexual harassment is, as well as the factors that limit their ability to respond effectively. Survey and questionnaire methodologies that are commonly used in the study of sexual harassment may be inappropriate tools for assessing the experiences of sexual harassment among black women. These methods are limited measures of the context, culture, and personal experience of harassment for black women and have not been designed to measure the impact of culture on the experience of sexual harassment.

The sexual abuse experienced by women belonging to an ethnic group is often tied to the economic and political oppression of that group. The political, economic, and social system that benefits from this oppression must be drastically altered to directly impact the lives of women who are the most vulnerable. However, enforcement of current laws prohibiting sexual harassment and education of employers and women are essential to reducing sexual harassment. Research designed to clarify the experiences of black women and the circumstances unique to them is essential. Knowledge gained from this research will be critical to the development of policies and interventions that reduce the impact of sexual harassment by decreasing the vulnerability and increasing the efficacy of black women in the workplace and by better educating employers of circumstances that pose the greatest risk for sexual harassment and methods by which they can promote appropriate behavior and improve reporting when sexual harassment occurs.

## REFERENCES

Bell, E. L. (1992). Myths, stereotypes, and realities of black women: A personal reflection. *Journal of Applied Behavioral Science, 28*(3), 363–376.

Brownmiller, S. (1975). *Against our will: Men, women and rape.* New York: Fawcett Columbine Books.

Christian, B. (1982). Black women novelists: The development of a tradition, 1892–1976. In P. Giddings (Ed.), *When and where I enter: The impact of black women on race and sex in america* (p. 14). New York: Bantam Books.

Crenshaw, K. (1992). Whose story is it, anyway? Feminist and anti-racist appropriations of Anita Hill. In T. Morrison (Ed.), *Race-ing justice, en-gendering power* (pp. 402–436). New York: Pantheon Books.

Davis, A. (1981). *Women, race, and class.* New York: Vintage Books.

Davis, A. (1990). *Women, culture, and politics.* New York: Vintage Books.

Douglass, F. (1969). *Narrative of the life of Frederick Douglass.* B. Quarles (Ed.), Cambridge, MA: Belknap Press.

Dziech, B., & Weiner, L. (1984). *The lecherous professor.* Boston: Beacon Press.

Franklin, J. H. (1969). *From slavery to freedom: A history of Negro Americans.* New York: Vintage Books/Random House.

Giddings, P. (1984). *When and where I enter: The impact of black women on race and sex in America.* New York: Bantam Books.

Hacker, A. (1992). *Two nations: Black and white, separate, hostile, unequal.* New York: Balantine Books.

Hotelling, K.(1991). Sexual harassment: A problem shielded by silence. *Journal of Counseling and Development, 69*, 497–500.

Hooks, B. (1981). *Ain't I a woman: Black women and feminism.* Boston: South End Press.

Kemble, F. A. (1961). *Journal of a residence on a Georgian plantation in 1838–1839.* New York and Scarborough, Ontario: New American Library.

Lerner, G. (1972). *Black women in white America: A documentary history.* New York: Vintage Books.

McKay, N. Y. (1992). Remembering Anita Hill and Clarence Thomas: What ready happened when one black woman spoke out. In T. Morrison (Ed.), *Race-ing justice, en-gendering power* (pp. 269–289). New York: Pantheon Books.

Painter, N. (1992). Hill, Thomas, and the use of racial stereotype. In T. Morrison (Ed.), *Race-ing justice, en-gendering* power (pp. 200–214). New York: Pantheon Books.

Paludi, M. A., & Barickman, R. B. (1991). *Academic and workplace sexual harassment.* Albany, NY: SUNY Press.

Sandler, B. R. (1990). Sexual harassment: A new issue for institutions. *Initiatives, 52*(4), 5–10.

Stanton, E. C., Anthony, S., & Gage, M. J. (1881). *History of woman suffrage, Vol. 2 (1861–1876).* Rochester, NY.

Wooley, S. C.(1992). Anita Hill, Clarence Thomas and the enforcement of female silence. *Women and Therapy, 12*(4), 3–23.

# CHAPTER 14

# SEXUAL HARASSMENT IN SCHOOLS

## Michele A. Paludi

It made me feel confused, whether I should tell or not. I didn't know if I was overreacting since this was a teacher I trusted and looked up to.

The experience was unnerving. I was rattled. I felt insecure and vulnerable at school, which should be a safe place for learning.

It made me feel low. Thought that I was dirt. I just wanted to die.

I was ashamed, thought it was my fault, and was worried that the school would take action against me—for "unearned" grades—if they found out about it.

Who was going to believe me? I was an undergraduate student and he was a famous professor. It was an unreal situation.

I…became quite skilled at glancing down department hallways to make sure he wasn't there before venturing forth, and pretending not to see him when we did cross paths. The whole experience has left me quite mistrustful of faculty in general and I still feel some trepidation when visiting the department.

The impact of this isolated incident on me has been enormous. It has changed my way of relating to the program. I used to think it could be a place of learning, mentoring, work and fun. Now, although there are still people there whom I trust and learn from, I am angry and insecure every time I'm in that building. I have heard that this professor has propositioned at least two other students, and I am silently furious.

(AAUW, 1993; Project on the Status and Education of Women, 1978)

As these accounts from students in junior high, senior high, and college affirm, sexual harassment in schools and colleges is a major barrier to individuals' career development as well as a traumatic force that disrupts and damages students' personal lives. Students' performance in coursework suffers, and many of them drop out of school altogether. Sexual harassment is invariably followed by stress reactions, including depression, anger, fear, feelings of helplessness and embarassment, and decreased motivation. College students' economic vulnerability is paramount. They may be dependent on financial aid to fund their education; they have loans to repay. As Koss (1990) suggested, experiencing sexual harassment transforms students into victims and changes their lives: "It is inevitable that once victimized, at minimum, one can never again feel quite as invulnerable" (p. 74).

I propose in this chapter to: (1) define sexual harassment and describe the incidence of sexual harassment of students in elementary, secondary, and higher education; (2) describe the impact sexual harassment has on students' lives; (3) describe sexual harassers; (4) identify students' responses to dealing with sexual harassment; and (5) offer suggestions for curtailing sexual harassment through the institution of school policies and panels to enforce them, training of teachers and students, and educational campaigns to inform the educational community of the nature and severity of the problem.

## DEFINING SEXUAL HARASSMENT IN THE SCHOOLS

### Legal Definition

Sexual harassment is clearly prohibited within the school and college/university system as a form of sexual discrimination, under Title IX of the 1972 Education Amendments (and, for employees, Title VII of the 1964 Civil Rights Act). The Equal Employment Opportunity Commission states in its Guidelines on Sex Discrimination:

> Unwelcome sexual advances, requests for sexual favors, and other verbal or physical conduct of a sexual nature constitute sexual harassment when (1) submission to such conduct is made either explictly or implicitly a term or condition of an individual's employment, (2) submission to or rejection of such conduct by an individual is used as the basis for employment decisions affecting such individual, or (3) such conduct has the purpose or effect of substantially interfering

with an individual's work performance or creating an intimidating, hostile, or offensive working environment. (p. 33)

This definition has been extended to academic environments.

Courts have called the first two conditions quid pro quo sexual harassment and the third condition hostile environment sexual harassment. The major elements of quid pro quo sexual harassment for school systems are as follows:

The sexual advances are unwanted.
The harassment is sexual.
The submission is explicitly or implicitly a term or condition of school status or is used as a basis for making decisions about the student's school status.

Hostile environment sexual harassment refers to behaviors in the classroom or in the school hallways or college dorms that reasonably interfere with a student's ability to learn.

Title IX of the Education Amendments prohibits discrimination on the basis of sex and covers all educational institutions that receive federal financial assistance and all federally funded educational programs in noneducational institutions. It also covers institutions whose students receive federal financial aid. Virtually all public and private institutions of higher education are covered as well as all public elementary and secondary schools. Private elementary and secondary schools are only covered if they receive federal funds. This federal statute is enforced by the Office of Civil Rights (OCR) at the U.S. Department of Education. According to the OCR, sexual harassment is defined as "verbal or physical conduct of a sexual nature, imposed on the basis of sex, by an employee or an agent of [an institution] that denies, limits, provides different, or conditions the provision of aid, benefits, services, or treatment protected under Title IX." This definition clearly covers sexual harassment of students by faculty and staff. OCR also interprets Title IX to cover peer sexual harassment of students (i.e., student-to-student sexual harassment).

## Behavioral Definition

Sexual harassment takes many forms—from sexist remarks and covert physical contact (patting, brushing against the bodies) to blatant propositions and sexual assaults. In recent years, researchers have developed five categories to encompass the range of sexual harassment (e.g., Fitzgerald, 1990): gender harassment, seductive behavior, sexual bribery, sexual coercion, and sexual imposition. These levels of sexual harassment correlate with legal definitions of sexual harassment and have been definitively discussed in preceding chapters. Behavioral examples of verbal sexual harassment include sexual innuendos, comments and sexual remarks; implied or overt threats related to students' grades; and sexual propositions or other pressures for sex. Behavioral examples of nonverbal sexual harassment include patting, pinching, and brushing up against one's body; leering, ogling; obscene gestures, and use of pornographic teaching materials in class discussions.

The most useful behavioral definition of sexual harassment has been offered by Fitzgerald and Omerod (1993):

> Sexual harassment consists of the sexualization of an instrumental relationship through the introduction or imposition of sexist or sexual remarks, requests, or requirements, in the context of a formal power differential. Harassment can also occur where no such formal differential exists, if the behavior is unwanted by or offensive to the [individual]. (p. 556)

There are four main elements in this definition:

1. The behavior is unwanted and unwelcome.
2. The behavior is sexual or related to the sex of the individual.
3. The behavior typically occurs in the context of a relationship in which one person has more formal power than the other.
4. The impact of the behavior, not the intent, is the most crucial to understanding whether sexual harassment has occurred.

With respect to students' experiences, Zalk, Paludi, and Dederich (1991) have argued:

> The bottom line in the relationship is POWER. The faculty member has it and the student does not. As intertwined as the faculty-student roles may be, and as much as one must exist for the other to exist, they are not equal collaborators. The student does not negotiate indeed, has nothing to negotiate with....
>
> All the power lies with the faculty member—some of it real, concrete, and some of it is imagined or elusive. The bases of the faculty member's almost absolute power are varied and range from the entirely rational into broad areas of fantasy. Professors give grades, write recommendations for graduate schools, awards and the like, and can predispose colleagues' attitudes towards students. (pp. 101–102)

## Definitional Problems

Many individuals are confused over the definition of sexual harassment, especially hostile environment sexual harassment. A major source of this confusion is the different experiences that girls and women typically have within our society than boys and men do (Doyle & Paludi, 1994). For example, Fitzgerald, Weitzman, et al. (1988) found that male faculty members typically do not label their behavior as sexual harassment despite reporting that they frequently engage in behaviors that meet the legal definition of sexual harassment. Kenig and Ryan (1986) reported that faculty men were less likely than faculty women to define sexual harassment as including jokes, teasing remarks of a sexual nature, and unwanted suggestive looks or gestures. In addition, women faculty were more likely than men to disapprove of romantic relationships between faculty and students.

Furthermore, students and teachers have substantially different definitions of sexual harassment. Fitzgerald, Weitzman, et al. (1988) reported that male faculty members who participated in their study denied the inherent power differential between faculty and students, as well as the psychological power conferred by this differential. Students, however, recognize this power differential.

The interpretation given to the professors' behavior by women students is not flattery or friendliness. As high school students in Minnesota outlined, there is a distinction between flattery or flirtation and sexual harassment (cited in Sandler & Paludi, 1993, p. 12):

| *Flirting* | *Sexual Harassment* |
| --- | --- |
| feels good | feels bad |
| makes me feel attractive | is degrading |
| is a compliment | makes me feel cheap |
| is two-way | is one-way |
| is positive | makes me feel helpless |
| I liked it | I felt out of control |

Adopting the "reasonable woman" standard for hostile environment sexual harassment claims requires an analysis of the differing perspectives females and males often have and a recognition that behavior many boys and men find unobjectionable may offend girls and women. It is the power differential and the individual's reaction to the behavior that are the critical variables.

## Consensual Relationships

Margaret Mead (1978) once argued that a new taboo is needed that demands that teachers and faculty make new norms, not rely on masculine-biased definitions of success, career development, and sexuality. One important change needs to be in the mentor-protegé relationship in which women are protegés and men are mentors (Haring-Hidore & Paludi, 1991). This common arrangement by which men are in positions of power within mentoring relationships (as mentors) and women are in more vulnerable positions (as protegés) suggests the possibility of sexuality and sex as significant and complex factors within such relationships. Mentors are seen as essential because they generate power. The introduction of sexuality and sex into mentoring relationships can have negative implications for achievement for women protegés. Women who are suspected of having "slept their way to the top" are castigated by others, sometimes unfairly when the accusation is false. Women who have sex with their mentors may be unjustly deprived of their achievements if the achievements did not depend on an unfair

advantage gained by a sexual mentoring relationship. Whether it is fair or not, achievements made in sexual mentoring relationships may never boost protegés' careers and may, in fact, detract from their careers because of the stigma attached by others (Haring-Hidore & Paludi, 1991).

Neither Title IX nor Title VII prohibits consensual sexual relationships; however, a number of institutions are developing policies on this matter. While consensual relationships may not always be unethical, they always cause problems. This happens, according to Sandler and Paludi (1993) for the following reasons:

> The situation involves one person exerting power over another.
> The seduction of a much younger individual is involved.
> Conflict of interest issues arise, e.g., How can a teacher fairly grade a student with whom they are having a sexual relationship?
> The potential for exploitation and abuse is high.
> The potential for retaliatory harassment is high when the sexual relationship ceases.
> Other individuals may be affected and claim favoritism.

Stites (in press) noted how including consensual relationships as part of the definition of academic sexual harassment has been met with considerable resistance. A few campuses (e.g., University of Iowa, Harvard University, Temple University) prohibit sexual relationships between faculty and students over whom the professor has some authority (e.g., advising, supervising, grading, teaching). A few other campuses have "discouragement policies," in which consensual relations are not strictly prohibited but discouraged (e.g., University of Minnesota, University of Connecticut, New York University Law School, Massachusetts Institute of Technology).

Recently the University of Virgina called for a total ban on all sexual relationships between faculty and student regardless of the professor's role vis-à-vis the student. However, the Faculty Senate approved a prohibition-only policy rather than the total-ban policy. Thus, this campus prohibits sexual relations between faculty and student when the faculty has some organizational power over the student. The case can be made, however, that a faculty member does not have to be the student's professor in order for that faculty member to be powerful and to potentially abuse that power over the student. All faculty members have an ethical and professional responsibility to provide a learning environment that is respectful of students and fosters the academic performance and intellectual development of students.

The fact that a student is defined as an adult by chronological age can in no way remove the obligation of a teacher or administrator to refrain from engaging in sexual harassment, and the student's adulthood is in no way a proxy for consenting to a relationship. The stories girls and women tell about their "consensual relationships" do not parallel romances or typical stories about sexual affairs; instead, they depict patterns of manipulation and victimization, responses identical to those girls and women who are sexually harassed in a nonconsensual relationship (Zalk, Paludi, & Dederich, 1991).

Is there such a thing as female students' informed consent in a sexual relationship with male faculty members? In answering this question, Stites asks us to think about power relations in the school setting that are stratfied by sex. The structure of educational institutions interacts with psychological dynamics to increase students' vulnerability to all forms of sexual harassment (Stites, in press). Professors have the power to enhance or diminish students' self-esteem. This power can motivate students to learn course material or convince them to give up. The tone and content of the student–professor interaction is especially important. Is the student encouraged or put down? Do the teachers use their knowledge to let students know how "stupid" they are, or to challenge their thinking? As Zalk, Paludi, and Dederick (1991) point out, this is *real power*.

## INCIDENCE OF SEXUAL HARASSMENT OF STUDENTS

Research has suggested that most students do not label their experiences as sexual harass-

ment despite the fact that the behavior they have experienced meets the legal definition of either quid pro quo or hostile environment harassment (Fitzgerald, 1990; Paludi & Barickman, 1991). A major interpretation of this research finding concerns individuals' lack of understanding of the definition of sexual harassment. Most students still report that sexual harassment doesn't occur unless there has been some physical assault. Yet, most sexual harassment experienced by students does not include assault or perhaps even touching. This finding has suggested to researchers that in order to collect incidence data on sexual harassment, one cannot simply ask the question, "Have you ever been sexually harassed?" Providing respondents with behavioral examples of sexual harassment facilitates more reliable responses (Paludi & Barickman, 1991).

The American Association of University Women (1993) used this methodological approach when collecting incidence data of adolescents' experiences with sexual harassment. In this study, 1,632 students in grades 8 through 11 from 79 schools across the United States were asked: "During your whole school life, how often, if at all, has anyone (this includes students, teachers, other school employees, or anyone else) done the following things to you *when you did not want them to?*"

1. Made sexual comments, jokes, gestures, or looks.
2. Showed, gave, or left you sexual pictures, photographs, illustrations, messages, or notes.
3. Wrote sexual messages/graffiti about you on bathroom walls, in locker rooms, etc.
4. Spread sexual rumors about you.
5. Said you were gay or lesbian.
6. Spied on you as you dressed or showered at school.
7. Flashed or "mooned" you.
8. Touched, grabbed, or pinched you in a sexual way.
9. Pulled at your clothing in a sexual way.
10. Intentionally brushed against you in a sexual way.
11. Pulled your clothing off or down.
12. Blocked your way or cornered you in a sexual way.

13. Forced you to kiss him/her.
14. Forced you to do something sexual, other than kissing.

Results suggested that four out of five students (81%) reported that they have been the target of some form of sexual harassment during their school lives. With respect to gender comparisons, 85% of girls and 76% of boys surveyed reported they have experienced unwelcomed sexual behavior that interferes with their ability to concentrate at school and with their personal lives. The AAUW study also analyzed for race comparisons. African American boys (81%) were more likely to have experienced sexual harassment than white boys (75%) and Latinos (69%). For girls, 87% of whites reported having experienced behaviors that constitute sexual harassment, compared with 84% of African American girls and 82% of Latinas.

The AAUW study also suggested that adolescents' experiences with sexual harassment are most likely to occur in the middle school/junior high school years of sixth to ninth grade. The behaviors reported by students, in rank order from most experienced to least experienced, were:

Sexual comments, jokes, gestures, or looks
Touched, grabbed, or pinched in a sexual way
Intentionally brushed against in a sexual way
Flashed or "mooned"
Had sexual rumors spread about them
Had clothing pulled at in a sexual way
Were shown, given, or left sexual pictures, photographs, illustrations, messages, or notes
Had their way blocked or were cornered in a sexual way
Had sexual messages/graffiti written about them on bathroom walls, in locker rooms, etc.
Forced to kiss someone
Called gay or lesbian
Had clothing pulled off or down
Forced to do something sexual, other than kissing
Spied on as they dressed or showered at school

Students reported that they experience these behaviors while in the classroom or in the hallways as they are going to class. The majority of harassment in schools is student to student. However, 25% of harassed girls and 10% of boys reported they were harassed by teachers or other school employees.

Bogart et al. (1992) reviewed sexual harassment complaints brought by students against teachers to the Massachusetts Department of Education. Among the complaints they reported were the following:

A science teacher measured the craniums of the boys in the class and the chests of the girls. The lessons in skeletal frame measurements were conducted one by one, at the front of the class, by the teacher.

The print shop teacher, who was in the habit of putting his arms around the shoulders of the young women, insisted, when one young woman asked to be excused to go to the nurse to fix her broken pants' zipper, that she first show him her broken zipper. She was forced to lift her shirt to reveal her broken pants' zipper. (p. 197)

Girls in nontraditional high school programs have reported the following experiences (Stein, 1986, cited in Bogart et al., 1992):

One female in diesel shop refused to go to lunch during her last two years of shop because she was the only young woman in the lunchroom at that time. When she went to the cafeteria, she was pinched and slapped on the way in, and had to endure explicit propositions made to her while she ate lunch.

A particular shop's predominantly male population designated one shop day as "National Sexual Harassment Day," in honor of their only female student. They gave her non-stop harassment throughout the day, and found it to be so successful (the female student was forced to be dismissed during the day), that they later held a "National Sexual Harassment Week." (p. 208)

These accounts provide a better picture than do simply percentages of the types of behaviors children and adolescents are experiencing at school.

With respect to the incidence of sexual harassment of college/university students, Dziech and Weiner (1984) reported that 30% of undergraduate women suffer sexual harassment from at least one of their instructors during their four years of college. When definitions of sexual harassment include sexist remarks and other forms of gender harassment, the incidence rate in undergraduate populations nears 70% (Paludi, 1990).

Bailey and Richards (1985) reported that of 246 women graduate students in their sample, 13% indicated they had been sexually harassed, 21% had avoided enrolling in a course to avoid such behavior, and 16% indicated they had been directly assaulted. Bond (1988) reported that 75% of the 229 women who responded to her survey experienced jokes with sexual themes during their graduate training, 69% were subjected to sexist comments demeaning to women, and 58% of the women reported experiencing sexist remarks about their clothing, body, or sexual activities.

Fitzgerald, Shullman, et al. (1988) investigated approximately 2,000 women at two major state universities. Half of the respondents reported experiencing some form of sexually harassing behavior. The majority of these women had experienced sexist comments by faculty; the next largest category of sexual harassing behavior was seductive behavior, including being invited for drinks and a backrub by faculty members, being brushed up against by their professors, and having their professors show up uninvited to their hotel rooms during out-of-town academic conferences or conventions.

Research by Paludi, DeFour, and Roberts (1994) suggests that the incidence of academic sexual harassment of ethnic minority women is even greater than that reported with white women. Dziech and Weiner (1984) and DeFour (1990) suggested that ethnic minority women are more vulnerable to receiving sexual attention from professors. Ethnic minority women are subject to stereotypes about sex, viewed as mysterious, and less sure of themselves in their careers (DeFour, 1990). Although all students are vulnerable to some degree, male teachers and faculty tend to select those who are most vulnerable and needy. For certain student groups the incidence of sexual harassment appears to be higher than for others (Barickman, Paludi, & Rabinowitz, 1992). For example, those vulnerable to harassment include:

Girls and women of color, especially those with "token" status

Graduate students, whose future careers are often determined by their association with a particular faculty member

Students in small colleges or small academic departments, where the number of faculty available to students is quite small

Female students in male-populated fields, e.g., engineering

Students who are economically disadvantaged and work part-time or full-time while attending classes

Lesbian women, who may be harassed as part of homophobia

Physically or emotionally disabled students

Women students who work in dormitories as resident assistants

Girls and women who have been sexually abused

Inexperienced, unassertive, socially isolated girls and women, who may appear more vulnerable and appealing to those who would intimidate or entice them into an exploitive relationship

Schools most likely to have a high incidence of sexual harassment are ones, according to research (Sandler & Paludi, 1993) that

Have no policy prohibiting sexual harassment

Do not disseminate the policy or report information regarding sexual harassment

Have no training programs for teachers, staff, and students

Do not intervene officially when sexual harassment occurs

Do not support sexual harassment victims

Do not quickly remove sexual graffiti

Do not give sanctions to individuals who engage in sexual harassment

Do not inform the school community about the sanctions for offenders

Have been previously all-male or have a majority of male students

Sexual harassment is thus a major form of victimization of women in higher education, even though it is still largely a "hidden issue" (as the Project on the Status and Education of Women called it in 1978). According to Fitzgerald and Omerod (1993): "It seems reasonable (if not conservative) to estimate that one out of every two women will be harassed at some point during her academic or working life, thus indicating that sexual harassment is the most widespread of all forms of sexual victimization studied to date" (p. 559).

Girls and women are more likely to be victims of sexual harassment. However, boys and men can be harassed. Their experiences are most commonly with other males—both male teachers and male peers—although they may be targeted, when in high school, by girls (AAUW, 1993; Sandler & Paludi, 1993). Saal, Johnson, and Weber (1989) pointed out that males frequently interpret females' behavior as sexual when it is not. Thus, males may misinterpret a female's behavior as being a sexual invitation and mislabel the behavior as sexual harassment.

## IMPACT OF SEXUAL HARASSMENT ON STUDENTS

Several reports have documented the high cost of sexual harassment to individuals (Koss, 1990; Paludi, in preparation; Rabinowitz, 1990). The outcomes of the harassment/victimization process can be examined from three main perspectives: study/work-related, psychological or emotional, and physiological or health-related (Fitzgerald & Omerod, 1993).

### Study/Work-Related Outcomes

Research has documented decreased morale and absenteeism, decreased school satisfaction, performance decrements, and damage to interpersonal relationships at school (Paludi, 1990).

### Psychological Outcomes

The emotional consequences of being harassed include depression, helplessness, strong fear reactions, loss of control, disruption of their lives, and decreased motivation (Rabinowitz, 1990).

### Physiological Outcomes

The following physical symptoms have been reported in the literature concerning sexual harassment: headaches, sleep disturbances, disordered eating, gastrointestinal disorders, nausea, weight loss or gain, and crying spells. Recently researchers and clinicians have argued that victims of sexual harassment can exhibit a "post abuse" syndrome characterized by shock, emotional numbing, constriction of affect, flashbacks, and other signs of anxiety and depression (Quina, 1990).

In recent years the label Sexual Harassment Trauma Syndrome has been applied to the effects of sexual harassment on physical, emotional, interpersonal, and career aspects of students' lives (Rabinowitz, 1990). The AAUW (1994) study reported that approximately one in four students who had been sexually harassed cut a class or did not want to attend school. In addition, one in four students became silent in their classes following the experience of harassment. With respect to the emotional aspects of sexual harassment, the AAUW study reported the following experiences, in rank order, among the students who were sexually harassed:

Embarassment
Self-consciousness
Being less sure of themselves or less confident
Feeling afraid or scared
Doubting whether they could have a happy
    romantic relationship
Feeling confused about who they are
Feeling less popular

Sexual harassment victims may experience a second victimization when they attempt to deal with the situation through legal and/or institutional means. Stereotypes about sexual harassment and victimization blame girls and women for the harassment. These stereotypes center around the myths that sexual harassment is a form of seduction, that girls and women secretly want to be sexually harassed, and that they do not tell the truth. As DeFour (1990) commented:

> The images and perceptions of women of color also increase their vulnerability to harassment. These images either portray the women as weak and thus unlikely to fight back if harassed, or they are perceived as very sexual and thus desiring sexual attention. Hispanic women have been described as hot-blooded…Asian women have been described as…submissive. However, they are also viewed by some as the exotic sexpot who will cater to the whims of any man. (pp. 48–49)

Students may not label their experiences as sexual harassment, despite the fact their experiences meet the legal definition of this form of victimization. Consequently, they may not label their stress-related responses as being caused or exacerbated by the sexual harassment. Their responses can be attributed by peers, teachers, and family to other events in their life—biological and/or social.

The responses of the trauma syndrome are influenced by disappointment in the way others react and the stress of harassment-induced life changes such as moves, loss of income, and disrupted school history (Paludi, 1990). Students and their families may also have to incur legal expenses, medical costs, and psychotherapy costs.

## WHO HARASSES?

Most individuals believe that sexual harassers are pathological, abnormal, and can easily be spotted. Fitzgerald and Weitzman (1990) reported, following their study of men on college/university faculties, that the stereotype that there is a "typical" harasser who can be identified by his blatant and obvious mistreatment of many women is a serious oversimplification of a complex issue and contributes to the misunderstanding in this area. Harassers are found in all types of teaching ranks. Fitzgerald and Weitzman also noted that,

although it may be painful to confront the reality that harassment can be perpetrated by teachers who are familiar to students, who have traditional family lives, and who appear to be caring and sensitive to their students, it must not be ignored. Research has thus suggested that there is no typical harasser. Individuals who harass typically do not label their behavior as sexual harassment despite the fact they report they frequently engage in initiating personal relationships with individuals. They deny the inherent power differential between themselves and their employees as well as the psychological power conferred by this differential that is as salient as the power derived from evaluation.

Pryor (1987) reported that the man who is likely to initiate severe sexually harassing behavior appears to be one who emphasizes male social and sexual dominance and who demonstrates insensitivity to other individuals' perspectives. Men faculty were also significantly more likely than women to agree with the following statements, taken from Paludi's "Atttitudes Toward Victim Blame and Victim Responsibility" survey (Paludi, in preparation):

> Women often claim sexual harassment to protect their reputations.
>
> Many women claim sexual harassment if they have consented to sexual relations but have changed their minds afterwards.
>
> Sexually experienced women are not really damaged by sexual harassment.
>
> It would do some women good to be sexually harassed.
>
> Women put themselves in situations in which they are likely to be sexually harassed because they have an unconscious wish to be harassed.
>
> In most cases when a woman is sexually harassed, she deserved it.

Lott (1993) and her colleagues have also found empirical support for a widely accepted assumption among researchers in sexual harassment; that sexual harassment is part of a larger and more general dimension of misogyny or hostility toward women and extreme stereoytpes of women, including the mythical images of sexual harassment—that sexual harassment is a form of seduction and that women secretly need/want to be forced into sex.

Paludi (1993) noted in her research on why boys and men sexually harass girls and women that the focus should not be on males' attitudes toward females but instead on males' attitudes toward other males, competition, and power. Many of the men with whom Paludi has discussed sexual harassment often act out of extreme competitiveness and concern with ego or out of fear of losing their positions of power. They don't want to appear weak or less masculine in the eyes of other males, so they will engage in "scoping of girls," pinching girls, making implied or overt threats, or spying on women. Girls and women are the game to impress other boys and men. When boys are being encouraged to be obsessively competitive and concerned with dominance, it is likely that they will eventually use violent means to achieve dominance (Paludi, 1993). Paludi also noted that boys are likely to be abusive verbally and intimidating in their body language. Deindividuation is quite common among adolescent boys, who, during class changes and lunchbreak "scope" girls as they walk by in the hall. These boys discontinue self-evaluation and adopt group norms and attitudes. Under these circumstances, group members behave more aggressively than they would as individuals.

The element of aggression that is so deeply embedded in the masculine gender role is present in sexual harassment. For many boys and men, aggression is one of the major ways of proving their masculinity, especially among those men who feel some sense of powerlessness in their lives (Doyle & Paludi, 1994). The male-as-dominant or male-as-aggressor is a theme so central to many males' self-concept that it literally carries over into their interpersonal communications, especially with female peers. Sexualizing a professional relationship may be the one area where the average man can still prove his masculinity when few other areas can be found for him to prove himself in control, or the dominant one in a relationship. Thus, sexual harassment is not so much a deviant act as an overconforming act to the masculine role in this culture (Paludi, 1990).

Can girls and women engage in sexual harassment? The data to date suggest that during adolescence girls may be likely to sexually harass boys, although the boys may misinterpret or mislabel their experiences, as suggested earlier. Women teachers and college/university professors are highly unlikely to date or sexually harass their students. As Fitzgerald and Weitzman (1990) concluded, although it is theoretically possible for women to harass men, it is, in practice, an extremely rare event.

## STUDENT RESPONSES TO SEXUAL HARASSMENT

Research (e.g., Paludi, 1990; Paludi & Barickman, 1991) suggests the following with respect to responses to sexual harassment. First, most students do not tell the harasser to stop. Their initial attempts to manage the initiator are rarely direct. Typically, harassers are more powerful—physically and institutionally—than the students, and sometimes the harasser's intentions are unclear. The first or first several harassing events are often ignored by victims, especially when they are experiencing hostile environment sexual harassment in which the behavior is more subtle. Students may interpret or reinterpret the situation so that the incident is not defined as sexual harassment. Many times, victims ignore the perpetrator.

The AAUW (1994) study reported that fewer than 1 in 10 students who had been sexually harassed told a teacher, although girls are twice as likely to report their experiences as boys. In addition, fewer than 1 in 4 students who had been sexually harassed told a family member about their experiences. The majority of adolescents who did report their experiences told a friend of theirs. Still, a sizable amount of students remained silent about sexual harassment.

Research suggests (e.g., Fitzgerald & Omerod, 1993; Paludi, 1990) that students fear retaliation should they confront the harasser. Students do not want their careers threatened. As Sandler and Paludi (1993) argue, students are serious about school; they do not enjoy experiencing sexual harassment. Malovich and Stake (1990) found that women students who were high in performance self-esteem and who held nontraditional gender-role attitudes were more likely to report incidents of sexual harassment than women who were high in self-esteem and who held traditional gender-role attitudes or women who were low in self-esteem. Brooks and Perot (1991) found that reporting behavior was predicted by the severity of the offense and by feminist attitudes on the part of the student.

Fitzgerald, Gold, and Brock (1990) constructed an empirically based system for classifying individuals' responses to sexually harassing behaviors. They classifed individuals' responses into two categories: internally focused strategies and externally focused strategies. Students who use internally focused strategies typically deny the event or relabel it so as not to appear as a victim. Fitzgerald, Gold, and Brock offered the following classification system for internally focused strategies:

*Detachment*   Student minimizes situation, treats it like a joke
*Denial*   Student denies behaviors; attempts to forget about it
*Relabeling*   Student reappraises situation as less threatening; offers excuses for harasser's behaviors
*Illusory Control*   Student attempts to take responsibility for harassment
*Endurance*   Student puts up with behavior because of not believing help is available or fearing retaliation

Externally focused strategies that might be used by students include the following categories (Fitzgerald, Gold, & Brock, 1990):

*Avoidance*   Student attempts to avoid situation by staying away from the harasser
*Assertion/Confrontation*   Student refuses sexual or social offers or verbally confronts the harasser
*Seeking Institutional/Organizational Relief*   Student reports the incident and files a complaint

*Social Support*   Student seeks support of others to validate perceptions of the behaviors
*Appeasement*   Student attempts to evade the harasser without confrontation; attempts to placate the harasser

Most incidents of sexual harassment in schools and colleges/universities are handled informally (Paludi & Barickman, 1991), suggesting that schools and colleges focus on supportive techniques to help victims of sexual harassment other than formal grievance procedures.

## IMPLICATIONS FOR EDUCATION AND POLICY

To effectively deal with sexual harassment in schools and colleges/universities, the following components are recommended: (1) an effective policy statement; (2) an effective grievance procedure, and (3) education/training programs for all members of the educational institution.

### Policy Statement

In order to deal with the issue of definitions of sexual harassment and promote the effective and equitable resolution of problems involving sexual harassment, it is necessary to have an explicit policy adopted by the school or college/university in compliance with the provision of Title IX, applicable to all units of the system. Such a policy allows the educational institution to uphold and enforce its policies against sexual harassment within its own community (including such severe penalities as loss of pay or position) without requiring victimized individuals to undertake the laborious, protracted, and costly process of seeking redress from the courts. The components of an effective policy statement for schools and colleges/universities are presented in Appendix 14-1.

The policy statement should be reissued each year by the school principal or college/university president and should be placed prominently throughout the school for all students, faculty, and nonfaculty employees. In addition, adding the policy statement to student handbooks is recommended.

## Grievance Procedures

Procedures for investigating complaints of sexual harassment must take into account the psychological issues involved in the victimization process, including students' feelings of powerlessness, isolation, changes in social network patterns, and wish to gain control over their personal and professional lives. Supportive techniques for working with victims of sexual harassment include the following:

Acknowledge students' courage by stating how difficult it is to label, report, and discuss sexual harassment.

Encourage students to share their feelings and perceptions.

Provide information about the incidence of sexual harassment. Also share the symptoms associated with the Sexual Harassment Trauma Syndrome.

Assure students that they are not responsible for their victimization.

Work with students in their search for the meaning in their victimization; support them while they mourn their losses.

Work with students in monitoring their physical, emotional, academic, and interpersonal responses to sexual harassment.

Provide a safe forum for students' expression of anger and resentment.

Work with students on ways to validate themselves so as to feel empowered.

Suggest a peer counseling group for students who need support for dealing with their experiences.

Recommendations for investigating complaints of sexual harassment in schools and colleges/universities are presented in Appendix 14-1.

## Education and Training

Several kinds of intervention may be instituted in order to challenge attitudes that perpetuate harassment in schools and colleges. Biaggio, Brownell, and Watts (1990) and Barickman, Paludi, and Rabinowitz (1992)

suggested that key individuals within the educational institutions can be targeted—residence hall advisors in dormitories, department chairs—for attendance at workshops at which they can be informed about the policy statement and procedures for dealing with harassment. In addition, new student orientations are another arena for disseminating information about institutional policies that prohibit sexual and gender harassment. Items relating to gender and sexual harassment can be placed on teaching evaluations (Paludi, in preparation).

Paludi and Barickman (1991) suggested the following educational interventions:

Include information about sexual harassment in faculty and student orientation materials.

Hold a "Sexual Harassment Awareness Week" and schedule programs around the issue of lesbian and gay harassment.

Require that student leaders attend workshops on sexual harassment.

Encourage sororities and fraternities to present programs on sexual harassment.

Include information on sexual harassment in packets for transfer students.

Report annually on sexual harassment.

Encourage faculty to incorporate discussions of sexual harassment in their courses.

For elementary and secondary schools, the following educational interventions can be recommended:

Encourage school groups to sponsor activities that foster awareness of sexual harassment, e.g., poster contests, writing contests, plays, presentations.

Discuss sexual harassment at parent-teacher conferences.

Send information home to parents about the school's sexual harassment policy and grievance procedures.

Check bathroom walls daily for sexual graffiti. Wash and/or paint the walls as needed.

Offer recognition for students who treat peers with respect and equity.

Train older students to teach younger ones about sexual harassment.

Paludi and Barickman (1991) also provide questions concerning sexual harassment for campuses to address. These questions can also be applied to elementary and secondary schools. For example:

Are there policies and effective procedures for dealing with sexual harassment?

Do the policies forbid peer harassment behaviors, or is it limited to harassment by teachers, administrators, and other staff?

Are the policies forbidding sexual harassment well publicized? Are they circulated periodically among students, staff, faculty, and administrators?

How do individuals in your school community learn whom they should see to discuss sexual harassment?

Are there specific individuals to whom individuals can go for help with sexual harassment issues?

Are remedies clear and commensurate with the level of violation?

Do you have procedures to inform new faculty, staff, and students about sexual harassment?

Do you have a task force or other structure that examines and reports annually on sexual harassment?

Are there regular workshops on sexual harassment, including peer harassment?

What services are available to individuals who have experienced sexual harassment?

Education/training must follow the development of an effective policy statement and grievance procedures (Paludi, 1993). The finding that more than half of the students in the AAUW survey did not know if their school has a policy on sexual harassment is indeed disturbing. Examples of training programs for students in elementary and secondary schools and in college are presented in Appendix 14-2.

The suggestions offered here are based on research and training experiences of the author as a consultant for schools and colleges. They are related to changing the educational system. In order to continue to address the prevention of sexual harassment, the following recommendations for researchers are offered so as to provide valuable information for investigative hearings and alleviate the double bind that

many students now face as they try to seek resolution for sexual harassment.

First, research should include students from general populations as well as specific populations, for example, students who have filed complaints and students who have sought counseling regarding sexual harassment. Within this framework, mediating and moderating variables such as age, perception of the meaning of the trauma, duration, response to the harassment, availability of resources to assist victims, social support, and school climate must be discussed in order to elucidate the conditions under which sexual harassment leads to the various outcomes that have been reviewed in this chapter.

As sexual harassment has become increasingly recognized as a social problem of enormous proportions, researchers have attempted to identify individual and organizational factors that place individuals at risk for this type of victimization. There has been considerable speculation in the literature that ethnicity or race minority status and sexual orientation may increase the risk of being sexually harassed (e.g., DeFour, 1990). Studies are needed that document lesbian women's experiences with sexual harassment. Biaggio (in press) has recently written that lesbians may experience sexual harassment differently and may be exposed to some unique forms of sexual harassment. For lesbians, sexual harassment may be experienced as an affront to their sexual orientation and may reinforce their sense of being an outsider. She also contends that while most victims of sexual harassment are often worried about being believed by others and about possible retaliation if they take formal steps to protest the behavior, for lesbians this may be an especially salient obstacle. Lesbians who are not "out" to other students or even to family members may be worried that perpetrators could retaliate by informing others of their sexual orientation. Such disclosure may result in rejection by family, friends, and coworkers.

DeFour (1990) suggested that ethnic minority women are more vulnerable to receiving sexual attention from employers. They are also subject to stereotypes about sex, achievement motivation, and career development. However, despite the intuitively reasonable argument that ethnic and race minority status heightens vulnerability, such an argument remains largely unexamined.

It is important to note that, similar to women's intentions to report a rape, intentions to report academic sexual harasssment vary according to ethnic group membership (Paludi, DeFour, & Roberts, 1994). Girls and women with the fewest resources to cope with victimization—for example ethnic minority girls and women, physically challenged girls—carry the most severe burden of fear (Riger & Gordon, 1981). Special attention must be paid to providing a safe place in the school or college/university setting for ethnic minority women to report academic sexual harassment, should they choose this option. Rowe (1990) noted that ethnic minority girls and women want their complaints defined as they wish them to be defined. She reported that many Asian American women and African American women view unwelcome sexualized behavior as racism, not sexism, and want it dealt with in those terms. Consequently, Rowe recommends the availability of several options for reporting for women based on their own definitions and explanatory models of sexual harassment.

Sexual harassment has a radiating impact and can thus affect the learning experiences of all girls and boys and women and men in a school or college. This radiating impact must be considered in the development of policy statements as well as in future research on the effects of sexual harassment.

Finally, rather than changing the level of analysis from the systemic to the individual, as is frequently the case among researchers, it is important to pursue an organizational or institutional level of analysis to explain the prevalence of sexual harassment, and to recognize more explicitly the contexts within which harassment is more likely to occur, to avoid victim blame.

Bond's (1988) plea for an ecological perspective for handling sexual harassment—educational, psychotherapeutic, legal, and sociocultural—is underscored. As Bond argued:

The use of an ecological perspective can move beyond finger-pointing to a more comprehensive understanding of a complex social problem that has been a critical barrier to… professional development for many years…. Continued development of an ecological approach will provide a more solid basis for developing policies and preventive interventions to reduce the negative impact sexual harassment has on…professional development. (p. 6)

Perhaps the most important step that school and college administrators can take to dealing with sexual harassment is to listen to student input when formulating their policies, procedures, and training programs. Teachers and administrators must decenter from their own perspectives and consider how their behavior and the school's policies and procedures are being interpreted by students. As indicated throughout this chapter, and as Demby (1990) argued, students can tell teachers and administrators the important things they need to know about sexual harassment. Students have dealt with sexual harassment. They know.

You may laugh or something because you're nervous and people are looking at you, but it does bother you—it affects your self-esteem.

I couldn't handle it anymore. I came home and said, "Mom, I'm sick of this. I'm sick of going to school every day and hearing this. I'm sick of getting no support from the school system. I'm going to do something about this because it's bothering me."

I think high school is something most kids look forward to—you see movies, read books about high school being the best time—and I'll always remember dark days, coming home, sitting on my bedroom floor sobbing.

Sexual harassment is unwanted and unwelcome sexual behavior which interferes with your life.

(Strauss, 1992; AAUW, 1993)

## REFERENCES

American Association of University Women (AAUW) (1993). *Hostile hallways: The AAUW survey on sex-*

ual harassment in America's schools. Washington, DC: Author.

Bailey, N., & Richards, M. (1985, August). Tarnishing the ivory tower: Sexual harassment in graduate training programs. Paper presented at the Annual Meeting of the American Psychological Association, Los Angeles.

Barickman, R. B., Paludi, M. A., & Rabinowitz, V. C. (1992). Sexual harassment of students: Victims of the college experience. In E. Viano (Ed.), *Victimization: An international perspective.* New York: Springer.

Biaggio, M. (in press). Sexual harassment and homophobia. In M. Paludi (Ed.), *Working 9 to 5: Women, men, sex, and power.* Albany, NY: SUNY Press.

Biaggio, M., Watts, D., & Brownell, A. (1990). Addressing sexual harassment: Strategies for prevention and change. In M. A. Paludi (Ed.), *Ivory power: Sexual harassment on campus.* Albany, NY: SUNY Press.

Bogart, K., Simmons, S., Stein, N., & Tomaszewski, E. (1992). Breaking the silence: Sexual and gender harassment in elementary, secondary, and postsecondary education. In S. Klein (Ed.), *Sex equity and sexuality in education.* Albany, NY: SUNY Press.

Bond, M. (1988). "Division 27 sexual harassment survey: Definition, impact, and environmental context. *The Community Psychologist, 21,* 7–10.

Brooks, L., & Perot, A. (1991). Reporting sexual harassment: Exploring a predictive model. *Psychology of Women Quarterly, 15,* 31–47.

DeFour, D. C. (1990). The interface of racism and sexism on college campuses. In M. A. Paludi (Ed.), *Ivory power: Sexual harassment on campus.* Albany, NY: SUNY Press.

Demby, L. (1990). In her own voice: One student's experiences with sexual harassment. In M. A. Paludi (Ed.), *Ivory power: Sexual harassment on campus.* Albany, NY: SUNY Press.

Doyle, J., & Paludi, M. (1994). *Sex and gender: The human experience.* Dubuque, IA: Brown/Benchmark.

Dziech, B., & Weiner, L. (1984). *The lecherous professor.* Boston: Beacon Press.

Fitzgerald, L. F. (1990). Sexual harassment: The definition and measurement of a construct. In M.A. Paludi (Ed.), *Ivory power: Sexual harassment on campus.* Albany, NY: SUNY Press.

Fitzgerald, L. F., Gold, Y., & Brock, K. (1990). Responses to victimization: Validation of an objective policy. *Jounal of College Student Personnel, 27,* 34–39.

Fitzgerald, L. F., & Omerod, A. (1993). Sexual harassment in academia and the workplace. In F. L. Denmark & M. A. Paludi (Eds.), *Psychology of women: Handbook of issues and theories.* Westport, CT: Greenwood.

Fitzgerald, L. F., Shullman, S., Bailey, N., Richards, M., Swecker, J., Gold, Y., Omerod, A., & Weitzman, L. (1988). The incidence and dimensions of sexual harassment in academia and the workplace. *Journal of Vocational Behavior, 32,* 152–175.

Fitzgerald, L. F., & Weitzman, L. (1990). Men who harass: Speculation and data. In M. A. Paludi (Ed.), *Ivory power: Sexual harassment on campus.* Albany, NY: SUNY Press.

Fitzgerald, L. F., Weitzman, L., Gold, Y., & Omerod, M. (1988). Academic sexual harassment: Sex and denial in scholarly garb. *Psychology of Women Quarterly, 12,* 329–340.

Haring-Hidore, M., & Paludi, M. (1991). Power, politics, and sexuality in mentor-protege relationships: Implications for women's achievement. In S. Klein (Ed.), *Sex and sexuality in education.* Albany, NY: SUNY Press.

Kenig, S., & Ryan, J. (1986). Sex differences in levels of tolerance and attribution of blame for sexual harassment on a university campus. *Sex Roles, 15,* 535–549.

Koss, M. P. (1990). Changed lives: The psychological impact of sexual harassment. In M. A. Paludi (Ed.), *Ivory power: Sexual harassment on campus.* Albany, NY: SUNY Press.

Lott, B. (1993). Sexual harassment: Consequences and realities. *NEA Higher Education Journal, 8,* 89–103.

Malovich, N. J., & Stake, J. E. (1990). Sexual harassment of women on campus: Individual differences in attitude and belief. *Psychology of Women Quarterly, 14,* 63–81.

Mead, M. (1978). A proposal: We need new taboos on sex at work. Reported in B. Dzeich & L. Winer (1984). *The lecherous professor.* Boston: Beacon Press.

Paludi, M. A. (Ed.) (1990). *Ivory power: Sexual harassment on campus.* Albany, NY: SUNY Press.

Paludi, M. A. (1993). Ethnicity, sex, and sexual harassment. *Thought and Action: The National Education Association Higher Education Journal, 8,* 105–116.

Paludi, M. A. (in preparation). *Sexual harassment of adolescents by peers and teachers.* Albany, NY: SUNY Press.

Paludi, M. A., & Barickman, R. B. (1991). *Academic and workplace sexual harassment: A manual of resources.* Albany, NY: SUNY Press.

Paludi, M. A., DeFour, D. C., & Roberts, R. (1994). *Academic sexual harassment of ethnic minority women.* Research in progress.

Pryor, J. (1987). Sexual harassment proclivities in men. *Sex Roles, 17,* 269–289.

Quina, K. (1990). The victimizations of women. In M. A. Paludi (Ed.), *Ivory power: Sexual harassment on campus.* Albany, NY: SUNY Press.

Rabinowitz, V. C. (1990). Coping with sexual harassment. In M. A. Paludi (Ed.), *Ivory power: Sexual harassment on campus.* Albany, NY: SUNY Press.

Riger, S., & Gordon, M. (1981). The fear of rape: A study in social control. *Journal of Social Issues, 37,* 71–92.

Rowe, M. (1990). People who feel harassed need a complaint system with both formal and informal options. *Negotiation Journal, 6,* 1–9.

Saal, F., Johnson, C., & Weber, N. (1989). Friendly or sexy? It may depend on whom you ask. *Psychology of Women Quarterly, 13,* 263–276.

Sandler, B., & Paludi, M. (1993). *Educator's guide to controlling sexual harassment.* Washington, DC: Thompson.

Stites, M. C. (in press). Consensual relationships. In M. Paludi (Ed.), *Sexual harassment on college campuses: Abusing the ivory power.* Albany, NY: SUNY Press.

Strauss, S. (1992). *Sexual harassment and teens.* Minneapolis, MN: Free Spirit.

Zalk, S. R., Paludi, M. A., & Dederich, J. (1991). Women students' assessment of consensual relationships with their professors: Ivory power reconsidered. In M. A. Paludi & R. B. Barickman. *Academic and workplace sexual harassment: A resource manual.* Albany, NY: State University of New York Press.

# APPENDIX 14-1

# POLICIES AND PROCEDURES FOR ADDRESSING SEXUAL HARASSMENT IN SCHOOLS

## COMPONENTS OF AN EFFECTIVE POLICY STATEMENT

1. Statement of Purpose
   Identify School's Position on Sexual Harassment
2. Definition
   Quote from Equal Employment Opportunity Commission's Definition of Sexual Harassment and OCR's definition
3. Behaviors that Constitute Sexual Harassment
   Illustrate Legal Definition
4. Statement of Importance
   Discuss Impact on Students and Schools
5. Statement of Student's Responsibility
   Discuss Methods Students Should Take to Report the Harassment

6. Statement of School's Responsibility
   Discuss Complaint Procedures
   Include:
       Due Process
       Confidentiality
       Amount of Time to Complete Investigation
7. Statement of Sanctions
   Illustrate Sanctions Commensurate with Type of Sexual Harassment
8. Statement of Sanctions for Retaliation
9. Statement Concerning False Complaints
10. Statement Concerning Peer Sexual Harassment
11. Statement Concerning Consensual Relationships
12. Identification of Individual(s) Responsible for Hearing Complaints
       Provide Office and Phone Numbers
       Provide Brief Biographical Statement

## WHO SHOULD INVESTIGATE COMPLAINTS OF SEXUAL HARASSMENT?

Each school and college will select the individual who will be responsible for hearing and investigating charges of sexual harassment. At some colleges this role is usually given to the Ombudsperson, Dean of Students, Affirmative Action Officer, or Sexual Harassment Committees or panels. In elementary or secondary schools this role is usually given to a guidance counselor or a Title IX compliance officer. The individual who is responsible for investigating complaints should meet the following criteria. She/he must:

- Have sufficient credibility in the area of sexual harassment, including knowledge and formal training in the legal, psychological, and physical aspects of sexual harassment
- Be readily accessible for students, faculty, employees, and administrators
- Have skill in relating to people and eliciting information from them
- Not be uncomfortable in discussing matters of sexuality and sexual deviancy, incest, battering, and rape
- Be fluent in languages in addition to English (or have a co-investigator who can meet this need)
- Be tenured (and a full professor, if at a college/university) to avoid potential problems with tenure and promotions review decisions
- Be sensitive and trained in eliciting information from children and adolescents, should the investigator be working in the primary or secondary school
- Report directly to the individual who will determine the school/college's response, i.e., administer sanctions (i.e., school principal or college/university president)
- Not permit any of the individuals in the complaint procedure to pressure her/him to reveal confidential information, to become their advocate, or to "take sides" in the final report of the investigation

- Be honest and candid, without permitting personal feelings to interfere with effectiveness
- Be sensitive to civil service rules, collective bargaining agreements, and other personnel rules
- Be prepared for discussions with all individuals involved to be very emotional and be a calming force for these emotional discussions
- Set up a "safe" atmosphere for the complainant, alleged harasser, and witnesses to discuss their perspectives without the fear of being ridiculed or judged
- Maintain a distance from all individuals involved in the complaint process so (1) a reasoned judgment can be made about whether to sustain the charge of sexual harassment and (2) she/he can be upheld as objective by individuals such as hearing officers, judges, and parties involved in complaint process
- Not use tape recorders or video recorders during interviews as part of the investigative process since these machines create unnecessary added stress for individuals
- Work well with the principal or president and not be viewed as adversarial.

## GENERAL GUIDELINES FOR INVESTIGATING COMPLAINTS OF SEXUAL HARASSMENT

While each school will set up its own complaint procedure that fits its unique needs, the following general guidelines should apply for all investigations of sexual harassment:

- **Investigators must make it clear to all parties involved in the investigative procedure that the school has an obligation to make the environment free of sexual harassment and free of the fear of being retaliated against for filing a complaint of sexual harassment.** Investigators must also state that they cannot ignore any complaint of sexual harassment.

- **Every complaint must be taken seriously by the individual(s) charged with investigating sexual harassment charges.**
- **Every complaint must be kept confidential.** The need for confidentiality is essential to protect the rights of those who filed the complaint, those against whom the complaint has been filed, and witnesses.
- **No conclusions about the veracity of the complaint should be made until the investigation is completed.** Investigators must not make determinations about the complaint based on the reputations of the individuals involved.
- **The investigation must be thorough and fair**. The school's policy statement and procedures must be followed at all times. There must be provisions, for example, for hearing complaints against the investigator. New procedures must not be developed during the course of an investigation.
- **Every step of the investigation must be completely and accurately documented and in a form that can be defended to others**. This procedure should be maintained for the in-house investigation and for subsequent lawsuits, for which all notes, reports, and written materials will be subpoenaed and be made part of the court record.
- **Investigations must be completed in a timely fashion.** A prompt investigation is necessary to obtain accurate and complete statements from all individuals involved in the complaint. A quick time frame also assists in the complainant's coping with the victimization. Time deadlines for individuals to respond to charges of sexual harassment must be rigorously observed.
- **The complainant must be interviewed in detail**. The following information must be obtained from the complainant in writing:
  - Detailed description of the behavior about which the indvidual is complaining (i.e., approximate date(s), times, frequency, location, circumstances, identity of alleged harasser)
  - Names of potential witnesses
  - Impact of behavior on complainant in terms of emotional, physical, or learning

- Whether individual has voiced her/his concern to alleged harasser and if so, the outcome of such objection
- The type of resolution the individual is seeking for her-/himself and for the alleged harasser.
- **The person complained about must be interviewed in detail.** The person must be shown the written complaint and documents given to the investigator. The following information must be obtained in writing from the individual against whom the complaint was filed:
  - Reaction to complaint
  - Interpretation of events mentioned in complaint
  - Understanding the impact of her/his behavior on complainant
- **All witnesses must be interviewed**. Witnesses identified by the complainant and by the alleged harasser should be invited to meet with the investigator. Witnesses should only discuss information related to the incidents about which they are assumed to have knowledge with respect to the complaint at hand. They must not be interviewed about information they have about previous victims, for example. The identity of the witnesses for the complainant must not be provided for the alleged harasser. Similarly, the identity of the witnesses for the alleged harasser must not be given to the complainant. This confidentiality will ensure that witnesses will come forth and participate in the investigative process without fear of retaliation.
- **All documents presented by the complainant, alleged harasser, and witnesses must be reviewed.** Documents include, but are not limited to letters or notes sent to an individual involved in the complaint process. Investigators must not seek out any additional records without the prior written consent from the individual(s) involved and only when these materials are deemed absolutely necessary to conduct the investigation.
- **Each complaint against the same individual must be handled independently.** The outcome of the investigation should never be

based on knowledge that the alleged harasser has had other complaints filed against him/her. Similarly, knowledge that the complainant has filed other complaints must not enter into the investigative process. Such information may be helpful in determining sanctions, however.

- **Provisions must be made for students who wish to wait until they receive a grade prior to filing a complaint.** This need may be met by instituting an anonymous complaint procedure whereby individuals do not have to sign their name to the complaint in order for it to be investigated. This complaint procedure works best when one or several students file a complaint against a teacher.

- **Closure must be provided for all parties involved in the complaint procedure.** Information regarding the status of the investigation and the completion of the investigation must be provided to all individuals involved in the complaint process.

# SAMPLE LESSON PLANS

## LESSON PLANS FOR TRAINING SCHOOL-AGE STUDENTS (K–12)

Total Time for Training Program: 3 Class Periods

### Overall Goals of Training Program

- Define quid pro quo and hostile environment sexual harassment.
- Discuss the physical and emotional reactions to being sexually harassed.
- Discuss peer sexual harassment.
- Discuss means of resolution for complaints of sexual harassment.

### Overall Objectives of Training Program

At the conclusion of this training program, students will be able to:
- Assess their own perceptions of sexual harassment
- Adequately label behaviors as illustrative of sexual harassment or not illustrative of sexual harassment
- Identify peer sexual harassment
- Describe the effects of sexual harassment on students
- State the proper procedure to follow if sexual harassment occurs

# Topics for Presentation and Discussion

*Lesson 1 Introduction to Program and Definition of Sexual Harassment (1 class period)*

*Objectives.* At the conclusion of this class, students will be able to:

- Assess their own perceptions of sexual harassment
- Adequately label behaviors as illustrative of sexual harassment or not illustrative of sexual harassment
- Identify peer sexual harassment
- State the difference between flirting and sexual harassment

*For Secondary School Students.*

*Introduction*
Trainer welcomes students to the class.
Trainer introduces her/him self to students.
Students introduce themselves and state one question they want to have answered in the training sessions.
Trainer writes these answers on the flipchart/chalkboard for all students to see.
Trainer summarizes students' responses.
Trainer states goals for training session.

*For Elementary School Students.*

*Introduction*
Trainer welcomes students to the class.
Trainer introduces her/him self to students.
Students introduce themselves and offer goal for training.
Trainer writes these responses on the flipchart/chalkboard for all students to see.
Trainer summarizes students' responses.
Trainer states goals for training session.

*For Secondary School Students.*

*Definition of Sexual Harassment*
Trainer distributes copies of sexual harassment case study.
Students read case study to answer trainer-directed questions.
Trainer lectures and leads guided discussion of sexual harassment.

Trainer makes summary comments from this unit.

*For Elementary School Students.*

*Definition of Sexual Harassment*
Trainer distributes copies of sexual harassment case study.
Students read case study to answer trainer-directed questions.
Trainer lectures and leads guided discussion of sexual harassment.
Trainer makes summary comments from this unit.
Trainer posts major points from lesson.
Trainer identifies goals of next class period.

*Lesson 2 What Are the Causes and the Impact of Sexual Harassment? (1 class period)*

*Objectives.* At the conclusion of this class, students will be able to:

- Assess their perceptions of the effects of sexual harassment on students
- Identify emotional, physical, and career development effects of sexual harassment
- Assess contributing factors to sexual harassment

*For Secondary School Students.*

*Presentation*
Trainer reviews major points from first class period.
Trainer discusses the interface of gender and power.
Trainer lectures on the impact of sexual harassment on students.
Trainer makes summary comments from this unit.
Trainer identifies goals of next class period.

*For Elementary School Students.*

*Presentation*
Trainer reviews major points from first class period.
Trainer lectures on the impact of sexual harassment on students.
Trainer presents case studies.
Trainer leads guided discussion with case studies.

Trainer makes summary comments from this unit.

Trainer identifies goals of next class period.

*Lesson 3 Stopping Sexual Harassment (1 class period)*

*Objectives.* At the conclusion of this class, students will be able to:

- Determine action to take if a person experiences sexual harassment
- Determine solutions to incidents of sexual harassment
- Examine the school's policy on sexual harassment
- Identify educational programs to help their school deal with sexual harassment
- Summarize major issues in sexual harassment identified in three class periods

*For Secondary School Students.*

*Presentation*

Trainer will review information from previous two classes by using flipchart/chalkboard.

Trainer will announce goals of final class period devoted to sexual harassment.

Trainer asks students to list ways they can work with their school in preventing sexual harassment.

Trainer posts these responses on the flipchart/chalkboard.

Trainer distributes copies of school's policy statement on sexual harassment.

Trainer introduces individual charged with implementing policy statement (optional).

Trainer leads guided discussion of policy statement.

Trainer asks students to list additional educational programs for their school.

*Conclusion to Training Program.*

Trainer reviews major points from three class periods.

Trainer asks students to reread case study and answer questions.

Trainer distributes copies of evaluation form.

Trainer meets individually with students who wish to speak to her/him privately.

*For Elementary School Students.*

*Presentation*

Trainer will review information from previous two classes by using flipchart/chalkboard.

Trainer will announce goals of final class period devoted to sexual harassment.

Trainer asks students to list ways they can work with their school in preventing sexual harassment.

Trainer posts these responses on the flipchart/chalkboard.

Trainer distributes copies of school's policy statement on sexual harassment for students' parents.

Trainer introduces individual charged with implementing policy statement (optional).

Trainer asks students to list additional educational programs for their school.

*Conclusion to Training Program*

Trainer reviews major points from three class periods.

Trainer asks students to reread case study and answer questions.

Trainer meets individually with students who wish to speak to her/him privately.

## LESSON PLAN FOR TRAINING COLLEGE STUDENTS

### Goals of Training Program

- Define quid pro quo and hostile environment sexual harassment.
- Discuss psychological issues involved in dealing with sexual harassment.
- Discuss the physical and emotional reactions to being sexually harassed.
- Provide a psychological profile of sexual harassers.
- Discuss peer sexual harassment.
- Discuss means of resolution for complaints of sexual harassment.

### Objectives of Training Program

At the conclusion of this training program, students will be able to:

- Assess their own perceptions of the definition, incidence, and psychological dimensions of sexual harassment
- Adequately label behaviors as illustrative of sexual harassment or not illustrative of sexual harassment
- Assess why students choose to report or not report their experiences of sexual harassment
- Identify peer sexual harassment
- Identify students' rights and responsibilities under Title IX
- Understand their college's policy statement against sexual harassment and grievance procedures for dealing with sexual harassment
- Design educational programs for their campus to deal with sexual harassment, including peer sexual harassment

## Topics for Presentation and Discussion

*Part 1—Introduction to Training Session and Goals of Seminar/ Workshop*

Students state their goals for the training session.

Faculty writes these goals on the flipchart/ chalkboard for all students to see.

Faculty summarizes goals of participants.

Faculty lectures on the major components from the training session.

*Part 2 Perceptions versus Realities in Sexual Harassment: Students' Views of Sexual Harassment*

Faculty asks students for their responses to case study or exercise.

Faculty posts students' responses on the flip-chart/chalkboard.

Faculty lectures on the similarities between the exercise/case and issues to be discussed on sexual harassment.
  Sexual harassment is illegal.
  A variety of responses exists for individuals dealing with sexual harassment.

Professors' power over students makes students modify their behavior for fear of retaliation.

Faculty distributes copies of sexual harassment case study.

Students read case study to answer trainer-directed questions.

Faculty summarizes students' responses to questions.

Faculty makes summary comments for this unit.

*Part 3 Definition of Sexual Harassment*

Faculty lectures and leads guided discussion of sexual harassment.
  Equal Employment Opportunity Commission definition
  Summary of case law on quid pro quo and hostile environment sexual harassment
  Behavioral examples of sexual harassment
  Peer sexual harassment
Faculty makes summary comments from this unit.

*Part 4 Incidence of Sexual Harassment among College Students*

Faculty lectures on the incidence of academic sexual harassment.
  Measurement considerations
  Underreporting of incidences
  Individuals at risk for sexual harassment
  Relationship between incidence and reporting
Faculty makes summary comments from this unit.

*Part 5 Impact of Sexual Harassment on Students and Campus*

Faculty lectures on the impact of sexual harassment on students.

Faculty lectures on the cost of sexual harassment for the college/university.

Faculty makes summary comments from this unit.

*Part 6 Causes of Sexual Harassment*

Faculty lectures on explanatory models of sexual harassment.

Faculty lectures on psychological profiles of harassers.

Faculty makes summary comments from this unit.

*Part 7 Preventing Sexual Harassment on Campus*

Faculty lectures on components of an effective policy statement for students.

Faculty distributes copies of college's policy statement against sexual harassment.

Faculty introduces college representative charged with enforcing policy statement.

Faculty discusses policy statement.

Faculty asks students to list potential educational programs for their college/university campus.

Faculty writes these responses on the flip-chart/chalkboard for all students to see.

Faculty makes summary comments from this unit.

*Part 8 Summary Comments and Review*

Faculty lectures on "myths and realities" of sexual harassment.

Faculty leads general discussion of sexual harassment of college students.

Faculty asks students to reread case study and answer questions.

Faculty reviews students' goals that were generated at the beginning of the session.

Faculty conducts question-and-answer period.

# CHAPTER 15

# SEXUAL HARASSMENT IN THE MILITARY

**Robert E. Niebuhr**

The 1991 Tailhook convention in Las Vegas of Navy aviation officers contributed to the increase in public awareness of sexual harassment and also provided a "wake-up call" to the military to increase efforts to monitor and reduce incidents of sexual harassment. The initial cursory investigation into the incident only highlighted the issue, resulting in the Pentagon and House Armed Services Committee conducting their own in-depth investigations. As a result, Navy Secretary Lawrence Garrett, Admiral Frank Kelso (the Chief of Navy Operations), and several other high-ranking officers were forced to resign (Eisaguirre, 1993).

As evidenced by the Tailhook incident, assimilation of female personnel into the military branches has resulted in stressful environments as the traditional male-dominated culture seeks to cope with change. A study of female integration at the U.S. Naval Academy (Gilroy et al., 1990) found that the climate of not accepting women as equals resulted in a culture in which steady, low-level sexual harassment passed as normal operating procedure. Both sanctioned and unofficial activities (e.g., company t-shirts with lewd acronyms, suggestive electronic mail messages, pornographic movies in the wardrooms at night) perpetuated the stereotypic male views of women as sex objects. It is probably not surprising that incidents such as Tailhook would occur given the culture that has developed and became entrenched over decades of a "macho" approach to gender relationships.

The definition of sexual harassment has its roots in Section 703(a) of Title VII of the Civil Rights Act of 1964, which prohibits discrimination of individuals on the basis of sex (as well as race, color, religion, or national origin). Out of this legislation, efforts have focused through the intervening years on increasing the awareness and reducing the occurrence of both sexism (gender discrimination/harassment) and sexual harassment. As Greenbaum and Fraser (1981) indicate, sex discrimination was not a part of the first draft of this landmark legislation, but was actually included at the last moment in an attempt to prevent passage of the Civil Rights Act. Members of the House of Representatives who opposed the legislation added the amendment in the hope that the inclusion of gender along with other prohibited classifications would hinder passage of the bill. However, the legislation, with the amended wording to include gender discrimination, was passed quickly with little discussion.

The first claims of sexual harassment were not litigated until almost 10 years after passage of the Civil Rights Act. The initial cases often resulted in a favorable finding for the defendant since the courts interpreted Title VII to be extremely limited in terms of relevance to sexual harassment cases. The first case to hold that sexual harassment violated Title VII occurred in *Williams v. Saxbe* (1976), in which the court ruled that not only was sexual harassment actionable under Title VII, but also that an employer is responsible for the sexual harassment acts of its supervisory personnel. Reviews of court cases on the interpretation of Title VII (Baxter, 1985; Woerner & Oswald, 1990) suggest that there is still a lack of consistency in court decisions, both in the definition of sexual harassment and in the appropriate steps organizations must take to handle sexual harassment decisions. Aside from the conditions that the conduct must be sexual in nature and be unwelcome, it appears that sexual harassment will be determined on a case-by-case basis, considering all the circumstances and issues that surround the alleged conduct (Baxter, 1985). As Morgenson (1989) concludes, the court decisions have clearly indicated that sexual harassment is wrong, with the result that organizations seem to have developed a somewhat warranted paranoia regarding the issues; future litigation in the sexual harassment arena may only be bounded by the imagination and creativity of the litigant (Woerner & Oswald, 1990).

The possibility of bringing sexual harassment issues under Title VII was extremely instrumental in the expansion of litigation in this area. A claim brought under Title VII makes available to claimants the resources and mechanisms of the Equal Employment Opportunity Commission (EEOC) and similar state agencies. The EEOC issued guidelines on sexual harassment in 1980; these guidelines provide the most current and explicit definition of sexual harassment:

> Harassment on the basis of sex is a violation of Sec. 703 of Title VII. Unwelcome sexual advances, requests for sexual favors, and other verbal or physical conduct of a sexual nature constitute sexual harassment when
>
> 1. submission to such conduct is made either explicitly or implicitly a term or condition of an individual's employment,
> 2. submission to or rejection of such conduct by an individual is used as the basis for employment decisions affecting such individual, or
> 3. such conduct has the purpose or effect of unreasonably interfering with an individual's work performance or creating an intimidating, hostile, or offensive working environment.

It is interesting to note that Secretary Casper Weinberger issued a Department of Defense sexual harassment policy on July 17, 1981, and the memorandum outlining the definition of sexual harassment (Korb, 1981) that was sent to the various services and defense agencies was almost a verbatim statement of the EEOC definition. In fact, the Department of Defense definition strengthened the EEOC statement by replacing the word "employment" in condition (1) with the words "job, pay, or career" and removing the word "unreasonably" in condition (3). The memorandum went on to require training on sexual harassment and the development of a monitoring/reporting system so that a report on sexual harassment issues could be provided annually to the Secretary of Defense.

The guidelines and federal court decisions generally recognize two distinct situations in which conduct may be viewed as sexual harassment. The first two EEOC guidelines characterize a quid pro quo situation, in which sexual cooperation is coerced by promises of rewards or threats of punishment. The third guideline characterizes an offensive work environment, in which sexually offensive behavior makes the work environment unfairly unpleasant. These two situational dimensions have been used by researchers to develop classification systems and instruments to measure and investigate sexual harassment issues (Fitzgerald & Hesson-McInnis, 1989; Till, 1980).

## RESEARCHING OCCURRENCES OF SEXUAL HARASSMENT IN THE MILITARY

While the public view of military life is probably a perception of a male-dominated culture, it is interesting to note that the military has actually been one of the most aggressive segments of our society with respect to researching the occurrences and causes of sexual harassment and developing mechanisms to reduce the incidents that have severely damaged their reputation. The following section provides a chronological review of a number of these research endeavors.

### Merit Systems Protection Board Surveys

One of the first efforts to examine sexual harassment on a large scale was the 1980 U.S. Merit Systems Protection Board survey of permanent, full-time federal employees (USM-SPB, 1981). This study was replicated by an almost identical survey administered in 1987 (USMSPB, 1988) to determine what changes had occurred in the federal workplace during the seven-year period.

Approximately 8,500 employees responded to the 1987 survey from across all federal agencies, including each branch of the military. Despite an apparent increase in sensitivity to the concept of sexual harassment, there was no change in the percentage of respondents who indicated that they had received unwanted and uninvited incidents of sexual

treatment. In both 1980 and 1987, 42% of all women reported that they had received some form of sexual harassment over the previous two-year period. The breakdown for the three primary military branches indicated that they were among the highest percentages reported in both surveys, as shown in Table 15-1.

The governmentwide average percentage of males in the survey who indicated they had been sexually harassed was 15% in 1980 and 14% in 1987, with a breakdown by military branch as shown in Table 15-2.

Using the 1987 database, Fain and Anderton (1987) examined the factors affecting the frequency of sexual harassment and suggested that women in lower-status positions due to race, age, or marital situation were more frequently harassed than those not in lower-status positions. Another study using the 1987 database (Niebuhr & Oswald, 1992a) reported that females were more likely to be sexually harassed if they were in male-dominated groups and/or were considered to be gender

**TABLE 15-1.** Prevalence Rate of Sexual Harassment of Women

| SERVICE BRANCH | PERCENTAGE AS VICTIMS | |
|---|---|---|
| | *1980* | *1987* |
| Navy | 44 | 47 |
| Air Force | 46 | 45 |
| Army | 41 | 44 |

*Source*: MSPB, 1988, p. 18.

**TABLE 15-2.** Prevalence Rate of Sexual Harassment of Men

| SERVICE BRANCH | PERCENTAGE AS VICTIMS | |
|---|---|---|
| | *1980* | *1987* |
| Navy | 12 | 16 |
| Air Force | 14 | 14 |
| Army | 16 | 11 |

*Source*: MSPB, 1988, p. 19.

pioneers in their jobs (i.e., one of the first females to be in a particular occupation or job category).

Both of these studies provide some evidence for the higher harassment rates experienced by females in military settings. Given the low female–male gender ratios in the service branches and the traditional male culture discussed earlier, it is not surprising that broad-based military surveys indicate a more severe problem with sexual harassment than would be indicated for the population as a whole.

## Department of Defense Survey

In response to a recommendation from the Task Force on Women in the Military, the Secretary of Defense mandated in 1988 that a survey be administered to examine the frequency of sexual harassment among the active-duty military and the effectiveness of existing programs to prevent, reduce, and eliminate sexual

harassment (Pryor, 1988). The survey of a 38,000-subject sample in 1988 and 1989 yielded a little over 20,000 usable responses, almost equally divided between males and females. The results of the survey (Martindale, 1990) reported on responses from the four Department of Defense branches (Air Force, Army, Marines, and Navy) as well as the Coast Guard.

In addition to providing responses on their experiences with being sexually harassed, the subjects also provided demographic information. Those respondents who had experienced sexual harassment in the year prior to the survey were asked questions regarding the circumstances surrounding the incident (e.g., type of harassment, description of perpetrator, working environment characteristics). Many of the survey items were similar to those developed for the Merit Systems Protection Board surveys. The following example items focus on the types of harassment received:

Have you received any of the following kinds of *UNINVITED AND UNWANTED* sexual attention *DURING THE LAST PAST MONTHS* from someone where you work in the active-duty military? (If you have served less than 1 year, answer for your entire service period.)

| *Type of Uninvited, Unwanted Sexual Attention* | *Never* | *Once* | *Once a Month or Less* | *2–4 Times a Month* | *Once a Week or More* |
|---|---|---|---|---|---|
| a. Actual or attempted rape or sexual assault | 1 | 2 | 3 | 4 | 5 |
| b. Pressure for sexual favors | 1 | 2 | 3 | 4 | 5 |
| c. Sexual touching, leaning over, cornering, pinching, or brushing against | 1 | 2 | 3 | 4 | 5 |
| d. Sexually suggestive looks, gestures, or body language | 1 | 2 | 3 | 4 | 5 |
| e. Letters, telephone calls, or materials of a sexual nature | 1 | 2 | 3 | 4 | 5 |
| f. Pressure for dates | 1 | 2 | 3 | 4 | 5 |
| g. Sexual teasing, jokes, remarks, or questions | 1 | 2 | 3 | 4 | 5 |
| h. Sexual whistles, calls, hoots, or yells | 1 | 2 | 3 | 4 | 5 |
| i. Attempts to get your participation in any other sexual activities | 1 | 2 | 3 | 4 | 5 |

In comparison with the MSPB results, the Department of Defense (DoD) survey found a greater degree of sexual harassment perceived among the active-duty military females than was reported in the two surveys of female federal government employees in the various military branches. The DoD survey result of 64% indicating at least one form of sexual harassment during the prior year was substantially higher than the 41–47% range found in either the 1980 or 1987 MSPB surveys.

A further analysis of the DoD survey data by Niebuhr (1994a) suggested that the organizational climate relative to sexual harassment, as suggested by the perceptual differences among males and females regarding leadership efforts to stop sexual harassment, might be a contributing factor to the degree of harassment perceived by females. The data in Table 15-3 indicate that the rank order of the service branches based on differing perceptions of males and females regarding this climate corresponds to the rank order based on the percentage of females reporting sexual harassment. The data might suggest that the greater the gender differential in perceptions of the sexual culture of an organization, the more likely it is that the organization will have greater problems with sexual harassment.

The average across the branches (62%) indicates more of a problem with sexual harassment in military settings versus nonmilitary settings (e.g., 42% as reported earlier in the federal employees surveys (MSPB, 1982, 1988). The findings are not completely unexpected given theoretical causal models of sexual harassment that suggest sexual harassment behaviors are due to a male's exercise of power over a female (Gutek, 1985; Tangri, Burt, & Johnson, 1982) or the degree of contact based on male–female ratios (Gutek, Cohen, & Konrad, 1990). Certainly, the "macho" culture discussed earlier and the male/female perceptual differences indicated here reinforce the power rationale for increased harassment activities. Additionally, the potential for more male contacts is simply a recognition that females in the military environment not only are often gender pioneers on their jobs, but also exist in mostly male-dominated work units.

Niebuhr and Oswald (1992b) found that the data from the DoD survey supported the contact hypothesis, in that a greater percentage of harassment occurred in large work units than in small ones for females in male-dominated work groups. It is interesting to note that the military service with the highest harassment percentage (71.7%) in the 1988 DoD survey has only about 4% females and during the survey period was using a recruiting slogan focusing on needing "a few good men." This combination of high "contact" and high male "power" orientation lends support to both the-

**TABLE 15-3.**  Relationships across the Service Branches

| | % OF RESPONDENTS INDICATING SENIOR LEADERSHIP MAKING REASONABLE EFFORT TO STOP SEXUAL HARASSMENT | | | % OF FEMALES REPORTING SEXUAL HARASSMENT[c] |
|---|---|---|---|---|
| | Males[a] | Females[b] | Difference | |
| Marines | 92.1 | 77.8 | 14.3 | 71.7 |
| Army | 91.6 | 81.8 | 9.8 | 62.6 |
| Navy | 94.5 | 85.8 | 8.7 | 60.5 |
| Coast Guard | 94.0 | 85.3 | 8.7 | 60.5 |
| Air Force | 91.5 | 86.0 | 5.5 | 52.6 |

[a]$n = 7,721$          [b]$n = 6,179$          [c]$n = 9,497$

oretical models and results in the most severe hostile environment for females among the military branches.

While the 1987 MSPB survey suggested that minority females are more likely than nonminority females to be sexually harassed in several areas (e.g., pressures for dates, gestures) (Fain & Anderton, 1987), the 1988 DoD survey found that race was not a factor if the total population mix is examined, as indicated in Table 15-4 (Martindale, 1990).

However, Niebuhr (1990) used a portion of the DoD database to examine the relationship between victim race and harasser race and found that black victims received a much greater proportion (30%) of their harassment from a different-race harasser than did white victims (17%). This relationship could simply reflect the fact, shown in Table 15-4, that there are proportionally more whites in the military, thus providing more sexual harassment contact opportunities (Gutek, Cohen, & Konrad, 1990) aimed at black victims from white harassers.

Martindale (1990) also reported that 17% of the male active-duty respondents indicated that they had experienced sexual harassment over the previous 12-month period. While this percentage is somewhat higher than found in the MSPB surveys (15% in 1980 and 14% in 1987), the differential is much less than discussed for the female population (64% versus 42%). In general, it appears that females, and not males, in military settings exist in much more hostile environments than do females in nonmilitary settings.

**TABLE 15-4.** Race of Victims Versus Active Force

| RACE | VICTIMS | ACTIVE DUTY |
|------|---------|-------------|
| White | 68% | 66% |
| Black | 27% | 29% |
| Other | 5% | 5% |

*Source:* Martindale, 1990.

In a follow-up examination of the data on the male respondents from the DoD study, Niebuhr (1994b) found that 30% of the male victims indicated that their harassment was perpetrated by other males (only 1% of the females indicated their harassment was from other females). It could be that fewer females in the military forces provides fewer "targets" for male perpetrators, thus resulting in more covert homosexual activity as often evidenced in male prison populations.

## Navy Surveys

Even before the Tailhook incident, sexual harassment had became a critical issue for the Navy (Carey, 1982). During the same period of time the Department of Defense was developing policies on sexual harassment and mechanisms to measure and control harassment behaviors, a Navy Women's Study Group found that more than half of 1,400 Navy women interviewed had been victims of some form of sexual harassment (Chief of Naval Operations, 1987). As a result of this study, the Navy Personnel Research and Development Center developed and administered the 1989 Navy Equal Opportunity/Sexual Harassment (NEOSH) Survey. The report on this survey (Culbertson et al., 1992) indicated that 5,619 surveys were returned (from a stratified random sample of more than 10,000 active-duty personnel), with 42% of enlisted women and 26% of female officers indicating that they had been sexually harassed at some time during the previous 12-month period. Very small percentages of male enlisted (4%) and male officers (1%) reported being sexually harassed during this period. The survey also included attitudinal items regarding gender and race/ethnic issues (e.g., "Navy women get lighter punishment than men who commit the same offenses"; "Many Navy women make sexual harassment claims that aren't true"). Also included were descriptive items on the types of sexual harassment occurring, the conditions under which the harassment happened, and the individual's response to the harassment incident (Culbertson et al., 1992).

In response to the survey results and continued publicity from specific sexual harassment cases (Donovan, 1990; Mitchell, 1990), the Secretary of the Navy (1989) restated the Navy policy of "zero-tolerance" for sexual harassment, formed another Navy Women's Study Group (Secretary of the Navy, 1990), and approved the administration of a second Navy-wide survey in the fall of 1991 on sexual harassment in the active-duty forces (Culbertson, Rosenfeld, & Newell, 1993). This second administration occurred during the period of time when public reports about the 1991 Tailhook Association Convention were beginning to surface.

The 1991 survey was almost identical to the 1989 survey except that additional items were added in some areas and an alternate version was developed to evaluate different methods of estimating rates of sexual harassment. The use of two versions was prompted by the hypothesis that the percentage of respondents indicating that they had been sexually harassed would vary with the methodology used to assess and calculate this percentage. As indicated earlier, the 1988 DoD indicated that 60.5% of females reported being sexually harassed over the prior one-year period. However, the data for the 1989 Navy survey (as summarized earlier) found only 42% of enlisted women and 26% of female officers indicated that they had been sexually harassed during the previous year. Culbertson and Rosenfeld (1994) hypothesized that the differences in findings was due to survey design differences. The 1988 DoD survey asked respondents about the rate of harassment experienced in any of nine categories (items were provided earlier in this chapter), and the sexual harassment rate was computed based on a positive response to any single or multiple occurrence(s) for any of these categories.

The 1989 Navy survey, however, calculated the sexual harassment percent from positive responses to either of two direct questions (During the past year, have you been sexually harassed while on duty? During the past year, have you been sexually harassed on base or ship while off duty?). Culbertson and Rosen-

feld (1994) suggested that the behavioral experiences approach (as used in the DoD survey) might result in inflated percentages since differences exist on the definition and measurement of sexual harassment (Culbertson & Rosenfeld, 1993; Fitzgerald, 1990; Gruber, 1990, 1992) and that some of the responses (e.g., a single occurrence of whistles or jokes) may not constitute a legally defined hostile work environment.

Additionally, recognizing that sexual harassment is an individual interpretation (Chapter 2; Terpstra & Baker, 1991), what one individual perceives as sexual harassment may not be perceived as sexual harassment by another. For example, Terpstra and Baker (1988) found that less than 50% of working females in one study agreed that whistles, repeated requests for dates, and sexual stares and looks were sexual harassment. In a recent study of almost 350 Navy enlisted personnel (Thomas, 1995) the subjects were given 16 short scenarios depicting a variety of sociosexual behaviors, ranging from mild behaviors to more severe situations (propositions, unwanted touching). As hypothesized, females were more likely to rate the behaviors as sexual harassment than were the males. Additionally, both males and females were more likely to rate the behaviors as interfering with work performance than they were to see the behaviors as sexual harassment. As is the situation among civilians discussed previously (Terpstra & Baker, 1988), many Navy personnel (both male and female) do not perceive that the milder forms of sexually inappropriate behavior are facets of sexual harassment. While they recognize that these behaviors damage the work environment, they are not aware that the Navy's definition of sexual harassment includes these behaviors.

While responding positively to behavioral items in a survey may indicate the behavior did occur, the individual may or may not have actually classified the behavior as sexual harassment. The result, in Culbertson and Rosenfeld's opinion, may be an assumption of precision in measurement that may in fact be illusory. A direct question asking respondents whether they have been sexually harassed leaves the interpretation of behavioral events up to the respondents rather than the researcher; this approach has been criticized for underestimating the degree of sexual harassment when the behaviors are not labeled as sexual harassment by the target (Barek, Fisher, & Houston, 1992; Fitzgerald et al., 1988).

The use of both methodologies for measuring sexual harassment in the 1991 Navy survey provided the comparative results shown in Table 15-5. As the data indicate, using the behavioral experiences methodology results in a much higher sexual harassment rate than the direct query method. These results may explain the differential results discussed earlier between the 1988 DoD survey and the 1989 Navy Survey and also suggest care in designing surveys and making comparisons across surveys (Culbertson & Rosenfeld, 1994).

In addition to evaluating this methodology problem, the Navy survey assessed the following areas (Culbertson, Rosenfeld, & Newell, 1993):

• Perceptions about sexual harassment
• The occurrence of sexual harassment
• Forms and frequency of sexual harassment behaviors
• Characteristics of victims and alleged perpetrators
• Actions and effects resulting from sexual harassment experiences

The findings of the 1991 survey were consistent with those of the 1989 survey regarding characteristics of victims and perpetrators and actions taken after the sexual harassment experience. Victims tended to more likely be junior women, work in mostly male environments, or be gender pioneers in their jobs. Race did not appear to be a factor in being a victim. Perpetrators were likely to be other individuals in the organizational environment (coworkers and supervisors). The most common actions in response to sexual harassment were to ignore the behavior, avoid the perpetrator, or tell the person to stop (Culbertson, Rosenfeld, & Newell, 1993).

## Defense Equal Opportunity Management Institute (DEOMI)

The Department of Defense has established a training and research institute at Patrick Air Force Base in Coco Beach, Florida to assist both active-duty and reserve units throughout the military branches in ensuring equal opportunity for all service personnel. In addition to providing training materials and instruction for individuals responsible for human resources development, the institute also has a research unit whose mission involves the examination of data that might suggest discriminatory activity.

With regard to the area of sexual harassment, the DEOMI research unit has made several analyses of the 1988 DoD Survey (Martindale, 1990) discussed earlier and provided input for a proposed new militarywide sexual harassment survey. In the early 1990s the research unit developed and refined a questionnaire to examine discriminatory environments within work units. Called the Military Equal Opportunity Climate Survey (MEOCS), the instrument measures perceived work environments with respect to racial/ethnic and gender relationships (Dansby & Landis, 1991; Landis, Dansby, & Faley, 1993). Using a structural-equation model of organizational commitment, the researchers have found linkages between gender discrimination/sexual harassing environments and respondents' commitment to a career in the military (Landis, Faley, & Dansby, 1992).

In a recent field study of more than 1,100 respondents from an active-duty military unit

**TABLE 15-5.** Sexual Harassment Rates (%)

|  | BEHAVIORAL ITEMS METHODOLOGY | DIRECT QUESTION METHODOLOGY |
| --- | --- | --- |
| Female enlisted | 74 | 44 |
| Female officers | 60 | 33 |
| Male enlisted | 21 | 8 |
| Male officers | 7 | 2 |

using a six-item gender discrimination scale from the MEOCS (e.g., one item states, "In meetings, usually the men are called upon to speak first"), researchers found a negative correlation between gender discrimination climate and both group cohesion ($r = -.23$; $p < .001$) and perceived group performance ($r = -.16$; $p < .001$) (Niebuhr, Krouse, & Dansby, 1994). While causation could not be determined from the data, it is apparent that the gender/sexual discriminating climates in military organizations are related to the cohesiveness and performance levels of work units.

The MEOCS instrument has been used in numerous survey administrations and currently a database of more than 290,000 respondents is available for research purposes (Dansby, 1995). An aggregation of the data at the work organization level (760 organizations) was used to examine the influence of the proportion of women in the organization (called the "sex ratio"). The result of this study was the finding that a relationship did not exist between the sex ratio and ratings of sexual harassment/discrimination climate by females (Tallarigo, 1994). As the percentage of women increased from less than 1% up to 50%, the female respondents' perception of a discriminatory climate did not substantially change ($r = .03$; $p = .421$). Although the percentage of females in the military has increased from 5.4% in 1976 to 11.7% in 1993 (DEOMI, 1994), the percentage of females in a work unit rarely exceeds 50% since there are presently no female-dominated career areas in the service branches. The sex ratio will range as low as 2–3% in combat occupations to 34% in medical and administrative fields (DMDC, 1993).

The sex-role spillover theory (Nieva & Gutek, 1981) and contact theory (Gutek, Cohen, & Konrad, 1990) would suggest that discrimination climates would improve as the ratio of females and males becomes more equal. A DEOMI reexamination of the 1988 DoD survey data (Niebuhr, 1994a) provides some support for this hypothesis. The study found that females' and males' perceptions of the degree of sexual harassment in the work environment were very different at low sex ratios but were essentially the same once the ratio was 50% or more.

It appears, from a female perspective, that the sexually harassing climate decreases as the percentage of females in the work unit increases (this is in contrast to the Tallarigo (1994) study reported earlier). The analysis of the DoD data also suggests that males may become more sensitive to the existence of sexual harassment as the percentage of females in the work unit increases. The shift in male perceptions and the convergence of male and female perceptions, interestingly, is similar to the finding of Tallarigo (1994) in the study of 760 military organizations. This convergence might suggest a more balanced "power" system (Gutek, 1985) operating in the sociosexual facet of the work climate.

In a recent DEOMI study using the 1988 DoD database, Faley (1993) suggested that the costs of sexual harassment in the military due to decreases in productivity and increases in absenteeism exceed $40 million annually. Including other cost factors, such as replacement costs due to turnover, increased use of medical/psychological service, and increased administrative costs, could raise this figure to the $200 million range. The analysis of the data focused on items that asked respondents questions dealing with the influence of sexual harassment on productivity, absenteeism, and sickness. The resulting costs were extrapolated to the entire military population and are provided in Table 15-6.

## THE MILITARY JUSTICE SYSTEM

While the discussion provided earlier focused on the definition of sexual harassment as determined through legislation and court decisions, it is important to recognize differences within the public and private enterprise environments. All employees within private enterprises and civilian employees within public enterprises have available to them both the EEOC claim process and civil law. In addition, civilian employees of the federal government have several other remedy processes

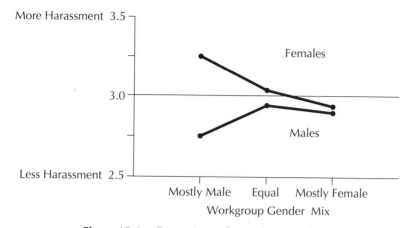

**Figure 15-1.** Perceptions of Sexual Harassment

**TABLE 15-6.** Costs of Sexual Harassment in the Military (by Grade and Harassed Sex)

| Dollar Value of Perceived Productivity Losses | MALE | FEMALE | TOTAL |
|---|---|---|---|
| Enlisted | $29,357,322 | $8,099,368 | $37,456,690 |
| Officers | $1,037,810 | $2,351,398 | $3,389,206 |
| TOTAL | $30,395,132 | $10,451,066 | $40,845,896 |
| Dollar Value of Sick Leave/Absences | | | |
| Enlisted | $276,080 | $1,523,458 | $1,799,628 |
| Officers | — | $102,203 | $102,203 |
| TOTAL | $276,080 | $1,625,751 | $1,901,831 |
| GRAND TOTAL | $30,671,212 | $12,076,817 | $42,748,029 |

available to resolve their work-related complaints of sexual harassment. However, they often do not use the formal remedies available and are unaware that some of these even exist (e.g., requesting an investigation by an outside agency such as the Merit Systems Protection Board [MSPB, 1981, 1988]). It is interesting to note that a civilian employee in a military organization may elect to file a sexual harassment complaint through the EEOC and then, if the EEOC claim is upheld, may choose to use the Uniform Code of Military Justice (UCMJ) remedies for action against a military supervisor (Howard, 1991).

Military personnel who have experienced sexual harassment would proceed internally through the claim process and actionable cases would be evaluated under the Uniform Code of Military Justice (UCMJ). While the definition of sexual harassment from EEOC legislation and federal court cases may not correspond exactly to the descriptions of sexual harassment behaviors provided within each branch of service, the root definition for the military, as indicated earlier, does rely on the EEOC definition. Each branch of the service has developed a policy and grievance procedure to handle cases of sexual harassment, a policy that often extends responsibility to nonwork situations (e.g., AR 600–20, 1988, provides the Army's policy on sexual harassment). Aspects of the UCMJ that can be used in the adjudication of sexual harassment claims include the following:

Articles 89, 91: Disrespect
Article 92:       Dereliction of Duty
Article 93:       Cruelty and Maltreatment
Article 117:      Provoking Speech or
                  Gestures
Article 120:      Rape
Article 127:      Extortion
Article 128:      Assault
Article 133:      Conduct Unbecoming
                  an Officer
Article 134:      The General Article—Con-
                  duct Prejudicial to Good
                  Order and Discipline...
                  Discredit the Armed Forces
Article 77:       Principals: May Apply to
                  Someone Who Observes Mis-
                  conduct But Neither Stops It
                  Personally Nor Reports It to a
                  Higher Authority

It should also be mentioned that sexual harassment cases dealing with rape, attempted rape, and sexual assault are a violation of criminal law and as such may be actionable through the criminal court system. For military personnel, whether the criminal court system is used will depend upon the victim's classification and the setting of the incident.

The military system for responding to sexual harassment claims has been criticized in a study by the National Women's Law Center (Reske, 1993). The study found the adjudication process was inadequate to address sexual harassment complaints and was a "patchwork" of ineffective procedures and policies. Following the Tailhook incident, Undersecretary of the Navy Dan Howard proposed to Defense Secretary Dick Cheney that debate be initiated to consider a specific article in the UCMJ that would deal specifically with sexual harassment (Greenlaw & Port, 1993). Because these are no standards specifically focusing on sexual harassment, the effectiveness of the organization in responding is very dependent on the discretion of the individual charged with investigating and resolving complaints. Since sexually harassed military personnel cannot sue for damages, victims are at the mercy of the local command structure to investigate and resolve issues of discrimination and harassment.

The study by Reske (1993) also found that victims may fear reprisals for reporting harassment, are likely to be regarded as troublemakers, and have limited rights to remedies even if their accusations are upheld. A DoD study by the Discrimination and Sexual Harassment Task Force (Dansby, 1995) examined a number of issues related to remedies (reporting, retribution, complaint systems, etc.).

## SUMMARY

Some aspects of the military work environment appear to lag behind the changes that have already occurred in the civilian sector of society. Principally, the inclusion of more females in the work force and the systematic development of EEO legislation and court decisions specifically focusing on sexual harassment are two areas in which additional focus is deemed necessary by the military hierarchy. Downsizing pressures on the military may slow the attrition rate of females into the service force, particularly at the officer level (Dansby, 1994).

In the light of the Tailhook incident the Navy proposed that the UCMJ be amended to deal specifically with sexual harassment. The Department of Defense has not perceived that this change is warranted at this time.

The survey work done by various military study groups or research units is a positive facet of the effort to deal with discriminatory and harassing environments. Careful effort has been expended at DEOMI to produce measures that can accurately reflect situations in which discriminatory and harassing practices are occurring. Since 1992 the measurement of sexual discrimination and harassment using the MEOCS instrument indicates that the military culture for females is improving (Dansby, 1994). Not in place, however, is a mechanism for taking these cultural findings and ensuring that remedies are provided to remove undesirable work climates. While policies, procedures, and training programs do create an aura of military concern about sexual harassment, a systematic proactive remedy system (based on perceived climates) and an uniformally applied judicial system for harassment are the missing pieces needed to provide more focus on the causes and solutions to sexual harassment in the military.

# REFERENCES

AR 600–20 (1988). *Army Command Policy (AR 600–20)*. Washington, DC: Government Printing Office.

Barek, A., Fisher, W. A., & Houston, S. (1992). Individual difference correlates of the experience of sexual harassment among female university students. *Journal of Applied Social Psychology, 22*, 17–37.

Baxter, R. H. (1985). *Sexual harassment in the workplace*. New York: Executive Enterprises.

Carey, S. H. (1982). *Sourcebook on sexual harassment*. Washington, DC: Department of the Navy.

Chief of Naval Operations (1987). *Navy study group's report on progress of women in the Navy*. Washington, DC: Department of the Navy.

Culbertson, A. L., & Rosenfeld, P. (1993). Understanding sexual harassment through organizational surveys. In P. Rosenfeld, J. Edwards, & M. D. Thomas (Eds.), *Improving organizational surveys* (pp. 164–187). Newbury Park, CA: Sage.

Culbertson, A. L., & Rosenfeld, P. (1994). Assessment of sexual harassment in the active-duty Navy. *Military Psychology, 6*(2), 69–93.

Culbertson, A. L., Rosenfeld, P., Booth-Kewley, S., & Magnusson, P. (1992). *Assessment of sexual harassment in the Navy: Results of the 1989 Navy-wide survey* (Report No. NPRDC TR 92–11). San Diego, CA: Navy Personnel Research and Development Center.

Culbertson, A. L., Rosenfeld, P., & Newell, C. (1993). *Assessment of sexual harassment in the active-duty Navy: Results of the 1991 Navy-wide survey* (Report No. NPRDC TR 94–2). San Diego, CA: Navy Personnel Research and Development Center.

Danovan, E. P. (1990, Nov. 5). Harassment found to be serious in Orlando. *Navy Times*, pp. 6–7.

Dansby, M. R. (1994, December). The military equal opportunity climate survey. Paper presented at the World-Wide Military Equal Opportunity Conference, Coco Beach, FL.

Dansby, M. R. (1995). Personal communication.

Dansby, M. R., & Landis, D. (1991). Measuring equal opportunity climate in the military environment. *International Journal of Intercultural Relations, 15*(4), 389–405.

DEOMI (1994). *Representation of minorities and women in the Armed Forces (1976–1993)*. Patrick Air Force Base, Coco Beach, FL.

DMDC (1993). *Semi-annual race/ethnic/gender profile of the Department of Defense*. DEOMI, Patrick Air Force Base, Coco Beach, FL.

Eisaguirre, L. (1993). *Sexual harassment*. Santa Barbara, CA: ABC-CLIO.

Equal Employment Opportunity Commission (EEOC) (1980). Guidelines and discrimination because of sex. (Sec. 1604.ii). *Federal Register, 45*, 74676–74677.

Fain, T. C., & Anderton, D. L. (1987). Sexual harassment: Organizational context and diffuse status. *Sex Roles, 5/6*, 291–311.

Faley, R. H. (1993). *Preliminary partial estimates of the annual dollar-value of overall lost productivity due to sexual harassment in the active-duty military*. DEOMI, Patrick Air Force, Coco Beach, FL.

Fitzgerald, L. F. (1990). Sexual harassment: The definition and measurement of a construct. In M. A. Paludi (Ed.), *Ivory power: Sexual harassment on campus* (pp. 21–44). Albany, NY: SUNY Press.

Fitzgerald, L. F., & Hessan-McInnis, M. (1989). The dimensions of sexual harassment: A structural analysis. *Journal of Vocational Behavior, 35*, 309–326.

Fitzgerald, L. F., Shullman, S. L., Bailey, N., Richards, M., Swecker, J., Gold, Y., Ormerod, A. J., & Weitzman, L. (1988). The incidence and dimensions of sexual harassment in academia and the workplace. *Journal of Vocational Behavior, 32*, 152–175.

Gilroy, J. E., Good, J., Seymour, H., Harper, G., Edwards, C., Fabry, K., & Ruth, D. (1990). *Report to the superintendent on the assimilation of women in the brigade of midshipmen*. Annapolis, MD: U.S. Naval Academy.

Greenbaum, M. L., & Fraser, B. (1981). Sexual harassment in the workplace. *The Arbitration Journal, 36*, 30–41.

Greenlaw, P. S., & Port, W. H. (1993). Military versus civilian judicial handling of sexual harassment cases. *Labor Law Journal, 44*, 368–374.

Gruber, J. E. (1990). A typology of personal and environmental sexual harassment: Research and policy implications for the 1990's. *Sex Roles, 26*, 447–464.

Gruber, J. E. (1992). Methodological problems and policy implications in sexual harassment research. *Population Research and Policy Review, 9*, 235–254.

Gutek, B. A. (1985). *Sex and the workplace: The impact of sexual behavior and harassment on women, men, and organizations*. San Francisco: Jossey-Bass.

Gutek, B. A., Cohen, A. G., & Konrad, A. M. (1990). Predicting social-sexual behavior at work: A contact hypothesis. *Academy of Management Journal, 33*, 560–577.

Howard, S. (1991). Organizational resources for addressing sexual harassment. *Journal of Counseling and Development, 69*, 507–511.

Korb, L. J. (1981). MEMORANDUM Subj: Department of Defense policy on sexual harassment. Washington, DC: Department of Defense.

Landis, D., Dansby, M. R., & Faley, R. H. (1993). The military equal opportunity climate survey: An example of surveying in organizations. In P. Rosenfeld, J. E. Edwards, & M. D. Thomas (Eds.), *Improving organizational surveys* (pp. 210–239). Newbury Park, CA: Sage.

Landis, D., Faley, R. H., & Dansby, M. R. (1992). *The effect of equal opportunity climate on commitment to a military career: An analysis using latent variables.* DEOMI, Patrick Air Force Base, Coco Beach, FL.

Martindale, M. (1990). *Sexual harassment in the military: 1988.* Washington, DC: Defense Manpower Data Center.

Mitchell, B. (1990, May 28). Incidents at Naval Academy spark investigations. *Navy Times*, pp. 10, 19.

Morgenson, G. (1989). Watch that leer, stifle that joke. *Forbes, 5*, 69–72.

Niebuhr, R. E. (1990). *An empirical analysis of the relationships and situations surrounding sexual harassment incidents.* DEOMI, Patrick Air Force Base, Coco Beach, FL.

Niebuhr, R. E. (1994a). *The relationship between organizational characteristics and sexual harassment.* DEOMI, Patrick Air Force Base, Coco Beach, FL.

Niebuhr, R. E. (1994b). An empirical examination of sexual harassment differences across the service branches. Paper presented at the Applied Behavioral Sciences Symposium, Colorado Springs, CO.

Niebuhr, R. E., Krouse, S. B., & Dansby, M. R. (1994). *Workgroup climates for acceptance of diversity: Relationship to group cohesiveness and performance.* DEOMI, Patrick Air Force Base, Coco Beach, FL.

Niebuhr, R. E., & Oswald, S. L. (1992a). The impact of workgroup composition and other work unit/victim characteristics on perceptions of sexual harassment. *Applied H.R.M. Research, 3*(1), 30–47.

Niebuhr, R. E., & Oswald, S. L. (1992b). The influence of workgroup composition on sexual harassment among military personnel. Paper presented at the Psychology in the Department of Defense Symposium, Colorado Springs, CO.

Nieva, V., & Gutek, B. A. (1981). *Women and work: A psychological perspective.* New York: Praeger.

Pryor, J. B. (1988). *Sexual harassment in the United States Military: The development of the DoD survey.* DEOMI, Patrick Air Force Base, Coco Beach, FL.

Reske, H. J. (1993). How the military investigates itself. *ABA Journal* (February), 39.

Secretary of the Navy (1989). *SECNAV INSTRUCTION 5300.26A: Department of Navy policy on sexual harassment.* Washington, DC: Department of the Navy.

Secretary of the Navy (1990). MEMORANDUM subj: Women's progress in the Navy—1990 update. Washington, DC: Department of the Navy.

Tallarigo, R. S. (1994). Perceptions of equal opportunity/treatment: How related to organizational sex ratios? Paper presented at the Sixth Annual Convention of the American Psychological Society, Washington, DC.

Tangri, S. S., Burt, M. R., & Johnson, L. B. (1982). Sexual harassment at work: Three explanatory models. *Journal of Social Issues, 38*, 33–54.

Terpstra, D. E., & Baker, D. D. (1988). Outcomes of sexual harassment charges. *Academy of Management Journal, 31*, 185–194.

Terpstra, D. E., & Baker, D. D. (1991). Sexual harassment at work: The psychosocial issues. In M. J. Davidson & J. Earnshaw (Eds.), *Vulnerable workers: Psychosocial and legal issues* (pp. 179–201). New York: Wiley.

Thomas, M. D. (1995). *Gender differences in conceptualizing sexual harassment* (Report No. NPRDC-TR–95–5). San Diego, CA: Navy Personnel Research and Development Center.

Till, F. J. (1980). *Sexual harassment: A report on the sexual harassment of students.* Report of the National Advisory Council on Women's Educational Programs, U.S. Department of Education.

U.S. Merit Systems Protection Board (USMSPB) (1981). *Sexual harassment in the federal workplace: Is it a problem?* Washington, DC: Government Printing Office.

U.S. Merit Systems Protection Board (USMSPB) (1988). *Sexual harassment in the federal government: An update.* Washington, DC: Government Printing Office.

*Williams v. Saxbe* (1976). 413 F. Supp. 654.

Woerner, W. L., & Oswald, S. L. (1990). Sexual harassment in the work place: A view through the eyes of the court. *Labor Law Journal, 41*, 786–793.

# CHAPTER 16

# CROSS-CULTURAL PERSPECTIVES ON SEXUAL HARASSMENT

## Azy Barak[1]

Cross-cultural comparisons of human behaviors are popular across a wide range of social disciplines. Beyond their obvious scientific importance, researchers find it curious, attractive, and intriguing to study and compare different cultures, in what probably reflects their own natural human curiosity. But cross-cultural comparisons are serious matters and require clear conceptualizations, special research designs, and methodological considerations, as well as coping with complex measurement issues (Berry et al., 1992; Brislin, 1993; Smith & Bond, 1993; Triandis, 1994). These considerations make cross-cultural research much more complicated than mere comparisons of data among countries or societies. Unfortunately, unsophisticated and raw comparisons among nations are typical in many social scientific publications. The reader is thus advised to practice much caution in interpreting the findings reported in

this chapter as far as having significance in terms of true cultural differences. However, the findings may offer a possibility to review and form initial impressions on sexual harassment as a social phenomenon across a number of countries and societies.

The term "cross-culture" has several connotations, at least as it is related to sexual harassment. First, it refers to similarities and differences of the sexual harassment phenomenon among different cultures, with "cultures" in most cases used as synonymous with *countries*. Second, it refers to *ethnic or racial aspects* related to sexual harassment. Third, it is associated with the *psychological meaning of culture*, that is, the social environment and climate of a given group of individuals. This chapter, although attempting to expand the cross-cultural understanding of sexual harassment, refers primarily to the first two aspects. Notwithstanding the importance of the psychological aspect, it is being left to be reviewed in other chapters of this volume. The meaning of the concept of culture is not expanded here over its normal and typical scientific use in studying international and interracial differences. Thus, the focus here is essentially on the differences among groups that share common social norms, standards, customs, values, symbols, education, and the like, *as being operationally delineated by their clear nationality or ethnicity.*

The term "sexual harassment" itself, as discussed in other chapters of this volume, is not used uniformly. Different researchers and writers have defined it differently and subsequently have used different operational definitions (i.e., measures) to collect data on the phenomenon. This obviously adds extra burden in comparing among research reports and necessitates taking extra precautions when interpreting findings and drawing conclusions. Moreover, since what is labeled by one researcher as sexual harassment can be labeled as sexual victimization, sexual aggression, or sexual assault (to mention just a few examples) by others, the current review has approached the topic very comprehensively. That is, although the term "sexual harassment" was searched for, in a number of instances the report does not limit the scope to only these studies that used the term "sexual harassment" but refers to related terms as well.

As with most cross-cultural assignments, collecting information for this review was arduous, due to the need to collect information from numerous countries, agencies, and individuals worldwide, on top of the obvious lingual difficulty. In order to collect the information, several databases were surveyed (including ABI/Inform, PsycLit, SocioFiles, MEDLINE, ERIC, and Cross-Cultural), and some 100 researchers and relevant agencies all over the world were contacted. In addition, the special volume of *Conditions of Work Digest* (vol. 11, no. 2) published by the International Labour Office (ILO) on the topic of sexual harassment in the workplace in various countries was a major source of information. This chapter thus reviews a broad and updated international scope of sexual harassment literature. However, in spite of the comprehensiveness of the review, it is by no means conclusive, because of several reasons: (1) The scientific study of sexual harassment is relatively new and has not been equally developed in all countries. Hence, the review is biased in the way that countries where science and research are developed are highly represented in comparison to other countries. This by no means has any implication on the existence, perceptions, or treatment of sexual harassment in the unrepresented countries. (2) In spite of the serious attempts, contacts have not been established with numerous countries and researchers. Reports on any aspect of sexual harassment or related subjects from only a limited number of countries are included here. (3) Because of the sensitivity of the subject of sexual harassment itself, research might be kept confidential by governments, organizations, and researchers. The current review refers only to knowledge made public in scientific journals, books, official reports, conference presentations, published technical abstracts, and so on, or where personal contacts have been successful. (4) Language and communication difficulties prevented access to more data resources. It is thus suggested to take the current review as allowing only a partial, possibly biased picture of the global view of the sexual harassment phenomenon.

The scope of this chapter, although aimed at a broad and comprehensive interdisciplinary review, is social scientific in nature. This means that most of the emphasis has been given to the understanding of sexual harassment behavior, its antecedents and consequences, and its possible change. Other issues, such as legal questions and legislature in general (except their relevance in prevention), as well as economic issues or other relevant aspects, are only briefly reviewed. In addition, while sexual harassment is a problem for both women and men and for many specific groups (e.g., homosexuals), this review refers only to the general harassment of women by men, which is the most frequent form of sexual harassment.

The information surveyed is reported here in four different categories by which the concept of sexual harassment could be classified to make practical sense. These categories are prevalence, ethnic perspectives, perceptions, and prevention. Following this review is a brief conceptual/methodological analysis, and some conclusions are subsequently offered.

## PREVALENCE OF SEXUAL HARASSMENT

In referring to actual prevalence of any behavior or social phenomenon, one should be very cautious in formulating the questions and obtaining the answers, especially in regard to some specific factors such as counting individual experiences versus social happenings, and the time period in question. As noted by Allison and Wrightsman (1993) concerning the statistics of rape and by Fitzgerald and Shullman (1993) concerning the parameters of sexual harassment, a clear distinction should be made between *prevalence* and *incidence rates*. While the former relates to frequency of appearance of a social phenomenon over a long period of time (or even without time limits at all) and to aggregated people's experiences, the latter refers to frequency of occurrences in terms of individual, personal experiences in a limited period of time. This methodological difference—and apparently not other, essential differences—may account for different rape as well as sexual harassment statistics. The studies reviewed here used different survey methods, different instructions given to respondents, and different time frames of the sexual harassment in question. In addition, unfortunately, these details in most cases were not made clear in the research reports as published. The statistical figures that follow should thus be addressed and interpreted with maximum caution to avoid erroneous conclusions.

The question of methodological flaws and complications is typical to this area of scientific research. For example, one of the most interesting observations concerning the relationship between culture and sexual abusive behavior was conducted by Sanday (1981), who collected extensive anthropological data on 95 (past and current) societies and classified them into three ordinal categories by the frequency rate of rape in each. In a second stage she examined the association between this "rape proneness" scale and 16 societal variables, which represented cultural norms, standards, and behaviors characterizing each society. These variables were rated by "expert judges" according to summarized descriptions elicited from historical, anthropological, and sociological literature. The societal descriptive variables included those related to sexual repression (e.g., attitude toward premarital sex), intergroup and interpersonal violence (e.g., ideology of male toughness), child rearing (e.g., proximity of father in care of infants), and ideology of male dominance (e.g., female political decision making). Correlations[2] computed between the ordinal category of rape proneness and each of the descriptive variables revealed mixed results: Some of the variables, especially in the intergroup and interpersonal violence category, showed significant correlations with rape rate (e.g., the higher the degree of interpersonal violence in society the higher rate of rape), while others had no significant relationships. However, if we take into account the fact that rape is considered to be a violent act in itself, thus confounding at least some of the descriptive variables, a possible contamination of these analyses makes it difficult to draw clear-cut conclusions. Sanday (1981, 1982), however, actually drew definitive conclusions from the study, such as "The correlates…strongly suggest that rape is the playing out of a socio-cultural script in which the expression of personhood for males is directed by, among other things, interpersonal violence and an ideology of toughness" (Sanday, 1981, p. 24), and "Sexual violence is one of the ways in which men remind themselves that they are superior. As such, rape is part of a broader struggle for control in the face of difficult circumstances. Where men are in harmony with their environment, rape is usually absent" (Sanday, 1981, p. 25). Sanday (1982) went on to make implications such as "The insights we can garner from the cross-cultural study of rape in tribal societies bear on the treatment of rape in our own. Ours is a heterogeneous society in which more men than we like to think feel that they do not have mastery over their destiny. They learn from the script provided by nightly television that violence is a way of achieving the material rewards that all Americans expect" (p. 542). It is interesting to note that on a related issue—violence against women in general and domestically within the family in particular—Levinson (1989) reported that these types of crimes prevail in most of the 90 societies he had studied. Wife beating was found as one type of female abuse that was similarly shared by 84% of the cultures. This finding seems to contradict Sanday's (1981) conclusion on the specific culture values–women abuse connection.

The research findings on prevalence of sexual harassment as collected and presented here were aimed at identifying some pattern related to culture, as long as culture could be defined along lines of nationality. However, as previously emphasized, since the methodological problems undermine valid conclusions, it is highly recommended to consider the following only as a general, descriptive, preliminary review.

## Prevalence of Sexual Harassment of Female University Students

Fitzgerald et al. (1988) developed the Sexual Experiences Questionnaire (SEQ), an instrument intended to measure respondents' personal incidents of sexual harassment. The SEQ consisted of a list of behaviorally based items, representing Till's (1980) typology of five sexual harassment severity levels (i.e., gender harassment, seductive behavior, sexual bribery, sexual coercion, and sexual assault). Respondents were anonymously asked to say for each item whether they had never experienced it, had experienced it once, or had experienced it more than once. It was possible to analyze the responses to the SEQ by items, total scores within each level of severity, and a total SEQ score.[3] Fitzgerald et al. (1988) administered the SEQ to large samples of uni-

versity (female and male)[4] students in two institutions in the United States. They found that various forms of sexual harassment prevailed in all samples, while the prevalence rates were significantly different along the severity level. Across samples, gender harassment was experienced[5] at least once in the range from some 20% who reported seductive remarks made by professors to a high of approximately 50% who experienced "differential" treatment by instructors due to gender. On the average, across items and samples, about 31% of female students experienced some kind of gender harassment at least once. Seductive behavior, across samples, was experienced at least once in the range from about 8% who encountered propositions from professors to some 20% who encountered unwelcome seductive behaviors. Across items and samples an average of approximately 14% of female students experienced some form of seductive behavior at least once. Sexual bribery, across items and samples, was experienced by approximately 2% of students at least once; *sexual coercion* was similarly experienced by some 2%. Sexual imposition and assault, across items and samples, was experienced by 4.5% of students at least once. In addition, a special item specifically and explicitly asked if respondents had been "sexually harassed" by professors or instructors. Students who answered positively ranged from 3.80% (undergraduate students in University 1) to 15.85% (graduate students in University 2), making a grand mean of 6.8%. In an additional U.S. study, Brooks and Perot (1991) administered the SEQ to a sample of 276 graduate students. Their findings revealed somewhat lower rates of sexual harassment than those reported by Fitzgerald et al. (1988). On the average, across items in the five categories, they found that 23.6%, 6.8%, 1.0%, 0.35%, and 0.9%, respectively, had experienced that behavior. Brooks and Perot (1991), however, also reported the percentage of students who experienced at least one item in each sexual harassment category (this information was not reported by Fitzgerald et al., 1988). They found that 62.7% reported they had experienced at least one item in the gender harassment level, 20.7% reported they had experienced at least one of the seduction level items, 3.6% had experienced at least one sexual bribery item, 1.1% experienced at least one threat item, and 5.1% experienced at least one sexual imposition and assault item.

The data on the prevalence of sexual harassment in U.S. universities as presented here was compared to an equivalent sample of Brazilian students by Fitzgerald and Gelfand (1994). In order to make this comparison, a random sample of 25% ($n = 434$) was drawn from the four samples used by Fitzgerald et al. (1988). This sample was compared with data collected from female students ($n = 389$) sampled from four universities in Brazil who responded to a Portuguese version of the SEQ. It should be noted that no special procedures were taken to control for equivalence of the two samples in terms of race, socio-economic status, and so on. This comparison revealed mixed results: On the one hand, American and Brazilian female students reported being exposed to a similar degree of gender harassment (32.3% vs. 34.2%, respectively, of mean response to items in this category), and of sexual coercion (3.0% vs. 2.4%, respectively). On the other hand, Brazilians reported higher mean rates of unwanted sexual attention than Americans (21.0% vs. 11.8%, respectively, of mean item responses in this category). The overall experiences of Brazilians were, however, more extensive: 77.8% of Brazilians experienced at least one item in the gender harassment category (68.0% Americans), 72.7% Brazilians experienced at least one unwanted sexual attention item (38.7% Americans), and 7.1% reported encountering at least one sexual coercion item (6.7% Americans). Overall, 89.3% Brazilians experienced *any* SEQ item, in comparison to 72.8% of Americans. Since this latter comparison (by single SEQ items) is probably less reliable (because it relies on item, not scale, responses), it seems that it is safe to say that the major difference in the two samples was found in the unwanted sexual attention category, and not in the other two. In addition, the respondents were asked to subjectively rate their experiences ("Have you been sexually harassed?"). While 6.1% of Bra-

zilians responded affirmatively to this question, 4.4% of Americans did. This difference was not found to bear statistical significance ($\chi^2 = 0.75$; $df = 1$; *ns*).

Barak, Fisher, and Houston (1992) studied sexual harassment of female students in a large-size Canadian university. The purpose of their study was to examine some individual differences that might correlate with sexual harassment experiences, but by using the SEQ they were able to survey the incidence rate of sexual harassment of female students.[6] Results showed lower rates of sexual harassment of the Canadian students than those reported by Fitzgerald et al. (1988) in the United States. Approximately 60% of the Canadian students responded positively to at least one of the SEQ items (in comparison to some 73% of American students). The same trend was found for all sexual harassment categories, as some 10–15% fewer Canadian students reported experiencing sexual harassment by university professors. However, when comparing *subjective* perceptions (i.e., "have you been sexually harassed by...") of experiences of sexual harassment, 4.3% of Canadians (vs. 4.4% of Americans) reported they have been sexually harassed. This complexity of the findings (that is, Americans reported higher rates of being in behaviorally defined sexual harassment situations than Canadians, while subjectively they reported almost identical rates) might be interpreted in light of different sampling procedures. While Fitzgerald et al. (1988) used large graduate and undergraduate samples from two universities, Barak, Fisher, and Houston (1992) used an undergraduate and relatively small sample ($n = 161$) of female students who took a human sexuality course. In light of Fitzgerald et al.'s (1988) and Brooks and Perot's (1991) findings of generally higher rates of sexual harassment among graduate students, the limited sample of Barak, Fisher, and Houston (1992) may have produced the differences, and not the actual differences between the two countries.

The SEQ was translated to Hebrew and anonymously administered to students in two independent surveys in a large Israeli university. In the first study (Avni, 1989), data were collected on 169 randomly selected female students who studied in four departments. In the second study (Goldstein & Yariv, 1991), data were collected from a larger random sample ($n = 789$) of female students representing all 10 faculties. Since there were some differences between the two samples, their collapsed parameters were compared with the SEQ findings mentioned above. The overall picture showed that the prevalence of sexual harassment was very similar to that reported in the United States, although some differences were noticed. On the average, gender harassment was reported by some 25%, and approximately 70% of the respondents indicated experiencing at least one incident of any form of sexual harassment. Although these figures are high, they are somewhat lower than those of the American and the Brazilian samples, and resemble more those of the Canadian sample. In the unwanted sexual attention category, some 32% responded affirmatively to at least one item (with an average of approximately 28% for this category, across items), a figure close to the American and Canadian samples, but substantially lower than the Brazilian one. The sexual coercion harassment type was encountered by an average of some 2.3% of the respondents, a figure close to the American and Brazilian samples.

Overall, in comparing the diverse findings of the four national samples, it seems that sexual harassment of university female students prevails in all these countries, but the *forms* of harassment might be slightly different. The general picture, that similar percentages of students have encountered any one specific kind of sexual harassment in the four countries, tells us that it is not the phenomenon of sexual harassment on campus that is different among the countries, but rather *the way it is being behaviorally manifested*, which is probably due to different behavioral standards related to different cultures. Another interesting comparison shows that 6.1% of Brazilian, 4.4% of American, 4.3% of Canadian, and 4% of Israeli female students, who were all administered equivalent forms of the SEQ, reported "they have been sexually harassed" at least once. That is, also in their subjective interpretations of sexual harassment and labeling of intergender episodes the general figures are relatively close to each other.

Some additional studies on the prevalence of sexual harassment among university students, though limited in sample size, materials, or comparative capacity, were conducted in several countries. For instance, Mazer and Percival (1989b), surveyed sexual harassment in a small Canadian university. They found the incidence of sexual harassment to be *higher* than previously undertaken research in the United States using similar questionnaires. However, as these researchers themselves acknowledged, several other characteristics (e.g., nature of sample) of the study other than nation could be responsible for these differences. In fact, in another survey on sexual harassment of Canadian female university students in another university, McDaniel and van Roosmalen (1992) reported prevalence findings that were very similar to those found in research in the United States. In Finland, Uhari et al. (1994) surveyed sexual harassment (among other forms of mistreatments) of local medical students and compared their findings to those revealed in an equivalent sample of American students. They found that although the Finnish students were less sexually harassed than their American counterparts, sexual harassment was still excessive. However, most incidents involved episodes of a sex discrimination nature (e.g., 12% of students felt they were denied opportunities because of their sex) and less of a sexual nature (e.g., 7% experienced unwanted sexual advances). Saroja (1990), in presenting 12 case studies of female university students in India, together with some more general observations, concluded that sexual harassment presented a major social problem.

## Prevalence of Sexual Harassment of Female Workers

While it is possible to compare sexual harassment incidents of female university students among countries, as in the preceding section, a sound and valid comparison of sexual harassment of women in the workplace is basically impossible. Although surveys of harassment in the workplace have been conducted in numerous countries, the use of different definitions of sexual harassment, different techniques of data collection, different questionnaires where used, different samples and sampling procedures, different questionnaire administration procedures, and different statistical procedures make the comparison of findings almost useless. In addition to these methodological considerations, two other essential factors add to the complexity of the comparisons, that is, the meaning and connotations of words (especially those related to sexual and intergender behaviors) in different languages and cultures and the social tolerance toward and acceptance of social surveys in various societies and cultures. These methodological hurdles almost make fruitless the mission of trying to compare the findings of sexual harassment surveys carried out in different countries. The findings reviewed here should thus be used and interpreted within these limitations.

## Australia

The Human Rights and Equal Opportunity Commission (HREOC) (1993) outlined many aspects of sexual harassment in the Commonwealth of Australia. While research on prevalence of sexual harassment was not reported, it was noted that hundreds of formal complaints and legal charges per year were filed, as well as thousands of inquiries. The Sex Discrimination Commissioner stated in this publication her conviction that "all women" were sexually harassed at work at some time. HREOC (1994) mentioned 360 complaints in 1993 handled at the federal level and many more at the state level. In a survey conducted in Perth, Western Australia, Savery and Gledhill (1988) and Savery and Halsted (1989) found that 80% of female workers reported they had been sexually harassed by coworkers, and 67% by superiors. Also workers' associations (e.g., Queensland Women's Sub-Committee, 1980) admitted that sexual harassment is widespread in the workplace. Holgate (1989), in a rather small sample of 21 women, found that more than 60% of them were exposed to various forms of sexual harassment.

## Austria

The International Labour Office (ILO, 1992) reported on a study carried out in 1986 in which 30.5% of more than 1,400 women sampled reported serious incidents of sexual harassment at work. The most frequent harassing behavior was being pinched or fondled (experienced by 18% of the participants) and being touched on the breasts (17%). Seven percent experienced attempts of sexual bribery, while more than 2% were targets of sexual blackmail.

## Belgium

Garcia (1992) reported on a survey of sexual harassment that found that 34% of women experienced any form of sexual harassment (compared to 12% of men). Most victims were single, and most harassers were work colleagues. Wijns (1991), apparently referring to the same data pool, reported that 33% of women had experienced some form of sexual harassment on the job. Of those sexually harassed, 51% had experienced ogling and leering, 42% insinuating comments, 19% sexual propositions, and 5% sexual violence.

## Canada

A survey conducted in British Columbia (Women's Rights Committee and the Vancouver's Women's Research Centre, 1980) revealed that 90% of women respondents reported some form of sexual harassment in the workplace. A national survey (Canadian Human Rights Commission, 1983) found that 49% of women had received unwanted sexual attention in the workplace. It should be mentioned that studies conducted on sexual assault in general in Canada (e.g., Brickman & Briere, 1984; Kinnon, 1981) have found similar general rates of rape and other sexual abusive behaviors to those in the United States. Similarly, a Canadian survey on children's sexual abuse (Badgley, 1984) found similar prevalence data to that of the United States, as well as with other kinds of sex offenses (Gunn & Minch, 1992; Painter, 1986). These findings are also similar to findings in minority Inuits (Seltzer & Langford, 1984). In a recent international comparison of sexual harassment, Gruber, Smith, and Kauppinen-Toropainen (in press) reported on a Canadian national telephone survey on sexual harassment, conducted in 1992, of women in the workplace, a year before the time the survey was taking place, in a large sample of 1,990 women. The authors reported various incidence rates of different sexual harassment experiences. For instance, 33% reported staring, 13% touching, and 3% sex bribery. One of the interesting findings of this research, however, was that geopolitical region did not make any difference in terms of rates as well as severity levels of sexual harassment. Another Canadian survey of sexual harassment in managerial and professional women (Burke & McKeen, 1992) also showed incidence rates similar to those found in the United States.

## Former Czechoslovakia

The ILO (1992) reported on two surveys on sexual harassment of working women in the former Czechoslovakia. In the first one, which was conducted before the 1989 political changes, 31% of women employed in health services and 20% of women employed in industry experienced sexual harassment. In the second study, conducted after the 1989 changes (which, among other social changes, brought about liberalization of pornography and censorship laws), 38.5% of women reported sexual harassment in terms of misuse of power by their boss, and 17.5% reported they had been exposed to physical sexual harassment.[7]

## Denmark

The ILO (1992) reported that in a national survey of working women conducted in Denmark in 1991, 11% responded positively to the question of whether they had been sexual harassed at work. In 66% of the cases of sexual harassment, male superiors were indicated as the harassers. (See additional findings on Denmark in the section on Russia and the former USSR.)

## Egypt

No report on sexual harassment in the workplace in Egypt was found. However, it is interesting that Egypt, as a country governed by very strict Islamic laws but yet greatly exposed to Western cultures, has the same sexual assault incidence rate as in any other country (Shaalan, El-Akabaouri, & El-Kott, 1983). It might only be extrapolated that the incidence rate of sexual harassment in the workplace is also similar to that of other countries.

## Finland

Kauppinen-Toropainen (1993) reported on a survey conducted in 1987 on 957 Finnish women representing a wide range of occupations. On the average, 36% experienced some form of sexual harassment at work (20% by superiors or coworkers and 16% by customers). There was a huge variance among occupations, from police women who rated highest, to production workers who rated lowest.[8] In studying 132 women from different occupations and workplace, Haavio-Mannila, Kauppinen-Toropainen and Kandolin (1988) found that 31% of them were sexually harassed in the period of 24 months prior to the study. Interestingly, they found a similar sexual harassment incidence rate in men. (See additional findings on Finland in the section on Russia and former USSR.)

## France

The ILO (1992) reported that a French government survey carried out in 1991 found that an average of 21% of female workers personally experienced sexual harassment. This general rate was different in various work sectors. Different types of sexual harassment were experienced in different frequencies, ranging from 63% who reported dubious propositions and gestures, 60% who experienced continued advances despite refusals, 48% who reported an overall sexually unpleasant environment, to 12% who reported some kind of sexual blackmail. Husbands (1992) reported that research in France showed that women who had been sexually harassed indicated that the harasser was an employer or supervisor (55%), a coworker (22%), or a client (27%).

## Germany

Sex related crimes prevail in Germany similarly to other Western countries (Clausen, 1987). Bustelo (1991) cited survey findings indicating that 59% of German women encountered some form of sexual harassment in the workplace. A study by Holzbecher et al. (1991) found that 6% of their women participants had to quit their job because of a sexual harassment problem.

## India

There are indications that the incidence of sexual assault is as prevalent or even higher in India than in many other countries. This might be due to the low status of women and social norms permitting or encouraging exploitation of women (Pandey, 1986, 1987). However, acknowledgment and awareness of the issue of sexual harassment and readiness to deal with it have been developing (Ram, 1981). Relatively low percentages of sexual harassment incidents are being reported, and only a limited number of studies in this area have been conducted (Pandey, 1986). Although not relying on empirical surveys, Kishwar (1992a, 1992b) reported that sexual harassment in the workplace in India is widespread. He also observed that women who worked in science institutions were exposed to sexual harassment more than other working women and attributed this to more power differential in that sector. He also argued that possible sexual harassment is the major reason why parents discourage their daughters' education. Also, Menon and Kanekar (1992) and Kanekar and Dhir (1993) report that sexual harassment in India is more endemic and more blatant than in Western countries. Giri (1990) found that Indian television commercials, in imitating ordinary television commercials from the United States, are portraying women as subordinates and sex objects for men, thus directly influencing sexual harassment behaviors.

## Israel

The first survey on sexual harassment in the Israeli workplace was conducted in 1986 on a large sample of female government employees (Shapira-Libai, 1987). Incidence rates varied from 1% who experienced sexual assault, 4% who went through sexual harassment accompanied with threats, 10% who were pressured to have intimate contacts, 31% who experienced unwanted physical touch, to 34% who encountered verbal sexual harassment. As in studies in many other countries, single and younger women had more experiences of sexual harassment. This study, however, was criticized on conceptual, methodological, and statistical grounds (Barak, 1989). Another study was conducted by Pinto (1989; reported also by Ellis, Barak, & Pinto, 1991) in a sample of female employees in four Israeli hospitals.[9] She found that 27%, on the average, experienced some kind of verbal harassment; some 16%, on the average, were exposed to seductive behaviors; more than 4% experienced some kind of sexual bribery; some 8% encountered threats for noncompliance with sexual propositions; and almost 8% went through sexual assault. However, only 11% of the respondents subjectively admitted they had been encountered sexual harassment at work when responding to a subjective rather than a behaviorally anchored item (i.e., "Have you been sexually harassed…").

## Italy

Bustelo (1991) reported findings that showed that 48% of Italian working women experience some form of sexual harassment at work. Giacobbe (1991) mentioned a national survey on this subject but did not reveal its findings, except that 70% of the women surveyed were in favor of a specific provision on sexual harassment in employment contracts.

## Japan

The Tokyo Metropolitan Government (1992) reported on a survey carried out in Tokyo in which 51% of the male and female respondents knew about sexual incidents in the workplace. Husbands (1992) mentioned empirical findings from Japan showing that 23.5% of women were sexually harassed by their boss, 14% by other superiors, 18.5% by experienced workers in their area, 16% by a colleague, and 8.5% by customers or clients (more than one option was possible). Do Rosario (1993) reported that sexual harassment of women at work was a widespread problem that apparently has to do with the thin line in this society between work and afterwork activities. Abe (1993) noted that the many cases of sexual harassment in Japan are a direct result of discrimination against women in the workplace.

## Luxembourg

A survey on sexual harassment in Luxembourg was conducted in a heterogeneous sample of 502 women (Ecker, 1993). It was found that 58% were subjected to sexual looks, 31% to whistling, 23% to remarks concerning their body or appearance, 8% to unwanted touches of the body, 5% to unwanted kisses, 5% to unwanted touching of the legs, 4% to unwanted touching of the breasts, 2% to pressures to have sex, and 1% to rape. As in most other research results, victims were usually single and young.

## Mexico

The problem of sexual harassment of women in the workplace has been acknowledged and conceptually analyzed by Garcia y Garcia (1991) in the framework of the Mexican society. However, no incidence rates of sexual harassment were found.

## Netherlands

The ILO (1992) reported on a government-initiated study carried out in the Netherlands in 1986 on sexual harassment in the workplace. It was found that 58% of women, on the average, experienced some kind of sexual harassment. De Bruijn and Timmerman's (1988) study of industry, office, and sales workers in a small sample revealed that the extent of sexual harassment was dependent on the type of work and working conditions. Junger (1987),

acknowledging sexual harassment in the workplace as a major psychological problem, found that women's experiences of sexual harassment were the best predictor of fear as well as anticipation of rape.

## New Zealand

MacKinnon (1992) reported on sexual harassment in New Zealand but did not offer detailed data on its extent. However, an interesting comparative study may shed light on relative proportions of sexual victimization between this country and the United States.

Koss, Gidycz, and Wisniewski (1987) administered anonymous questionnaires to a large sample of female and male students enrolled in various academic institutions in the United States, asking about various experiences of sexual aggression. Women were asked to respond as to victimization experiences, and men were ask to respond to the same items (with slight change in wording) concerning their aggression toward women.[10] Interestingly, in using the same questionnaire and a representative university student sample, Gavey (1991) reported sexual victimization prevalence in New Zealand as equal to that reported by Koss, Gidycz, and Wisniewski (1987) in the United States. For instance, sexual coercion was experienced by 10.7% of the New Zealand women, in comparison to 11.9% of the American women, and attempted rape was experienced by 11.2% of New Zealand women, in comparison to 12.1% of the American women. This finding is intriguing since in New Zealand there is no ethnic composition equivalent to the United States and, as Gavey (1991) noted, there was no social awareness of various types of sexual aggression as existed in the United States.

## Northern Ireland

Kremer and Curry (1986) found that 22% of women in Northern Ireland had experienced sexual harassment at work. Kremer and Marks (1992), in studying employers' and unions' responses to sexual harassment, noted that harassment was widespread, as revealed by their data.

## Norway

The ILO (1992) reported that a Norwegian survey (of a relatively small and highly non-representative sample) carried out in 1988 had found that 90% of women experienced unwanted sexual touching in the workplace (41% many times, 40% sometimes, 9% once), 65% experienced pressure to have sex (9% many times, 38% sometimes, 18% once), and 21% experienced rape or attempted rape.

## Pakistan

No report on sexual harassment at work in Pakistan was found. However, Mehdi (1990), describing changes of laws concerning sex crimes from solely Islamic laws to more modern laws, referred to sexual assault in Pakistan (including of women in the workplace) as a prevalent problem.

## Portugal

A large national survey of sexual harassment on the job was conducted by the Portuguese Commission of Job Equity using a representative sample of 1,022 working women (Amân-cio & de Lima, 1992). Across different forms of sexual harassment behaviors it was found that 5.7% had frequently been victims of sexual harassment, 9.4% had experienced it sometimes, and 19.1% had seldom experienced it. These results were similar for temporarily hired women and permanent workers, as well as across different regions of Portugal. As in other countries, rates of sexual harassment were higher in single and younger women. Most sexual harassment incidents (some 55%) were initiated by colleagues, about 32% by superiors, and approximately 10% by clients/customers.

## Russia and the Former USSR

No sexual harassment prevalence data were found for Russia and the former USSR. However, the related sexual offense behavior of rape was thought to be as pervasive in the former USSR as in Western countries and to have similar characteristics and correlates (Sperling, 1990). Also, Hahn (1992) noted that sexual harassment of Soviet Jewish women in the workplace was common, and there was indication that this minority group was exposed to sexual harassment more extensively than other minorities or the mainstream. Some additional and more relevant data may be obtained in a study that aimed at comparing factors contributing to sexual harassment among cultural groups (Kauppinen-Toro-painen & Gruber, 1993). The researchers of this study grouped countries together and compared data from the former USSR (professional and simple workers sampled in Kamaz, Russia and Tallinn, Estonia), Scandinavia (Copenhagen, Denmark and Helsinki, Finland), and the United States (Michigan). In comparing means of a scale of "women-unfriendly experiences" (which included unwanted touching and sexual jokes), it seems that former USSR participants scored the lowest (3.20 on a 7-point scale) among these groups (3.90 and 4.75 for the Scandinavian and American groups, respectively). This difference was noticeable especially among simple workers, and not among professional workers. Gruber and Kauppinen-Toropainen (1994) reported, however, that the main differences attached to the sexual harassment experiences had to do with organizational variables rather than individual or national ones.

## Spain

The ILO (1992) reported on a survey conducted in 1986 in Madrid by the workers' union in a wide sample of working women. Verbal harassment was experienced by 84% of the women in their workplaces, 55% reported sexual looks or gestures, 27% experienced imposed sexual advances (e.g., pressure for sexual dates, unwanted touching), and 4% reported they had been subjected to attempted sexual intercourse.

## Sweden

A survey was carried out by the Swedish Ministry of Labor in a wide sample that represented various workers' unions from both the private and public sectors (Jämställdhetsom-budsmannen, 1987). Findings showed that an average of 17% of the respondents indicated they had experienced some kind of sexual harassment in the workplace. This figure changed from one union to another. Verbal harassment and unwelcome touching were experienced by 70% of women. Close to 33% had received unwanted sexual requests.

## South Africa

No report on sexual harassment in the workplace in South Africa has been found, and the subject is yet to be extensively studied in this country, along with other sexuality-related subjects (Theron, 1989; Zubber, 1992). Studies on rape and other sexually abusive behaviors in South Africa, however, have found similar general characteristics of these subjects to those found in North America (Levett, 1989; Levett & Kuhn, 1991; Vogelman, 1990).

## Switzerland

No survey on the extent of sexual harassment in the Swiss workplace has been found. However, Barone (1991), representing the national workers' union position, has referred to sexual harassment as a prevalent problem.

## United Kingdom

Sexual harassment in the United Kingdom could be documented as far back as the middle of the nineteenth century with distressful experiences of female cotton workers in Lancshire (Benenson, 1993). More recently the ILO (1992) reported that in 1987 a survey on sexual harassment was carried out by a government office. Seventy-three percent of women indicated they had experienced some form of sexual harassment in the workplace. Verbal sexual harassment was the most common form (48%), then sexist and patronizing behavior (45%) and unwanted touching (34%). Another survey reported by the ILO (1992), conducted in 1991, studied a more restricted sample of employment agencies' clients. It found that 47% of women reported they had been sexually harassed. Unwanted touching was experienced by 43%, suggestive remarks by 41%, sexual propositions by 32%, suggestive looks by 10%, and personal comments about the body by 6%. In Leeds a survey

of women in various occupations found that about 50% had been sexually harassed on the job (Leeds Trade Union and Community Resource and Information Centre, 1983). Reid (1991) mentioned surveys conducted in the United Kingdom that showed that some 20% of women suffered from some form of sexual harassment on the job; this rate increased to 96% in nontraditionally female areas. Green et al. (1993) observed extensive sexual harassment of women medical laboratory workers in Scotland. However, in another survey (Phillips, Stockdale, & Joeman, 1989) only 16% of women reported experiencing sexual harassment on their job. Bustelo (1991) indicated a rate of 51% who had experienced some form of sexual harassment in the United Kingdom. Nash (1989) cited a British survey that found that 25% of women were sexually harassed in the workplace. Stanley (1987) found that sexual harassment is typically experienced by public service workers (i.e., police officers, garage attendants, road workers, grocery clerks, shopkeepers, and taxi/bus drivers). Rubenstein (1991a) noted that sexual harassment in the United Kingdom was as extensive as in other European countries. A survey of nurses and nursing students (Finnis & Robbins, 1994) found that 66% (46% within the last year only) of the nurses and 35% of the students were sexually harassed on the job. Most of the harassment incidents were initiated by patients.

## United States

Research on sexual harassment in the United States is probably the most extensive of all countries. The reason for that is not because sexual harassment is more problematic or prevalent in the United States than in other countries, but apparently because of general social attitudes that favor research related to women's issues, the influence of women's equal opportunities movements, as well as financial resources. In any case, the American activists and researchers first publicly noted the existence of sexual harassment in the workplace and have since extensively contributed to its study from various perspectives.

Data on incidence rates of sexual harassment in the workplace in the United States can be obtained from numerous studies (see also Chapter 5). Only three large-scale surveys are reviewed here. In a survey of more than 10,000 female government employees, the U.S. Merit Systems Protection Board (USMSPB, 1981) found that 33% of the respondents reported repeated sexual remarks, 26% unwanted touching, and 15% various forms of pressures for dates; close to 10% had been pressured for sexual cooperation; and 10% had been exposed to sexy phone calls and to written notes over a two-year period. Overall, it was reported that 42% of this sample of working women has suffered some form of sexual harassment in the workplace. Similar results were found in a follow-up survey (USMSPB, 1988). In another well-known survey, conducted by telephone interviews with more than 800 women, Gutek (1985) found that 53% of women had encountered some form of sexual harassment in the workplace. For instance, over 7% were expected to take part in sexual activities as a part of work, and 24% were exposed to unwanted physical touch. These surveys found that most sexual harassment incidents were originated by peers or coworkers (69% in USMSPB, 1988, and 56% in Gutek, 1985), and less by supervisors (31% in USMSPB, 1988, and 44% in Gutek, 1985). A recent survey (Newman, 1993) compared sexual harassment prevalence data in six different states in the United States and found some significant differences among them. For instance, women in Texas reported the lowest rates of sexual harassment. While the reasons for these differences are unknown, they could at least direct researchers' attention at additional investigations. (See additional findings on the United States in the sections on New Zealand and on Russia and the former USSR.)

## Summary

As stated before, due to several serious methodological limitations, the comparison of the phenomenon of sexual harassment across countries is impossible. It should be underlined that it would be completely erroneous to compare the different figures among countries in an attempt to identify significant patterns of prevalence rates. Factors such as sampling procedures, questioning methods, terms used, time length the questions referred to, anonymity and confidentiality of disclosures, vocabulary and connotative meanings of questionnaire items and instructions, statistical analyses employed, and so on make this (however intriguing) contrasting impossible. It will not be risky to contend that even what seem to be significantly higher reported percentages of sexual harassment in one study than those in another do not necessarily mean more prevalent occurrences of sexual harassment. Thus, one who would try to assert that sexual harassment is more common in say, Spain than in Sweden would commit a severe error, and any interpretation that followed would hence be meaningless.

Given these limitations and precautions, not much can be validly concluded from this review. It is obvious, however, that all of the research on sexual harassment has been conducted and reported in developed, industrialized countries. This may reflect the importance of social and/or ethical issues in these countries in contrast to other countries, as well as natural distribution of resources to meet the countries' economic and social needs. Also, the sexual harassment of women at work is a relatively widespread phenomenon across countries, continents, cultures, languages, and societies. However, the *form* or the *type* of sexual harassment being carried out might be different in different countries. This observation is similar to Levinson's (1989) findings on family violence across cultures—that family violence was similarly prevalent in all societies, but *the form* of violence was different in different societies. Levinson (1989) also found some social correlates for wife beating. As far as types of sexual harassment are concerned, the social or culturally related factors are yet unknown and need to be further examined, but one could speculate on how cultural norms affect the probability of occurrence of wife beating or other forms of sexual harassment.

## RACE, ETHNICITY, AND PREVALENCE OF SEXUAL HARASSMENT

An interesting cross-cultural perspective of sexual harassment has to do with its differential impact on different racial or ethnic groups. The relationship between ethnicity and incidence of sexual harassment is important because it may be related to the general question of the antecedents of sexual harassment.

Many theoreticians of sexual harassment, as well as those of sexual assault in general, have argued for a major effect of the power drive in originating (or at least contributing) to the incidence of sexual harassment (for a review on this issue see Barak, Pitterman, & Yitzhaki, in press; Cleveland & Kerst, 1993). Since control, mastering, patronizing, and degrading—which result from and are indicative of power differential and power motives—exist in relation to ethnic groups as well, comparing empirical data of sexual harassment among these groups is intriguing. The argument here is that sexual harassment might basically express more general control and humiliating drives of behavior, in comparison to sex drives (e.g., Hoffman, 1986; Stringer et al., 1990; Wise & Stanley, 1987). Assuming that minority (i.e., ethnic) groups are overpowered by majority (or mainstream) white groups, there should be significantly higher incidence rates of white (harasser)–ethnic (victim) sexual harassment than other possible combinations, other things being equal. These differences should thus be reflected in sexual harassment prevalence data, where higher incidence rates of sexual harassment among ethnic groups than among a mainstream group are hypothesized (O'Brien, 1989; Paludi, 1993).

An example of these dynamics for sexual harassment (as well as other forms of sexual exploitation) was described by Pape (1990) in analyzing sexual victimization of black women by white men in colonial Zimbabwe. Another example of this possible trend was shown in observing the high incidence rates of sexual violence toward refugee women, who represent an ethnic minority in the accepting country (see Van-Willigen, 1992, for an example of this phenomenon in the Netherlands). An additional example was supplied by Cole and Boyle (1986), who reported that sexual harassment was found to be much more extensive in Australian aboriginal women than in white women. Yet another example is seen in the extensive sexual assault cases in Soweto (South Africa), which, like other forms of crimes, were not reported mainly because of the inferior social status of the black group (Strijdom & Schurink, 1979). It should be stressed, however, that there was no specific indication in these last two studies as to the identity of the offenders. In referring to the black minority group in the United States, Ellis (1981) argued for much resemblance of race and sex discrimination. Since she considered sexual harassment as related to sex discrimination, she also contended that the experience of sexual harassment would be higher in black women than white women because of general attributions made of black women as sexually available and sexually promiscuous, as well as their higher economic vulnerability. Similar arguments were made by Farley (1978). An additional explanation for possible higher sexual harassment incidence rate of minorities (i.e., blacks) than whites and less use of remedies (i.e., reporting) was given by Gwartney-Gibbs and Lach (1992). These authors, arguing from a sociological perspective, proclaimed that blacks in typical nonblack jobs might experience sexual harassment in the same way women in general do in traditionally male-dominated occupations. This argument is similar to that used by Wyatt (1992) to hypothesize about higher rape and attempted rape incidents among black than among white women. However, her data, based on a sample of 248 women in Los Angeles County in California, did not support this hypothesis. In an additional study of sexual assault, George, Winfield, and Blazer (1992), studying a large (n = 1,157) representative sample of women in North Carolina, found that race (black versus white) was not related to the likelihood of sexual assault. Sorenson and Siegel (1992), in a large-scale survey in Los Angeles, found that lifetime prevalence of sexual assault of whites was 2.5 times that of Hispanics (19.9% versus 8.1%, respectively).

In the workplace and in educational institutions, Chan (1987) noted that female Asian Americans were exposed to extended sexual harassment, including harassment in their workplaces, and emphasized the unique features of this phenomenon in terms of antecedents, not in terms of consequences. She contended that the stereotype of the Asian American women is of an exotic sexual object who is available, passive, and subservient. This social perception could contribute to sexual harassment behaviors toward them. Similarly, Staples (1993; see also D. Bell, 1991, and E. L. Bell, 1992, for diverse opinions on the relationships of race and sexual abuse) underlined the role of the image of black women as sensual and sexual in contributing to their sexual harassment experiences, in addition to blacks' history of slavery (see also Chapter 13). Still in the same vein, Segura (1992), who studied sexual harassment in the workplace of Chicanas (women of Mexican descent), described social stereotypes that reinforce sexual harassment of this minority group and reported that 33% of the respondents in her sample had been sexually harassed. It should be noted that, although this ethnic group is characterized by a combination of traditional and Anglo-acculturated sexuality and sex-role attitudes (Pavich, 1986), social stereotypes of female Chicanas usually incorporate a notion of inferiority to whites in general and to men in particular.

While the general argument of higher prevalence of sexual harassment in minority groups in comparison to mainstream groups is difficult to directly and strictly test—especially in testing hypothesized causal relationships—cumulated research evidence may shed some light on its validity.

## Research

The USMSPB (1981, 1988) research findings did not support the racial differentiation hypothesis: Fain and Anderton (1987), in reanalyzing the survey data of federal employees in the United States, indeed found that some types of sexual harassment were significantly more extensively experienced by the nonwhite minority women than by white women. The differences found, however, were small. For instance, unwanted pressure for sexual favours was experienced by 7.9% of nonwhite women in contrast to 6.6% of white women, unwanted sexual suggestive looks or gestures were experienced by 21.8% of nonwhite respondents as opposed to 19.4% of white ones, and unwanted pressure for dates was encountered by 12.3% of nonwhites and 9.2% of whites. The other four forms of sexual harassment studied (actual or attempted rape or sexual assault; unwanted deliberate touching, leaning over, cornering, or pinching; unwanted letters or phone calls of a sexual nature; and unwanted sexual teasing, jokes, remarks, or questions) were experienced equally in both groups. Also, in this study there was no indication of the identity of the harassers in terms of their race.

In a study of United States military personnel, Niebuhr and Boyles (1991) compared the prevalence of sexual harassment of female soldiers among various ethnic groups. They too found no support for the ethnicity hypothesis. As a matter of fact, white enlisted women experienced a higher degree (90.3%) of various sexual harassment behaviors than did nonwhite enlisted women (75.4%).[11]

Results that conflicted with the latter two studies were found in a study by Mansfield et al. (1991). While these researchers were primarily interested in examining issues concerning sexual harassment and the traditionality of women's jobs (comparing women who work as school secretaries with women who work either as transit workers or as skilled tradeswomen), they used ethnic group (i.e., blacks vs. whites) as one of their independent variables. Personal experiences of sexual harassment were measured by a subjective, yes/no single item. They found that across occupational groups 16.6% of white women reported they had been sexually harassed in contrast to 48.6% of black women.[12] These incidence rates could be misleading, however, since they represent responses to a general, subjective, yes/no question and not ratings of actual (behaviorally described) incidents as in other studies. Black women thus could have responded to this item inaccurately, bringing their overall frustration feelings and experiences of race discrimination into it. Another possibility is that the race variable showed significant effects on sexual harassment because it was confounded with the occupational group variable (traditional vs. nontraditional), which has long been proven to have significant effects on sexual harassment. It is impossible to examine these artifacts with the data as published.

A large-scale survey of sexual harassment in American public high schools (AAUW, 1994) also addressed ethnicity. It was found that 87% of white girls, 84% of black girls, and 82% of Hispanic girls were sexually harassed in school (by anybody, including peers, and with any form of sexual harassment behavior). While closer examination of the results, when broken down by form of sexual harassment, revealed some ethnic group differences, these differences were inconsistent in their directions. It seemed, however, that the educational and emotional impact of sexual harassment was different for the ethnic groups: blacks were found to be more vulnerable in terms of the consequences of sexual harassment than either whites or Hispanics (who had experienced a similar impact). The results of this survey clearly showed, however, that gender differences, not ethnicity, were the major factors in experiencing sexual harassment, being involved in sexual harassment conduct, or suffering from sexual harassment.

It is interesting to note that Koss, Gidycz, and Wisniewski's (1987) survey of sexual victimization in the United States did find significant differences in prevalence of sexual victimization by ethnic group, *but not in the hypothesized direction* (as outlined above). For instance, rape was reported by 40% of Native American women, 16% of white women, 12% of Hispanic women, 10% of black women, and 7% of Asian women. On the average, approximately 10% of the nonwhite (minority) women were raped. This, in contrast to the 16% rape rate of white women, is just in reverse to the direction hypothesized. The rape incidence rate in this survey hence did not indicate that women members of minority or ethnic groups were exposed to more sexual violence than the female members of the majority (white) group.

## Summary

Various arguments have been made to support the hypothesis that women of ethnic minority groups would experience higher rates of sexual harassment than women in a mainstream group. The basic and most common rationale behind this argument is that sexual harassment is a behavior that manifests power drives: Since a majority group's members would strive to suppress a minority group's members, this attitude would be reflected in their sexual abuse of women. In addition, several authors showed how social stereotypes of specific ethnic groups might increase sexual harassment behaviors toward their own women members. However, most of the studies reviewed here did not support this argument. This disconfirmation holds for both sexual abuse and offense in general, as well as sexual harassment in the workplace in particular. As a matter of fact, there is some evidence that female members of ethnic groups experience *lower* (or at least similar) rates of sexual harassment than women of the mainstream group.

## PERCEPTIONS AND INTERPRETATIONS OF SEXUAL HARASSMENT BEHAVIORS

As reviewed and underlined throughout this volume, sexual harassment is a complicated phenomenon, one that incorporates both objective (behaviorally or legally based) definitions as well as subjective perceptions and interpretations. Definitions of concepts and terms such as "hostile environment," "unwelcome advances," or "sexual intention," which are common in definitions of sexual harassment, are heavily dependent on people's perceptions, labeling, attributions, judgments, and interpretations of incidents. These cognitive processes are all subjective and heavily dependent on personal as well as social and environmental norms. Investigating and understanding these conceptions and processes of sexual harassment are highly important because of several reasons. First, they could be directly associated with the development and escalation of a sexual harassment incident (e.g., Williams & Cyr, 1992). Second, they are related to reactions to sexual harassment experiences (e.g., Bingham & Scherer, 1993). Third, they are directly related to legal definitions, considerations, and ruling (e.g., Mechling & Mechling, 1985; York, 1989). Fourth, they may shed light on psychological and social processes, with special relevance to possible cases of misinterpretations and miscommunications that might be crucial in sexual harassment prevention (e.g., Barak, in press; Pineau, 1989; Stockdale, 1993). Since societal norms and standards play a significant role in these processes, it seems only logical that cross-cultural comparisons could enhance our understanding of the perceptual processes. These comparisons might hence be very valuable.

Subjective views of sexual harassment involve cognitive processing of information, which includes verbal processing. In this context, even terms, language, and verbal associations and connotations involved with sexual harassment–related vocabulary are culture-specific and sometimes present problems. This naturally holds true if various nationalities and ethnic groups that have different social norms are to be considered. Ramsey and Stefanou-Haag (1991), for example, discussed the lingual complexity of sexual harassment as a term and showed how "sexual harassment," and some of its related terms, is quite diverse in 10 languages used even in a restricted territory of South Australia. Distinctive cultural groups might thus be even more different in their perceptions of and relation to what might objectively be termed as sexual harassment. Stockert (1985), for instance, in reviewing sexual harassment incidence in the University of Hawaii, which is characterized by a multicultural community under a common legal system, argued how different perceptions and attributions made by distinctive international

student groups make prevention of sexual harassment on campus very complicated. This complexity certainly makes legislation, education, and research on sexual harassment difficult in typical multicultural societies.

The subject of human judgments of what might constitute sexual harassment, how people differ in their cognitive processing of it, and variables that might interact with these processes has attracted numerous investigators. Since these cognitive processes rely heavily on socialization (i.e., acculturization) and environmental influences (e.g., Scupin, 1992), it seems that the study of cultural correlates of sexual harassment is crucially important. It is beyond the scope of this chapter to review the exhaustive literature on perceptual processes related to sexual harassment (see Chapter 2), but some highlights of the cumulative knowledge in this area in regard to different cultures are included here. Thus, the focus of this section is to allow some comparisons of findings across cultures concerning the perceptions and judgments of sexual harassment. This review is divided into comparisons among countries, as well as comparisons among ethnic groups. However, since research on sexual harassment is limited, some related research on perceptions of sexual assault in general is included too.

## Judgments of Sexual Harassment Acts in Different Countries

As most of the sexual harassment research has been conducted in the United States, it is interesting to compare some of the major findings on judgments of sexual harassment incidents there with equivalent research in other countries. In most cases these studies were conducted independently, by using local terms, descriptions of behaviors, and questionnaires. The comparisons hence can be made in regard to the conceptual conclusions, not to the data themselves.

The internal structure of the concept of sexual harassment, as evidenced by people's judgments and experiences, has been a topic of several research attempts. For instance, Fitzgerald and Hesson-McInnis (1989), in a study involving university students in the United States, asked participants to judge similarity of sexual harassment incidents in terms of seriousness. When subjected to a multidimensional scaling technique, the data revealed a two-dimensional structure, rather than Till's (1980) unidimensional system of five levels of severity of sexual harassment. The dimensions consisted of severity *level* and *type* of sexual harassment, composed of quid pro quo versus environmental forms of harassment. The structure of sexual harassment was also studied in a cross-cultural framework by Gelfand, Fitzgerald and Drasgow (in press), this time using women's reports of actual sexual harassment experiences. These researchers compared factor analyses of women's responses to the SEQ items in the United States (both in university female students and in working women) and in Brazil (university female students only). They found a stable structure of the construct of sexual harassment in all three samples, composed of the three factors of gender harassment, unwanted sexual attention, and sexual coercion. Barak (1994) reported that an analysis of SEQs of university female students in Israel revealed a similar structure.

One of the most consistent findings in the U.S. research is the significant differences between men and women in labeling incidents as sexual harassment, judgments of their severity, and attributions of responsibility. This has been found in sexual harassment of university students (e.g., Bursik, 1992; Hunter & McClelland, 1991; Malovich & Stake, 1990; McKinney, 1992; Saal, 1990), as well as in sexual harassment of employees on the job (e.g., Gutek, Morasch, & Cohen, 1983; Jones & Remland, 1987, 1992; Popovich et al., 1992; Saal, 1990; Thacker & Gohmann, 1993). The consistent gender differences found in U.S. research can be compared with studies utilizing the gender variable in other countries. In India, Menon and Kanekar (1992) found that men put more blame on a woman victim in a hypothetical incident of sexual harassment in the workplace than did women. This effect was the most salient one in all judgment-related variables investigated.

The results of this study were successfully replicated (Kanekar & Dhir, 1993), with the gender difference overshadowing all other independent variables. In Israel, research also found consistent gender differences in judgments of sexual harassment incidents, when using written vignettes as stimulus materials to portray these incidents (Neer & Krimolovski, 1991). However, a recent international comparison had different results. In a cross-national investigation, DeSouza et al. (1994) compared perceptions and judgments of written descriptions of two university sexual harassment episodes among participants in four countries: Australia, Brazil, Germany, and the United States. The vignettes were translated into the respective languages, along with the rating instruments, and administered to undergraduate students. However, in contrast to the former studies, results revealed that while gender differences in rating the sexual harassment episode in terms of severity and guilt were ample in the American sample, they were absent in all other three countries. Also, Fitzgerald and Gelfand (1994), in comparing personal sexual harassment labeling and definitions of behaviors, found no gender differences in Brazil, in contrast to the United States.

It seems that international findings concerning judgments made on sexual harassment, as well as other sexual assault behaviors, are quite diverse. For instance, lack of gender differences in judgments of sexual harassment in countries other than the United States is consistent with a study conducted by Smith, Tritt, and Zollmann (1982), who examined raters' perceptions of rape victims and compared judgments made in Germany with those made in the United States. Yet, a study comparing attitudes and judgments toward rape between the United States and India (L'Armand, Pepitone, and Shanmugam, 1981) found opposite findings to those of DeSouza et al. (1994). Although the vignettes used in the 1981 study described rape incidents (rather than sexual harassment of students as in DeSouza et al., 1994), while there generally was a strong gender effect for the Indian participants, there was almost no effect of this variable in American participants. An important methodological comment in this regard was made by Krahe (1985), who, in reviewing and analyzing numerous German studies on perceptions of sexual assault, argued that raters' (or observers') gender differences could be interpreted and understood only in context of several other independent variables that characterize the victim, the assailant, and the rater. This viewpoint was supported in another German study (Hassebrauck, 1986), which also found complex interactions with raters' gender in interpreting rape incidents. Similarly, an investigation in Sicily, Italy (di Maria & di Nuovo, 1986) of judgments of sexual offense indeed found gender differences, but also evidence for significant interactions with age, as well as with level of education. In the same vein, a study conducted in India (Kanekar, Kolsowalla, & D'Souza, 1981) found that there was no main effect of gender differences on judgments of rape incidents, but, rather, gender differences interacted with victims' characteristics in affecting these judgments. Also, results of a South African study on attitudes toward and judgments of rape (Levett & Huhn, 1991) showed complex interactions of gender differences, basically related to characteristics of the offender. Generally, it seems that one should not generalize about cross-national variations concerning gender differences before carefully examining possible interactions of gender with other relevant variables in affecting judgments of sexual harassment.

Another factor that has repeatedly been found to correlate with perceptions, interpretations, and other judgments of sexual harassment is the type or severity level of incidents. For instance, findings of U.S. research have consistently shown that the more objectively explicit, physical, or hostile an incident is, the more it is labeled as sexual harassment, by both men and women (cf. Fitzgerald & Shullman, 1993). In a related vein, a consistent correlation was found between severity level of sexually harassing cases experienced by women and subjective rating of being exposed to sexual harassment in the workplace or in the uni-

versity (e.g., Fitzgerald et al., 1988). This factor too has been investigated in different countries, where researchers were interested to know which perpetrators' behaviors would be considered by women and/or men as sexual harassment. A study in Tokyo, Japan by the Tokyo Metropolitan Government (1992) examined what behaviors men and women would consider to be sexual harassment. It was found, for instance, that 81% of respondents labeled touches of the body (including hand) as sexual harassment, and 60% of them regarded jokes and comments about a person's body as harassment (71% of men and 52% of women!). In Luxemburg, Ecker (1993) also found that judgments regarding sexually harassing behaviors were differential. While 95–100% thought rape, touching of breasts, asking for sex for promotion, and pressures to have sex should be considered sexual harassment, 40–50% thought the same about exhibiting pornographic materials in the workplace or telling "dirty" stories and jokes, and 20–30% thought so of sexy looks or whistling. In a survey of a national sample of women in Portugal (Amâncio & de Lima, 1992), sexual harassment was perceived by about 30% of the respondents to include comments regarding dress and personal appearance; by 37% to include comments on physical attributes; by 50% to include comments on a specific part of body; by 50% to include "undressing with one's eyes"; by 76% to include personal invitations with "second intentions"; and by almost all respondents to include direct sexual invitations, touches, grabbing and kissing, fondling, and assault. In comparing perceptions of behaviors in the United States and *Brazil*, Fitzgerald and Gelfand (1994) also found a strong, consistent effect of type and severity level of behavior and judgments of sexual harassment. In Northern Ireland, Kremer and Marks (1992) showed that while among trade union officers there was consensus regarding what should be regarded as sexual harassment, there was little agreement among employers. There were also differences between union officers and employers in the degree of leniency/strictness (in terms of offense involved or punishment deserved) they related to various forms of potentially sexually harassing behaviors. Similarly, Theron (1989) reported difficulties in South Africa in defining what incidents constituted sexual harassment because of different interpretations and attributions of behaviors. Based on New Zealand's conceptions, Crosthwaite and Swanton (1986) pointed out difficulties in defining sexual harassment in terms of specific acts and offered a definition based on considering (or ignoring) another person's interests, in the framework of workplace norms.

The question of what is labeled as sexual harassment was examined in several studies carried out in Israel. In a survey of female hospital employees, Pinto (1989) found that the higher the level of sexual harassment severity, using Till's (1980) categorization system, the higher was the correlation between personal sexual harassment experiences and subjective labeling of these experiences as sexual harassment (e.g., a Pearson correlation of .47 between personal experiences of sexual comments and subjective perceptions of being sexually harassed, versus a correlation of .83 between personal experiences of sexual assault and subjective perception of sexual harassment). Similarly, Goldstein and Yariv (1991) found this pattern of correlations in surveying Israeli university female students: a Pearson correlation of .20 between experienced verbal harassment and perceived sexual harassment, .34 between unwelcome sexual advances and perceived sexual harassment, and .53 between sexual assault and perceived sexual harassment. In two experimental studies conducted in Israel using men and women as "judges," Laufer (1991) using written vignettes, and Parzan and Kaplan (1991), using videotaped episodes, found that the more physically offensive the harasser's behavior was, the more it tended to be labeled and interpreted as sexual harassment.

In a study of university students in Canada, Barak, Fisher, and Houston (1992) also found that subjective interpretation of incidents as sexual harassment relied heavily on severity level of the incidents, but the effect of this factor was moderated by personality and attitudes of respondents. In another study of university students in Canada, Mazer and Percival (1989) found that subjective labeling and judgment of and attitudes toward sexual harassment were not related to personal experiences of sexual harassment. In another Canadian study, Valentine-French and Radtke (1989) examined some factors that may be responsible for attribution of responsibility in incidents of sexual harassment. They found that women attributed more responsibility to the harasser than did men, and that less traditional gender-role persons attributed less responsibility to the victim than did more traditional individuals. These findings are similar to those found on perceptions of rape in a British study (Howells et al., 1984). In another Canadian study that focused on perceptions and attributions, Summers (1991) found that the degree of feminist orientation of female complainants intervened with judgments of the causes (and potentially the sincerity and reliability) of their complaints.

## Race/Ethnicity and Judgment of Sexual Harassment

The question of whether ethnicity, representing a subculture, has a role in determining labeling, perceptions, attributions, or other judgments of sexual harassment incidents is intriguing. First, incorporating ethnic-related process research and relying on accumulated knowledge of ethnic effects may shed additional light on the perceptual and evaluation process related to sexual harassment. Second, by better understanding this process, investigators might develop a better focus on practical implications for both further research and prevention of sexual harassment. However, only a handful of studies, out of many conducted on human judgments of sexual harassment incidents, have included race, ethnic, or minority group of any kind as one of their independent variables. Although reasons for this omission could be political and not scientific (cf. Scarr, 1988), this topic remains to be thoroughly investigated in future research to achieve these ends. This is especially needed when the nature of the dependent variable in question—judgment of sexual harassment incidents—is heavily loaded by stereotypes, myths, and social norms that themselves are highly related to ethnicity. It thus seems that the inclusion of ethnic group, as well as other important independent variables (e.g., gender, gender-role attitudes, personality traits), in studying perceptions of sexual harassment (Reid & Comas-Diaz, 1990) is crucially important.

A brief highlighting of relevant research on sexual assault in general is worthwhile. As noted by Wyatt (1992), beliefs associated with rape could be highly mediated by race, ethnic group, or other sources of cultural differences. She argued that it is common for African American women to hear they are likely to be rape victims, regardless of actual rape statistics. This belief certainly interacts with black women's attributions and judgments of offenses of a sexual nature, although research has yet to determine precisely how. In a related vein, Ugwuegbu (1976) examined effects of racial similarity (black vs. non-black) on attributions of personality traits (positive and negative) to rape victims and defendants. She found that race similarity played a significant role in interpreting incidents and in judging both individuals, in such a way that dissimilar race created more negative attributions for both victims and offenders. Another effect of ethnic group on judgments (i.e., attribution of guilt) of rape victims and defendants was investigated by Bagby and Rector (1992) in Canada. These researchers were interested in the similarity/dissimilarity of victim's versus defendant's versus perceiver's ethnic group (English and French Canadians) on judgments. They found that the racial factor indeed made a significant contribution to these judgments. In a study in the United States, Wyatt (1992), comparing black and white women's rape and attempted rape incidents in terms of their disclosure and their impact of the incident, reported that perception of the assault incident seemed to be very different in these two groups according to victimization criteria. This difference, she claimed, could be responsible for significant differences in the reporting of those incidents in the two ethnic groups.

Only two studies addressing the mediation of ethnicity and judgments of sexual harassment were found. Reilly, Bernstein, and Cote-Bonanno (1992) studied a wide sample of high school students, adult students, and teachers, which included several ethnic groups (i.e., Caucasians, African Americans, Hispanics, Asians, and Native Americans), on perceptions of sexual harassment. Specifically, respondents were asked to determine which of 10 listed behaviors should be considered as sexually harassing behavior. While *across behaviors* ethnic group was not found to have a significant effect, different ethnic groups judged specific behaviors differently. For instance, a statistically significant difference of 75% versus 92% of Asians and Caucasians, respectively, judged "work hours conditioned on sexual favours" to be sexually harassing behavior. As another example, while only 42% of Native Americans thought "comments about physical attributes" to be sexually harassing, 71% of Hispanics did so. In an additional study, Neuman (1992) examined ethnicity, gender, and age as related to subjective definitions of sexual harassment. He found that ethnic group (i.e., all nonwhite respondents combined, including blacks, Asians, and Hispanics) had a significant effect on most of the nine offensive behaviors studied. For example, while 35.2% of nonwhites judged "persistent emphasis on sexuality" *not* to be defined as sexual harassment, only 17.2% of white respondents thought the same way. As another example, while 30.6% of nonwhites defined "unwanted sexual advances" as not being sexual harassment, only 10.2% of whites defined it similarly. On the average, across the nine offensive behaviors examined, the gap between nonwhites' and whites' judgments was approximately 15%, in that the former used more lenient definitions of sexual harassment than the latter. Interestingly, a similar gap of 15% (across ethnicity) was found between men's and women's perceptions, men using more lenient definitions of sexual harassment than women.[13]

## Summary

The research reviewed here has shown that cultural-related processes of perception and judgment of sexual harassment are complex. First, perceptions of *the structure of sexual harassment* seem to be independent of cultural differences, at least as is supported by research in Brazil, Israel, and the United States. This research showed consistent structure composed of factors of gender harassment, unwanted sexual attention, and sexual coercion. Second, apparently the dimension of *severity of sexual harassment* exists in all countries studied, where people differentiate among more and less harassing episodes by the degree of imposition they include and the level of negative consequences and impact they might have for the victims. The judgments of the harassing behaviors on this continuum, however, might be different in different cultures. What might be considered as no harassment or light harassment in one country or ethnic group might be rated differently in another country or ethnic group. Third, it seems that gender differences in judgments of sexual harassment are not consistent across cultures. However, the effects (or lack thereof) of this variable are not yet clear. Fourth, and most important, it seems that ethnic group—as more specifically defined, an expression of culture—may play a significant role in perceptions and judgments of sexual harassment. This variable has been overlooked in most sexual harassment perception research, and it is highly recommended that it be included as a crucial moderator variable in future research, if perceptual processes are to be better understood. It might be the case that ethnic group membership is a more "clean" definition of cultural membership, thus showing clearer effects than country membership, hence the results found. Overall, it seems that cultural background, either as related to nationality or to ethnicity, has some role in determining subjective definitions, perceptions, attributions, and other cognitive processes in relation to sexual harassment.

## PREVENTION OF SEXUAL HARASSMENT

As reviewed elsewhere in this volume, a variety of approaches and methods have been proposed and applied in dealing with sexual harassment. These various approaches put emphasis on different factors that could deter potential harassers, avoid sexual harassment escalation, or merely lower the probability of sexual harassment occurring in the first place by applying primary prevention measures. There is no doubt, however, that the major emphasis has been put upon legal deterrence, assuming that formal and strict legislation, provision of efficient grievance procedures, and determining relatively severe punishment would be very effective in significantly reducing the prevalence of sexual harassment in the workplace as well as in educational institutions (cf. Rubenstein, 1993). These basic approaches, with the salience of the legal ones, are characteristic of many countries. The typical examples are reviewed here. However, some other attempts have been made at combating sexual harassment, focusing on education of men and women and changing social norms. Some examples of these are reviewed here as well.

## Legal and Policy Approaches

As just mentioned, legal approaches to prevent occurrence of sexual harassment by attempting to deter possible harassers are the most frequent ones. The reason for this visible emphasis is not necessarily because of the success of legal remedies or the existence of policies in deterring social problems, including sexual harassment (Riger, 1991). Apparently, due to the clear legal aspect of sexual harassment, the reason for this emphasis is because the subject has long been handled by legal professionals and bodies. One should not downplay the importance of legal policies in formulating clear standards of accepted and unaccepted behaviors and thus communicating desired social values. However, the effectiveness of such approaches in actually deterring potential offenders and preventing undesired behaviors is questionable. Nonetheless, national laws, as well as local regulations, that directly or indirectly relate to sexual harassment exist in many countries. Since laws and regulations related to sexual harassment are quite similar in most areas of the world, only examples will be supplied here.

Many countries developed legislation concerning sexual harassment as a part (or a section) of a broader legal act dealing with gender discrimination. On the federal level in the United States, for instance, there are several laws that can be related to sexual harassment; for a comprehensive review see Chapter 4 and Lindemann and Kadue, 1992. In the United Kingdom the law that most refers to sexual harassment is the Sex Discrimination Act of 1975. This legislature refers to discrimination on the basis of employee's sex as related to his or her hiring, terms, promotion, and dismissal. As in the case of Title VII in the United States, although it was not originally designed to outlaw sexual harassment, it can and is used to do so (see review of the application of this law, and other legal aspects in the United Kingdom in Gay, 1991; see comparison of the legal approaches in the United States and the United Kingdom in Lipper, 1992). In Canada, with its own complex political and legal system, the main federal legislation relevant to sexual harassment is the Canadian Human Rights Act. This legislation is very general, however, does not include clear legal definitions and procedures, and generally applies only to federal employees. Some of the 10 Canadian provinces (which, according to the Canadian system, are basically responsible for labor laws) have legislated specific laws, such as the Ontario Human Rights Code, the Quebec Charter of Human Rights and Freedom, and the Newfoundland Human Rights Code (see review of legal aspects of sexual harassment in Canada by Aggarwal, 1992). In Australia, a country that also has federal as well as state legislative levels, the federal Sex Discrimination Act of 1984 and its 1992 amendments constitute the basic definitions and legal procedures

concerning sexual harassment. In addition, in recent years, all but one of the Australian states have legislated specific laws concerning sexual harassment. In Israel the Law of Employment Equal Opportunities of 1988 refers to forbidden discriminatory acts by employers, including discrimination on the grounds of sex, with special reference to sexual harassment. However, the law has no definitions or details of what constitutes sexual harassment in the workplace. Anti-discrimination in employment laws, which explicitly refer to sexual harassment, also exist in some other countries, including Austria (the Anti-Discrimination Act of 1991), Ireland (the Employment Equality Act of 1977), and New Zealand (the Human Rights Commission Act of 1977).

In many other countries there is no legislation that refers to sexual harassment directly or explicitly, yet there are other relevant laws and legal remedies on a national level (e.g., government-issued guidelines) that are used to legally protect employees against sexual harassment. For instance, in Sweden the Equal Opportunities Act of 1991 (which does not refer to or define sexual harassment as such), the Employment Security Act of 1984, and the Penal Code of 1962 have all been used to protect against sexual harassment and have been used in court cases. In the Netherlands an amendment to current laws specifically addressing sexual harassment is in legislative processes. However, a series of other laws have been used in this country for legal protection of employees against sexual harassment, including the Men and Women (Equal Treatment) Act of 1980, some titles of the Civil Code of 1989, the Working Environment Act of 1980, and some titles in the Penal Code.

In reviewing and comparing the legislation in 23 industrialized countries, Husbands (1992) showed how different nations have adopted different legal approaches in coping with sexual harassment. Although much has been found to be common to all or most of these countries, some meaningful differences have been detected as well. Of the 23 countries surveyed, only 9 had statutes that specifically defined or mentioned the term sexual harassment. Among those countries that did use explicit definitions, there were differences in terms of their breadth. Broad definitions, including both quid pro quo and hostile environment types of sexual harassment, were found in some countries (e.g., the United States, Australia), while others (e.g., France) used narrower definitions. In addition, Husbands (1992) found differences in terms of what constituted sexual harassment definitions (e.g., acts of perpetrator, response of victim); type of laws (i.e., equal opportunity laws, labor laws, tort laws, or penal laws); in emphasis put on prohibition versus affirmative duty to act; in issues of liability, remedies, and sanctions; and in legal procedures. Husbands concluded that the differences found among the countries surveyed represented differences in cultural attitudes, as well as in legal systems. However, to what degree the findings of these comparisons actually represent differences in attitudes is an important empirical sociological question yet to be answered.

The establishment of the European Communities provided additional codes to be adopted by its members. The Commission of the European Communities issued an official recommendation to its members "on the protection and dignity of women and men at work" in 1991. This recommendation listed legal, informative, and educational action items concerning sexual harassment for the member countries. Along with this recommendation the Commission adopted a Code of Practice to be implemented by the member communities (Sanglas, 1991). Rubenstein (1988, 1991b, 1992) analyzed legal aspects of sexual harassment and showed how the European Communities' Code and Directives, in addition to the Code of Practice and Recommendations, could enhance protection and remedies in sexual harassment cases.

In addition to national- or state-level legislative attention, sexual harassment has been given legal consideration in many countries on a local level too, including city level, specific organizations (business or school), or professional associations. As previously mentioned, states in the United States, as well as states in Australia and provinces in Canada, have developed their own legislation, in accordance with national statutes, to adjust rulings for specific endemic conditions or emphases. In addition, quite a few cities around the world have developed their own laws, either to make up for missing national legislation or to complete the law where there are certain legal gaps. In Germany, for instance, in order to fill in for the lack of a specific legal remedy for sexual harassment in the workplace of the national legislation, the state (and city) of Berlin legislated in 1990 a local Anti-Discrimination Act that specifically addresses this problem. Also, in Japan there is no specific national legislation dealing with sexual harassment (locally nicknamed "*seku hara*"), and it took several court rulings, based on more general antidiscriminatory laws and regulations, to develop a legal approach to sexual harassment. Responding to this legal gap, several cities, headed by Tokyo, developed local legislation that has been successfully used in legal cases (Abe, 1993; do Rosario, 1993). According to Labour Canada (Sexual Harassment Clauses, 1991) 41% of workplaces in Canada of 500 or more workers have some form of local provision on sexual harassment. In some cases, cities have taken the initiative in developing and presenting local sexual harassment policies as a way to stress the importance of this issue and extend the utility of the policy to be an informative and educational vehicle, beyond its legal value. For example, the city of Newcastle (England, UK) was the first British city to develop local policies and guidelines to tackle sexual harassment (and other kinds of violence) in the workplace (Adams & Bray, 1992). Likewise, local sexual harassment policies have also been developed in numerous work organizations and schools in many countries. As advocated by Rubenstein (1991a), who represented the British as well as the European Communities approach, local policies were highly recommended on top of national legislation. However, as a survey in the United Kingdom (Davidson & Earnshaw, 1990) showed, although most employers were aware of the illegality of sexual harassment, they were ignorant of many crucial aspects of the law (e.g., their liability). However, although the issue of sexual harassment in the United Kingdom has not kept pace with the United States, British companies have clearly shown an increased consciousness of the problem in recent years (Lipper, 1992). It seems that developing local guidelines and procedures is still a necessity.

Professional associations too have developed policies, guidelines, and specific sections in ethical codes to stress the illegality and the minimum tolerance of sexual harassment. This appears to be a growing trend in many countries. In the United Kingdom, for example, the British Sociological Association (1987) published its explicit definitions and guidelines, as did the Canadian Psychological Association (Byers & Price, 1986) in Canada. Similar to workplaces, many educational institutions worldwide have developed their own sexual harassment policies and guidelines (Perry, 1993). Although this is characteristic of U.S., Canadian, and British universities (see Paludi, Chapter 14, and 1990, for reviews on university policies in the United States), it seems that increasing numbers of universities in other countries are following suit, including those in many European countries, South Africa, India, Japan, and more.

One of the other resources that has taken an active role in combating sexual harassment is workers' labor unions. While this trend is less typical for the United States, as fewer employees there are unionized and labor unions are less powerful, it is common to most European countries, as well as in other nations (e.g., Kadar, 1983). The role of labor organizations could be regarded as twofold: protecting their members from a common occupational hazard and protecting the work environment from a poisonous atmosphere in order to enhance workers' welfare. In some countries, labor unions have taken a very active role in attempting to combat and prevent sexual harassment. In Italy, for instance, where there is no legal definition of sexual harassment,

explicit legislation is absent, and laws only indirectly relate to it, the Italian Federation of Labor (CGIL) has been very active in protecting employees and in dealing with sexual harassment cases (Giacobbe, 1991). In many European countries, as well in some other nations (e.g., Canada), provisions on sexual harassment have been part of collective bargaining and agreements. Examples can be found from the Heineken beer factory in the Netherlands, to the Air Canada airline in Canada, to port authorities in Spain (see samples of agreements in ILO, 1992).

Many businesses and organizations have developed their own policies on sexual harassment. This has been done in order to fill in a gap in national or local legislation, to refer to concrete concerns characterizing a workplace, to promote education of employees, or to correct possible liability problems (e.g., Howard, 1991). This is a growing trend across nations and cultures, especially in countries (or states) where liability is enforced (Husbands, 1992). Publications on sexual harassment aimed at business owners or employees that stress this financial issue apparently have produced much result (e.g., Nash, 1989, and Anonymous, 1993, in the United Kingdom; Gray, 1985, in Canada; Lan, 1991, in Japan; Oleck, 1993, in the United States).

## Ethnicity and Legal Procedures

Since legislation is equal and universal, it is legally complicated and politically sensitive in that it includes and takes into consideration special attributes and conditions related to cultural matters, such as special considerations related to ethnic minority groups. This might present certain difficulties in making the legal steps efficient. For instance, legal considerations in combating sexual harassment necessitate grievance procedures exclusively created to fit this problem's unique characteristics, including complete privacy, confidentiality, nonthreatening interrogation of incident, maximum removal of fear of revenge, and so on. Most legislation has accordingly defined such procedures. However, it seems that these procedures have overlooked some typical difficulties of minority groups, such as characteristics typical to women themselves (Riger, 1991) and to certain ethnic groups. A recent example may demonstrate this special complexity: As highlighted by several authors in regard to the black minority group in the United States following the Anita Hill–Clarence Thomas case, sexual harassment grievance procedures (including filing a complaint, interrogations, hearings, testimonies, etc.) are not sensitive to the interaction of race and the influential element of privacy versus publicity (Fraser, 1992), to ethnic employment inequality in general (Gwartney-Gibbs & Lach, 1992), to ethnic social stereotypes (Patterson & Teeple, 1992; see also Chapter 13), and to the possible politization of the case involved (Stone, 1992). Hence, it is apparent that cultural issues might be salient in using the law as a remedy, since using grievance procedures for a minority woman incorporates special considerations that are not applicable for a mainstream-group woman. These may include some additional precautions to avoid racial discrimination and interculture miscommunication, better understanding and sensitivity to values, standards, or beliefs typical of various minority groups, and appropriate training of personnel responsible for grievance procedures.

## Educational and Informative Interventions

Many have acknowledged that legislative and legal policies and procedures are insufficient remedies and apparently have minimal effectiveness in combating sexual harassment. For instance, in comparing the sexual harassment incidence rates revealed in the two large-scale surveys conducted with U.S. federal employees (USMSPB, 1981, 1988), data showed that the extent of the problem had not changed over a time interval when much legal action was taken. Indeed, one should be cautious in generalizing conclusions based on these specific surveys, conducted at these specific time points, at specific workplaces. However, because of the multifactorial nature of sexual harassment, its universality, and its extensive-

ness, it seems that it is naive, if not unprofessional, to hold that legal actions can eliminate, prevent, or even significantly decrease sexual harassment. This view has been shared by researchers across nations and was stressed, for example, by Barak (1992) in Israel; Carr (1991) in Canada; Hemming (1985) in Scotland; Garvey (1986), Howard (1991), and Popovich (1988) in the United States; Kishwar (1992a) in India, and Larsen (1989) in Denmark. This does not mean in any way that legislation is unimportant or unnecessary, but that it is insufficient to effectively combat sexual harassment. As proposed by Fitzgerald (1993), primary prevention, by equalizing proportions of men and women in workplaces (including nontraditional ones), could prove to be a major action to eliminate sexual harassment.

Many researchers, like those cited here, have called for inclusion of educational reforms, large-scale and continuous informative campaigns, individual and small-group training of both men and women, as well as some other actions to combat sexual harassment. Such steps have actually been taken in various countries (e.g., Australia, Belgium, Canada, Israel, the United States). Unfortunately, these attempts have not always been publicized—probably because of the confidential and sensitive nature of the topic—and have been only rarely reported in professional publication outlets. Likewise, there has been only limited research on their application and impact.

Informative and educational campaigns have been initiated in several countries, by state or local government agencies, as well as by activist groups (e.g., women's movements). Much work in this regard has been done, for instance, in Australia. The offices of the Human Rights and Equal Opportunity Commission (HREOC) of this country, backed up by the Sex Discrimination Act of 1984, have initiated publication and distribution of a number of booklets, posters, and flyers, as well as a training package on sexual harassment and a biannual newsletter (named AGENDER). These massive, multimethod interventions, on top of law enforcement both at the federal and state level, seem to have more impact than legislation itself, however progressive and applied this legislation is.

Educational interventions aimed to change people's attitudes toward and behaviors of sexual harassment, as well as to develop employees' awareness to the problem, coping options, and the use of legal policies, have been developed and published also by Barak (in press) in Israel and Beauvais (1986), Kaufman and Wylie (1983), Licata and Popovich (1987), and Paludi (1990) in the United States. These reports showed that educational interventions—based on different conceptual approaches and with various emphases— might be quite effective in achieving their goals. Some other ideas on the educational aspects of sexual harassment have been proposed by Smith (1994) in the Netherlands, who called for intervention focused on communication between men and women as a means to resolve sexual harassment complaints as well as to change the workplace environment.

## Summary

Many attempts have been made at the elimination and prevention of sexual harassment as a major social problem that threatens workplaces' climate and employees' welfare and affects the well-being of educational institutions and students. These attempts have been similar in many countries, in putting a major emphasis on relevant legislation. While some countries have developed a legal act specifically tailored to fit sexual harassment in the workplace (or educational institutions), many have used existing laws (e.g., human rights acts, labor laws) for the same purpose. The cultural correlates of existence or absence of sexual harassment–related legislation are still an open empirical question. The degree of imposition of the law in different countries is yet unknown, although legal complaints and court rulings have been on the rise in most countries. However, the effectiveness of legal remedies is still questionable, and there are good reasons to believe that laws, regulations, and policies have been insufficient to effec-

tively combat sexual harassment. Further steps have been proposed, such as steps at primary prevention by equalizing proportions of men and women in workplaces, but these proposals do not to seem to be followed around the world yet, apparently because of social forces beyond the issue of sexual harassment. Educational and informative steps have been proposed too in a number of countries, and it seems that their massive application may prove effective in reducing the prevalence of sexual harassment.

## SUMMARY AND CONCLUSIONS

As mentioned earlier, the very nature of this chapter necessitated exhaustive literature searches and correspondence with numerous individuals and agencies in order to obtain the needed materials. However, because of language barriers, difficulties in making contacts, limited opportunities to approach unpublished research in many countries, as well as the sensitivity of the subject of sexual harassment itself, the current review was limited to available reports only. It is by no means complete, nor does it pretend to be representative of what the picture of sexual harassment actually is worldwide. For instance, the prevalence of sexual harassment of university students is reviewed in only four countries (Brazil, Canada, Israel, and the United States) and is just briefly noted in two more countries (Finland and India). This does not mean that there is no research, writing, or concern about sexual harassment of university students in other countries, but just that materials were only available from these countries. Prevalence of sexual harassment in the workplace, however, was covered over many more countries because of the availability of the materials, and not because this population was studied more extensively than students (as a matter of fact, it seems that the opposite is true).

Research on judgments, perceptions, interpretations, and attributions of sexual harassment was available from many more countries than were prevalence data. The reason for that, one may speculate, is that the cognitive research aspect of sexual harassment is less legally, morally, socially, or emotionally loaded than other aspects—such as incidence rates, correlates, antecedent factors, or consequences—so publications and communications are more open and receive more legitimacy.

The review of the prevalence of sexual harassment shows that it is widespread across nationalities and ethnic groups. As stressed here, the degree to which sexual harassment, or any of its forms, is extensive cannot be determined without committing a severe methodological error. Although numerous researchers used the term "sexual harassment" in their studies and reports, many of them referred to different conceptual and/or operational definitions of this construct, so any comparison among them would be erroneous and speculative. Moreover, even findings of studies that used similar or even identical definitions or the same questionnaires are basically incomparable, for many reasons. The most apparent limitation on comparing results is the language barrier. Words, terms, idioms, and examples do not have the same meaning in different languages. Thus, even if researchers use very strict and sophisticated translation/reverse translation techniques, they still might miss the essence of a term in question. Similarly, cultural groups might be different in their willingness to expose themselves, their experiences, feelings, or behaviors; hence the responses to a questionnaire might be confounded by this variable too, significantly moderating statistical findings. These serious limitations, together with the variety of questionnaire administration procedures employed (e.g., personal interviews, telephone interviews, anonymous surveys), type of sample used (e.g., working women in general, female employees in specific organization/s), sampling method (e.g., arbitrary, completely random, stratified by any factors), time period in which sexual harassment is under investigation (in some research the period refers to "last six months in current job," while in others to "last five years"), and disclosure or return

rates, might all be responsible for large portions of the existing between-group variance, rather than true cultural differences. Consequently, one cannot and should not refer to differences in sexual harassment prevalence data between countries superficially and make any deductions concerning these comparisons. The reported incidence rate of 84% in Spain is by no means larger than the 34% in Portugal despite what seems to be a great arithmetic difference.

Given this precaution, a possible generalization one can make is that *sexual harassment in the workplace and educational institutions—however defined and measured and in whatever form or type—prevails widely in all societies*. This is, of course, assuming that the countries reviewed here actually represent *all* countries, an assumption that is not necessarily correct. The second generalization that might be made is that *sexual harassment has different faces and is manifested in different ways in different countries*. One could speculate on how what seem to be culture-specific standards interact with different behaviors, that is, why gender harassment is more prevalent than unwanted sexual attention in the United States, while unwanted sexual attention is less different in extent than gender harassment in *Brazil*. However, since the different types of sexual harassment were measured under the same conditions within countries, it seems that this generalization is more valid than the first one. Related to this latter finding, it is highly recommended that researchers not only start using accepted standards for measuring sexual harassment, but also start reporting it in an accepted, multifaceted structure (e.g., Fitzgerald's conception). This will enable more informative and comprehensive descriptions as well as more understanding of sexual harassment in different places.

An additional generalization one could make from this review is that—despite quite convincing theoretical arguments—*the incidence rate of sexual harassment is not higher in ethnic groups* (i.e., Blacks, Asians, Hispanics, Natives) *than in mainstream groups* (mostly whites), at least as most research in the

United States has shown. Because in these studies the data collection on sexual harassment was conducted under equivalent conditions in all ethnic groups in a single country (so many of the possible methodological flaws are minimized), it seems that drawing conclusive inferences is more legitimate in this case. However, it should be stressed that the lack of dissimilarity of sexual harassment in various ethnic groups may be true for overall, total comparisons of *sexual harassment prevalence*, but not in other terms of comparison, such as motivations for sexual harassment or personal harm made. Hence, it might still be speculated that sexual harassment of women in ethnic groups represents the more general motivation of oppression (as some have hypothesized), while sexual harassment of women in the mainstream group could be more sexually motivated. If this is the case, sexual harassment prevalence data might be similar (as they actually appear to be), but sexual harassment behaviors would represent different psychosocial processes. Only further research will shed light on this question.

Another generalization that could be drawn from the ethnic-related research, following quite consistent findings, is that *ethnicity does make a significant difference as far as labeling, judgments, and interpretations of sexual harassment–related behaviors are concerned.* The reason behind this finding is still to be investigated, but one could speculate on how behavioral standards, social norms, cultural values, or ethnic group–specific beliefs, myths, and stereotypes contribute to the development of differential conceptions of sexual harassment. This speculation, if tested in sound empirical research, could further illuminate some intriguing questions of the culture–sexual harassment connection.

One last generalization that could be derived here has to do with the important aspect of prevention of sexual harassment. Although only generally and briefly reviewed here, it seems to be that *the major means—and almost the sole means in many places—of attempting to prevent sexual harassment is legal deterrence.* In some countries—and this

seems to be a growing trend—specific legislation, or at least specific sections of more general legislation, has been made to directly refer to sexual harassment. This might include federal or state legislation, or more local statutes in the form of city, association, or specific organization guidelines. Usually these legal acts have been accompanied with specific grievance procedures that consist of already existing services and authorities or custom-made ones. In different countries, nonspecific laws have been applied to cover the illegality of sexual harassment, and growing numbers of court rulings serve as valid grounds for legal steps. In these countries either specific guidelines and procedures have been established to enforce the law, or existing legal channels have been used for this purpose. The judiciary approach, however, in all of these different legal applications, across nations and localities, is meant not only to punish sexual harassment offenders, but is also—perhaps primarily—designed to prevent sexual harassment from appearing in the first place, by deterring possible offenders. This approach at prevention of sexual harassment, which is none other than the general legal approach of any felony prevention, assumes that people fully know the relevant laws, understand them well, and act rationally in order to avoid punishment or to obey normative rules. These assumptions, or parts thereof, might be valid or invalid. But the efficiency of the legal approach of prevention of sexual harassment might be challenged on the basis of two main reasons. First, people who break laws usually are certain that they would not be reported, and/or that they would not be charged, and/or that they would not be convicted. In comparing sexual harassment prevalence data across countries and cultures with actual numbers of formal charges and convictions made, (again, across nations and localities), one could easily see that sexual harassment offenders do in fact act rationally, since they actually would not be reported, charged, or convicted. Hence, the deterrence factor of legal approaches to preventing sexual harassment is quite limited in reality. Second, the legal approach assumes that people are usually aware of their behaviors and their behaviors' consequences and are in full control of their actions. This assumption might also be challenged. In many cases, people behave automatically and mechanically and do not prejudge and plan their actions, and their common, accepted behaviors are distorted by powerful internal drives, as well as reinforced by environmental factors. These might be the context of the antecedents for sexual harassment as well (Pryor, LaVite, & Stoller, 1993), although the specific nature of these antecedents is still to be examined (Barak et al., in press).

This negative evaluation of the effectiveness of legal approaches at prevention does not mean that legislation is unneeded. Societies need legislation primarily to set values and standards for their members, and sexual harassment–related laws (and awareness of them by the populace) might well serve this end. However, it is highly unprofessional and naive to advocate legal procedures as the sole or main remedy in combating sexual harassment.

Other, less massive approaches at preventing and combating sexual harassment have been adopted in several countries. These include *organizational interventions* such as equalizing proportions of men and women in workplaces, stricter job definitions, and pre-screening job applicants on the basis of their sexual harassment history. Other approaches, advocated for or actually executed in several countries, underline *training and education* of individuals and groups on the topic of sexual harassment as a possible efficient way to combat it. Assuming that the legal approaches have indeed been unsuccessful in achieving their goal because of the factors outlined here, it seems that organizational and educational interventions might help close the psychosocial gap left in judiciary approaches. It is striking to note that while legal approaches are seen from one country to another, and international attempts are common (e.g., by the International Labour Office or by the European Communities), there seems to be a deficiency of attempts on the psychosocial dimension.

Because, as this review shows, sexual harassment represents a social problem that has no cultural borders, international, cross-cultural cooperation on these approaches could prove very useful.

The process of the world's shrinkage and globalization is rapid, due to many features and needs. Cultures in their "true" anthropological sense are almost nonexistent, and national and ethnic cultures (as well as languages, melodies, fashion, or food cuisine) are in the process of integrating and mixing (e.g., Brown, 1991; Falk, 1992; Featherstone, 1990; Robertson, 1992). On the other hand, terms such as "the American culture" or "the German culture" refer to the overestimation of a society's unidimensionality, while downplaying the multifaced specific ingredients of these cultures. Some of the findings reviewed here show, for instance, that subcultures, or ethnic groups, may maintain unique attributions related to sexual harassment. Because of these factors, investigators have to practice much caution in conducting and interpreting research that relates to cross-cultural aspects of sexual harassment (Barak, 1994). Moreover, it seems that studying sexual harassment across nations is legitimate as long as it leads to international cooperation and sharing of knowledge in dealing with this social problem that has no obvious country-specific roots or correlates. However, because of general methodological difficulties, as well as specific ones, it could be quite erroneous and misleading to compare sexual harassment data among nations by using translated questionnaires or other common research methods (Barak, 1994). It is suggested here to adopt Kim's (1990) thoughtful proposal of the indigenous psychology paradigm in studying sexual harassment across cultures. This approach calls for application of local, culture-specific methods in investigating a psychological construct. Once converted to the conceptual level, the findings could be compared interculturally. It seems that employment of this approach might significantly enhance our knowledge of cross-cultural perspectives of sexual harassment.

# NOTES

1. *Author's Note*: Work on this manuscript was supported by The Canada-Israel Foundation for Academic Exchanges. I am indebted to Lori Horner for her help in preparing this manuscript. I am also thankful to numerous individuals and agencies worldwide who supplied me with local materials on sexual harassment.

2. The scales of measurement of the variables correlated were either categorical or ordinal. However, Sanday (1981) mistakenly reported Pearson's correlations. Her findings might therefore be distorted.

3. The SEQ has two equivalent versions, for sexual harassment of university students and for sexual harassment of employees at the workplace. Following extensive research (see Chapter 3), the SEQ has been changed slightly in format, item content, and subscales. The current subscales consist of Gender Harassment, Unwanted Sexual Attention, and Sexual Coercion.

4. The following figures refer to sexual harassment of women only.

5. It is assumed here, as well as in most related research, that if respondents reported incidents, they actually experienced these incidents, although verification data are regularly not available on the genuineness of the personal reports.

6. Some of these findings were not reported in the article and were obtained by subsequent analyses.

7. No further findings were reported by ILO (1992) to make comparison of the two surveys possible.

8. These figures are not reported in the article but were computed based on frequencies reported in it.

9. These figures are not reported in the original report and were determined on the basis of the published findings.

10. The findings of Koss, Gidycz, and Wisniewski (1987) refer to sexual victimization prevalence the respondents have experienced after the age of 14 and not limited to incidents in university or workplace.

11. These figures were not reported in the original article but were computed based on the published results.

12. These figures are not reported in the article but were computed based on frequencies reported in it.

13. This figure is not reported in the original report and was determined on the basis of the published findings.

# REFERENCES

Abe, H. (1993). Fighting against sexual harassment at the workplace. *Asian Women Workers Newsletter, 12*(4), 9–10.

Adams, A., & Bray, F. (1992). Holding out against workplace harassment and bullying. *Personnel Management, 24*(10), 48–53.

Aggarwal, A. P. (1992). *Sexual harassment in the workplace* (2d ed.). Toronto: Butterworths.

Allison, J. A., & Wrightsman, L. S. (1993). *Rape: The misunderstood crime*. Newbury Park, CA: Sage.

Amáncio, L. B. Q., & de Lima, M. L. P. (1992). *Assédio sexual no mercado de trabalho* [National survey on sexual harassment in the job market]. Lisbon, Portugal: Center for Investigation and Social Studies, Ministry of Employment and Social Security. [Portuguese]

American Association of University Women (AAUW) (1994). *Hostile hallways: The AAUW survey on sexual harassment in schools*. Washington, DC: AAUW Educational Foundation.

Anonymous (1993). Female brickie wins settlement. *Pesonnel Management, 25*(2), 10.

Avni, N. (1990). Me'afyenim psichologiim vedemografiim shel hatrada minit shel studentyot [*Psychological and biographical characteristics of sexual harassment of female students*]. Master's thesis, Tel Aviv University, Tel Aviv, Israel. [Hebrew]

Badgley, R. (1984). *Report to the federal committee on sexual offenses against children and youth*. Ottawa, Canada: Federal Department of Justice and Health and Welfare.

Bagby, R. M., & Rector, N. A. (1992). Prejudice in a simulated legal context: A further application of social identity theory. *European Journal of Social Psychology, 22*, 397–406.

Barak, A. (1989). Hatrada minit bemekom ha'avoda: Mada ve'agada. [Sexual harassment in the workplace: Science and legend]. *Mash'abei Enosh, 17*, 23–26. [Hebrew]

Barak, A. (1992). Combatting sexual harassment. *American Psychologist, 47*, 818–819.

Barak, A. (1994, August). Sexual harassment in cross-cultural perspectives: Implications from a series of studies in Israel. In J. B. Pryor & A. Barak (Co-Chairs), *Cross-cultural perspectives on sexual harassment*. Symposium conducted at the Annual Convention of the American Psychological Association, Los Angeles.

Barak, A. (in press). A cognitive-behavioral educational workshop to combat sexual harassment in the workplace. *Journal of Counseling and Development*.

Barak, A., Fisher, W. A., & Houston, S. (1992). Individual difference correlates of the experience of sexual harassment among female university students. *Journal of Applied Social Psychology, 22*, 17–37.

Barak, A., Pitterman, Y., & Yitzhaki, R. (in press). An empirical test of the role of power differential in originating sexual harassment. *Basic and Applied Social Psychology*.

Barone, A. M. (1991). Quelle politique syndicale face au harcélement sexual? [Which trade union policy with regard to sexual harassment?]. *Revue Syndicale Suisse, 83*, 2–9. [French]

Beauvais, K. (1986). Workshops to combat sexual harassement: A case study of changing attitudes. *Signs, 12*, 130–145.

Bell, D. (1991). Intraracial rape revisited: On forgoing a feminist future beyond factions and frightening politics. *Women's Studies International Forum, 14*, 385–412.

Bell, E. L. (1992). Myths, stereotypes, and realities of Black women: A personal reflection. *The Journal of Applied Behavioral Science, 28*, 363–376.

Benenson, H. (1993). Patriarchal constraints on women workers' mobilization: The Lancshire female cotton operatives 1842–1919. *British Journal of Sociology, 44*, 613–633.

Berry, J. W., Poortinga, Y. H., Segall, M. H., & Dasen, P. R. (1992). *Cross cultural psychology: Research and applications*. Cambridge, England: Cambridge University Press.

Bingham, S. G., & Scherer, L. L. (1993). Factors associated with responses to sexual harassment and satisfaction with outcome. *Sex Roles, 29*, 239–269.

Brickman, J., & Briere, J. (1984). Incidence of rape and sexual assault in an urban Canadian population. *The International Journal of Women's Studies, 7*, 195–206.

Brislin, R. W. (1993). *Understanding culture's influence on behavior*. Fort Worth, TX: Harcourt Brace Jovanovich.

British Sociological Association (1987). Sexual harassment. *Network, 37*(January), 13.

Brooks, L., & Perot, A. R. (1991). Reporting sexual harassment: Exploring a predictive model. *Psychology of Women Quarterly, 15*, 31–47.

Brown, D. E. (1991). *Human universals*. New York: McGraw-Hill.

Burke, R. J., & McKeen, C. A. (1992). Social-sexual behaviours at work: Experiences of managerial and professional women. *Women in Management Review, 7*(3), 22–30.

Bursik, K. (1992). Perceptions of sexual harassment in an academic context. *Sex Roles, 27*, 401–412.

Bustelo, C. (1991). Sexual harassment: Nature, scope, and consequences for women. In I. M. de Vries (Ed.), *Report EC seminar sexual harassment at work* (pp. 21–23). The Hague, The Netherlands, Ministry of Social Affairs and Employment.

Byers, E. S., & Price, D. (1986). Guidelines for the elimination of sexual harassment. *Canadian Psychology, 27*, 371.

Canadian Human Rights Commission (1983). *Unwanted sexual attention and sexual harassment: Results of a survey of Canadians*. Ottawa, Canada: Author.

Carr, R. A. (1991). Addicted to power: Sexual harassment and the unethical behaviour of university faculty. *Canadian Journal of Counselling, 25*, 447–461.

Chan, C. S. (1987). Asian-American women: Psychological responses to sexual exploitation and cultural stereotypes. *Women and Therapy, 6*(4), 33–38.

Clausen, G. (1987). Vergewaltigung: Erforschung einer geheimen dimension des alltags [Rape: Exploration of a secret dimension of everyday life]. *Gruppendynamyk, 18*, 217–227. [German]

Cleveland, J. N., & Kerst, M. E. (1993). Sexual harassment and perceptions of power: An under-articulated relationship. *Journal of Vocational Behavior, 42*, 49–67.

Cole, M., & Boyle, H. (1986). The aboriginal struggle: An interview with Helen Boyle. *Race and Class, 27*(4), 21–33.

Crosthwaite, J., & Swanton, C. (1986). On the nature of sexual harassment. *Australasian Journal of Philosophy, 64*, 91–106.

Davidson, M. J., & Earnshaw, J. (1990). Policies, practices and attitudes toward sexual harassment in UK organisations. *Personnel Review, 19*(3), 23–27.

De Bruijn, J., & Timmerman, G. (1988). Ongewenste intimiteiten en verschuivende machtsverhoudingen [Sexual harassment and changing power relations between the sexes]. *Amsterdams Sociologisch Tijdschrift, 15*, 291–309. [Dutch]

DeFour, D. C. (1990). The interface of racism and sexism on college campuses. In M. A. Paludi (Ed.), *Ivory power: Sexual harassment on campus* (pp. 45–52). Albany, NY: SUNY Press.

DeSouza, E. R., Pryor, J. B., Fitness, J., Hutz, C., Kumpf, M., Lubbert, K., Pesonen, O., & Erber, M. W. (1994, August). Gender differences in the interpretation of sexual harassment: A cross-cultural perspective. In J. B. Pryor & A. Barak (Co-Chairs), *Cross-cultural perspectives on sexual harassment*. Symposium conducted at the Annual Convention of the American Psychological Association, Los Angeles.

di Maria, F., & di Nuovo, S. (1986). Judgments of aggression by Sicilian observers. *Journal of Social Psychology, 126*, 187–196.

do Rosario, L. (1993). Petite lady lawyer fights sex harassment. *The Eastern Economic Review, 156*(32), 86.

Ecker, V. (1993). *Rapport final: Evaluation d'ensemble des résultats des travaux par rapport aux objectifs initiaux* [Final report: General evaluation of results with respect to initial objectives]. Unpublished paper. [French]

Ellis, J. T. (1990). Sexual harassment and race: A legal analysis of discrimination. *Journal of Legislation, 8*, 30–45.

Ellis, S., Barak, A., & Pinto, A. (1991). Moderating effects of personal cognitions on experienced and perceived sexual harassment of women at the workplace. *Journal of Applied Social Psychology, 21*, 1320–1337.

Fain, T. C., & Anderton, D. L. (1987). Sexual harassment: Organizational context and diffuse status. *Sex Roles, 17*, 291–311.

Falk, R. (1992). *Explorations at the edge of time*. Philadelphia: Temple University Press.

Farley, H. (1978). *Sexual shakedown: The sexual harassment of women on the job*. Toronto: McGraw-Hill.

Featherstone, M. (Ed.) (1990). *Global culture: Nationalism, globalization and modernity*. London: Sage.

Finnis, S. J., & Robbins, I. (1994). Sexual harassment of nurses: An occupational hazard? *Journal of Clinical Nursing, 3*, 87–95.

Fitzgerald, L. F. (1993). Sexual harassment: Violence against women in the workplace. *American Psychologist, 48*, 1070–1076.

Fitzgerald, L. F., & Gelfand, M. (1994, August). Sexual harassment in Latin America: Prevalence and perceptions in Brazil. In J. B. Pryor & A. Barak (Co-Chairs), *Cross-cultural perspectives on sexual harassment*. Symposium conducted at the Annual Convention of the American Psychological Association, Los Angeles.

Fitzgerald, L. F., & Hesson-McInnis, M. (1989). The dimensions of sexual harassment: A structural analysis. *Journal of Vocational Behavior, 35*, 309–326.

Fitzgerald, L. F., & Shullman, S. L. (1993). Sexual harassment: A research analysis and agenda for the 1990s. *Journal of Vocational Behavior, 42*, 5–27.

Fitzgerald, L. F., Shullman, S. L., Bailey, N., Richards, M., Swecker, J., Gold, Y., Ormerod, M., & Weitzman, L. (1988). The incidence and dimensions of sexual harassment in academia and the workplace. *Journal of Vocational Behavior, 32*, 152–175.

Fraser, N. (1992). Sex, lies, and the public sphere: Some reflections on the confirmation of Clarence Thomas. *Critical Inquiry, 18*, 595–612.

Garcia, A. (1992). Une étude sur le harcélement sexuel en Belgique [A study on sexual harassment in Belgium]. *Chronique Féministe, 44*, 11–17. [French]

Garcia y Garcia, B. E. (1991). El hostigamiento sexual en la mujer trabajadora: Un problema de discriminación visto de soslayo [Sexual harassment of the working woman: A problem of bias and discrimination]. *Revista Mexicana de Psicologia, 4*, 175–183.

Garvey, M. S. (1986) The high cost of sexual harassment suits. *Personnel Journal, 65*, 75–78, 80.

Gavey, N. (1991). Sexual victimization prevalence among New Zealand University students. *Journal of Consulting and Clinical Psychology, 59*, 464–466.

Gay, V. (1991). Sexual harassment: Legal issues, past and future developments. In M. J. Davidson & J. Earnshaw (Eds.), *Vulnerable workers: Psychological and legal issues* (pp. 203–221). New York: Wiley.

Gelfand, M. J., Fitzgerald, L. F., & Drasgow, F. (in press). The structure of sexual harassment: A confirmatory analysis across cultures and settings. *Journal of Vocational Behavior*.

George, L. K., Winfield, I., & Blazer, D. G. (1992). Sociocultural factors in sexual assault: Comparison of two representative samples of women. *Journal of Social Issues, 48*, 105–125.

Giacobbe, I. (1991). Case: The policy of CGIL—the Italian federation of labour. In I. M. de Vries (Ed.), *Report EC seminar sexual harassment at work* (pp. 33–34). The Hague, The Netherlands, Ministry of Social Affairs and Employment.

Giri, R. A. (1990). *The image of women in the American and Indian TV commercials: A comparative analysis*. Unpublished report, Tribhuvan University, Nepal. [ED329503]

Goldstein, R., & Yariv, A. (1991). *Tofa'at hahatrada haminit shel studentiot al yedei seggel acaddemi bacampus* [The phenomenon of sexual harassment of female students by academic staff on campus]. Unpublished seminar paper, Department of Psychology, Tel Aviv University, Tel Aviv, Israel. [Hebrew]

Gray, S. (1985). Sexual harassment: A compensable injury. *Canadian Dimension, 19*(1), 23.

Green, G., Barbour, R. S., Barnard, M., & Kizinger, J. (1993). "Who wears the trousers?": Sexual harassment in research settings. *Women's Studies International Forum, 16*, 627–637.

Gruber, J. E., & Kauppinen-Toropainen, K. (1994, August). Sexual harassment experiences and outcomes: A comparison of American and European women. In J. B. Pryor & A. Barak (Co-Chairs), *Cross-cultural perspectives on sexual harassment*. Symposium conducted at the Annual Convention of the American Psychological Association, Los Angeles.

Gruber, J. E., Smith, M. D., & Kauppinen-Toropainen, K. (in press). An exploration of sexual harassment experiences and severity: Results from North America and Europe. In B. A. Gutek, A. H. Stromberg, & L. Larwood, *Women and Work* (6th ed.).

Gunn, R., & Minch, C. (1992). Sexual assault in Canada: A social and legal analysis. In E. C. Viano (Ed.), *Critical issues in victimology: International perspectives* (pp. 166–173). New York: Springer.

Gutek, B. (1985). *Sex and the workplace*. San Francisco: Jossey-Bass.

Gutek, B., Morasch, B., & Cohen, A. (1983). Interpreting social-sexual behavior in a work setting. *Journal of Vocational Behavior, 22*, 30–48.

Gwartney-Gibbs, P. A., & Lach, D. H. (1992). Sociological explanations for failure to seek sexual harassment remedies. *Mediation Quarterly, 9*, 365–373.

Hall, J. D. (1992). "The mind that burns in each body": Women, rape, and racial violence. In M. L. Anderson & P. H. Collins (Eds.), *Race, class, and gender: An anthology* (pp. 397–412). Belmont, CA: Wadsworth.

Hahn, D. F. (1992). Soviet Jewish refugee women: Searching for security. *Women and Therapy, 13*, 79–87.

Hassebrauck, M. (1986). Verantwortungszuschreibungen nach vergewaltigungen: Der einfluss von tatwahrscheinlichkeit, sozialem ansehen und physischer attraktivitat [Attribution of responsibility for rape: The influence of likelihood of rape, social acceptability, and physical attractiveness]. *Gruppendynamik, 17*, 421–428.

Haavio-Mannila, E., Kauppinen-Toropainen, K., & Kandolin, I. (1988). The effect of sex composition of the workplace on friendship, romance, and sex at work. In B. A. Gutek, A. H. Stromberg, & L. Larwood (Eds.), *Women and work* (vol. 3, pp. 123–137). Newbury Park, CA: Sage.

Hemming, H. (1985). Women in a man's world: Sexual harassment. *Human Relations, 38*, 67–79.

Hoffman, F. L. (1986). Sexual harassment in academia: Feminist theory and institutional practice. *Harvard Educational Review, 56*, 105–121.

Holgate, A. (1989). Sexual harassment as a determinant of women's fear of rape. *Australian Journal of Sex, Marriage and Family, 10*, 21–28.

Holzbecher, M., Braszeit, A., Müller, U., & Plogstedt, S. (1991). *Sexuelle belästiging am arbeitsplatz.* [Sexual harassment at work]. Stuttgart, Germany: Ministry of Youth, Family, Women, and Health. [German]

Howard, S. (1991). Organizational resources for addressing sexual harassment. *Journal of Counseling and Development, 69*, 507–511.

Howells, K., Shaw, F., Greasley, M., Robertson, J., Gloster, D., & Metcalfe, N. (1984). Perceptions of rape in a British sample: Effects of relationship, victim status, sex, and attitudes to women. *British Journal of Social Psychology, 23*, 35–40.

Human Rights and Equal Opportunity Commission (1993). *Inquiry into sexual harassment in the Australian defence force.* Sydney, Australia: Author.

Human Rights and Equal Opportunity Commission (1994). *Agender: Sex discrimination newsletter.* Sydney, Australia: Author.

Hunter, C., & McClelland, K. (1991). Honouring accounts for sexual harassment: A factorial survey analysis. *Sex Roles, 24*, 725–751.

Husbands, R. (1992). Sexual harassment law in employment: An international perspective. *International Labour Review, 131*, 535–559.

International Labour Office (ILO) (1992). Combating sexual harassment at work. *Conditions of Work Digest, 11*(1).

Jämställdhetsombudsmannen (1987). *Sexuella trakasserier: Sexuella trakasserier mot kvinnor i arbetslivet* [Sexual harassment: Sexual harassment in the workplace]. Stockholm, Sweden: Author. [Swedish]

Jones, T. S., & Remland, M. S. (1987). Effects of employment relationship, response of recipient and sex of rater on perceptions of sexual harassment. *Perceptual and Motor Skills, 65*, 55–63.

Jones, T. S., Remland, M. S. (1992). Sources of variability in perceptions of and responses to sexual harassment. *Sex Roles, 27*, 121–142.

Junger, M. (1987). Women's experiences of sexual harassment. *British Journal of Criminology, 27*, 358–383.

Kanekar, S., & Dhir, V. L. (1993). Sex-related differences in perceptions of sexual harassment of women in India. *The Journal of Social Psychology, 133*, 119–120.

Kaufman, S., & Wylie, M. L. (1983). One-session workshop on sexual harassment. *Journal of National Association for Women Deans, Administrators, and Counselors, 46*, 39–42.

Kauppinen-Toropainen, K. (1993). Sexual harassment at the workplace. In OECD Panel Group, *Women, work and health* (pp.153–158). Helsinki, Finland: Ministry of Social Affairs and Health.

Kauppinen-Toropainen, K., & Gruber, J. E. (1993). Antecedents and outcomes of woman-unfriendly experiences: A study of Scandinavian, former Soviet, and American women. *Psychology of Women Quarterly, 17*, 431–456.

Kim, U. (1990). Indigenous psychology: Science and applications. In R. W. Brislin (Ed.), *Applied cross-cultural psychology* (pp. 142–160). Newbury Park, CA: Sage.

Kinnon, D. (1981). *Report on sexual assault in* Canada. Ottawa, Canada: Canadian Advisory Council on the Status of Women.

Kishwar, M. (1992a). Sex harassment and slander as weapons of subjugation. *MANUSHI: A Journal about Women and Society, 68*, 2–15.

Kishwar, M. (1992b). Sexual harassment: Ways to obtain redressal at the workplace. *MANUSHI: A Journal about Women and Society, 69*, 17–18.

Koss, M. P., Gidycz, C. A., & Wisniewski, N. (1987). The scope of rape: Incidence and prevalence of sexual aggression and victimization in a national sample of higher education students. *Journal of Consulting and Clinical Psychology, 55*, 162–170.

Krahe, B. (1985). Die zuschreibung von verantwortlichkeit nach vergewaltigungen: Opfer und tater im dickicht der attributionstheoretischen forschung [The blame for the responsibility of rape: Victim and culprit in the theoretical attributional research]. *Psychologische Rundschau*, *36*(2), 67–82. [German]

Kremer, J., & Curry, C. (1986). *Attitudes toward women in Northern Ireland*. Belfast, Northern Ireland: Equal Opportunities Commission for Northern Ireland.

Kremer, J., & Marks, J. (1992). Sexual harassment: The response of management and trade unions. *Journal of Occupational and Organizational Psychology*, *65*, 5–15.

Lan, S. (1991). Sexual harassment: An international problem—Japanese businessman produces video to prevent lawsuits. *Japan Times Weekly International Edition*, *31*(45), 8.

L'Armand, K., Pepitone, A., & Shanmugam, T. E. (1981). Attitudes toward rape: A comparison of the role of chastity in India and the United States. *Journal of Cross-Cultural Psychology*, *12*, 284–303.

Larsen, H. H. (1989). Seksuel chikane i arbejdslivet [Sexual harassment in work life]. *Nordisk sexologi*, *7*, 23–35. [Norwegian].

Laufer, S. (1990). *Hashpa'at ramat tchunat hacharada shel hanivdeket umidat ha'iyum basituatzia al offen tyug hasituatzia* [The influence of the level of female participant's trait anxiety and the level of situation's threat on labeling of the situation]. Unpublished paper, Department of Psychology, Tel Aviv University, Tel Aviv, Israel. [Hebrew]

Leeds Trade Union and Community Resource and Information Centre (1983). *Sexual harassment of women at work*. Leeds, England: Author.

Levett, A. (1989). A study of childhood sexual abuse among South African university women students. *South African Journal of Psychology*, *19*, 122–129.

Levett, A., & Kuhn, L. (1991). Attitudes toward rape and rapists: A white, English-speaking South African student sample. *South African Journal of Psychology*, *21*, 32–37.

Levinson, D. (1989). *Family violence in cross-cultural perspective*. Newbury Park, CA: Sage.

Licata, B. J., & Popovich, P. M. (1987). Preventing sexual harassment: A proactive approach. *Training and Development Journal*, *41*(5), 34–38.

Lindemann, B., & Kadue, D. D. (1992). *Sexual harassment in employment law*. Washington, DC: The Bureau of National Affairs.

Lipper, N. R. (1992). Sexual harassment in the workplace: A comparative study of Great Britain and the United States. *Comparative Labor Law Journal*, *13*, 293–342.

MacKinnon, A. (1992). *Sexual harassment in the workplace: The Public Service Association response*. Wellington, New Zealand: Public Service Association.

Malovich, N. J., & Stake, J. E. (1990). Sexual harassment on campus: Individual differences in attitudes and beliefs. *Psychology of Women Quarterly*, *14*, 63–81.

Mansfield, P. K., Koch, P. B., Henderson, J., Vicary, J. R., Cohn, M., & Young, E. W. (1991). The job climate for women in traditionally male blue-collar occupations. *Sex Roles*, *25*, 63–79.

Mazer, D. B., & Percival, E. F. (1989a). Ideology or experience? The relationships among perceptions, attitudes, and experiences of sexual harassment in university students. *Sex Roles*, *20*, 135–147.

Mazer, D. B., & Percival, E. F. (1989b). Students' experiences of sexual harassment in a small university. *Sex Roles*, *20*, 1–22.

McDaniel, S. A., & van Roosmalen, E. (1992). Sexual harassment in Canadian academe: Explorations of power and privilege. *Atlantis*, *17*, 3–19.

McKinney, K. (1992). Contrapower sexual harassment: The effects of student sex and type of behavior on faculty perceptions. *Sex Roles*, *27*, 627–643.

Mechling, E. W., & Mechling, J. (1985). Shock talk: From consensual to contractual joking relationships in the bureaucratic workplace. *Human Organization*, *44*, 339–343.

Mehdi, R. (1990). The offence of rape in the Islamic law of Pakistan. *International Journal of the Sociology of Law*, *18*, 19–29.

Menon, S. A., & Kanekar, S. (1992). Attitudes toward sexual harassment of women in India. *Journal of Applied Social Psychology*, *22*, 1940–1952.

Nash, T. (1989). Labour pains: Is it safe to go to work? *The Director*, *42*(12), 106–110.

Neer, O., & Krimolovski, B. (1991). *Hashpa'at mino shel hanivdak, matzavo hamishpachti, mikum hasituatzia vechumrat hahatrada al hatfisa hasubyektivit shel hahatrada haminit* [The influence of participant's gender, marital status, location of the situation and severity level of harassment on subjective perception of sexual harassment]. Unpublished manuscript, Tel Aviv, Israel: Department of Psychology, Tel Aviv University. [Hebrew]

Neuman, W. L. (1992). Gender, race, and age differences in student definitions of sexual harassment. *Wisconsin Sociologist*, *29*, 63–75.

Newman, M. A. (1993). Career advancement: Does gender make a difference? American *Review of Public Administration*, *23*, 361–384.

Niebuhr, R. E., & Boyles, W. R. (1991). Sexual harassment of military personnel: An examination of power differentials. *International Journal of Intercultural Relations*, *15*, 445–457.

O'Brien, E. M. (1989). Date rape: Hidden epidemic makes campuses unsafe for women. *Black Issues in Higher Education*, *6*(19), 6–10.

Oleck, J. (1993). An ounce of prevention: The chains figure they need formal policies on harassment. *Restaurant Business, 92*(2), 53.

Painter, S. L. (1986). Research on the prevalence of child sexual abuse: New directions. *Canadian Journal of Behavioral Science, 18*, 323–339.

Paludi, M. A. (1990). *Ivory power: Sexual harassment on campus.* Albany, NY: SUNY Press.

Paludi, M. A. (1993). Ethnicity, sex, and sexual harassment. *Thought and Action, 8*, 105–116.

Pandey, R. (1986). Rape crimes and victimization of rape victim in free India. *Indian Journal of Social Work, 47*, 169–186.

Pandey, R. (1987). In search of causes of rape in India. *Indian Journal of Social Work, 48*, 103–121.

Pape, J. (1990). Black and white: The "perils of sex" in colonial Zimbabwe. *Journal of Southern African Studies, 16*, 699–720.

Parzan, L., & Kaplan, A. (1991). *Hahashpaot haemotzyonalyot hashlilyot shel hatrada minit kematzav shel choser onim* [The negative effects of sexual harassment as a helplessness condition]. Unpublished paper, Department of Psychology, Tel Aviv University, Tel Aviv, Israel. [Hebrew]

Patterson, O., & Teeple, G. B. (1992). Race, gender and liberal fallacies. *Society-Societe, 16*, 1–4.

Pavich, E. G. (1986). A Chicana perspective on Mexican culture and sexuality. *Journal of Social Work and Human Sexuality, 4*(3), 47–65.

Perry, N. W. (1993). Sexual harassment on campus: Are your actions actionable? *Journal of College Student Development, 34*, 406–410.

Phillips, C. M., Stockdale, J. E., & Joeman, L. M. (1989). *The risks in going to work: The nature of people's work, the risks they encounter and the incidence of sexual harassment, physical attack and threatening behaviour.* London: The Suzy Lamplugh Trust.

Pineau, L. (1989). Date rape: A feminist analysis. *Law and Philosophy, 8*, 217–243.

Pinto, A. (1989). *Bechinat hakesher bein hitnasuiot matridot levein haha'aracha hasubyektivit shel midat hahatrada haminit ota chova isha: bdika bacontext ha'irguni* [A study of the correlation between sexual harassment experiences and the subjective perception of the sexual harassment extent experienced by women at the workplace]. Unpublished Master's thesis, Faculty of Management, Tel Aviv University, Tel Aviv, Israel. [Hebrew]

Popovich, P. M. (1988). Sexual harassment in organizations. *Employee Responsibilities and Rights Journal, 1*, 273–282.

Popovich, P. M., Gehlauf, D. N., Jolton, J. A., Somers, J. M., & Godinho, R. M. (1992). Perceptions of sexual harassment as a function of sex of rater and incident form and consequence. *Sex Roles, 27*, 609–625.

Pryor, J. B., LaVite, C. M., & Stoller, L. M. (1993). A social psychological analysis of sexual harassment: The person/situation interaction. *Journal of Vocational behavior, 42*, 68–83.

Queensland Women's Sub-Committee (1980). *Sexual harassment in the workplace: ACOA policy and associated documents on sexual harassment in the workplace.* Queensland, Australia: Administrative and Clerical Officers' Association.

Ram, K. (1981). Women's liberations in India. *Social Alternatives, 2*, 6–10.

Ramsey, E., & Stefanou-Haag, E. (1991). On lies and silence: Cross cultural perspectives on the construction of women's oppression through linguistic omission. *Working Papers on Language, Gender, and Sexism, 1*, 31–42.

Reid, B. (1991). Case: British rail policy. In I. M. de Vries (Ed.), *Report EC seminar sexual harassment at work* (pp. 29–31). The Hague, The Netherlands: Ministry of Social Affairs and Employment.

Reid, P. T., & Comas-Diaz, L. (1990). Gender and ethnicity: Perspectives on dual status. *Sex Roles, 22*, 397–408.

Reilly, L. B., Bernstein, J. D., & Cote-Bonanno (1992). *Study to examine actions perceived as sexual harassment.* Trenton, NJ: Division of Adult and Occupational Education, New Jersey State Department of Education. [ED 359378]

Riger, S. (1991). Gender dilemmas in sexual harassment policies and procedures. *American Psychologist, 46*, 497–505.

Robertson, R. (1992). *Globalization: Social theory and global culture.* London: Sage.

Rubenstein, N. (1988). *The dignity of women at work: A report on the problem of sexual harassment in the member states of the European Communities.* Luxembourg: Office of the Official Publications of the European Communities.

Rubenstein, M. (1991a). Devising sexual harassment policy. *Personnel Management, 23*(2), 34–37.

Rubenstein, M. (1991b). Relationship between the Resolution, Recommendation and the Equal Treatment Directive. In I. M. de Vries (Ed.), *Report EC seminar sexual harassment at work* (pp. 13–15). The Hague, The Netherlands: Ministry of Social Affairs and Employment.

Rubenstein, M. (1992). *Preventing and remedying sexual harassment at work: A resource manual* (2d ed.). London: Industrial Relations Services.

Rubenstein, M. (1993). Sexual harassment in the workplace: A review of the legal rights and responsibilities of all parties. *Public Personnel Management, 22*, 123–135.

Saal, F. E. (1990). Sexual harassment in organizations. In K. R. Murphy & F. E. Saal, *Psychology in organiza-*

*tions: Integrating science and practice* (pp. 217–239). Hillsdale, NJ: Erlbaum.

Sanday, P. R. (1981). The socio-cultural context of rape: A cross-cultural study. *Journal of Social Issues, 37*(4), 5–27.

Sanday, P. R. (1982). The social context of rape. *New Society, 61*(1037), 540–542.

Sanglas, L. F. (1991).The EC Recommendation and Code of Practice on the protection of the dignity of women and men at work. In I. M. de Vries (Ed.), *Report EC seminar sexual harassment at work* (pp. 17–19). The Hague, The Netherlands, Ministry of Social Affairs and Employment.

Saroja, K. (1990). A study of counselling needs of female postgraduate students of the University of Agricultural Studies: A case study approach. *Indian Journal of Behaviour, 14*(4), 28–32.

Savery, L. K., & Gledhill, A. C. (1988). Sexual harassment of women in industry and commerce by co-workers: Some Australian evidence. *Personnel Review, 17*, 34–37.

Savery, L. K., & Halsted, A. C. (1989). Sexual harassment in the workplace: Who are the offenders? *Equal Opportunities International, 8*(2), 16–20.

Scarr, S. (1988). Race and gender as psychological variables: Social and ethical issues. *American Psychologist, 43*, 56–59.

Scupin, R. (1992). *Cultural anthropology: A global perspective.* Englewood Cliffs, NJ: Prentice-Hall.

Segura, D. A. (1992). Chicanas in white-collar jobs: "You have to prove yourself more." *Sociological Perspectives, 35*, 163–182.

Seltzer, A., & Langford, M. A. (1984). Forensic psychiatric assessments in the Northwest Territories. *Canadian Journal of Psychiatry, 29*, 665–668.

Sexual harassment clauses (1991). *The Worklife Report, 8*(3), 4–6.

Shaalan, M., El-Akabaoui, A. S., & El-Kott, S. (1983). Rape victimology in Egypt. *Victimology: An International Journal, 8*, 277–290.

Shapira-Libai, N. (1987). Hatrada minit ba'avoda klapei nashim besherut hamedina [Sexual harassment at work against civil service women]. *Ma'amad Ha'isha, 16*, 1–30. [Hebrew]

Smith, A. R. (1994). Phrasing, linking, judging: Communication and critical phenomenology. *Human Studies, 17*, 139–161.

Smith, P. B., & Bond, M. H. (1993). *Social psychology across cultures: Analysis and perspectives.* Boston: Allyn & Bacon.

Smith, R. J., Tritt, K., & Zollmann, A. (1982). Sex differences in the social perception of rape victims in West Germany and the United States. *The Journal of Social Psychology, 117*, 143–144.

Sorenson, S. B., & Siegel, J. M. (1992). Gender, ethnicity, and sexual assault: Findings from a Los Angeles study. *Journal of Social Issues, 48*, 93–104.

Sperling, V. (1990). Rape and domestic violence in the USSR. *Response to the victimization of Women and Children, 13*(3), 16–22.

Stanley, L. (1987). Essays on women's work and leisure and "hidden" work. *Studies in Sexual Politics, 18*, 1–61.

Staples, R. (1993). Sexual harassment: Its history, definition and prevalence in the Black community. *Western Journal of Black Studies, 17*, 143–148.

Stockdale, M. S. (1993). The role of sexual misperceptions of women's friendliness in an emerging theory of sexual harassment. *Journal of Vocational Behavior, 42*, 84–101.

Stockert, N. A. (1985). Sexuality and sexual harassment. In J. C. Naughton, S. G. Karel, & N. A. Stockert (Eds.), *Health care for the international student: Asia's and the Pacific* (pp. 85–89). Washington, DC: National Association for Foreign Student Affairs.

Stone, D. A. (1992). Race, gender, and the Supreme Court. *American Prospect, 8,* 63–73.

Strijdom, H. G., & Schurink, W. J. (1979). Victims of serious crimes in Soweto. *Humanitas, 5*, 39–45.

Stringer, D. M., Remick, H., Salisbury, J., & Ginorio, A. B. (1990). The power and reasons behind sexual harassment: An employer's guide to solutions. *Public Personnel Management, 19*, 43–52.

Summers, R. J. (1991). Determinants of judgments of and responses to a complaint of sexual harassment. *Sex Roles, 25*, 379–392.

Thacker, R. A., & Gohmann, S. F. (1993). Male/female differences in perceptions and effects of hostile environment sexual harassment: "Reasonable" assumptions? *Public Personnel Management, 22*, 461–472.

Theron, A. (1989). Women as victims of sexual harassment in the workplace. *South African Journal of Sociology, 20*, 216–223.

Till, F. (1980). *Sexual harassment: A report on the sexual harassment of students.* Washington, DC: National Advisory Council on Women's Educational Programs.

Tokyo Metropolitan Government (1992). *Koyo biyodo o kangaeru. 5: Sexual harassment he nanda ro?* [Thinking about equal employment: 5. What is sexual harassment?]. Tokyo: Author. [Japanese]

Tokyo Metropolitan Government (1992). *Koyo biyodo o kangaeru. 6: Romu kanritoshiteno sexual harassment* [Thinking about equal employment: 6. Sexual harassment—a labor relations issue]. Tokyo: Author. [Japanese]

Triandis, H. C. (1994). *Culture and social behavior.* New York: McGraw-Hill.

Ugwuegbu, D. C. E. (1976). Black jurors' personality trait attributions to a rape case defendant. *Social Behavior and Personality, 4*, 193–201.

Uhari, M., Kokkonen, J., Nuutinen, J., Vainionpaa, L., Rantala, H., Lautala, P., & Väyrynen, M. (1994). Medical student abuse: An international phenomenon. *Journal of the* American *Medical Association, 271*, 1049–1051.

U.S. Merit Systems Protection Board (1981). *Sexual harassment in the federal workplace: Is it a problem?* Washington, DC: Government Printing Office.

U.S. Merit Systems Protection Board (1988). *Sexual harassment in the federal government: An update.* Washington, DC: Government Printing Office.

Valentine-French, S., & Radtke, H. L (1989). Attributions of responsibility for an incident of sexual harassment in a university setting. *Sex Roles, 21*, 545–555.

Van-Willigen, L. H. (1992). Incidence and consequences of sexual violence in refugees: Considerations for general health care. *Nordisk Sexologi, 10*, 85–91.

Vogelman, L. (1990). *The sexual face of violence: Rapists on rape.* Johannesburg, South Africa: Raven.

Wijns, M. (1991). Case: The policy of the Belgian government. In I. M. de Vries (Ed.), *Report EC seminar sexual harassment at work* (pp. 35–37). The Hague, The Netherlands, Ministry of Social Affairs and Employment.

Williams, K. B., & Cyr, R. R. (1992). Escalating commitment to a relationship: The sexual harassment trap. *Sex Roles, 27*, 47–72.

Wise, S., & Stanley, L. (1987). *Georgie porgie: Sexual harassment in everyday life.* New York: Pandora.

Women's Rights Committee and the Vancouver's Women's Research Centre (1980). *Sexual harassment in the workplace: A discussion paper.* Vancouver, BC, Canada: British Columbia Federation of Labour.

Wyatt, G. E. (1992). The sociocultural context of African American and White American women's rape. *Journal of Social Issues, 48*, 77–91.

York, K. M. (1989). Defining sexual harassment in workplaces: A policy-capturing approach. *Academy of Management Journal, 32*, 830–850.

Zubber, K. (1992). The socialization of human sexuality. *South African Sociological Review, 4*, 27–49.

# AUTHOR INDEX

# SUBJECT INDEX